Reading the Church Fathers

Other Books from Sophia Institute Press by James L. Papandrea:

What Really Happens After We Die (There Will Be Hugs in Heaven)

How Christianity Saved Civilization ...
and Must Do So Again (with Mike Aquilina)

From Star Wars to Superman: Christ Figures in
Science Fiction and Superhero Films

Other Books on the Early Church by James L. Papandrea

The Early Church (33–313): St. Peter, the Apostles, and Martyrs

A Week in the Life of Rome

The Earliest Christologies: Five Images of Christ in the Postapostolic Age

Handed Down: The Catholic Faith of the Early Christians

The Wedding of the Lamb: A Historical Approach to the Book of Revelation

Novatian of Rome and the Culmination of Pre-Nicene Orthodoxy

Trinity 101: Father, Son, Holy Spirit

James L. Papandrea

Reading the Church Fathers

A History of the Early Church and the Development of Doctrine

SOPHIA INSTITUTE PRESS
Manchester, New Hampshire

This book is an expanded version of *Reading the Early Church Fathers: From the Didache to Nicaea* (Paulist Press, 2012).

Cover design by Joshua Facemyer, Impressus Art LLC (ImpressusArt.com).

On the cover: *The Four Fathers of the Latin Church*,
by Jacob Jordaens (1593-1678), public domain.

Sophia Institute Press
Box 5284, Manchester, NH 03108
1-800-888-9344

www.SophiaInstitute.com

Sophia Institute Press® is a registered trademark of Sophia Institute.

paperback ISBN 978-1-64413-656-0
ebook ISBN 978-1-64413-657-7

Library of Congress Control Number: 2022930856

SPA POD 2026

Tradition means giving votes to the most obscure of all classes, our ancestors. It is the democracy of the dead. Tradition refuses to submit to the small and arrogant oligarchy of those who merely happen to be walking about.

— G. K. Chesterton, *Orthodoxy*

Contents

Acknowledgments

I would like to thank those who went before me in the study of early Christianity; although the reader may notice that the footnotes for this volume emphasize the primary sources (and this is intentional, since I believe the primary sources are the place to begin), nevertheless I recognize that I stand on the shoulders of my predecessors in the field. I especially want to thank those who taught me to love the early Church and to appreciate the importance of historical theology: my professors at Fuller Theological Seminary, including James E. Bradley, Marianne Meye Thompson, Ralph Martin, and Colin Brown; my dissertation advisers, Dennis E. Groh and Robert Jewett, and Northwestern professors James Packer and John Wright; my colleagues in the field, including Mike Aquilina, David Eastman, Peter Steiger, Young Kim, Helen Rhee, Jared Ortiz, and David Wilhite; and my PhD students Carol Korak, Peter Smith, and Jessica Lee. I would like to thank all my students, including the Holy Family Bible Journey group and the students at Garrett-Evangelical Theological Seminary, for their patience and helpful input. Last but far from least, I want to thank those colleagues, friends, and conversation partners who have always supported me, encouraged me, challenged me, debated with me, and taught me so much about the grace of God, including Rich and Karin Vetrano, George Kalantzis, Stephanie Perdew, Glenn Murray, Paul Jarzembowski, Graziano Marcheschi, and my bandmates in *Remember Rome*. Getting to this point would not have been possible without each of you, and I have valued our conversations immeasurably. Most recently I want to thank my friend and fellow historian Roberto Pacheco for his careful reading of the first edition, and his thoughtul feedback for this revision. I've taken the opportunity to make use of the last decade of teaching experience and research to round out the book with some much-needed additions, which I am confident will make it even more useful as an introduction to early Christianity. May God bless those who read it, and may it draw them closer to God through Christ, in the spirit of James 4:8, "*Draw near to God, and he will draw near to you.*"

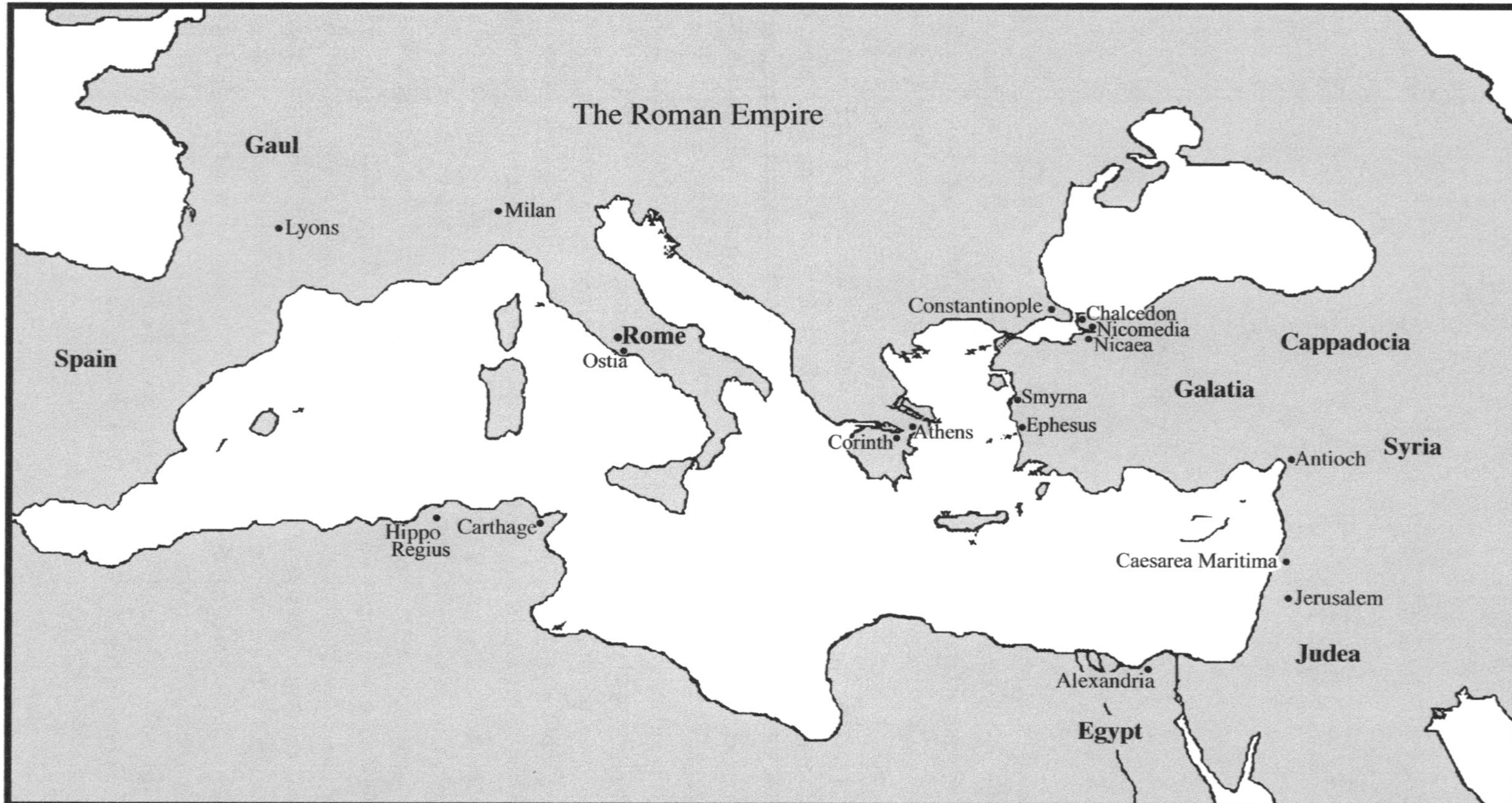
The Roman Empire
Gaul
Milan
Lyons
Spain
Rome
Ostia
Hippo Regius
Carthage
Constantinople
Chalcedon
Nicomedia
Nicaea
Cappadocia
Galatia
Smyrna
Ephesus
Athens
Corinth
Antioch
Syria
Caesarea Maritima
Jerusalem
Judea
Alexandria
Egypt

Reading the Church Fathers

1

What Do You Mean by *God*?

Introduction

Therefore, since we are surrounded by so great a cloud of witnesses …

—Hebrews 12:1

The author of the letter to the Hebrews describes the life of faith in Christ as running a marathon. It's a long haul that requires perseverance and keeping one's eye on the finish line. But along the way there are those who cheer us on, who encourage us, and included in that "cloud of witnesses" are those who went before us in the Faith — our ancestors and spiritual mothers and fathers who handed down the Faith to us — some of whom gave their lives to witness to the Faith. All religion is received, and all religion is "conservative" in the sense that it preserves something down through the generations. We do not invent the Faith, we accept it from those who came before us. Indeed, Judeo-Christian faith teaches that Truth is not found "within," as if one individual's truth could be different from another. Rather, Truth is revealed to humanity by God, through holy people, who produced holy writings, and lived holy lives. Their witness is what we receive as our Tradition.

The Christian Faith begins with Jesus Christ and His apostles, of course. The first century of the Christian era saw the flourishing of the Roman Empire, as well as the birth of the Church and the writing of the documents that would become the New Testament. The Empire would try to suppress the Church, but the Church would eventually convert, and then outlive, the empire, as it has all other empires that have tried to kill it. This book is meant to introduce you to the history of the Church, and the vast treasury of writings produced by its early leaders. This is the era of the Church "Fathers," the name given to those leaders of the early centuries who produced the writings that make up our received tradition. There are Church

"Mothers," as well, and we will meet those who have come down to us through their witness. We often refer to the Church Fathers by a name and a place. When you see a reference to someone like Augustine of Hippo, for example, it usually means that St. Augustine was the bishop of the city of Hippo. There are some exceptions, such as Clement of Alexandria, who was never bishop of Alexandria, but we refer to him that way to distinguish him from St. Clement of Rome. In any case, when you see *someone of someplace*, it usually refers to a bishop. As it turns out, many of the early Christian writings that still exist are from bishops, not because they used their power to suppress other writings, but because they were the authoritative teachers of their time and place, handing on to their flock what they had received from the teachers who came before them.

The period of the Church "Fathers" is known as the *patristic* period. Therefore the study of *patristics* refers to the study of the history and theology of the early Christian Church. We will begin our study with the "postapostolic" age which, as the name suggests, begins where the apostolic age ends, with the leadership of those whom the apostles had chosen to succeed them. In fact, we can already see the second generation of Church leaders in the pages of the New Testament, in people like Mark, Luke, and Timothy, to name just a few. Therefore, the postapostolic age has something of an overlap with the New Testament, and in fact there is no well-defined line of division between the age of the apostles and the next phase of Church history. At the very least, we have to acknowledge that some apostles lived longer than others, thus the second generation of leadership begins earlier in some places than in others.

Therefore, our exploration begins in the late first century, and though we will not focus on any of the documents that would come to be included in the New Testament, a few of the documents we will examine were written before the latest of the New Testament writings. One must keep in mind that the "New Testament" as we know it was not yet a standardized collection even in the second century, and while the formation of the New Testament canon is a subject for another chapter, we will begin to ask the question why some of the earliest Christian writings were not included in the Christian Bible.

The postapostolic age encompasses two phases of the history of the Church. The first phase is often referred to as the age of the *apostolic fathers*. The second is the age of the *apologists*. Each will be explained as we come to it, however for now it is important to note that just as there is overlap between the apostolic (New Testament) age and the postapostolic age, there is also an overlap and no clear dividing line between the time of the apostolic fathers and the apologists within the postapostolic age. Therefore, we will not concern ourselves with attempting to define these stages of Church history by a strict time frame. In general, the postapostolic age runs from the last decades of the first century to the last decades of the second century, or about AD 80 to AD 180. This latter date is a turning point because the first true theologians emerge at the end of the second century, beginning a new era in the history of the Church. After that, the age of the early theologians takes us up to the early fourth century, leading to the Council of Nicaea in AD 325. This time is a watershed in Christian history, for reasons that will become evident below.

The Origin of Christianity in Context

When one reads the New Testament, it is relatively easy to see that from the very beginning, the movement Jesus started was in conflict with the leaders of His own religion of Judaism. At first, that conflict was an internal struggle between two competing ways of understanding God's revelation. Both sides were forced to face their irreconcilable differences when the temple in Jerusalem was destroyed in AD 70. After that point, the sacrifices ended and the priesthood eventually died out, and Judaism itself had to figure out how to continue as a religion without the sacrificial system that was once central to its faith.

The vast majority of Jewish faithful followed the Pharisees, the experts in the Jewish law who became the Rabbis. They made the written word of God, the *Torah*, the new center of their faith. However, a minority of Jewish believers went a different way. They followed the disciples of a man called Jesus of Nazareth, and these disciples taught that Jesus was Himself the *living* Word of God. Those who took this path, of course, would eventually be called Christians, but we have to keep in mind that the concept of "Christianity," as a separate religion, did not exist in the beginning. In the first century, the movement Jesus started was known simply as "The Way" (Acts 9:2, cf. John 14:6), and it was only after the destruction of the Jewish temple that Christianity would finally become a separate religion.

All this is to say that Christianity and Rabbinic Judaism are twin siblings from the same parent (Temple Judaism). As such, there was a lot of sibling rivalry, especially at the beginning when Christianity was still seen as a sect within Judaism. During that time, Christians continued to worship in the synagogues with their Jewish family and neighbors, but they also met in the evenings and/or at dawn on Sunday mornings to do something that would horrify their fellow Jews. They worshiped Jesus. This became the greatest bone of contention between the more traditional Jews and the earliest followers of Jesus. A traditional Jew would wonder how one could worship Jesus, and still say one is a good Jew — for Judaism must be monotheistic (Deut. 6:4). For the followers of Christ, their liturgical practice would put them on the defensive theologically, forcing them to try to figure out a way to justify the apparent oxymoron of Christian monotheism. The result was the development of doctrine in the early Church, and the answer to the question of Christian monotheism was the doctrine of the Trinity.

Therefore, much of the dialogue between Christians and Jews in the early decades centered around the Christian conviction that Jesus fulfilled the prophecies of the Old Testament. Many Jews were convinced by these arguments and converted to Christianity. Many were not convinced and continued to believe that what the Christians were doing was a form of polytheism, and blasphemy against God. Some even felt justified in following in the footsteps of the pre-conversion Saul (the apostle Paul) as they participated in persecution against their Christian neighbors (Acts 17:5–9). But the persecution of the Church by Jews would give way to persecution by the Roman Empire when the Romans began to take notice of the Church as something separate from Judaism. Ironically, as long as Christianity was seen as a sect within Judaism, the Romans left it alone, either reasoning that it was part of an ancient religion and was probably not a threat, or failing to notice that it even existed. Once Christianity was out from under the umbrella of Judaism, it became perceived as something new, and therefore potentially dangerous.

At the same time, certain strains of Greco-Roman philosophy were coming to the conclusion that there was really only one God, or perhaps one High God above all other "principalities and powers." As Christianity emerged as a separate religion from Judaism, it inherited some of the cultural aspects of Greek philosophy. There were many aspects of Greek philosophy that Christianity rejected, as one might expect, but there were certain points at which philosophy could be seen to agree with Hebrew wisdom, and these the Christians adopted and adapted.

It was once the trend for some scholars to argue that Christianity was at first essentially Jewish, but later was corrupted by "Hellenism," or the influence of Greek philosophy and even religion.[1] However, that has now been debunked as an erroneous view of the way the Church developed in the first century. The truth is that

[1] The myth of "pre-hellenized" Christianity was started by Adolf von Harnack, a very influential patristics scholar who wrote sweeping overviews of the whole patristic era. The problem was that he had a surface knowledge of a wide swath of time and texts but lacked depth in very many of them, and consequently made many erroneous assumptions that led him to false conclusions. He started the trend of looking for a pristine Jewish version of Christianity that had not yet been "ruined" by the attempt to contextualize (in his mind, sell out) the Gospel to Greco-Roman culture for the sake of the evangelization of the Gentiles. See Edward T. Oakes, S.J., *Infinity Dwindled to Infancy: A Catholic and Evangelical Christology* (Grand Rapids: Eerdmans, 2011), 114. The best treatment debunking the myth of pre-hellenized Christianity is in Paul L. Gavrilyuk, *The Suffering of the Impassible God: The Dialectics of Patristic Thought* (Oxford: Oxford University Press, 2004).

Christianity was a marriage of Hebrew thought derived from Judaism with the best of Greco-Roman philosophy. There was no pristine, pre-hellenized version of Christianity, but rather the early Christians understood that some aspects of philosophy could support and help interpret what God had revealed to humanity through the Hebrew faith. In fact, the first Christian apologists were all philosophers! At least through the first two centuries of the history of the Church, the Fathers assumed that revelation and philosophy were not necessarily at odds, and that human reason could be guided by God to discern which aspects of philosophy should be accepted and which should be rejected. The late second-century catechist, Clement of Alexandria, would say that what the Hebrew Scriptures had done for the Jews, philosophy had done for the Gentiles — that is, prepare them for the coming of Christ.[2]

The Same God?

One question that is likely to come up in any setting where people are learning about their faith is this one: Do Christians, Jews, and Muslims worship the same God? As we will see, a case could be made for more than one right answer, but the thoughtful leader will first respond with another question: What do you mean by *God*? We use the word *God* frequently (sometimes even as an expletive), and we use it as though we can assume that it means the same thing to everyone in our audience. But the truth is that the word *God* can mean different things to different people, especially as globalization puts us in touch with a more diverse group of people than ever before in history. So it is no longer the case (if it ever was) that a person can stand in front of a congregation, say the word *God,* and assume that everyone knows what that word means in the mind of the speaker.

Within the Christian context, the word *God* can have at least three distinct meanings. It can mean the Holy Trinity, that is, the Godhead as historically understood by the Christian Church, as a result of Christian experience and interpretation of Scripture (modeled by the apostles, whose writings came to be added to the Christian Bible). The word "God" can also mean specifically the First Person of the Trinity, called YHWH in the Old Testament, and God the Father by Jesus. Finally, the word "God" can also refer to Divinity itself, the very essence of the Divine.

Therefore, to answer the question above, we first have to clarify which of these three meanings of the word "God" are in play. If we mean the Holy Trinity, then the answer would be no, Jews and Muslims do not think of the One God as triune. If we mean God the Father, then a case could be made that Jews, Christians, and

2 Clement of Alexandria, *Miscellanies,* 1.5; see also Clement of Alexandria, *The Instructor,* 1.6, 1.11.

Muslims are all talking about the same God when they refer to YHWH, the Father, or Allah. The same could be true for the third definition, Divinity itself. The differences between these religions, then, come down to the ways God is said to have been revealed to humanity. This is not to minimize those differences, nor to attempt to reduce all monotheistic faith to a common denominator. As St. James reminds us, simply believing in the One God is not necessarily a sign of faith in God, since the demons also believe in the same God (James 2:19).

As Christians, we are used to saying that Jesus Christ is God. Is this statement true? Again, before we can answer that, we have to ask: What do you mean by *God*? If *God* means the Trinity, then no, Jesus Christ is not the Trinity. He is the Second Person of the Trinity, but not all three Persons of the Trinity. If *God* means the Father, then again the answer is no, Jesus Christ is not the First Person of the Trinity, He is the Second Person, He is the Son. And while the Father and Son are God, the Father is not the Son and the Son is not the Father. So then, the only sense in which we can say that Jesus Christ is God, is in the sense that Jesus Christ is divine. As we will see, this will be clarified in terms of His divine nature, which does not diminish His true humanity at all, but the point for the moment is that it *is* appropriate to say that Jesus Christ is God, as long as everyone knows what you mean by *God*.

As we read in the first chapter of the Gospel of John, Jesus Christ is the incarnation (the embodiment) of the eternal *Logos*. This is a Greek term we normally translate with the English *Word*. Jesus Christ is the *Word of God*. We will discover more about what this means in the coming chapters. For now, it is enough to point out that when we speak of God, we often need to be more specific. In this book, the First Person of the Trinity will usually be referred to as the Father (since this is the term that Jesus used as the new substitution for the divine Name: YHWH); the Second Person of the Trinity will be referred to as Jesus, Christ, Jesus Christ, the Son, or the Word; and the Third Person of the Trinity will be referred to as the Holy Spirit.

It is interesting to see how, even in the text of Scripture, the meaning of the word "God" can shift. Notice John 1:1, "In the beginning was the Word, and the Word was with God, and the Word was God." The term *God* is used twice in that sentence, and each time it means something different. It would be legitimate to translate that sentence this way: "In the beginning was the Word, and the Word was with the Father, and the Word was divine." Do you see how even John, in his Gospel, assumes that his audience will get the nuance of the meanings of the word "God"? And yet in our world, we cannot make that assumption. Therefore, one of the goals of this study in reading the Church Fathers is for the reader to learn to be more precise with language about God and the Christian Faith. Differences of language that may seem subtle can often have implications for major differences of doctrine. Therefore, we should be as clear as possible whether we are talking about the Trinity, or one Person of the Trinity. And we should make sure our audience receives the meaning we intend.

The Attributes of God

Before we begin to read the writings of the Church Fathers, we should also clarify some of the philosophical assumptions they shared about who God is, and what God is like. Note that these assumptions can be found in both Greco-Roman philosophy and the Hebrew Scriptures. These are not so much an adaptation of Jewish faith to Greek culture, as they are the very places where Hebrew and Greek thought overlap.[3] In what follows, the word *God* refers to Divinity itself, or more precisely, what we call the attributes of divinity, which all three Persons of the Trinity have in common. What is the essence (or in Latin, the *substance*) of divinity? How are we to describe God, and how are we to talk about God so that we can all agree we are talking about the *same* God? Because if we describe God in a way that is not at least consistent with the descriptions of God that have been revealed and handed down to us, then we run the risk that we are describing a *different* god, one that obviously does not exist. Following are the attributes of God that are shared and assumed by the Church Fathers and make up the patristic consensus of the doctrine of God.

God Is One, and All-Sufficient

The *Shema,* sometimes called the creed of Judaism, is arguably the very foundation of all monotheistic belief. It comes from Deuteronomy 6:4, "Hear, O Israel: the LORD our God, the LORD is one." (When you see the word *Lord* in all caps, that's telling you that in the Hebrew, the word is the divine name, YHWH.) So although other cultures might believe in many gods, for the Hebrews there is only one God. In other places in the Old Testament, God is called *El-Shaddai,* which means something like, "God All-Sufficient." Again, in contrast to polytheistic cultures, who believed that male gods needed to partner with female gods to create life, the God of the Hebrews is all-sufficient to create life, and all that exists, without needing a divine consort. In fact, it must be the case that God needs nothing at all, since any need would be a lack, and therefore a deficiency.

[3] On the attributes of divinity, see Hippolytus, *Against Beron and Helix*. Although there is significant debate over the authorship of these fragments, it is not necessary to settle the matter for our purposes, since the text at least demonstrates the early Christian assumption that these philosophical descriptions of the attributes of God are consistent with Judeo-Christian monotheism.

It is worth noting at this point that although we call the First Person of the Trinity *Father,* we should not project human maleness onto God, and we should not read into this any kind of deficiency in God in the sense of lacking what we might think of as positive female traits. God is, on one hand, neither male nor female because God is incorporeal, and yet on the other hand, God is both male and female, since God is all-sufficient and completely self-sufficient, and since both males and females are made in God's image (Gen. 1:27). Having said that, since this is a book about the Tradition, and for the sake of clarity, we will maintain the traditional pronouns for God, with the understanding that grammatical gender does not necessarily imply bodily sex.

God Is Omnipresent, and Uncircumscribable

In the Judeo-Christian worldview of the Church Fathers, there is only one God. In fact, there is room for only one God, since God is everywhere (Ps. 33:5; 139; Isa. 6:3). The polytheistic religions that assume the existence of multiple gods usually ascribe roles or a kind of division of labor to the gods. There is a god of love and a god of war. There is a god of healing and a god of partying. The Greeks and Romans had gods for just about everything, which means that each god has to stay out of the others' way. Each god has to defer to the others' sphere of influence. But with the God of the Jews and Christians, there is no room for any other gods, because the one God takes up all the space, so to speak. God defers to no other being, and God does not have to stay out of anyone's way. Since God is all-sufficient, there is no need for any other gods. And as the Church Father Tertullian wrote, those who believe in many gods necessarily choose which gods to worship, and by doing so, they choose not to worship other gods. If those other gods are real, why are people not afraid of offending them by failing to worship them?[4]

Since there is only one God, that God must be omnipresent — everywhere all at once.[5] This means that God does not have to move from one place to another, and God can be present in any place, and is present in every place simultaneously. God is unlimited, and cannot be contained within any part of creation, since God is the Creator and is "bigger" than creation. Another way to say this is that God is *uncircumscribable.* To "circumscribe" something means to draw a boundary around it, and yet no boundary can contain God. Since God is omnipresent, God is therefore also uncircumscribable.

[4] Tertullian, *Apology,* 13.

[5] See, for example, Theophilus of Antioch, *To Autolychus,* 2.3.

God Is Omnipotent, and Eternal

Often written simply as *almighty*, the omnipotence of God means that God is all-powerful. The God who is not limited by any boundaries in creation is also not limited in power over creation. This is because God is the Creator of all that is, the Unmoved Mover of all existence, the Uncaused First Cause in every chain of cause and effect. And because God is Creator (and Sustainer) of all existence, God is the one being who exists outside of creation — and existed before creation. And so we say that God is eternal, because it is impossible for nothing to turn into something, and so it would be impossible for creation to come into being without a Creator, and yet it would be impossible for that Creator to come into being from nothing, therefore God has always existed (Ps. 90:1–4; 102:24–27; 2 Macc. 1:25).[6]

God has neither beginning nor end. Many other religions have believed in *immortal* beings who came into being but would live forever. But God is not immortal only, God is eternal, because God had no beginning. The Church Fathers believed that any being who had a beginning would also have an end — any being who could be "born" into existence would also eventually die. And so they reasoned that God cannot die or cease to exist.

God Is Simplex, and Incorruptible

Since God cannot die, it would be impossible for God to decay or be diminished or corrupted in any way. For the Church Fathers, any being who is born must grow, and any being who can die must get old. But God has no beginning to His existence, and therefore does not grow; and God has no end to His existence, and therefore cannot suffer entropy or decay. To say this is to say that God is incorruptible. Furthermore, any being that is corruptible is corruptible precisely because that corruption would mean a breaking down into smaller parts, and/or a breaking apart of constituent parts. But since God is incorruptible, God cannot be made up of parts at all. Therefore, God is *simplex*, meaning that Divinity is one single substance (essence) throughout, with no division of parts or smaller components of any kind. This also means that there can be no degrees of divinity — a being cannot be partly divine, nor could one being be more or less divine than another. There is only one divine being, and that is God, who is Divinity itself, one single substance with no component parts.

[6] See Theophilus of Antioch, *To Autolychus*, 1.4, 2.3, and John of Damascus, *Exposition of the Orthodox Faith*, 1.3–1.4. It was assumed by the Church Fathers that eternality is also interdependent with the attributes of perfection, incorruptibility, and immutability (see below). See also, Augustine of Hippo, *On the Trinity* 4.19.

God Is Omniscient

Since God is all-powerful, everywhere at all times, and eternal, therefore God is also all-knowing (Sir. 42:18–20).[7] God is not bound by time, and therefore does not see the universe as we see it, from within. God sees it all at once, and knows every detail of what we would call the past, present, and future. The early Christian apologist Tatian wrote:

> Why do you divide time, saying that one part is past, and another present, and another future? For how can the future be passing when the present exists? As those who are sailing imagine in their ignorance, as the ship is borne along, that the hills are in motion, so you do not know that it is you who are passing along, but that time remains present as long as the Creator wills it to exist.[8]

In other words, we may think that we are moving along through time, but God, who is outside of time, is not, and therefore God can see everything at once. God never lacks knowledge of anything, and never needs to learn anything. God is never caught by surprise.

The question of God's omniscience naturally leads to questions about the problem of evil, God's providence, and the relationship between grace and free will. There was less consensus on these questions among the Church Fathers, so it will have to be left for later to deal with some of these issues. For now, it is enough to say that, especially in the early centuries of the Church, the question of evil was answered with the conviction that God is not responsible for evil, that evil is not a created thing but rather the rejection of God's will (the absence of good), and that evil exists in the world because of the misuse of human free will. In other words, God does not cause everything that happens, but God does allow some things to happen that are against His will, because God has gifted human beings with free will (this is part of what it means to be made in the image of God), and that freedom of will includes the freedom to reject God and choose to bring evil into the world.

God Is Omnibenevolent, and Perfect

Since God is neither born and grows, nor ages and dies, it is assumed that there is no potentiality in God. The idea of potential in divinity would imply that God was once less than He is, or could be more than He is — but for the Church Fathers, that would also leave open the possibility that God could someday be less than He

7 Theophilus of Antioch, *To Autolychus*, 2.3.

8 Tatian, *Address to the Greeks*, 26, translation in Alexander Roberts and James Donaldson, eds., *Ante-Nicene Fathers*, vol. 2 (reprint, Peabody, MA: Hendrickson, 2004), 76. The word translated "time" is *aiwn*.

is now. But because God is omnipotent, omniscient, and eternal, God is therefore also perfect (Deut. 32:4; Ps. 18:30–31; 19:7–8). Perfection means that God has always been at the maximum of whatever God is and does, and has never been less so. God does not grow, and God does not learn, because it would be impossible for the omnipotent Creator to grow, or the omniscient and eternal Sustainer to learn. There is no room for growth. There is no potential in God because potential would effectively negate all of the other attributes. That's the meaning of the word "all" in *all-powerful* and *all-knowing*.

The concept of perfection is defined, in part, in terms of holiness. To say that God is perfect is to say that God is absolute holiness — that is, absolute purity. It also means, as we have seen with God's all-sufficiency, that God is absolute actualization — maximum creative activity, lacking nothing whatsoever. And since evil is the lack of good, God is completely without evil. God is maximum good. We say that God is *omnibenevolent*, or all-good. Or as John said, God is love (1 John 4:8). Of course, to be precise, it is not that we have a standard for what is good that is apart from God, by which we can measure God's goodness. Rather, God is the standard for what is good. Whatever God is, is good. Whatever God wills is good. If God were to be, or to will, something else, then *that* would be good. Yes, God is good. But really, good is whatever God is.

God Is Immutable

All of the divine attributes we've seen so far come together in the attribute of immutability, that is, that God does not change.[9] There are several reasons for this. As we have seen, change would negate perfection, since the very possibility of change requires some kind of potential in God. In order to change, God would have to have some direction in which to change, and the difference between what God was and what God becomes would be a deficiency — a gap between what is worse and what is better, and that gap is, by definition, an evil. Another reason that God must be immutable is that change is a function of time, and God is not circumscribed by time. Since God is outside of time, He cannot be measured by time. God is what God is, without regard for past, present, or future. And since God is omnipresent, God does not need to move around, which would be another kind of change.[10] But God is everywhere

[9] The best treatment of this subject is Thomas Weinandy, O.F.M. Cap., *Does God Change?* (Petersham, MA: St. Bede's, 1985). On the immutability of God, see Augustine of Hippo, *The Literal Meaning of Genesis*, 8.20–23.

[10] See Theophilus of Antioch, *To Autolychus* 1.4, 2.4; John of Damascus, *Exposition of the Orthodox Faith* 1.3–1.4; and Hippolytus, *Against Beron and Helix*. Any apparent movement

at once, and so has access to everything in the universe without needing any kind of movement other than the movement of His will.

The Scriptures of both the Old and New Testaments are clear that God does not change (Ps. 102:27; Sir. 42:21; Mal. 3:6; Heb. 13:8; James 1:17). We also read that God does not change His mind (Num. 23:19; 1 Sam. 15:29). In fact, the Jewish philosopher Philo of Alexandria argued that for God to change His mind would negate omniscience.[11] But what about those passages where it says that God "repented," or changed His mind?[12] The Church Fathers always maintained that the Scriptures have a way of anthropomorphizing God, that is, ascribing human traits to God as a way of talking about the relationship between God and the people. However, these anthropomorphisms were not meant to be taken as a "literal" description of God, but rather as a way of describing the perspective of the people. In the Septuagint (the Greek translation of the Old Testament used by Jesus, the apostles, and the earliest Christians, indicated by the abbreviation LXX) the text is "softened" to say more directly what the Hebrew version had said in figures of speech. For example, where the Hebrew text of Exodus 32:14 says, "So the Lord changed his mind about the punishment he had threatened to inflict on his people," the LXX (Septuagint) reads, "And the Lord was prevailed upon [i.e., through prayer] to preserve his people."[13] What had appeared by a figure of speech to be an indication that God might have a plan B, is explained as all part of God's eternal providential plan. This is how the Church Fathers would have interpreted any text that seems to allow for change in God. Because God is omniscient, God cannot be surprised, and God never needs a plan B.

It is important to understand that the whole concept of God's immutability is built on the foundation of the Hebrew idea of God's faithfulness, based on passages such as Psalms 100 and 136, which repeat the phrase, "his mercy endures forever." The point of God's immutability is that God is eternally unchanging in His love and compassion for humanity. Furthermore, God keeps His promises, and so God is trustworthy. As we read in Psalm 18:26–27, "Toward the faithful you are faithful;

---

or change in God is, in reality, a movement or change in us, and the relationship between ourselves and God as seen from our perspective, see Augustine of Hippo, *On the Trinity* 5.16.

[11] Philo of Alexandria, *Quod deus*, 70. Referenced in Gavrilyuk, *The Suffering of the Impassible God*, 44–45.

[12] For a list of passages that would appear to contradict each other, see Gavrilyuk, *The Suffering of the Impassible God*, 38.

[13] Gavrilyuk, *The Suffering of the Impassible God*, 39.

to the honest man you are honest; Toward the pure, you are pure; but to the perverse you are devious." Are we really to believe that God changes from faithful to devious, from one day to the next? No — God is faithful, in the sense of unchanging, but He is also unchanging in His opposition to sin and injustice. So in a way, what you bring to the table is what you have to eat. Since God is immutably holy, He is also immutably opposed to whatever is unholy. God remains the same, but the human perspective changes depending on the human situation.

Imagine a single bare light bulb shining in an otherwise darkened room. The light makes a starkly defined circle on the floor, surrounded by shadow. You may walk into the light, and you may walk out of the light, but the light does not change. You may walk right up to the bare bulb and feel its warmth, or you may walk into the cold dampness of a dark corner, but the light does not change. You may look at something that is illuminated by the light, or you may turn away from the light and look into the darkness, but the light does not change. This is something like what we mean when we say that God does not change. The human experience of a relationship with God may feel like it changes, but that's because we change, and we sin, and we repent. But God does not change. The sun seems to move in the sky, rising and setting, but that's just from our point of view, because we are really the ones who are moving.

God Is Impassible

Because God does not change, therefore God is also impassible, meaning that God does not suffer.[14] This is because suffering is a kind of change. Also, suffering implies that the victim of suffering is being acted upon by an outside superior power, and that the suffering is involuntary.[15] Yet there is no greater power than God. Any suffering implies a change in circumstances, from better to worse. Also, suffering is, by definition, a lack of something good, and since God does not lack anything good, or need anything, God cannot be said to suffer. In fact, God is so all-powerful and all-sufficient that God cannot be said to be affected by any force or entity, and God is never compelled, coerced, or made to do anything. God keeps promises because of His faithfulness, and answers prayers because of His mercy, but God is never obligated to anyone or anything, except in the sense that God is faithful and unchanging. We cannot even say that God needs humanity to express His mercy, since that would make

[14] The best treatment of this subject is Thomas Weinandy, O.F.M. Cap., *Does God Suffer?* (Edinburgh: T & T Clark, 2000).

[15] The idea of voluntary suffering is an aspect of the Incarnation, but it is not an attribute of divinity.

God dependent on creation in order to be fully divine. In other words, we cannot ever imply that God needs creation in order to be God.[16]

God's impassibility means that God is never passive. God is never acted upon but is always the actor. And since God is immutable, God is immutably active, never less than fully active, with no potential in the level of God's activity. God's activity is always creative, so we could say that God is always creating. In fact, since God is eternal, there is really no difference between God creating, or sustaining, or even redeeming. It is all God's creative activity. Another way to say this is that God can never suffer because God is always healing. If we were to ask about the passages in Scripture that say God "grieves," the answer would be the same as for those that say God changes his mind. This is a projection of human emotions onto God meant to explain the human experience of God from the human perspective. Human beings suffer when we feel pain or loss, but in God there is no pain or loss. Human suffering is heightened when we experience regret for the past, or fear for the future, but since God is eternal, He has no regrets and no fears. Human suffering is, in part, a significant limitation of our freedom, but God is unlimited, and to ascribe suffering to God is to put a limit on God of one kind or another. God is not simply incapable of suffering, God is beyond suffering.[17] And in this way, God is able to alleviate human suffering (Rev. 21:4).

Misunderstanding God's Immutability

Unfortunately, many theologians of the twentieth and twenty-first centuries have misunderstood the concept of divine immutability, with very confusing results. They have read into the idea a host of perceived problems that early Jews and Christians would not recognize as having anything to do with divine immutability.[18] Therefore, it is important to be clear about what the doctrine of divine immutability does *not* say about God. The fact that God is immutable does not mean that God is static, aloof, or uncaring. In fact, it is just the opposite. God is immutably and eternally at the maximum of activity, love, and mercy. There is no potential for more of these because in God they

[16] Thomas Weinandy, O.F.M. Cap., "God and Human Suffering: His Act of Creation and His Acts in History," in *Divine Impassibility and the Mystery of Human Suffering*, ed. James F. Keating and Thomas Joseph White, O.P. (Grand Rapids: Eerdmans, 2009), 111.

[17] David Bentley Hart, "Impassibility as Transcendence: On the Infinite Innocence of God," in *Divine Impassibility and the Mystery of Human Suffering*, ed. James F. Keating and Thomas Joseph White, O.P., 300.

[18] One of the best treatments (and critique) of the contemporary theologians' misunderstanding of divine immutability is Gavrilyuk, *The Suffering of the Impassible God*. See also Fr. Thomas Weinandy's two books, *Does God Change?* and *Does God Suffer?*.

are eternally "turned up to eleven" as it were. God is never less than fully active, in fact God *is* pure activity. God is never less than fully loving, because God *is* love. A god who could change would have to change for the worse, since God is, and has always been, ultimate in every good thing. Far from being a limitation, God's immutability means that He is unlimited, but also consistent. God is faithful and trustworthy in unchangeable love (cf. Ex. 34:7; Ps. 106:7, 119:41).

Misunderstanding God's Impassibility

Since immutability and impassibility go hand in hand, the same contemporary theologians have also gravely misunderstood the doctrine of divine impassibility.[19] They read it as though it implies, again, a lack of compassion in God. Many make the mistake of limiting the definition of the word *compassion,* to the facile "suffer along with," which hardly captures the full range of meaning, especially in the biblical languages. Compassion cannot be reduced to "misery loves company," for this is self-centered.[20] The truth is quite the opposite in fact, because real compassion requires impassibility, if the one showing compassion is not to be overwhelmed by the pain of the one who is suffering. If God were not impassible, then God would be powerless over suffering.[21]

Another way to say this is that when one is sick, one does not need another sick person to commiserate with — one needs a doctor, and preferably one who is not sick herself. God does not need to be passible to have mercy on humanity any more than a physician needs to have a disease in order to heal a patient. The Good Samaritan did not hire thugs to beat him up and throw him into the ditch with the injured man, but rather he pulled the man out of the ditch and paid the innkeeper to nurse him back to health. Only one who is not in the ditch can pull someone else out.

The Church Fathers would say that projecting human emotions on God is an attempt to make God in our image. God does not need to have human feelings like pain in order to love humanity. More precisely, God is not susceptible to the negative aspects of human emotion, Old Testament anthropomorphisms notwithstanding. God is not happy with us one day and angry with us the next — any difference we may perceive in our relationship with God over time is the result of us changing, not God. God does not have more love or compassion for any of us, simply because we

[19] Paul L. Gavrilyuk, "God's Impassible Suffering in the Flesh: The Promise of Paradoxical Christology," in *Divine Impassibility and the Mystery of Human Suffering,* ed. James F. Keating and Thomas Joseph White, O.P., 137, 143.

[20] Gavrilyuk, *The Suffering of the Impassible God,* 12.

[21] Gavrilyuk, "God's Impassible Suffering in the Flesh," 140–141. See also Tertullian, *Against Praxeas* 29.

suffer — God's love and compassion were already at the ultimate and will always be consistently so. God's love is not measured by our standards, and in fact it's not about feelings at all, it's about God's active presence. So the immutability and impassibility of God are not limitations on divine imminence, but expressions of God's faithful, consistent, reliable, and trustworthy unlimited giving of Himself.

Sacrificing Immutability and Impassibility for Sentimentality

Nevertheless, with all of these caveats in mind, there are still those who misconstrue these important patristic doctrines, and it will be imperative to be clear about what the Church Fathers meant (and what they did not mean) as you read the early Christian documents. Perhaps the most influential of the contemporary theologians who misunderstand these doctrines is Jurgen Moltmann, who famously wrote, "Were God incapable of suffering in any respect, and therefore in an absolute sense, then he would also be incapable of love."[22] To be fair to Moltmann, you can see that he qualified the statement with the phrases, "in any respect," and "in an absolute sense," however it has become commonplace among those who came after him to boil the sentence down to the very succinct maxim, "a god who cannot suffer is a god who cannot love." In addition to destroying the very definition of love by equating it with suffering, this pithy phrase has the ultimate effect of putting exactly the kind of limits on God that the contemporary theologians would want to avoid.

To say that God must suffer is to say that God must be susceptible to change, and this is to make God subject to time, and therefore circumscribed by creation. This is exactly what process theologians have done, with the addition of ascribing potential to God, such that God might grow, learn, or improve. It is important to clarify this as you begin a journey through the early Church and the Church Fathers because for some theologians writing today, God is neither omniscient, nor perfect. Often, they have come to this conclusion because they have decided that an eternally perfect and omniscient God would have created a better world than we seem to have. But that is putting the cart before the horse. If God is not eternally perfect, then the very concept of holiness loses its meaning. And to propose that God is circumscribed by creation in the sense that He is bound by the passage of time, is to describe a panentheistic god, not the God of the Hebrew and Christian Scriptures. But God is not fickle or capricious like the gods of the Greco-Roman pantheon. The point

[22] Jurgen Moltmann, *The Crucified God: The Cross of Christ as the Foundation and Criticism of Christian Theology* (San Francisco: Harper and Row, 1974), 230, quoted in "Introduction: Divine Impassibility in Contemporary Theology," in *Divine Impassibility and the Mystery of Human Suffering*, ed. James F. Keating and Thomas Joseph White, O.P., 3.

of passages like Malachi 3:6, is that our God is always faithful to keep covenant promises and never fails to love humanity completely. To speculate on a patristic answer to the Moltmannian maxim, I believe that the Church Fathers would reply, "A god who is not immutable is a god who is not trustworthy."

The Divine Sweater

All of these assumed attributes of God are interdependent, and mutually supportive. The fact that there is only one God is directly related to the fact that this God is omnipresent, omnipotent, and eternal — and this, in turn, means that God is omniscient, perfect, and omnibenevolent. In the same way, the Church Fathers reasoned God must be *simplex*, and incorruptible. The attributes are not separate things, but rather like a sweater knitted from a single thread, and that thread is what we call the substance of Divinity. In fact, St. Augustine, the fifth century bishop of Hippo in North Africa, wrote that God does not "have" attributes, as if we could somehow imagine these attributes as things distinct from God Himself — no, God does not "have" anything, God simply is what and who God is.[23] So these attributes are not possessions of God, but rather describe God's very being.

Having said that, we should notice that all of these attributes are really what we would call *apophatic*, or in the Latin, they come to God by the *via negativa* (the negative way). In other words, they describe God by saying more about what God is *not*, than about what God *is*. This means that we must maintain a certain humility which admits that our finite minds could never really know what God is, but we can approach some measure of knowledge of God by describing what God is not. And so when we say God is one, omnipresent, omnipotent, and eternal, we are saying that God is not limited by anything in creation, and that God is uncreated — there is no beginning to His existence. God is not limited by a need for any other gods, God's will and power are not subject to any limitations, and God's influence is not limited by any boundaries of space or time. In fact, miracles would be completely impossible if God were not bringing power from outside of the tangible world's physical laws. We cannot know the "size" of God, but we can know that God is uncircumscribable. When we say that God is omniscient, we are saying that God is not limited in terms of knowledge or wisdom. We cannot know what God does know, but we can say what God doesn't know, which is nothing. When we say that God is perfect, and omnibenevolent, we are saying that God is not accountable to the judgment or scrutiny of any other being — not that God is morally neutral, but that goodness itself is defined by God, and evil is the absence of good, or the rejection of God and

[23] Augustine of Hippo, *On the Trinity*, 5.8.9.

God's will. God is *Im*mortal because He cannot die, God is *In*corporeal because He is pure spirit and without a physical body, God is *In*visible because He can't be perceived with the senses, and God is *In*compresensible because we can never fully understand Him.[24]

The same can be said when we come to God's immutability and impassibility. These words tell us that we can trust God because we know something about what God is *not* like. God is immutable because God is not fickle or a trickster, or in any way untrustworthy (like many of the gods of the Greco-Roman pantheon). God is impassible because God is not limited in any way by any created boundaries. God's impassibility means that God is transcendent, and therefore cannot be acted upon by any outside force that would compel God to respond in any way. Because God is uncreated, God is in a completely separate category of existence from creation. Everything that exists is either Creator or creation; there are no degrees of createdness. And only God (the Trinity) is Creator, and therefore uncreated. Everything else that exists is created.

However, the Church Fathers believed that if we pull at one end of the thread, the whole sweater will unravel. If God is not in a category of His own, apart from creation, then God could not be the Creator, since whatever is created could not be the ultimate Source and origin of all creation, let alone sustain or redeem it. And if God is bound by the passage of time, then that would put God within time, and therefore within creation, and that would make God a creature, who needs things, rather than the Creator who gives what creation needs. God cannot be a receiver of anything, because God is the source of everything.[25] And if God could suffer, then God would need to be saved. But God cannot need salvation, because God is Savior. Therefore the Church Fathers would say that is inappropriate to describe God in any way that implies that God is enhanced by, or benefits from, historical realities. God acts in history, but history does not act on God. So, God's compassion and mercy are not a "suffering with" the sinner, but rather forgiveness, redemption, and salvation of the sinner by overcoming the very thing that distances the sinner from God. God's compassion is demonstrated in salvation, not in wallowing in the very things from which people need to be saved.[26]

But we should remember that the Church Fathers never thought of immutability or impassibility as implying that God is uncaring, inactive, or distant. God's immutability means that He is ultimate love, and unceasing action. God's impassibility

[24] Gavrilyuk, "God's Impassible Suffering in the Flesh," 139.

[25] Weinandy, O.F.M. Cap., "God and Human Suffering," 109.

[26] Weinandy, O.F.M. Cap., "God and Human Suffering," 112–113.

means that He is unfazedly immanent (and imminent). So it is not as though God cannot be in solidarity with humanity — as we will see, this is exactly what God does in the Incarnation — but in our quest for precision of language, there are better ways to speak of God's solidarity and compassion than to ascribe passibility, and mutability, since emphasizing divine immanence at the expense of divine transcendence puts limits on the power of God to heal and redeem creation and save humanity.

How to Read Early Christian Texts

Before we can begin to examine the various writers and documents of the postapostolic age and beyond, we need to pause for a moment to address the differences between the writings of the early Church and modern literature. It is tempting to read early Christian documents as though they always give us the facts as they were, however, often the authors are presenting more of a wish list than a news report. We must keep in mind that most of the early Christian writers were not consciously writing history for our benefit, they were writing for the people of their own time, to convince them of something. Therefore, the following caveats will be helpful to keep in mind while reading the patristic documents.

Don't assume uniformity across the empire, or uniformity of development.

Just because a certain document includes evidence of a particular belief or practice, one cannot generalize that belief or practice as if it were universally held by the whole Church. As long as the Church was not legally recognized, communication could be somewhat limited between cities, and especially between the eastern and western halves of the empire. Even where communication was easy, Christians in different areas did not necessarily agree. Proof of this is in the New Testament itself, where many of the earliest Christian documents (the letters of Paul) would not exist if it were not for conflict and disagreement. Therefore, one must take the origin of a document into consideration when one is trying to determine what the Church believed and practiced. In reality, the old impression of the early Church (based on Acts 2:44), that it was characterized by a uniformity that was eventually lost and never regained, is probably far from the truth. In fact, as it happened, it was most likely quite the opposite. For example, there was certainly a significant amount of diversity of liturgical practice within the early Church that over time went through a kind of standardization as the boundaries of what was acceptable were drawn.[27] And of course, much like documents in the New

[27] I am indebted to Paul Bradshaw for this insight, and for the idea of creating a list of caveats for reading patristic texts. See his more specialized list for reading early liturgical texts, "Ten Principles for Interpreting Early Christian Liturgical Evidence," in *The Making of*

Testament, many of our patristic documents would never have been written had it not been for the reality of disagreements and controversies.

In addition to diversity across the empire, we also have to acknowledge a diversity across time. In other words, we cannot assume that traditions developed at the same rate from one place to another. For example, if we can determine that the shift from an evening *agape* meal to Sunday morning Eucharist had taken place by the mid-second century in Rome, for example, that does not necessarily mean that it had also developed in Antioch by the same time. The end result is the same: just because a document provides evidence of a belief or practice at a particular place and time in history (assuming that the document can even be dated with accuracy), that does not necessarily mean that the same belief or practice was held in other places at the same time, or in other times at the same place.

Don't assume that something is new the first time it is mentioned.

Unfortunately, there are many early Christian documents that we no longer possess. Some were lost to the decay of time; others were deliberately destroyed. In fact, there may be more documents that we *don't* have, than that we do. The documents available to us are called *extant*, which simply means that they still exist. But the fact that there are many missing pieces of the early Christian puzzle means that we cannot assume that a lack of mention of something in the extant sources is definitive proof that it did not exist. Silence is not proof of absence, though it may be one piece of evidence in that direction. We also cannot assume that the early Christian writers told us everything, or even tried to. Often the beliefs and practices most universally agreed upon in the early Church are the very ones that no one bothered to write about. Why take up precious parchment or vellum writing down what everyone already agrees about? For the most part, issues are discussed precisely because they are not agreed upon.

Therefore, if something shows up for the first time in a certain document written at a certain time, we cannot assume that it did not exist in the Church before then. In fact, it is safer to assume that it was not new, since as we will see, the early Christians were often skeptical of anything new, and to be accepted, an idea had to have at least an air of age to it.[28] On the other hand, it is also possible that an author will exaggerate the length of time a particular practice has been around in order to enhance its credibility.

Jewish and Christian Worship, ed. Paul F. Bradshaw and Lawrence Hoffman (Notre Dame, IN: University of Notre Dame Press, 1991), 3–21.

[28] Theophilus of Antioch, *To Autolycus*, 3.29.

Don't assume that a tone of certainty is evidence of agreement.

Since the main reason for writing was often to enter into debate and convince someone of a particular point of view, the authors of early Christian documents will naturally write as though what they are saying is the only reasonable point of view. However, here we need to read between the lines and recognize that if, for example, St. Ignatius of Antioch says that everyone knows there should be only one bishop in each city, there is obviously some disagreement on that point or he wouldn't bother to write it. If everyone really did know it, they would not need Ignatius to tell them. Therefore, if an early Christian writer takes the attitude that "everyone knows this is how it's always been done," you can be sure that someone was out there doing it differently.

When reading patristic texts, always ask yourself why the text was written. Who is the opponent? What is the agenda? In order to properly interpret a document, we must keep these things clear in our minds, especially when the authors resort to ridicule and name-calling (and they do).

Don't assume that the content of early Christian documents is raw information.

Remember that reading patristic texts is not like reading a contemporary history. The aim of early Christian authors was never just to report the facts, but to convince and convert. We must assume that even when they are reporting historical events, the documents already contained at least one layer of interpretation. This is because the ultimate goal of early Christian authors was to promote a Christ-centered view of history, and while it is certainly the case that they believed Christ to be Truth incarnate, this conviction did not lead them to create unbiased accounts. On the contrary, their accounts are biased because they are first and foremost statements of faith. Therefore, early Christian texts of the postapostolic period and beyond are not to be treated as divinely inspired. They are the product of sincere, but evangelistically motivated Christians attempting to interpret the inspired texts and the events of history, both of which they believed to be products of God's providence. But, to put it bluntly, they could be wrong at times. A case in point is Irenaeus of Lyons, who was a brilliant theologian and a pioneer in the interpretation of Scripture, but nevertheless had his Roman history wrong, and thought that Jesus had lived in the time of Claudius.[29] Eusebius of

[29] Irenaeus of Lyons, *Demonstration* [or *Proof*] *of the Apostolic Preaching*, 74. See also Irenaeus of Lyons, *Against Heresies*, 2.22.5–6, where Irenaeus relates a tradition that Jesus' ministry lasted only one year. See also 3.21.3, where Irenaeus says that Jesus' ministry lasted ten years and that he was in his forties when he died, demonstrating that he is in many cases only passing on what he has heard, even if that means including contradictory oral tradition.

Caesarea, the first Christian historian, combined oral and written records to create his *Ecclesiastical History*, but at times he simply reports competing traditions, and leaves the contradictions up to the reader to decide.

For our purposes, we will still focus on the patristic documents as the *primary sources*, that is, as the best record of the history of the early Church, and we will take them as reliable in the absence of contradictory evidence. Eusebius is an especially valuable source, and often he is our only source of information about the Church Fathers and their writings, sometimes preserving documents (or fragments of documents) that are otherwise not extant. We simply have to keep in mind that he was a fourth-century writer, in the East, who seemed to have as his agenda a desire to promote the glory of the Constantinian dynasty. Therefore, we take his word with a grain of salt when he is transmitting traditions from the first centuries of the Church, or from the West, or from sources hostile to his cause. At one point this bishop of Caesarea was even questioned as to the orthodoxy of his faith (that he might have leaned toward Arianism), and so this, too, must be kept in mind.

Don't assume that people in the ancient world are less enlightened than modern people. Ever since the Enlightenment, there has been a kind of modernist arrogance which assumes that the later one lives in time, the more "advanced" one must necessarily be. This is partly based on the realities of the Scientific and Industrial Revolutions, but when reading ancient texts, the reader has to keep in mind that this does not mean that in the realms of philosophy or theology, the reader is automatically superior to the author. It is true, on the one hand, that ancient authors had their biases, agendas, and to a certain extent, outdated worldviews — but on the other hand, the modern world is hard pressed to come up with very many who can match the Doctors of the Church. So when it comes to the Church Fathers, the reader should approach the text as a student, open to learning from the wisdom of the geniuses and spiritual giants of the early Church.

Always beware of approaching the text with condescension, as if the document is a quaint artifact to be read as a curiosity only. Never presume to think that you read with a neutrality that allows you to be an unbiased judge over the content. Beware of what Henri de Lubac warned of, when he wrote, "We think that we can affirm tolerance is making progress. What we don't realize is that a new intolerance has taken the place of the old one."[30] As Edward Oakes has commented, "No one is more prejudiced than someone who thinks he is without prejudices."[31]

[30] Henri de Lubac, *Paradoxes of Faith*, trans. Earnest Beaumont (San Francisco: Ignatius Press, 1987), 161.

[31] Oakes, S.J., *Infinity Dwindled to Infancy*, 115.

Don't assume that anyone in the text looks like you.

When you read the ancient Christian documents, I hope you will read them with a sense of familial connection, that is, that you will see yourself as part of the legacy whose inheritance is this deep well of tradition. The early Church tradition belongs to all Christians, whether Orthodox, Catholic, or Protestant. This is your heritage.

On the other hand, the world of the Church Fathers was a very different world from our own. So in that sense, while it may be tempting to project yourself into the text and see the people there as being like you, in many ways they are not. This is why we are taking the time to learn about their assumptions about God and the way they wrote their documents before we start actually reading. An important case in point is the issue of race, racism, and slavery. The truth is that skin color was not much more important to people in the ancient world than hair color. Only rarely is it even mentioned in the patristic texts, but it is almost never connected to any kind of prejudice, let alone slavery. In reality, we have no idea of the skin color of the authors of our documents because no one bothered to write it down. So we cannot assume we know who in the early Church might look like us, and we can be sure that what we think of as white skin was probably not the majority.

Finally, you will read about slavery in the Roman world, and you will be disappointed to learn that some of the early Christians owned slaves. From our perspective we would wish that their Christian Faith would prevent them from participating in such an evil system, but they were a persecuted minority in an empire where they could never dream of the idea of "changing the world." Social transformation was not on their radar, but they did pioneer a morality that rejected and critiqued prostitution, the sexual abuse of slaves, and the sexual abuse of minors. Nevertheless, it would not be until the third century when we have an extant theologian making a case against slavery from the doctrine of the *imago Dei.*[32]

The point for the moment is that slavery in the ancient world was a very different thing from what it would become later, in the history of the Americas and in our own country of the United States. As I hinted above, one of the most important differences was that slavery in the ancient world was not based on any assumptions that connected skin color to a person's status. Slavery in the ancient world was based on the rights of conquest, not on any belief that skin color indicated degrees of humanity.

[32] Novatian, *On the Trinity,* 1.10. Novatian says, "humanity must be free, since slavery is inconsistent with the dignity of the image of God." Translation of the complete works of Novatian by the present author in James L. Papandrea, *Novatian: On the Trinity, Letters to Cyprian of Carthage, Ethical Treatises* (Corpus Christianorum in Translation Series) (Turnhout, Belgium: Brepols, 2015).

In other words, if the Romans conquered the Greeks in a war, the Romans took Greeks into slavery. But if the tables were turned, Romans could (theoretically) just as easily end up as slaves to conquering Greeks. Another way that a person might become a slave was as punishment for a crime. This means that as you read about slaves and masters, you must resist the temptation to imagine the slaves as having darker skin than their owners. It is certain that most slaves in the Roman world were not of African descent, and it is likely that many slave owners had darker skin than their slaves. A person could be any color and that would not have anything to do with his or her social class.

In addition to working within a household or on a farm or ranch, slaves did many of the same jobs that free people might do. In fact, the consolidation of land outside of Rome into large slave-run estates meant that the city had an increasingly large population of freeborn workers (including former farm hands) who were unemployed or underemployed, and who resented the slaves whom they perceived were taking jobs away from them. Many of the slaves were not Italians, and yet if they were the slaves of citizens, they had a track toward citizenship, and even upward mobility. Freedmen of citizens were citizens, and although they could not rise into the equestrian class, their sons could. Therefore, the situation of slavery was not considered permanent, and many slaves could look forward to manumission and even some measure of upward mobility. Obviously, this is not to imply that slavery was a benefit. Slaves were still always at the mercy of their owners and susceptible to sexual abuse, physical punishment, and the separation of families.

This is also not to imply that the ancient world was without racism. Racism existed, but it was not based on skin color, or in fact on anything one could see. On any given day there could be hundreds of people milling around and walking through the Roman forum, and apart from the way they dressed, you might not know by looking at them who were the free, the slaves, the rich, or the poor. However, you could tell by listening to them. Racism in the ancient world was not based on what you looked like, it was based on what you sounded like. A person who spoke Greek and Latin well would be considered civilized. A person who could not speak Greek or Latin, or perhaps spoke with a distinctive accent, would be considered a "foreigner," or even a "barbarian," and could well be discriminated against. So racism, such as it was in the ancient world, was based on where one came from — that was one's "race."

But it's important to recognize that Christian tradition is not the product of only one culture. It was global from the beginning, and was unified, not by ethnic traits, but by a common commitment to identify with Christ through worship, creed, and sacrament, and by a common attempt to live a life of gratitude toward God by "paying forward" the mercy God has shown, as Jesus taught in His parable of the unmerciful servant (Matt. 18:21–35). This means that no one group in existence can claim any special ownership of the gospel, except in the sense of a historic connection going back through time to the apostles and Jesus Himself. To remain in the Church is to inherit the legacy of the apostles, regardless of one's ethnic, cultural, national, social, or economic background.

And so that brings us back to the issue of social location — where you come from. As a reader, it's important to know as much about where the text, and the author, come from, so that you can read between the lines and understand the meaning in the document. But with that in mind, it is still possible to put yourself into the world of the early Church, and connect with the people you meet there — they are your ancestors in the Faith; they are your cloud of witnesses.

2

What Do You Mean by *Church*?

What's a *Church*?

In the Gospels, there are two times when Jesus used the word *church* (the Greek word is *ekklesia*). In Matthew 16:18, Jesus said to St. Peter, "And so I say to you, you are Peter, and upon this rock I will build my church, and the gates of the netherworld shall not prevail against it." Two chapters later (18:17) Jesus refers to the church as a group of people who would exercise discipline over its members, even to the point of excommunicating a member who remains obstinate. In the book of Acts and the rest of the New Testament, the word *church* is used many times to describe the universal body of the followers of "The Way" (the Church) or the local congregations meeting in various cities (the churches).[1]

To be precise, Jesus probably did not use the Greek word *ekklesia,* because He was probably not speaking Greek when He was speaking to His disciples. He was probably speaking Aramaic. No one really knows what Aramaic word Jesus would have used here, but we know it wasn't the word for synagogue, otherwise Matthew would have used that word when writing the Gospel in Greek. Whatever the Aramaic word was, the author of our first Gospel believed that *ekklesia* was the best Greek word to translate it. And *ekklesia* is not a building, nor even an institution, but it can mean anything from a political party to a military regiment. It is a group of people with a mission, grounded in a common worldview. And that's what Jesus was starting.

So the first thing we have to remember when we think of the beginnings of the Church is that there were no "churches" in the sense of church buildings, built specifically for Christian worship.[2] One could not walk down the street and see "*a*

[1] Throughout the present book, the word *Church* is capitalized when it refers to the universal Church, and not capitalized when it refers to a local congregation or city church, i.e., the Christians in a particular place.

[2] The earliest use of the word *church* to refer to a place of worship seems to be in Clement of Alexandria, *The Instructor,* 3.11, written in the late second century. However, even here it

church." Christians met in homes, in groups small enough to fit into one room of a house or apartment. As the group of Christians in any given city grew to the point where they all could no longer fit into one house, the group divided between two or more houses.[3] Therefore, *the Church* was not yet a tangible entity, but more of a concept. It was the Body of Christ, understood to be the extension of the Kingdom of God on earth, and it existed wherever people gathered at the table of Christ, in the name of Christ (Matt. 18:20).

Initiation into the Church was, of course, by Baptism, and thus Baptism formed the boundary of the Church. In other words, the Church was the worldwide community of the baptized, and the local expression of the Church was a group of the baptized in a particular city. Baptism required catechesis, so the local communities of Christians quickly devised methods for training initiates and preparing them for Baptism. This would eventually evolve into the catechetical "school," which could be very informal, or in the larger cities it could be a more formal program, something like the philosophical schools of the time. Early Christian catechesis focused more on ethical concerns than theology, and from the very beginning it was extremely important to draw the lines of distinction between the morals of the Church and the morals of the rest of Greco-Roman culture and society.[4] Baptism was considered a serious commitment, one that required a significant lifestyle change (especially for former pagans) and therefore could not be undertaken without preparation.[5] Baptism also required sponsorship, that is, the endorsement of someone already within the Church to vouch for the new convert's sincerity and readiness to accept the moral expectations of a baptized Christian.

---

does not refer to a church *building*, but to a dedicated worship space, probably a converted home.

3 Early house-church divisions may have been along ethnic (language) lines, socioeconomic lines, or geographic lines in the larger cities.

4 See Justin Martyr, *1 Apology*, 16.8.

5 The word *pagan* is used here without the pejorative connotation it might have had in the early Church. The English word comes from the Latin *pagani*, which referred to the country dwellers, those outside of the urban areas. In the time after Christianity was legalized, some claimed that the only people who held on to the Greco-Roman mythologies were the people in the rural areas, since many cities were coming to have a Christian majority in their population. It is, admittedly, also used somewhat anachronistically when applied in the early centuries of the Church. In the present context, it simply refers to anyone who was not Christian or Jewish, and it assumes that participating in the traditional Greco-Roman worship would be considered a form of idolatry for Jews and Christians.

Since the Church was understood to be the extension of God's reign on earth, and since the conflict between Church and culture would soon force the Church into an "us versus them" position, the boundary lines of the Church became tied not only to the initiation of Baptism, but also to the goal or culmination of initiation, the table of the Eucharist. In other words, what Baptism initiated one into, was the mystery of the Incarnation of Christ, celebrated — but also participated in — at the eucharistic table. The table of the Lord *was* the Kingdom of God on earth, the down payment of the Christian's heavenly inheritance. Therefore, salvation itself, as participation in Christ, was embodied in the Eucharist, and so the Church came to be defined by the table. And since salvation was found at the table of the Eucharist, and the Eucharist was found in the assembly of the Church, the early Christians believed that there was no salvation outside the Church.[6]

The Church in the Apostolic Age

Near as we can tell, it was in the year AD 33 that a series of events took place that would change the world forever. Jesus gathered His disciples around a table in an upper room, instituted a sacred meal, and told all of His followers to "do this in remembrance of me" (Luke 22:19; 1 Cor. 11:24). The next day He was executed by crucifixion, and on the third day after that, He overcame death and rose to life again. Forty days later, He ascended into the heavenly realm, taking with Him His human body — glorified, and yet still showing the scars of His sacrifice. Ten days after that, His Holy Spirit entered all of His followers and filled them with grace and divine power, transforming them from frightened sheep without a shepherd to bold evangelists. Immediately they were persecuted, and the deacon Stephen became the first victim of anti-Christian violence — the first martyr. But not very long after that, the chief persecutor was converted to the movement and Saul the Pharisee became Paul the evangelist. And so the Church was thrust upon the world, and the world hated it, from embarrassment.

In about the year AD 42, Peter came to Rome and found the Church there already established, but in need of a leader. No doubt Roman Jews who had been in Jerusalem almost a decade earlier remembered hearing him preach that first Christian homily (Acts 2:14–41). As the leader of the apostles, he was welcomed in Rome as its first apostolic overseer. In the year AD 50, he would have traveled back to Jerusalem for the first council of the Church (Acts 15; Gal. 2).

Paul wrote the letters that would become a major part of the New Testament in the fifties and sixties of that first century. The first Gospels were also probably being written at this time. Although many scholars would date the writing of the Gospels

[6] Ignatius of Antioch, *Letter to the Philadelphians*, 3.3.

later, the fact that the deaths of Peter and Paul are not recorded in the book of Acts places the writing of Acts (and Luke before it) prior to the mid-sixties. Both Peter and Paul were martyred in Rome sometime between the years AD 64 and AD 68. Their tombs are, of course, still there to this day, directly under the altars of the basilicas that are dedicated to them.

The rest of the New Testament was written in the second half of the first century, with the apostle John living the longest — according to tradition into the second century. But the fact that the apostles spread out and died at different times means that the transition of leadership from the people who knew Jesus personally to those who didn't was not consistent in terms of time or geography. We know that the apostle Paul chose his successors in various cities and commissioned them with the laying on of hands (1 Tim. 4:14). Therefore, it is reasonable to assume that, as tradition tells us, Peter and the other apostles similarly chose their own successors, which not only mirrors the way in which Jesus appointed those whom He sent out, but also effectively established what would become the sacrament of Holy Orders, or ordination. Thus the selection of the second generation of leaders, at least in the case of the successors of the apostles, was based on an apprenticeship model. What this shows us is that there has always been a hierarchy of authority in the Church, which both served to maintain unity across the Church, but also tolerated a measure of diversity of practice from one city to another.

In those places where the local churches were founded without an apostolic evangelist, the succession of leaders may have been accomplished by vote of the baptized members. Eventually, all the local churches would move to election as the method for selecting leaders. The point is that from the very beginning, the Church was both universal and local (see 1 Cor. 1:1–3).

Since the leadership of the Church was founded on discipleship, the teachings of Jesus and the apostles were handed down from one generation of leaders to the next with an emphasis on unity of doctrine across the Church. Catechesis, preaching, and liturgy reinforced the teachings to prevent them from becoming "diverted to myths" (2 Tim. 4:3–4). We can already see evidence in the New Testament documents of "false teachings" and "other gospels" that are perceived as distorting the message that Jesus and the apostles delivered. The word *heresy,* meaning a divergence from what is correct — a kind of going off on a tangent — is used to describe these alternative teachings.

The word *orthodoxy,* meaning correct teachings or doctrine (literally, "correct praise") is used to describe the accepted teachings handed down from Jesus and the apostles to their successors. *Heresy* and *orthodoxy* are the nouns used to refer to the teachings themselves. The adjectives are *heretical* and *orthodox* respectively. (Note that *orthodox* and *orthodoxy* are spelled with a lowercase letter *o*, as opposed to *Orthodox* with a capital *O* which refers to the eastern Christian communions after the split of West and East in the eleventh century). The word *orthodox* can also be used to describe those who affirm and promote the orthodox teachings, while those who teach heresy are referred to as heretics. But note that to be a heretic means more than simply being wrong about something. Many people can be innocently mistaken. To be a heretic is to teach heresy, to lead the innocent astray, and to refuse to come back within the boundaries of orthodoxy when confronted by leaders in the Church. As the author of *2 Clement* wrote, "Now if they alone were doing these things, it could be endured, but now they persist in teaching evil to innocent souls."[7] The danger of heresy is, of course, that people's salvation is at stake. To believe the wrong things about the Savior is to put one's faith in a *different* savior — one who doesn't exist and cannot save. And if enough people were to follow a heretic, that would cause a *schism*, or a split of the Church.

All of this leads us to two important points about the early Church. First, despite the insistence of some to speak of "proto-orthodoxy," or "pre-orthodoxy," there was never a time in the history of the Church without a consensus over what orthodoxy is. It is not the case that orthodoxy is an invention of the fourth century, that it has anything to do with the legalization of Christianity, or that it coincides with the ecumenical councils or with the Church's later connection to the Roman Empire. We can already see by the way Paul and the other apostles clarify the difference between true and false teachings that there is an orthodoxy in every generation of the Church, and that each generation's orthodoxy is built on the foundation of the previous generation's orthodoxy. This is not to say that doctrine doesn't develop — it does develop over time — by which we mean that it comes to be more fleshed out and clarified. Doctrine develops, but it does not evolve — in other words, it does not change so much that what is heresy in one generation could be orthodoxy in the next, or vice versa. This never happened. And therefore, there is no Church prior to orthodoxy, since from the beginning each generation of the Church has a consensus about what orthodoxy is, and by contrast what heresy is.

The second point is that there is, in each generation of the Church's history, a majority that adheres to the teachings that were faithfully passed down from the previous generation. In this book, we will refer to this majority consensus as the "mainstream" Church. (This is not to be confused with the term "mainline," which in the contemporary situation refers to the major Protestant denominations.) The

[7] *Second Clement*, 10.5, translation in Michael W. Holmes, ed., *The Apostolic Fathers: Greek Texts and English Translations* (Grand Rapids: Baker Academic, 2007), 151.

mainstream Church is the orthodox Church which teaches the orthodox doctrines. And while there was significant room for a diversity of liturgical and devotional practices in the early Church, the very unity of the Body of Christ was seen as residing in the unity of acceptance of the orthodox doctrines and was (at least theoretically) guaranteed by the discipleship and apprenticeship model of the choosing and commissioning of the successors to the apostles as Church leaders.

The history of the Church is in many ways the history of the teachings that were passed down from the beginning, including the interpretation of the Scriptures, and then adding the writings of the Church Fathers, all of which become the Tradition of the Church. The early Church was not a *sola scriptura* Church, which becomes obvious when we see that for most of the first century the Christian Bible was the Old Testament (the Greek version, the Septuagint), and that even when the New Testament was becoming compiled, most Christians only ever heard the Scriptures read as part of the liturgy — lay Christians never owned their own Bibles, and did not read them privately. And even when the New Testament was written and compiled, it was seen as a collection of the Tradition of the Church, such as it was up until that point. And then each generation of Church Fathers relied on previous generations of Church Fathers for authoritative interpretations of Scripture. Therefore Scripture is a part of the Tradition of the Church, and while it may be thought of as set apart from the rest of Tradition in the sense that it is inspired in a way that makes it infallible and authoritative for the whole Church, there was never a time when Scripture was separate from Tradition, or when Tradition could be set aside as though it did not include Scripture.

As we begin to think about the history of interpretation and the development of doctrine, there are three observable laws (as I have called them) of historical theology.[8] They are:

1. *Heresy forces orthodoxy to define itself.* This means that often orthodoxy is assumed, but not clarified, until it is challenged by an alternative interpretation or teaching. It is often only after this challenge that the orthodox position is clarified, over against the heretical teaching, which facilitates the development of doctrine over time.

2. *Orthodoxy is the middle way between the extreme alternatives.* The history of interpretation is like a pendulum. When an alternative interpretation or teaching goes to an extreme, there is a "center of gravity" in the mainstream that wants to pull it back to the center. However, there are always those who would overreact to

[8] I first wrote about the three laws of the development of doctrine in my 2012 book, *Trinity 101: Father, Son, Holy Spirit* (Liguori, MO: Liguori, 2012).

the alternative, and by doing so go to the other extreme and create another alternative. Orthodoxy is always the middle between the extremes, not in the sense of a compromise, but in the sense of the refusal to avoid mystery and paradox by creating either-or answers to important questions. For example, as we will see, one of the most important tasks of the early Church was to elaborate on Peter's answer to Jesus' question, "Who do you say that I am?" (Matt. 16:15). This is the question of christology. And as we will see in the chapters that follow, there were those who would answer the question by saying that Jesus was human, but not divine (one extreme). Then there were those who would answer the question by saying that Jesus is divine but not human (the other extreme). The orthodox answer, however, was that Jesus is both divine and human. Taking the middle way in this sense means rejecting the simplistic either-or answer in favor of the both-and answer. It means embracing paradox and mystery, and it means refusing to rule out some Scripture passages in favor of others. Those who taught the extreme positions were asking *which* Scripture passages were true — those that spoke of His humanity, or those that spoke of His divinity. The mainstream Church refused to ask *which* ones were true, but rather asked *how* it could be explained that both sets of Scripture passages are true.[9]

3. *Christology informs soteriology* (and vice versa). Christology (what we believe about Jesus Christ) and soteriology (what we believe about salvation) are interdependent. In other words, what we teach about the Savior has implications for the way we assume that the Savior saves — how salvation works. If we embrace one of the extremes, we will come to a view of salvation that does not align with what Scripture or the Church Fathers taught. As we will see, to say that Jesus was human but not divine leaves Him as little more than an example to follow, and rules out any possibility that He is the embodiment of divine intervention. On the other hand, to say that He was divine but not human either makes Him a second god or confuses Him with God the Father, and rules out any possibility of Him truly being one of us, or representing us in any real way. As the mainstream Church concluded, it is only by being both human and divine that He is able both to represent us as one of us, and also save us. We will explore all of these concepts in depth as we track the development of doctrine through the centuries of the early Church.

The Church in the Empire and the Beginning of Persecution

Somewhere around the year AD 49, the Roman emperor Claudius heard that there was some sort of conflict in the Jewish quarter of Rome. What was probably a conflict between Christian Jews and non-Christian Jews was perceived by the Romans

[9] Hippolytus, *Against Noetus*, 3–4.

as an internal dispute among the Jews — and in a way, it was. To prevent any possible unrest, Claudius expelled all Jews from the city of Rome, including, of course, Jewish Christians.[10] This is why the apostle Paul encountered Priscilla and Aquila outside of Rome — they had been forced to leave with all the rest (Acts 18:2). But this left the Christian community in the city of Rome in the hands of newly converted Gentiles. Those who had been Christian the longest, who knew the stories of Jesus, and who understood the tradition and roots in Judaism were now gone. This may have been the occasion for the writing of the Gospel of Mark, since the Gentile Christians who remained would need to know the stories. In any case, the fact that the Jews had left Rome, but some Christians remained, demonstrated that Christianity was not simply a Jewish sect. Therefore, even before the final split between Judaism and Christianity that took place after AD 70, the Romans began to notice the existence of the Church.

The first impressions of the Church on its Roman neighbors were not good, mainly because of misunderstandings. Hearing that Christians ate the Body of Christ and drank His Blood, some believed they were cannibals. Hearing married Christians call each other "brother" and "sister" led to rumors about incest. The fact that the Christians met at dawn left some thinking they were another mystery cult, like the ones that already existed in Roman society, or worse, a seditious political faction, and with the distasteful additions of cannibalism and incestuous orgies.[11] Roman writers thought that Christianity was bad for society, and called it a "destructive superstition."[12] The Roman historian Suetonius would call the Church "a new and mischievous superstition."[13]

In general, therefore, the Roman attitude toward the Church, once the Romans realized it existed, was unfavorable. Those in the Roman government feared that it might be subversive, like the movement of the Zealots in Judea. The Zealots, born out of the annexation of Judea to Syria as a Roman province in AD 6, would eventually provoke the Romans into the war that led to the fall of Jerusalem and the destruction of the temple in AD 70.[14] So one can see how the Romans would view any new

[10] Suetonius, *Life of Claudius*, 25.4. It is not the case that all Jews left Rome. Many would have been slaves, and thus owned by Romans, and others simply refused to leave and stayed out of sight for a while, or passed as Gentiles. Many did leave, however, including St. Paul's friends Aquila and Priscilla.

[11] Athenagoras, *A Plea for the Christians*, 3; Theophilus of Antioch, *To Autolycus*, 3.4; Tertullian, *To the Nations*, 1.7.

[12] Tacitus, *Annals*, 15.44.

[13] Suetonius, *Life of Nero*, 16.

[14] The annexation of Judea to Syria took place in the year AD 6. It coincided with the appointment of Quirinius as proconsular legate ("governor") of Syria, and resulted in a census,

"movement" as suspicious. In addition, the average Roman would have worried that people who refused to worship the gods of Rome would anger those gods, causing them to remove their protection from the Empire. Ironically, the Christians, who worshiped only one God as opposed to many, were called "atheists."[15]

At the same time, the Roman emperors were enjoying their ability to be treated as gods themselves. Julius Caesar, who was assassinated to prevent him from becoming emperor, was still proclaimed a god by the senate after his death (even if somewhat reluctantly). When his nephew and heir Octavian became the first emperor, it was natural that he be considered the "son" of a "god." So when Jesus came into the world during the reign of Octavian (who had come to be called Augustus), and the Christians said that Jesus was *the* Son of God, this was in direct competition to the emperor, who was called a son of a god. The next emperor, Tiberius, apparently reasoned, "Why wait until you're dead to be deified? A son of a god is a god, right?" Therefore, he demanded to be called *dominus,* or "lord." So when Jesus was conducting His ministry during the reign of Tiberius, and His followers called Him Lord, this was in direct competition to the lordship of the emperor. By the time the emperor Domitian reigned at the end of the first century, he demanded to be called *dominus et deus,* or "lord and god." So when the fourth Gospel recorded that Thomas called Jesus "my Lord and my God" (John 20:28), the Church held this up as their way to say, *Jesus* is Lord and God, *not* that one in Rome who claims to be lord and god! In the minds of many, this pitted the Kingdom (or empire) of God against the Empire of the Romans. As we will see, the emperors will eventually try to force their Christian subjects to choose between Christ and Caesar (see Luke 23:2; John 19:12, 15).

Around midnight on the night of July 18th, in the year AD 64, a fire broke out in the city of Rome. It leveled a major part of the center of the city. Coincidentally (or not), the emperor Nero had plans on his desk for a new palace to be built on that spot. Naturally, rumors began to circulate that he had started the fire to make room for his new "Golden House." Nero needed a scapegoat to divert attention away from himself. He blamed the fire on the Christians, and many people were happy to vent their frustration on the Church, though most did not believe they were guilty.[16]

---

which was apparently the catalyst for the rebellion. See below regarding the Quirinius Problem.

[15] The reader must also keep in mind that the members of the Church were not yet called "Christians." I use the term here strictly for convenience.

[16] Timothy D. Barnes, "Pagan Perceptions of Christianity," in *Early Christianity,* 1, ed. Ian Hazlett (Nashville: Abingdon, 1991), 231. Barnes notes that the fact that Nero could even

Thus the first persecution of Christians at the hands of the Romans began. Anyone admitting to being a Christian was charged with the crime of arson and could be executed. Many people died in the circus of Nero on the Vatican hill, which is now the site of St. Peter's Basilica.[17] The apostles Paul and Peter were martyred at about this time, and Peter himself was crucified in Nero's circus.[18] The important thing to note is that the persecution set a precedent for the future attitude of the Romans toward the Church. Though this persecution was limited to Rome, and was temporary, the official position of the Roman government was that Christians were to be seen as enemies of the state.

In the year AD 81, the emperor Domitian came to the throne, and in AD 95 he began persecuting the Church.[19] According to tradition, Domitian had his own cousin, the senator Flavius Clemens, executed for "atheism." It is likely (though not certain) that this refers to Christianity, though the actual motivation for the execution might have been anything from a desire to confiscate his property to the removal of possible rivals for succession of the Flavian dynasty. As the story goes, Clemens's wife, Flavia Domitilla, was subsequently exiled, leaving land to the Roman Christians that would eventually be used for the catacombs named after her.[20] It was also at this time that the apostle John was exiled to the Island of Patmos,

---

attempt to blame the fire on the Christians shows that public opinion was already against them.

17 Note that the Colosseum was not built yet. In fact, the Colosseum now stands in the area that was leveled by the fire. It was built about fifteen years later.

18 According to tradition, St. Peter was crucified upside down. When he found out that he was to die in the same manner as the Lord, he begged that he was not worthy and should die some other way. His executioners mockingly agreed, nailing him to the cross upside down (see John 21:18–19).

19 It is impossible to know to what extent Domitian was personally involved in persecution, especially in the provinces. See Timothy D. Barnes, *Tertullian: A Historical and Literary Study* (Oxford: Clarendon Press, 1971), 150. On the other hand, Tertullian and Eusebius both attest to Domitian as a persecuting emperor. See Tertullian, *Apology*, 5; and Eusebius of Caesarea, *Ecclesiastical History*, 4.26.9.

20 Cassius Dio, *Roman History*, 67.14.1–2 refers to the execution of Flavius Clemens and the subsequent exile of his wife, Flavia Domitilla, on a charge of atheism. This may refer to Christianity, but it is not certain. Some argue that it refers to a conversion to Judaism, though there may still have been confusion of the two in the minds of the Romans. Tradition associates the couple with the catacomb of Domitilla in Rome, and also possibly as the former masters of a freedman who would become known as bishop Clement of Rome. The later *Acts of Nereus and Achilles* make Domitilla the niece of Clemens, probably in an attempt to present her as a virgin, though this error would find its way into later writers, including Jerome.

where he would write the book of Revelation.[21] But even at this time, persecution was sporadic and regional. Christians continued to worship, though at some times and places they had to meet in secret. However, the early Christians never hid in the Roman catacombs, as some legends (not to mention movies) suggest. The catacombs were legally registered burial grounds, so the Romans knew exactly where they were. They may have had funeral services at a burial site, and there are some chapels in the catacombs that attest to this, but the cramped quarters, the lack of light and fresh air, not to mention the smell of decaying bodies, would make regular worship (let alone hiding out for any length of time) impossible.

In the early second century, a Roman governor named Pliny wrote from his province in the East to ask the emperor Trajan for advice on what to do about the Christians. Trajan, who was emperor from AD 98 to 117, wrote back and confirmed that although Christians deserved to be executed, Pliny should not try to seek them out. If any were accused, he should interview them and ask them whether they were Christians. He should not take the accuser's word for it, since anyone might accuse someone to avoid paying a debt or to settle a conflict. Therefore, the accused were given a chance to speak for themselves, and if anyone denied being a Christian, proving it was as simple as swearing an oath to the emperor and making some act of worship of the traditional gods, perhaps as little as throwing a pinch of incense on a pagan altar. If there was still some question about a person's sincerity, they could be required to curse Christ, since even Pliny believed that a true Christian would never do that.[22] If anyone was willing to do this, they were to go free. If they were not willing, they could be tortured, or sent into exile having all their property confiscated, or possibly sent to the mines, which was essentially a slow death sentence. If they were Roman citizens, they were sent to Rome. Otherwise, they were sentenced to death, which could come by beheading (if the governor wanted to be merciful), crucifixion, burning at the stake, or being thrown to the wild beasts in the arena. According to

[21] While there is ongoing debate over the date and authorship of the book of Revelation, it is this author's conviction that the document was in fact written by the apostle John in the year AD 95. See James L. Papandrea, *The Wedding of the Lamb: A Historical Approach to the Book of Revelation* (Eugene, OR: Wipf & Stock/Pickwick, 2011), 16–27.

[22] Pliny the Younger, *Epistles*, 10.96–97 (to Trajan, with Trajan's reply). Pliny implied that he was following an earlier order of Trajan to outlaw Christian assembly, however there is no extant evidence of such a law. Some have argued that the Christians in Pliny's province were considered guilty of illegal assembly, and not that the name of "Christian" alone was enough to have them executed. However, if that were the case, then simply making a loyalty sacrifice or denouncing the Faith would not suffice to remove the charge.

Eusebius of Caesarea, no distinction was made for age or sex.[23] The important thing to note here is that by the second century, we have two important milestones in the history of persecution. First, we have gone from requiring a crime, like arson, to accuse someone, to simply the name of Christian being a capital offense.[24] Second, we see the use of pagan sacrifice as a test of loyalty to the state.

The irony which Tertullian would later point out is that the Romans were torturing prisoners to try to make them *deny* the accusation they were charged with, not admit it.[25] A denial of the charge would result in acquittal, and a Christian would only be punished if he or she refused to deny the Faith.

In the middle of the second century, Antoninus Pius (ruled AD 138–161) made conversion to Judaism illegal, which would set a precedent for similar laws against Christian evangelism.[26] It was during Pius's reign that Polycarp would be burned at the stake, shortly after a dream in which he saw his pillow on fire. Justin Martyr wrote his first *Apology* as an open letter to Antoninus. It is impossible to know whether Antoninus was personally invested in the persecution, but it is clear that it continued during his reign.[27]

[23] Eusebius of Caesarea, *Ecclesiastical History*, 6.5, 8.8. Eusebius is known as the first Christian historian and was writing in the fourth century.

[24] Tertullian, *Apology*, 2–4, 10. Tertullian (writing around the turn of the third century) does say that the name of Christian implies the crimes of "sacrilege and treason." This is significant because it makes Christianity, as a form of treason, a capital offense. The apocryphal *Acts of Apollonius* mentions a law which stated that it was illegal for anyone, anywhere, to be called a Christian. See *Acts of Apollonius*, 23–24. The document may not be reliable on this point, and probably reflects the author's perception of public opinion rather than imperial policy. Note that Hermas's *The Shepherd* says that martyrs suffer "for the sake of the name." See *The Shepherd*, 9.9, 10.1. It is not clear here whether "the name" means the name of Jesus, or the name "Christian," and much depends on the dating of the document to determine whether it would be too early for followers of Jesus even to be called Christians, however the important point to note is that by the time of the early second century, believers are called "Christians," (Pliny used the word) and it appears that the name was first used as an insult by the enemies of the Church, which strongly implies that the name "Christian" emerged at the same time that it was becoming a crime.

[25] Tertullian, *Apology*, 2, 49. The Romans also tortured the slaves of people suspected of being Christians, to try to get them to accuse their masters; Justin Martyr, *2 Apology*, 12.

[26] See Timothy D. Barnes, *Early Christianity and the Roman Empire* (London: Variorum, 1984), 40–41.

[27] As Barnes correctly points out, we do not know to what extent some emperors endorsed persecution, or for that matter, to what extent their orders were even carried out in the provinces. Therefore we cannot assume uniformity of enforcement across the empire, even when we have imperial edicts authorizing the persecution of the Church. No doubt

Marcus Aurelius (who reigned from AD 161 to 180) issued an edict in AD 167 ordering pagan sacrifice in the emperor's honor as a test of loyalty.[28] Refusing to make such a sacrifice was an act of treason.[29] Though he did not specifically target Christians (he didn't understand that Christians could not just add Jesus to the league of gods in the pantheon), pagan sacrifice became tied to patriotism. Justin Martyr wrote his second *Apology* to Marcus Aurelius and was subsequently beheaded. Also during Marcus Aurelius's reign, the Martyrs of Lyons and Viennes met their end at the hands of an angry mob in Gaul in AD 177, and the Scillitan Martyrs were the victims of a massacre in North Africa in AD 180.

After Septimius Severus became emperor in AD 193, he traveled to the East to survey his empire. There he saw the famous Christian school in Alexandria, which was attracting so many people to Christianity that Severus saw it as a threat to traditional religion and to the stability of the empire. Persecution began in earnest in Alexandria in about AD 201.[30] It would be Septimius Severus, in AD 202, who would issue the first imperial edict that specifically mentioned Christians, that they should be sought out, arrested, and executed.[31] He made conversion to Christianity illegal

---

many Christians were martyred without the emperors' knowledge, and even under emperors who did not endorse persecution. On the other hand, there were also provinces governed by men who did not persecute Christians, even when the emperors encouraged it. A governor's primary goal was to keep the peace, and if the Christians and pagans in his province could coexist peacefully, he had the luxury of looking the other way. In general, the farther from Rome a governor was, the more flexibility he had to deviate from the emperor's current programs. See Barnes, *Tertullian*, 149, 155. It cannot go without mentioning at this point, that the temple erected in the Roman forum dedicated to the deified Antoninus was later converted into a church.

[28] Eusebius of Caesarea, *Ecclesiastical History*, 4.13.1–7. Because Christians refused to participate in the sacrifices, some martyrdoms resulted, though this was an indirect result of the edict.

[29] Barnes, *Early Christianity and the Roman Empire*, 44, 49–50.

[30] Eusebius of Caesarea, *Ecclesiastical History*, 6.41. In the early part of his reign, Severus appeared to be tolerant of the Church. This made some Christian writers reluctant to blame the persecution on him. Tertullian even tried to paint him as a friend of the Church in order to convince the governor of North Africa to discontinue persecution. See Tertullian, *To Scapula*, 4.3–6.

[31] Paul Keresztes, *Imperial Rome and the Christians* (Lanham, MD: University Press of America, 1989), 11–13. The edict is mentioned in the *Historia Augusta, Septimius Severus*, 17.1, though the reliability of the *Historia Augusta* has been challenged. See Geoffrey D. Dunn, *Tertullian* (New York: Routledge, 2004), 17. Dunn does not accept the historicity of the edict, based on favorable comments Tertullian makes about Severus in *To Scapula*. However, this was an apologetic document and it would not have served Tertullian's

(based on the precedent of Antoninus's edict) and tried to close down the catechetical schools. Many people took this as fulfillment of predictions of a "tribulation" in the book of Revelation.[32] Another significant milestone in the history of persecution had been reached, since now Christians could be sought out and rounded up.[33] This is exactly what happened to Perpetua and her catechism classmates.[34] Even though there would not be a systematic, empire-wide persecution of the Church until the middle of the third century, it was nevertheless the case that the Christian leaders and writers of the early Church were conducting their ministry in a world that wanted them dead (Matt. 10:22).

Clement of Rome

Clement was probably born around AD 30 and was the bishop of Rome from AD 88 to 97, though Eusebius of Caesarea wrote that he became bishop in the year AD 93.[35] According to tradition, he was a disciple of the apostle Peter, and was chosen personally by Peter to succeed him, though he did not succeed Peter directly. Irenaeus of Lyons, writing about a century later, said that Clement was the third leader of the church in Rome after Peter.[36] Traditional lists of the bishops of Rome (popes) name Peter as the first, then Linus, Anacletus, and then Clement. There is a Clement mentioned by Paul in Philippians 4:3, and although there is no way to be certain whether it is the same Clement, Eusebius says it is. It seems hard to imagine that there was *another* Clement mentioned by Paul as someone who helped him while he was under house arrest in Rome, unless the Clement mentioned by Paul was the Roman senator I have already mentioned, Flavius Clemens. According to tradition, bishop Clement of Rome was a freed slave from the household of Domitian's cousin, Flavius Clemens. As we noted

---

purpose to criticize Severus. Note that Eusebius mentions the closing of the catechetical school in Alexandria. Eusebius of Caesarea, *Ecclesiastical History*, 6.3. In the end, the change in policy from Trajan's reply to Pliny (advising that Christians should not be sought out) to the situation in the early third century (when Christians like Perpetua were rounded up) is unexplainable without the edict of AD 202.

32 Eusebius of Caesarea, *Ecclesiastical History*, 6.7. See Papandrea, *The Wedding of the Lamb*, 156–159.

33 Tertullian, *Apology*, 7.

34 Enforcement of the edict apparently targeted recent converts, such as Perpetua. See Barnes, *Early Christianity and the Roman Empire*, 40. Perpetua and Felicitas were martyred in Carthage in AD 203. Even though Perpetua was from the aristocracy, the right of Roman citizens to appeal to the emperor had all but disappeared by this time.

35 Eusebius of Caesarea, *Ecclesiastical History*, 3.15–16.

36 Irenaeus of Lyons, *Against Heresies*, 3.2.

above, Domitian had his cousin executed, probably for his faith, and it is reasonable to believe that upon his death Flavius Clemens's will provided for the release of his slaves, as even many non-Christian Romans did this. Then a newly freed slave could take his master's name, and so this very first of the early Church Fathers is known to us as Clement. It is interesting to note that if this scenario was in fact the case, then Clement was the bishop of Rome *while still a slave*! This is certainly possible, and it demonstrates the fact that in the early Church, the office of bishop was not a position of power, or something to which only the wealthy could aspire.

But was he really the *bishop* of Rome? Did the office of bishop even exist at this early date? The answer is yes and no. When we read the earliest Christian literature, including the letter of Clement to the Corinthians, there are two Greek words used for those who lead and preside in worship. One is the word *presbyteros* (which means *elder*, but is often translated *priest*) and the other is *episkopos* (which means *overseer*, but is usually translated *bishop*). On the surface, it seems that these two terms are used interchangeably. Upon closer inspection, we can see that the two words overlap in meaning, but are not complete synonyms, though some early authors use them as though they are.[37] The point is that in the first century, the Church did not have the familiar three-tier hierarchy of bishop, priest, and deacon. Rather, it had a two-tier hierarchy of presider and assistant.[38] St. Paul's letter to the Philippians, in the New Testament, and Clement's letter to the Corinthians both use what appears to be the earliest phrase referring to what we would today call the "clergy." That phrase is "bishops and deacons."[39]

[37] As late as the turn of the fifth century, Chrysostom said that the terms are interchangeable, and that a priest or bishop could even be called a deacon, because the word "deacon" means servant. See John Chrysostom, *Homilies on Philippians*, 1. See also Alistair C. Stewart, *The Original Bishops: Office and Order in the First Christian Communities* (Grand Rapids: Baker Academic, 2014), 6–8, 15–17, 18, 22–24, 48, 354. Building on the work of Lampe and Brent, Stewart makes a somewhat compelling case for the priority of the word *episkopos* as the original term for house-church pastors. He further argues that the term *presbyteros* came into use as multiple house-church pastors formed citywide or regional councils, thus becoming the "elders" of the Church in that place. He cites the pre-Christian meaning of the term *presbyteros* as referring to "senior members of guilds and associations in the Hellenistic cities." Stewart adds nuance to the work of his predecessors on this topic, and corrects some aspects of their theories that are based on erroneous assumptions, though he still fails to take the influence of direct apostolic appointment and succession seriously enough.

[38] Stewart, *The Original Bishops*, 354.

[39] See Phil. 1:1. In some English translations, the phrase will be rendered, "overseers and ministers."

However, it is important to keep two things in mind. First of all, in the early Church, there is no equivalent to the English word *clergy*. In our contemporary context, we may have in mind a clear division of who the clergy are, as opposed to laity, but that was not necessarily in the minds of the early Christians. In addition, the word *clergy* is related to the word *clerk* and comes from a time in English (British) culture when the ministers of the churches were the ones who kept the town records, because often they were the only ones in town who could read. In the early Church, the rate of literacy was actually higher than in the Middle Ages, and yet we know from several early documents that literacy was not required of a leader in the Church. Where the bishop could not read, a lector was chosen to read the Scriptures. In any case, the early Church has no concrete term like *clergy* for the collective body of its leaders. The second thing to keep in mind is that for most of the first century, many towns and cities in the empire only had one house-church — only one congregation of Christians who would understand themselves as being the church in that place. And whenever there is only one congregation in town, then even under a three-tier system, the bishop and the priest are the same person.

Clement tells us that the apostles appointed "bishops and deacons," because they knew that there would be "strife over the bishop's office."[40] In other words, the apostles knew that if they didn't appoint their own successors before they died or left town, then there would be confusion and division over who would succeed them as the authorities in the Church. The apostle Paul reminded Timothy that he was also commissioned by a council of elders who laid hands on him, ratifying Paul's choice (1 Tim. 4:14), and he gave Titus the authority to appoint house-church pastors, which are referred to in that letter as both bishops and priests (Titus 1:5–7). We get the same sense from the document known as the *Didache*, which we will examine in another chapter.

That means that a house-church pastor in the first century could be called an "elder" (priest), or an "overseer" (bishop). But it appears that in the earliest decades of the Church's history, the most usual term for what we would call a house-church pastor would have been the word *bishop*. In fact, in the Septuagint (LXX), the Greek Old Testament in use by Jesus and the apostles, as well as by the earliest Christians, the word *shepherd* (in places where God and His anointed are described as being shepherds to the people of Israel) is a form of the word *episkopos*.[41] God promises to be (or appoint someone to be) a *bishop* (overseer) for the people. A bishop is therefore a shepherd, and that is the meaning of the word *pastor*. So it seems that

[40] Clement of Rome, *1 Clement*, 42.4, 44.1, in Holmes, *The Apostolic Fathers*, 101, 103.

[41] Stewart, *The Original Bishops*, 32; cf. Jer. 23:2; Ezek. 34:11.

the leadership of the Church at this time is made up of house-church pastors, who are normally called bishops (overseers) but who can also be called priests (elders) because of their role in presiding over the liturgy, and then assisting the bishops in the liturgy and leadership of the local church is the order of deacons.

Such is the state of the *language* about the hierarchy in the time of Clement. However, in Clement's letter we can see that the three-tier hierarchy is already developing, because when Clement actually does refer to the hierarchy of leadership in the Church, he compares it to the three levels in the Old Testament: high priest, priest, and levite.[42] This means that although local church leadership exists in two tiers, bishop and deacon, Clement understands the universal Church as having a leadership of three levels, which he refers to as high priest, priest, and deacon, and naturally he sees himself in the role of high priest, as the successor of Peter. So the office of bishop as a regional authority with jurisdiction over multiple pastors did exist, they just had not started calling it "bishop" yet. What we think of as the bishop was, for a while apparently, referred to as the high priest. Or at least that's how Clement described it.

Nevertheless, it is important to remember that all bishops always remain priests, so that even as the office of bishop as we know it emerges, the bishop is one of the priests, and (as we will discuss in the next chapter) the leader of a citywide or regional council of priests. But as long as there is only one congregation in any city, there is only one priest there, and that priest is, by default, also the bishop.

We have to keep in mind that whatever development took place in Rome, we cannot assume that the development was the same, or happened at the same rate, in the other cities. By the time of Clement, the city of Rome had several house-churches, perhaps as many as seven to ten congregations. Clement, as the bishop of Rome (or as he would perhaps call himself, the high priest of Rome), functioned as the chair of the council of priests in the city, and in that role, was charged with corresponding by letter with the Christians in other cities. As we will see, one of the earliest Christian documents outside of the New Testament is one of those letters.

After the fire of AD 64, some of the land in the destruction zone — land owned by Flavius Clemens — was rebuilt to include a house and a warehouse. According to tradition, it was in one of these buildings that Clement himself led a house-church until his exile from Rome. Today the church of San Clemente (St. Clement) stands on the site, and visitors can venture down into the excavations under the medieval basilica and explore the fourth-century church, and below that, the first-century house and warehouse where Clement presided. It is truly holy ground to stand in

[42] Clement of Rome, *1 Clement*, 40.5.

a place where Christian worship has been conducted continuously for over one thousand nine hundred years.[43]

Finally (according to tradition), Clement was eventually banished from Rome by the emperor Trajan, and sentenced to hard labor in the mines in the east, which was essentially a death sentence, since the convicts were literally worked until they dropped dead. But Clement shared the Gospel with fellow prisoners and guards alike and converted many. However, this led to increased visibility, which in turn led to his martyrdom. He was thrown into the Black Sea, tied to an anchor. Legend says that in the ninth century, St. Cyril found his body and brought it back to Rome, where it is buried in the church that bears Clement's name. The final details of Clement's death, as well as the story of the repatriation of his remains, may be legend, but he was exiled from Rome in about the year AD 97, which ended his term as the leader of the church there. He died about two or three years later.

In some ways, Clement of Rome is a transitional figure. He is one of the earliest of the second generation of Church leaders, and yet his life is almost entirely within the first century, and he lives during a time when one or more apostles were still alive, and there were still a number of people around who knew the apostles personally. The apostle John would actually outlive Clement by a few years, and Clement's letter to the Corinthians was written at the same time as, or shortly before, the book of Revelation.

1 Clement

This document, called *First Clement* (*1 Clement*), is a letter written by Clement on behalf of the church in Rome to the Christians in the Greek city of Corinth, the same city to which the apostle Paul wrote the Corinthian letters in the New Testament, but now forty years later. Although Clement's name is not in the text (it is written on behalf of the church of Rome), it is universally attributed to him by the Church Fathers who came after him. We can date the letter of *1 Clement* quite confidently to the year AD 95, the same year as the book of Revelation, though perhaps earlier in that year. In the letter, we can see that Domitian has begun his persecution, but it must have been early in the persecution, since Clement still believes government leaders are appointed by God, and advocates praying for them.[44]

The letter is written in the form of an ancient epistle of negotiation. Just as there was division in Corinth in Paul's time, so now there is still division, and Clement

[43] See James L. Papandrea, *ROME: A Pilgrim's Guide to the Eternal City* (Eugene, OR: Cascade Books, 2012), 83–91.

[44] Clement of Rome, *1 Clement*, 1.1, 7.1, 60.4–61.2.

writes in an attempt to reconcile the factions. Therefore, the letter is much more practical in tone than its apocalyptic cousin, the book of Revelation. Apparently, there was some conflict in Corinth over the authority of some priests.[45] We can't be sure what the real issue was, though it may have been a dispute over the selection of their bishop (or "high priest").[46] If a bishop's selection was being challenged, this might be evidence of a transition in the office of bishop from one who was handpicked by an apostle (in this case, Paul) to one who would have to be elected. The factions seem to be along generational lines, with tension between older and younger members of the church.[47] This would be consistent with a development in the office of bishop, since older members might want to make sure the previous bishop's closest disciple was chosen, while younger members might have wanted to elect someone else. On the other hand, it is also possible that the division in Corinth was over the question of whether ordination was for a term or for life. Younger members of the church of Corinth may have wanted older leaders to step down. In any case, Clement does not give the details of the dispute because he says he is sending negotiators to do the real work of reconciliation, and the letter is simply to set the stage.[48] Clement writes with urgency, though, because the threat of schism is causing some to doubt the Faith,[49] and it is an embarrassment to the cause of evangelization.[50]

Historically, one of the most important things about *1 Clement* is the tone of authority with which Clement writes. He assumes that the Christians in Corinth, who have their own leaders, should listen to the bishop of Rome and accept his advice. The reason that this is so is based on the fact that Peter was the first apostolic overseer in the church of Rome and that his authority as Jesus' right-hand man and leader of the apostles (Matt. 16:18–19; John 21:15–17) is transferred to his successors in the city.[51] This concept of the transfer of authority from apostles to bishops is known as *apostolic succession.* The assumption is that the first bishops of the Church were consecrated by the apostles, who handed down the mantle of authority, and

[45] Clement of Rome, *1 Clement*, 47.6.

[46] Clement of Rome, *1 Clement*, 44.

[47] Clement of Rome, *1 Clement*, 3.3; see also *1 Clement*, 38.2, where the division is described in terms that are reminiscent of 1 Corinthians 12:22–26.

[48] Clement of Rome, *1 Clement*, 63.3–4.

[49] Clement of Rome, *1 Clement*, 46.9.

[50] Clement of Rome, *1 Clement*, 46.9, 47.7.

[51] Clement of Alexandria would later remark that Peter is preeminent among the apostles because he is the only apostle for whom Jesus had paid his tax (Matt. 17:27); Clement of Alexandria, *Who Is the Rich Man That Shall Be Saved?*, 21.

conferred the anointing of the Holy Spirit, through the imposition ("laying on") of hands. Subsequent generations of bishops would in turn be ordained and consecrated by their predecessors in the succession, keeping the line of authority intact. In addition, whatever a bishop teaches is assumed to have been learned from his predecessor in the same city, who learned it from his predecessor, in an unbroken line going all the way back to the original disciples, and to Jesus Himself. Therefore, any bishop should be able to trace his line of succession — both the content and the authority of the teaching office — like a pedigree, back to the founder of the church in the city where he is bishop. If one wants to rest assured that a bishop's teaching will not lead the faithful astray, simply ask whether that bishop's teaching (and hence his authority) can be traced back to an apostle. If so, one can be confident that the bishop in question is on the same page, so to speak, with the other bishops, the apostles, and ultimately, with Jesus.[52]

However, what happens when two bishops disagree? The bishop with the higher authority (both theologically and ecclesiastically) will be the one who can trace his succession back to one of the original apostles. If both of them can, then the one with the greater authority will be the one who can trace his succession back to one of the inner circle of Jesus' closest disciples: Peter, James, and John. Ultimately, though, since Peter was made the leader of the disciples, Peter trumps all others, even Paul. Therefore, since the church of Rome claimed an unbroken chain of succession going back to Jesus through Peter, it eventually just became easier to ask whether any church was in agreement with Rome. The important point to note is that even before the office of bishop in general developed into the regionally authoritative role (the metropolitan) that it would eventually become, the church of Rome was already coming to be seen as the church with which anyone had to agree if they wanted to be considered part of the universal Church.

One has to understand that the worldview of the early Church was not like today. We live in such a technology-driven culture that we are conditioned to believe that whatever is newer is automatically better. This was not the belief in the ancient world. To them, whatever is older is better, because it's established, and has stood the test

[52] On apostolic succession, see Irenaeus of Lyons, *Against Heresies*, 2.9.1, 3.1.1, 3.3.1–2, 3.4.1, 4.26.2–4, 4.33.8; see also Tertullian, *The Prescription against Heretics*, 19–21, 23 (an answer to the objection that Peter was rebuked by Paul), 28, 32, 36–37. Note that in chapter 37, Tertullian says that the Scriptures do not belong to the heretics, but to those who still hold the "deed" to them, which comes from the "original owners," the apostles. In chapter 28, Tertullian also says that the Holy Spirit guarantees that the Church will not go astray, based on Jesus' promise to Peter in Matthew 16:18–19.

of time.[53] If something new comes along to challenge what already exists, the new thing is suspect. So in Clement's world, the tradition is always more trustworthy than the innovation. Therefore, since the oldest teaching is always the most reliable, and since the authority of the church of Rome was seen as going back to the original leader of the apostles, the church of Rome, and whoever is in leadership there, assumes an authority, even over the bishops of other cities.

Of course, this certainly doesn't mean everyone accepted this unconditionally. But it is remarkable that we can see from the late first century, already a bishop of Rome is writing to other churches with a tone of authority as though he speaks for Peter. In fact, Clement believed the Corinthian Christians should listen to him as though he were Peter, even implying that this letter should be taken as inspired.[54] Therefore, *1 Clement* is our earliest witness to the claim of apostolic succession.[55]

So why wasn't this letter included in the New Testament? Clement, as a possible disciple of Peter, could have been seen as a secondary apostle, much like Mark or Luke. Clement refers to Paul's letters and the book of Hebrews as Scripture (especially reminding his Corinthian audience of Paul's famous love chapter in 1 Cor. 13).[56] In fact some did treat this letter as Scripture and advocated including it in the Christian canon.[57] But in the end it did not stand the test of time. The letter is quite long compared to the New Testament letters and has little theological content. Surprisingly, when Clement wanted to talk about the Resurrection, instead of mentioning the empty tomb, he used the allegory of the phoenix, the mythical bird that rises from its own funeral ashes every five hundred years.[58] Finally, the fact that Clement sees the Roman government as ordained by God must have worked against acceptance of his letter in times of persecution.[59] While it is true that the letter of Philemon is also a personal letter without a lot of theology, and yet that was included in the New Testament, Clement is not Paul, and he was just not close enough to Jesus to merit this letter being included in spite of its disadvantages.

[53] Theophilus of Antioch, *To Autolycus*, 3.29.

[54] Clement of Rome, *1 Clement*, 63.2.

[55] Clement of Rome, *1 Clement*, 42, 44.

[56] Clement of Rome, *1 Clement*, 49.5.

[57] For example, Polycarp of Smyrna, and Clement of Alexandria; see Clement of Alexandria, *Stromata*, 4.17. In fact, Clement's letter continued to be read as part of liturgy on certain holy days in Alexandria, at least through the second century. See Eusebius of Caesarea, *Ecclesiastical History*, 4.23.

[58] Clement of Rome, *1 Clement*, 25. The phoenix was apparently a popular Christian symbol early on, as evidenced by catacomb paintings and early church apse mosaics.

[59] Clement of Rome, *1 Clement*, 60.4–61.2.

2 Clement

The document known as *Second Clement* (*2 Clement*) may not have been written by Clement of Rome. It only exists in three manuscripts, and in those three manuscripts it is always placed next to *1 Clement*, and attributed to the same source. It could be that it is another letter written from Rome on behalf of the church at Rome, but perhaps by one of Clement's successors. Scholars are uncertain about the date it was written but estimate it around the turn of the second century, that is, around the year AD 100. *Second Clement* is not really a letter, but more of a homily. In fact, it has been called "the oldest surviving complete Christian sermon outside the New Testament."[60] On the other hand, it may have originated as a catechetical lecture. The author urges his audience to, "pay attention to what is written, in order that you may save both yourselves and your reader."[61] So we see that the document was not meant to be read by individuals, but to be read aloud in an assembly, where most people would hear it read. This would be the case for many of our patristic documents, as well as Scripture, since most people in the early Church did not own their own copies of biblical or other texts.

The primary concern of *2 Clement* is to warn the reader against false teachers, specifically those who deny the reality of Christ's humanity (see 1 John 4:1–3). These false teachers are said to be leading Christians astray, putting their salvation at risk.[62] There are also warnings about the persecution, and a reminder to resist apostasy.[63] The author states that to deny Christ is to "undo" one's Baptism.[64] It is clear from this and other similar writings that the early Christians were aware of the possibility of the loss of salvation after Baptism, which could happen because of continuing in sin, following a heresy, or in times of persecution by denial of the Faith.[65] Baptism was considered the "seal" of Christ, but the seal could be broken by post-baptismal sin.[66] Not that Baptism could actually be "undone," but the actions of a person after Baptism could lead to the loss of salvation. This is one of our earliest examples of the problem of post-baptismal sin, the low tolerance for transgressing the moral expectations of a baptized Christian, and the problem of how to "reinstate"

60 Holmes, *The Apostolic Fathers*, 132.

61 *2 Clement*, 19.1, translation in Holmes, ed., *The Apostolic Fathers*, 163.

62 *2 Clement*, 10, 15. The false teachers in question are the docetics, see chapter 6, below.

63 *2 Clement*, 3, 6.

64 *2 Clement*, 6; cf. Hermas, *The Shepherd*, 72.3–4.

65 On the belief that salvation could be lost, see *Didache*, 16; Hermas, *The Shepherd*, 74.5, 95.2; Irenaeus of Lyons, *Against Heresies*, 5.9.3. Irenaeus says that the Holy Spirit, once received, can be driven out.

66 *2 Clement*, 6.9, 7.6, 8.6.

someone to membership in good standing after serious sin. We will return to these issues in a future chapter.

The author of *Second Clement* knew Matthew's Gospel, and probably Luke's. There is a quotation of Matthew 9:13 which is called Scripture: one of the earliest, if not the earliest verbatim quote of a New Testament passage as Scripture.[67] The author also refers to Ephesians, Hebrews, and 1 Peter as authoritative. *Second Clement* quotes at least four sayings of Jesus that are not found in the New Testament, one of which is also referred to as Scripture in *1 Clement.*[68] Another is also quoted by the very same false teachers this author is writing against.[69]

In one place, the author of *2 Clement* quotes Jesus as saying, "Even if you were gathered together with me in my very bosom, yet if you did not keep my commandments, I would cast you off, and say to you, 'Depart from me! I don't know where you come from, you who do evil.'"[70] In another place, after quoting Matthew 10:16, where Jesus says, "You shall be as lambs in the midst of wolves," *2 Clement* continues, "But Peter answered and said to Him, 'What if the wolves tear the lambs to pieces?' Jesus said to Peter, 'After the lambs are dead, let them fear the wolves no longer, and as for you, do not fear those who, though they kill you, are not able to do anything else to you, but fear the one who, after you are dead, has the power to cast soul and body into the flames of hell.'"[71] Thus the author connects these sayings of Jesus to the context of persecution, bookending it with Matthew 10:28. However, we do not know where these additional quotations come from.

In *2 Clement,* we can already see the traditional top three spiritual disciplines of prayer, fasting, and almsgiving, but in an interesting hierarchy. The author writes, "Fasting is better than prayer, while charitable giving is better than both, and love covers a multitude of sins, while prayer arising from a good conscience delivers

[67] *2 Clement,* 2.4.

[68] *2 Clement,* 11.2–4; cf. *1 Clement,* 23.3. This saying of Jesus is not found in the Gospels, but mirrors elements in other early patristic writings in its condemnation of those who are "double-minded." Note that St. Paul also quotes a saying of Jesus that we do not find in the Gospels. In Acts 20:35, he tells his audience that Jesus said, "It is more blessed to give than to receive."

[69] *2 Clement,* 12; cf. *Gospel of Thomas,* 22. The gnostics, who probably produced the *Gospel of Thomas,* were mostly docetic in their christology, meaning that they denied the real humanity of Jesus Christ.

[70] *2 Clement,* 4, translation in Holmes, *The Apostolic Fathers,* 143. The second part of this is like Matthew 7:23, but the first part has no biblical parallel.

[71] *2 Clement,* 5.2–4 (cf. Matt. 10:28), translation in Holmes, ed., *The Apostolic Fathers,* 143–145.

one from death. Blessed is everyone who is found full of these, for charitable giving relieves the burden of sin."[72] The author has taken the passage from 1 Peter 4:8, and connected it directly to almsgiving (which is reasonable, given the context in 1 Pet. 4). Later patristic writers will say "almsgiving covers a multitude of sins," and so we see here the early assumption that almsgiving is an act of love, and can be a form of penance.

Second Clement also contains one of the earliest references to the doctrine of universal resurrection after the New Testament — a doctrine we will see come to be explained in great detail by the apologists of the second century. This is another way that the author is refuting the false teaching of a Christ who had no flesh. Not only did Christ have true humanity with a real human body, but His Resurrection was a bodily Resurrection, which means that humanity will be raised bodily as well, and we will all be judged in the flesh.[73]

Finally, we can also see in *2 Clement* a hint of something we see in some later fringe documents (the apocryphal acts, which we will look at in a later chapter), which is an implied expectation that all serious Christians should be celibate.[74] In fact, such an expectation is described in terms similar to what we find in later heretical documents.[75] It was probably for this reason, and due to the unknown authorship, that this document was not considered for inclusion in the New Testament. In addition, depending on how one dates this document, it could be considered too late to be apostolic or to be included in the canon.

Just as we have a word to refer to what we believe about Christ — christology — and we have a word for what we believe about salvation — soteriology — we also have a word to talk about what we believe about the Church: *ecclesiology*. And we can see that already in the first century, the apostolic age, the people who made up the Church were working through their own self-identity as members of the Body of Christ. Through the writings of the apostles and the earliest of the Church Fathers, the Church was beginning the process of defining itself and clarifying its boundaries. If we were to ask the question why the Church must have boundaries, the answer would have a lot to do with what we can observe about the interdependency of christology

[72] *2 Clement*, 16.4 (cf. 1 Pet. 4:8), translation in Holmes, ed., *The Apostolic Fathers*, 159.

[73] *2 Clement*, 9.1–6.

[74] *2 Clement*, 12.1–6.

[75] The author of *2 Clement* seems to be quoting something that Clement of Alexandria referred to as the *Gospel of the Egyptians*, though we only have fragments of what this document might have contained. See Clement of Alexandria, *Stromata*, 3.13.92. There are also similarities to the gnostic *Gospel of Thomas*.

and soteriology. Jesus Christ founded the Church to reconcile believers to God in a way that would lead to eternal life, that is, salvation. But from the very beginning, the apostles and subsequent leaders of the Church were convinced that heresy, that is, an incorrect understanding of God and God's self-revelation in Christ, would not lead to salvation. So it was always the conviction that souls were at stake, and that heresy and schism would lead the innocent astray, which is to say, they would lead people away from God and eternal life. The remedy for heresy, indeed the path to salvation, was through the Church, which was already being defined according to its sacraments, especially Baptism and the Eucharist. The way to remain in Christ (John 15) is to remain in the Church, understood as the Mystical Body of Christ at the table, receiving the eucharistic Body of Christ (John 6).

3

Christianity, the Next Generation: The Apostolic Fathers

Apostolic Succession and the Development of the Hierarchy

As we have already noted, the second generation of leadership of the Church was simply the continuation of the discipleship and apprenticeship model that Jesus Himself instituted. This means that the content of the Church's teaching was always seen as that which was handed down from teachers to students, and the authority of the Church was, by default, structured on the choosing and commissioning of leaders by their predecessors. In other words, Jesus chose His disciples, and they in turn chose their disciples, and handpicked those who would take over for them, either when they moved on to a new area, or when they died.

By the end of the first century, all of the apostles had died, though some traditions say that John may have lived into the first few years of the second century. This is certainly possible, though he would have been about eighty-five or ninety years old at the turn of the century. The point is that the second generation of Church leaders, beginning with people like Timothy, and Titus, and going through to the bishops Ignatius of Antioch and Polycarp of Smyrna, were all people who had known one or more of the apostles personally, and had been their students. Those second-generation leaders who are outside of the New Testament, but who are still in the time when people had met the apostles, are a subset of the Church Fathers, often referred to as the "Apostolic Fathers." These include Clement of Rome, whom we have already met, as well as the leaders and writings we will look at in this chapter.

As we look at the development of the hierarchy in the postapostolic age, we can see two phases, the first morphing into the second slowly, sometimes imperceptibly at the time, and certainly in different ways and at different times in different places. The first phase is what we see in the New Testament. The apostles chose and commissioned their successors, both on the level of the local congregation and in some cases with a regional authority. In that context, the Greek terms that we translate as "bishop" (*episkopos*) and "priest" (*presbyteros*) overlap in meaning and are often treated as basically synonymous. The standard designation for those who would lead the Church (apart from the apostles themselves) is the phrase "bishops and deacons" (Phil 1:1).[1] Therefore, the first phase of Church leadership is already a hierarchical structure which looks like this:

- Apostles (itinerant missionaries with regional and/or universal authority)
- Bishops (pastors of local congregations, sometimes called priests)
- Deacons (assistants to the pastors)

The apostles were considered to be inspired authorities, on the level of the Old Testament prophets (Rev. 18:20), and of course we know that their writings would come to be called Scripture (2 Pet. 3:15–16).[2] They commissioned and sent their disciples to lead local congregations, and chose their immediate successors, who would have regional authority after them, as the inheritors of their teaching. Some of these disciples of the apostles were to become seen as apostles themselves. One could argue that Paul fits into this category, but certainly also Mark, Luke, Timothy, and Titus. Some, like the author of at least two of the Johannine letters, were called *presbyters*, which at the time probably meant *elders*, but which can also be translated *priests*, because of the assumed liturgical leadership that would come with that position.[3] The apostles were itinerant, moving around as they established and supported various local Christian groups. They had authority over those local churches (especially the ones they had founded) and over the resident leaders there, partly because they had appointed and commissioned these second-generation church leaders, but for many of the apostles they also had authority because they had known and learned from Jesus — they had been His disciples.

[1] Sometimes translated "overseers and ministers," but the Greek terms are the terms for *bishops* and *deacons*.

[2] *Didache*, 11.3.

[3] As we have noted above, the Greek word *presbyteros* can be translated either "elder" or "priest." However, in some documents, the term seems to have a technical meaning referring specifically to the second generation of Church leaders, the ones whom the apostles chose to succeed them. Alistair Stewart has argued that their official title would be "bishop" (*episkopos*), but that they also take on the title of *presbyter* when they become members of a council of priests, or a *presbytery*. See Stewart, *The Original Bishops*, 6–8, 15–17, 18, 22–24, 48, 354. The letters of 2 John and 3 John are by a John who calls himself "the Elder," and who may not be the apostle John but another John, possibly his successor. See Papias, *Exposition on the Sayings of the Lord*, 4–7, and Irenaeus of Lyons, *Against Heresies*, 2.22.5, 5.5.1. Note that Papias believed that the book of Revelation was also by this John the Elder, though this was a minority opinion within the mainstream Church.

The resident pastors are referred to in the New Testament, *1 Clement*, and the *Didache* as bishops (*episkopos, overseer*) and sometimes also as priests (*presbyteros, elder*). In Justin Martyr, the leader is called a presider (*proestos*, sometimes translated *president*).[4] This term can refer to teachers of philosophy, and the nature of Justin's document (that it was written for non-Christians) may mean that Justin chose that word because it would make sense to outsiders, and so does not prove that the term was used for Church leaders internally.[5] However it does show us that by Justin's time (the middle of the second century) local Christian congregations could be seen (at least by outsiders) as philosophical schools, and the *presider* or bishop/priest would be the one with the authority to teach and with the responsibility to safeguard the content of the local church's teaching against corruption. Therefore, the early bishops were the leaders of worship, with the authority over teaching (whether done themselves or delegated). They are also sometimes called teachers, and they are the ones who read and explain the letters from the apostles, passages from the Gospels, and generally encourage the faith of the group.[6]

At this point we should also distinguish between the leader and the host of a local congregation. Most local church groups met in homes or apartments, and while the host would be the person whose home it was, that does not necessarily mean that the host is also the bishop (i.e., the presider). Very likely, the host was considered a patron of the church in that place, but the bishop of that congregation was someone chosen for the position, not simply by virtue of offering up the space. Therefore we cannot assume that simply because a house-church is said to be meeting in a certain person's home, that this same person was the one presiding over the sacraments. The bishop (presider) would be someone in succession from the apostles and previous leaders; the host would be someone who had the wealth and/or space to invite the church into a place for meals and worship. The bishop might also be the host, but most of the time was probably not.

When the church in any city grew to the point where all the Christians there could no longer fit into one house, or when multiple congregations arose in different

[4] John Meyendorff, *Imperial Unity and Christian Divisions: The Church AD 450–680* (Crestwood, NY: St. Vladimir's Press, 1989), 39, cf. also 42–43.

[5] Stewart, *The Original Bishops*, 20, 24.

[6] Hermas, *The Shepherd*, 3.5.1, 13.1, 102.2. In *The Shepherd*, the leaders are called teachers. As long as the terms bishop and priest are somewhat interchangeable, the resident pastor was of course the teacher of the house-church. Once the office of bishop emerged as an "overseer" of the other priests, the teaching authority would ultimately rest with the bishops, but would be granted to the priests for their churches, as long as their teaching was consistent with the bishop.

parts of a larger city, or among different ethic (language) groups, the bishops or presiders would have to meet together periodically to compare notes, share letters, and support each other.[7] There is some evidence that they may have even shared the yeast to make the eucharistic bread, so that the bread they shared was truly *one* bread, in the sense that it had come from a single starter.[8] In any case, the point is this: as long as there is only one house-church meeting in a city, there is no need for much distinction between the terms *bishop* and *priest* because the only priest in town is also the bishop. But as soon as you have more than one congregation in a city, you necessarily have a council of pastors, and that council needs a leader, if only to avoid serious division.[9]

If one of the pastors had been the disciple of an apostle, then naturally that person would be the representative of the council — the *de facto* council chair — since that person would already be seen as having a measure of authority above the rest by virtue of his direct connection to Jesus Christ through an apostle. In cases where there was no one in the city who had personally known an apostle, then the position would go to the one who was closest to an apostle in terms of a teacher-student line of succession. This is, in part, what we mean by apostolic succession. If no member of the council could claim any particular connection to an apostle, then in those cases (probably in smaller towns and more rural areas) a process of election emerged. And as time went on, and it became more difficult to determine who was closest to a direct line of succession, election became the norm. Whenever it became necessary to correspond with the Christians in another city, the leader of the council wrote

[7] Stewart, *The Original Bishops*, 18. Note that in *The Martyrdom of Justin*, Justin Martyr tells the Roman authorities that the Christians of Rome do not have a single meeting place because there are too many of them to fit into one space. At about the same time (mid-second century) Polycarp of Smyrna visited Rome, and met with the Christians from Asia Minor, who were presumably meeting in separate house-churches, conducting liturgy in their native language(s). This shows that in Rome, at least, the Christians there were divided by ethnicity/language. More important, the Christians from Asia Minor were celebrating Easter on a different day from the native Western Christians, and this was tolerated at this time. See Eusebius of Caesarea, *Ecclesiastical History*, 5.24.

[8] Eusebius of Caesarea, *Ecclesiastical History*, 5.24. Here in a fragment from Irenaeus of Lyons, Irenaeus says that the leaders in Rome before Victor passed around the Eucharist. Some have speculated that this may refer to the *fermentum*, or the yeast, used to make the bread.

[9] We can see the mention of a council of priests, even in the third century; see Hippolytus, *Against Noetus*, 1.

the letter on behalf of the whole church in that city, speaking for all the members of the council.[10]

At some point the word *bishop* came to be used primarily for the one pastor who was the chair of the council, while the word *priest* (*presbyter*) came to be associated with the members of the council, as members of a *presbytery*.[11] This development probably happened sooner in places like Rome, where it would be more clear that one of the pastors was in the direct line of succession from an apostle (in this case, Peter), and therefore would have authority over the other pastors. We can see this development (though not yet the shift in terminology) in the way Clement of Rome refers to his office using the analogy of the Old Testament high priest.[12] In other places where election became the norm early on, the position of council chair may have developed from one of representation to one of authority.[13]

As we have already seen, Clement wrote *1 Clement* with an air of authority even over the Christians in Corinth, based on Rome's association with Peter. So although the word *bishop* does not yet seem to designate the specific office of leader of the council of priests, that office does exist. The person who holds that office in Rome is seen as the successor of the apostle Peter, who was the first apostolic *overseer* in the capital city. It is important to note, however, that at this point in history, even when church leadership becomes an "office," it is still not a "job." Church leaders do not make a living leading the Church, and their leadership in the Church does not exempt them from having to participate in regular secular society — and for Clement, that meant that he would have had to keep up his duties as a slave, while also

[10] See Hermas, *The Shepherd*, 8.3. As long as the apostles were alive, they functioned as something more like the bishops of today, as the authority over a region, or over a group of churches. For example, as the apostle Paul was the authority over the churches he founded, or the apostle John over the churches of Asia Minor (mentioned in Rev. 1–2). By the time the apostles were gone, there were likely multiple house-churches in each city, so that as the office of bishop developed, the bishop would again have authority over multiple churches, but within a city rather than regionally. Eventually, certain cities would be designated as *metropolitans*, the bishops there having authority over a region, even over the other bishops in that region.

[11] Stewart, *The Original Bishops*, 6–8, 15–17, 18, 22–24, 48, 354.

[12] We can also see this in the *Didache*, 13, where the prophet (apostle) is called a high priest.

[13] Even where the office of bishop is an authority over the rest of the priests, it was always assumed that the bishop remained a priest and in that sense was "first among equals." In the third century, Cyprian of Carthage assumes that bishops are priests, and that bishops and priests are co-presiders of the sacraments. Cyprian of Carthage, *Epistles*, 51.7, 54.20.

acting as the bishop of Rome.[14] Clement of Rome is therefore a transitional figure, in which we can see that the office of bishop exists, although it was not called "bishop" yet, at least not in any sense that the title distinguished one person from the other pastors in the city.

Although it happened at different paces in different places, by the time of Ignatius of Antioch in the early second century, we can see the second phase in the development of the Church's hierarchy. Two important things have happened to move the process along. First, the apostles died. With the death of John around the turn of the century, there were no more apostles left, and only a few remained who knew them personally. Even these so-called "elders" were not given the same inspired or prophetic status as apostles, and with the controversy over Montanism, which we will consider below, prophecy never became a leadership position within the Church (cf. 1 Cor. 12:7–11). The second thing that happened was the growth of the Church to the point where there were multiple church meeting places in virtually every city. This meant that the leaders of the individual congregations within each city had to keep in touch, and the leadership of each city had to try to keep in touch with the leadership in other cities, in order to make sure that the Church stayed unified.

However, staying unified requires maintaining a unified body of teaching. If different pastors are teaching conflicting interpretations of Christ and the Scriptures, the Church will split. Therefore, as Ignatius knew, it is not enough to have a council of priests, there must also be a centralized authority for when disputes arise. The office of bishop (as we think of it) emerged as that authority. The word *bishop* (*episkopos*) came to be used exclusively for the leader of the council of priests, the one whose responsibility it was to protect the integrity of the teaching. The bishop in each place was still one of the priests and continued to serve as the leader of a local congregation, but the bishops took the place of the apostles as their successors in

[14] Clement of Rome, *1 Clement*, 40.5–41.1. It does not appear that church leadership becomes an occupation (with pay) until the late second century. By the time of Tertullian, writing at the turn of the third century, he can criticize some heretics because their leaders have to have secular jobs to make a living. The implication is that if their sects were legitimate, they would be able to support their leaders. Tertullian, *The Prescription against the Heretics*, 41. According to the *Didascalia Apostolorum*, 8–9, when bishops do receive pay for leading their churches, they are to consider themselves as sharing the resources of the church with the needy. It appears that offerings were collected and entrusted to the bishop, who distributed money to those in need, keeping some for himself as a salary. The *Didascalia* also includes a schedule of clergy stipends, however this represents a later development, no earlier than the third or fourth century.

the role of *overseers*, in the sense of having an authority over the other priests. The primary difference between the first phase and the second phase is in the terminology. Clement of Rome compared himself to a high priest with authority over the other priests, but the Church did not yet have a specific word for this office of *high priest*. In the second phase, and only a little more than a decade later, Ignatius of Antioch would specifically name the office of *bishop*, and compare the authority of the bishop over the priests to the authority of God over the apostles.[15]

Therefore, in the second phase, we still have a hierarchy of three levels, however now it looks like this:

- Bishops (regional or citywide overseers with authority over local priests)
- Priests (presiders in local congregations, with authority delegated by bishops)
- Deacons (assistants to the bishop)

The bishop has replaced the apostle as overseer, but is not itinerant, he is local to his *see*, which is the sphere of his influence.[16] He is the pastor of all the Christians in that town or city. The bishop may be one of the resident pastors (especially early on), and he is the chair of the council.[17] In the letters of Ignatius of Antioch, we can see him arguing for the ideal of one bishop per city,[18] but the fact that he feels the need to argue for it means that this was not always the reality. In some larger cities, it is entirely possible that when the church got large enough there could have been more than one intra-city council (perhaps based on language), each with its own chair, and possibly each with its own catechetical school.[19] This could cause confusion over who the bishop of that city really was, or whether there could be more than one bishop (under the newer definition of the word) in one place. Clearly Ignatius knew that having more than one bishop in a city could cause division, and in a case where the two bishops disagreed, it could force every Christian in that city to choose between them, creating not one church, but two.

[15] Ignatius of Antioch, *Letter to the Ephesians*, 3; *Letter to the Magnesians*, 3.1, 6.

[16] The term *see* comes from the Latin for seat, *sedes*. See Meyendorff, *Imperial Unity*, 152.

[17] Ignatius of Antioch, *Letter to the Ephesians*, 2, 20; *Letter to the Magnesians*, 2, 7; *Letter to the Trallians*, 2–3; *Letter to the Philadelphians*, 4.

[18] Ignatius of Antioch, *Letter to the Philadelphians* 4.1; *Letter to the Trallians* 3.1. Note that the word for *bishop* here is singular.

[19] Note that in the middle of the second century, Justin Martyr, though not a bishop, was the leader of a philosophical (catechetical?) school in Rome. It appears to be just one of a number of such schools, though we do not know how many, nor do we know whether each school had a different teaching authority over it. It is possible that at the beginning, some cities developed with a separate bishop for each language group, though this would be precisely the kind of development that Ignatius was trying to prevent.

Even when there were multiple priests functioning as presiders over multiple congregations in a city, it seems that as long as they could, the bishops tried to keep all the Christians together for the sacraments, or the *mysteries* of the Church. In practice this might mean that they gathered all Christians together in one place for Baptisms, or perhaps even for the Eucharist, at least until the number of Christians became too great to do so. In some places, it is possible that individual house-churches may have met on Sunday mornings for a liturgy without the Eucharist. Then Christians from across the city would gather in a larger place in the evening for a eucharistic "*agape* meal" presided over by the bishop.[20] When they could no longer bring all the Christians in a city together in one place, then the bishops delegated the authority to preside over the sacraments to the local priests. Then the sacrament of the Eucharist became part of Sunday morning worship, and the *agape* meal continued in the evening, without the sacrament, as a way to share resources and fellowship. This seems to be the case in Rome by the middle of the second century, based on the liturgy of Justin Martyr.[21] We know from the correspondence between the pagan governor Pliny the Younger and the emperor Trajan (forty years earlier), that a law against the meetings of "secret societies" had forced Christians in Asia Minor to discontinue the evening meetings. This could very well be another reason for moving the sacrament of the Eucharist from the evening meal to the morning pre-dawn meetings.

Of course, it would be required that the local priests maintain the acceptable teachings and stay within certain liturgical boundaries in order for them to remain a part of the universal Church. To this day, any local priest only has permission to teach and preside as long as that permission is granted by the bishop. Based on the concept of apostolic succession, the unity of the Church is guaranteed by the consistency of its teaching, which in turn in guaranteed by the integrity of the teaching office. The responsibility for this integrity rested (and still rests) with the bishops.

Baptisms were generally done in groups, once a year at Easter, when the bishop would initiate all the candidates of the city, with the assistance of the deacons. The bishops may have also held some authority over burials, at least we know this was

[20] Acts 20:7–12 may indicate an early tradition of evening Eucharist, which would be understandable considering the fact that the Last Supper was in the evening; see Ralph P. Martin, *Worship in the Early Church* (Grand Rapids: Eerdmans, 1964), 33.

[21] Justin Martyr, *1 Apology*, 67. Note also that in the *Martyrdom of Justin*, it is clear that there are multiple church meetings in Rome. Justin does not actually say that the eucharistic liturgy he describes took place in the morning, but we assume that it did, since this was about forty years after the time of Pliny's letter, when the Christians in his province had moved the Eucharist to Sunday morning.

so by the third century. Once the church of a city could acquire and control land for burials, the bishop or his appointee would manage the cemetery and (we assume) the bishop would conduct the burials. Marriage at this time was not a ritual of the Church, but was a legal contract. However, a tradition of going to the bishop for a blessing emerged, and Ignatius advised that all Christian couples should get the bishop's permission to marry.[22]

Deacons always assisted the bishops, not only in liturgy, but also in the visitation and distribution of resources to the sick and needy. In general, the deacons represented the bishop, and part of the deacons' responsibilities included visiting the sick and keeping the bishop informed of the needs of the people in his see.[23] The deacons would continue to serve as assistants to the bishops for many matters of church administration, including the distribution of alms to the poor, but they would also eventually serve as assistants to the priests in liturgy, since their liturgical role is to assist the presider, whether that person is the bishop, or a priest to whom the bishop has given liturgical authority. In some places, the deacons also functioned as ushers, or *doorkeepers*, with the responsibility of questioning unknown visitors before they were allowed into the assembly where they would receive the Eucharist.[24] We learn from Justin Martyr that the deacons are also charged with taking the eucharistic elements to shut-ins and prisoners.[25] Eventually, the deacons would help distribute the eucharistic elements.[26] Therefore, there must be enough deacons, "in proportion to the number of the congregation of the people of the church."[27] Therefore, in one sense church leadership came to be defined as the three *orders* of bishop, priest, and deacon. However, in another sense, the deacons were not considered what we might call *clergy*, (a term that didn't exist back then) since their role in liturgy was

[22] Ignatius of Antioch, *Letter to Polycarp*, 5.2.

[23] *Didascalia Apostolorum*, 16. As the Christian population in a city grew, the deacons could also be charged with communicating with the bishop on behalf of the people, acting as a secretary to the bishop, so that the bishop's time did not become consumed by the needs of individuals.

[24] *Didascalia Apostolorum*, 12. However in Rome, there was a separate office of doorkeeper.

[25] Justin Martyr, *1 Apology*, 65, 67. The deacons were to act on behalf of the bishops in visiting the sick and shut-ins. According to the *Didascalia*, they would also bring food to those in prison, and were authorized to bribe the guards to treat the Christian prisoners well. They might also use church money to ransom kidnapped Christians or even buy the freedom of Christian slaves or prisoners. *Didascalia Apostolorum*, 18–19.

[26] Cyprian of Carthage, *On the Lapsed*, 25.

[27] *Didascalia Apostolorum*, 16. As we will see below, the church of Rome in the third century had seven deacons, which corresponded to the division of the city into regions.

limited and they never had the authority to preside over the sacraments.[28] At some point, the role of deaconess emerged, primarily as one who would assist women as they went through Baptism. We will have more to say about this in another chapter.

It was always assumed that every Christian has a responsibility, by virtue of his or her Baptism, to uphold the expectations that Jesus and the apostles set down for a follower of "the Way." This includes love of neighbor and care for the poor. In other words, we might say that it was assumed that lay people were to be involved in ministry, though the early Church did not necessarily make such a distinction as *lay* versus *clergy*. In many cases bishops did give the authority of teaching to lay catechists (one thinks of Justin Martyr and Tertullian), and there are hints of lay people involved in ministries of healing.[29] It was the persecution of the Church by the Roman empire that eventually forced a distinction between *clergy* (those who were most targeted by authorities) and *laity*.

Metropolitans and the Primacy of Rome

In the early Church, the office of bishop developed out of necessity. One could say that the bishops were charged with the ministry of breaking down some boundaries and safeguarding some others. The bishops led the Church in breaking down the boundaries of what, today, we would call race and class. Anyone, of any ethic background or any social status, was welcome in the Church (Gal. 3:28–29), and the Christians reached out in charity to the vulnerable both inside and outside of the Church. On the other hand, to preserve the integrity and the unity of the Church, the bishops were also the shepherds of the Church's teaching (doctrine), liturgy (specifically the sacraments), and moral expectations (discipline).

As the primary teaching authority of the Church, the bishop would normally be in charge of the school of catechesis, and even when there were lay teachers such as Justin Martyr, the bishop held the authority over the content of what was taught.[30] Before the third century, there may have been more than one catechetical school

[28] See Ignatius of Antioch, preface to the *Letter to the Philadelphians*, and the *Martyrdom of Polycarp*, 6. On the restriction of presiding to bishops and priests, see also the *Apostolic Tradition*, 8, 28. On the other hand, deacons (and deaconesses) did play a more central role in Baptism in some places. See the *Didascalia Apostolorum*, 16.

[29] *Apostolic Tradition*, 14.

[30] Tertullian is also an example of a lay teacher, though his relationship to the hierarchy is unclear. On the assumption that teachers (at least in some places) could be lay or clergy, see the *Apostolic Tradition*, 19. On the episcopacy as teaching office, see Irenaeus of Lyons, *Against Heresies*, 3.3.3. In the early Church, pre-Baptism catechesis focused more on morality (how to live as a Christian) than theology (what to believe). Apparently, the

in some large cities, each having its own lead catechist. Justin Martyr had his own students in Rome in the mid-second century and admitted to his captors that there were other *schools* of Christians — though he would not name names or give up their locations. But this was not a faction in opposition to the bishop. It may not even have been a formal school of catechesis. We usually assume that Justin was teaching Christianity as a philosophy for those who were philosophically minded, but it could be that what he really had was just one of several individual congregations in Rome. If that was the case, then Justin was the host, and the catechist, but apparently not the priest/presider.

Even in the early third century Hippolytus may have been the leader of the Greek-speaking Christians in Rome, perhaps with their own school. More likely, he was the bishop of a smaller town near Rome. But Hippolytus openly criticized the bishops of Rome, and in doing so, he proved Ignatius of Antioch's point, that having more than one teaching authority in a city would eventually lead to disagreement and schism. In Hippolytus's case it seems that his own disciplinary authority was clashing with that of the bishops of Rome, leading to conflict over excommunication and Reconciliation (we will look at the details of this controversy in a later chapter). And so Ignatius had concluded that the unity of the Church depended on the authority of a single bishop. The development of the office of bishop as a singular point of authority in a given city is sometimes referred to as *monoepiscopacy*.[31]

Cyprian of Carthage (bishop AD 249–258), would follow Ignatius on two important, and interdependent, points. First, there must be only one bishop in a city.[32] This is because multiple authorities would threaten unity. More than one bishop would ultimately mean more than one church. As soon as two bishops disagreed on matters of theology or church discipline, every Christian in that city would be

---

early bishops thought it was more important to emphasize the behavioral commitments that new converts were making, assuming they would learn their theology after Baptism.

[31] The most comprehensive of the recent major studies on the monoepiscopacy is Allen Brent, *Hippolytus and the Roman Church in the Third Century: Communities in Tension Before the Emergence of a Monarch-Bishop* (Leiden: Brill, 1995). However, there are some problems with this study, not least of which is the lack of regard for the obvious influence of apostolic succession and the nature of the early hierarchy as discipleship/apprenticeship. See also Stewart, *The Original Bishops*. It is the present author's opinion that both of these works, while brilliant, suffer from a refusal to accept the evidence of Petrine leadership in Rome and its effect on the office of bishop there.

[32] Cyprian of Carthage, *Epistles*, 40.2; *On the Unity of the Catholic Church*, 5; see also Ignatius of Antioch, *Letter to the Philadelphians*, 2.2, 6.2; Ignatius of Antioch, *Letter to the Smyrnaeans*, 9.1.

forced to choose between them. As we have seen, the very definition of heresy is that it is a factioning, a separation from the mainstream majority. Thus, as Ignatius had said, nothing could be considered valid that was done without the authority of the bishop of the city.[33]

The other point on which Cyprian agreed with Ignatius was that there could be no salvation outside of the Church.[34] These issues are related because the Church was defined in terms of the sacraments, which were under the authority of the bishop.[35] In any given city, to be *in* the church meant to be in communion with the bishop.[36] Thus if there were more than one bishop, it would appear that there was more than one church. In practice, if one bishop was reconciling those excommunicated by another bishop, excommunication becomes meaningless (not to mention ineffective as a deterrent to sin). As we have seen, this was in fact happening in the time of Hippolytus. Part of Hippolytus's complaint seems to have been that people whom he had excommunicated (presumably in his town) were being reconciled and receiving communion in Rome.

To be excommunicated meant to be excluded from communion, barred from the table of the Eucharist. The Eucharist was, among other things, a symbol of the unity of the Church and the communion of the saints.[37] There is only one Eucharist, and outside the Church there is no valid Eucharist, in fact no valid sacraments at all.[38] If one was not in communion with the bishop, one could not receive the Eucharist, let alone receive a blessing on a marriage, or expect a Christian burial in the catacombs or cemeteries near the saints. Therefore the unity of the Church was dependent on the unity of its sacraments, and the unity of the sacraments was dependent on the singular authority of the episcopacy.

[33] See also Irenaeus of Lyons, *Against Heresies*, 3.2.2, and *Didascalia Apostolorum*, 9.

[34] Cyprian of Carthage, *Epistles*, 72.21; *On the Unity of the Catholic Church*, 6. The importance of this question was extended to the sacraments, since the authority to administer the sacraments came from the bishop through ordination. Cyprian of Carthage, *Epistles*, 75.3, 8. See also Ignatius of Antioch, *Letter to the Philadelphians*, 3.3. In reality, this view was universally held in the early Church. The question was not whether there was the possibility of salvation outside the Church, the question was how to define the Church.

[35] Cyprian of Carthage, *On the Unity of the Catholic Church*, 7.

[36] Ignatius of Antioch, *Letter to the Philadelphians*, 8.1. For Ignatius, Reconciliation meant returning to the bishop.

[37] Cyprian of Carthage, *Epistles*, 51.21, 53.2, 54.5.

[38] Cyprian of Carthage, *Epistles*, 75.3, 8; *On the Unity of the Catholic Church*, 13, 17. See Ignatius of Antioch, *Letter to the Ephesians*, 5.2, 20.2; *Letter to the Philadelphians*, 4.1; *Letter to the Smyrnaeans*, 8.1. We will see this same principle applied to Baptism in the baptismal controversy.

The bishops naturally had authority over the ordination of priests and deacons, and eventually also the election of their fellow bishops.[39] In other words, in those places where the succession was not clear, the council of priests would elect one from among them to be the bishop (sometimes also allowing the laity to vote). But eventually, regional bishops were gathering and electing the priests who would join their ranks.[40] In this way, the new bishops and priests could be guaranteed to be within the direct succession from the apostles. We have already seen how ordination begins with the choosing and commissioning of the disciples of the apostles (1 Tim. 4:14). Ordination was therefore seen as the first line of defense in maintaining the integrity of the sacraments and the teaching of the Church. Thus, the only valid sacraments were those performed by the ordained, and the only valid ordinations were those within the chain of apostolic succession.[41]

By the end of the third century, the bishops of certain major cities were emerging as having a level of authority above the smaller surrounding cities.[42] These *metropolitans* (or as we might call them, archbishops) would eventually have veto power even over ordinations in the other cities under their jurisdiction. When bishops met in regional councils, the metropolitan bishop functioned as the chair of that council, just as the city bishop functioned as the chair of the local council. By the end of the patristic era, five traditional metropolitan churches had emerged: Jerusalem, Rome, Antioch, Alexandria, and eventually Constantinople.[43] And although Jerusalem was the mother church, Rome was seen as the primary church, the metropolitan of metropolitans, with authority over all of the other bishops.[44] This is why Clement of Rome could write with such assumed authority to the church in Corinth, a place he had never been.

It is important to note at this point that the Church, on every level, was understood to be a kind of household. And in the Roman world, the head of a household

[39] Cyprian of Carthage, *Epistles*, 40.2, 51.8, 54.5–6; see also *Apostolic Tradition*, 1.9.6–8.

[40] David Rankin, *Tertullian and the Church* (Cambridge: Cambridge University Press, 1995), 191, 195.

[41] Cyprian of Carthage, *Epistles*, 48.2, 75.3, 75.8; *On the Unity of the Catholic Church*, 10.

[42] Tertullian, *On Modesty*, 1.7–8. Tertullian mentions "bishops of bishops." Note that Ignatius had said only bishops had the authority to convene a council. Ignatius of Antioch, *Letter to Polycarp*, 7.

[43] Some consider Carthage and Caesarea Maritima to have had minor metropolitan status. In any case, an important point to note is that unless one counts Carthage, Rome was the only metropolitan in the West.

[44] This was codified in the ecumenical councils of the fourth century, as well as at the Council of Serdica in 343. There it was affirmed that the bishop of Rome has authority even over the other metropolitans. See Meyendorff, *Imperial Unity*, 59–65.

(an extended family) was called the *paterfamilias*, the *family-father*. Therefore, when every local pastor was called bishop, he was considered the *father* of those whom he taught and led — certainly of those whom he had converted and baptized — on St. Paul's precedent (1 Cor. 4:14–15; Philem. 10). And when the terminology changed, and the word *bishop* came to be used of the citywide or regional authorities, they continued to be seen as both the shepherd, and the father, of their sees.[45] Of course, the priests, the presiders over local congregations, also came to be called *father*, because they were the father of the household of the local assembly. The English word *pope* (as well as the word *patriarch*) is simply a form of the Greek and Latin words for father.

It seems that by the third century, words that we might translate as *pope* were becoming titles specific to the metropolitan bishops. Stephen of Rome was called pope, and at the same time the Christians of North Africa considered Cyprian of Carthage to be their pope.[46] In the fourth century, Eusebius of Caesarea referred to the bishop of Alexandria as a pope.[47] But in the fifth and sixth centuries (at least in the West) the term came to be used exclusively for the bishop of Rome.

Since the bishop in any major city was considered the successor of the apostle(s) who founded the church there, the bishop of Rome was considered the successor of Peter. Every bishop was invested with the authority to forgive sin (John 20:21–23), but Peter was the one with the keys (Matt. 16:19).[48] It should come as no surprise, then, that Rome emerged as the primary metropolitan. Irenaeus of Lyons, writing in the late second century, expressed a growing consensus that all churches should agree with Rome, at least on matters of doctrine.[49] Tertullian accepted the primacy of Rome, and so did Cyprian, though as we will see he did not want to submit to Stephen of Rome on matters related to the sacraments.[50] Both Stephen and Cyprian

[45] See the *Martyrdom of Polycarp*, 12.2, where Polycarp, the bishop of Smyrna, is called "the father of Christians."

[46] Cyprian of Carthage, *Epistles*, 73.

[47] Eusebius of Caesarea, *Ecclesiastical History*, 7.7.

[48] Cyprian of Carthage, *Epistles*, 26.1. Clement of Alexandria had said that Peter was the preeminent apostle because Jesus had paid his tax for him (Matt. 17:27). Clement of Alexandria, *Who Is the Rich Man That Shall Be Saved?*, 21. On the bishops as recipients of the apostles' authority, specifically the authority of "binding and loosing" granted by Jesus in Matthew 18:18, and interpreted as the authority to absolve sin and excommunicate, see the *Didascalia Apostolorum*, 5.

[49] Irenaeus of Lyons, *Against Heresies*, 3.3.2.

[50] Tertullian, *The Prescription against the Heretics*, 36; Cyprian of Carthage, *Epistles*, 28, 42, 51.6–8, 54.14, 62.1, 70.3, 71.1–3; see also the letter of Firmilian in Cyprian of Carthage, *Epistles*, 74.3–6, 24; cf. Michael M. Sage, *Cyprian*, Patristic Monograph Series, vol. 1 (Cambridge, MA: Philadelphia Patristic Foundation, 1975), 301.

accepted the concept of apostolic succession, however Cyprian thought it only applied to the teaching office of the Church (doctrine), not to Church discipline.[51] Eventually, however, the metropolitans, and especially Rome, would come to have authority over the other cities on all matters. As we will see, Dionysius of Rome followed the lead of his predecessor Clement, and took the initiative to write a letter of correction to a fellow bishop. And when the heretic Paul of Samosata refused to vacate his see, the emperor Aurelian — a pagan — enforced the authority of Rome.[52] Eventually, the first ecumenical Council of Nicaea in AD 325 would declare Rome to be the primary metropolitan. This was reaffirmed at the Council of Serdica in 343 and the second ecumenical Council of Constantinople in 381.

Thus the developing hierarchy, combined with an urgent concern for unity, led to the singular authority of the episcopacy, with the assumption that the authority of the bishop *is* the authority of the Church.[53] In fact, the three-level hierarchy of bishop, priest, and deacon was seen as somewhat analogous to the Trinity, with its primary authority, and therefore its unity, invested in and dependent upon the one at the top of the hierarchy, while at the same time maintaining a certain equality,

[51] Cyprian of Carthage, *Epistles*, 72.13, 73.1–3, 73.9–10, 75.5. See also the letter of Firmilian in Cyprian of Carthage, *Epistle*, 74.16–17. Cyprian, like some other bishops, questioned the limits of Rome's authority over other cities. While most (if not all) would have accepted that all churches should agree with Rome on matters of doctrine, some questioned whether they had to submit to Rome on other matters. Cyprian argued that each bishop is the highest authority in his own area but is free of the authority of other bishops. Thus, the councils of Carthage need not submit to the bishop of Rome. After all, Peter had deferred to Paul on the issue of the Gentiles; see Cyprian of Carthage, *Epistles*, 62.1, 70.3, 71.3. Cyprian argued that truth takes precedence over Tradition; see Cyprian of Carthage, *Epistles*, 72.13, 73.2–3, 9; and the letter of Firmilian in Cyprian of Carthage, *Epistles*, 74.19. Firmilian argued that the Romans do not always agree among themselves, so he reasoned that the Roman bishops might err; see the letter of Firmilian in Cyprian of Carthage, *Epistles*, 74.3, 6; see also Cyprian of Carthage, *Epistles*, 73.1. Therefore, the bishops, even the bishops of Rome, must be teachable and ultimately submit to the consensus of the greater Church (cf. 1 Cor. 14:29–30); see Cyprian of Carthage, *Epistles*, 70.3, 73.10. This attitude was confirmed by a council in Carthage, which criticized Stephen for setting himself up as a "bishop of bishops." Nevertheless, the idea of metropolitans was firmly entrenched; cf. Tertullian, *On Modesty*, 1.7–8. Firmilian summed it up when he wrote, as if to Stephen, "for while you think that all may be excommunicated by you, you have excommunicated yourself alone from all." See the letter of Firmilian in Cyprian of Carthage, *Epistles*, 74.24, translation in *Ante-Nicene Fathers*, vol. 5, 396.

[52] Eusebius of Caesarea, *Ecclesiastical History*, 7.30.

[53] Cyprian of Carthage, *Epistles*, 9.1, 3–4, 10.2, 11.2, 26.1; *On the Unity of the Catholic Church*, 5.

at least between bishop and priest.[54] Therefore, it was understood that there was an ontological equality between bishops and priests, even while acknowledging a hierarchy of authority.[55] In the end, the need for consistency between cities (not just within cities) would drive the Church toward a hierarchy which included "bishops of bishops" (metropolitans), and one singular authority as the primary metropolitan, the bishop of Rome.

Ignatius of Antioch

Ignatius, bishop of Antioch in Syria, was born around AD 50. According to tradition, he was a disciple of the apostle John. Since John is said to have lived to the end of the first century, this is certainly possible. Ignatius had been arrested for spreading the Faith, at about the same time that Pliny was corresponding with Trajan. However, the governor of Syria was sending Ignatius to Rome for trial and execution. On his way to Rome, his guards allowed him to meet with other Christians, and he even stayed briefly in Smyrna with his friend, the bishop Polycarp. Ignatius wrote seven letters during that time, mostly to the Christians in cities along the way. One of the letters mentions a bishop of Ephesus named Onesimus, who, according to tradition, is the same Onesimus mentioned in Paul's letter to Philemon (Philem. 1:10; Col. 4:9).[56] He would have been about seventy years old by this time. Ignatius's letters were written about AD 107 or 108, and he was martyred shortly after writing them, probably in AD 108. Tradition tells us that he died in the Colosseum in Rome. The letters of Ignatius, with a brief description of significant content, are listed below.[57]

Ignatius wrote with authority, but also with great humility. He could have claimed authority as the bishop of what was emerging as one of the great metropolitan cities

[54] It is interesting to note that in the *Didascalia Apostolorum*, 9, the deaconess is compared to the Holy Spirit.

[55] *Didache*, 15; Clement of Rome, *1 Clement*, 41–42, 44; Cyprian of Carthage, *Epistles*, 45.2, 51.7, 54.12, 75.5; *On the Unity of the Catholic Church*, 6, 11, 23; see also the anonymous *Against Novatian*, 3, 7–8, 12.

[56] Ignatius of Antioch, *Letter to the Ephesians*, 1.3. The belief that the Onesimus of Philemon became bishop of Ephesus provides another possible reason why the letter to Philemon was included in the New Testament.

[57] There are long versions, middle versions, and short versions of the letters. Scholarly consensus is that the middle versions are the authentic (original) versions. The long versions were embellished later, and the short versions were abbreviated summaries made much later. The best translations of the letters are in Kenneth J. Howell, *Ignatius of Antioch and Polycarp of Smyrna: A New Translation and Theological Commentary* (Zanesville, OH: CHResources, 2009), and the scholarly standard in Holmes, *The Apostolic Fathers*.

of the Church. But instead he took a position of humility, implicitly emphasizing his role as a confessor, and soon to be martyr, over his role as a bishop (but cf. the opening greeting of the *Letter to the Trallians*).[58] In fact, on several occasions he makes a point to say things like, "I am not commanding you, as though I were someone important";[59] "I do not think myself qualified for this, that I, a convict, should give you orders as though I were an apostle";[60] "I do not give you orders like Peter and Paul."[61] But he knew that his reputation would precede his letters, that he was one who was willing to sacrifice his life for the Faith — and for his flock in Antioch — and this was a kind of authority that, as we will see, was available to all Christians.

On the other hand, Ignatius was a bishop, and he was a strong advocate for the newly emerging office of bishop and its authority. This authority was primarily meant to maintain the unity of the Church. For Ignatius, to oppose the bishop was to threaten to split the Church.[62] In fact, he wrote that to disobey a bishop was to disobey God,[63] and that Christians must listen to the bishop as though it were the Lord Himself.[64] Calling himself "a man set on unity," he believed that the unity of the Church required a limit of one bishop per city, since more than one bishop in a city could lead to disputes, and inevitably to division.[65] Of course, Ignatius is preaching what he thought was the ideal, and the very fact that he feels he has to say it with such urgency means that it is not always happening that way. There must have been some cities at the time where confusion over the title *bishop* or controversy between multiple catechetical schools may have led to division or factioning. Or perhaps it may be more likely that heretical groups like the docetics (whom we will meet below) were claiming to have their own bishops. It is easy to see, however, that Ignatius feared such a situation would lead to schism.

Ignatius is the first person we know of to use the Christian application of the word *catholic*.[66] It is often said that the word *catholic* originally meant *universal*. However

[58] See Howell's critique of Holmes's translation in Howell, *Ignatius of Antioch and Polycarp of Smyrna*, 40–43. See below for the definition of a confessor and the role of the martyrs.

[59] Ignatius of Antioch, *Letter to the Ephesians*, 3.1, in Holmes, *The Apostolic Fathers*, 185.

[60] Ignatius of Antioch, *Letter to the Trallians*, 3.3, 5.2, in Holmes, *The Apostolic Fathers*, 217.

[61] Ignatius of Antioch, *Letter to the Romans*, 4.3, in Holmes, *The Apostolic Fathers*, 229.

[62] Ignatius of Antioch, *Letter to the Magnesians*, 6.2.

[63] Ignatius of Antioch, *Letter to the Ephesians*, 5.3; see also *Letter to the Magnesians*, 6.13; *Letter to the Trallians*, 7; *Letter to the Smyrnaeans*, 9.

[64] Ignatius of Antioch, *Letter to the Ephesians*, 6.1.

[65] Ignatius of Antioch, *Letter to the Philadelphians*, 4.1; see Holmes, *The Apostolic Fathers*, 243.

[66] Ignatius of Antioch, *Letter to the Smyrnaeans*, 8.

the phrase *catholic church* in Ignatius (in Greek, *katholike ekklesia*) may simply be a reference to Acts 9:31, which refers to the "Church throughout all..." (*ekklesia kath holes...*). The *catholic Church* is the "Church throughout all" the world, which gives us the meaning of the universal Church.[67] However, the Church's unity was already threatened by teachers of alternative interpretations of the Person of Christ. Therefore, while the word "catholic" refers to the whole, or universal Church, in Ignatius it already also meant the *true* Church as opposed to any alternative expressions. The concept of the "universal" Church would be used to exclude those who were considered outside the Church, as the word was employed in the attempt to set the boundaries of what was correct Christian teaching. In other words, the teaching of the *catholic* Church would not lead one astray. The same could not be said for the teachings of those who separated themselves from the universal Church — and that included anyone who was not in unity with the bishops, the successors of the apostles. So although we rightly say that *catholic* means universal, it is possible to speak of the *catholic* church in a given place, such as Antioch, meaning the congregations that are orthodox, or united with the mainstream universal Church, as opposed to those who may be meeting separately and without the approval of the bishop.[68]

The primary threat to unity in Ignatius's letters seems to be the same false teachers mentioned in the first letter of John in the New Testament, and in *2 Clement*. They were teaching that Jesus was not really human but was pure spirit (cf. 1 John 4:1–3). The implications of this teaching will be discussed below, however the problem for Ignatius was that these "false teachers" were holding their own meetings, separate from the rest of the Church, and without the sanction of the local bishop (or possibly claiming to have their own bishop; see 1 John 2:19).[69] In a Jewish context, any

[67] The word *katholicos* may be a compound word made from *kath holos*. The point is that Ignatius has not coined a new term here, since it is clear that he is using the word on the assumption that he doesn't have to explain it, and he expects his audience already to know what it means. This is especially true given the suspicion with which the early Christians viewed innovation. It seems likely that his audience would recognize the term as having come from the passage in Acts. I am indebted to my fellow historian Dr. Roberto Pacheco of Florida International University (Miami) for these insights.

[68] Howell, *Ignatius of Antioch and Polycarp of Smyrna*, 33–37.

[69] For Ignatius, to be outside the authority of the bishop is to be outside of the Body of Christ; Ignatius of Antioch, *Letter to the Ephesians*, 5; *Letter to the Magnesians*, 7; *Letter to the Trallians*, 2–3; *Letter to the Philadelphians*, 3–4, 7; *Letter to the Smyrnaeans*, 8. Ignatius wrote that only bishops have the authority to convene a council, *Letter to Polycarp*, 7; note that Irenaeus also condemned unauthorized meetings, Irenaeus of Lyons, *Against Heresies*, 3.2.2.

ten men could form a synagogue, however Ignatius was arguing against a Christian version of this system. As long as the Church was still defining itself, meetings, worship, and especially the teaching of the Church must be more controlled in order to prevent the propagation of incorrect interpretations that would lead the innocent astray. In this sense, the "false teachers" are *heretics*, in the truest sense of the word. *Heresy* comes from a Greek concept meaning "to separate," so for Ignatius, there is no difference between (theological) heresy and schism. Ignatius says that no group can call itself *church* without the bishop, priests, and deacons.[70] Therefore, whoever does not meet with the authorized assembly has separated himself from the Church,[71] so there should be no gatherings without the consent of the bishop.[72]

As I have hinted above, and as we will see in more depth later, the Church was defined in terms of the sacraments, especially the Eucharist, and so it is not surprising that Ignatius connects the Eucharist to the office of the bishop, saying that the only true Eucharist is that which is presided over by the bishop.[73] There can be only one Eucharist, and to divide the table is to divide the Church.[74]

Finally, in Ignatius's letter to the Romans, he anticipates his arrival in Rome and his own death. He begs his Roman brothers and sisters not to try to interfere with his martyrdom.[75] In humility, he says he is only beginning to be a disciple of Jesus, a process that will be completed in his martyrdom. However, there is a more practical reason why he cannot afford to be rescued. Though he does not say it in the letter, he knows that if he were to appear alive after his scheduled execution, many people might assume that he had denied the Faith to save his life, and this would be discouraging to the faithful. There was nothing to do but see it through, believing that those who follow Christ in death will follow Him in resurrection.

We know from Polycarp's letter (below) that soon after Ignatius's death his letters were copied and circulated as a collection, much like the letters of Paul and the four Gospels were.[76] So why weren't Ignatius's letters included in the New Testa-

[70] Ignatius of Antioch, *Letter to the Trallians*, 3.1.

[71] Ignatius of Antioch, *Letter to the Ephesians*, 5.3.

[72] Ignatius of Antioch, *Letter to the Magnesians*, 6.2, 7.1; *Letter to the Trallians*, 2.2; *Letter to the Philadelphians*, 2.2, 6.2, 7.2; *Letter to the Smyrnaeans*, 8.1–2, 9.1.

[73] Ignatius of Antioch, *Letter to the Ephesians*, 5.2, 20; see also *Letter to the Smyrnaeans*, 8, where it is clear that the bishops could delegate the authority to preside over the Eucharist to priests under their authority.

[74] Ignatius of Antioch, *Letter to the Ephesians*, 20.2; *Letter to the Philadelphians*, 4.1; *Letter to the Smyrnaeans*, 8.1.

[75] Ignatius of Antioch, *Letter to the Romans*, 2.1, 4.1, 5.2, 6.3, 7.2.

[76] Polycarp of Smyrna, *Letter to the Philippians*, 13.2.

ment? They have a reliable authorship (though this has been debated at times), and no objectionable content, yet for various reasons the later writers, especially the theologians, did not quote them as authoritative. In other words, they did not come to be treated as Scripture, in the sense of inspired, they did not catch on as books to be read in worship, and so they did not stand the test of time. By the time the New Testament canon was being standardized, they had gone by the wayside.

Letter to the Ephesians (written while at Smyrna)

Ignatius affirms the authority of bishops, along with the council of priests. He says that just as Jesus Christ has the mind of the Father, the bishops have the mind of Christ. Every Christian must listen to the bishop as one would listen to the Lord himself. But anyone who is not in good standing (in union) with the bishop is not in union with God and is outside of the fellowship of the true Eucharist. The "one bread" of the Eucharist is the "medicine of immortality."

In terms of christology, Ignatius affirms the two natures of Jesus Christ: His true humanity and His true divinity, against those who would deny one or the other. He specifically mentions Mary as the one who gave Christ His humanity.

Letter to the Magnesians (written while at Smyrna)

Again Ignatius mentions the bishop as the leader of a council of priests. To be united with the bishop is to be united to Christ. But to do anything without the sanction of the bishop would be wrong and divisive. He warns against "strange doctrines" (docetism, the denial of Christ's humanity) and "antiquated myths" (adoptionism, the denial of Christ's divinity), the two alternative interpretations of the Person of Christ that are, in the end, deceptions.

Letter to the Trallians (written while at Smyrna)

One looks in vain for a nice, neat, trinitarian analogy for the hierarchy of the Church. In this letter, Ignatius compares the bishop, priests, and deacons, to the Father, the apostles, and Jesus Christ, respectively. Here he seems to be emphasizing the deacons and advocating respect for them among the Trallians. In any case, when referring to all of the orders of clergy together, he says, "Without these, no group can be called a church,"[77] and, "Whoever does anything without the bishop and council of [priests] and deacons does not have a clean conscience."[78]

[77] Ignatius of Antioch, *Letter to the Trallians,* 3.3, in Holmes, *The Apostolic Fathers,* 217.

[78] Ignatius of Antioch, *Letter to the Trallians,* 7.2, in Holmes, *The Apostolic Fathers,* 219.

Ignatius calls docetics "atheists," and rhetorically asks them, if Christ's suffering was an illusion (as they taught) then why are these chains real? If Christ didn't really die, why does the martyr have to die? He ends by asking the Trallians to pray for him, so that he may be found worthy to be a martyr.

Letter to the Romans (written while at Smyrna)

Ignatius treats the Roman Christians somewhat differently than the recipients of the other letters, in that he seems to spend more time praising than admonishing the church at Rome. Furthermore, the mention of the apostles Peter and Paul (and in that order) and the reference to the church at Rome presiding (that is, exercising authority) speaks to the emerging primacy of Rome.[79]

Ignatius spends much of this letter reassuring the Roman Christians that he goes to his death willingly, and that they should not try to rescue him. "Let me be food for the wild beasts," he writes, "through whom I can reach God. I am God's wheat, and I am being ground by the teeth of the wild beasts, so that I may prove to be pure bread."[80] So he thinks of his martyrdom in eucharistic terms. Just as Jesus suffered to become the Bread of Life for us, so the bishop will suffer and be ground down only to rise up in resurrection. He even says that if he should change his mind later and beg to be rescued, the Roman Christians are not to listen to him at that time.

Letter to the Philadelphians (written while at Troas)

Here Ignatius emphasizes the importance of having a single point of authority in any given city. The bishop is the shepherd, and the shepherd's job is to keep the sheep safe from the wolves. Of course, in this analogy, the wolves are the heretics, who threaten to lead people astray, and away from the true Church and the Eucharist. This is a serious problem, since, "if any follow a schismatic, they will not inherit the kingdom of God. If any hold to alien views, they disassociate themselves from the passion. Take care, therefore, to participate in one Eucharist, for there is one flesh of our Lord Jesus Christ, and one cup that leads to unity through his blood; there is one altar, just as there is one bishop, together with the council of [priests] and the deacons."[81]

It is interesting to note that we have in this letter a very early reference to the sacrament of Reconciliation. For those who are temporarily taken in by a heretic and find themselves within a schismatic movement, all that is required to return to

[79] Howell, *Ignatius of Antioch and Polycarp of Smyrna*, 43–46.

[80] Ignatius of Antioch, *Letter to the Romans*, 4.1, in Holmes, *The Apostolic Fathers*, 229.

[81] Ignatius of Antioch, *Letter to the Philadelphians*, 3.3–4.1, in Holmes, *The Apostolic Fathers*, 239.

the true (catholic) Church is to be reconciled to the bishop. Ignatius says, "all those who repent and enter into the unity of the church will belong to God," and "the Lord, however, forgives all who repent, if in repenting they return to the unity of God and the council of the bishop."[82] To return to the bishop is to return to the Church, and to return to the Church is to return to God. For Ignatius, it's all about the unity of the Church, and he calls himself "a man set on unity."

Letter to the Smyrnaeans (written while at Troas)

This letter continues the warning against the dangers of docetism. To deny Christ's flesh is to deny Christ (1 John 4:1–3). Ignatius not only affirms the real humanity of Jesus, but also the real bodily Resurrection, and shows how the denial of Jesus' humanity has serious implications for the theology of the Eucharist. Specifically, the docetics deny the Real Presence of Jesus Christ in the Eucharist because they start by denying the physical presence of Jesus Christ in the world at all. The letter also contains perhaps the earliest mention of an important problem with docetism, which is that the denial of flesh and blood in Christ leads to the refusal to care for the bodies of the poor. The docetics "have no concern for love, none for the widow, none for the orphan, none for the oppressed, none for the prisoner or the one released, none for the hungry or thirsty."[83] Therefore no meetings can be allowed without the sanction of the bishop because without the bishop, teaching can be corrupted and the sacraments are invalid.

Letter to Polycarp (written while at Troas)

On one level this seems like a personal letter to a friend and fellow bishop, and in some ways Ignatius seems to have some authority over Polycarp. However, parts of the letter are clearly written to be read aloud to Polycarp's flock and encourage them to put their trust in their bishop and show him respect. Ignatius described Divinity as being outside of time — the invisible who became visible, the intangible who became tangible, the impassible who became passible and suffered for our sake.[84]

Polycarp of Smyrna

According to tradition, Polycarp was also a disciple of the apostle John, along with Ignatius, and John personally appointed him as the bishop of Smyrna (modern-day

[82] Ignatius of Antioch, *Letter to the Philadelphians*, 3.2, 8.1, in Holmes, *The Apostolic Fathers*, 239, 243.

[83] Ignatius of Antioch, *Letter to the Smyrnaeans*, 6.2, in Holmes, *The Apostolic Fathers*, 255.

[84] Ignatius of Antioch, *Letter to Polycarp*, 3.

Izmir, in Turkey).[85] In fact, Polycarp seems to be the last one to have known any of the apostles personally.[86] Not much is known about his early life, but as bishop of Smyrna he was the mentor and teacher of Irenaeus of Lyons, whom he would later send as a missionary priest into Gaul (modern-day France), to assist the bishop of Lyons. Polycarp himself traveled to Rome to meet with the bishop there to discuss the proper way to calculate the date for the celebration of Easter. They agreed to disagree, but parted amicably.[87] Shortly after that, Polycarp was martyred, in about AD 156.

Letter to the Philippians

This is the only writing we have from Polycarp, written shortly after Ignatius died, in about AD 110. Polycarp assumed Ignatius had been martyred but wondered if the Christians in Philippi had heard any of the details of his death. The letter itself functions as a kind of cover letter for the collection of copies of Ignatius's letters that Polycarp is sending along.[88] Following his friend Ignatius, Polycarp warns of the heretics who are denying the reality of Christ's humanity. He quotes 1 John 4:2–3, that those who deny that Christ came with real flesh are "antichrists." These also denied the resurrection, claiming that spiritually they were already living the resurrection life (see 2 Tim. 2:17–18).

The letter includes a message of hope in the midst of persecution, much like we find in the book of Revelation, though without the apocalyptic symbolism. The point is that those who follow Jesus in death will follow Him in resurrection.[89] This is the promise that should give Christians the strength to resist the temptation to deny the Faith to save their lives. Finally, Polycarp encourages his audience to pray for those who persecute them.[90] He would soon have the opportunity to practice what he preached.

The Martyrdom of Polycarp

This is the oldest of the martyr documents that we have. It is actually a letter from the church of Smyrna telling the story of Polycarp's martyrdom. It is probably also the

[85] Eusebius of Caesarea, *Ecclesiastical History,* 5.20; Tertullian, *The Prescription against Heretics,* 32.

[86] Irenaeus of Lyons, *Demonstration of the Apostolic Preaching,* 3; *Against Heresies,* 5.5.1.

[87] Eusebius of Caesarea, *Ecclesiastical History,* 4.14. The bishop of Rome was Anicetus, bishop from AD 155 to 166.

[88] Howell, *Ignatius of Antioch and Polycarp of Smyrna,* 68.

[89] Polycarp of Smyrna, *Letter to the Philippians,* 2.1–2.

[90] Polycarp of Smyrna, *Letter to the Philippians,* 12.3.

most historical of all the martyr documents, possibly based on the actual proceedings or other eyewitness account(s) and having been embellished with fewer legendary elements than some of the later martyr acts. Still, this embellishment meant that the martyr documents in general would not be seriously considered for inclusion in the New Testament.

According to the story, Polycarp had a vision or a dream in which he saw his pillow on fire. By this he knew he was to be burned at the stake. At first, he tried to avoid arrest, but when the soldiers came for him, he did not resist, he only asked to be allowed to pray. The account also relates the story of one Quintus, who volunteered for martyrdom. This is a cautionary tale because Quintus eventually lost his nerve and denied the Faith to save his life. So the Church did not advocate volunteering for martyrdom. Polycarp is presented as the calm and rational middle way (and the faithful imitator of Jesus Himself) between the extreme enthusiasm of rushing to martyrdom and the cowardice of running from it.

Like Jesus coming into Jerusalem, Polycarp was led into the city on a donkey. At his interrogation, he was of course given the chance to deny his faith to save his life. To go free, he would have had to curse Christ and swear an oath to the emperor, saying, "Caesar is lord." When he refused, the Roman official tried to provoke him, yelling at him, commanding him to denounce his Christian community by saying, "Away with the atheists." Polycarp turned to the crowd of pagan accusers, pointed to *them*, and said, "Away with the atheists!" And so his fate was sealed. After his death, his bones were retrieved and kept to be venerated as holy relics.

The Martyr Documents

The word *martyr* is simply the Greek word for *witness*. In the Church, it became the technical term for one who dies as a witness to the Faith. As we have seen with the *Martyrdom of Polycarp*, one of the types of literature we encounter in the postapostolic age is the *martyr document* or *martyr acts*. They chronicle the experience of the martyrs as they faced their accusers and executioners.

When Christians were brought before the Roman officials and asked whether they were Christians, they knew this was a moment of truth, and a matter of life or death. Christians could save their lives by denying the Faith, but they knew the words of Jesus in Matthew 10:33, "But whoever denies me before others, I will also deny before my heavenly Father." So to save one's life was to lose eternal life (Matt. 16:25). But to lose one's life for Jesus' sake was seen as a guarantee of eternal life.[91]

[91] *Martyrdom of Polycarp*, 2.

Martyrdom was therefore seen by the early Christians as a kind of baptism in one's own blood. Therefore, martyrdom was believed to "wash away" any sin, including previous apostasy.[92] Even before there was a formalized sacrament of Reconciliation, martyrdom was the ultimate penance.[93]

The Church also remembered the words of Jesus in Matthew 10:19–20, "When they hand you over, do not worry about how you are to speak or what you are to say. You will be given at that moment what you are to say. For it will not be you who speak, but the Spirit of your Father speaking through you." They took Jesus at His word, believing that anyone who admitted to being a Christian at the risk of physical life was therefore filled with the Holy Spirit. Christians who confessed their faith to the Romans were called *confessors*. These confessors sometimes lived to tell of their experience, but even if they were eventually martyred, during the time they were in prison awaiting execution, they were treated as though they were prophets. They were invested with a kind of prophetic authority, implicitly given to them by the people, though not necessarily endorsed by the bishops. People would come to visit the confessors in prison to get advice, and they became, in effect, the first spiritual directors. Eventually, people started asking them for reassurance that their own sins were forgiven, so the concept of confessor became expanded to mean someone to whom one might go to confess one's sins. The point is that confessors and martyrs were treated almost as though they were a new set of apostles, and the stories of their heroic confessions and deaths became beloved devotional material in the early Church.[94]

The martyr documents have two main parts. Some of them contain both parts, but some contain only one part or the other. The first part is a record of the interrogation and confession. These tend to be very matter-of-fact, straightforward dialogue between the "accused" and the Roman magistrate. These may very well be based on actual court proceedings and are probably quite historical. The second part is the account of the martyr's death. These include details of the imprisonment, torture, and execution, and often a public death in the circus or arena. Some of these are embellished with legendary material, and the later ones become somewhat apocalyptic. Included are such elements as prophecies, miracles of protection (the first attempt the kill the martyr rarely works), as well as out-of-body experiences complete with

[92] See also Hermas, *The Shepherd*, 24, where it says that the flames of martyrdom purify. This could also be a reference to Purgatory.

[93] *2 Clement*, 20.

[94] For an excellent overview of this genre, see Helen Rhee, *Early Christian Literature: Christ and Culture in the Second and Third Centuries* (New York: Routledge, 2005).

the smell of incense, and even painless death.[95] The martyr is depicted as a hero, like an athlete winning a contest, or a soldier victorious in battle.[96] However, in the end they do die, so the victory is not in cheating death. The victory was in the refusal to deny the Faith, and it is seen as a victory over the devil.

Martyrdom was understood as a birth to new life; therefore, the date of a person's martyrdom was celebrated annually as his or her "birthday."[97] The martyr documents were used in these celebrations, along with the reading of Scripture. Often a martyr was celebrated with a *feast*, or what amounted to a picnic that was held as close to the burial site as possible. Being close to the martyr's remains was like being close to the martyr. And since one could be certain that the martyr was in Heaven with God, and because the doctrine of the resurrection of the body assumed an eternal connection between the remains of the martyrs' bodies (their relics) and their spirit, that meant that being close to the martyr was like being closer to God.[98] Later, when it was more difficult to be physically close to one's favorite martyr, parts of their remains could be taken to other places so that the people there could feel closer to God. These *relics*, from the Latin word *relicum*, meaning "remainder," or "something left behind," could be body parts such as bones, or personal effects such as a piece of clothing or even a lock of hair.

Since martyrdom was believed to guarantee salvation, one could be absolutely certain that anyone who died for the Faith was in fact in Heaven with Christ, and even though the word *saint* (holy one) originally meant any Christian, many people came to believe that the only way one could be sure that another person had made it to Heaven was if they had died a martyr's death.[99] Therefore, it became a tradition to call someone a saint only when you could be sure. These people, the "saints

[95] The lack of crying out in pain was seen as a kind of transfiguration of the martyr. See *Martyrdom of Polycarp*, 2.

[96] Clement of Rome, *1 Clement*, 6–7; *Martyrdom of Polycarp*, 18. However, volunteering for martyrdom was frowned upon. Since one might risk failing in the end (especially under torture) and losing one's salvation, it was better not to seek martyrdom, but to do as Jesus did, and wait to be arrested. Polycarp was seen as a model, since he neither ran to martyrdom, nor ran from it; see *Martyrdom of Polycarp*, 1, 4.

[97] Ignatius of Antioch, *Letter to the Romans*, 6.1.

[98] *Martyrdom of Polycarp*, 18; *Apostolic Constitutions*, 6.6 (6.30).

[99] There was a saying in the ancient world, "Call no man blessed while he lives." This meant that as long as one was still alive, there was still time for something to go wrong. As we will see, the early Christians believed that one could lose one's salvation by committing serious sins after Baptism; therefore, the only way to know for sure if another person who had passed on had, in fact, persevered to the end, would be to know that the person had died in the manner that would erase all sin — through martyrdom.

for sure," were in Heaven with God, and had the Lord's ear, and therefore they could be called on to intercede for those on earth as their confessors in Heaven. Although there was no official process of canonization in the early Church, a martyr's status as a saint was ensured for posterity when the martyr's tomb was marked for visitation, and then when a shrine or eventually a basilica was built over it.[100] Eventually, the relics of the martyrs became the very thing that sanctified the altar of a church building.

We will look at a few more of the martyr documents as they come up in our exploration of the postapostolic age. Many of the important writers of this time period were in fact martyred, sometimes because their writings made them more visible to the Romans. But they recognized that the danger of martyrdom was part and parcel of a Christianity that stood against the culture. As Ignatius of Antioch said on his way to Rome to be executed, "Christianity is greatest when it is hated by the world."[101]

Papias of Hierapolis

Papias was a contemporary and a colleague of Polycarp. It was said that he knew the daughters of the apostle Philip.[102] Some later writers said he knew John the apostle, though he does not seem to have claimed this himself. He is also said to have personally known some people whom Jesus had healed, who were still alive when he was young. These stories of secondhand connections to Jesus must, of course, be taken with a grain of salt, since they may have been invented by people who were devoted to Papias in order to increase the credibility of his teachings.

Exposition on the Sayings of the Lord

This is the only document we have from Papias, and it does not exist in its entirety. In it, Papias interprets the so-called millennium of the book of Revelation as a literal one-thousand-year reign of Christ on the earth. Using 2 Peter 3:8 ("with the Lord one day is like a thousand years, and a thousand years like one day"; cf. Ps. 90:4) as his interpretive key, he reasoned that the seven days of creation in Genesis are a metaphor for the whole of human history.[103] He taught that there would be four thousand years from the time of creation until the coming of Christ, then another two thousand years between the advent of Christ and His return. This makes six thousand years, with the

[100] Meyendorff, *Imperial Unity*, 92–93.

[101] Ignatius of Antioch, *Letter to the Romans*, 3.3, in Holmes, *The Apostolic Fathers*, 229.

[102] Eusebius of Caesarea, *Ecclesiastical History* 3.39.9.

[103] That the concept of a day need not be interpreted as a literal day of twenty-four hours, see Irenaeus of Lyons, *Against Heresies*, 2.22.2.

seventh thousand years as a millennial "sabbath."[104] The majority of the Church did not accept this interpretation, which is probably why this document was not accepted as authoritative by the early Church (and why most of it is lost to us). However, a similar view was shared by a fringe group known as the Montanists (see below), and Papias's interpretation influenced the theologians Irenaeus and Tertullian.[105] Not only was Papias's interpretation eventually rejected by the majority of the Church, this kind of interpretation almost got the book of Revelation itself excluded from the canon.

The Epistle of Barnabas

If this document was written by someone named Barnabas, it was not the Barnabas of the New Testament. The authorship is unknown, but we can date the writing to shortly after the last rebellion in Judea, about AD 135.[106] The "epistle" is really an ethical treatise, possibly for catechesis, and somewhat like the ethical section of the *Didache*. It has a heavy emphasis on good works as evidence of devotion to God. The questionable authorship was probably enough to disqualify this document from the New Testament, though there is some questionable theology in it as well.[107]

The Shepherd of Hermas

The actual title of this document is simply *The Shepherd*, but it is traditionally attributed to one Hermas, supposedly the brother of bishop Pius I of Rome (bishop from AD 140 to 155). The premise of the writing is that Hermas was given a vision, much like the vision of the book of Revelation. The "shepherd" is not Jesus, but a guardian angel, who brings the message of the vision to Hermas.[108]

The majority of the book is an allegory of a tower, which represents the Church. The tower is still being built, and as stones are added to the structure, Hermas realizes that the stones are people (cf. 1 Pet. 2:4–8). Some are ready to be built into the tower, but others are not ready, and are set aside. This is not a problem, as long as

[104] Assuming the birth of Christ in 6 or 5 BC, if this interpretation had been correct, we all would have been convinced of it by 1995. Papias was followed in this interpretation by the author of the *Epistle of Barnabas* as well as Justin Martyr, Irenaeus, and Tertullian; see *Epistle of Barnabas*, 15; Justin Martyr, *Dialogue with Trypho*, 80; and Irenaeus of Lyons, *Against Heresies*, 5.28.2–3, 5.35.1–2.

[105] Eusebius of Caesarea, *Ecclesiastical History*, 3.28, 5.33.4.

[106] Barnabas, *Epistle*, 16.4.

[107] See for example Barnabas, *Epistle*, 4.6–8, where the author seems to go much further than Paul on the subject of the rejection of Israel and the validity (or non-validity) of the covenant. Also, the emphasis on works suggests a possible adoptionist origin.

[108] Hermas, *The Shepherd*, 25.1–5.

these stones become ready before the tower is finished, because after that time it will be too late to be added to the tower.[109] The end of the age of the Church will come when the tower is finished, and then Jesus will return. Jesus does stop by a few times in the vision, though, to see how the building is coming along. He is described as a man who is taller than the tower.[110] However, it is all very vague, and Jesus is never actually identified by name. Jesus is called the "angel of justification,"[111] while the shepherd is referred to as the "angel of repentance."[112] There is also a confusing cast of characters reminiscent of some of Jesus' parables, such as the parable of the ten bridesmaids (Matt. 25:1–13).

Hermas seems to be using the allegorical vision to critique what he perceives as hypocritical behavior in the Church. The problems include doubt (or not practicing what one preaches, in some translations called "double-mindedness"),[113] anger,[114] and wealth, which leads one to postpone one's Baptism for worldly reasons.[115] Also criticized is fear, which leads to apostasy in times of persecution.[116] Hermas warns that while those who denied their faith in a previous persecution might be forgiven,[117] presumably because they did not understand the implications, those who deny the Faith in any future persecution could not be forgiven.[118] Clearly, Hermas was concerned

[109] Hermas, *The Shepherd*, 13.5.

[110] Hermas, *The Shepherd*, 83.1.

[111] Hermas, *The Shepherd*, 33.6.

[112] Hermas, *The Shepherd*, 25.7, in Holmes, *The Apostolic Fathers*, 503.

[113] Hermas, *The Shepherd*, 12.3, 39.5–7, 98.1.

[114] Hermas, *The Shepherd*, 34.1–2.

[115] Hermas, *The Shepherd*, 15.3, 108.1–2. Often in the early Church, a man who hoped to continue an upwardly mobile public career (which often included the military) would postpone his Baptism until retirement. This was because of the strict moral expectations of the baptized, and the conflict presented when the requirements of a government job included participation in pagan sacrifice, or the authority over capital punishment. This created a situation in which there were times and places when the churches were made up of more aristocratic women than men, since women had less to lose with regard to their status in society.

[116] Hermas, *The Shepherd*, 37.4, 98.3. In *The Shepherd*, 14, Hermas also says that those who deny Christ in persecution often do so to protect their property.

[117] Hermas, *The Shepherd*, 6.8, 96.3. Note that this implies that there were some in the Church who were known to have denied the Faith in a previous persecution, yet reconciled to the Church. Hermas mentions one by name, a certain Maximus, *The Shepherd*, 7.4.

[118] Hermas, *The Shepherd*, 6.7–8, 103.6. For Hermas, it is a foregone conclusion that there will be more persecution. Given the affinity of the structure of *The Shepherd* to the book of Revelation, it is clear that Hermas believed Revelation to be predicting greater persecution in the future; see *The Shepherd*, 22.1. Of course, he turned out to be right.

that the Reconciliation of some who had denied the Faith to save their lives would lead others to deny the Faith, thinking that they, too, could be reconciled later.

According to Hermas, the remedy for these problems is faith,[119] self-control,[120] and charity. He believes it is God's will for the rich and the poor to live in a kind of symbiotic relationship, whereby the rich help the poor by giving them resources, and the poor help the rich by giving them a ministry (i.e., almsgiving).[121] He probably saw it as a Christian version of the patron-client relationship that existed in Roman society. By that system, wealthy patrons offered favors to their clients, who in turn could be asked to do anything from providing an entourage to voting for whomever the patron supported. In this way, someone of a lower economic status who might not otherwise have friends in high places could, if he got into trouble, hope to rely on the influence of an aristocratic patron. In return, the patron had someone to do his dirty work for him. Hermas apparently saw a divinely appointed patron-client system at work between the rich and poor. If you are wealthy, Hermas says, God made you rich specifically to help the poor.[122]

There are many reasons why this document is not included in our New Testament. In general, there seems to be a consensus that by now we are just too far from the apostolic period to ascribe any kind of inspiration to a text. In spite of that, several of the early theologians did quote from *The Shepherd*, including Irenaeus of Lyons. Even if they didn't see it as inspired, it remained popular devotional reading for centuries. But on the whole, it is simply too long and too obscure to have stood the test of time, let alone gain a tradition of reading in liturgy. In addition, it never mentions Jesus by name, so it was probably seen as insufficiently christocentric. In fact, the theology of *The Shepherd* may tend toward another early heresy, the opposite of the one we have already seen. While *2 Clement*, Ignatius of Antioch, and Polycarp all seem to be opposing a heresy that denied the real humanity of Jesus, *The Shepherd* seems to lean in the other direction, denying or diminishing the divinity of Christ, as if He were only an angel (i.e., a created being).[123] Jesus is never called Lord, nor is

[119] Hermas, *The Shepherd*, 48.3–4.

[120] Hermas, *The Shepherd*, 65.5.

[121] Hermas, *The Shepherd*, 50–51.

[122] Hermas, *The Shepherd*, 17.5, 50.8–9, 51.10.

[123] It is true that the Greek word *angelos* simply means *messenger*, and that in other contexts it is perfectly acceptable/orthodox to refer to Jesus Christ as *angel*, however here the "angel of justification" (Jesus) does not seem to be described in any way that is significantly different from the "angel of repentance" (the Shepherd). It may be possible to interpret these two angels as both referring to Jesus Christ, but this would seem to force orthodoxy into the text, and at the very least the later Church did see the need to doctor the

He presented as a Savior, per se, and it seems to be possible to earn salvation by good works alone.[124] In fact, for Hermas good works are everything, and salvation comes through self-control. He basically says that if you enjoy something, it must be a sin.[125]

The Shepherd enjoyed a resurgence of popularity in the fourth century, though this was because it emerged in an edited version which was corrected to make it more acceptable. Specifically, the term *Logos*, referring to Christ, was inserted where the original had used the word *spirit*.

The late first and early second century saw the development of the office of bishop as a citywide, and then regional, authority, understood to be in succession from the apostles, and carrying on their teachings. This time period of the "apostolic fathers" also saw the first generation of important Christian documents outside of the New Testament, which give us a bit of a window into the development of the hierarchy, the clarification of the two natures of Jesus Christ against the early versions of the alternative christological understandings, and the importance of the sacrament of the Eucharist for the self-identity of the Church. In these documents, we also become witnesses to the escalation of persecution and the early Church's understanding of martyrdom and the communion of the saints.

text for orthodoxy. Most likely, what the author had in mind was more of an adoptionist interpretation, perhaps that the two angels represented the Son and the Spirit, yet both with the assumption that they were created beings, leaving divinity for the Father alone.

[124] Hermas, *The Shepherd*, 69.5.

[125] Hermas, *The Shepherd*, 65.5.

4

Early Worship and the Sacraments

Early Christian Worship

Much could be said about worship in the early Church, and it should go without saying that many whole books have been written on the subject.[1] Here we can only give an overview of early Christian worship, especially as it relates to the extant texts. For instance, there are some examples of early Christian hymns, such as are contained in the New Testament itself: Colossians 1:15–20, Philippians 2:6–11, Ephesians 5:14, to name a few, and we will see below that there is a second verse to the Ephesians hymn included in Clement of Alexandria's *Exhortation to the Greeks*.[2] In addition, there are two documents from the postapostolic age that appear to include Christian songs, or at least poems. There are also written statements of faith that resemble early creeds, as well as some hints at "orders of worship" and instructions for presiders. Finally, there are early liturgical books, such as the *Liturgy of St. James*, and the *Liturgy of St. Mark*, however these will have to remain outside the scope of the present study since the only manuscripts we have for these come from the Middle Ages, and the question of what they may have looked like within the time of the Church Fathers is too complicated to enter into here.

There has been a lot of scholarly debate about the extent to which the practice of worship in the early Church was based on Jewish practice (and in fact over what the

[1] For some good introductions to early worship, I recommend the books on early worship by Paul Bradshaw and Andrew McGowan, as well as Edward Foley's *From Age to Age: How Christians Have Celebrated the Eucharist* (Collegeville, MN: Liturgical Press, 2016), and Mike Aquilina's *The Eucharist Foretold: The Lost Prophecy of Malachi* (Steubenville, OH: Emmaus Road, 2019); see also Martin, *Worship in the Early Church*, 11–12, 19, 24–27, 57–60.

[2] There is some scholarly debate over whether these passages are, in fact, hymns, in the sense that they were songs sung by early Christians. See the section on Early Christian Hymns in Papandrea, *Trinity 101*.

first-century Jewish practice was), but it is clear that early Christian worship always included the reading of Scripture, prayer, some form of melodic or chanted praise (hymns), and instruction, which meant the interpretation of Scripture and exhortation to live according to Christian morality. In addition, the sacramental acts of Jesus, as well as the disciples' understanding of His life, death, and Resurrection, all resulted in the institution of sacraments, but even these have their Jewish precedents.

What Do You Mean by *Worship*?

In the early second century a Roman governor named Pliny the Younger wrote a letter to the emperor Trajan (reigned AD 98–117), in which Pliny told the emperor that the Christians have a habit of singing songs to Christ "as to a god." Later, the first Christian historian, Eusebius of Caesarea, wrote in his *Ecclesiastical History*, "All the psalms and hymns which were written by faithful Christians from the beginning sing of the Christ as the Word (*Logos*) of God and treat him as God."[3] We can see that from the very beginning of the Church (including in the New Testament itself) there was never a time when Christians did not believe in the divinity of Jesus Christ. But what would it mean, especially for Jewish Christians, to *worship* Jesus?

The very word *worship* implies an acknowledgment of the *worthiness* (worth-ship) of the object of worship. The Christian concept of worship was, of course, founded on the assumptions of Hebrew religion, and so worship for the early Church meant two things: submission, and service (see Deut. 6:13, quoted by Jesus in Matt. 4:10).[4] In other words, the one who worships is submitting to the providence of God, desires to do the will of God, and asks for the intervention of divine power to that end. Therefore, to worship Christ is to include Jesus in the conceptual definition of the God who is worthy to be the object of submission, and who is powerful enough to protect and empower the devotee. In a practical sense, to worship Christ in the early Church meant praying to Him and asking for His presence and intervention (see Acts 7:59–60 and the prayers of the early martyr acts), calling Him *Lord* in confessions of faith that make Him the object of faith (see Rom. 10:9–13; 1 Cor. 12:1–3; 15:3–5), conducting sacraments in His name, and singing hymns in praise of His divinity.

It is arguably the case, depending on how one looks at it, that the most obvious and accessible aspect of worship is the singing of hymns of praise. However, we have

3 Eusebius of Caesarea, *Ecclesiastical History*, 3.33.1–3, 5.28.5–6. Translation in Loeb Classical Library, vols. 153 and 265, Eusebius of Caesarea, *The Ecclesiastical History*, vol. 1, trans. Kirsopp Lake (Cambridge: Harvard University Press, 1926), 519.

4 For a more detailed discussion of this, see James L. Papandrea, *Handed Down: The Catholic Faith of the Early Christians* (El Cajon, CA: Catholic Answers Press, 2015), 171–174.

to keep in mind that singing praise to someone is not in and of itself an act of worship. What matters is the content of the lyrics. In other words, *The Ballad of Davey Crockett* is not a hymn worshiping the folk hero. Worship hymns specifically ascribe divine attributes to the object of praise and assume an attitude of submission. To anticipate the point, there will be times in the history of the Church when hymns will be sung in praise of Mary or other saints, but this is not an act of worship, it is primarily an act of gratitude toward God for what God has done through these humans, as well as an acknowledgment of their praiseworthy attributes that make them worthy of imitation.

The next logical question would be to ask what the music of the early Church sounded like. In most cases, we have no idea. It should be noted, however, that the early Church did not have our refined modern distinction between intoned reciting, chanting, and singing. Like the debate over worship in general, there is considerable debate about whether and to what extent Christian hymn singing followed the practice of the synagogue (see Matt. 26:30). However, it is clear that there was never a time in Christian worship without some form of singing/chanting and it would seem obvious that the assumption that worship must include sung praise comes from Jewish worship. The music itself, however, may have been significantly influenced by Greek and Roman music, especially in the cities.[5] St. Paul encourages his people to sing "psalms and hymns and spiritual songs" (Eph. 5:19; see 1 Cor. 14:15, 26; Col. 3:16), but we don't know whether these were three distinctly defined kinds of music, or if perhaps Paul was just listing things to cover all the possibilities.[6] It seems that early Christian singing was like melodic chanting, and it was most likely all in unison, without any harmony or polyphony of any kind. A hymn would usually have been sung as a call and response, possibly based on a psalm or some biblical parallelism, with the leader singing a line alternating with the assembly echoing the same line, or repeating a refrain.[7] At the beginning, in the house-churches, it seems that anyone

[5] See Charles Cosgrove, "Music at Christian Social Meals" in *Music at Social Meals in Greek and Roman Antiquity* (forthcoming, Cambridge University Press).

[6] Cf. Tertullian, *Apology*, 2.6, 39.

[7] Early Christian melodies probably used a limited number of notes orbiting around a tonic, something close to a Phrygian (pentatonic) scale, and not unlike medieval chant. Their musical intervals were not exactly like ours, so most of their scales would probably sound like minor keys to us, though they eventually developed the use of different modes for different liturgical purposes or seasons. The Oxyrhynchus hymn, from the third century, is our earliest example of Christian music with notation. It has a range of one octave. See Ralph P. Martin, *A Hymn of Christ* (Downers Grove, IL: InterVarsity Press, 1997), 4, 7. See Tertullian, *Apology*, 2.6, 39, and Eusebius of Caesarea, *Ecclesiastical History*, 2.17.22;

might bring a song (1 Cor. 14:26) which was then led by the one who composed it. Tertullian mentions this around the turn of the third century, though we are not quite sure how widespread this practice was by that time.[8] At some times and places, the singing of spontaneous hymns may have been seen as a charismatic gift, and of course it may be the case that some early speaking in tongues was intoned or chanted, again blurring the distinctions between speaking and singing — though clearly the apostle Paul discouraged any kind of charismatic utterances that would be disruptive (1 Cor. 14:26–28). If and when instruments were used, it would have been only to help the singers with the melody, as they did not yet have chords as an accompaniment as we would expect. It could be that the references to "harps" in Revelation's scenes of heavenly worship are a reflection of the use of lyres in early worship.[9] On the other hand, instruments such as flutes, horns, and cymbals would have been frowned upon because of their use in pagan worship.

The Sacraments

The early Church did not have the set list of seven sacraments that would emerge in the Middle Ages. However, all of the rituals existed in the postapostolic age in one form or another. The one possible exception is marriage. Although it is true that a ritual of Matrimony does not seem to have emerged until after the legalization of Christianity in the fourth century, Ignatius of Antioch assumes that couples should get the bishop's blessing, and at least in some places this probably took on a quasi-ritual or at least public character, since it would be necessary to discern whether the couple was really free to marry according to the Church's expectations. Anointing of the Sick is already mentioned in the New Testament (James 5:14–15), but again we

---

see also Martin, *Worship in the Early Church*, 40–41; and *A Hymn of Christ*, 3–4, 6, 13. Possible examples of antiphonal singing in the Bible include Ezra 3:11; Nehemiah 12:24, 31; and Revelation 22:17; cf. also *Didache*, 10.6, and Justin Martyr, *Dialogue with Trypho*, 63.

8 Tertullian, *Apology*, 39.

9 See for example Rev. 5:8; 14:2; 15:2; see also *Odes of Solomon*, 14.8, 26.3. These songs may have been accompanied by a lyre, though probably not by flutes, horns, or percussion instruments, because those were used in the pagan mystery cults, and the Christians did not want to be mistaken for these cults or be perceived as imitating them. Martin, *Worship in the Early Church*, 41. The lyre was something like a cross between a guitar and a small harp, though not for the purpose of playing chords or accompaniment, but rather simply for plucking the melody as a reference for the singers. Cf. also 1 Sam. 16:23; but see Clement of Alexandria, *The Instructor*, 2.4, where Clement allows the use of the harp, but not the playing of songs or tunes that are "secular" (love songs) or that imitate the chromatic melodies of pagan music.

don't know what (ritual) form that may or may not have taken in the earliest centuries of the Church. It may be that in this case, it was more a component of home visitation than corporate worship.

Ordination is based on Jesus' own commissioning of the apostles whom He sent out, and in Paul's day included the imposition of hands to confer the power of the Holy Spirit and the authority to teach and preside over the sacraments (1 Tim. 4:14). A more formal rite of ordination must have emerged as the hierarchy moved from the first phase (when the apostles were still alive) into the second phase, when there was a need to publicly consecrate new church leaders.[10] When the apostles (and their disciples) were no longer around to handpick Church leaders or simply commission their own disciples to succeed them, bishops were elected by the council of priests (in some places, with the ratification of the laity).[11] A newly elected bishop would be consecrated by other bishops from the region.[12] Eventually, however, the election of bishops came to be reserved for fellow bishops, as the elevation of a bishop shifted from the priests choosing one of their own to lead them, to the bishops choosing one from the lower rank to join them.[13]

Baptism

Baptism and Confirmation were originally one ritual. When one reads the book of Acts, one gets the impression that there was no consistency in how these were done, however, the Church quickly recognized the need to unify Baptism, and in the post-apostolic documents we can see that the Confirmation (laying on of hands) immediately followed the Baptism with water. Baptism itself was the sign of identification with Christ and an affirmation of the faith of the one being baptized, or the faith of the parents in the case of a child or infant. Although most converts in the New Testament would have naturally been adults, conversion was not the individual decision it would become with the Protestant Reformation. In the early Church, whole extended

[10] Ordination is a ritual by the time of Tertullian, *The Prescription against the Heretics*, 41.

[11] *Apostolic Tradition*, 2. In the *Apostolic Tradition*, which contains layers of material that cannot be dated with any certainty, it appears that early on, lay people participated in the elections. However, this could simply mean that the priests voted, and the laity ratified the vote by an acclamation of assent in liturgy.

[12] *Apostolic Church Order*, 16; see also *Didascalia Apostolorum*, 4.

[13] When it came to choosing a bishop, it was seen as better if he were unmarried, but if he were married, he must have been married only once. If he were married, his wife must also have been a believer and be morally above reproach. He should have been at least fifty years old, unless the congregation in a particular city were so small that no one over fifty was acceptable, then a younger man might have been chosen; *Didascalia Apostolorum*, 4.

families converted together, and Roman cultural norms would dictate that the children (even adult children) could be expected to follow the decision made by the head of the household. (See Acts 16 for New Testament examples of whole households being baptized, and cf. Luke 19:8–10.) Thus the Baptism did not require the personal faith of the one being baptized, and in fact the reality of vicarious faith even allowed for the short-lived practice of Baptism for the dead (1 Cor. 15:29). The Confirmation of the Baptism was the imposition of hands to confer the indwelling of the Holy Spirit. In most places, the Baptism/Confirmation was accompanied by an anointing with oil. Depending on the time and place, the anointing could be done at the beginning of the ritual, at the end, or both.

A time of catechesis preceded Baptism, in which the convert learned the expectations of the church community with regard to morality and behavior. The earliest tradition seems to be that the catechesis lasted three weeks, though we don't know how far back that goes. The three weeks was eventually extended to forty days, and later it could be as much as a year or more. By the third century, some places may have required a three-year catechism, but as soon as Christianity became legalized in the fourth century, there were too many converts to have such extended pre-baptismal courses, and the catechesis was streamlined, then reduced, until it all but went away. As the centuries wore on, the more the Church influenced the culture, and the culture was perceived to be grounded on the morals of the Church, the more the sense of urgency about the baptismal commitment to a countercultural lifestyle decreased.

The main goal of pre-baptismal catechesis (for adults) was to clarify the serious nature of the lifestyle commitment that was Christian Baptism. Sponsors would be expected to vouch for the catechumen's sincerity of faith and readiness to enter the life of the Church, and adults or heads of households might be expected to stand in a congregation and make a public statement of faith or respond affirmatively to elements of the creed in an interrogative (question and answer) format. Therefore, catechumens would have been taught a statement of faith, probably a version of what would become the Apostles' Creed.[14] They also must have learned a few important prayers, such as the Lord's Prayer (the *Our Father*). However, teaching theology, per se, was not the priority of catechism in the early Church.

It was assumed that the catechumens had been listening to the Scriptures read and explained in the first half of the liturgy, and that the newly baptized Christian

[14] For examples of excerpts from creeds in the postapostolic age, see Ignatius of Antioch, *Letter to the Ephesians*, 7.2, 8.2; *Letter to the Trallians*, 9.1–2; *Letter to the Smyrnaeans*, 1.1–2; and Aristides, *Apology*, 15.

would learn to understand the sacraments over time; the point being that one could not learn about the Eucharist, for example, until one had begun to receive it. In some places the Church would develop an extended post-Baptism course called the *Mystagogia*, meant to help believers understand the sacraments (the *mysteries*). In other words, doctrine is something one absorbs over time, after one has been initiated. To prepare for Baptism, what was required was a commitment to the moral expectations of the Church, which for anyone converting from Roman culture, would mean significant lifestyle changes.

To get ready for the Baptism, a person was expected to fast for one, or preferably, two days (Friday and Saturday, if we assume the Baptism was conducted on a Sunday).[15] The tradition of a precautionary exorcism also became part of the baptismal preparation, and even part of the ritual. Remnants of this exorcism remain today in those traditions that include a renunciation of Satan. Many baptismal rites also included a vigil the night before the Baptism. In obedience to Christ (Matt. 28:19), Baptism was always done in the name of the Father, Son, and Holy Spirit.[16] New Testament references to Baptism as simply "in the name of Jesus" and the like are not quoting the actual baptismal ritual but are using a shorthand form. The earliest known church manual, the *Didache*, explains the acceptable methods for Baptism:

> Now concerning baptism, baptize as follows: after you have reviewed all these things, baptize in the name of the Father and of the Son and of the Holy Spirit in running water [i.e., outdoors, not in standing water]. But if you have no running water, then baptize in some other water; and if you are not able to baptize in cold water, then do so in warm. But if you have neither, then pour water on the head three times in the name of the Father and Son and Holy Spirit.[17]

This demonstrates that while there were clear preferences for how a Baptism should be done, the method of applying the water was not something that could render a Baptism invalid.[18]

Infants born into Christian homes would be baptized soon after their birth, and there was some debate over whether it should be immediately (due to fears about infant mortality and the possible danger of a child dying unbaptized) or on the eighth day, in imitation of Jewish circumcision rituals, since in one sense the

[15] *Didache*, 7; Justin Martyr, *1 Apology*, 61.

[16] Justin Martyr, *1 Apology*, 61.

[17] *Didache*, 7.1–3, in Holmes, *The Apostolic Fathers*, 355.

[18] Clement of Alexandria, *Exhortation to the Greeks*, 10.

Baptism was seen as an initiation into the Church, analogous to Jewish circumcision. Overall, though, it seems as though the preference for Sunday, as the day of worship with the congregation, would decide the debate in favor of the first Sunday of the newborn's life. As infant Baptism became more and more prevalent (that is, with the reality of multi-generation Christian families), the rites of Baptism and Confirmation eventually became separated, though only in the West. By the third century, the Baptism took on more of the sense of the initiation into the Body of Christ, the Church, and the Confirmation (the imposition of hands to signify the indwelling of the Holy Spirit) was postponed. This may have been so that the confirmation could wait until a perceived age of reason, something like what would develop in Judaism as the Bar Mitzvah, but it also may have had to do with the fact that while the authority to baptize would be delegated to priests (and possibly deacons), the authority to confirm remained with the bishops, who found it more practical to separate and postpone the rite. After the legalization of Christianity in the fourth century, infant Baptism overtook adult Baptism as the most common in the West, and by the fifth century it was normative.[19] However, in the East (and sometimes in the West), Christian parents who hoped their sons would aspire to very lucrative secular careers (which might be frowned upon by the Church) simply did not have them baptized, and sometimes this led to the postponement of Baptism until middle age or even retirement.

It seems that, in general, Baptisms could be done at any time (Acts 8:36). But given the logistics of forming catechism classes and the desire for an appropriate day on which to conduct Baptisms, it seems that they were most often done at Easter, Epiphany, and Pentecost, and in some places also at Christmas and on the feasts of the saints.[20] Rome and North Africa showed an early preference for Easter, and eventually it became most common to do all Baptisms at Easter, with a vigil of Scripture readings and prayer the night before. This lasted until after the legalization of Christianity, when there were simply too many people requesting Baptism to do them all at Easter, or even on a few specific days. The emperor Constantine himself commissioned a baptistery to be built at the Cathedral of San Giovanni in Laterano (St. John in Lateran) in Rome.[21] The original intention, it seems, was for all Baptisms in Rome to be done at this baptistry, and at Easter. But by the end of

[19] Paul F. Bradshaw and Maxwell E. Johnson, *The Origins of Feasts, Fasts, and Seasons in Early Christianity* (Collegeville, MN: Pueblo/Liturgical Press, 2011), 111.

[20] Bradshaw and Johnson, *The Origins of Feasts, Fasts, and Seasons in Early Christianity*, 82–83, 149, 162.

[21] For details on this, see Papandrea, *ROME*, 182–184.

the fourth century, there were so many Baptisms being conducted in Rome, that they were taking place virtually every day of the year.[22]

Baptism was described as the "seal" of eternal life.[23] Theologically, going under the water and coming back up symbolized dying and rising with Christ (Rom. 6:3–4).[24] But Baptism was no mere symbol, certainly not a symbol of something that had already happened, such as a personal faith commitment or decision to join the Church. Baptism was considered an act of God, by which God forgave original sin, and all personal sin up until the time of Baptism. However, Baptism was never believed to wash away future sin.[25] Therefore, post-baptismal sin was a real problem, and many people believed that the sins Christians committed after Baptism could not be forgiven without some kind of significant repentance.[26] It was universally assumed that one could lose one's salvation, especially by committing serious sin(s) after Baptism.[27] "Serious sins," or "mortal sins" (see 1 John 5:16–17) included apostasy, idolatry, murder, and adultery. Eventually that category would be expanded to include any sin that broke one of the Ten Commandments, and then later this became the basis for the medieval list of "seven deadly sins."

Some early writers would talk of the possibility of forgiveness for *one* post-baptismal sin,[28] especially for new converts, but the strict application of Hebrews 6:4–6 and 10:26–29 led to the very real expectation that once baptized, a Christian was not supposed to sin at all. Not surprisingly, this led some, especially men, to postpone Baptism (and Church membership) until all wild oats were sowed. Especially the men of the aristocracy, who knew that joining the Church would conflict with their careers, often waited until retirement to join their wives as baptized members.

[22] Innocent I, *Letter to Victricium*, 9, cited in Bradshaw and Johnson, *The Origins of Feasts, Fasts, and Seasons in Early Christianity*, 83–84.

[23] *2 Clement*, 7.6, 8.6; Hermas, *The Shepherd*, 11.5, 72.3–4, 93.4; see also 2 Cor. 1:22; Eph. 1:13; 4:30; 2 Tim. 2:19; cf. Rom. 4:11, in which Paul refers to circumcision as a seal. Note also that in the book of Revelation, the mark of the beast is contrasted with the ones who are marked for God. No doubt the concept of being marked for God refers to Baptism.

[24] In Mark 10, the concepts of "cup" and "baptism" are used symbolically to refer to Jesus' death. We can see in this how the early Christians connected the sacraments to sacrifice.

[25] Hermas, *The Shepherd*, 32.4, 49.2, 60.3–4; Justin Martyr, *1 Apology*, 61.

[26] For example, see the *Didascalia Apostolorum*, 5, 20.

[27] Hermas, *The Shepherd*, 6.5, 32.4, 33.3, 41; Irenaeus of Lyons, *Demonstration of the Apostolic Preaching*, 3; Cyprian of Carthage, *Epistles*, 54.13, 75.16; *On the Unity of the Catholic Church*, 20–21; and the anonymous *On Rebaptism*, 12.

[28] Hermas, *The Shepherd*, 29.8, 31.6; Clement of Alexandria, *Miscellanies*, 2.13; *Who Is the Rich Man That Shall Be Saved?*, 39–40.

Eventually, the reality that human beings cannot stop sinning simply because they are baptized would contribute to the development of the sacrament of Penance and Reconciliation. It is worth noting at this point that the concept of penance begins with the idea that almsgiving was an act of faith in God's providence that both overcame sin and brought grace to the giver through the prayers of the recipients (see Tob. 4:10; 12:9; Sir. 3:30; 29:12; Matt. 6:4).[29]

Eucharist

A sacrament (Latin: *sacramentum*) is a "sacred mystery," and the Eucharist was often called *the* "Mystery of the Church."[30] The word *Eucharist* means "thanksgiving," and from the very beginning of the Church it was seen as a ritual act of thanks for the sacrificial Passion of Christ, as well as a prophetic act of anticipation of the heavenly banquet. Both the setting, as part of a meal, as well as the ritual of bread and cup itself, is based on the Jewish Passover meal, the Sabbath meal, and of course the Last Supper of Jesus, when He gave the command for His disciples to "do this in memory of [Him]." This command appears only in Luke 22:19 (but is repeated by Paul in 1 Cor. 11:24; see the whole episode in Matt. 26:20–29; Mark 14:17–25; and Luke 22:14–23), nevertheless it is clear that the apostles understood that it should be repeated regularly, as we see in Acts 2:42–47.

At first, the *Lord's Supper* was part of an actual meal called the *agape*, or love feast (see 1 Cor. 11:18–22). This meal was most likely held on Sunday evenings in the earliest decades of the Church's existence. We are told that Sunday was chosen because it was on Sunday morning that Jesus rose from the dead, and as the Eucharist was considered a re-presentation of His Passion, it was only fitting that it should take place on the day of the Resurrection.[31] However, there is some debate over this, including whether we should assume that early Christians defined the day in the

[29] The early Church Fathers were unanimous that almsgiving was a form of penance that would contribute to atonement for post-baptismal sin. Some of the Church Fathers quoted 1 Peter 4:8 ("love covers a multitude of sins") and went so far as to say that *almsgiving* covers a multitude of sins. See, for example, *2 Clement*, 16:4; Hermas, *The Shepherd*, 50–51; and Clement of Alexandria, *Who Is the Rich Man That Shall Be Saved?*.

[30] For example, see *Didache*, 11.

[31] *Epistle of Barnabas*, 15.9; Justin Martyr, *1 Apology*, 66–67. Cyprian would feel the need to justify that, even though the Last Supper of Jesus was in the evening, it is appropriate to celebrate the Eucharist in the morning because the Resurrection occurred in the morning. Cyprian of Carthage, *Epistles*, 62.16. Sunday became, in effect, the Sabbath of the New Covenant, but it would not be called that until the fourth century, so that early Christian writers tend to continue to use the word "Sabbath" to mean Saturday, and use

Jewish sense, that is, from sundown to sundown. This becomes an issue because if that is the way early Christians defined a day, then, after sundown on Sunday would have been considered the beginning of Monday.

If we look at the worship scene in Acts 20:7–12, it seems obvious that "the first day of the week" is Sunday, and it is still considered Sunday at midnight when poor Eutychus falls out of the window. If it is correct to assume that Luke is a Gentile (tradition makes him Greek), then it is reasonable to imagine that he has in mind a Greek or Roman definition of a day, which does not end at sundown, and that this whole event happened on a Sunday evening. It is theoretically possible that the eucharistic meal was held before sundown on Sunday, but the preaching went all night, into what Jewish believers would consider the beginning of Monday. The problem with this, or any possible pre-sundown meal (including the Friday Sabbath meal) is that everyone who had to work for a living would be expected to work until sundown, and therefore they would miss the meal. Therefore, it seems most likely that the majority practice was to have the *agape* meal on Sunday evenings after sundown.[32] It is possible that different scenarios were happening in different places, for a while at least. In any case, we should also keep in mind that in some places the eucharistic meal was celebrated daily, and in other places it was celebrated every day except the fast days (Wednesday and Friday, see below). Some places would develop the tradition of daily Eucharist during certain seasons of the year.[33] Eventually the movement was in the direction of some kind of worship every day, wherever possible.

In any case, by the time of Ignatius at the turn of the second century, the ritual of the Eucharist had become separated from the meal and moved to Sunday morning.[34]

"the Lord's Day" to mean Sunday. See Bradshaw and Johnson, *The Origins of Feasts, Fasts, and Seasons in Early Christianity*, 12, 25–26.

[32] Some have speculated that Jewish Christians may have simply added the Eucharist to their Sabbath meal, or that the ritual elements of the Sabbath meal morphed into the Eucharist, however, since the Sabbath meal was celebrated before sundown on Friday (before the official beginning of the Sabbath), this would mean that anyone who worked a full day on Friday could not participate. It is more likely that for some Jewish Christians, a Saturday evening meal (after sunset, so that it counted as Sunday) either replaced the Sabbath meal or was celebrated in addition to it. But for all those working with a Greek or Roman definition of a day, the meal would have been on Sunday evening.

[33] Bradshaw and Johnson, *The Origins of Feasts, Fasts, and Seasons in Early Christianity*, 34.

[34] This assumption is based on evidence in the letter of Pliny to Trajan, where it seems clear that the evening Eucharist had been discontinued due to Trajan's law against the meeting of "secret societies." In its place, an *agape* meal without the Eucharist may have been held, but the Eucharist was moved to the morning. Ignatius seems to speak of the Eucharist and

Pliny the Younger told the emperor that in his province the Christians met before dawn on Sunday, and again in the evening for a meal, though they had discontinued the evening meeting because of his decree against assembly.[35] It is possible that the persecution, with suppression of gatherings, was one reason for the movement of the Eucharist from the more visible evening meetings to more discreet morning (predawn) meetings. It could also be that the very abuse that the apostle Paul criticizes in 1 Corinthians chapter 11 contributed to the need to separate the liturgy from the meal. But the primary reason for the separation may have had more to do with the logistics of serving communion to the growing Christian community in any given city. In other words, as the number of Christians increased in any place, and it became more difficult for all of them to gather in one place for a meal, the bishops were forced to let go of the ideal of having all Christians in the city together in one place for the sacrament, and had to delegate to the priests the authority of presiding over the Eucharist in their individual house-church meetings, so that the sacrament could be celebrated in the smaller group settings.

In many places, the *agape* meal continued on as an evening "potluck" gathering for fellowship, prayer, and praise, and was one of the ways in which the early Christians shared resources and fed the poor. It also continued in the tradition of memorial meals, or *refrigeria,* which became the feasts of the saints (see below). The combination of the Eucharist within its original context of a meal probably lasted the longest in these memorials at the catacombs and cemeteries.

The writers of the postapostolic age did not have a highly developed eucharistic theology, however there was a general consensus that what happens in the Eucharist is much more than a mere symbol or a memorial.[36] As we have noted

---

the *agape* meal as two different things. Ignatius of Antioch, *Letter to the Smyrnaeans* 8.1–2. See also Clement of Alexandria, *The Instructor,* 2.1. In the *Apostolic Tradition,* 25–27, we can see a separation of the Eucharist (in the morning) from the meal (in the evening).

35 Pliny the Younger, *Letter to Trajan.* In order for the morning meeting and evening meal to be on the same day (the eighth day) it would have to be Sunday morning, and Sunday evening. However, that assumes a Greek or Roman reckoning of the day. With a Jewish reckoning of the day, the evening meal would have to come before the morning meeting.

36 It was only the gnostics who interpreted the Eucharist as strictly symbolic. Since they did not believe in the real flesh of Christ, they could hardly see the Eucharist as in any way the Real Presence of Christ's flesh. The gnostics interpreted John 6 metaphorically, but the majority of the Church did not. Even Irenaeus, who is famous for interpretation using typology, did not see the Eucharist as a metaphor, except as the miraculous fulfillment of multiple types (the manna, the feeding of the multitudes). For Irenaeus, the eucharistic bread *becomes* the Body of Christ; see Irenaeus of Lyons, *Against Heresies,* 5.2.2–3.

above, the Eucharist was seen as a reenactment of the Passion of Christ (1 Cor. 11:26), much like the Jewish Passover meal, in which a past event is mystically made present. However, the Church's eucharistic theology comes primarily from John, chapter 6, the Bread of Life discourse, in which Jesus refers to His Body as *true food* and His Blood as *true drink*. Early Christians associated the Eucharist with the Incarnation of Christ, so that the Eucharist becomes in a way a new Incarnation.[37] Just as the Word *became* flesh, the eucharistic bread and wine *become* the Flesh and Blood of Christ.[38] In fact, the early Christian writers are unanimous in making a point to say specifically that the eucharistic elements *become* the Body and Blood of Christ.[39] Therefore, the Eucharist was never thought of as a symbol or memorial only, but a mystery, and the early Christians knew that whatever was happening in the ritual, it was a miracle of incarnation, in which Christ was present as the Word made flesh.

It is interesting to note that, unlike the doctrine of the Trinity and other important issues, there was never any real debate over eucharistic theology in the early Church. The Church Fathers adamantly defended the Real Presence of Christ's Body and Blood in the sacrament, against those docetics and gnostics who would deny the reality of Jesus' Flesh and Blood. But the definition of what would later come to be called *transubstantiation* was not debated until the Middle Ages, when philosophical concerns raised questions about the nature of reality itself. So even when a controversy arose over the Church's understanding of the Eucharist (beginning in the ninth century), it was less a debate over whether the eucharistic elements were the Real Presence of the Body and Blood of Christ, and more a debate over what it means for something to be *real*.[40] But the definitions of terms notwithstanding, the

37 Justin Martyr, *1 Apology*, 66.

38 Although the early Christian writers do use the language of "becoming" for the Eucharist, they are not actually using it in the same way that it is used of the Incarnation. "The Word became flesh" (John 1:14) means that the Word acquired a human nature and came to exist in human form and live a human life. It does not mean "the Word changed into flesh," in the sense of ceasing to be divine. However, when the language of "becoming" is used of the Eucharist, it *does* mean that the bread and wine change into the Body and Blood of Christ, not in their tangible aspects, but in their intangible essence. Nevertheless, in a very real way, they cease to be bread and wine.

39 See, for example, Ignatius of Antioch, *Letter to the Smyrnaeans*, 6; Justin Martyr, *1 Apology*, 66; Irenaeus of Lyons, *Against Heresies*, 4.18.5, 4.33.2, 5.2.2–3; see also John of Damascus, *Exposition of the Orthodox Faith*, 4.13.

40 For a detailed discussion of the Church's eucharistic theology and the medieval debate, see Papandrea, *Handed Down*, 121–163.

early Church Fathers and medieval Scholastics were all in agreement that the bread and wine become the Body and Blood of Christ, which then exist as the deepest and truest reality of what is received, regardless of the fact that the sensory aspects (like appearance and taste) of the elements remain that of bread and wine.[41]

Just as Baptism and Confirmation were originally one rite, so it was with the Eucharist and confession of sins. It was always assumed that the Eucharist should be preceded by confession, and that eucharistic prayers should include some form of penitential act.[42] Confession of venial (smaller) sins was part of the regular liturgy of the Eucharist, and forgiveness of these sins was assumed to be covered by the grace of the sacrament. However, serious sins required some form of verbal confession (based on James 5:13–19) and any sin that was publicly known was public enough for a public confession (Matt. 18:15–17). Later, those who committed serious sins like apostasy could be expected to confess publicly in front of the congregation before Reconciliation.

Since the table of the Eucharist was believed to be the foretaste of the heavenly banquet, and therefore an earthly expression of the Kingdom of God, it was directly connected to membership in the Body of Christ. To be at the table is to be in the Church, and to be out of favor with the Church required being excluded — or excommunicated — from the communion table.[43] Therefore, excommunication emerged very early as a form of discipline within the Church (1 Cor. 5).[44] Reconciliation to the Church meant being readmitted to the table, but since the bishop held the authority over the sacraments, Reconciliation meant returning to the bishop.[45] As we noted above, this is one reason why it became important to limit the number of bishops to one per city. If there was more than one bishop in a city, a person who was excommunicated by one bishop could try to receive the Eucharist from the other bishop. If bishops did not enforce each other's excommunication, then the unity of the Church was threatened. For most people, though, every Eucharist was also a reconciliation service, in which daily sins were confessed, and access to God through Christ was granted.

[41] The underlying reality of the Body and Blood of Christ will come to be referred to as the *substance* of the elements, while the sensory aspects (the outward appearance, etc.) will come to be called the *accidents*, in that they are "accidental," that is, not a part of the essence of the elements. The Body and Blood of Christ are said to exist under the veil of the accidents of the elements.

[42] *Didache*, 14.1. On the Eucharistic prayers, see Meyendorff, *Imperial Unity*, 71–72.

[43] Meyendorff, *Imperial Unity*, 40.

[44] Clement of Rome, *1 Clement*, 57.2; cf. 1 Cor. 5:1–11.

[45] Ignatius of Antioch, *Letter to the Philadelphians*, 8.1.

In the middle of the second century, we have something like a very detailed order of liturgy preserved for us in Justin Martyr's *1 Apology*. It includes all the elements of liturgy, even taking up a collection (see 1 Cor. 16:2), though he does not mention singing (yet we know that Christians were singing from other sources). Since Justin was writing to try to explain Christian worship to non-Christians, we cannot assume too much about the universality of the form or language used by Justin, but it is significant that already by the mid-second century he can talk in general terms about what Christians do in worship — and that what we see there is remarkably similar to orders of worship we are still familiar with.

Prayer, Devotion, Feasts, and Fasts

Christian Prayer

The first thing to keep in mind is that early and medieval Christians did not sit down to pray. For the most part, Christians prayed standing, in what is known at the *orans* position. The word *orans* is simply the Latin word for praying, but the implied position is standing, with arms raised up. Some Christians stood in a *cruciform* position, with arms outstretched, in imitation of the bodily position of Jesus on the cross. This would be the case in worship, as well as in small group prayer, since even wealthy homes did not have a lot of chairs around, and even when Christianity was legalized and the first basilicas were built, they did not have pews.

Kneeling was considered a position of penitence, so for much of the Christian year (depending on the place), kneeling was not allowed unless one was doing penance after confession, because it was seen as something that negated the celebration that should naturally come with gratitude (remember that *Eucharist* means "thanksgiving"). In actual practice, the expectation for kneeling varied a lot, but by the time of the first ecumenical Council of Nicaea in AD 325, the bishops there thought it necessary to mandate that everyone must stand for prayer on Sundays and throughout the season of Pentecost.[46]

People in the early and medieval Church did not own their own Bibles, nor did they read the Bible on their own. The Bible of Jesus, the apostles, and the earliest Christians was what we would call the Old Testament, translated into Greek, and known as the Septuagint (abbreviated LXX), because of a tradition that it was translated by seventy scholars, working independently, who all (miraculously) came up

[46] Tertullian admits to variations of practice in *On Prayer*, 23.1–2; see Council of Nicaea (AD 325), canon 20; Bradshaw and Johnson, *The Origins of Feasts, Fasts, and Seasons in Early Christianity*, 17, 26, 72.

with the exact same translation. We cannot call it the *Hebrew Bible*, however, because although it was the Bible of the Jewish religion, it did contain some books that were not written in Hebrew, but were originally in Greek, or perhaps were originally written in Hebrew, but only existed in Greek translation. This includes the books sometimes referred to as *apocryphal*, or more accurately, *deuterocanonical*. We can see that Jesus read these books from the many places in His own teaching when He refers to them.[47] We will look at the addition of the New Testament to the Christian Bible in detail in a later chapter.

In the early Church, individual congregations meeting in homes would have, maybe, one copy of a limited collection of biblical documents. Like the synagogue tradition, these would be kept in a safe place, where they were treated with reverence. If one member of the congregation was designated as the *lector* (reader), then that person might keep the Scriptures at home. We know this because during times of persecution, when Roman soldiers went looking for holy books to burn, they often raided the homes of the bishops and the lectors. Even throughout the Middle Ages, most people did not own their own Bibles, though in large part this was because very few people could afford the price of a hand-copied manuscript. Those who could afford it, and who could read, would commission, not whole Bibles, but collections of readings, especially the psalms, and collections of prayers. In the Middle Ages, wealthy people with a heart for spirituality, a lot of free time, and the ability to read would often imitate the monks by praying the daily offices. And although that is getting ahead of ourselves a bit, the point is that in the early and medieval Church, *prayer* usually meant *reading* something, especially Scripture. Spontaneous prayer was done, of course, but it was normally left up to the bishops and priests. This was not a hard-and-fast rule, as there is evidence in the early Church that even eucharistic prayers sometimes had room for improvisation, but the point is that in the early and medieval Church, most people *heard* Scripture read, and *prayed* Scripture from written prayers.

Prayer was always thought of as going hand in hand with fasting (see Acts 13:3; 14:23). Early Christians were told to fast on Wednesdays and Fridays, often specifically to distinguish Christians from (non-Christian) Jews who fasted on other days,

[47] See for example, Sir. 27:6, which Jesus paraphrases in Matt. 7:16–20; Sir. 28:1–4, which becomes the parable of the unmerciful servant; and Sir. 29:10–12, which is behind Jesus' statements about storing treasure in Heaven, e.g., Matt. 6:19–21; cf. also Tob. 4:15 (Matt.7:12); Jth. 11:19 (Matt. 9:36); and 1 Macc. 1–2 (Matt. 24:15–16); also Paul, in Eph. 6 (the armor of God), probably has in mind Wisd. 5:17–22. Jesus' statement that "the Sabbath was made for [humanity]" (Mark 2:27) could also be a reference to 2 Macc. 5:19.

and who could not fast on Fridays because of the Sabbath meal.[48] Some especially pious people continued the Friday fast through Saturday.[49] However, there does not seem to be any universal consensus on what *fasting* meant (no food at all? water only? bread and water allowed?), or about when the fast ended (sundown? midnight? dawn the next day?). The latter question was, of course, dependent on whether one was working with the Jewish or Roman understanding of when a day begins and ends.[50] In any case, there was a wide diversity of practice across the Church on this point. For many people, fasting went hand in hand with kneeling, since fasting was also seen as a penitential act, and therefore some advocated praying while kneeling on the fasting days.[51]

Early Devotion to Mary and the Other Saints

As we have already noted, it was very early in the history of the Church, and a direct result of the earliest persecutions, that Christians began celebrating the anniversaries of the martyrs' deaths as holy days of observance. It is important to note that the celebration of the feast days of the saints, that is, the tradition of a memorial meal with some form of worship and prayer at the tombs of the martyrs, was not a tradition imposed by the hierarchy, but was in fact, a grassroots movement from the beginning. Starting as a continuation of the Roman tradition of the *refrigerium*, these celebrations quickly became "the heart of the annual calendar for most ordinary worshippers."[52] They were something that the common people could understand and engage in without worrying about complex theological or christological concepts, in part because the heart of the message was a concrete story of imitation of Christ through self-sacrifice, rather than a theoretical or moralizing homily. The feasts of the martyrs became so important that eventually, if one fell on a fast day, the fast could be suspended by the bishop so that the people could celebrate.[53] To this day, bishops in the United States often suspend the Lenten fast if St. Patrick's Day falls on a Friday.

48 *Didache*, 8.1. Note that in texts which contrast Christian fasting from Jewish fasting, the "hypocrites" mentioned would be the so-called Judaizers, who argued that Christians should keep the Jewish law.

49 Bradshaw and Johnson, *The Origins of Feasts, Fasts, and Seasons in Early Christianity*, 17.

50 Bradshaw and Johnson, *The Origins of Feasts, Fasts, and Seasons in Early Christianity*, 19.

51 Tertullian, *On Prayer*, 23; see also Bradshaw and Johnson, *The Origins of Feasts, Fasts, and Seasons in Early Christianity*, 30.

52 Bradshaw and Johnson, *The Origins of Feasts, Fasts, and Seasons in Early Christianity*, xv.

53 Egeria, *Pilgrimage Diary of Egeria* , 27.5, cited in Bradshaw and Johnson, *The Origins of Feasts, Fasts, and Seasons in Early Christianity*, 34.

As we saw in the *Martyrdom of Polycarp,* Christians also venerated the bodily remains of a saint, referred to as their *relics* (from the Latin word that means "remains"). In part this was based on the respect that Christians already had for the human body (which comes from Judaism) and the Judeo-Christian aversion to cremation. But reverence for relics has its deeper theological roots in the doctrine of the resurrection, with its assumptions about the eternal connection between body and spirit.[54] In other words, those who die in Christ are more than ever alive in Christ, and their spirits are with Him in Paradise (Luke 23:43). Believers can be closer to Christ by getting closer to the saint, which means being in physical proximity to the saint's relics. So when we are told in *The Martyrdom of Polycarp* that his relics were put in a special place, it means a *martyrium,* a marked or embellished tomb that could be visited by believers who wished to make a pilgrimage there, especially on his feast day.

The feast of the martyrs was a real meal, complete with picnic-type food, and wine.[55] For a while, some Christians continued the Roman tradition of the libation, which meant that there was hole in the top of the tomb, or even a tube running down into the grave, where the family or other devotees could pour some wine, so that the saint or deceased loved one could share in the toast, so to speak. It is not that Christians thought the deceased needed food or drink in the afterlife, but rather it was a gesture of connectedness, an affirmation of the belief in the communion of the saints. The celebration also included a reading of the written account of the saint's martyrdom (the martyr acts), if there was one, and some combination of Scripture, prayers, and songs. Christians prayed to the saints, asking for their intercession. But just as singing praise to someone is not in and of itself an act of worship, so prayer to someone is not necessarily an act of worship. When praying to the saints, the early and medieval Christians were primarily asking the saints to pray for them, reasoning that if a fellow believer here on earth can pray for another (James 5:16), how much better to ask for the prayers of one who is in Paradise with Jesus and who has His

[54] For a detailed treatment of the doctrine of the resurrection in the early Church, see James L. Papandrea, *What Really Happens After We Die? (There WILL Be Hugs in Heaven)* (Manchester, NH: Sophia Institute Press, 2019). Note that because the martyrs were said to have been "baptized in their own blood," their sins are completely forgiven, and the purification of Purgatory for them would be minimal at most, and one need not wonder whether they are already in the heavenly realm.

[55] On the early Christian practice of the *refrigerium,* and worship at the cemeteries, see Ramsay MacMullen, *The Second Church: Popular Christianity A.D. 200–400* (Atlanta: Society of Biblical Literature, 2009).

ear?[56] Other martyr documents and patristic texts also attest to the early practice of prayer to the saints.[57] In fact, there is graffiti at one of the catacombs in Rome, in the very place where the memorial feasts were held, that ask for the prayers of the saints, including Peter and Paul. Christians also prayed for the souls of the dead, though it was widely believed that the martyrs did not need such prayers, because their place in Heaven was guaranteed by their martyrdom.[58] In this tradition of devotion to the saints and asking for their intercession, there was no fear of confusion over idolatry, because, as we have seen, worship (submission and service) was clearly reserved for God alone (God in Christ), and the devotion showed to the saints was a reverence born of respect, and a desire to imitate those who had perfectly imitated Christ.

If a bishop or priest were present, a memorial feast might include the Eucharist, and often, in the case when there was a marble coffin, or *sarcophagus*, present, the sarcophagus lid served as the eucharistic table. This may seem strange to us at first, but the doctrine of the Resurrection implied a strong connection between the Incarnation, the crucifixion, and the Resurrection. As we have noted above, the Eucharist was considered to be a re-presentation of all of these, as well as an anticipation of the final resurrection of all believers. In other words, having a tomb as the altar of the Eucharist was a visceral lesson about the connection of the Church on earth to the Kingdom of Heaven. Note that in the book of Revelation, the souls of the martyrs are waiting, "underneath the altar" (Rev. 6:9). Of course, in the text this is a reference to the heavenly altar of the New Jerusalem, but that's precisely the point. The earthly altar table of the Eucharist is an image and foreshadowing of the heavenly altar table. And this was the start of the tradition of having relics under the altar tables of the churches, once the legalization of Christianity allowed for the building of basilicas. The churches of Rome would have altars that look like sarcophagi (because they are) and mosaics in the apses above that depict scenes of

[56] For a more detailed treatment of prayer to the saints, see Papandrea, *Handed Down*, 167–177.

[57] See, for example, the *Diary of Perpetua*, as well as Athanasius of Alexandria, *On the Incarnation of the Word*, 57; Cyril of Jerusalem, *Catechetical Lectures*, 23.9 (*On the Mysteries*, 5.9); and Gregory of Nazianzus, *Orations*, 24, cited in Bradshaw and Johnson, *The Origins of Feasts, Fasts, and Seasons in Early Christianity*, 181–182, 202–203.; cf. also Tob. 12:12, for an example of the belief in intercessory prayer, though in this example it is the intercession of the archangel Raphael.

[58] See, for example, Cyprian, *Epistles*, 33.3, 36.2, cited in Bradshaw and Johnson, *The Origins of Feasts, Fasts, and Seasons in Early Christianity*, 175. Note that when patristic writers speak of the "sacrifices" at the tombs, they mean Masses, that is, the Eucharist, not pre-Christian or pagan sacrifices.

Christ's second coming and other heavenly scenarios, so that the believer who raises her eyes up above the eucharistic table is looking into Heaven much like the apostle John in the book of Revelation.

When worshipers left the memorial feast, they often brought home with them what we would call *contact relics*, that is, handkerchiefs, articles of clothing, vials of oil, or other items that had been touched to the saints' relics or tombs. These were thought by some to have healing power, and for many former pagans, they probably made a convenient replacement for the amulets of protection that they were no longer allowed to wear.[59]

In the fourth century, when Christianity became legalized, the feasts became full-blown festivals, which included free food for the feeding of the poor.[60] This was the early version of the parish festival, commemorating a saint who came from that congregation. The tradition of naming churches in honor of a saint has its roots in the connection of a martyr to the place where the saint worshiped or presided. The fourth century also saw the official creation of the "church building," that is, a basilica built specifically for Christian worship. The first of these were shrines built directly over the tombs of saints such as Peter and Paul. When church buildings were built within the city walls, some of the relics of the martyrs were brought into the cities from the cemeteries and placed in (under) the altar tables. By the seventh century, the movement, or *translation*, of relics into the church buildings became commonplace. In Rome, when invasion and piracy threatened the security of the catacombs, an effort was made to bring all of the relics of the martyrs into the city. In the year AD 609, the Pantheon was consecrated as a church building, and it is said that twenty-eight wagonloads of human remains were brought from the catacombs, to be entombed there.[61]

With the legalization of Christianity, however, the reality of martyrdom diminished significantly. This led to a new kind of martyrdom, which we will explore below, but which will allow for a new kind of saint. The new martyrdom will be *asceticism* — not giving up one's life, but giving up the worldly lifestyle to live more faithfully in imitation of Christ. This voluntary renunciation of the world and its comforts and pleasures will be seen as a kind of "dying to the world daily," and will produce a new batch of saints who did not die for the Faith, but who lived for the Faith in ways that most could never imitate.

[59] See, for example, Ambrose of Milan, *Epistles*, 22, cited in Bradshaw and Johnson, *The Origins of Feasts, Fasts, and Seasons in Early Christianity*, 182–183, 185.

[60] Bradshaw and Johnson, *The Origins of Feasts, Fasts, and Seasons in Early Christianity*, 182.

[61] Bradshaw and Johnson, *The Origins of Feasts, Fasts, and Seasons in Early Christianity*, 184; see also Papandrea, *ROME*, 33–36.

However, although the persecution had to end before sainthood could be extended beyond martyrdom, this was never the case for Mary, the mother of Jesus. She was not martyred, but was always considered a saint (and later she will be called the Queen of the Saints, and the Queen of Heaven), the point being that she was considered holy from the beginning.[62] As we will see below, a second-century document known as the *Protevangelion of James* attests to the very early belief in the Immaculate Conception and Perpetual Virginity of Mary. The Immaculate Conception is a doctrine built on the tradition that Mary's own birth was miraculous (though not virginal), in that she was born exempt from the effects of original sin, which resulted in her living her whole life without any personal sin. The greeting of the archangel Gabriel, acknowledging Mary as "full of grace" (Luke 1:28, often translated "favored one," but it means *entirely sanctified*), and which would eventually become part of the *Hail Mary* prayer, contributed to the belief in Mary's sinlessness. This went hand in hand with her Perpetual Virginity, that is, not only was she a virgin at Jesus' birth (and remained physically a virgin even through the delivery), but also that she remained a virgin all her life and had no other children after Jesus. Both of these doctrines were energized by the grassroots devotion of the laity, but by the fourth century, to deny them was considered a heresy.[63]

In two of the catacombs in Rome there are early paintings of Mary with the baby Jesus.[64] In the catacombs of Priscilla, visitors can see what is probably a second-century fresco depicting Mary holding Jesus on her lap, with a prophet pointing to a star.[65] This is the earliest "Madonna and Child" in existence, though the concept was probably adapted from even earlier portrayals of the visitation of the Magi. There are actually quite a few grave markers and sarcophagi from the early Church which are inscribed with this scene. They show a seated Mary, with the infant Jesus on her lap, giving audience to a procession of Magi bearing gifts.

The first official feast of Mary was the feast of Mary, Mother of God (in Greek: *Theotokos*), celebrated on August 15th. We don't know when this started, but it was probably already being celebrated (at least in some places) by the third century, and most likely even earlier, since there is no recorded debate over any of this at this

[62] For a detailed treatment of early and medieval devotion to Mary, and the Marian doctrines, see Papandrea, *Handed Down*, 177–192.

[63] Epiphanius of Salamis, *Panarion*, 79, mentioned in Bradshaw and Johnson, *The Origins of Feasts, Fasts, and Seasons in Early Christianity*, 203.

[64] Bradshaw and Johnson, *The Origins of Feasts, Fasts, and Seasons in Early Christianity*, 197.

[65] See Papandrea, *ROME*, 73–74.

time.[66] In the fourth century, Gregory of Nazianzus would write, "If anyone does not believe that Holy Mary is the Mother of God, he is severed from the Godhead."[67] A third century papyrus has been found with the oldest known prayer to Mary, calling her the Mother of God. The prayer is referred to as the *Sub Tuum Praesidium* (Under Your Protection). There are various translations of the Greek text, and a Latin translation. One possible translation of the prayer, taking both Greek and Latin into account is my translation:

> *Holy Mother of God, uniquely pure and blessed,*
> *We take refuge under your compassion.*
> *Do not ignore our prayers in our time of need,*
> *But free us from danger.*[68]

The "danger" in question was, of course, the persecution, probably at the time of Decius. The first recorded apparition, or vision, of Mary was also in the third century.[69] Eventually, pilgrims to Jerusalem would be shown a tomb that had been prepared for Mary (she was never buried there), and this seems to have prompted the August 15th date to incorporate the commemoration of her *Dormition* (death), and her *Assumption.*[70] As noted above, Mary did not die a violent death but died peacefully in the presence of the apostles (according to tradition). Then, because she was sinless and therefore could not suffer the corruption of decay, she was taken (*assumed*) into Heaven, body and soul. Later, several documents emerged presenting the (highly embellished) story of Mary's death and assumption, presumably to counter apocryphal stories that, like Enoch and Elijah, she had never really died. In any case, this is why there could be no actual tomb of Mary, and no bodily relics. Now August 15th is the feast of Mary's Dormition and Assumption, though the eastern church seems to focus on the Dormition, while the West focuses on the Assumption.[71] The feast of Mary, *Theotokos*, was moved to December 26th (in the East) and January 1st (in the West).

66 Bradshaw and Johnson, *The Origins of Feasts, Fasts, and Seasons in Early Christianity*, 198–201.

67 Gregory of Nazianzus, *Letter to Cledonius the Priest Against Apollinarius*, in *Nicene and Post-Nicene Fathers*, vol. 7, ed. Philip Schaff and Henry Wace (repr., Peabody, MA: Hendrickson, 2004), 439.

68 First published in James L. Papandrea, *Praying a Christ-Centered Rosary: Meditations on the Mysteries* (Notre Dame, IN: Ave Maria Press, 2021).

69 *Life of Gregory the Wonderworker*, 4, mentioned in Bradshaw and Johnson, *The Origins of Feasts, Fasts, and Seasons in Early Christianity*, 203.

70 Bradshaw and Johnson, *The Origins of Feasts, Fasts, and Seasons in Early Christianity*, 207.

71 See, for example, John of Damascus, *Three Sermons on the Dormition of the Virgin*.

As we will see, there will be a controversy over the title "Mother of God" (*Theotokos*) for Mary, but in the end, ecumenical councils will affirm that it is appropriate, in that it affirms the divinity of Christ whom Mary held in her womb. But it is important to remember that neither the title, nor the Marian doctrines that go with it, were new in the fifth century when the controversy emerges. All of this finds its genesis in the popular piety of the laity, and in the *Protevangelion of James*, along with the background for other Marian feasts, such as the Nativity of Mary (celebrated on September 8th) and the Presentation of Mary in the temple (celebrated on November 21st). It is ironic, therefore, that the Protestant Reformation, with its emphasis on the priesthood of the laity, would eventually mean the removal of exactly those aspects of Christian devotion that had come from the laity. This includes devotion to Mary, though to be precise the original reformers, including Martin Luther, accepted the doctrine of her Perpetual Virginity.

Easter and Lent

In the early Church, Easter was called the *Pascha*, which is the Greek word for Passover (*pesach*). This means that the first Christians simply referred to Easter as Passover (much like Pentecost was originally a Jewish holiday).[72] However, the meaning of the word *Pascha* for Christians quickly morphed into something that came to refer to Jesus' passion (in Greek: *pathein*). Since the early and medieval Christians tended to think of the passion, death, and Resurrection of Jesus as one event that made salvation possible, Easter Sunday was originally thought of as Passion Sunday, combining Jesus' death with His Resurrection in one celebration.

One of the longest-lasting debates of the early Church — one which was never truly resolved — is the question of how to determine the date for celebrating the Passion and Resurrection of Christ. Should *Easter* be celebrated on Passover, since the passion event took place at the time of Passover, or should it be celebrated on a Sunday, since Jesus' Resurrection was on a Sunday (Matt. 28:1; Luke 24:1)?[73] Those who advocated for a date based on Passover were mostly in the East, though there is evidence to suggest that this was the original way it was done. The day of Passover is the fourteenth of the Hebrew month Nisan, and so the advocates for this

[72] The origin of the English word "Easter" is a matter of debate, with various theories based on supposed etymologies of the word. The word "Easter" does not occur in the Bible, though some translations use the English term to translate "Passover" when it refers to Christian Easter, as in Acts 12:4.

[73] For a detailed discussion of this controversy, see Bradshaw and Johnson, *The Origins of Feasts, Fasts, and Seasons in Early Christianity*, 39–47.

way of determining Easter were called *Quartodecimans* (fourteeners). But doing this required converting the date on the Jewish calendar to a date on the Roman calendar, which in practice resulted in confusion over which date was the right date. Plus, the Christians had to wait until the Jewish leaders in Jerusalem confirmed the date for Passover, which meant that those farthest from Jerusalem might not get the news about which date was chosen until after the day had come and gone. Those who maintained that the date must be on a Sunday argued that Easter should be the first Sunday after the vernal equinox. However, they could not always agree on the date of the equinox. Others (perhaps in an attempt at a compromise?) argued in favor of the first Sunday after the Passover.

In the second century there were Christians from the East living in Rome. They were celebrating Easter according to the Quartodeciman tradition, while the rest of Rome was celebrating on a Sunday. The bishop of Rome, Victor (bishop AD 189–199), tried to force everyone to conform to the Sunday celebration (with threats of excommunication), but Irenaeus traveled to Rome from Lyons and advised him to let them continue with their tradition.[74] Victor took Irenaeus's advice and it was agreed that the two traditions could exist side by side. However, by the fourth century, the emperor Constantine did not think so, and encouraged everyone to get on the same schedule. He attended the Council of Arles in AD 314, which decreed that the bishop of Rome should send out a letter each year, with the date of Easter that all Christians should use.[75] In the controversy leading up the Council of Nicaea in AD 325, Constantine thought that unity on the date of Easter was the most important topic of conversation (over the doctrine of the Trinity!). The very first canon (decree) of the Council of Nicaea was to declare that all churches everywhere must follow the Roman practice. The universal Church did fall in line with regard to celebration on a Sunday, but eastern Christians still tend to use the Jewish (lunar) calendar and calculate from Passover, which results in the reality that we still do not all celebrate Easter on the same day.

In many places, the celebration of Easter has always included what is called a *vigil*, a service of prayer and Scripture readings that goes through the night leading up to Easter morning, based on the idea of watchfulness, from such Scripture texts as the parable of the bridesmaids (Matt. 25:1–13). Some places actually celebrated Easter at midnight, based on the belief that the Resurrection had taken place at midnight,

[74] Eusebius of Caesarea, *Ecclesiastical History*, 5.24.9–14. The implication that some of Victor's predecessors in Rome had been of the Quartodeciman tradition seems to support the claim that this was the earlier practice.

[75] Bradshaw and Johnson, *The Origins of Feasts, Fasts, and Seasons in Early Christianity*, 59.

even though no one came to the empty tomb until dawn. In general, though, the celebration of Easter expanded from one day that included the commemoration of the passion, death, and Resurrection to a celebration of three days, referred to as *Triduum*. Perhaps this began as an attempt to incorporate both ways of determining the date, bringing together those who would celebrate on Passover with those who insisted on Sunday. We do know that by the fourth century, Jerusalem had processional liturgies in which pilgrims remembered the events of the passion and Resurrection by standing in the places where tradition said these things had happened. This would have been expanded to incorporate the chronology of events, eventually including a Palm Sunday procession, and all of this would have spread to other places (in various forms) with the return of pilgrims to their home cities.[76] This development led to the concept of Holy Week. In some places (including Rome) the Passion was celebrated on the Sunday before Easter, but later, in the Middle Ages, that became Palm Sunday.[77]

It is important to note at this point that, as soon as there is a commemoration of specific events in the life of Jesus, we naturally see the creation of a *lectionary*, that is, a specified cycle of Scripture readings meant to go with the events being celebrated. There were many lectionaries created in the early and medieval Church, and many were only regional. Nevertheless, the idea that individual churches should have a set of readings appropriate for the day caught on and furthered the emerging idea of a Christian calendar.

Lent seems to have begun, not so much as a time of repentance, but more as a time of preparation and catechesis for the people who planned to be baptized (at any time of year), and in fact it was probably the attempt to limit Baptisms to Easter that eventually got Lent permanently attached to the time leading up to Easter.[78] As we have noted, early pre-baptismal catechesis was originally three weeks, and there is evidence that what we now call Lent also began as a three-week time of preparation. It was later expanded to forty days, with various ways of counting the days for fasting. Pentecost began as a time of post-baptismal celebration and catechesis, commemorating the Resurrection, Ascension, and the coming of the Holy Spirit.[79]

[76] Bradshaw and Johnson, *The Origins of Feasts, Fasts, and Seasons in Early Christianity*, 63, 65, 114–115, 192.

[77] Bradshaw and Johnson, *The Origins of Feasts, Fasts, and Seasons in Early Christianity*, 117.

[78] Bradshaw and Johnson, *The Origins of Feasts, Fasts, and Seasons in Early Christianity*, 81, 91–99, 107–108, 112–113.

[79] Bradshaw and Johnson, *The Origins of Feasts, Fasts, and Seasons in Early Christianity*, 70–71, 74.

Eventually, though, as Easter Sunday came to be all about the Resurrection, and the Ascension got its own day (the fortieth day), Pentecost (which means "the fiftieth day") came to be focused on the coming of the Holy Spirit.[80]

Christmas and Advent

Early Christians believed that Jesus died on Passover, the fourteenth of Nisan (probably in the year AD 33), which as western Christians calculated, would have been on March 25th. Eastern Christians made the same calculation and ended up on April 6th. They all seemed to agree, however, that it was only fitting that the Son of God, who lived a perfect human life in perfect obedience to the Father's will, would also live a perfectly "whole" life — that is, a number of days that added up to a whole number of years. This is based on a tradition that Moses died on his birthday. For Jesus, that would mean that He came into the world on the same day He left it. However, the Incarnation (when "the Word became flesh," John 1:14), did not occur at Jesus' birth, but rather at His conception, when the angel came to Mary and announced God's plan to her. This is called the Annunciation, and it assumes that as soon as Mary agreed to it, she became pregnant. Therefore, because it was seen as fitting that Jesus left the world on the same day that He came into it, the early Christians concluded that the conception of Jesus took place on the same date as the crucifixion: March 25th for the western Christians, April 6th for the easterners. Thus, it becomes a simple math problem to determine the date of the Nativity. Jesus must have been born (a perfect) nine months after His conception. For the westerners, this meant that Jesus was born on December 25th.[81] For the East, it meant January 6th. By the fourth and fifth centuries, however, each tradition had migrated to the other side of the empire and although the generalization remains, neither one became universal.[82] In the East, Christians actually celebrated both Jesus' birth and His Baptism on January 6th.[83]

[80] Bradshaw and Johnson, *The Origins of Feasts, Fasts, and Seasons in Early Christianity*, 74.

[81] This is a bit of a generalization and the distinction of West from East should not be pushed too far here. There is evidence that some westerners followed the more eastern tradition, and vice versa. It seems that the December 25th tradition begins in Rome, certainly by the third century at the latest, and moves out from there, along with North Africa. However, this "Western" tradition may not have made its way to Gaul until the fourth century. Bradshaw and Johnson, *The Origins of Feasts, Fasts, and Seasons in Early Christianity*, 135–136, 152–153.

[82] Bradshaw and Johnson, *The Origins of Feasts, Fasts, and Seasons in Early Christianity*, 129.

[83] Bradshaw and Johnson, *The Origins of Feasts, Fasts, and Seasons in Early Christianity*, 137, 157. There may have been a felt necessity to separate the celebration of Jesus' birth from His Baptism after the Council of Nicaea, since the Arians apparently celebrated His Baptism

It has been argued that the date for Christmas (or indeed the invention of the holiday itself) was originally intended to supplant a pagan holiday. As we can see, however, the dates for Christmas are dependent on Passover and the Annunciation, and so are not dependent on any Roman holiday that may occur near it on the calendar. It is true that some early Christian writers noted how the conception and birth of Christ fall on the vernal equinox and winter solstice,[84] respectively, and it should come as no surprise that pre-Christian cultures had festivals at these times of the year, but to say any more than that is to assume causality from coincidence. The truth is that Christmas was being celebrated in the West (at least in Rome) by the third century, which is much too early for the Church to want to "baptize" a Roman holiday, since that would have been seen as a form of imitating the pagans.[85] Furthermore, the Roman holiday usually cited as the precedent for Christmas is the Day of Sol Invictus, instituted by the emperor Aurelian in the year AD 274 — at least a full half century *after* we know that Christmas was being celebrated in Rome.[86]

January 6th came to be known as *Epiphany*, which implies a revelation of divine glory. This concept was still vague enough to include Jesus' birth and His Baptism, but for the most part, the West would celebrate January 6 as Christ's revelation to the Gentiles (the Magi).[87]

Advent probably began as a celebration of the Annunciation and Visitation (Luke 1:26–56), complete with feasts dedicated to Mary. In some places, the Annunciation was originally celebrated on the Sunday before Christmas. In other places, Baptisms were done on Christmas, and so like Lent, Advent emerged as a time for pre-baptismal

---

as His birth, that is, as His adoption by the Father. Thus the mainstream bishops would want to emphasize that Jesus' Incarnation came before His Baptism. See Bradshaw and Johnson, *The Origins of Feasts, Fasts, and Seasons in Early Christianity*, 143–145, 148.

84 See, for example, Pseudo-Chrysostom, *De solstitiis et aequinoctis* (early fourth century), cited in Bradshaw and Johnson, *The Origins of Feasts, Fasts, and Seasons in Early Christianity*, 125.

85 Hippolytus mentions the celebration of Christmas, *Commentary on Daniel*, 4.23, a text which also tells us that Jesus died on March 25th. There is considerable debate over this text, which is admittedly cobbled together from fragments. However, part of the reason some scholars reject it is precisely because it mentions Christmas, which they assume must be a later development. As with many documents (including some in the New Testament), the argument over the authorship and date of this document easily becomes a chicken and egg question, since assumptions about content drive conclusions about authorship and date, and vice versa.

86 Bradshaw and Johnson, *The Origins of Feasts, Fasts, and Seasons in Early Christianity*, 124.

87 Bradshaw and Johnson, *The Origins of Feasts, Fasts, and Seasons in Early Christianity*, 153–154, 156–157.

catechesis and fasting.[88] This means that Advent, like Lent, may have started out as three weeks long. At its longest it eventually developed into the same length as Lent (six weeks or forty days) but was shortened to four weeks by Pope St. Gregory the Great (bishop AD 590–604).[89]

Didache

The word *didache* means "teaching" and is actually a short form of the full Greek title of this document, which is translated, *The Teaching of the Lord to the Gentiles, by the Twelve Apostles*. The authorship of this document is unknown, but as the title suggests, it claims to transmit tradition that comes from Jesus Himself through the apostles. It is entirely possible that the content is based on apostolic preaching, and in any case that was the assumption, and so it gained widespread acceptance in the early Church as a document that was both useful for Church leaders and edifying for the laity.

Since we do not know who wrote it down in its final form, we cannot be sure when it was written. The author (or authors, if the work is a compilation) seems to know the Gospel of Matthew, which means that it was probably written after Matthew, though we don't know exactly when that was written, either. The lack of reference to any persecution could indicate a date before AD 64, when persecution began in Rome, or at least before AD 95, when the persecution spread to the East. This would make this the earliest Christian document outside of the New Testament, perhaps even earlier than *1 Clement*. The advice for discerning true from false prophets (apostles) would suggest that it was written while some of the apostles were still alive and traveling, and perhaps the Church at large was dealing with the problem of people claiming to be apostles who were not. The author refers to the itinerant prophets as "high priests," and so it may reflect the same hierarchical situation as *1 Clement*, where the office of bishop is emerging, but it is not called that yet.[90] It was certainly written before the letters of Ignatius of Antioch, since in the *Didache* the word "bishop" still seems to refer to local pastors rather than citywide or regional authorities.[91] And it must have been written before the time of Justin Martyr (fl. AD 145–165) and Theophilus of Antioch (bishop AD 169–183), both of whom refer to the text in their writings.[92]

88 Bradshaw and Johnson, *The Origins of Feasts, Fasts, and Seasons in Early Christianity*, 158–159, 163, 176, 210.

89 Bradshaw and Johnson, *The Origins of Feasts, Fasts, and Seasons in Early Christianity*, 165.

90 *Didache*, 13.

91 *Didache*, 15, in which clergy are referred to as "bishops and deacons."

92 Kenneth J. Howell, *Clement of Rome & the Didache: A New Translation and Theological Commentary* (Zanesville, OH: CHResources, 2012), 58–59, 65–66.

With all of this in mind, we can say that the document was probably written in the second half of the first century.

The Didache is primarily a manual for the Church. It consists of two main parts, one for instructing those preparing for Baptism, and one for Church leaders. The first part is based on a Jewish teaching called the "Two Ways" (Deut. 30:15, 19). As indicated above, early Christian catechesis was not so much concerned with teaching theology, as it was with teaching morality. Since the ethical expectations of the Church would result in a radical change of lifestyle and rejection of many aspects of the culture, a convert needed to know how to behave as a Christian before initiation. The Church could not afford to have its members hindering its evangelization efforts with embarrassing conduct, but more important, since it was understood that one could lose one's salvation through post-baptismal sin, it was imperative to instruct converts in proper behavior before their Baptism.[93] Therefore, the initiate is instructed in the "Two Ways" of life and death and encouraged to choose the way of life. The motivation for, and urgency of, this teaching is explained at the end of the book. Jesus would return soon, and the believer must be ready.[94]

Beyond the question of the internal integrity of the Church and its members, there was also the question of the identity of Christians in the view of those outside. As we will see in the writings of the apologists, the concept of who or what a Christian is was often defined in terms of "what we don't do." The things Christians don't do (according to the documents) included such culturally acceptable practices as adultery, prostitution, pedophilia, and the exposure and abortion of babies. In the Roman Empire, it was acceptable to abort a pre-born child, or even to "expose" a newborn, to leave her outside to die, if she was unwanted.[95] The *Didache* shows that from the very beginning of its existence the Church has opposed abortion as a form of infanticide.[96] Consistent with its countercultural morality, the Church taught

[93] On the belief that the grace of Baptism could be lost, see Cyprian of Carthage, *Epistles,* 54.13; *On the Unity of the Catholic Church,* 20–21. Cyprian wrote almost two centuries after the *Didache,* however he is expressing what was considered a traditional belief.

[94] *Didache,* 2, 16; see also the apocryphal *Apocalypse of Peter,* 25.

[95] For more on this topic, see Mike Aquilina and James L. Papandrea, *How Christianity Saved Civilization, And Must Do So Again* (Manchester, NH: Sophia Institute Press, 2018), 35–55. Most of the abandoned children were probably girls, since girls were often perceived as a financial burden. Many of the children exposed in this way were probably taken and raised to be slaves (including prostitutes); see *Epistle to Diognetus,* 5.6.

[96] *Didache,* 2.2; see also Juvenal, *Satire IV.* Writing at about the same time as the *Didache,* Juvenal, a non-Christian Roman writer, criticized the practice of abortion as a convenience of the wealthy class to avoid the "burden" of having children. His motivation for this

that Christians were not to engage in these practices and that abortion, no less than exposure, constituted a form of murder.[97] In fact, some Christian writers pointed out that in spite of the false accusation of incest directed at Christians, Romans ran the risk of unintentional incest when they exposed their daughters who could then be taken by slave traders and raised to be prostitutes.[98]

Because of the lack of identifiable apostolic authorship, the *Didache* was seen by most early Church Fathers as worthwhile for devotional reading and liturgical instruction, but not worthy of inclusion in the canon. A few did consider it Scripture, but not enough to sway the majority. Parts of it were, however, used by bishops as a manual on how to perform Baptisms and preside over the Eucharist.

Protevangelion of James

The word *Protevangelion* (sometimes spelled "*Protoevangelium*") is like saying the "pre-gospel." This is the prequel to the gospel story, and details not only the birth of Jesus, but the birth of Mary as well. It claims to be by the same author as the New Testament letter of James, the "brother of the Lord" (Gal. 1:19), but was probably actually written in the second century to emphasize the divinity of Jesus against the Ebionites (see below). However, in the process it sounds like Jesus' birth was so divine that it makes him seem almost docetic.

In this document we find the foundation of the doctrine of the Immaculate Conception of Mary. Also, with regard to her Perpetual Virginity, we are told that the brothers and sisters of Jesus mentioned in the Gospels (Matt. 13:55; Mark 6:3)

---

critique is very different from the Christian critique, however it shows how prevalent and acceptable abortion was at the time, but even Juvenal called it murder. Apparently, oral drugs could be used to cause a miscarriage. But even if a baby was born, under Roman law it could be legally disposed of, for no other reason than it was unwanted. However, at times the Roman government tried to encourage the wealthy to have more children, since many couples were opting to limit their children so that their fortunes would not be dispersed. This was seen as a threat to the empire because it resulted in a decrease in population. If the prevailing attitude among Roman aristocracy was that children were a burden, the early Christians responded to this by saying that having children is the very purpose of marriage; see Justin Martyr, *1 Apology*, 29.

[97] *Epistle of Barnabas*, 19.5, 20.2; Athenagoras, *A Plea for the Christians*, 35 (note that Athenagoras also condemns capital punishment); Clement of Alexandria, *The Instructor*, 2.10, 3.4 (note that Clement criticized the Romans who, he says, would save a baby animal to keep as a pet, but expose their own child); Tertullian, *Apology*, 9; *Apostolic Church Order*, 6. The early Christian writers, exemplified by Tertullian, did not see a difference between abortion and infanticide; see also *Apostolic Constitutions*, 7.1 (7.3).

[98] Justin Martyr, *1 Apology*, 27.

are actually his stepbrothers and stepsisters, children of Joseph from a previous marriage. Mary remains a virgin after the birth of Jesus, not only because she remains celibate, but because Jesus' miraculous birth left her physically as though she had never been pregnant.

Finally, there is another interesting connection to the tradition of Christian holy sites. To the western mind, when we read in the New Testament that Jesus was laid in a manger because there was no room in the inn, we usually picture a freestanding wooden stable or similar structure. However, according to the *Protevangelion*, Jesus was born in a cave. The Church of the Nativity in Bethlehem is built over a cave, where early tradition tells us our Savior came into the world.[99]

Sibylline Oracles

The Sibyl was a Greco-Roman female medium. She supposedly had mystical visions inspired by the gods, and pronounced oracles, or prophecies, based on those visions. These oracles were then written down and consulted later after significant events, something like the way the writings of Nostradamus are supposed to have predicted certain disasters. Jewish apologists wrote their own versions of these oracles, presenting them as older prophecies of current events. Following their lead, some Christians modified the Jewish versions, rewriting them to appear to be pre-Christian predictions of Christ. They seem to be intended to look like the book of Revelation, except the predictions of the life of Christ are not even subtle, let alone symbolic. While the majority of the Church did not accept these as real prophecy, they do seem to have been used as devotional poetry. Books 1, 6, and 8 of the *Sibylline Oracles* may have been used in Christian worship, though book 8 has some heretical (adoptionist) leanings. Book 6 especially may be an early Christian hymn, and includes a reference to the Eucharist, comparing the advent of Christ to the nourishment of bread.[100]

[99] Eusebius also speaks of the tradition of passing down the location of holy sites from one generation to another. See Eusebius of Caesarea, *Ecclesiastical History*, 7.18–19. Eusebius specifically mentions that the location of the home of the woman with a hemorrhage could be pointed out, and he also knows of statues and paintings of Jesus and the apostles, as well as the location of the episcopal "throne" of James.

[100] This close connection between the Incarnation and the Eucharist was typical of the early apologists and theologians. The manna in the wilderness is the bread that came down from Heaven, and is interpreted as a foreshadowing of the coming of Christ (see John 6). This was the basis for early eucharistic theology, in which authors such as Justin Martyr and Irenaeus connected the Incarnation ("the Word *became* flesh," John 1:14; emphasis added) with the Eucharist, using the same language of *becoming* to describe their understanding that the elements of bread and wine *become* the Flesh and Blood of Christ.

Odes of Solomon

Sometimes called an early Christian hymnal, the *Odes* are written like a Christian version of the Psalms. They are allegorical to the point of being mystical, and even use some surprising feminine images for God, including presenting God as a nursing mother, providing life-giving milk for her children.[101] The Virgin Mary has a somewhat prominent role in Ode 33.[102] We also get an interesting glimpse of prayer in the *Odes*, which suggests that at least on some occasions, Christians prayed in a cruciform position, standing, with arms outstretched to the sides, in imitation of Christ on the cross.[103]

Church Order Documents

In the first few centuries, before the legalization of Christianity, the Church tolerated a great amount of liturgical diversity. However, in the third century, and certainly by the fourth century, the Church started to work toward a greater unity through standardization of practice. In addition, the ease of travel and communication once Christianity was legalized (and especially with the growing popularity of pilgrimages to the Holy Land) highlighted differences from one city to another, which could sometimes be an embarrassment.

We have several Church order documents, some of which go back to the third century in their original form, that outline Church practice and liturgy. When reading these documents, the student of early Christianity should take them as the product of particular communities, and while the leaders of these communities (the writers of the documents) would certainly like to think that all Christians should follow their lead and do as they do, the fact that this was not happening is proven by the very existence of the document. If everyone was practicing their Christian Faith the same way across the empire, these documents would not have been necessary.

[101] *Odes of Solomon*, 19, 28, 36; note also that in Clement of Alexandria, *Who Is the Rich Man That Shall Be Saved?*, 37, Clement refers to God as both Father and Mother.

[102] *Odes of Solomon*, 33.5–6.

[103] *Odes of Solomon*, 27, 42.1–2; see also Clement of Rome, *1 Clement*, 2.3. The usual prayer position seems to be the so-called *orans* position (*orans* is simply the Latin word for prayer). This would be standing, with arms out, though not necessarily stretched out as in a cruciform position, with head and hands raised; Clement of Alexandria, *Miscellanies*, 7.7. Note that Clement says there is some movement of the feet, possibly a swaying back and forth, though it's not clear, and he may be saying that at the end of prayer, the true Christian "sets the feet in motion," meaning that prayer leads to action out in the world. According to Tertullian, *Apology*, 16, and the *Didascalia Apostolorum*, 12, the one who prays should face east.

Therefore, the documents are evidence, more of the process of standardization, than of universal acceptance of any particular liturgical practice. In addition, these documents were continually updated, so that in their present form they represent an amalgam of material from the third and fourth centuries.

Apostolic Tradition

Traditionally attributed to Hippolytus, this document may in fact go back to the third century in its original form, however, in its present state it certainly contains layers of later material.[104] It contains instructions for liturgy and ordination, including descriptions of the various Church offices, as well as references to an early form of the Liturgy of the Hours and making the Sign of the Cross.[105]

This community expected that new converts would go through a three-year catechism, which included regular exorcisms.[106] The teachers might be clergy, but they could also be lay people.[107] At the end of the catechumenate, sponsors attested to the candidate's sincerity and morality, at which time the candidate was baptized, which also included an exorcism performed by the bishop.[108] An interrogative version of the creed was used as a statement of faith, in which the candidates would respond in the affirmative to the questions, "Do you believe ..."[109] The Baptism was sealed with the Sign of the Cross on the forehead, ears, and nose.[110] It is assumed that children and infants were also being baptized.[111] If a catechumen was martyred before being baptized, the martyrdom would count as a baptism in his or her own blood (cf. Luke 12:50).[112] Just as the "good thief" might hope to be with Jesus in Paradise (Luke 23:42–43), the sincere believer who died without the chance of Baptism was not without that same hope.[113]

[104] A good overview of the problem is in J. A. Cerrato, "The Association of the Name Hippolytus with a Church Order Now Known as The Apostolic Tradition," *St. Vladimir's Theological Quarterly* 48:2 (2004): 179–194.

[105] *Apostolic Tradition*, 41.5–17, 41.13, 42.1. The signing of oneself with the cross probably meant tracing a cross on one's forehead with the thumb of the right hand.

[106] *Apostolic Tradition*, 17, 20.3.

[107] *Apostolic Tradition*, 19.1. It would be assumed that even in the case of lay teachers, the bishops held the final authority over the content of the teaching.

[108] *Apostolic Tradition*, 15, 20.

[109] *Apostolic Tradition*, 21.

[110] *Apostolic Tradition*, 20.8; see also Cyprian of Carthage, *On the Unity of the Catholic Church*, 18.

[111] *Apostolic Tradition*, 21.4.

[112] *Apostolic Tradition*, 19.2; see also *On Rebaptism*, 11.

[113] Cf. Cyprian of Carthage, *Epistles*, 72.22.

A newly baptized Christian's first Eucharist included milk and honey, to symbolize the hope of eternal Paradise.[114] The *Apostolic Tradition* contains an early version of a eucharistic prayer, but also says that the prayers were not static, and could be embellished *ad lib* by the presider, as long as the theology contained in the prayers was orthodox.[115] Members of the community were expected to fast before receiving the Eucharist.[116] In the assembly, men and women were separated, and were discouraged from greeting each other with a kiss.[117] The reverence with which the eucharistic elements were handled is consistent with early eucharistic theology that assumed a miraculous change had taken place, analogous to the Incarnation itself, and so the bread and wine had become the Body and Blood of Christ.[118]

With regard to ordination, it is stated that a (male) confessor does not need to be ordained (by the imposition of hands) but can be considered a priest because of the presence of the Holy Spirit.[119] This is an interesting concession to that prophetic authority invested in the confessors by the laity. It has echoes of Cyprian's dilemma of wanting to control the confessors without offending the people who saw them as prophets (see below). The *Apostolic Tradition* also clarified that although a deacon is ordained, he is not counted as a member of the council of priests, and he is not to preside over the sacraments, though deacons did help distribute the elements.[120] Thus the deacons fall into an in-between area, considered ordained, but not authorized to preside over the sacraments. Lay offices mentioned by the *Apostolic Tradition* are subdeacon, lector (reader), healer, and consecrated virgin.[121] Bishops are said to be chosen by the people.[122] This may be a reference to a time when lay people participated in the selection of a bishop, though it may also only mean that the people acknowledged their assent when the new bishop's name was announced in the consecration liturgy.[123]

[114] *Apostolic Tradition*, 21.27.
[115] *Apostolic Tradition*, 4 (Eucharistic Prayer), 9.4–5.
[116] *Apostolic Tradition*, 36.
[117] *Apostolic Tradition*, 18.
[118] *Apostolic Tradition*, 37–38.
[119] *Apostolic Tradition*, 9. As we have seen, this is based on the assumed prophetic authority granted by the presence of the Holy Spirit in the confessor (Matt. 10:19–20).
[120] *Apostolic Tradition*, 8.2–3; see Cyprian of Carthage, *On the Lapsed*, 25.
[121] *Apostolic Tradition*, 11–14.
[122] *Apostolic Tradition*, 2.
[123] See Cyprian of Carthage, *Epistles*, 40.2, 51.8, 54.5–6.

Didascalia Apostolorum

The *Didascalia Apostolorum,* sometimes called the *Catholic Didascalia,* is written as advice for bishops, claiming to come directly from the twelve apostles, who had supposedly gathered in Jerusalem to write it.[124] It mentions Peter and Matthew by name, as if to invoke their authority against heresy.[125] Heresy is defined as blasphemy of the Holy Spirit, because of its inherent rejection of Scripture.[126] Specific heresies mentioned are the Ebionites, those who reject marriage (possibly Encratites or other ascetic or docetic gnostics), and vegetarians.[127]

With regard to Church discipline, bishops are instructed to accept all who repent by showing them mercy.[128] This may be an implicit argument against the rigorists, such as Hippolytus, or Novatian (see below). The bishop is described as the physician of the Church, so for the bishops to withhold Reconciliation would be like a doctor withholding medicine from the sick. To forgive is to follow the example of Christ, but to fail to reconcile a sinner is to commit spiritual murder.[129] Repentant sinners should not be shunned, since that might cause them to give up hope. Rather, they should be sought out like the shepherd who leaves the flock of ninety-nine and goes after the one lost sheep (Matt. 18:3–7).[130] Even the sin of idolatry can be forgiven, because God wants all to be saved, and God has given the keys of Reconciliation to the bishops (Matt. 16:19; 18:18; John 20:23).[131] To be excommunicated is to be cast out of the Kingdom of God, therefore it is to be avoided, or considered a last resort, since if anyone should die in a state of excommunication that person was assumed to be damned.[132] Although this document does not specify, it might be assumed that one who died in a state of excommunication could not be buried with the Christian

[124] *Didascalia Apostolorum,* 10, 24.

[125] *Didascalia Apostolorum,* 10, 24.

[126] *Didascalia Apostolorum,* 25. In reality, as we have seen, the "heretics" also claimed to be faithful to Scripture. This was especially true at the Council of Nicaea, when the Arians complained about the addition of the word *homoousios* (which is not found in Scripture) to the creed. Thus the *Didascalia* is presenting the perception that orthodoxy is biblical and heresy is not, though it is not really that simple.

[127] *Didascalia Apostolorum,* 23, 26.

[128] *Didascalia* Apostolorum, 6–7.

[129] *Didascalia Apostolorum,* 6; see also *Against Novatian,* 1, and Cyprian of Carthage, *Epistles,* 51.19.

[130] See *Against Novatian,* 15, and Cyprian of Carthage, *Epistles,* 51.15.

[131] *Didascalia Apostolorum,* 5, 11.

[132] *Didascalia Apostolorum,* 11; see also *On Rebaptism,* 13.

community. The only time a person should be excommunicated is when he or she is unrepentant, or if the sin is repeated after Reconciliation.[133]

Of course heretics and schismatics cannot be reconciled as long as they remain unrepentant, since they effectively excommunicate themselves by separating from the Catholic bishops.[134] In what appears to be a remark directed at Novatian (see below), the document specifically mentions "puritans and sticklers for holiness" who "covet the primacy and dare to make a schism."[135] In fact, anyone who so much as prays with the excommunicated is thereby excommunicated.[136] However, if heretics or schismatics come back to the Church, they are not to be rebaptized, but are only to be reconciled with the imposition of hands.[137] Their prior Baptism is considered valid because one Baptism is enough, and to be rebaptized would "undo" the Baptism.[138] Penance is described in terms of a time of fasting lasting anywhere from two to seven weeks.[139] There is also an interesting connection made between fasting and almsgiving, with the recommendation that one might fast and give the money one would have spent on food to the poor.[140] Reconciliation was done by the bishops who would lay their hands on the penitent sinner, which was understood as restoring the Holy Spirit to the person.[141]

In what appears to be an earlier layer of tradition, there is no allowance made for post-baptismal sin.[142] This point seems to contradict the anti-rigorist argument, since all post-baptismal sin is described as "deadly sin," assuming salvation is thereby lost.[143] To keep oneself holy by refraining from sin was to keep the seal of Baptism

[133] *Didascalia Apostolorum*, 10.

[134] *Didascalia Apostolorum*, 25.

[135] *Didascalia Apostolorum*, 23, translation in Hugh R. Connolly, *Didascalia Apostolorum* (Oxford: Clarendon Press, 1929).

[136] *Didascalia Apostolorum*, 15.

[137] *Didascalia Apostolorum*, 10.

[138] *Didascalia Apostolorum*, 24, 26.

[139] *Didascalia Apostolorum*, 6.

[140] *Didascalia Apostolorum*, 19.

[141] *Didascalia Apostolorum*, 7, 10.

[142] *Didascalia Apostolorum*, 5.

[143] *Didascalia Apostolorum*, 20, translation in Connolly, *Didascalia Apostolorum*; see also Cyprian of Carthage, *Epistles*, 48.4, 54.13, 75.15, and *On the Unity of the Catholic Church*, 20–21. Cf. *On Rebaptism*, 12. There may be a pre-Augustinian doctrine of election/perseverance in Cyprian. He quotes Matthew 15:13, saying that if those in the (invisible) Church are planted, they could not be rooted up.

unbroken.[144] Even so, all sins are cancelled by martyrdom.[145] Thus we seem to have evidence of an early stage in the development of this document, when it was still believed that one could successfully refrain from post-baptismal sin, and a later stage of development from after the controversy over the lapsed (see below), when the goal is Reconciliation and rigorism is denounced.

Unlike the community that produced the *Apostolic Tradition*, this community did not have lay teachers, only the clergy were allowed to teach. Lay people were only allowed to speak "in refutation of idols and concerning the unity of God."[146] Of course whenever we read of such prohibitions we must always recognize the possibility that lay people were actually teaching, and that the author(s) of the document wanted that practice to change.

Baptisms could be delegated to priests, or even deacons and deaconesses, however the "seal," or post-baptismal anointing (the Confirmation), must be performed by a bishop or priest.[147] Once baptized, the believer is encouraged to attend worship regularly, and the author criticizes those who are too busy with the affairs of the world, or who cannot wait to leave the assembly and go to the theater.[148] Men and women sit separately, as in the *Apostolic Tradition,* however the *Didascalia* further specifies that worshipers face toward the east for prayer.[149] The Eucharist is described as a sacrifice, replacing the sacrifices of the Old Testament, just as Baptism replaced circumcision.[150] In addition to the regular church meetings, the Eucharist was also being celebrated in the cemeteries, including liturgies for the dead.[151] This refers to more than simply funeral services, as we have seen: it includes celebrations on the anniversaries of the deaths of the martyrs and other beloved dead.[152]

The role of the deacon is described in some detail in the *Didascalia*. In this community the deacons also function as the ushers, or doorkeepers. This means that it is their job to make sure that the people sit in their proper places, according to age or rank of office.[153] They are even charged with questioning visitors to make sure

[144] *Didascalia Apostolorum,* 16.

[145] *Didascalia Apostolorum,* 20.

[146] *Didascalia Apostolorum,* 15.

[147] *Didascalia Apostolorum,* 16; see also Cyprian of Carthage, *Epistles,* 72.9, and the *Apostolic Constitutions,* 1.2 (1.16, 1.20).

[148] *Didascalia Apostolorum,* 13.

[149] *Didascalia Apostolorum,* 12.

[150] *Didascalia Apostolorum,* 9, 11; see also Cyprian of Carthage, *Epistles,* 62.9.

[151] *Didascalia Apostolorum,* 26.

[152] *Apostolic Constitutions,* 6.6 (6.30).

[153] *Didascalia Apostolorum,* 12.

that no one receives the Eucharist unless he or she is a baptized member in good standing with their home church. The deacons also visit the sick, the needy, and the confessors in prison.[154] If possible, they should bribe the guards to gain better treatment of Christian prisoners, and they can use the church's money to buy the release of slaves.[155] The deacons provide the line of communication between the lay people and the bishop, keeping the bishop informed of the needs of the people, but also apparently limiting access to the bishop to prevent the office from becoming too focused on administration.[156] Therefore the number of deacons in a city church should be proportionate to the number of people.[157]

The *Didascalia* specifies that a bishop should be at least fifty years old, if possible, and it is desirable (though not required) that he be able to read.[158] A bishop may be married, as long as his wife is a believer.[159] It is expected that a bishop draw a salary from the offerings of the church, however he must share the offerings with the widows, orphans, and any others who need support.[160] The faithful are instructed to give their alms to the bishop, rather than directly to the needy. The bishop will decide who is most in need, and will dispense the alms accordingly.[161] In actual practice, the deacons would have distributed the alms, but the bishops retained the authority to determine who would receive support, and how much.[162] Finally, the bishop is charged with appointing the other clergy.[163]

Apostolic Church Order

This document is very much like the other two, even combining elements from them with the *Didache*, except that it is written more like a dialogue, as if the apostles are speaking and their actual words were recorded. It claims to be from the apostles through Clement of Rome, though it is clearly much later. In the list of apostles, it even confuses the two names for Peter (*Peter* from Greek; *Cephas* from Aramaic) and treats the two names as if they refer to two different apostles. The document may contain

[154] *Didascalia Apostolorum*, 16, 18–19.

[155] *Didascalia Apostolorum*, 18–19.

[156] *Didascalia Apostolorum*, 9, 11, 16.

[157] *Didascalia Apostolorum*, 16.

[158] *Didascalia Apostolorum*, 4.

[159] *Didascalia Apostolorum*, 4. Obviously this was written before clergy celibacy was assumed or enforced.

[160] *Didascalia Apostolorum*, 8–9. It may be that priests were paid as well.

[161] *Didascalia Apostolorum*, 9.

[162] See *Apostolic Church Order*, 22.

[163] *Didascalia Apostolorum*, 9.

anti-gnostic elements, since the dialogue style seems similar to some gnostic texts, and it forbids the practice of women participating in presiding over the sacraments, which was considered a gnostic practice.[164]

In this document we learn that the office of reader is considered the evangelist of the church.[165] Deacons are not allowed a second marriage.[166] Celibacy is advocated for priests.[167] Bishops might be married, though celibacy is advised as the better path. However, if a bishop is married, he may not be married a second time (1 Tim. 3:2).[168] Like the *Didascalia*, it is advisable that a bishop should be literate, but even if he is not, he is the ultimate authority over the teaching and discipline of the local church.[169]

Apostolic Constitutions

This late fourth-century text rounds out our examination of the Church order documents. More than any of the others, it is a compilation of layers of material from different time periods, including portions from the earlier Church order documents, and it exemplifies the attempts at standardization in the post-Constantinian Church. It contains the standard advice that bishops ought to be married only once and at least fifty years old (though if no one of age can be found suitable, a younger man might be chosen).[170] An important characteristic for a bishop is the ability to read the Old Testament and discern which laws apply to the Church and which do not.[171] In the document, it is assumed that bishops have the authority to judge civil cases (a right given to them by the emperor Constantine), and it is assumed that bishops have authority even over the aristocracy in their area.[172] As the teaching authority in the Church, the bishop is described as a mediator between God and the faithful (in the context of worship) and as a father to the faithful, he is to be honored as God's representative on earth.[173]

[164] Here I am indebted to the research of my colleague, the Rev. Dr. Stephanie Perdew. I am grateful for her willingness to share some of her research from her Ph.D. dissertation. See Stephanie Perdew (Van Slyke), *Ministry for Women? Gender and Authority in the "Apostolic Church Order"* (PhD Diss., Garrett-Evangelical Theological Seminary, 2012).

[165] *Apostolic Church Order*, 19.

[166] *Apostolic Church Order*, 20.

[167] *Apostolic Church Order*, 18.

[168] *Apostolic Church Order*, 16.

[169] *Apostolic Church Order*, 12, 16.

[170] *Apostolic Constitutions*, 2.1 (2.1–2).

[171] *Apostolic Constitutions*, 2.2 (2.5).

[172] *Apostolic Constitutions*, 2.3 (2.11).

[173] *Apostolic Constitutions*, 2.4 (2.26–27).

The leaders of the Church are compared to the Trinity, though surprisingly, the Father, Son, and Holy Spirit are compared to the bishop, deacon, and deaconess, with the priests compared to the apostles. Ordained bishops, priests, and deacons are expected to remain celibate if they were single when ordained. They may be ordained if married, but only once, and they may not remarry, even if widowed.[174] Here the deaconesses function as liaisons between the clergy and the women of the congregation.[175] Deaconesses are expected to be consecrated virgins or widows.[176] The council of priests is compared to the Sanhedrin and the Senate, and a relative scheme of payment of church leaders is outlined, including the lay offices.[177] Priests and deacons may be ordained by one bishop, but a new bishop must be consecrated by at least two other bishops.[178]

The document includes a description of worship in a Constantinian basilica, in this case a cathedral (the basilica associated with the bishop of the city). It is comparable to the description of worship given by Justin Martyr in his *First Apology*, written in the mid-second century. The bishop is seated on a *cathedra* (*throne*, or chair) in the middle of the eastern end, with multiple priests on either side. The deacons stand by, ready to assist in the Eucharist. The laity sit opposite them, men separated from women and children, with the widows and consecrated virgins in front. After readings from the Old Testament, a cantor sings one or more psalms, and the people sing a refrain. Then the book of Acts and/or Pauline epistles are read. Then all the people stand while the Gospel is read by a priest or deacon. After the Gospel reading, there were apparently multiple short homilies by all the priests in attendance, and then finally by the bishop. After this, the catechumens and penitents are excused, and the deacons prepare the Eucharist. The faithful exchange the kiss of peace, but only men with men and women with women. Then a deacon leads intercessory prayer, after which the bishop begins the eucharistic prayers. Finally, the elements of the Eucharist are shared while the ushers watch the door so that no one who is an unbeliever, or uninitiated, can come in.[179] Also provided are instructions for an all-night Easter vigil, with the Baptism of the catechumens at dawn.[180]

[174] *Apostolic Constitutions*, 6.3 (6.17).
[175] *Apostolic Constitutions*, 2.4 (2.26–27).
[176] *Apostolic Constitutions*, 6.3 (6.17).
[177] *Apostolic Constitutions*, 2.4 (2.28).
[178] *Apostolic Constitutions*, 3.2 (3.20).
[179] *Apostolic Constitutions*, 2.7 (2.57); see also 7.2 (7.25) for an example of a eucharistic prayer.
[180] *Apostolic Constitutions*, 5.3 (5.19).

The *Apostolic Constitutions* also contains familiar anti-rigorist arguments, including the mention of both Peter and Paul as having been forgiven by God for denial and persecution of the Faith respectively.[181] However, in this case, excommunication seems to be more of a tool of discipline than a last resort.[182] Rebaptism is condemned as an attempt to crucify the Lord a second time.[183] Infant Baptism in encouraged, based on the words of Jesus in Matthew 19:14, "Let the children come to me, and do not prevent them; for the kingdom of heaven belongs to such as these."[184]

In this community, believers were expected to pray the *Our Father* (Lord's Prayer) three times a day, and give one tenth of their net income to the widows, the poor, and the strangers.[185] Also included are recommended prayers for morning, evening, and mealtime.[186] It is clear that by this time the Church enjoys legal status, and perhaps there is even a sense that the Church is starting to experience the phenomenon of nominal Christianity, people joining the Church for reasons other than a faith commitment. This might explain the high expectations for the faithful, even to the point of being unrealistic. In fact, we noted that in the early centuries of the Church, catechism emphasized morality over theology. However, in the post-Constantinian Church, the emphasis will shift to include teaching orthodox theology as preparation (and prerequisite) for Baptism.[187]

Finally, it is interesting to note that in the *Apostolic Constitutions*, we come to the point where *the church* refers to a building.[188]

[181] *Apostolic Constitutions*, 2.3 (2.12, 14, 18, 20, 24).
[182] *Apostolic Constitutions*, 2.3 (2.16).
[183] *Apostolic Constitutions*, 6.3 (6.15).
[184] *Apostolic Constitutions*, 6.3 (6.16).
[185] *Apostolic Constitutions*, 7.2 (7.24, 29).
[186] *Apostolic Constitutions*, 7.5 (7.47–49).
[187] *Apostolic Constitutions*, 7.3 (7.39).
[188] *Apostolic Constitutions*, 8.4 (8.34).

5

Apology Not Accepted

The Apologists

The apologists are a group of early writers who wrote *apologies*, or a justification of the Faith to those outside the Church. In this context, an *apology* is not meant to express regret for something, but to give a rationale for it, in the spirit of 1 Peter 3:15, "Always be ready to give an explanation to anyone who asks you for a reason for your hope." Most of the apologists were philosophers who had converted to the Church, and then taught Christianity as a philosophy. Their writings were meant to try to explain Christianity and its value to the very people who persecuted the Church, but because they were writing to non-Christians, they preferred to make their case from philosophical arguments rather than from Scripture. It is not as though they never referred to Scripture, just that they recognized that Scripture was not authoritative for their primary audience, so an appeal to Scripture would not be convincing.[1] In addition, there was still no universal consensus about which of the early documents should be included in the Christian Bible. On the other hand, the apologists did quote extensively from the Old Testament when they were writing for a Jewish audience.

For the sake of clarity, the writings of the apologists can be contrasted with the writings of the theologians, who will be the subject of a later chapter. The audience of the apologists is made up of non-Christians, those outside the Church. Since the apologists are converts from philosophy, and still consider themselves philosophers, they believe in the value of philosophy for demonstrating the truth of the Christian Faith. This is partly based on an assumed optimism about the capacity for human reason to grasp ultimate truth. In contrast, the theologians will be skeptical of philosophy, believing human reason to be so fallen that it can only lead one down the wrong path. For them, philosophy is the root of all heresy. What is needed is revelation, and human reason must be subject to it. Also, the focus of the theologians

[1] See the introduction to Tertullian's *On the Soul's Testimony*.

will shift from an external audience to an internal audience. The theologians were writing for fellow Christians, to warn them of the dangers of heresy within the Church, and to teach correct doctrine. Therefore they will claim that they do not rely on philosophy (though to a certain extent they still do), rather they will intentionally support every argument with Scripture. Chronologically, the apologists overlap with the theologians, the last of the true apologists being Minucius Felix, and the first of the theologians being Irenaeus of Lyons, so even though Irenaeus came before Minucius, we will have to wait to meet Irenaeus until later. Also, some of the later writers will emulate the early apologists and write apologies meant for a pagan audience, sometimes in response to specific critiques of the Church written by pagan philosophers, but by the third century, the threats of persecution from the outside and heresy from within will shift the emphasis to the exposition of orthodoxy.

The writings of the apologists have much in common with each other, as they used many of the same arguments to try to convince their readers of the validity of the Christian Faith. These arguments fall into two types, or themes, based on philosophical categories: Christianity is *truth*, and Christianity is *virtue*.

To show that Christianity is *truth*, the apologists often criticize Greco-Roman religion and denigrate it by comparison. To the modern sensibility, it doesn't seem like a good idea to try to convince someone of the truth of your religion by telling them that their religion is ridiculous, and yet this is what they did. The apologists go on at length about how the traditional mythologies of Greece and Rome are silly superstition. They argued that the idols the Romans worship could not be real gods for three reasons: 1) The idols were made by humans, while the real God made humans; 2) The idols require sacrifices from humans, while the real God gives to humans what we need;[2] and 3) The idols made of gold and silver need to be guarded by humans, to prevent them from being stolen, but the real God guards (protects) humans.[3] Some precedent for these arguments can already be found in the Old Testament (see Wisd. 13:10–19; 14:15–22; 15:14–17). The apologists would also point out that if you were to climb Mt. Olympus, you would find it deserted.[4] Therefore, the gods of Greece and Rome are not gods at all, but are either completely fictitious, or they are demons, or they are mere humans who have been proclaimed to be gods after their death.[5]

2 For example, see Justin Martyr, *1 Apology*, 10.

3 For example, see Justin Martyr, *1 Apology*, 9.

4 Theophilus of Antioch, *To Autolycus*, 2.3.

5 As proof of this, the apologists will point out that one of the newest additions to the Roman pantheon was Antinous, the young boy whom the emperor Hadrian had seduced.

Another tactic the apologists used to show that Christianity is *truth* was to argue that Christianity was older than Greek philosophy. In a world where the more ancient teaching is often assumed to be the better one, the apologists showed that the Hebrew prophets predate the philosophers, and then demonstrated the continuity between the prophets and the Church.[6] In fact, they claimed that anything good that the philosophers said was actually plagiarized from the prophets.[7] Therefore, the apologists reasoned that Christianity is the best philosophy, the most rational, and the logical conclusion of all good philosophy. It is superior to Greek philosophy because it combines the best of both sources of truth, revelation from God and human reason.

To show that Christianity is *virtue*, the apologists argued that Christian morality is a higher standard than that of Roman society, and is in fact the best way to achieve the good life. In spite of the rumors, Christians do not practice incest or cannibalism.[8] In fact, they do not even practice the immoralities that the Romans indulge in. As I have indicated above, the Church saw itself as countercultural in its morality, especially since in times of persecution it could not afford to give its neighbors any more reasons to be suspicious of it. However, this may have worked against the Church, since the claim of superior morality was of course a critique of Roman society, and the refusal to participate in accepted Roman activities (including entertainment) could be seen as antisocial, or even unpatriotic.[9] For example, the patron-client system was used by wealthy men to entice boys into sexual relationships. Clement of Alexandria, when listing the Ten Commandments, actually has eleven, inserting the phrase, "Thou shalt not seduce boys" into the Decalogue.[10] We

---

When Antinous drowned in the Nile (possibly a suicide), Hadrian had him proclaimed a god; see Justin Martyr, *1 Apology*, 29, Clement of Alexandria, *Exhortation to the Greeks*, 6.

6 Theophilus of Antioch, *To Autolycus*, 3.1, 3.4, 3.29.

7 Justin Martyr, *1 Apology*, 23, 44, 59, 60; Clement of Alexandria, *Exhortation to the Greeks*, 6.

8 Theophilus of Antioch, *To Autolycus*, 3.4.

9 Ironically, when Athenagoras argued that Christians were morally superior to the rest of the Romans, he said, in effect, "If you don't believe us, just ask our slaves." Athenagoras, *A Plea for the Christians*, 32. Obviously, one of the ways in which the Church was not critical of Roman society was in its capitulation to the slave culture, though Christians would have argued that they treated their slaves better than the average Roman. The Church always treated the enslaved as equal and valued people made in the image of God, but it was only later that the Church gained the courage to critique slavery as an institution.

10 Clement of Alexandria, *Exhortation to the Greeks*, 10. See Meyendorff, *Imperial Unity*, 11.

have also already noted how the Church criticized the culture for allowing abortion and child exposure — in fact there was never a time when the Church did not condemn abortion as a form of murder. The apologists went on to argue that even the stories of the gods have them committing acts of murder and adultery, so not only do the Christians behave better than the Romans, but they behave better than the *gods* of the Romans!

Finally, sometimes the apologists felt the need to claim a superiority to Judaism as well. In AD 135, the last of the Jewish rebellions resulted in the Romans expelling all Jews from Jerusalem, which left some Romans thinking that Jews were rebellious and violent by nature. The apologists wanted to assure their Roman rulers that the Church was not a threat to the empire. To do that, they made a point to show that Christianity was separate from Judaism. Unfortunately, in the attempt to distance Christianity from Judaism and show that the Church was not treasonous, some of the apologists laid the foundation for later anti-Semitism. Wanting to make the case that Romans and Christians were on the same "peace-loving" page, the apologists downplayed the role of the Romans in Jesus' death, laying all of the blame at the feet of His Jewish enemies.

The point that the apologists hoped the Romans would get was that Christianity, far from being a danger to the empire, was actually good for it. Christians do not kill, they do not steal, they are faithful to their marriages, they pay their taxes, and they pray for the empire and its leaders.

The *Apology of Aristides*

Aristides was an Athenian philosopher converted to Christianity. He wrote an apology to be given to the emperor Hadrian, who was traveling through Greece in AD 125 or 126.[11] Aristides argues that Christianity is better than the traditional Roman religion because it is historical, while Greco-Roman religion is mythological. He also has an interesting version of an "intelligent design" argument, saying that creation implies a Creator.[12] According to tradition, he actually received a response from the emperor. A letter from Hadrian is preserved in Eusebius's *Ecclesiastical History*, however the letter may not be authentic.[13]

11 Eusebius of Caesarea, *Ecclesiastical History*, 4.3.

12 Cf. also Theophilus of Antioch, *To Autolycus*, 1.5. Theophilus said that when you see a ship sailing into harbor, you assume that there must be a pilot. Therefore the universe must also have its pilot, who is God.

13 Eusebius of Caesarea, *Ecclesiastical History*, 4.9.

The *Epistle to Diognetus*

The author of this letter is unknown.[14] It is written to a Roman official named Diognetus, who had apparently asked for more information about the Christian Faith. The reply is the standard apologetic fare, including pointing out how ridiculous the mythological gods are, as well as an assurance that the Christians are not like the Jews. Unlike the Jews, who have a different diet than the Romans, the only thing that sets Christians apart from Roman society is better morals. If the felt need to show the difference between Christians and Jews comes from a context of recent Jewish rebellion, that could place the writing of the document shortly after AD 135. The atonement of Christ is explained in terms of the *wonderful exchange*, in which He took the punishment of humanity, and humanity in turn received His immortality.[15] The author concludes that the truth (and divine origin) of Christianity should be sufficiently demonstrated by the fact that the martyrs are willing to die for it.[16]

Justin Martyr

Born somewhere between AD 110 to 114, Justin was a Greek philosopher from Samaria, living in Ephesus. As one might guess, *Martyr* was not his last name, it describes his fate. At a time when philosophers were becoming more and more accepting of various forms of monotheism, he began a personal quest of exploring different philosophical systems to determine which one was the best. He was impressed with the way Christians interpreted Christ as the fulfillment of Hebrew prophecy, and with the high moral standards of the Church. However, his conversion to Christianity came by the testimony of the martyrs.[17]

Sometime between AD 130 and 132, Justin joined the Church, and became its greatest advocate since the apostles. Like the other apologists, he understood Christ according to the philosophical concept of the *Logos*, the Word of God (following John 1). He moved to Rome, where he taught Christian philosophy out of his apartment over a public bath. It is possible that his *school* was also a house-church, though if that were the case, he was the host, but not the presider. As far as we know, he was not ordained, but would have been considered a lay catechist. However, the teachers of other systems of philosophy in Rome were envious of his success in converting people to Christianity, and they conspired against him. He was martyred in AD 165.

[14] It has been suggested that the author may be an apologist named Quadratus. A fragment of his apology is preserved in Eusebius of Caesarea, *Ecclesiastical History*, 4.3.1–2.

[15] *Epistle to Diognetus*, 9.

[16] *Epistle to Diognetus*, 7.7.

[17] Justin Martyr, *2 Apology*, 12.

First Apology

Justin's *First Apology* (*1 Apology*) was written in the AD 150s, addressed to the emperor Antoninus Pius.[18] Interestingly, Justin takes an antagonistic attitude with the emperor, saying in effect, "You can kill us, but you can't hurt us" (cf. Matt 10:28).[19] He even threatens the emperor with eternal punishment if he should continue harassing the Church.[20] In contrast, Justin says a good emperor would not persecute the Church, since that's what the Jews did in the early days, so the Romans should not do such a "Jewish" thing as persecute Christians.[21] A good emperor would recognize that the Church is good for the empire, and would want more people to be like the Christians.[22] A good emperor would recognize the truth in what people are willing to die for, since no one would die for a myth.[23]

Probably the most interesting aspect of Justin's *First Apology* is toward the end where he explains to the emperor what Christians do in their meetings.[24] Here we have, from little more than a century after Christ, an "order of worship" that looks remarkably similar to liturgy today. All the major liturgical elements are there, including the reading of the Gospels, a homily, prayers of intercession, the eucharistic prayers, the sacrament of the Eucharist (with the elements taken out to those who could not be there), and an offering, all of which shows that the basic structure of Christian worship has not changed much in almost two thousand years.[25] The only thing Justin doesn't mention is singing, but we know from other sources that singing was also part

[18] Justin mentions that Jesus was born 150 years earlier, which, assuming the birth of Jesus at 5 BC, would put the writing of *1 Apology* at AD 145. However, there are other internal clues which point to a slightly later date, showing that either Justin's statement was meant to be approximate, or he already had the current calendar's miscalculation in mind.

[19] Justin Martyr, *1 Apology*, 2, 45.

[20] Justin Martyr, *1 Apology*, 45, 68.

[21] Justin Martyr, *1 Apology*, 31, 36.

[22] Justin Martyr, *1 Apology*, 12.

[23] Justin Martyr, *1 Apology*, 45.

[24] Justin Martyr, *1 Apology*, 67.

[25] Although Justin does not mention singing, it must be assumed that early Christian worship included singing (or chanting). Pliny's letter to Trajan, written about forty years earlier, does mention the singing of hymns to Christ. It is also interesting to note that in Justin's description of early worship, the term he uses for *presider* (sometimes translated *president*) is not the New Testament term *presbyter* (priest) but rather the Greek word, *proestos*, which means simply, the leader — the one who stands in front. He may have used this word because he expected his non-Christian audience would not understand the Christian technical terms for the Church's presiders.

of liturgy from the very beginning. It is important to keep in mind that this description of early liturgy was written for a non-Christian, so it may be simplified, and the Greek term that Justin uses for the presider (*proestos*) is not necessarily one that was used within the Church. Traditionally, this word is translated *president*, but it has the connotation of more of a group leader or master of ceremonies than an organizational leader, therefore it is better to translate it *presider.* We also have to keep in mind that Justin was describing liturgy in Rome specifically, and as we have already seen, there was a certain amount of tolerance for diversity of practice from one city to another.

Second Apology

The *Second Apology* (*2 Apology*) was written to Marcus Aurelius, the son and successor of Antoninus Pius, and a self-proclaimed philosopher. No doubt Justin thought he could appeal to Marcus Aurelius as a fellow philosopher. It is relatively short, and even sounds a bit desperate, explaining that no man (not even an emperor) should be honored above the truth,[26] and anyone who persecutes Christians must be possessed by demons.[27] Not long after the letter was written, Justin would be executed.

Dialogue with Trypho

Trypho is probably a fictional character, invented for the purpose of the *Dialogue.* He is presented as a sincere but misguided Jew who meets the philosopher Justin and enters into a debate over the proper interpretation of the Old Testament. The *Dialogue* is apparently meant as an apology for a Jewish audience, hoping to convince them that Jesus was in fact their Messiah. However, most of its readers were probably actually Christians, who either hoped to use the contents as ammunition in debate with Jews, or who simply read it for edification and for the encouragement of their own faith. It is full of quotations from the Old Testament, as one would expect, and, also as one would expect, the philosopher wins the debate by producing the more convincing arguments. It can be a bit confusing, however, since it actually begins with a narrative about another dialogue which led to the philosopher's (Justin's) own conversion to Christianity.

On the Resurrection

Though this document no longer exists in its entirety, there is enough available in manuscript fragments to get the sense of Justin's teaching on the resurrection of the

[26] Justin Martyr, *2 Apology*, 3.

[27] Justin Martyr, *2 Apology*, 7.

body.[28] Justin is arguing for the Pauline understanding of the future resurrection (1 Cor. 15), as opposed to a Greek philosophical view of the afterlife. Against such a view, Justin argues that we are not destined to be disembodied spirits, but that at the resurrection, our bodies will be reunited with our spirits.[29] Salvation, he says, is for the whole human, not the spirit only. Since Jesus was raised and ascended in the flesh, so will we be.

It is clear from the text that Justin had encountered the objection that human bodies will have decayed. Yet he argues from the principle of the conservation of matter that even when decayed, all the elements of the body remain, though they may be scattered. Therefore, like an artist who creates a mosaic from individual tiles, God can put the body back together again, since He is the one who made the body in the first place. The important concept here is that for Justin, the body is an essential part of our humanity (against a docetic or gnostic anti-body dualism, see below), and to be saved into the Kingdom without the body would be to lose part of our humanity.

The Martyrdom of Justin

This martyr document describes the martyrdom of Justin and others in Rome, therefore it was obviously not written by Justin himself, but was written after his death. Like most of the martyr acts, the confessors' dilemma is presented as a choice between following human laws and the following the law of God. When Justin was interrogated, the Roman officer tried to find out where the Christians were meeting, but Justin simply said that they meet wherever they can, since there are too many Christians in Rome to meet all in one place.[30] Justin and his companions refused to make the required sacrifice, and so they were led outside the city walls and beheaded. Some of the Christians were able to take Justin's body and bury it.

Tatian

Tatian lived from about AD 110 to 172, and was a student of Justin Martyr in Rome. He is often accused of heresy by later writers, and there are problematic elements in his writings, but there is not enough of his writings extant for us know with any

[28] For a general treatment of the teaching of the early Church on the doctrine of the resurrection, see Papandrea, *What Really Happens After We Die*.

[29] See also Justin Martyr, *1 Apology*, 8, 18, 52.

[30] The martyr document does mention the location of Justin's school, "above the baths of Martin."

certainty whether he would really have been considered a heretic in his time.[31] He did leave Rome after the death of Justin, and seems to have gone back to his hometown in Syria, where he taught an extreme asceticism that advocated celibacy for all Christians.

Address to the Greeks

In this apology, Tatian attempted to explain Christ as *Logos* to a philosophical audience. However, his explanation is problematic because he imagined that the pre-incarnate Word of God existed in two phases, the first phase of which made the *Logos* nothing more than the wisdom of the Father.[32] The *Logos* then went from being the wisdom of the Father to being the Word of the Father, at which point, as he describes it, the *Logos* became "a work of the Father." Tatian used the same language to describe this "work of the Father" that he used to describe creation. In doing so, he made it sound like the *Logos* was created. For this reason, it can be said that he probably had more influence on future heresy than on future orthodoxy.[33]

Diatessaron

Tatian is most famous for his *Diatessaron*, an attempt at a harmonization of the four Gospels, written about AD 170. Only fragments remain, but we can tell from the fragments that he used the four canonical Gospels, and based the structure on the chronology of John's Gospel. Other writers also attempted to write one gospel that collated the information from all four, but the practice didn't catch on, probably because Irenaeus would soon sing the praises of the fourfold canonical Gospels.[34] The

[31] Eusebius of Caesarea, *Ecclesiastical History*, 4.29. The accusations against Tatian by later writers are contradictory. Jerome called him the founder of a sect known as the Encratites, however the Encratites already existed before Tatian left Rome. Eusebius is probably correct in saying that Saturninus was the real founder of the Encratites. Others, including Irenaeus, have accused Tatian of gnosticism, but there is nothing to support this in his extant writings.

[32] Tatian, *Address to the Greeks*, 5.

[33] In spite of the later accusations of gnosticism, Tatian's christology was more likely an influence on adoptionism and Arianism, both of which saw Christ as a created being who was not eternally coexistent with the Father. See James L. Papandrea, *Novatian of Rome and the Culmination of Pre-Nicene Orthodoxy* (Eugene, OR: Wipf & Stock/Pickwick Publications, 2011).

[34] Irenaeus of Lyons, *Against Heresies*, 3.11.8. For Irenaeus, the four Gospels are the four pillars of the Church, and since there are four winds and four corners of the earth, there also must be four Gospels — no more, no less. Irenaeus explains the symbolism of the four Gospels that emerged in the Church, based on the biblical images of the four "living creatures" (cherubs): Matthew is the man, emphasizing Jesus' humanity; Mark is the

importance of the *Diatessaron* is in the fact that it demonstrates that only the four canonical Gospels were considered authoritative.

Melito of Sardis

Melito was another student of Justin Martyr, who became bishop of Sardis in Asia Minor. Like his teacher, he wrote an apology addressed to the emperor, Marcus Aurelius, though only a fragment of it survives.[35] In it, he argued that the empire should not persecute the Church since both empire and Church were "born" at about the same time.

Homily on the Passover

Melito is best known for his *Homily on the Passover*, or sometimes known simply as *On the Passover*. It is actually an Easter homily, but as we noted above, the early Christians did not have the word *Easter*, but rather referred to the celebration of the Resurrection by the term *Pascha*, which comes from the word for Passover. The homily was apparently originally delivered around AD 176. In it, Melito connects the passion of Jesus to the Exodus in the Old Testament. Unfortunately, this is probably the most anti-Judaic of the postapostolic documents. Following the *Epistle of Barnabas*, Melito believed that the covenant in the Old Testament was no longer valid.[36] He says that the Scriptures and traditions of the Jews now belong to the Church, implying that the Jews no longer deserve them. In his interpretation, the bitter herbs of the Passover represent the bitterness of the Jews who rejected their Messiah, and he claims that Jerusalem fell and the temple was destroyed because the Jews killed Jesus.

Athenagoras

Athenagoras was an Athenian philosopher who converted to Christianity. His conversion to the Faith is said to be the indirect result of the apostle Paul's preaching in

---

eagle, representing the Holy Spirit and prophecy; Luke is the calf, symbolizing Christ's role as priest and sacrifice; and John is the lion, which represents Christ's royal power. See also Eusebius of Caesarea, *Ecclesiastical History*, 6.25; cf. Ezek. 1:5–10; 10:20–22; Rev. 4:7. These four creatures became standard symbols of the four Gospels/evangelists, as can be seen in the apse mosaics of the churches in Rome.

35 The fragment of Melito's apology is preserved in Eusebius of Caesarea, *Ecclesiastical History*, 4.26.

36 Note that Clement of Alexandria wrote that the "new song" of Revelation 5:9 and 14:3 is a reference to the New Covenant. Clement of Alexandria, *Exhortation to the Greeks*, 1; see also Papandrea, *The Wedding of the Lamb*, 102–104.

Athens (Acts 17). According to the story, Athenagoras had heard about Paul's ministry in Athens, and set out to disprove the Christianity that Paul preached. Athenagoras was especially interested in refuting the Christian understanding of the resurrection of the body, in favor of the philosophical belief in the immortality of disembodied souls. However, when he actually read the apostle Paul's letters, he was convinced of the truth of Christianity and joined the Church.

On the Resurrection of the Dead

Athenagoras's attempt to find a way to discredit Christianity had failed, and in the process, it had changed him. The result was a treatise that defends the very belief he set out to disprove. It appears to be heavily influenced by Justin Martyr's writing on the same subject.

A Plea for the Christians

Sometimes translated as *A Supplication for the Christians*, this apology was written about AD 177, and was addressed to the emperor Marcus Aurelius and his son (the next emperor) Commodus. Athenagoras tried to explain the relationship between God the Father and Jesus the Son as similar to the relationship between the emperor and his heir. They rule jointly, and the son carries the father's authority, yet the father is the source of that authority, and in that sense has authority over the son (though they represent one power). While the analogy ultimately falls short of adequately describing the Trinity, it was ahead of its time as a way to try to explain both the unity of the Father and Son and the distinction between the divine Persons.

Theophilus of Antioch

Born around AD 115, Theophilus was bishop of Antioch in Syria from about AD 168 or 169 until his death, though accounts differ as to whether he died in AD 181 or 188. Antioch was emerging as one of the most influential centers of Christian thought, and Theophilus (as a successor of Ignatius in the same see) contributed to that. Antioch had been the headquarters of the original mission to the Gentiles and was the place where followers of Jesus were first called *Christians* (Acts 11:26). At first it was a derogatory term used by the enemies of the Church to try to insult them, as if to say they were the slaves of an executed man. But Christians liked thinking of Jesus as their master, and so the name stuck. Theophilus refers to this in his writings, saying that the name Christian means more than just a follower of Christ — it means one who is also anointed like Christ.[37]

[37] Theophilus of Antioch, *To Autolycus*, 1.1, 1.12.

To Autolycus

Theophilus's only remaining work, this document is a compilation of a series of three letters written to a pagan friend named Autolycus. We can date the correspondence to the early AD 180s, since by this time Marcus Aurelius was dead, yet Commodus had not been emperor long enough to escalate persecution. Therefore, we seem to be in a short lull in the persecution, when Theophilus, like Clement of Rome, can say that the emperor rules by God's will. In trying to convince Autolycus of the truth of Christianity, Theophilus argued that just because the blind cannot see, does not mean the sun doesn't shine.[38] He also followed Aristides in arguing for a Creator based on a version of an argument from intelligent design. Since a ship sailing on the sea implies a captain, therefore the universe must also have its pilot, who is God the Creator.[39]

While the Church has always conceived of God in the divine unity that is the relationship of Father, Son, and Holy Spirit (Matt. 28:19), the *doctrine* of the Trinity was still in the early stages of development, or clarification, at this time. In fact, Theophilus was the first that we know of to attempt to put a name on the Trinity, calling God a *Triad*, or *Triados* in Greek. A generation later, Tertullian would be the first to use the word *Trinity* in Latin (*Trinitas*). Theophilus's theology has its problems, however, since he seems to follow Tatian in dividing the pre-incarnate existence of the *Logos* into two phases, based on the analogy of the Word of God with a spoken word. In the first phase, the Word was *in* the Father (like a thought in the Father's mind), and in the second phase the Word was *emitted*, or "spoken forth." This is connected to the concept of God creating by speaking, as in Genesis chapter 1. Thus, the *Logos* goes from being *in* the Father to being *with* the Father. The problem with this is that even though both phases exist before the creation of the universe, in the first phase the Son of God does not seem to have His own distinct existence, but only exists as the wisdom of the Father. This implies a change in the very being of the *Logos* (going from internal to external relative to the Father), which would contradict the early Christian consensus that divinity is *immutable*, as we noted above. Therefore, Theophilus's way of dividing the pre-Incarnation existence of the Word into two phases did not survive in later theology. However, Theophilus should probably not be called a heretic, since it would be unfair to hold him to later standards of orthodoxy, but it is likely that his thoughts about the preexistent *Logos* influenced later heresies, including Arianism (see below).[40]

[38] Theophilus of Antioch, *To Autolycus*, 1.2.

[39] Theophilus of Antioch, *To Autolycus*, 1.5.

[40] It is assumed that the *heresies* were sincere attempts to interpret Scripture, many of them motivated by the admirable conviction that no matter how one understands Christ, one

One interesting feature of Theophilus is a distinction he made between *worship*, which is reserved for God alone, and *reverence*, which can be legitimately directed toward the emperor. In making this distinction, he was attempting to clarify why Christians cannot participate in the imperial cult, but he also must have had in mind the distinction Christians understood between the worship of God and the reverence shown to Mary and the other saints. This distinction also anticipated the conclusions of a later debate over the proper use of religious icons. Later councils would clarify that it is acceptable to show reverence to icons, but not to worship them.

Clement of Alexandria

In some ways Clement is a transitional figure between the apologists and the theologians, because he wrote for Christians as well as for non-Christians, and he did use Scripture to support his arguments. He was a priest, but not a bishop, yet we call him Clement "of Alexandria" to distinguish him from Clement of Rome.[41] Born around AD 150 to 160, Clement is yet another example of the philosopher who set out to find the best philosophy and ended up a Christian. When he sought out someone who could teach him about Christianity, he found a man named Pantaenus, who was the leader of a well-known school of Christian philosophy in Alexandria, Egypt — much like Justin Martyr had in Rome — but here it is usually referred to as a *catechetical school*, or a school of Christian catechesis. Clement followed Pantaenus

---

cannot compromise monotheism. However, it was not long after the writing of the apostolic documents we call the New Testament that the Church started to produce varying (and often mutually exclusive) interpretations of those documents. Often it was the case that the position that would come to be confirmed as *orthodox* was not defined until it was forced to be by opposing alternative interpretations. In each generation of the Church's development, the orthodox response was a refutation of the alternatives by an increasingly refined defense of the conclusions of the previous generations. Thus each generation's orthodoxy becomes the foundation for future generations. This does not mean that no one ever challenged the conclusions of a previous generation, as we can see with Tatian and Theophilus. But it does mean that when the dust had settled, the Church defined orthodoxy in such a way as to preserve consistency with the consensus of previous generations. The Church's Tradition, then, is the collective contribution of the early Church to the interpretation of Scripture. Put more simply, Tradition interprets Scripture, and does so in a way that uses the consensus of the previous generations to refute the current alternatives (2 Pet. 1:20). Therefore the history of the Church, specifically the history of the development of doctrine, is the history of the interpretation of Scripture.

41 Eusebius said that Clement of Alexandria's name was Titus Flavius Clemens, though there still may be some confusion with Clement of Rome. See Eusebius of Caesarea, *Ecclesiastical History*, 6.13.

to Alexandria, joined the church there, and eventually succeeded Pantaenus as the head of the school in about AD 190. As leader of the school in Alexandria, he would be the teacher and predecessor of Origen, whom we will meet later. When persecution came to Alexandria at the beginning of the third century, Clement left and went to Jerusalem, then Antioch, and eventually Cappadocia in Asia Minor. He died there in about AD 215.

Exhortation to the Greeks

Sometimes known as *Exhortation to the Heathen*, or by its Greek name, *Protreptikos*, this is an apologetic defense of Christianity as a philosophy. Clement says that the Greek philosophers were right to reject the old pagan mythology, but that they were wrong to trade it for atheism. For Clement, superstition is one extreme, and atheism is the other. True religion is found in the middle between the extremes.[42] He said that Socrates believed in one God, and his disciples would have proclaimed the same if they had not been afraid to share his fate.[43] Clement's explanation of Christian monotheism is in many ways a summary of the *Logos* christology of the apologists up to his time. While he does not add much to the refinement of doctrine, per se, his *Exhortation to the Greeks* is an excellent epitome of the state of Christian theology in the age of the apologists.

Finally, in this document, there is an interesting quote of an early Christian hymn. The same hymn (based on Isa. 52:1–2) is quoted in Ephesians 5:14, though Paul only gives us the first stanza. Clement provides the second verse:[44]

Verse 1: Awake, O sleeper
Arise from the dead
And Christ will give you light

Verse 2: Christ, the sun [*sic*] of resurrection
Who existed before the morning star
With his light he gives life

[42] Clement of Alexandria, *Exhortation to the Greeks*, 2. Clement said that "superstition" (or paganism) is the worship of too many gods, but atheism admits to no gods at all. The happy medium between the two dangerous "extremes of ignorance" is monotheism.

[43] Clement of Alexandria, *Exhortation to the Greeks*, 6.

[44] Clement of Alexandria, *Exhortation to the Greeks*, 9, translation by the present author. The word I've translated as *light* in the second verse is actually the word *beams*. Apparently, a popular analogy for the Trinity in the early Church was the image of the sun, the beams of light from the sun, and the heat from the sun.

The Instructor

This is a catechetical manual, often known by its Greek name, *Paidagogos*. It must have been written for use in the catechetical school at Alexandria to prepare candidates for Baptism. True to the times, catechesis was not instruction in theology, but in morality. It is important always to keep in mind that conversion to Christianity could mean a drastic change from the lifestyle that people were used to, especially for the wealthy. Therefore, catechesis had to do more with behavior than belief. Church leaders of the postapostolic age assumed the faithful would get their theology from the liturgy after their Baptism, and also from post-baptismal catechesis, or *Mystagogia*, in places where that was happening. But before Baptism, what was needed was to learn how to live as a follower of Jesus, before making the commitment to join the Church. In Clement's words, Christ is our Instructor, and we are His students, though *students* here is meant more in the sense of children going to school than what we might think of as adult learners.

With regard to moral expectations, however, Clement goes to the extreme, and it is difficult to imagine that everything he preached was actually followed. To his credit, he advocates living simply, and caring for the poor. But for him (like Hermas) every luxury is a sin, including gourmet food, imported wine, and colorful clothing. In truth, the very fact that he urges so strongly and goes to such extremes probably tells a story of much more conformity to culture among the Christians than he would like.

We can also see in Clement of Alexandria a very strict approach to sexuality. He strongly promoted the idea that sex (even within marriage) is only for procreation, and here we are already seeing an association of all sexuality with sin.[45] This was, at least in part, a reaction against the hedonistic approach to sexuality and rejection of children found in some of the gnostic sects (see below), and would contribute to a western bias that celibacy is a higher calling than marriage.[46] Although popular opinion often blames these views on Augustine (two hundred years later), it can actually be traced to Clement, who for all his talk about the middle way, goes to the opposite extreme from these gnostics when it comes to sexuality. Clement's own

[45] Clement of Alexandria, *The Instructor*, 2.10. See also the *Apostolic Constitutions*, 6.5 (6.28). This attitude was at least partially a reaction to the promiscuity and rejection of childbearing in some of the gnostic sects. Since it came to be believed that heretics avoided having children but advocated an orgiastic lifestyle, the Church would promote the opposite view, that sex, even within marriage, was only for the purpose of having children; cf. also Athenagoras, *A Plea for the Christians*, 32–33, in which Athenagoras even worries about the kiss of peace, saying that only one kiss was allowed, a second kiss crossed the line into sin.

[46] For example, see Novatian, *On the Benefit of Purity*, 7.

student Origen would demonstrate the unhealthy consequences of his attitudes toward sex, as we will see. But in the second century, the affirmation of apologists like Justin and Athenagoras that the body is part of the whole human, that it is part of God's good creation, and that it will be redeemed along with the soul in the resurrection, is at odds with the negative attitudes toward sexuality of writers like Clement. We can probably blame the extreme hedonism and pedophilia within Roman culture for the fact that the Church in the West would choose to distance itself from society by following Clement's lead.[47]

Miscellanies

As the name suggests, this is not a unified work, so much as a collection of thoughts on various subjects, most of which have to do with comparisons of Christianity to the various systems of philosophy in the Greco-Roman world, and the heresies that existed on the fringes of the Church. It is sometimes referred to by its Greek name, *Stromateis* or *Stromata*. The approach is what we might call *internal apology*, since it was written with an apologetic tone, yet it was intended for a Christian audience. Here Clement famously says that philosophy is to the Greeks what the Old Testament is to the Jews, a "schoolmaster" (think headmaster, or even truant officer) to bring them to Christ.[48]

Note that older editions (including online translations) of *The Instructor* and *The Miscellanies* have some sections that are not translated into English. Nineteenth-century editors apparently felt that the sections having to do with sexuality were not for the eyes of the lay person, so those sections are only given in Latin. The *Fathers of the Church* series, however, does have the full English translation.

Who Is the Rich Man That Shall Be Saved?

This is a homily on Jesus' words in Matthew 19:24, "It is easier for a camel to go through the eye of a needle than for one who is rich to enter the kingdom of God." Clement's interpretation is that spiritual wealth is different from worldly wealth. A person can be poor in the eyes of the world, yet rich in the things of God. In the same way, a person can be rich in the eyes of the world, yet poor in relation to God. In fact, material wealth has the potential to distract one from focusing on God. However, it is not as though no wealthy person can be saved ("for human beings this is impossible, but for God all things are possible," v. 26), especially since if everyone were poor, who would give to the poor? Clement is clearly influenced by Hermas's *The Shepherd*, and its concept

[47] See Meyendorff, *Imperial Unity*, 10–12.

[48] Clement of Alexandria, *Miscellanies*, 1.5; see also *The Instructor*, 1.6, 1.11.

of the symbiotic relationship of rich and poor. Therefore, the rich person who will be saved is the one who gives to the poor. In fact, throughout the early and medieval Church, almsgiving would be considered a form of penance, and one of the primary spiritual disciplines, along with prayer and fasting.

Minucius Felix

It is unclear whether Minucius lived and wrote closer to the middle of the second century (like most of the other apologists) or the turn of the third century. It all depends on whether similarities in his writings with those of Tertullian lead us to believe that Tertullian had read Minucius, or the other way around, though it is possible that they may have been contemporaries. There are traditions that they were both lawyers, and both from Rome, though perhaps Minicius remained there. The greatest difference between Minucius and the apologists who preceded him is that while they all wrote in Greek, Minucius wrote in Latin, making him one of the earliest Christian Latin writers. In any case, with Minucius (and Tertullian, to the extent that he wrote an apology) we come to the end of the age of the apologists. The practice of writing apologetics would continue in authors like Arnobius of Sicca (d. ca. AD 330), Lactantius (ca. AD 260–ca. AD 325), and even John of Damascus (AD 675 or 676–749), who repeats much of what was written before him. But the era of Christian philosophers was coming to an end, at least until the Middle Ages.

Octavius

This early Latin document was written between AD 205 and 210, or possibly later (if Minucius borrowed from Tertullian), or some say around AD 166 (if Tertullian borrowed from Minucius). Like Justin Martyr's *Dialogue with Trypho*, it is written as a conversation between a Christian named Octavius and a non-Christian, in this case a pagan named Caecilius, with Municius himself in the role of moderator.

Caecilius begins by arguing from the uncertainty and injustice in the world, that there could not be one God who is sovereign. If there were, he reasons, Socrates would never have had to drink the poison. Furthermore, he says it is foolish to worship a man who was crucified, and it is dangerous to ignore the gods. After the usual litany of supposed atrocities perpetuated by Christians in their secret rituals, Caecilius goes on to question the doctrine of the resurrection of the body. Then Octavius responds that one should look to the order of creation for evidence of the sovereign Creator. He goes on to shame the pagan gods by the drama of their own stories, and to observe how disrespecting them causes no fear of retaliation. Finally, Octavius clarifies that it is not Christians who are guilty of atrocities, but the pagans, who abort and expose their own children, and as others had already pointed out, they run the risk that one of their own exposed daughters will be rescued by the pimps, who will raise them to be prostitutes and unknowingly sleep with their own fathers. After a brief explanation of the doctrine of the resurrection, Caecilius admits defeat and converts to Christianity.

The Case of the Montanists

Tertullian will be introduced in detail later, in the chapter on the theologians, however we should mention at this point that he did write an apology for the Faith. In addition, he is also known for his association with a fringe group called the Montanists. This group came into conflict with the bishops of the early Church over the authority to preach, and were called heretics by some, though it is not at all clear whether they held to any particular doctrinal heresies.[49]

In the postapostolic age, a kind of prophetic authority, which was invested by the grassroots of the laity in certain people like the confessors, existed side by side with the apostolic authority of the ordained hierarchy, and which was based on apostolic succession, the succession of bishops from apostles. In the second century, a movement emerged which forced the Church's hand in enforcing apostolic authority over against the claim that laypeople might prophesy new revelation. The movement was known at the time as the *New Prophecy* but is now generally referred to as Montanism. It is named after its founder, a Phrygian named Montanus, who with his daughters claimed to be prophets speaking with the voice of the Holy Spirit.

The Montanists were an ascetic faction within the Church, whose leaders practiced certain charismatic gifts such as ecstatic speech (though there is no evidence that they practiced glossolalia in the modern Pentecostal sense) as well as ecstatic dancing, and who taught that the return of Christ was imminent. As we will see, Tertullian would eventually associate with the Montanists in North Africa, which may simply mean that he was the (lay) host of a house-church that read Montanist writings and exhibited certain charismatic gifts. But although it is often said that Tertullian "became" a Montanist, it is not clear that they were a schismatic group. We should not necessarily assume that the movement considered itself as having

[49] On Montanism, see William Tabbernee, *Fake Prophecy and Polluted Sacraments: Ecclesiastical and Imperial Reactions to Montanism*, Supplements to *Vigiliae Christianae*, vol. 84 (Leiden: Brill, 2007); and William Tabbernee, "Montanism and the Cult of the Martyrs in Roman North Africa: Reassessing the Literary and Epigraphic Evidence," in *Text and the Material World: Essays in Honour of Graeme Clarke*, ed. Elizabeth Minchin and Heather Jackson, 299–313, *Studies in Mediterranean Archeology and Literature* 185 (Uppsala: Astrom Editions, 2017). I am grateful for email conversations with Dr. Tabbernee, as well as with my friends Dr. David Eastman, and Dr. David Wilhite.

separate congregations or meetings apart from the mainstream Church.[50] And we certainly cannot assume that any of Tertullian's writings reflect a particularly Montanist teaching or point of view.[51] It is more accurate to say that the Montanists were a rigorist, prophetic reform movement within the Church.[52] In any case, their rising popularity would prove to be their downfall, since anyone who claims to have a direct connection to God, and to speak with the voice of the Holy Spirit, presents a problem for the unity of the Church.[53] How does the Church prevent a person or group who claims prophetic authority from preaching heresy — something that would divide the Church? Also, the Montanists followed Papias's interpretation of the book of Revelation (also followed by Irenaeus and Tertullian), which included an interpretation of the so-called millennium that the majority of the Church would reject. The result was an uncertainty about the usefulness of the book of Revelation, and significantly, a growing suspicion of any claims of prophecy as a challenge to both the authority and the unity of the Church.

Consequently, two things happened in the postapostolic age. First, prophecy as an *office* of the Church (see Rom. 12:6–8; 1 Cor. 12:4–11) came under the authority of the bishop, just like teaching and preaching. As it turned out, preaching replaced prophecy as the proclamation and interpretation of revealed truth, or perhaps it is

[50] Tabbernee, *Fake Prophecy and Polluted Sacraments*, 404, 417–418, 422; Tabbernee, "Montanism and the Cult of the Martyrs in Roman North Africa," 303. The Montanists did have their own separate congregations in some places in the East, possibly with their own separate hierarchy, but we do not know that they had any particular kind of structure that would facilitate a connectional unity, and there is no evidence that they had their own congregations in North Africa at the time of Tertullian. See Tertullian, *On the Soul*, 9.4.

[51] Tabbernee, "Montanism and the Cult of the Martyrs in Roman North Africa," 304.

[52] Tabbernee, *Fake Prophecy and Polluted Sacraments*, 408. See also Rankin, *Tertullian and the Church*, 41, 44.

[53] Tabbernee, *Fake Prophecy and Polluted Sacraments*, 407–408. The opposition to Montanism in Tertullian's time would have been mostly that they claimed to have "new prophecy," and for the mainstream, the word "new" was the problem. To the bishops, they were not speaking for the Holy Spirit, but were preaching false prophecy, the very novelty of which betrays its falsehood (protestations of Tertullian that it never contradicts Scripture notwithstanding). Also, to whatever extent the Montanist prophecies included ecstatic speech, it was prohibited from worship by Paul (1 Cor. 14:28), and seemed to be opposed to the very idea of revelation being handed down from the apostles by Tradition. Also, it was rumored that they prophesied for money, and it was widely believed that their predictions did not come true, making them false prophets according to biblical criteria. Finally, the very fact that they had a name for themselves (New Prophecy) meant to some that they were not Christian. It was also charged that they followed a different canon, or had additional books, but of course the canon was not settled in Tertullian's time.

more accurate to say that prophecy, such as it was, came to be subsumed under the concept of preaching.[54] The other thing that happened was the development of local church leadership *as a vocation* distinct from the laity. These two things are, of course, interrelated.

The concept of apostolic succession assumes that there will always be a hierarchy in the Church. And it was generally accepted that there was a necessary relationship between hierarchy and unity. The Montanists, on the other hand, seemed to bypass the authority of the hierarchy, and for them authority was invested based on perceived gifts of the Holy Spirit, rather than on the basis of a connection to (or authorization from) previous leaders.

Montanism is often portrayed as an egalitarian movement in opposition to the developing hierarchy of the mainstream Church. The fact that there were at least two women (Montanus's daughters) in prominent leadership roles gives the impression that they rejected a male-only hierarchy. In reality, though, leadership within the New Prophecy was based on gifts of the Spirit, and while they certainly must have believed that the gifts of the Spirit were available to women as well as men, only those who had the gift of prophecy could be leaders.[55] In the end, it is more likely that having women in leadership of a rigorist group like the Montanists reinforced the development of a male-only clergy in the mainstream, rather than existed as a reaction against it. They must have believed that the immanent return of Christ made a structured hierarchy unnecessary.

[54] According to the *Apostolic Church Order*, 19, the office of *evangelist* was the person who reads the Gospel. Other lists of church officers include *readers*. Even though the authority of the teaching office would be reserved for the bishops (and delegated to the priests), it was acknowledged that the bishop might be illiterate. Therefore, the evangelist was the reader. With regard to prophecy, we can already see that in the *Didache*, it is assumed that itinerant "prophets" are preachers. See *Didache*, 13.

[55] See Tabbernee, *Fake Prophecy and Polluted Sacraments*, 408, 423. Tabbernee assumes that the fact that the Montanists had female prophets means that they also had female preachers. This is probably true, since prophecy and preaching were often conflated in the early Church. However, it is not clear that a woman could be a preacher, or in any leadership role, in the Montanist movement without also being a prophetess, and to whatever extent the Montanists did allow women to lead, this would be seen as a schismatic departure from the mainstream apostolic succession, and from Tradition. In addition, there is no evidence that being a preacher necessarily made one a presider, and just as there were lay catechists in the mainstream Church who did not preside over the sacraments, there is no evidence that women, even within the Montanist movement, ever presided over sacraments. Tertullian, in fact, criticized the concept.

A synod was held in Rome in AD 177 to discuss what to do about the New Prophecy. Irenaeus (when he was still a priest) was present at this synod, and some believe that he supported the Montanists, and was able to convince the bishop of Rome, Eleutherius (bishop AD 175–189), that the Montanists were not a threat to orthodoxy or unity.[56] Eusebius tells us that similar synods had already been held in the East, however there the Montanists were declared heretics.[57] Eleutherius's successor, Victor (bishop AD 189–199), at first tolerated the Montanists until the actions of Tertullian's nemesis Praxeas convinced him to change his mind.[58]

Accusations against the Montanists accumulated. It was said that Montanus claimed that he *was* the Holy Spirit, and although this is probably unfounded, it may have been the claim of a later Montanist leader named Militiades.[59] The opponents of Montanism said it was not the Holy Spirit who spoke through Montanus at all, but that the ecstatic trances of the New Prophecy were evidence of demonic possession.[60] Montanists were accused of giving their own leaders more authority than the Scriptures, however Tertullian denied this accusation. They were also accused of encouraging women to abandon their husbands and then call themselves virgins. They were criticized for wearing expensive jewelry and for prophesying for money.[61]

[56] See Tabbernee, *Fake Prophecy and Polluted Sacraments*, 33–35. Irenaeus was sent to Rome to advocate for moderation with regard to the Montanists. They had been considered suspect in Gaul, but not to the point of requiring excommunication. Rome must have had Montanists, perhaps even a Montanist house-church made up of immigrants from Phrygia. Irenaeus may have been submitting the Gaul synod's decision to Pope Eleutherius so that they would be on the same page with whatever Rome was doing about it. Irenaeus was probably arguing against excommunication, just as he would later in the Quartodeciman controversy. It was Eusebius who said that Irenaeus's name was appropriate for such a peacemaker. Eusebius of Caesarea, *Ecclesiastical History*, 5.24.18.

[57] Eusebius of Caesarea, *Ecclesiastical History*, 5.16. Note that these synods are some of the earliest councils of the Church. See also Tabbernee, *Fake Prophecy and Polluted Sacraments*, 409. Some Montanists had been accused of Sabellianism (modalism), but this could not have been the case with the Montanists in North Africa, since Tertullian was orthodox, and wrote *Against Praxeas* in opposition to modalism.

[58] Tertullian, *Against Praxeas*, 1.5.

[59] Rankin, *Tertullian and the Church*, 51.

[60] Eusebius of Caesarea, *Ecclesiastical History*, 5.16–17. The apologist Quadratus is quoted by Eusebius as saying, "The false prophet speaks in ecstasy." Translation in Lake, *Eusebius*, vol. 1, 485.

[61] Eusebius of Caesarea, *Ecclesiastical History*, 5.18. The latter point, that the Montanists were accused of prophesying for money, may actually be evidence of one of the earliest cases of church leaders receiving stipends for their ministry. The accusation may even be the result of sour grapes on the part of mainstream clergy who were jealous that the leaders

Finally, it was said that when predictions of Christ's immediate return proved untrue, both Montanus and his daughter Maximilla had committed suicide.[62]

Hippolytus accused the Montanists of being modalists (on modalism, see below), and it is theoretically possible that Montanists in Rome had fallen under the influence of the modalist teacher Noetus. However, it seems impossible that North African Montanism was modalist, given Tertullian's acceptance of the movement, and his refutation of modalism in *Against Praxeas*.[63] Perhaps some eastern Montanists had leaned toward modalism, which could explain why they were declared heretics by the eastern councils when the Roman bishops were reluctant to condemn them.[64] On the other hand, if they did become schismatic in the East, it could have been because they were excommunicated as heretics.[65] In other words, in the places where Montanists did have their own separate congregations, it may only have been because they were kicked out of the mainstream house-churches.

The conflict between the Montanists and the mainstream Church was not really a conflict between an institutionalized, hierarchical, male-dominated organization and an anti-institutional, egalitarian resistance. It was the conflict between apostolic authority and the unbounded expression of charismatic gifts. The Montanists were not anti-hierarchy, per se, but would have opposed any structure that appeared to suppress the Spirit. Tertullian said that Montanists were followers of the Holy Spirit, not of humans.[66] The majority of the bishops would have argued, however, that anyone can *claim* to speak for the Holy Spirit, but without a centralized authority to oversee the Church's teaching, disagreements would soon lead to division. Thus

---

of the New Prophecy were getting paid in the time before leadership in the mainstream Church was an occupation.

[62] Eusebius of Caesarea, *Ecclesiastical History*, 5.16. They are compared to Judas, who betrayed Christ and then killed himself. According to Epiphanius of Salamis, Maximilla had claimed that she would be the last prophet; see Epiphanius of Salamis, *Panarion*, 48.2.

[63] Hippolytus, *Refutation of All Heresies*, 8.12, 10.22; see also Eusebius of Caesarea, *Ecclesiastical History*, 2.8; and Lewis Ayres, *Nicaea and Its Legacy: An Approach to Fourth-Century Trinitarian Theology* (New York: Oxford University Press, 2004), 101.

[64] On the other hand, the Roman bishops were at first reluctant to condemn Noetus and his followers, and Hippolytus had accused bishops Zephyrinus and Callistus of being modalists themselves. In the end, the excommunications of Noetus and Sabellius show that the Roman bishops were not modalists, and Tertullian's association with the Montanists makes the charge impossible to pin on them as well.

[65] Tertullian, *On Monogamy*, 1; see Rankin, *Tertullian and the Church*, 38. Note that the so-called *Tertullianists* were fourth-century Montanists in North Africa. However, if they were descendants of Tertullian's followers, it is unlikely that their theology was heterodox.

[66] Tertullian, *Against Praxeas*, 13.

the primary issue became one of Tradition (that is, the teaching that is received from those who came before, which includes Scripture) versus ongoing revelation, and these were seen as potentially mutually exclusive since it was only a matter of time before some self-proclaimed prophet claimed the authority of the Holy Spirit to contradict the Scriptures or the received Tradition.[67] For the mainstream Church, the Tradition defined the boundaries of orthodoxy, therefore any teaching outside of the Tradition (or outside of the succession of bishops) was suspect and probably heresy. But the Montanists were claiming direct access to God, and the power that such claims gave to those outside the hierarchy was perceived as dangerous to the unity of the Church.

Tertullian valiantly defended the New Prophecy. He tried to reassure the bishops that the Holy Spirit would never introduce a novelty."[68] The role of continuing revelation was to aid the Church in interpreting Scripture, and so the Holy Spirit would never contradict the Tradition.[69] Prophecy was meant to fill in the gaps of Scripture, giving answers to questions that the apostles never addressed. In fact, the Montanists believed that one could not correctly interpret Scripture without prophecy. And here is precisely the rub. For the Montanists, interpretation without ongoing prophecy would leave too many unanswered questions and would leave the interpreter too much room for speculation, thus leading to heresy. For the mainstream Church, on the other hand, interpretation outside of the authority of apostolic succession would lead to heresy, because it would be too easy for an interpreter to fool himself into thinking that his own agenda was endorsed by the Holy Spirit. The Montanists trusted their own discernment of spirits. The rest of the Church trusted the bishops in succession from the apostles.

Therefore, the mainstream Church was defined as the Church of the bishops. In order to safeguard the teaching office and the disciplinary authority of the episcopacy, and thereby preserve the unity of the Church, it was implicitly decided that the charismatic gift of prophecy had either ended with the apostolic age, or if it was to continue, it would continue through the bishops and the preaching of the Church. Preaching took the place of prophecy in the life of the Church, and it was reserved for the ordained clergy.[70] This aided in the development of the concept of Church

[67] Eusebius of Caesarea, *Ecclesiastical History*, 5.16.

[68] Tertullian, *On Monogamy*, 3; see Tabbernee, *Fake Prophecy and Polluted Sacraments*, 416. Tertullian would argue that accusations of false prophecy were untrue, and were really the result of the prophets telling people what they didn't want to hear.

[69] Tertullian, *Against Praxeas*, 30; *On Monogamy*, 3; see Rankin, *Tertullian and the Church*, 48.

[70] Rankin, *Tertullian and the Church*, 172–174.

leadership as a vocation, and the third century would see the beginning of stipends for bishops and priests, turning what was a volunteer role into a profession.[71] It also reinforced the existing practice of limiting leadership roles to men.

The Role of Women

Several groups on the fringes of the Church had allowed women to occupy leadership roles. It was said that Marcion (see below) allowed women to baptize. Irenaeus complained that some gnostics allowed women to participate in presiding over their eucharistic liturgy.[72] As we have seen, Montanism also accepted the preaching of women, provided they had the gift of prophecy. However, even Tertullian did not allow that women should teach or administer the sacraments.[73] He criticized the apocryphal *Acts of Paul and Thecla,* in which Thecla baptized herself when Paul refused to baptize her.[74] As we will see in the next chapter, the apocryphal acts of the second and third century had become popular with women because they often portrayed women as the protagonists who had a life, and even a ministry, apart from the authority of a male. However, they were the product of heterodox groups, written to promote their agenda of asceticism, rejection of marriage, and rejection of the authority of the bishops in succession from the apostles.

Because of all this, the mainstream attitude toward women in leadership was that to allow women to teach, debate, or preside over sacraments is unacceptable, because this is what the heretics do.[75] While the early bishops admitted that there were female disciples of Jesus, they maintained that there were no female *apostles,* because Jesus never sent women out on mission (it would have been dangerous to their safety to

[71] With regard to the separation of clergy from laity, by the third century, the clergy were spatially segregated from the laity in the assembly. The third century would also see the development of a paid clergy, which assumed that clergy could be a profession supported by the laity. See the *Didascalia Apostolorum,* 9, 12.

[72] Irenaeus said that the gnostic liturgy included a magic trick, in which water was poured from a large cup into a smaller cup without spilling. In this ritual, there were said to be women assisting; see Irenaeus of Lyons, *Against Heresies,* 1.13.2.

[73] Tertullian, *On Baptism,* 17.5; *On the Veiling of Virgins,* 9.1; see Rankin, *Tertullian and the Church,* 175.

[74] Tertullian, *On Baptism,* 17.5. Some have speculated that the *Passion of Perpetua and Felicitas* is a Montanist document; see Barnes, *Tertullian,* 77–78.

[75] Tertullian, *The Prescription against the Heretics,* 41; see also *Didascalia Apostolorum,* 15; *Apostolic Church Order,* 26. There women are not to stand in the assembly (to preach or to preside). In the *Apostolic Constitutions,* 3.1 (3.9), it is argued that if women were meant to baptize, then Jesus would have been baptized by his mother Mary, rather than by John the baptist.

do so).[76] Therefore the clergy orders, which were defined by their role in liturgy, were not open to women, and there is no evidence of a diversity of practice on this point.[77] Bishops, priests, and deacons had to be men, and the role of women was to learn and pray.[78] It is possible that in some places women were allowed to instruct the newly initiated, but this would be limited to women teaching other women.[79] This was, of course, reinforced by cultural norms that gave authority to men, however it was not made necessary by them. There were pagan cults with female priesthoods, and the Church was not afraid to be countercultural in other aspects. However, the existence of female priesthoods in the mystery cults only reinforced the Church's aversion to the idea of a woman as presider. Therefore this was not simply a case of excluding women in order to conform to a patriarchal culture. The issue was that the Church was differentiating itself from pagan culture and from heretical groups.

There were a few lay orders that were open to women, though we would not consider them *clergy*, because they had no role in liturgy. The one exception to this seems to be the deaconesses, whose responsibility it was to prepare women for Baptism by anointing them.[80] Since it would not be appropriate for a male bishop to anoint the body of a woman before Baptism (especially when Baptism was done in the nude, or when it came to include the changing of clothes into a symbolic white robe), a deaconess would perform the pre-baptismal anointing, though the bishop would still pronounce the Baptism in the name of the Trinity and anoint the newly baptized woman's head afterward. In some places, a curtain would have hung over the baptismal font, concealing the woman to be baptized from the bishop's view. A deaconess might also visit a sick woman if there were no men in the home to chaperone, or if the visit by a man would cause a scandal.[81]

Widows were supported by the Church, from the offerings of those who could afford to give.[82] In return, they made up a kind of order, whose ministry it was to

[76] *Didascalia Apostolorum*, 15; *Apostolic Constitutions*, 3.1 (3.6).

[77] Meyendorff, *Imperial Unity*, 50.

[78] *Apostolic Tradition*, 10.

[79] *Didascalia Apostolorum*, 16. The point being made seems to be that women who have been Christian for a time can help the newly baptized women adapt to the Church's expectations of morality and modesty.

[80] *Didascalia Apostolorum*, 16.

[81] *Didascalia Apostolorum*, 16. It is possible that the visitation of the sick might include helping the person bathe or accomplish other personal tasks which would make it impossible for a man to visit a woman.

[82] Justin Martyr, *1 Apology*, 67; Clement of Alexandria, *The Instructor*, 3.12. See also the letter of Cornelius of Rome in Eusebius of Caesarea, *Ecclesiastical History*, 6.43, in which

pray for the Church, and especially for those who had given alms to pay for their support.[83] They might also visit and pray over the sick (probably only women) with the permission of the bishop.[84] They were expected to communicate to the clergy when they became aware of any Christian in need, and were especially charged with being discreet.[85] However, the early documents say that they are not to presume to teach others, and if their visitation becomes a distraction, it is better for them to stay at home and pray than become busybodies and gossips.[86] It is unclear whether there was an actual initiation rite for the order of widows, but the stated ideal was that widows should be over fifty years old, so that they would not be tempted to remarry.[87]

The order of consecrated virgins seems to be an early version of monasticism, before the emergence of the tradition of living apart from society. There may be some evidence that there were male virgins, however for the most part, the order of virgins would have been made up of women who chose a celibate life to dedicate themselves fully to God.[88] In doing so, they were a living witness to an eschatology that waited for the imminent return of Christ. They represented the pure bride of the Church waiting for her groom (Matt. 25:1–13). There may have been an initiation ceremony that mirrored a wedding, in which the virgins pledged themselves to Christ. The order of virgin provided a viable life alternative for a woman who did not feel called to the vocation of marriage, and especially in the centuries before the cloistered convent, gave women an autonomy in society that they might not be able to have otherwise. With the support of the Church, the virgins could have a sense of security without living under the direct authority of a man. Of course, they were expected to submit to the authority of the bishop, and they probably did not live alone. But they were given a place of honor in worship, sitting up front. It

---

Cornelius writes that in the middle of the third century there were over 1,500 widows and other needy people supported by the church in Rome.

83 *Didascalia Apostolorum*, 14–15. The *Didascalia* states that widows should know who gave the money, so that they can pray for that person by name, but they should not divulge the name to anyone.

84 *Didascalia Apostolorum*, 15; *Apostolic Church Order*, 21.

85 *Apostolic Church Order*, 21.

86 *Didascalia Apostolorum*, 15.

87 *Didascalia Apostolorum* 14. The *Didascalia* does say that a second marriage is allowed for younger widows (1 Tim. 5:14), presumably to relieve some of the burden on the church, since the widows received support from the offerings. However, a younger, remarried widow would not be considered a member of the order of widows.

88 *Apostolic Tradition*, 14.

may be that in some places, the order of deaconess was only open to consecrated virgins. Eventually, the development of monasticism replaced the order of virgin, and some women, such as Melania and Paula (see below), would have enough money and power to make pilgrimages to the Holy Land and establish whole monastic communities.[89]

[89] For both men and women, after the end of persecution, asceticism and monasticism becomes the new martyrdom. By the same token, heresy and schism would become the new apostasy.

6

Logos Christology and Theology in the Postapostolic Age

Clement of Alexandria was on to something when he said that true religion can be found in the middle between the extremes.[1] As the Church read the Septuagint and the writings of the apostles, it was inevitable that diverging interpretations would emerge, some of which were mutually exclusive. And as it turned out, these diverging interpretations (which we now call *heresies*) can be described as two extremes, existing on the fringes of what, for lack of a better term, we are calling the *mainstream* Church in the middle.[2] This mainstream Church is represented by the majority of bishops and other Church Fathers throughout the centuries, which is not simply a case of majority rule, but rather demonstrates the way in which the mainstream was affirming that set

1 Clement of Alexandria, *Exhortation to the Greeks*, 2.

2 It is a difficult thing to distinguish that element within the universal Church that would come to be called orthodoxy, without relying on anachronisms. While admitting that history is written by the winners of the debates, and terms such as *orthodoxy* and *heresy* can only be defined in hindsight, this treatment takes the approach that, on one hand, what comes to be the orthodox definition of doctrine represents the majority position in any given age of the Church (see Tertullian, *The Prescription against the Heretics*, 1), and at the same time, accepts by faith the reality of Providence and the work of the Holy Spirit in guiding the outcome of doctrinal debates (Matt. 16:18). It must be admitted that at some times and places, the orthodox position was not, in fact, the majority, such as was the case in Augustine's North Africa, or the eastern empire of the fourth century under the emperor Constantius. However, in the bigger picture of worldwide Christianity, it was still true that what came to be defined as orthodoxy was the position held by the majority of bishops. Therefore, while admitting the limitations of such usage, I will fall back on the concept of a "mainstream" Church, when that seems to be the most useful designation, to denote the trajectory of orthodox doctrine that ran from the apostles through the ecumenical councils. Furthermore, I maintain that this "mainstream" Church represents a middle way between the extreme (and mutually exclusive) alternative interpretations that emerged in the history of the Church.

of interpretations most consistent with the interpretations of previous generations (apostolic succession).

So, for example, when it came to answering Jesus' question, "Who do you say that I am?" one extreme interpretation was to affirm His divinity, but deny His humanity and say that He was pure spirit. The other extreme interpretation was to affirm His humanity, but deny His divinity and say that He was only a man. The mainstream (majority) Church affirmed both the humanity and the divinity of Christ, refusing to diminish either, and thereby defended the middle against the extremes. So when we say that the mainstream is the *middle way*, we do not mean that in the sense of a compromise, but in the sense that the middle way embraces a "both-and" answer to the question, rather than an "either-or" answer. The "both-and" answer may be paradoxical, but that is precisely the point, since the Church Fathers would argue that orthodoxy embraces mystery, while heresy tries to avoid it by opting for the more simplistic, and therefore deficient, answer.

Docetics, Marcionites, and Gnostics

In the church at Corinth, the apostle Paul had had to deal with a problem of division between two groups of people, whom we will call the philosophical and the charismatic (1 Cor. 1:10–4:20).[3] The philosophical group was probably only a handful of people in the church at Corinth — maybe just a couple of families. They were wealthy and prided themselves on their education and their reading of Greek philosophy. Therefore, they considered themselves wise, that is, more enlightened, than the others. They reasoned that since idols are not really gods, there is no moral problem with eating meat from an animal that had been sacrificed to an idol. And this was a very practical issue for them, since they were wealthy and moved in aristocratic

[3] It is entirely possible that there were more than two groups, and that the different divisions mentioned in 1 Corinthians reflect multiple factions. In fact, there are many theories that attempt to explain the historical situation in Corinth, and what is presented here is just one of them, arguably the simplest, which attempts to place everyone in Corinth into one of two groups. However, theories that propose more than two or three different groups probably overestimate the size of the Corinthian church in the mid-first century. It is clear from Clement of Rome, *1 Clement*, 38, that similar divisions of rich/poor, wise/humble, strong/weak still existed in Corinth even in the early nineties of the first century. Contemporary scholarship on the letter of 1 Corinthians also includes theories that suggest the document we know as 1 Corinthians is actually a composition of fragments from more than one letter. While my interpretation assumes that 1 Corinthians is a single letter, it must be acknowledged that it is probable that the Corinthian correspondence as a whole originally included more than two letters (2 Cor. 10:9).

circles, and so they were still getting invited to the pagan feasts their non-Christian friends were holding (1 Cor. 8:10), and they were being served meat that may have been sacrificed to idols.

The other group was numerically larger, but from the lower economic classes and so probably couldn't even afford meat on a regular basis.[4] Eating or not eating idol meat was not a choice they had to make very often, since they were not as likely to get invited to pagan banquets where meat that had been sacrificed to idols would be served. They are probably the charismatics Paul addressed in 1 Corinthians 14.[5] They were disturbed by the fact that the wealthy among them were going to pagan banquets and would eat meat that had been part of a pagan sacrifice. This became an even more urgent problem when the philosophical group treated the Christian *agape* meal (including the Eucharist) like one of their pagan banquets. Since they didn't really have to work for a living, they could gather in the afternoon, eat all the best food that was brought and help themselves to extra servings of wine. When the working class (including slaves) finished their day at sundown, they would arrive at the Christian gathering to find all the best food eaten and their wealthier (and supposedly wiser) brothers and sisters drunk (1 Cor. 11:17–22). Poorer members of the congregation, who could not bring much but relied on others bringing more than they needed, may have been embarrassed by the gluttony of some. In fact, wealthy folks treating the *agape* meal like it was happy hour may have been part of the reason that the sacrament of the Eucharist became separated from the fellowship meal. In any case, those who considered themselves wise thought the charismatics were superstitious and therefore foolish for worrying about whether meat had been sacrificed to an idol. Paul responded to this by turning the concepts of wisdom and foolishness upside down — human wisdom is foolishness to God and the wisdom of the Cross seems like foolishness to Jews and Gentiles alike. Paul admits that those who call themselves wise have a strong faith and that in a way the faith of the others is weaker, however he also turns this distinction on its head by saying that even he (Paul) is weak, but God has chosen the weak to shame the strong. By responding in this way, Paul was calling into question the value of philosophical

[4] I am indebted to my colleague, Dr. K. K. Yeo, for this insight.

[5] The philosophical group never would have practiced speaking in tongues, since charismatic worship would violate the Stoic principle that virtue entailed suppression of the passions. The philosophical Christians of Corinth may have complained to Paul about disorder in worship, prompting Paul to address the issue. However, Paul had corrections for both sides of the disputes.

wisdom, or indeed anything that would allow some Christians to see themselves as above the others, and above responsibility to others.

The important thing for our observations on christology and theology in the postapostolic age is that the philosophical group was made up of Gentile Christians, converts from paganism, who did not feel the need to completely distance themselves from their pagan roots. They may have seen themselves as disciples of Apollos rather than Paul, and may have valued the eloquent philosophical style of speech of Apollos over the down-to-earth approach of the former Pharisee (Acts 18; 1 Cor. 1:12; 3:4–6). In Greek culture, it could easily be assumed that the more eloquent the speech, the more true the content, and so Paul himself might have been looked down upon by this group.

All of this was typical of some early Christian converts from paganism, who apparently were not concerned to shed all the elements of their former religion. This included a certain philosophical concept called *dualism*, which when brought into the Church, directly affected a person's understanding of Christ. Philosophical dualism goes back to the teachings of Plato and assumes that whatever exists in the material world is somehow not as real as that which exists in the spiritual realm.[6] The things of the physical realm were considered to be mere shadows of the true realities that exist in the spiritual realm. An extreme version of this went so far as to say that whatever is of the spiritual realm is good, but whatever is of the physical world is inherently evil.[7] If one applies this extreme dualism to Christ, one would have to conclude that Christ could not really become human, since pure spirit (the divine *Logos*) cannot touch evil matter (flesh). Therefore, there were some within the early Church who came to believe that Christ only *seemed* to be human, but was really some kind of phantom, or just a vision (cf. Matt. 14:26; Mark 6:49). The Greek verb for "to seem," or "to appear," gives us the word *docetism*. Docetism was the belief that spirit is "light" and flesh is "darkness," and therefore Jesus was not really flesh and blood, but only appeared to be.[8]

Docetics reasoned that if Christ was not really human and His body was only an illusion, then the Resurrection was not a real bodily resurrection, but simply another vision of Christ, though perhaps without the illusion of human

[6] Hippolytus, *Refutation of All Heresies*, 1.16.

[7] Philo of Alexandria seems to have taken the concept of dualism further than Plato, and therefore he may be one of the links from Platonic dualism to docetism. The Neopythagoreans also taught an extreme dualism which may provide part of the explanation for docetism.

[8] Hippolytus, *Refutation of All Heresies*, 8.3.

appearance. They further reasoned that since Christ was, in effect, always in a "resurrected" state, those who follow Him are also already living the resurrection life, and therefore they denied any future resurrection. In the letters of Ignatius of Antioch, Ignatius opposed this error that led the docetics to believe they were already living in a post-resurrection state, and had achieved the transcendence that Christ promised. Two people who taught this idea are mentioned by name in 2 Timothy 2:16–18. Therefore, since Hymenaeus and Philetus taught that "the resurrection has already taken place," they apparently denied the future resurrection based on a rejection of the flesh, and so are probably the earliest docetics we know of by name.[9]

Since docetics taught a strict separation between the spiritual and the physical, many saw themselves as primarily spiritual beings untouchable by the corruption of the flesh. This made them believe they were immune to evil and therefore what they did with their bodies could not affect their spirits. I do not mean to suggest that the wealthy and educated in Paul's Corinth were docetics, but this kind of philosophy would have allowed them to eat meat sacrificed to idols, and we know that later it would also allow some docetics to justify all kinds of immorality based on the assumption that their spirits were exempt from moral responsibility or accountability (cf. 1 Cor. 6:12).

Therefore, this extreme dualism could naturally lead to a hedonistic lifestyle that ignored or even abused the human body, which may be part of what Paul was referring to when he said that they did not correctly understand the body (1 Cor. 11:29).[10] Paul obviously believed that what one does with one's body *does* affect one's spirit, but even if idol meat does not directly affect the one who eats it, it does affect others, who are part of the same Body of Christ, the Church (1 Cor. 6:12–20).

[9] Early Christian writers tended to trace all docetism back to Simon Magus (Acts 8:9–24) and the Nicolaitans (Rev. 2:6, 15), however there is no evidence of a direct connection between these New Testament figures and later heretics. It does seem that the Nicolaitans were libertines, but that in itself does not necessarily make them docetics. Some also connected the Nicolaitans to the deacon Nicolas, mentioned in Acts 6:15, but this is pure speculation based on the similarity of the name. See Irenaeus of Lyons, *Against Heresies*, 1.23.1–4, 1.26.3; Hippolytus, *Refutation of All Heresies*, 6.14–15, 7.24; and cf. Epiphanius of Salamis, *Panarion*, 21, 25.

[10] There is probably an intentional triple meaning in this statement of Paul: 1) The human body matters, and what you do with your body does affect your spirit (1 Cor. 6:19–20); 2) The Church is the Body of Christ, and the philosophical group was disrespecting their brothers and sisters in Christ, fellow members of the Body of Christ; and 3) The Body of Christ in the eucharistic bread.

Ironically, a docetic philosophy led some others to attempt to deny the flesh and live an ascetic lifestyle that punishes the body, rejecting physical pleasure (1 Cor. 7:1; Col. 2:20–23). Not surprisingly, Paul advocates the middle way, that is, to respect the body as the temple of the Holy Spirit: do not punish it, but also do not indulge it.

Pagan converts to Christianity were also susceptible to what Paul calls superstition. Since they were used to the idea of worshiping multiple deities, it was easy for them to accept the worship of angels and other supposed heavenly "authorities and powers," as well as the practice of certain aspects of the occult, including magic and astrology. We can see Paul dealing with this in his letter to the Colossians. Some of the Christians in Colossae were apparently being led to incorporate elements of paganism with their (docetic) version of Christianity (Col. 2:8–19). This merging of elements from different religious systems is called *syncretism* and might be thought of as the "salad bar" approach to spirituality. It allows one to choose which parts of each system to accept based on preformed assumptions, or simply what feels most comfortable, and of course it allows the person to reject aspects of one tradition or another based on the authority of one's own preference.[11] Sometimes evidence of syncretism in the New Testament is called *proto-gnosticism*, because it is the precursor to the development of gnosticism in the second century.[12] We can definitely see the seeds of gnosticism in the docetics of the New Testament, however it is too early to call this real gnosticism. We can, however, understand this progression as an equation. Gnosticism is the result of the combination of docetism and syncretism, that is, docetism plus syncretism equals gnosticism.[13]

Docetics did not have a problem with the idea of worshiping Christ. Coming from a background of polytheism, the limitation of worship to one God was not necessarily a priority for them, and they wouldn't have worried about the doctrine of the Trinity because they could simply worship Christ as another God alongside the Father. Therefore, they were perfectly comfortable with the concept of the divinity of Christ. However, their docetism led them to deny the real humanity of Christ. In their way of thinking, He could not become human, because He could not become flesh. Therefore, in response to the docetics, Paul had emphasized the true humanity of Christ and His real flesh and blood (Col. 1:22). He did that by talking about the

[11] Irenaeus of Lyons, *Against Heresies*, 2.14.2.

[12] At one time some speculated that gnosticism pre-dated Christianity, however now it is clear that gnosticism emerged within the Church as the result of the combination of docetism and syncretism, and then as it evolved, it eventually separated from the Church.

[13] Hippolytus, *Refutation of All Heresies*, 5.1. For possible references to early gnosticism (called "false knowledge"), see 1 Cor. 8:1; 1 Tim. 6:20.

cross. He wrote that our sins were nailed to the cross along with Jesus' body, and so if He had no body, we are still dead in our sins (Col. 2:12–14). In addition, Paul implies that since Christ is the new Adam, He must be human as Adam was human (1 Cor. 15:44–49).[14] If Christ is to be the Savior of humanity, He must be truly human. This is because, if He is to be the mediator between God and humanity, He cannot represent humanity unless He is really one of us (1 Tim. 2:5–6). So Paul connects our very salvation with the humanity of Christ — if He was not human, He could not save humans. This was the basis for later arguments against docetism and gnosticism (*what is not assumed is not saved*).[15]

Pauline texts which affirm the humanity of Christ are of course numerous, however one stands out as a direct confrontation of docetism. In Colossians 2:9, Paul expands on a point made in the hymn quoted earlier in the letter, specifically Colossians 1:19. There it says that all the "fullness" dwelt within Christ. In Colossians 2:9, Paul explains that it is the fullness of deity, or divinity itself, that dwells within the Person of Christ. Of course, the docetics would not have a problem with this idea. But the other shoe drops when Paul finishes the sentence: "For in him the whole fullness of deity dwells *bodily*" (emphasis added). In other words, in this one verse Paul affirms both the divinity and the humanity of Christ. He is divine, but He also has a real human body, with real flesh and blood. Therefore, His Incarnation is an act of solidarity with us, and in His death He died as a representative of humanity, dying our death so that we could live His life (2 Cor. 5:21).

As we have noted, the apostle John also confronted docetism. In 1 John 4:2–3, he wrote, "every spirit that acknowledges Jesus Christ come in the flesh belongs to God, and every spirit that does not acknowledge Jesus [i.e., His humanity] does not belong to God. This is the spirit of the antichrist that, as you heard, is to come, but in fact is already in the world." So to deny the humanity of Jesus is to deny His Incarnation, and therefore to be "anti-Christian."

The legacy of the docetics of the first century emerges in the second century in the Marcionites, and then the gnostics.[16] As we saw in the letters of Ignatius of Antioch, Ignatius was aware of those who taught that Christ was human in appearance only,

[14] Gordon D. Fee, *Pauline Christology: An Exegetical and Theological Study* (Peabody, MA: Hendrickson, 2007), 516–517.

[15] For example, see Irenaeus of Lyons, *Against Heresies*, 2.22.4; Tertullian, *Against the Valentinians*, 26; and Novatian, *On the Trinity*, 10.6; see also Larry W. Hurtado, *Lord Jesus Christ: Devotion to Jesus in Earliest Christianity* (Grand Rapids: Eerdmans, 2003), 514.

[16] Polycarp of Smyrna, *Letter to the Philippians*, 7.1. Polycarp connected the docetics of his time (the first half of the second century) with the "antichrists" of 1 John 4:2–3; cf. Epiphanius of Salamis, *Panarion*, 41.1.

and that He did not have real flesh and blood.[17] Thus they denied the reality of Jesus' human nature. Second-century docetics apparently argued from Romans 8:3 and Philippians 2:7–8 that Jesus only appeared in the "likeness" of flesh, not in real flesh.[18] They further argued from 1 Cor. 15:50 that flesh and blood cannot be redeemed.[19] They apparently applied to Jesus what the angel Raphael says about himself in Tobit 12:6–22: "Although you were watching me, I really did not eat or drink anything — but what you saw was a vision" (v. 19). Therefore, their dualism led them to reject the concepts of physical incarnation and bodily resurrection in Christ. Also, since they were primarily converts from paganism, they were willing to accept the possibility of multiple deities without feeling the need to preserve the oneness of God.

The most famous docetic was Marcion, however he was apparently the disciple of one Cerdo (also known as Cerdon), who was later called the "founder of the Marcionite error."[20] We know very little about Cerdo, other than the fact that he was teaching in Rome in the AD 130s.[21] According to his opponents, he taught that the God of the Old Testament was actually a different God from the Father of Jesus revealed in the Gospels.[22] He said that the Old Testament God was a God of justice and punishment, but that the God and Father of the Lord Jesus Christ was a higher God, a God of love and mercy. In fact, Old Testament claims that the God of the Hebrews is the only God were presented as the prideful and ignorant boastings of a less-than-omniscient deity.[23] Based on a literal interpretation of anthropomorphisms of God in the Old Testament, Cerdo had reasoned that the God described there could not be the true Supreme Being, but must be an inferior deity, or *demiurge*.[24] This demiurge was the creator of the world, but that was precisely the problem. The material world was evil, or at least included evil, which meant that this creator demiurge was also the creator of evil (using Isa. 45:7 as a proof text).[25]

[17] Ignatius of Antioch, *Letter to the Trallians*, 10; *Letter to the Smyrnaeans*, 4.2.

[18] Tertullian, *On the Flesh of Christ*, 16. Tertullian responded that it was the (virtual) likeness of *sinful* flesh in which Christ came. In other words, he had real flesh, but no real sin.

[19] Novatian, *On the Trinity*, 10.9. Novatian responded that Paul was talking about the sins of the flesh, not the human body per se.

[20] Eusebius of Caesarea, *Ecclesiastical History*, 4.10, 4.11.2; cf. Epiphanius of Salamis, *Panarion*, 41.

[21] Eusebius of Caesarea, *Ecclesiastical History*, 4.10–11.

[22] Eusebius of Caesarea, *Ecclesiastical History*, 4.10–11.

[23] Irenaeus of Lyons, *Against Heresies*, 1.5.4. See also Hurtado, *Lord Jesus Christ*, 257.

[24] Hurtado, *Lord Jesus Christ*, 255.

[25] Arland J. Hultgren and Steven A. Haggmark, eds., *The Earliest Christian Heretics: Readings from Their Opponents* (Minneapolis: Fortress Press, 1996), 106.

It was said that Marcion embraced Cerdo's teaching because he was obsessed with the problem of evil, and Cerdo's theology provided a solution that made the God of the Old Testament responsible for evil, while exonerating the "real" God whom Jesus revealed.[26] Part of Marcion's motivation for rejecting the Old Testament may also have been a desire to distance himself from Judaism, following the second Jewish revolt and the fall of Jerusalem in AD 135.[27]

After a time of study with Cerdo, Marcion became a teacher in his own right, gaining followers and teaching his own brand of docetism. According to early tradition, Polycarp, the bishop of Smyrna, once met Marcion and called him to his face "the firstborn of Satan."[28] None of Marcion's writings are extant, however some fragments of his teaching are preserved in Tertullian's *Against Marcion*, which is our primary source for understanding his thought.[29] Consistent with his teacher, Marcion taught that it was a mistake to associate Jesus with the Messiah promised in the Old Testament prophets. In reality (he taught), Jesus did not come as a representative of the God of the Old Testament but came to rescue humanity from that God. The God who had created the world was keeping humanity imprisoned in the material realm (and in physical bodies) and Jesus came to free humans from this prison. Jesus was not born as a baby nor did he grow up, but appeared on earth as an adult shortly before His Baptism.[30] He was not human, but was a spirit who never actually suffered on a cross.[31]

By about AD 140, Marcion — who still considered himself a Christian — had published a list of the documents he thought should be included in the Christian Bible. Marcion's canon included only one Gospel, the Gospel of Luke, but with significant edits. He removed all references to Jesus' birth (his version of Luke began with Luke 3:1) and also any references to Jesus' Father as Creator, or to Jesus as the

[26] Tertullian, *Against Marcion*, 1.2.1–3.

[27] Hurtado, *Lord Jesus Christ*, 554.

[28] Eusebius of Caesarea, *Ecclesiastical History*, 4.14.7.

[29] We must always be careful when we use a writer's theological opponent(s) as a source for understanding his thought. We cannot assume that the opponents' assessment is completely accurate or fair. On the other hand, for those mainstream documents written during the life of the opponent, too much exaggeration would put credibility at risk.

[30] Hippolytus, *Refutation of All Heresies*, 10.15; cf. Epiphanius of Salamis, *Panarion*, 42.

[31] Tertullian, *On the Flesh of Christ*, 5; Hippolytus, *Refutation of All Heresies*, 8.3; see also Hurtado, *Lord Jesus Christ*, 556–557. It is possible that Marcion did believe in the crucifixion, however he would have rejected the idea that Jesus suffered, or that His suffering had any atoning significance. The death of Christ would have been interpreted by Marcion as a demonstration of the true goal of humanity, to escape the prison of the flesh.

fulfillment of Old Testament prophecy. He included some portions of Paul's letters that did not make Jesus sound too human.[32] The Old Testament itself, not surprisingly, was excluded completely. Because his canon was unacceptable to the majority of the bishops, it forced the Church to step up its efforts at coming to a consensus about which documents would be included in the Christian Bible, a topic which will be addressed the next chapter.

Marcion was excommunicated from the church of Rome in AD 144 by bishop Pius I (bishop of Rome AD 140–155), at which point he seems to have separated from the Christian community and started a schismatic movement, his followers (the *Marcionites*) continuing his teaching until we lose track of them.[33] Since Marcion's dualism led him to advocate a strict asceticism, including a requirement of celibacy for all members, their inability to pass their beliefs on to second generation members may have contributed to their eventual extinction.

Apparently, Marcion allowed up to three baptisms for believers; the result of a strict asceticism that was unrealistic in actual practice. If one could not live up to the expectations of the group after the first Baptism, up to two more baptisms were allowed. Also, because Marcion's asceticism probably prohibited the drinking of wine, but more importantly, because his docetism meant he did not believe Jesus had any real blood, the Marcionites rejected the use of wine in their Eucharist. If they practiced a Eucharist at all, they used water only.[34] Their docetism also led

[32] The letters of Paul have an inherent distinction between *flesh* and *body*. For Paul, *flesh* has a negative connotation, not because it belongs to the material world, but because of its connection to sin and temptation. There is no similar negative connotation with the word *body* in Paul, and in fact for Paul the Church is the Body of Christ. Marcion would have applied Paul's specific pejorative use of *flesh* to the human body in general.

[33] Hurtado, *Lord Jesus Christ*, 551–552.; cf. Irenaeus of Lyons, *Against Heresies*, 1.27.4.

[34] Ignatius of Antioch, *Letter to the Ephesians*, 5, 20; *Letter to the Smyrnaeans*, 6.1–2. Ignatius presents the issue as though the docetics rejected the Eucharist, but some probably actually had their own Eucharist, in which they rejected the use of wine because they did not believe Jesus had any blood. When Ignatius says they rejected the Eucharist, he means that they separated themselves from the unity of the one legitimate Eucharist of the Church under the authority of the bishop. The use of water instead of wine in the Eucharist is referred to as *aquarianism*. Ignatius is not directly addressing Marcionites (since Marcion did not arrive on the scene until after the time of Ignatius), however Cyprian also confronts the practice of aquarianism. Apparently, those who practiced it claimed that they did not want anyone to smell wine on their breath, which might lead to their condemnation during persecution. But Cyprian considered this an excuse, and chastised them for being ashamed of the Blood of Christ. Cyprian said that the sacrament must contain wine, not water alone, since Jesus used wine (and even turned water into wine), and Melchizedek

the Marcionites to believe that their members had transcended their sexuality (cf. Gal. 3:28), so some speculate that they may have allowed women to administer the sacraments, something that would have distinguished them from their mainstream counterparts. Finally, they seem to have followed a platonic view of the afterlife that included reincarnation, rather than resurrection.[35] This is, of course, consistent with the docetic rejection of the physical in favor of the spiritual. For the Marcionite, the goal of a blessed afterlife would be the freedom of the spirit from the body, like a snake shedding its skin. Whoever did not achieve this transcendence would be reincarnated into another body.

As I suggested above, docetism plus syncretism results in gnosticism; and the gnostics created a blend of polytheism and Christianity that would take docetism even further than Marcion, eventually turning it into a whole new religion, complete with various systems of mythology and cosmology.[36] Like earlier versions of docetism, gnostics had no problem with the idea of multiple deities, but their dualism prevented them from believing that Christ could really be human. While all gnosticism was basically docetic, the hallmark of gnosticism (and the main difference from pre-gnostic versions of docetism) was a belief in secret *knowledge* (in Greek: *gnosis*).[37]

True gnosticism seems to begin with Menander (see the chart, *The Gnostic Family Tree* at the end of this chapter), who taught that salvation required learning secret knowledge, which was supposedly brought to earth by Jesus.[38] This knowledge included

---

used wine. In fact, the Old Testament calls wine the "blood of the grape" (Gen. 49:11; Isa. 63:2), so no wine means no Blood, which means no salvation; Cyprian of Carthage, *Epistles*, 62.

[35] Eusebius of Caesarea, *Ecclesiastical History*, 4.7, 11; see also Hultgren and Haggmark, eds., *The Earliest Christian Heretics*, 112–115; cf. Epiphanius of Salamis, *Panarion*, 42.

[36] Irenaeus of Lyons, *Against Heresies*, 2.14.1–2. Some have called Marcion a gnostic, however Marcion does not seem to have subscribed to the idea of secret knowledge, the hallmark of gnosticism. Therefore it is more accurate to call Marcion a docetic, not a gnostic. By calling gnosticism "a whole new religion" I do not mean to imply that it was a unified or connected organization. It is more appropriate to speak of the many gnostic systems that existed side by side with no uniformity.

[37] Since Marcion's belief system did not include this secret knowledge, he cannot be called a gnostic. Technically speaking he was a docetic, but not a gnostic. Marcionite docetism continued in Marcion's followers and existed alongside gnosticism throughout the second century.

[38] Irenaeus of Lyons, *Against Heresies*, 1.23.5; see also Hippolytus, *Refutation of All Heresies*, 5.2. Hippolytus knew of some gnostics who said that the secret knowledge was handed down through James, but other gnostics claimed their teaching came from Thomas, Philip, or even Judas. This teaching was probably an answer to Irenaeus's critique that if

the revelation that the world was created by a lower order of deity, angelic beings known as *aeons*, and that the God of the Old Testament was simply one of these *aeons*.[39] Carpocrates, who is sometimes called the "father of the gnostics," also taught that the world was created by angels and that salvation would entail an escape from this world.[40] Therefore, the way to realize one's potential was to despise the material world and even flaunt a disregard for its values and its taboos. In fact, the Carpocratians were said to end their meetings with orgies.[41] They believed that the only way to end the cycle of reincarnation was to try everything that the physical world had to offer (and they did mean everything).[42] In this way one could disregard the material realm by "getting it out of one's system." Only when a person had had every possible earthly experience could he or she hope to finally transcend the material world.

Within gnosticism there were two main approaches to christology.[43] The first was a truly docetic christology, which envisioned Christ as purely spiritual, with

---

there was a secret knowledge, the bishops would know it, since they were the successors of the apostles; cf. Epiphanius of Salamis, *Panarion*, 22. It may also have been an attempt by the gnostics to create a (fictional) apostolic succession of their own.

39 Irenaeus of Lyons, *Against Heresies*, 1.24.1–2; Hippolytus, *Refutation of All Heresies*, 7.16.

40 Eusebius of Caesarea, *Ecclesiastical History*, 4.7; Irenaeus of Lyons, *Against Heresies*, 1.25.1; cf. Epiphanius of Salamis, *Panarion*, 27; see also Hippolytus, *Refutation of All Heresies*, 7.20. Hippolytus believed that there was some interdependence of influence between Ebionite *angel christology* and the Carpocratians. While Hippolytus may be confused about certain aspects of distinction between *angel christology* and what Carpocrates taught, one interesting aspect of Carpocratian gnosticism seems to be the belief that the reason Jesus could bring secret knowledge to earth was because He was able to remember His past lives, as well as His conversations with God the Father in the time before His journey to earth. Many of the philosophers had believed in reincarnation, and Plato had taught that the reason we make mistakes (sin) in this life is that we cannot remember the lessons learned in our past lives. Plato seemed to believe that if we could only remember the time before this present life, we would not sin. Apparently, Carpocrates picked up on this idea and incorporated it into his christology.

41 Clement of Alexandria, *Miscellanies*, 3.2.5–10; see also Epiphanius of Salamis, *Panarion*, 26.42. According to Epiphanius, the gnostics had a secret handshake so that they could recognize fellow gnostic "swingers." It entailed tickling the palm of the other person while shaking hands. Note that these libertine gnostics practiced orgies, but rejected children. They prohibited procreation, believing that sexuality was for pleasure only. The mainstream Church's response to this was to take the opposite position, that sex was for procreation only.

42 Hippolytus, *Refutation of All Heresies*, 7.20.

43 For a more detailed treatment of gnostic christology, see James L. Papandrea, *The Earliest Christologies: Five Images of Christ in the Postapostolic Age* (Downers Grove, IL: IVP Academic/InterVarsity Press, 2016).

no tangible body. Just as the docetics of the first century had taught, the Marcionites and those gnostics who held this belief assumed a dualism which could not accept any real contact between the spiritual (pure good) and the material (inherently evil). Those who believed in a docetic Christ tended to advocate an ascetic lifestyle, probably because their extreme dualism led them to believe that the only valid response to the material world was to reject it completely. Gnostics who taught a docetic christology included Menander, Saturninus, and some followers of Valentinus.

Saturninus was from Antioch in Syria and was the founder of a sect called the Encratites.[44] The name *Encratites* comes from the word for self-restraint, and referred to their ascetic lifestyle, which was influenced by Marcion.[45] They were vegetarians and advocated celibacy for all members.[46] Like the Marcionites, they only used water without wine in the Eucharist and they may have only used oil without water for Baptism.[47] But unlike Marcion, they completely rejected Paul's letters as well as the book of Acts, apparently believing that there was not enough in these documents that was useful for promoting a docetic christology.[48] They were also called Severiani, after Severus, one of the disciples of Saturninus.[49]

The other gnostic approach to christology was, for lack of a better term, a "hybrid christology," still based on an extreme dualism, but allowing for some kind of tangible

[44] Hippolytus, *Refutation of All Heresies*, 8.13; Eusebius of Caesarea, *Ecclesiastical History*, 4.7.; cf. Epiphanius of Salamis, *Panarion*, 23, 47.

[45] Hippolytus, *Refutation of All Heresies*, 7.16; Eusebius of Caesarea, *Ecclesiastical History*, 4.28–29.

[46] Irenaeus criticized vegetarianism as a sign of ingratitude toward God for the gift of meat; Irenaeus of Lyons, *Against Heresies*, 1.28.1. The asceticism of the Encratites, and in some cases the Ebionites, probably influenced several of the early Apocryphal Acts, which present marriage as sinful because it involves sexual intercourse. See Epiphanius of Salamis, *Panarion*, 30. These second-century documents often portray the apostles preaching a message of abstinence for all true believers, to the extent that for them following Christ means rejecting marriage. See the *Acts of Thomas* (which has gnostic elements) and also the *Acts of Paul and Thecla* (which does not seem to be gnostic, though it does advocate celibacy as the only true Christian calling).

[47] For their use of water without wine in the Eucharist, see Hippolytus, *Refutation of All Heresies*, 8.13, and Epiphanius of Salamis, *Panarion*, 47.1.5–7. For the possible use of oil without water in Baptism, see the *Acts of Thomas*.

[48] Irenaeus of Lyon, *Against Heresies*, 3.2.2; cf. the gnostic *Letter to Flora*; see also John Behr, *The Way to Nicaea: The Formation of Christian Theology, Volume 1* (Crestwood, NY: St. Vladimir's Seminary Press, 2001), 40.

[49] See Epiphanius of Salamis, *Panarion*, 45.

body of Jesus.[50] According to these gnostics, He was still not really human and His body was not really "material," rather it was described as an ethereal, or "luminous" body. This seems to be a concession to account for elements in the Gospel story that show Jesus as tangible. For some gnostics, this allowed them to admit that Jesus was born, grew up, and even appeared to die, though they did not all agree on whether His birth was a virginal birth or whether His death was something more than an illusion.[51] Proponents of this hybrid christology made a distinction between Jesus and *the Christ,* allowing some aspects of a "bodily" existence for Jesus, but not for *the Christ.* In this way, they preserved *the Christ* as entirely docetic while avoiding having to explain away references to his body in the text of the Gospels. Specifically, *the Christ* was immutable and impassible, but Jesus was subject to change.[52] Still, Jesus' "death" was not a passion, in the sense of a sacrifice that included real suffering; it was only meant to reveal His true, non-human self, as He shed His body. This would have been understood as a lesson on the true nature of all humans, who were really spiritual beings trapped in material bodies.

A teacher named Cerinthus seems to have added the idea that it was the immutable Christ who descended on Jesus at His Baptism, but left Him just before His death on the cross.[53] Cerinthus's christology would influence later gnostics, includ-

[50] Irenaeus of Lyons, *Against Heresies,* 1.6.1, 1.7.2; see also Novatian, *On the Trinity,* 10.6.

[51] Some gnostics who held a hybrid christology (for example Apelles) did reject the birth of Jesus altogether, saying that Christ simply created for Himself a "soulish" or spiritual body; see Irenaeus of Lyons, *Against Heresies,* 1.26.1; Tertullian, *On the Flesh of Christ,* 10; and Hippolytus, *Refutation of All Heresies,* 7.15, 7.21. Irenaeus and Hippolytus knew of some gnostics (including Cerinthus) who allowed for a kind of resurrection of Christ, though it was only the resurrection of this "soulish" body.

[52] This is similar to, but not the same as, the mainstream tendency to assign impassibility to the divine nature of Christ, and passibility to His human nature. The mainstream Church did not separate Jesus from the Christ as two entities, and of course the human nature of Christ was truly human. The gnostic separation of Jesus from the Christ was specifically meant to avoid attributing any real humanity to Him, even the part called *Jesus.* It must also be noted that the tendency among some contemporary theologians (especially of the schools of thought associated with the "quest for the historical Jesus") to speak of Jesus and "the Christ of faith" as two separate entities does have affinities with gnosticism — though in the contemporary context it is usually (and ironically) a veiled attempt to diminish the divinity of the "real" Jesus. For more on this, see Luke Timothy Johnson, *The Real Jesus: The Misguided Quest for the Historical Jesus and the Truth of the Traditional Gospels* (San Francisco: Harper, 1996).

[53] Irenaeus of Lyons, *Against Heresies,* 1.7.2; Hippolytus, *Refutation of All Heresies,* 7.21; see also Hultgren and Haggmark, eds., *The Earliest Christian Heretics,* 34–35; cf. Epiphanius of Salamis, *Panarion,* 28. This may sound similar to Ebionite christology (see below), however

ing Basilides and Valentinus. Other gnostics who also taught a hybrid christology included Carpocrates and Apelles.

Basilides was from Alexandria, the ancient world's incubator of philosophy and gnosticism.[54] Like the Carpocratians, he taught that the only way to inner peace was by indulging all the desires of the flesh and leaving nothing unfulfilled. He seems to have expanded the early forms of gnosticism into a more complex cosmology that would in turn influence others to expand it even further. Basilides's system included the personification and deification of biblical and philosophical concepts or virtues, such as wisdom (*sophia*) and mind (*nous*).[55] In fact, *the Christ* was understood as simply another name for the divine *nous*. Basilides's followers celebrated the feast of Jesus' Baptism, emphasizing this as the point at which the divine *Nous*, or *the Christ*, descended to earth and entered into Jesus.[56]

In addition to the concept that the world was created by angels, Basilides taught that there were three hundred sixty-five levels in the heavens, each one created by a different angel. The last angel was the God of the Old Testament, who created the lowest level of the universe, or the world as we know it. Salvation is an escape from the physical world (and from the prison of the body) and an ascent through the levels of

---

even those Ebionites who admitted to a preexistent Christ maintained that this Christ was a created being, while the gnostic version saw the Christ as a divine being. It is true that in gnostic hybrid christology the Christ might be described as an angel, but remember that for gnostics angels are divine beings, albeit a lower level of divinity. The closer we look as these alternative christologies, the more difficult it becomes to distinguish between some of the intricacies of their systems. For example, the difference between the Ebionite understanding of a created angel and the gnostic understanding of a lower order of divine being called angel can be hard to pin down. In the gnostic system, even these lower divinities are often described as born out of some prior procreative act, so that we cannot simply say that ascribing divinity to them means that they are eternal. The main difference seems to be in the difference between creator and created. For the Ebionites (and indeed the mainstream Church), angels are created beings and are not creators. For the gnostics, even if the divine angels (or *aeons*) have a beginning to their existence, they are the offspring of divine nature, and are therefore the creators of what comes after them. Therefore, the point is not whether Christ is called an angel, but whether he is understood to be divine or created, or some combination of the two.

54 Eusebius of Caesarea, *Ecclesiastical History*, 4.7; cf. Epiphanius of Salamis, *Panarion*, 24.

55 Virtually every philosophical concept becomes deified in the gnostic system, and yet these deities are so personified as to be made in the image of humanity, including procreation by coupling. Irenaeus criticized the gnostics for anthropomorphizing their deities, even while they rejected the God of the Old Testament because of the anthropomorphisms found there; Irenaeus of Lyons, *Against Heresies*, 2.13.3.

56 Hippolytus, *Refutation of All Heresies*, 7.15.

the universe to the highest Heaven.[57] At each level of the heavens, the angelic creator of that level would have to be appeased in order to pass and ascend to the next level. Basilides taught that *the Christ (nous)* had come from the highest heaven to teach the secret knowledge (*gnosis*) that would allow the gnostic believer to ascend past the angels and through the levels of the heavens, to reach the highest heaven.[58] The secret knowledge was supposedly handed down from Christ through Matthias (cf. Acts 1:21–26), which was meant to explain why none of the mainstream Christian bishops knew about it.[59] Their sect was organized like the mystery cults of the Roman Empire — secret societies with secret initiation rituals and protection of the essentials of the group from outsiders.[60]

Basilides also taught that Christ had magically switched forms with Simon of Cyrene when Simon was conscripted to carry the cross, and that Christ stood nearby and watched, laughing while Simon was crucified in His place.[61] This is apparently meant to protect Christ from the passion (and therefore from mutability), however it is not entirely clear why Christ would laugh at Simon. It was probably a way of ridiculing the Pauline concept of atonement, which required a human body of Jesus on the cross. Since gnostic salvation was understood as an escape from the physical world, gnostics rejected the concept of atonement as suffering or sacrifice. Jesus did not come to die for our sins, He came to bring the secret knowledge that would allow humanity to ascend to the highest heaven and transcend the physical realm.

[57] Since salvation was thought to be an escape from the body, even those gnostics who believed in some kind of resurrection of Jesus did not assume that Jesus' Resurrection implied a resurrection for humans. The Pauline doctrine of the resurrection of the body (1 Cor. 15) is antithetical to gnostic dualism. Cf. Epiphanius of Salamis, *Panarion*, 44.1–4.

[58] In the *Apocryphon of James*, Jesus says, "I have taught you what to say before the archons." Translation in James Robinson, ed. *The Nag Hammadi Library* (San Francisco: Harper, 1978; paperback ed., 1990), 33. Though it is clear that the secret knowledge must have included some kind of "password" to ascend through the heavenly "tollbooths," there is no extant gnostic document that records any of the secrets. However, it probably had to do with knowing and reciting the names of the *aeons* (or *archons*), which are an important feature of Basilidean and Valentinian gnosticism.

[59] Irenaeus had criticized the gnostics on the grounds that they had no apostolic succession. Their response was apparently to claim that they had their own succession of teaching, which originated with Jesus through Matthias; Irenaeus of Lyons, *Against Heresies*, 3.3.1–2; Hippolytus, *Refutation of All Heresies*, 7.20.1. Other gnostics taught that the secret knowledge was handed down through James; see Hippolytus, *Refutation of All Heresies*, 5.2.

[60] Epiphanius of Salamis, *Panarion*, 24.5.4–5.

[61] Irenaeus of Lyons, *Against Heresies*, 1.24.3–7.

Unfortunately, the extant gnostic documents never actually say what the secret knowledge is, although immortality is promised to those to whom it is revealed.

Gnostic documents such as the *Infancy Gospel of Thomas* portray Jesus as a magician, not motivated by compassion for humanity (as in the canonical Gospels) but with an arrogance and an attitude that only the illuminated elite were worthy of Him. The good news is not heard as a public proclamation for all, but a secret revelation for the select few.[62] This elitism contributed to the eventual separation of the gnostics from the mainstream Church, as they rejected and ridiculed the authority of those who led the Church (see 1 John 2:19).[63] Gnostics in general believed that martyrdom was foolish, and the followers of Basilides would have said that this was because the martyrs were really only following in the footsteps of Simon of Cyrene, not Jesus.

Sethian gnosticism is the name given to a sect of gnostics who believed that the real hero in the human story is Seth, the third son of Adam and Eve.[64] With some influence from Hebrew wisdom tradition, Sethian gnostics accepted certain aspects of the Old Testament as the story of a struggle between good and evil, with humanity caught in the middle as helpless hostages. To them the God of the Old Testament is not just inferior, he is evil and antagonistic toward his creation, including humanity. Good angels, the *aeons*, fight on behalf of the true Supreme Being (the God and Father of Jesus) against the demiurge's demons, or *archons* (cf. "principalities," Rom. 8:38). In their fall from grace in the garden of Eden, Adam and Eve lost the original knowledge (*gnosis*). But the *aeons* restored this knowledge to Seth, who began the tradition of passing it down through the generations. The story of the flood is then interpreted as an attempt by the God of the Old Testament to wipe out humanity, except that a few are saved by the true Father God and His *aeons*. Thus, Seth is seen as the ancestor of the true gnostics and Jesus was believed to be either a descendant or a reincarnation of Seth. Jesus' descent to earth is seen as a mission to rescue humanity from its Creator, and since the earth is the realm of evil, this descent is interpreted as a descent into hades.[65]

The most famous gnostic teacher is Valentinus. Probably from Alexandria, born around the turn of the second century (ca. AD 100), he came to Rome in about AD

62 Irenaeus of Lyons, *Against Heresies*, 1.6.2; Hurtado, *Lord Jesus Christ*, 459, 462.

63 Hurtado, *Lord Jesus Christ*, 458, 477; cf. *Gospel of Thomas*, 3.

64 Irenaeus of Lyons, *Against Heresies*, 1.29; Hippolytus, *Refutation of All Heresies*, 5.9–12; cf. Epiphanius of Salamis, *Panarion*, 39–40.

65 Hurtado, *Lord Jesus Christ*, 634. The second-century *Apocryphon of John* and the *Gospel of Judas* are Sethian documents. Note that in the *Gospel of Judas*, Judas is actually an *archon* (demon), so it is not as though he is the hero of the story; see April D. DeConick, *The Thirteenth Apostle: What the Gospel of Judas Really Says* (London: Continuum, 2007).

137 or 138. The height of his activity as a gnostic teacher was during the time that Pius I was bishop (AD 140–155).[66] Valentinus taught a hybrid christology and lived a libertine lifestyle, as did most of his followers. He seems to have left Rome for Cyprus in about AD 160 and probably died there around AD 175.

The followers of Valentinus did not call themselves Valentinians, they called themselves *Spirituals*.[67] Following an earlier trend, they believed that the true *gnosis* was only meant for a spiritual elite. Valentinus taught that there were three kinds of people: spiritual, soulish, and physical.[68] The Spirituals believed that they were actually a higher order of being than the rest of humanity, each one a divine spark, but fallen and trapped in a body.[69] The *gnosis*, and therefore salvation, was meant for them. The soulish were an intermediate level. There may be a lower form of salvation available to the soulish, but not the full ascent to the highest heaven, perhaps a version of reincarnation. The physical people had no hope of salvation. Their fate was to remain in the physical realm forever, probably on a never-ending cycle of reincarnation. This combination of fatalistic predestination and elitism meant that the Valentinian gnostics saw themselves as the Spirituals, they saw the non-gnostic Christians as the soulish, and the Jews and pagans as the purely physical people.

Valentinus expanded the gnostic cosmology to its furthest extent. He taught of a primordial heavenly realm, called the *pleroma* (the *fullness*). Within this *pleroma* there were many *aeons*, one of whom was *Sophia*, who was the mother of the God of the Old Testament.[70] For Valentinus, the God of the Old Testament was at least incompetent and probably evil. Though there are multiple versions of the myth, the world was created either by mistake, or as the result of an ill-fated attempt by *Sophia* to become a creator without the help of a divine male consort. The result of this pre-mundane debacle was the creation of the physical world, with all its imperfections. Another *aeon*, also a son of *Sophia* and therefore the brother of the God of the Old Testament, was Christ, who came down into the physical realm to

66 Eusebius of Caesarea, *Ecclesiastical History*, 4.11; cf. Epiphanius of Salamis, *Panarion*, 31.

67 Hurtado, *Lord Jesus Christ*, 525.

68 Irenaeus of Lyons, *Against Heresies*, 1.6.2. This seems to be based on the ancient anthropology that understood the human as being made up of three parts: the spirit (or rational soul), the soul (or animal soul), and the body. The spirit, or rational soul, was thought to include the mind, while the animal soul was simply the "life force" that drove the instincts, bodily functions, and physical desires of the human.

69 Irenaeus of Lyons, *Against Heresies*, 1.25.2, 2.19.3, 2.32.3.

70 Hultgren and Haggmark, eds., *The Earliest Christian Heretics*, 82.

unite with Jesus and pass along the secret knowledge so that the Spirituals could ascend back to the *pleroma*. This was based on the assumption that the Spirituals were originally sparks of divinity that had cooled and fallen from the *pleroma*, like cinders from a bonfire, and so salvation for them meant getting back to the highest heavenly realm from which they had come. The so-called *Gospel of Truth* may have been written by Valentinus himself.[71] In it, we are told that salvation is knowledge and the only real sin is ignorance.[72] In fact, the true goal of the gnostic is to know *oneself* (i.e., that one is a divine spark), as if to say that knowledge of self is what liberates, or saves, one from ignorance.[73] The implication is that Christ is not unique in His divinity and that all Spirituals equally come from the *pleroma* and are destined to return to it. The "good news" for them was that they are divine. Whatever relationship Jesus has with the true supreme God that He calls His Father, the gnostic believed that he or she shared that same relationship and the same divine nature.[74]

Valentinian gnosticism eventually split into two factions. The western group (probably the majority) followed Valentinus's disciples Heracleon, Ptolemy (leader of the Ptolemaeans), and Apelles.[75] They remained true to Valentinus's hybrid christology, teaching that there was a distinction to be made between *the Christ* and Jesus.[76] Christ is pure divine spirit, impassible and intangible. Jesus had a body, though it was a "luminous" body and not truly human. Because of this, He could eat and drink, but did not need to relieve Himself. The Christ spirit united with Jesus at His Baptism, but left Him before the crucifixion, so the connection between Christ and Jesus is only temporary and only for the purpose of His mission of passing on the secret knowledge.[77] Apelles explained that Christ had a cosmic body that was crucified, and thus He was able to show His wounds during His post-Resurrection appearances.

[71] It would be impossible to know what the original version of the *Gospel of Truth* was like, since the text that is part of the Nag Hammadi collection is a later, and certainly edited, version. It is important to note that the gnostic gospels were written no earlier than the second century, at a time when the gnostics were already separating themselves from the mainstream Church (1 John 2:19), and so the gnostic gospels were never considered for inclusion in the New Testament canon. Irenaeus called them a deception and a fantasy; Irenaeus of Lyons, *Against Heresies*, 1.8.1.

[72] Hurtado, *Lord Jesus Christ*, 473, 484.

[73] Hurtado, *Lord Jesus Christ*, 587.

[74] Irenaeus of Lyons, *Against Heresies*, 1.25.2, 2.19.3, 2.32.3.

[75] Hippolytus, *Refutation of All Heresies*, 7.26; cf. Epiphanius of Salamis, *Panarion*, 44.

[76] Hurtado, *Lord Jesus Christ*, 256.

[77] Irenaeus of Lyons, *Against Heresies*, 1.7.2.

However, His body dissolved back into the cosmic elements from which it was made before the Ascension, since it could not ascend into Heaven.[78] The eastern faction, on the other hand, followed Valentinus's disciples Theodotus, Marcus, Axionicus, and Bardesanes. They moved toward a purely docetic christology.

The two types of gnostic christology, docetic and hybrid, are related to two very different lifestyle responses. Those who taught a purely docetic Christ responded with an ascetic lifestyle. For them Christ had no real contact with the material world, and the believer's response should be to distance oneself from the physical as much as possible. Therefore, they tended to be ascetic, celibate, and even vegetarian. On the other hand, those who believed in a hybrid Christ tended to go to the opposite extreme from the ascetics and adopt a hedonistic approach to life and morality.[79] They apparently believed that Jesus could have some contact with the material world and still transcend it. They further believed that they were already living a resurrected life, and reasoned that since they transcended the physical realm, what they did with their bodies could not affect their souls, so they allowed themselves every indulgence.

Following is a summary of general gnostic beliefs (that is, beliefs that most gnostic groups seem to have had in common) by the time that the gnostics were separating from the mainstream Church:[80]

- Belief in many deities, including various biblical and philosophical names, concepts, and virtues personified. These deities were often expressed as male-female pairs who procreated, resulting in the creation of more deities. Angels are also considered divine beings and are worshiped by some gnostics, which also implies the belief in degrees of divinity.
- Evil is not the consequence of human sin, but is part of creation.
- The God of the Old Testament is not the Father that Christ preached.
- Salvation is not from sin, but from ignorance and from the material world. Therefore salvation is not a redemption of creation, but rescue from it.[81]
- There is no atonement as the mainstream Church understood it; Christ did not come to offer forgiveness, but enlightenment.

[78] Hippolytus, *Refutation of All Heresies*, 7.26; cf. Epiphanius of Salamis, *Panarion*, 44.

[79] Irenaeus of Lyons, *Against Heresies*, 1.6.2–4, 2.14.5.

[80] See Hultgren and Haggmark, eds., *The Earliest Christian Heretics*, 37–38; see also Hurtado, *Lord Jesus Christ*, 483–484; cf. Epiphanius of Salamis, *Panarion*, 26. The reader must keep in mind, however, that there was great diversity of thought among those we now call gnostics, and we should not assume that there was one consistent gnostic movement.

[81] Hurtado, *Lord Jesus Christ*, 367–368.

- Salvation is an ascent back through the many levels of the universe to the highest Heaven.
- Jesus' death (for those who believed He had "died") was not a substitution or a sacrifice, but simply a way of revealing His true, non-human self.
- Jesus' Resurrection (if there was one) does not foreshadow the bodily resurrection of humans, but shows that the *spiritual* person, or gnostic, is already resurrected.
- A predestinarian caste system meant that only the spiritual person had a divine origin and could transcend this world and ascend to the highest heaven. The Spirituals are actually a divine spark (albeit fallen and embodied) and as such, they are no different in essence from Christ Himself.[82] The soulish people were predestined to some lower order of salvation, the physical to eternal reincarnation.
- Gnostic christology falls into two main types:

  Docetic

  Christ is pure spirit, a phantom who only seemed to be human, but was in no way tangible.

  Those who held to this type of christology tended to follow an ascetic lifestyle.

  Hybrid

  There is a distinction made between Jesus and *the Christ.*

  The Christ is pure spirit, but Jesus had a "luminous," "ethereal," or "cosmic" body (somewhat tangible, though not really human).

  The Christ united with Jesus at His Baptism, but left Him before the crucifixion.

  Those who held to this type of christology tended to follow a hedonistic, or libertine, lifestyle.

To the outsider, perhaps the most obvious difference between mainstream Christianity and emerging gnosticism was that the Christians would tell you their good news, and then invite you to join. The gnostics would require you to join (and progress to a level that proved you were a *Spiritual*) before telling you their secrets. As gnosticism separated from the Church, different gnostic groups wrote their own gospels: to distinguish themselves from mainstream Christianity, to try to discredit the apostles of whom the bishops of the mainstream Church were the successors, and to remove any mention of Jesus' humanity, or any connection with the Old Testament. In these gnostic writings, Jesus does not suffer, and if He appears to die, it is all an illusion

[82] Irenaeus of Lyons, *Against Heresies*, 1.25.2, 2.19.3, 2.32.3.

meant to teach us that our ultimate goal is to escape from this body, this world, and from the one who created them. There are a wide variety of gnostic writings available today, and it is not our purpose to survey them all, but a sample of the most well-known ones will suffice. It is important to point out that these gnostic documents were never considered for inclusion in the New Testament. In spite of some popular accounts that wish to sensationalize the fringe and claim that the Catholic Church is hiding something from us, these are not "lost books of the Bible." They were written precisely because the communities that produced them were separating from the Church, so the last thing the Church would have ever done would be to include these documents in its canon. Thus it is clear that the ones which claim apostolic origin or authorship are pseudonymous.[83] Finally, when one reads these documents one has to keep in mind that often the version we have is from as late as the fourth century, and so it has gone through a lot of revisions, and there is no way to know what was actually in these documents in their original versions in the postapostolic age.

Infancy Gospel of Thomas

The document is meant to supply the story of Jesus that is not in the New Testament Gospels. It is the story of Jesus as a child, however this is a story of a wizard child, who does magic tricks to confound the adults in His life, and when the other children do anything that bothers Him, He strikes them dead. Yes, you read that right. Jesus kills children in this story. This is a Jesus who is disrespectful of His teachers, and even His parents. Some commentators charge the author(s) with anti-Semitism, since Jesus seems to have a disdain for Jewish teaching and tradition. This would be consistent with the docetic view of the Old Testament, and in fact, the docetics and gnostics tended to be more anti-Judaic than the mainstream writers.

There is a famous story in this document, in which Jesus makes birds out of clay on the Sabbath. When He is confronted with the fact that He is doing work on the Sabbath, He tells the birds to come to life and fly away, and of course they do. On the surface, it may seem like a harmless, precious story of Jesus as a child. However, the scene is part of the greater attitude of disrespect that Jesus shows toward elders in the document. Even more important, it is a picture of a docetic Jesus, who is not really human, and in fact looks down on humans and treats them with disgust. It is far cry from the New Testament Gospels that show how Jesus' miracles were

[83] Irenaeus of Lyons, *Against Heresies*, 3.11.9. Irenaeus, writing in the late second century, knew that the gnostic gospels (especially the so-called *Gospel of Truth*) were recent productions.

motivated by compassion, and that they were all *signs* that taught an important lesson or pointed people to God.

Gospel of Thomas

The *Gospel of Thomas* is simply a list of supposed sayings of Jesus. There is no story to speak of, and not surprisingly, it doesn't tell us anything about Jesus' life, especially that He was Jewish. Since gnostics did not believe in Jesus' humanity, the story of his life (if they thought He had one) is not important. Jesus is not presented as the fulfillment of Old Testament prophecy, as we would find in the New Testament Gospels. However, there are some similar sayings as we find in the New Testament, but often they are changed or twisted in ways that distort the meaning. Obviously, the authors of the gnostic gospels knew of the four canonical Gospels and could mine them for the sayings of Jesus.

Like most gnostics, the writer(s) of the *Gospel of Thomas* believed that the secret knowledge was only for a select few. This only served to exacerbate the growing rift between the gnostics and the mainstream Christians. It may be that the gnostics separated themselves out of the mainstream Church before they were asked to leave, but in any case, by the time this document was written there was already some division and rivalry between the mainstream bishops and the leaders of the gnostic factions. In fact, in the *Gospel of Thomas* Jesus makes a disdainful remark about "those who lead you." The apostles Peter and Matthew are presented in a negative light, but Thomas (the doubter) is held up as *the* apostle. In short, we can see that this is a document originally written during the time of separation from the Church.

In all the gnostic writings, we are never actually told what the secret knowledge is. It has something to do with the realization of each person's divinity. It probably also has something to do with knowing the names of all the gods and angels in their elaborate mythology. There seems to be a sense in which the ascent to the *pleroma* would require appeasing the angelic gatekeepers at each of the many levels of the heavens. Perhaps knowing their names would function as a kind of password to get through the heavenly tollbooth. We will never know, because in the *Gospel of Thomas*, when the apostles ask Thomas to tell them what secrets Jesus told him, he responds with the second-century equivalent of, "I could tell you, but then I'd have to kill you."[84]

[84] *Gospel of Thomas*, 13. Thomas actually says to the other disciples, "If I tell you one of the things which he told me, you will pick up stones and throw them at me; a fire will come from the stones and burn you up." Translation in Robinson, *The Nag Hammadi Library*, 128.

Gospel of Philip

It seems that the gnostics claimed to have their own version of apostolic succession. Just as the *Gospel of Thomas* was supposed to have come from the apostle Thomas, the *Gospel of Philip* was supposed to come from a tradition that goes back to Philip. Of course, the bishops of the Church knew that these documents had no connection to the apostles whatsoever, and in fact that is what sets them apart from the New Testament documents (see the chapter below, regarding the criteria for inclusion in the canon).[85] However, it is curious how in our own time some people have chosen to give more historical credence to the gnostic gospels than they do the canonical Gospels. The *Gospel of Philip* is one such document that has gained popularity in recent years.

True to its gnostic agenda, the *Gospel of Philip* holds up a fourth "Pauline" virtue — in addition to faith, hope, and love, there is knowledge. Here we are also told that Jesus' adoptive father Joseph the carpenter unknowingly made the cross on which Jesus was hung. But this is all part of the gnostic attitude that the crucifixion is just an illusion, and entailed no real suffering for Jesus. As mentioned above, in one version of the gnostic story, Jesus dupes Simon of Cyrene into getting crucified in His place, and stands by laughing.

The *Gospel of Philip* is the source of speculation about a relationship between Jesus and Mary Magdalene. In the story, Mary Magdalene is called the "companion" of Jesus, and it says that Jesus loved her more than the other disciples, and that He would "kiss her on her . . ." and then there is a gap in the text.[86] How one fills in the blank will determine the extent of the relationship. Of course, even if it said something scandalous, there is no historical validity to this document.

There is one redeeming feature in the *Gospel of Philip*, an analogy that is used to encourage its readers to practice what they preach. The works of one's life are compared to the child of a woman who had an affair. Though she may proclaim to the world that she loves her husband, her baby will look like her lover. In the same way, we may proclaim our love for God, but if we secretly love anything other than God, our works will bear the resemblance of our true love.

Judaizers and Ebionites

At the other extreme from the docetics was a group known to us as the Judaizers. Just as the docetics were Gentile (formerly pagan) Christians who were apparently comfortable retaining elements of paganism, the Judaizers were Jewish Christians who wanted to retain much of their Judaism. We can see them most clearly in Paul's

[85] Irenaeus of Lyons, *Against Heresies*, 3.3.2, 2.11.9.

[86] Robinson, *The Nag Hammadi Library*, 148.

letter to the Galatians. The Judaizers advocated following the whole Law and requiring Gentiles effectively to become Jews in order to become Christians. They are famous for demanding circumcision of men who wanted to enter the Church. Knowing that this would restrict his mission, Paul opposed this faction. He called them "some people ... from James" (Gal. 2:12). This does not imply that they had the approval of James, who was the leader of the church in Jerusalem, it only means that they came from Jerusalem. They may have been Pharisees, like Paul, who were converted to Christianity, but who did not see the Law in a new light as Paul did (Acts 15:5). Paul calls them "false brothers" (Gal. 2:4) and said that they preached a different gospel, which was antithetical to the true gospel and which would not lead to salvation (Gal. 1:6–9). Eventually, in about the year AD 50, a council was held in Jerusalem, the first council of the Church, where it was decided that Gentile men would not be required to be circumcised in order to be baptized, nor would Christians have to follow the Jewish dietary laws (Acts 15:1–21).

Although there is no direct evidence in the New Testament that the Judaizers denied Jesus' divinity or rejected the worship of Christ,[87] they would probably have understood Jesus as Messiah strictly in Old Testament terms. Since most Jewish believers did not expect messianic prophecies to be fulfilled by a divine being,[88] the Judaizers would have understood him as an anointed man, but still a mere human, much like the judges, kings, and prophets of the Old Testament. Therefore, they would most likely have rejected the idea of a divine nature in Christ. Jesus would be seen as a messenger of God, but not really the incarnation of God. Paul's response to this was to argue that believing in a Christ who was human only would be to put one's trust in the flesh, rather than in the spirit (Gal. 3:1–5). In other words, the Judaizers (and possibly some of the Galatian Christians) were putting their trust for their salvation in the Law (human effort), rather than in God's grace (divine intervention).

[87] Hurtado, *Lord Jesus Christ*, 166. However, the Church Fathers said that they were the original adoptionists.

[88] There are some hints in the Old Testament that the Messiah would be more than human, such as Daniel 7:13, however it was not until after the life, death, and Resurrection of Jesus that these began to make sense in a Christian context. There were also some hints in extra-biblical Jewish prophetic writings that the Messiah would be more than human, or even super-human (such as 2 Esdras 13), however these were not universally accepted nor were they consistently interpreted. The average Jewish believer would not have expected the Messiah to be a divine being, and even the followers of Jesus did not understand his divinity until after the Resurrection. This is, in part, why He was killed — He surpassed all expectations and in the end was not the kind of Messiah that the people expected, or even wanted.

Paul's response to the Judaizers is similar to his response to the docetics, in that he goes right to the cross. Paul is adamant that if one adds any requirements for salvation (such as following the Law), one makes the cross insufficient and ineffective, and if that is the case then Christ died for nothing (Gal. 2:21). Either the cross is enough for salvation, or it isn't. And if one needs to be circumcised, or follow dietary restrictions, then the cross is not enough. In fact, Paul went further, saying that if you advocate following the whole Law (circumcision), you are cutting yourself off from Christ (Gal. 5:2–4; note the ironic play on words with the concept of "cutting off").

What is most important for our purposes is that Paul emphasized the divinity of Christ against those who might diminish or deny it.[89] We have already seen Colossians 2:9, in which we are told that the fullness of deity dwells within Him (cf. also Heb. 1:3–8). In addition to this, Paul affirms that Christ was present in the days of the Old Testament, and therefore preexisted His Incarnation (1 Cor. 10:4; cf. 1 Cor. 8:6; John 1:1).[90] This preexistence demonstrates that He is more than a mere human. His Incarnation is then understood in terms of a descent from an exalted state to a state of humility (2 Cor. 8:9; Phil. 2:6–8). Furthermore, His death was the ultimate humiliation, a sacrifice for our sin (Rom. 8:3; 1 Cor. 5:7–8).[91] However, Jesus was raised from death (restored to his rightful place, Phil. 2:9–11), and in fact His Resurrection will lead to our own (Rom. 6:5–14; 1 Cor. 15:16–28). All this clarifies that Jesus was not a mere human and that the birth, life, death, and Resurrection of Jesus was the result of divine intervention. In His Incarnation, He is the very embodiment of divine intervention.

Whether or not the Judaizers who were the opponents of Paul actually denied the divinity of Christ cannot be known for certain, but the Church Fathers believed they did, and saw them as the predecessors of a group who did deny the divinity of Christ, a group who called themselves the Ebionites.[92] According to tradition, the

[89] Behr, *The Way to Nicaea*, 53, 57–59.

[90] Hurtado, *Lord Jesus Christ*, 119.

[91] Hurtado, *Lord Jesus Christ*, 127.

[92] Ignatius of Antioch, *Letter to the Magnesians*, 8–10; *Letter to the Philadelphians*, 6–9; cf. Epiphanius of Salamis, *Panarion*, 30. There was also a group called the Nazareans, mentioned by several early writers. Some have assumed that this was a separate group of Jewish Christians, however it is more likely that they are two names for the same group of people; see Jerome, *Epistle*, 112; but cf. Epiphanius of Salamis, *Panarion*, 29–30. Epiphanius mistakenly thinks the Ebionites were named after a person called Ebion, who was originally a Nazarean, yet he talks about them as if the Ebionites split from the Nazareans, making two separate groups. The name Ebionite does not derive from a

Ebionites were born out of the Jerusalem church after the fall of Jerusalem in AD 70, when the temple was destroyed and the sacrifices discontinued.[93] They chose their name *Ebionites* (which means "the poor ones") to emphasize the supposed poverty of Jesus and their belief that they were following in His footsteps.[94] Just as the Judaizers were Jewish Christians who wanted to maintain a strictly Jewish understanding of Jesus as prophet-Messiah, the Ebionites were also predominantly Jewish Christians who emphasized the Law and who saw Jesus as an anointed human, whose mission it was to show the way to perfect obedience. Philosophically, the Ebionites were also concerned to safeguard the immutability of God, which led them to reject the divinity of Christ.[95] In other words, the Ebionites could not

---

person, so Epiphanius is certainly mistaken. Still, it must be said that the label "Ebionite" as it came to be used is an umbrella term for any group that denied the divinity of Christ. We cannot assume that all early Christians who leaned in this direction agreed on all points, nor did they constitute a separate, organized ecclesial body. When there were individual house-churches that leaned in this direction, it would be just as likely to have been because they followed a particular Ebionite leader, as that they were organized around Ebionite christology.

93 Cf. Epiphanius of Salamis, *Panarion*, 30.2.7. Although Epiphanius is mistaken on other points of Ebionite origins, this seems plausible given the connection of the Judaizers to the Jerusalem church; see Hultgren and Haggmark, eds., *The Earliest Christian Heretics*, 116.

94 Some early Church writers thought the name was actually first used as an insult by their opponents, as if it meant that they were intellectually poor, or that they had a poor view of Christ; see Eusebius of Caesarea, *Ecclesiastical History*, 3.27. However, it is more likely that they chose the name for themselves. The belief that Jesus was poor probably comes from His own words in Matthew 8:20, "Foxes have dens and birds of the sky have nests, but the Son of Man has nowhere to rest his head." While this may be an argument for the fact that Jesus was not married, it does not mean that He was homeless. It simply means that He was itinerant. In fact, as the son of a skilled laborer, He came from the working class and would not have been what we would call poor, in the sense of malnourished. Even during His ministry, He seems to have lived with Peter's family, and made His headquarters there (Matt. 4:13). Note that the christologies which overemphasize the humanity of Christ also tend to understand salvation in terms of following His example.

95 Eusebius of Caesarea, *Ecclesiastical History*, 6.16. As we have noted in the first chapter above, there was a general consensus among the orthodox and heretics alike that part of the very definition of divinity included the concept of immutability, the conviction that God does not change. This was based on the assumption that what is divine is also eternal and therefore uncreated. To be uncreated must also mean immutable, since mutability is related to corruptibility; see Theophilus of Antioch, *To Autolycus*, 1.4, 2.4.

reconcile the obvious human changes that Jesus experienced (Luke 2:40) with their assumption of divine immutability, so they reasoned that there could be no divine nature in Jesus.

The earliest Ebionite teacher on record is known to us as Theodotus the Elder (also known as Theodotus the Tanner or Theodotus the Cobbler or Shoemaker).[96] He was excommunicated from the church at Rome by bishop Victor (bishop of Rome from AD 189–199), on the charge that he was teaching that Christ was a mere human.[97] A disciple of Theodotus the Elder was another Theodotus, called the Younger (or Theodotus the Banker),[98] and his disciples called themselves Melchizedekians, teaching that Christ was subject to a higher priest, the Melchizedek of Genesis chapter 14 (cf. Heb. 5–7).[99]

In the primary sources written by their opponents, the term *Ebionite* eventually came to be used as a catch-all for any christology that emphasized the humanity of Christ to the exclusion of the divine nature. There were apparently two main forms of Ebionite christology: *angel christology*, which speculated that Jesus was indwelt by an angel, or archangel, and *spirit christology*, which emphasized the role of the Holy Spirit as empowering Jesus. The latter seems to have been the point of view of the majority of Ebionites, however they believed the Holy Spirit to be a created being, not a divine Person of the Trinity.[100]

[96] Hippolytus, *Refutation of All Heresies*, 7.22–24, 35–36, 10.23–24. According to Hippolytus, Theodotus taught that Jesus had been converted from a life of promiscuity; cf. Epiphanius of Salamis, *Panarion*, 54. Epiphanius said that Theodotus had denied Christ to save his life during a persecution, and that he later taught that Christ was not divine as an excuse for his apostasy. Epiphanius implies that Theodotus gained followers because his christology allowed people to deny Christ in times of persecution, since they believed he was only a man.

[97] Eusebius of Caesarea, *Ecclesiastical History*, 5.28.6.

[98] Hippolytus, *Refutation of All Heresies*, 7.24.

[99] Aloys Grillmeier, *Christ in Christian Tradition, Volume 1: From the Apostolic Age to Chalcedon (451)* (New York: Oxford University Press, 2004), 78. Other known disciples of Theodotus were Asclepiodotus and Symmachus; cf. Epiphanius of Salamis, *Panarion*, 55.

[100] For a more detailed treatment of the two types of Ebionite/adoptionist christology, see Papandrea, *The Earliest Christologies*; see also Grillmeier, *Christ in Christian Tradition, Volume 1*, 46. Note that this is not to be confused with the orthodox tendency to interpret Old Testament appearances of the "angel of the Lord" as the pre-incarnate Christ. Ebionite angel christology denied Christ's preexistence, therefore he could not be present in the Old Testament. Hermas's *The Shepherd* is one possible example of angel christology. In this second-century document, Christ is described as an angel, and salvation is by keeping the law; see Hermas, *The Shepherd*, 69.5.

The Ebionites used a version of Matthew's Gospel, possibly in Hebrew or Aramaic, but edited to exclude any reference to the divinity of Jesus, and probably also without the story of His miraculous birth.[101] Although some (*angel christology*) did seem to accept a version of the virgin birth, most Ebionites believed that Jesus was born naturally from Mary and Joseph.[102] They may have had their own versions of the birth narrative, but interpreting the "virgin" of Isaiah 7:14 to mean simply "young woman."[103] They may also have had their own written gospels that no longer exist, but which would have presented Jesus as a prophet and emphasized following the Jewish Law.[104]

For the Ebionites, Jesus was an ordinary man who achieved extraordinary status through personal discipline and righteousness.[105] Because He was perfectly obedient to God and fulfilled the whole law, He was rewarded with God's anointing at His Baptism, and with a spiritual indwelling.[106] The Baptism of Christ was seen as the moment of His adoption by God, probably based on the way Jewish proselyte

[101] Cf. Epiphanius of Salamis, *Panarion*, 30.3.7. The so-called *Gospel of the Nazareans* may have been an Aramaic version of Matthew, while the so-called *Gospel of the Hebrews* may have been the edited version of Matthew in Hebrew. Epiphanius refers to a *Gospel of the Ebionites*, though it is not clear whether that is the name of a gospel they used, or simply a reference to one of these other gospels no longer extant. On the other hand, Eusebius says that they rejected the Gospel of Matthew altogether, though this probably is a reference to their rejection of the way Matthew connects Jesus to Old Testament messianic prophecies; see Eusebius of Carsarea, *Ecclesiastical History*, 6.17.

[102] Eusebius of Caesarea, *Ecclesiastical History*, 3.27. That the mainstream Church interpreted Isaiah 7:14 as a miraculous conception, see Justin Martyr, *1 Apology*, 33; and Irenaeus of Lyons, *Against Heresies*, 3.21.6–10. Irenaeus says that since Adam had no father, Jesus (the second Adam) also had no biological father.

[103] Eusebius of Caesarea, *Ecclesiastical History*, 5.8. Although it is true that the Hebrew word for *virgin* could be translated simply as "young woman," the Greek of the LXX makes it clearer, and in any case, the mainstream Church believed in the virgin birth as the only valid interpretation of the text. To the point, in the ancient world, where respectable people did not go on dates without a chaperone, it could be assumed that any unmarried young woman was also a virgin. Virginity itself was a criterion for eligibility for marriage, so to reduce the meaning of the text (as the Gospel has it) to "young woman" is to reduce it to redundancy.

[104] Eusebius of Caesarea, *Ecclesiastical History*, 6.16. See also n. 101, above.

[105] Grillmeier, *Christ in Christian Tradition, Volume 1*, 77.

[106] Hippolytus, *Refutation of All Heresies*, 7.22. In the case of *angel christology*, some may have believed that the spiritual indwelling was proactively effected at Jesus' conception (by God's foreknowledge of His perfect obedience), rather than His Baptism, which may be why they accepted the idea of a miraculous birth.

baptism was understood as effecting an adoption into the family of Abraham.[107] When He is called God's "beloved son" at His Baptism, that is when the Ebionites believed Jesus *became* a son of God. Therefore, to the Ebionites, Jesus is not *the* Son of God, but *a* son of God by adoption. What is more, He is not *the* Christ, but rather *a* christ, having earned the anointing and the title by perfectly obeying the law. This is another reason why most Ebionites were not normally interested in the Gospel accounts of Jesus' birth. It was not until His Baptism that He arrives at His (adopted) sonship.[108] Therefore, the Ebionite view of Christ, along with successive versions in the third and fourth centuries, is generally called *adoptionism.*

Ebionites believed that at Jesus' adoption He received the Holy Spirit, implying that He did not have the Holy Spirit before that time.[109] In general, the Ebionites envisioned a Jesus who was anointed and indwelt by a preexistent spiritual entity, either the Holy Spirit, or the *Logos,* or by an angel, in the case of *angel christology.*[110] However, the indwelling entity was understood to be a created being (even when it was thought to be the Holy Spirit), and this indwelling was only temporary. The Spirit/*Logos*/angel indwelt Jesus from the time of His Baptism until the cross, when Jesus the mere man was left alone (their interpretation of the cry of dereliction, Matt. 27:46).

Since Jesus was seen as an ordinary human who earned divine adoption by achieving righteousness, the Ebionites reasoned that any human could follow His example and achieve the same status — in fact, salvation would require it.[111] The mainstream critique of Ebionite christology was that, in essence, Jesus required adoption in order to receive salvation Himself, and if we want to receive salvation, we would have to follow His example and earn our own adoption through perfect righteousness.[112] Rather than saying, as the mainstream Church did, that we are adopted sons and daughters of God, but that Jesus is the *natural* Son of God (the Son of God by nature), the Ebionites' claim was that Christ is not ontologically

[107] Martin, *Worship in the Early Church,* 90.

[108] Grillmeier, *Christ in Christian Tradition, Volume 1,* 67. Although He was rewarded with an exalted status and adopted sonship, He was not thought to have been made divine at His Baptism. See Hippolytus, *Refutation of All Heresies,* 7.23. Some Ebionites may have believed that Jesus was rewarded with divine status after the Resurrection, perhaps at the Ascension. Later, the Arians would extend the exalted status of Jesus to a kind of divinity.

[109] Athanasius of Alexandria, *Against the Nations,* 46.1.

[110] Hippolytus, *Refutation of All Heresies,* 7.22–24. Hippolytus says the Ebionites believed that Jesus "received Christ," who descended on Him like a dove.

[111] Hippolytus, *Refutation of All Heresies,* 7.12–13, 22.

[112] Irenaeus of Lyons, *Against Heresies,* 3.19.1; Hippolytus, *Refutation of All Heresies,* 7.22.

different from the rest of humanity. This places Christ on the receiving end of grace, along with the rest of created humanity. He was adopted, just as we might be, so therefore His uniqueness among humanity is only as a pioneer, not as a divine giver of grace.[113] He received the Holy Spirit; He does not give the Holy Spirit. He was elevated by His indwelling; He did not descend to an incarnation. It should come as no surprise, then, that the Ebionites rejected the letters of Paul, who emphasized grace over the Law against their theological predecessors the Judaizers.[114] They preferred to hold up as the true apostles those who were considered to be Jesus' relatives. This was probably at least partly due to the Judaizers' connection with the Jerusalem church where James, the "brother of the Lord," was a leader. In any case, it began a tradition of speculation about the descendants of Jesus' family that sometimes continues to this day.

Because Jesus was considered to be a mere human, the Ebionites tended to see resurrection as simply a metaphor for eternal life. Jesus was "raised" only in the sense that He transcended this earthly life after His physical death. Since the Ebionites also did not believe that the Blood of Jesus held any saving significance, they (ironically, just like the docetics) rejected the use of wine in the Eucharist, using water only.[115] This practice would come to be called *aquarianism*.

We have no documents that we can be sure are the products of the Ebionite movement, apart from a few possible fragments. However, there are some that seem to have been favored by Ebionites. These include the later *Clementine Homilies*, and possibly Hermas's *The Shepherd*. There is also a group of documents called the *Apocryphal Acts*, that seem to have been used by heretics on both extremes, but they fit well within the context of Ebionite legalism.[116]

The Apocryphal Acts

The Apocryphal Acts claim to be the stories of certain apostles and their missions after the Ascension of Jesus. They combine traditional material about the lives of the apostles with legend and outright fiction. In reality, they tend to be documents of propaganda, promoting an agenda of extreme legalism and asceticism. Like Tatian, these authors believed that all sin ultimately comes from lust, and therefore many of the apocryphal

[113] Hippolytus, *Refutation of All Heresies*, 7.22.

[114] Irenaeus of Lyons, *Against Heresies*, 1.26.2.

[115] Irenaeus of Lyons, *Against Heresies*, 5.1.3; cf. Hippolytus, *Refutation of Heresies*, 8.13.

[116] Epiphanius of Salamis, *Panarion*, 30. On the apocryphal acts, see Rhee, *Early Christian Literature*.

acts advocated celibacy for all Christians, even going to the extreme of supposing that conversion to Christianity must mean a rejection of marriage.

A common theme in the Apocryphal Acts is the conversion of a wealthy woman by the apostle's preaching. But the problem is that the woman is either married or engaged. In converting to Christianity she rejects her husband or fiancé, who (understandably) becomes upset. The husband or fiancé conspires with local authorities to persecute the apostle, who flees, leaving the newly converted noblewoman to endure humiliation, risking torture, and even execution. Therefore, the real heroes of these stories are not the apostles, but the women. The stories were probably popular with women at the time because they were stories of women who found a way to have some personal power and reject the need to be under the familial authority of a man. So even though the woman in the story suffers, she is portrayed as having preserved her nobility and her integrity by rejecting the advances of men.

The Apocryphal Acts present the world as a battleground. Spiritual warfare rages all around, and the pagan idols, far from being benign blocks of wood and stone, are actually demons. These demons will attack if opposed, and the only way to gain power over them is through self-control, which means a rejection of lust and the suppression of sexual desire. If one is chaste, then the Sign of the Cross will overcome the demons. This worldview leads the authors of the Apocryphal Acts to present a radical separation from society as the only valid form of Christianity. As is the case with the gnostic writings, there are many Apocryphal Acts, however a few of the more well-known will suffice as examples.

The Acts of Paul and Thecla

The *Acts of Paul and Thecla* is probably the most famous of the Apocryphal Acts. It is originally part of a larger document called the *Acts of Paul*. However, in the story, the real hero is not Paul, but Thecla, a woman who is converted when Paul preaches "the word of God about self-control." This is the good news that Paul preaches, a salvation by asceticism. In the story, Paul has his own version of the beatitudes: "Blessed are they that have wives as not having them" (a reference to 1 Cor. 7:29, but taken out of context). Therefore, in this document, Baptism is only for those who are ready to be celibate, and the resurrection is only for those who can keep themselves chaste. At first Paul does not think Thecla is ready for Baptism, so when she becomes separated from Paul, she baptizes herself (though not in the name of the Trinity).

There were apparently some in the early Church who used this document to support the idea of female presiders, at least with regard to Baptism, since Thecla performed her own. Tertullian argued against this interpretation by discrediting the document's authorship, saying that it was written by an eastern priest who was removed from his position for having forged the document.[117]

As the story continues, Thecla is persecuted, but survives the attempts on her life. She becomes a hermit, and lives out her years in a cave. In one version of the story, some men come to her cave to try to rape her, but she escapes, leaving behind her veil. This veil then becomes a relic. There is also an interesting hint at an early expression of the belief in Purgatory, when a woman who befriends Thecla asks her to pray for her dead daughter.[118] According to the story, when Thecla died, her body was taken to Rome to be buried near Paul. There is a catacomb named after her in Rome, and to this day some people believe she was a historical person and consider her a saint. Devotion to Thecla as a saint grew, including pilgrimages to the supposed site of her cave in Syria.

The Acts of Thomas

In this story, Thomas does not want to go to India, so the risen Jesus appears and sells Thomas as a slave to someone who happens to be going to India. Thomas then preaches the message that Jesus has sent him to preach, which amounts to the conviction that following Jesus means leaving one's spouse. Marriage is described as "filthy intercourse," and the opposite of holiness. In one scene, we find out that sexual intercourse prevents one from receiving the Eucharist, as a certain man's "lust" causes his hands to wither when he touches the bread (cf. 2 Sam. 6:6–7). The man's hands were then healed with what appears to be one of the earliest references to holy water.[119] The point of the story seems to be that all sex is sinful, and as such, it corrupts the Eucharist, and must be kept apart from it. This is interesting because one of the earliest justifications for a celibate clergy in the western church was the belief that one had to abstain from sexual intercourse for twenty-four hours before receiving the Eucharist. Since a priest says Mass every day, he must be on a permanent fast from sex, and therefore cannot be married.

Even within marriage, sexual intercourse is presented in this document as unacceptable for Christians, and while the mainstream Church said that procreation was a legitimate reason to have sex, the *Acts of Thomas* describes children as a nuisance, and not worth the trouble, as if to try to talk its readers out of wanting to have children. Perhaps in a world where infant mortality was high, and death in childbirth significantly lowered the average life expectancy of women, this was meant as a

[117] Tertullian, *On Baptism*, 17.

[118] See also the *Diary of Perpetua*, 7–8.

[119] See also the *Apostolic Constitutions*, 8.4 (8.29).

justification for choosing not to have children. Still, it is not the procreation, but the sexual intercourse that is the problem. In one scene, there is an interesting vision of hell, with one of the earliest Christian portrayals of hell that includes all of the traditional elements, such as caverns, fire, sulfur, smoke, and stench — and yet there is a special place in hell for people who had a physical marriage.

The story includes the martyrdom of Thomas, who is taken up to a mountaintop and killed with a spear. Later, the king who had him killed goes up to the mountain to try to find Thomas's bones, hoping to use them to cure his son who is ill. Thomas appears to the king and rebukes him for not believing him while he was alive. In any case, the bones are not there, they had been taken to the West by Thomas's disciples. Today, pilgrims to the church of Santa Croce in Gerusalemme in Rome can see the relic of Thomas's finger bone, presumably the very finger that touched the wounds of Jesus.

The Acts of Peter

The *Acts of Peter* is worth reading for one story, made famous by the classic film, *Quo Vadis* (1951). In this account, Peter has been talked into leaving Rome to avoid the persecution of the emperor Nero. He is walking out of Rome along the Appian Way, when he sees the risen Jesus coming toward him, heading into Rome. As Jesus approaches, Peter asks him, *Quo vadis, Domine?* (Where are you going, Lord?). Jesus replies that He is going to Rome to be crucified again. By this Peter knew that it was his destiny to return to Rome where he would be martyred by crucifixion. To this day, there is a small chapel on the Appian Way at the site where Peter's vision of Jesus is supposed to have taken place. The place where Jesus stood is marked by marble footprints.

The Orthodox Middle

Against the two extremes of docetics and gnostics on the one hand, and Ebionites on the other, the mainstream writers of the postapostolic age argued for both the humanity and the divinity of Christ.[120] One could not emphasize one and diminish the other; one had to accept both (see the chart, *Christology and Theology in the Second Century* at the end of this chapter). Saying anything else would not be faithful to the teaching of the apostles. As I have indicated, the writers of the second century, many of them philosophers, explained the Person of Christ in terms of the *Logos*, the Word of God, and therefore their understanding of Christ is generally called *Logos christology*.

While the two natures of Christ presented something of a paradox for the Church, the apologists were convinced that both extremes of docetic/gnostic and Ebionite

[120] Clement of Alexandria, *Exhortation to the Greeks*, 1, 10.

were each in their own way an unfaithful interpretation of the Person of Christ. Against the docetics and gnostics, the mainstream emphasized the humanity of Jesus. They argued that His real humanity was proven by His birth as a baby, and especially by His suffering and death.[121] And while we might expect them to say the Resurrection of Jesus proves His divinity, they actually used it as a proof of His humanity, since He was raised with a body, which could eat and be touched.[122] There was an assumption, though not yet fully articulated, that in order to be the Savior of humanity, Christ had to be human. Clement of Alexandria called Him the *champion* of humanity, reminiscent of the ancient practice of representative warfare, by which one person could fight for the whole army (as in the story of David and Goliath). In this case, Christ is the champion who fights for the human race. He achieves victory through death, and in the end wins our salvation. Therefore, to deny the flesh (humanity) of Christ is to deny Christ (1 John 4:1–3).[123]

Against the Ebionites, the apologists emphasized the divinity of Christ. They believed He must be divine, otherwise He could not be a Savior, since salvation required divine intervention.[124] They maintained that Jesus Christ is the incarnation of the preexistent Word (*Logos*) of God, the agent of creation.[125] When God *said*, "Let there be light" (Gen. 1:3), that was the Father creating by His *Word*. When God said, "Let *us* make human beings in *our* image" (Gen. 1:26, emphasis added), that was the Father speaking to his *Logos*.[126] In fact, Christ can be seen in the Old Testament, whenever God is said to be visible.[127] The *Logos* was the inspiration of the prophets.[128] His miraculous virgin birth also demonstrates his divinity.[129] Finally, the Son is equal in divinity to the Father.[130]

[121] Ignatius of Antioch, *Letter to the Magnesians*, 11.1; see also Irenaeus of Lyons, *Against Heresies*, 3.19.3.

[122] *2 Clement* 9.1; Ignatius of Antioch, *Letter to the Smyrnaeans*, 12.2.

[123] Ignatius of Antioch, *Letter to the Smyrnaeans*, 5.2.

[124] Irenaeus of Lyons, *Against Heresies*, 3.20.3.

[125] Clement of Alexandria, *Exhortation to the Greeks*, 1, 11.

[126] Theophilus of Antioch, *To Autolycus*, 2.18.

[127] Justin Martyr, *1 Apology*, 36, 44, 62, 63. Since God is invisible, anyone in the Old Testament who thinks they are seeing God is really seeing the pre-incarnate Christ. Also, since the Divine is omnipresent, it was believed that God the Father could not be localized, or *circumscribed*, in one place. Therefore, any time the "angel of the Lord" appears in a place, and is presented as divine, it was assumed to be the pre-incarnate Christ; see Theophilus of Antioch, *To Autolycus*, 2.22.

[128] Clement of Alexandria, *Exhortation to the Greeks*, 1, 9, 10.

[129] Ignatius of Antioch, *Letter to the Smyrnaeans*, 12.2.

[130] Clement of Alexandria, *Exhortation to the Greeks*, 10–11.

The apologists of the second century established the orthodoxy of the two natures of Christ, which of course was consistent with the apostolic documents that would become the New Testament. However, they did not yet have a well-defined concept of the Holy Spirit, and in fact some described the Trinity in ways that blurred the distinction between the Holy Spirit and the pre-incarnate Christ.[131] Therefore, a more fully developed doctrine of the Trinity would have to wait until the third century. In fact, there are two documents which seem to represent mainstream responses to the extremes, but which demonstrate how the state of theological debate was in flux, since these documents work so hard to refute one extreme that they waffle back and forth, sometimes making concessions to the position they argue against, sometimes leaning a bit toward the opposite extreme. One is the *Protevangelion of James,* which we have already examined. The other is the *Epistula Apostolorum.*

The Letter of the Apostles

More often known by its Latin name, *Epistula Apostolorum,* this is not a letter from any of the original apostles, but a second-century response against gnosticism. It was written sometime after AD 135, but before the AD 180s, since in it Jesus tells the apostles He is returning in 150 years. It contains numerous historical errors, including mistaking Cephas (the Aramaic version of Peter's name) for another apostle beside Peter. Interestingly, though, the document locates the "Place of the Skull" (Golgotha) as the place of Jesus' *burial.* The Gospels say only that Golgotha was the place of the crucifixion, but this document corresponds with the tradition that locates Golgotha as the general area of both the crucifixion and the tomb of Christ. This entire location is now the site of the Church of the Holy Sepulcher in Jerusalem.

The *Epistula* was clearly written to emphasize Jesus' humanity against gnostic docetism. Jesus is born as a baby and is raised in the flesh. After the Resurrection, His feet make footprints, and the disciples touch His body. In this account, Peter, not Thomas, touches His wounds. On the other hand, at times Jesus sounds more like the Jesus of the *Gospel of Thomas* than the Jesus of the New Testament Gospels.

From Apology to Theology

With the last decades of the second century, we come to the end of an era. We leave the postapostolic age and make the transition from Christian apology to Christian theology. Another way to look at it is that apologetics have shifted from an external focus (trying to convince non-Christians of the validity of Christianity) to an internal focus (warning

[131] For example, see Hermas, *The Shepherd,* 78.1, though this particular example is a document that may lean toward adoptionism.

Christians against heresy). This internal apologetic blossoms into real theology as the emergence of heresies on the fringes of the Church force the mainstream bishops and theologians to more clearly define what correct belief is. In doing so, the theologians turn away from philosophy and turn to the Scriptures as the source of authority for supporting their interpretations. Thus we enter the age of the theologians, but before we look at them in detail, we will take a look at the Christian Scriptures.

Christology and Theology in the Second Century

Judaizers and Ebionites

Mostly Jewish Christians, Ebionites are considered the legacy of the so-called Judaizers of Galatians.

Jesus was an anointed prophet, but a mere human.

Jesus was indwelt by the Holy Spirit or an angel, but only temporarily.

The adoption of Jesus as a son of God takes place at his Baptism.

Jesus is the recipient of grace and the Spirit, not the giver of grace or the Spirit.

The resurrection is a metaphor for eternal life.

Ebionite Christology
Affirms Jesus' Humanity
Denies Jesus' Divinity

Practical responses

- Require adherence to all Jewish laws
- Emphasis on following Jesus' example, as opposed to a salvation by atonement
- Some took asceticism to the extreme
- Most probably rejected the worship of Jesus
- Possible emphasis on "social gospel," less on devotional life

Objections of opposition

- How could Jesus be a Savior if not divine? (Salvation requires divine intervention.)
- Jesus is described as divine in the New Testament (Col. 2:9).
- Jesus claimed a unique relationship to God.

The Apologists (and Irenaeus)

Jesus is both fully divine and fully human.

In his divine nature, he is the preexistent agent of creation.

Jesus was fully human, with real flesh (1 John 4:1–3), even after the Resurrection.

Jesus was uniquely filled with the Holy Spirit all his life, not just from his Baptism.

The Resurrection was a real, bodily resurrection.

Logos Christology
Affirms Jesus' Humanity
Affirms Jesus' Divinity

Practical responses

- Refusal to ignore any Scripture texts, even in the face of paradox or apparent contradiction
- It is appropriate to worship Jesus Christ
- Potential balance of devotion and service

Note: Both the Ebionites and the gnostics envision a Jesus who is not unique among humanity. For the Ebionites, Jesus is not unique because he is not divine; for the gnostics, Jesus is not unique because we are all divine.

The mainstream accepted the paradox of a Jesus who is ***both*** one of us ***and*** unique among us — uniquely filled with the Holy Spirit and uniquely one with the Father.

Docetics and Gnostics

Mostly Gentile Christians, retaining elements of their former paganism

Based on extreme dualism: matter is evil, only the spiritual is good

Therefore, Christ could not have real flesh, and Jesus only seemed to be human.

Gnosticism assumes salvation is by secret knowledge.

Some gnostics believed that Jesus had a tangible but "ethereal" body (hybrid Christology).

The Resurrection was a mystical vision in which Christ was revealed in his true (nonhuman) nature.

Docetic Christology
Denies Jesus' Humanity
Affirms Jesus' Divinity

Practical responses

- Worship of angels
- Lifestyle of extremes — either
- Asceticism: self-denial, or
- Libertinism: self-indulgence
- Emphasis on personal belief, little social responsibility

Objections of opposition

- How can Jesus represent humanity if not human? (What is assumed is not saved; salvation requires human representation.)
- Jesus is described as human in the New Testament (Luke 24:36–43).
- Jesus ate, even after the Resurrection.

The Gnostic Family Tree* with Christology Types

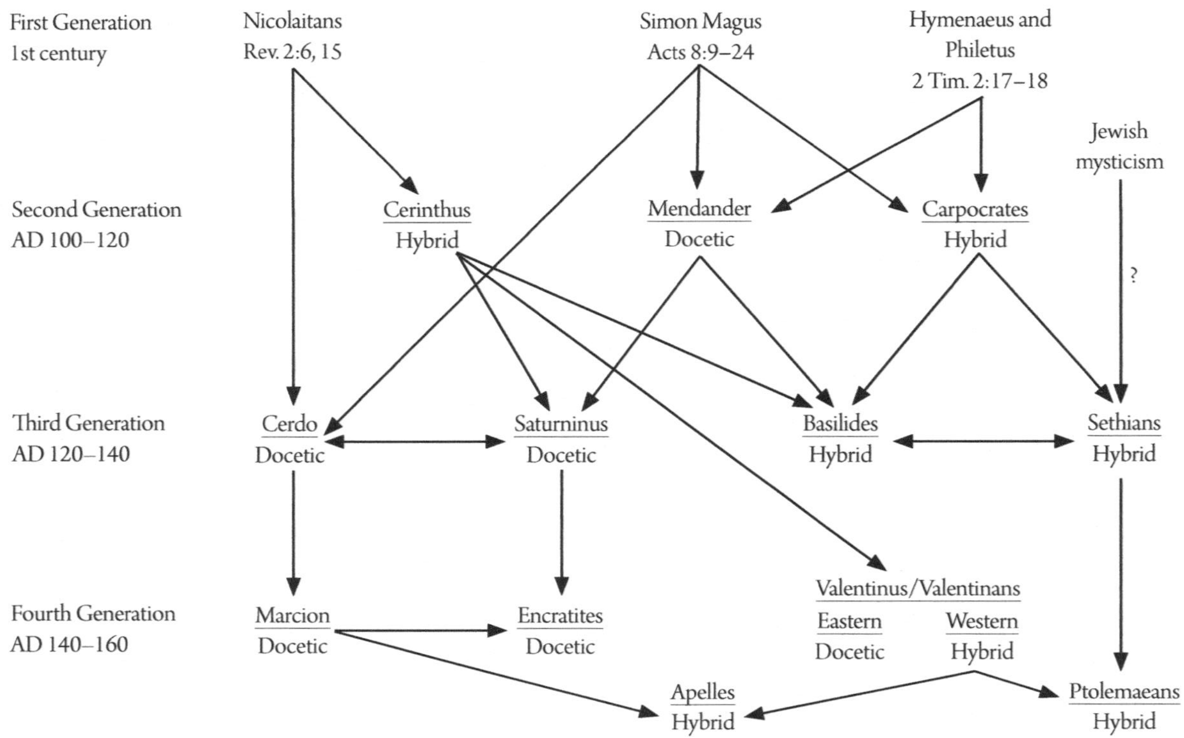

*According to ancient sources. Evidence for a link back to Simon and the Nicolaitans is lacking.

7

The Christian Canon and the New Testament

How Did the Church Get Its Bible?

The word *canon* means a standard, or rule, by which other things are measured. The New Testament canon is therefore the authoritative handbook for the Christian Faith and life. It is, at one and the same time, a compendium of the earliest apostolic teaching and tradition, and also the standard by which the doctrines and ongoing traditions of the Church are measured and evaluated. The phrase, *new testament,* is simply another way of translating the concept of a New Covenant (cf. Jer. 31:31–34; which is 38:31–34 in the LXX). What we call the New Testament is the collection of many of the earliest Christian writings, which came to be treated as inspired and authoritative, and were ultimately added to the Jewish Scriptures to make up the Christian Bible. The idea of a standardized "table of contents" of the Christian Bible actually developed over time in the early Church, on criteria that will be outlined below, and so is a product of the early Church Fathers, and a part of the Church's Tradition.

Historically, there have been two ways to look at Scripture as the primary authority for the Church. One way is to say that what is not prohibited in Scripture is allowed in the Church. In general, the early Christians realized that Scripture, while inspired, was not exhaustive, and so they took this approach. The other approach assumes that whatever is not commanded by Scripture is not allowed in the Church. This approach was tested in some of the rigorist movements of the early Church, but it is mainly a product of certain branches of the Protestant Reformation, and is related to the concept of *sola scriptura,* "Scripture alone." However, the early Church had no concept of *sola scriptura*. This is partly because the earliest Christians did not yet have the New Testament, and therefore no specifically Christian Bible, but even when they did, the Bible itself never teaches a doctrine of *sola scriptura,* and so the concept itself is self-contradicting. In fact, as we will see, the Christians of the early centuries would come to the conclusion that *sola scriptura non satis est*

(Scripture alone is not enough). In other words, since the orthodox mainstream and heretics alike were all interpreting the same Scriptures, but with mutually exclusive interpretations, the Church Fathers found that they had to go beyond Scripture to interpret Scripture.

The Bible of the very first Christians was, of course, what we call the Old Testament. After all, the first Christians were Jews. However, it would not be accurate to call their Bible the *Hebrew Scriptures,* since Jesus, the apostles, and the earliest Christians used the *Septuagint,* which was the Old Testament translated into Greek, including the seven deuterocanonical books (what some call the apocrypha): Tobit, Judith, 1 and 2 Maccabees, Wisdom, Sirach, and Baruch, as well as additions to the book of Daniel and a shorter version of the book of Jeremiah.[1]

The Septuagint is often abbreviated by the Roman numeral for seventy, LXX, because of a tradition that it was translated from Hebrew by seventy Jewish scholars, who, although they worked independently, came up with the exact same translation by the providence of God. However, from the very beginning Christians interpreted the Old Testament differently than their Jewish counterparts, and so it was inevitable that specifically Christian sacred writings would emerge (in part as commentary on the Jewish Scriptures) and that some of those writings would become accepted authoritative interpretations of the Old Testament in light of the life and ministry of Jesus. The production of these Christian writings naturally led to their addition to the Christian canon, giving the Church its Bible. But this did not happen overnight. The development of the New Testament went through four stages, over a period of almost four centuries. However, before we can get to that, it is important to demonstrate the necessity of understanding the wider context in which the New Testament was written and compiled.

[1] It is not clear whether Sirach was originally written in Hebrew or Greek. There is some question as to whether the early Rabbis considered the book of Judith to be inspired, but it was considered so by the early Church Fathers, referenced by Clement of Rome in *1 Clement* 55, and it was included in Jerome's canon. Also, there may have been some Jews who downplayed the significance of the books of the Maccabees, but these quickly became important for the Church, since the story is one of persecution. This is especially true of 2 Maccabees, where we see episodes of martyrdom (6:18–7:42), resurrection (7:9, 11, 14, 23; 14:46), the intercession of saints (15:11–16), and prayers for the dead (12:39–46), all of which demonstrates that at least some Jews believed in these concepts before the coming of Christ. It is worth noting that the tradition of Hanukkah comes from 2 Maccabees.

The Importance of the Church Fathers for Understanding the New Testament

One of the greatest problems in Christian scholarship is the study of the New Testament in isolation from the study of the early Church and the Church Fathers. Often the New Testament is studied with a kind of tunnel vision that scrutinizes every iota (literally) of the internal text but fails to look outside the text for its historical context. In doing this, it is worse than missing the forest by focusing on the trees, it is missing even the trees due to obsessive focus on the leaves. We must never forget that it was the Church Fathers who decided which books would be included in the Christian canon, and so what they have to say about it must inform our discussion of the authorship, dating, and theological content of the New Testament texts themselves. In addition to this, the study of the historical context of the Roman Empire, including Roman records, can tell us a great deal about the background of the New Testament documents. As an illustration of the dangers of studying the New Testament documents without sufficient attention paid to the Church Fathers and the historical context, I offer six serious problems in New Testament scholarship and interpretation that have sadly (and unnecessarily) shifted the focus of discussion toward, at best, a majoring on the minors, and at worst, something that ends up cutting the heart out of the Gospel. These problems are all the result of nineteenth- and twentieth-century academics who failed to consult the Church Fathers and the Tradition when studying the New Testament. I cannot emphasize enough: most of these issues simply did not exist before the modern age, and would have been considered ridiculous in the early and medieval Church. It should go without saying that whole books could be (and have been) written on each of these topics, so our survey here will be brief, only to call attention to them, and I would encourage further study in the books mentioned in the footnotes.

The Quirinius Problem

Almost all English language Bibles translate Luke 2:2 using the word "first," in a phrase such as, "this was the *first* census taken when Quirinius was governor of Syria" (emphasis added). The problem with this translation is that Quirinius did not become governor (technically proconsular legate) of Syria until the year AD 6, when Judea became a Roman province (as opposed to a client kingdom) and was annexed to the province of Syria. There certainly would have been a census taken at this time, to assess not only population, but to estimate potential taxes. This is the census mentioned by Luke in Acts 5:37. In fact, it seems that the militaristic faction known as the *Zealots* was born out of the protest against this very census.

However, Luke has just told us in chapter 1 that all this happened, "in the days of Herod, King of Judea" (Luke 1:5). But Herod died in 4 BC. So how can Jesus be born *both* "in the days of Herod" (before 4 BC) *and* at the time of the "first" census under Quirinius (after AD 6)? It's impossible. Sadly, most New Testament scholars are content to assume that 1) Luke didn't know what he was talking about, and 2) the inspiration of Scripture (to the extent that they believe in it) does not include dates. Some scholars, refusing to give up on the inspiration of Scripture, have tried to suggest that perhaps Quirinius was governor of Syria twice, both during the time of Herod's reign, and later. But we know from Roman records that he was not. When Herod was still alive and king over Judea, Quirinius was proconsul in Galatia. In any case, this kind of speculation is not necessary.

As it turns out, Luke did know what he was talking about. Assuming that it is true that Jesus was born while Herod was still alive (Matthew also says as much), we can see that the census of AD 6 under Quirinius *cannot* be the one mentioned in Luke 2. So why does Luke bother to mention Quirinius? It turns out that the Greek word *prote*, in Luke 2:2 can mean either "first" or "before." Translators — without consulting the historical context — usually choose the most common meaning, "first," and end up with the phrase as it's usually translated. However, in this case, it should be translated "before," so that the verse should be translated, "this census was *before* Quirinius was governing Syria." Luke's point would then be to distinguish the census that was taken around the time of Jesus' birth from the more famous one that caused an uprising in AD 6. In other words, Luke is saying that Joseph and Mary had to travel to Bethlehem because of a census, but he's clarifying, as if to say: "Do you remember that big census we had when Quirinius became governor of Syria? Well, it's not that one — it was before that."

At the time of Jesus' birth — when Herod was still alive and king of Judea — the proconsul of Syria was one Sentius Saturninus, who held the office from 9 to 5 BC. Tertullian knew this, and mentions a census conducted by Saturninus on behalf of the emperor in the year 6 BC.[2] Although the logistics of a census requiring the kind of travel that we read was forced on Joseph and Mary is unclear, whatever compelled them to go to Bethlehem could not have been the census ordered by Quirinius but must have been a census taken at least ten years earlier. And although there are no extant Roman records of the specific census in question, we know that such enrollments were ordered at that time. All this is to say that if New Testament translators would check their history, they would know how to translate Luke 2:2 correctly. And

[2] Tertullian, *Against Marcion*, 4.19. Justin Martyr also mentioned the census, but he was reading Luke the way most do today, and so he assumed that Quirinius was governor of Syria at the time of Jesus' birth. Justin Martyr, *1 Apology*, 34.

they would know that Luke *did* know what he was talking about, and his witness can be trusted with regard to dates.

The Myth of Acceptable Pseudonymity

As soon as this hypothesis was suggested (it did not exist before the modern era), it was almost immediately accepted without any real critical review. It spread across the field of New Testament studies like a California brush fire, and it quickly became a litmus test of serious scholarship. The myth suggests that certain New Testament books (primarily select letters of Paul) were not written by the author named in the text (they are pseudonymous), but that this is acceptable because this was a common practice in the ancient world, and Christians would have been fine with the idea that the content came from a disciple of the apostle, or a school of thought associated with the apostle, or just someone who wanted to honor the apostle (or gain credibility for the document) by putting the apostle's name on it. Usually the reasoning goes something like this: the document sounds too much like the later Church to be written early enough to be within the lifetime of the apostle. But that's a circular argument, because there is no reason why it could not be the case that the document sounds like the later Church precisely because the later Church patterned itself after what was written in the document. The whole myth is based on preconceived assumptions about how quickly the structure of the Church could (or could not) develop. Then those assumptions are used to declare — without any real evidence — that the document in question could not have been written by the apostle whose name is in it. Then, minute distinctions of vocabulary and style (of the assistant who took dictation!) are used as further "proof" that the same apostle who wrote Romans (for example) could not have written Ephesians or the Pastoral Epistles.

However, when one looks at the evidence in the early Church, one finds that none of this is true.[3] In those cases where a document was considered pseudonymous, the Church Fathers rejected it as a forgery and not worthy of Christian reading. As we will see below, the primary criterion for a document to be included in the New Testament was apostolic authorship, so any document thought to be written by someone

[3] E. Earle Ellis, "Pseudonymity and Canonicity of New Testament Documents," in *Worship, Theology and Ministry in the Early Church: Essays in Honor of Ralph P. Martin*, ed. Michael J. Wilkins and Terence Paige, 212–224, *Journal for the Study of the New Testament Supplement Series* 87 (Sheffield: JSOT Press, 1993), 217–219. I first wrote about this *Myth of Acceptable Pseudonymity* in James L. Papandrea, *The Early Church (33–313): St. Peter, the Apostles, and Martyrs* (Notre Dame, IN: Ave Maria Press, 2019), xxvi–xxvii; see also Brant Pitre, *The Case for Jesus: The Biblical and Historical Evidence for Christ* (New York: Image, 2016), 62–65.

other than an apostle or close associate of an apostle would not be included, and anyone who was thought to have fictitiously put an apostle's name on their document would be considered a fraud.[4]

Of course, there were pseudonymous documents in the ancient world. But the mistake made by those who promote this myth is to assume that this would have been acceptable within the Church. It would not. Any document the early bishops thought to be pseudonymous would have been considered a fabrication, just like the gnostic gospels. The early Church Fathers would have said that forging a document under someone else's name is exactly what the heretics do! In the end, the very fact that the documents we have made it into the New Testament means that the Church Fathers were convinced that their authorship was authentic. The lesson to be learned is that we must let the people who chose the documents for the New Testament tell us what they believed about who wrote them.

So the next time someone tells you that some of the New Testament documents attributed to Paul were not written by him, or that early Christians accepted the idea that a document could be both pseudonymous and authoritative, ask them to show you the evidence from the historical context of the letters, the early Church. They can't, because there is none. If the myth were true, there would be evidence in the documents of the early Church Fathers saying things like, "We know that letter is not by Paul, but it's okay, we can still include it in our canon" or, "Lots of people write documents and put someone else's name on them, and we're fine with that." Of course, when you look at the early Church Fathers, what you find is the opposite.

The Myth of the Anonymous Gospels

But what about when the author's name is not actually in the body of the text of a document? When I was in seminary, I learned, as most people do, that the four canonical Gospels are really anonymous, because the names Matthew, Mark, Luke, and John, are not "in" the text, and so were added later. But this is another case of a myth that got started without critical scrutiny, caught on because people wanted it to be true, and became a kind of dogma of New Testament studies. I am embarrassed to admit that I believed this myth a lot longer than the other ones, but we now know, thanks to brave scholars who are willing to be myth-busters, that the four Gospels were never

[4] A case in point is Tertullian's assessment of the apocryphal *Acts of Paul*. He says that since it was not actually written by Paul or some eyewitness of Paul's life, but was written much later, it is a fraud, and therefore not authoritative; see also Irenaeus, *Against Heresies*, 4.33.8.

anonymous.[5] While it is true that the names of the authors are not in the part of the text that has chapter and verse numbers, it is not true that the names of the authors were not part of the original document. Remember that the chapter and verse divisions were created only very recently in the big picture, and when you actually look at the evidence from the early Church, there was never a time when the Gospels circulated without the authors' names on the manuscripts. The names of the authors were always part of the document, and there are no examples of any manuscripts of the Gospels without the authors' names on them.

As Simon Gathercole, and more recently Brant Pitre (*The Case for Jesus*) have noted, there is no evidence that the Gospels ever circulated without their titles (with the authors' names), there is no evidence that the authorship of the four Gospels was ever disputed, or that any manuscript of any of the four Gospels ever circulated with any other name on it.[6] And in any case, if someone was going to invent a fictitious author for a life of Jesus, they would not choose people like Mark and Luke, who were not eyewitnesses to the event.[7] Also, there are no canonical lists from the mainstream Church that include any more or less than the four Gospels we have in our New Testament, and there are no canonical lists that suggest any other authors or that the Gospels were anonymous.

So the next time someone tells you that the Gospels were anonymous, ask them to show you evidence of a manuscript or a canonical list that supports that theory. There is no such evidence.

The Myth of Q

This myth is based on two assumptions that, like the ones above, are not supported by the evidence in the early Church. The first assumption is that Matthew and Luke could not have had direct access to each other's Gospels, and that a lot of time would have had to pass before either one of them could have read the Gospel written by the other. So, when observing the fact that there is a lot of material in Matthew and Luke that is exactly the same, it is taken for granted that it was impossible that Luke simply copied from Matthew, or the other way around. The other assumption underlying this is that Jesus could not have predicted the fall of Jerusalem (as He does in the Gospels)

[5] See Simon J. Gathercole, "The Titles of the Gospels in the Earliest New Testament Manuscripts," *Zeitschrift für die neutestamentliche Wissenschaft und die Kunde der älteren Kirche,* 104 no. 1 (2013): 33–76; and Pitre, *The Case for Jesus,* 12–38.

[6] Ibid.

[7] Pitre, *The Case for Jesus,* 9, 12–23, 43, 53.

and so therefore these Gospels must have been written (or at least edited into their present form) after the year AD 70, when Jerusalem fell.

To take the latter assumption first, we can dismiss it quickly as an assumption that can only be born from a lack of faith in Christ. To say that Jesus could not have predicted the fall of Jerusalem is to deny His divine personhood as the Son of God. However, if one should argue that good scholarship does not require that one be a believer, I maintain that it actually would not require a person to be the Son of God to see the fall of Jerusalem coming. One would only have to be politically savvy enough to predict that the zealot uprisings and guerrilla warfare that had been going on for a quarter of a century would eventually antagonize the Romans into crushing the rebellion, which would naturally lead to a siege of Jerusalem. And it would not take a prophet to predict who would win that war — and this is what happened in AD 66 to 70.

In any case, the point is that apart from this skepticism about Jesus' ability to predict the fall of Jerusalem, there is no reason at all to date the synoptic Gospels after the 60s.[8] In fact, the Church Fathers tell us that Matthew wrote his Gospel while Peter and Paul were still alive. Luke, too, must have written his Gospel before AD 70, since there is no conceivable reason why the book of Acts, written by Luke *after* his Gospel, would not include the martyrdoms of the two most important apostles, Peter and Paul, except that they had not happened yet. Since Peter and Paul were executed in Rome under the emperor Nero, who died in the year AD 68, Luke's Gospel could not have been written later than that. Finally, there is no reason why Luke, who was not an eyewitness to the events of Jesus' ministry, could not have simply copied parts of Matthew's Gospel.

Nevertheless, these faulty assumptions have led scholars to embrace the myth of the hypothetical existence of another written Gospel source, called Q, which is supposedly a lost source from which both Matthew and Luke copied their common material. But it must be emphasized: not only is there no *need* for such a source because the assumptions behind it are unfounded, there is also no *evidence* for such a source anywhere in the early Church.[9] No Church Father ever alludes to any document that could be this mysterious proto-gospel. And although scholars have made their whole careers speculating on the contents of this Q source, it simply never existed. It is an unnecessary hypothesis meant to answer an unnecessary question, one that is based on unfounded assumptions.[10]

[8] Pitre, *The Case for Jesus*, 90–94.

[9] Pitre, *The Case for Jesus*, 97.

[10] For the best introduction to the problem, see Mark Goodacre and Nicholas Perrin, eds., *Questioning Q: A Multidimensional Critique* (Downers Grove, IL: InterVarsity Press, 2004).

This question, often called the "synoptic problem," is the question of the origin and chronological order of the writing of the Gospels. But it is only a problem if one begins with the assumption that Matthew and Luke could not have been written while Peter and Paul were still alive (as the Church Fathers tell us they did), and that one of them could not have copied from the other (which they clearly could have). So the next time someone tells you that there was another (otherwise unknown) gospel behind the canonical Gospels, ask them to show some evidence from the early Church that such a gospel existed. And if they insist that Matthew and Luke could not have been written before AD 70, ask them why — ask them why Luke could not have simply copied from Matthew (or the other way around) — and then ask the questions posed by Brant Pitre: If these Gospels, with the prediction of the fall of Jerusalem, were really written after the fact, why didn't the narrator point out that Jesus' prediction came true, as we see in other non-canonical texts that were written after a similar kind of fulfillment? And why would an author, writing after the fact, have Jesus tell His followers to pray that these tragic events wouldn't happen in winter, when they would have known by then that they happened in the summer?[11]

The Myth of the Rapture

Another hypothetical answer to an unnecessary question is the concept of the *rapture*. It must be stated up front that the concept of the rapture, as popularly understood in Evangelical and Fundamentalist circles, is not found anywhere in Scripture, and no one before the late eighteenth century ever even thought of the rapture, let alone believed in it. The concept is a product of a certain strain of Fundamentalist eschatology (speculation about the end times). In their attempt to force Old Testament books such as Daniel and Ezekiel into overly literal interpretations of the book of Revelation, some interpreters found they could not reconcile everything, and to make a long story short, ended up needing to create a two-stage second coming of Christ, in which Christ would return temporarily, to remove those already saved from the coming trials (which were meant to convince the holdouts), only to return later for the "real" second coming. The rapture is meant to refer to the "taking up" of those who are already saved at the time of Jesus' "first" second coming.

In part, this is based on the common mistake of reading the book of Revelation as though almost everything predicted there is still in our future. However, as I have demonstrated elsewhere, the book of Revelation looks back on the fall of Jerusalem, and then predicts things like the fall of Rome which, although they were in the future

[11] Pitre, *The Case for Jesus*, 92–94.

for John and his audience, are clearly in our past.[12] This mistake leads interpreters to look for a future worldwide persecution of the Church (tribulation), when in fact that was already going on when the book was written, and although John's message there is "it's going to get worse before it gets better," the point is that to look for these events to be repeated in our future misses the real meaning of the text. In any case, there is no two-stage second coming of Christ spoken of anywhere in Scripture, or in the Church Fathers. But when one begins with this erroneous interpretation of the book of Revelation, one eventually gets stuck in the task of trying to reconcile it with other Scriptures, and the solution some found was to invent a temporary arrival of Christ before the actual end of things. These interpreters then read 1 Thessalonians 4:13–18 as though it was about *that* arrival of Jesus, even though that text says nothing about it being a temporary visit distinct from the actual second coming. In any case, it is from this passage that they get the word *rapture* (from the Latin for "caught up").

The next thing they did was to take Jesus' words in Matthew 24:37–41 out of context and read this, too, as though it refers to the first of two second comings. In this passage, Jesus refers to the flood at the time of Noah as a kind of foreshadowing of his second coming. Just as at the time of the flood, people laughed off Noah's warnings and yet when the flood came, many were "carried . . . away" (Matt. 24:39), Jesus warns His audience that something similar is coming. He goes on to say that His own return will be so unexpected that "two men will be out in the field; one will be taken, and one will be left. Two women will be grinding at the mill together; one will be taken, and one will be left" (Matt. 24:40–41). From this they get the idea of being "left behind," as though Jesus meant that the one "taken" is being taken up to Heaven, in the sense that 1 Thessalonians 4:17 says that people will be "caught up." However, the context actually shows that what Jesus meant was that of these pairs of people, the one "taken" is taken *away*, just as those who scoffed at Noah were swept away (Luke's Gospel says *destroyed*). So to be "taken" is not taken up to Heaven, but it is to be lost. And to be "left" is not left behind, but rather left alive, that is, spared. They have read it to mean the exact opposite of what Jesus intended, and they did so because they had to force it to fit within their invented scheme of a two-stage second coming. Had they consulted the Church Fathers, though, they would have seen that the early Christians did not interpret the book of Revelation in this way, nor did they ever see in Scripture anything like a "rapture."

[12] See Papandrea, *The Wedding of the Lamb*.

The Search for the "Historical Jesus"

The so-called Quest for the Historical Jesus is a complicated story, which unfolds in several phases. It is not my intention here to try do justice to the history of something that is fascinating, but only as the story of an exercise in futility. I should also point out that in many ways this is old news, which only goes to show how something that is the latest fad at one time can prove in the end to be little more than a huge waste of time.[13]

Just like the myth of Q, this story begins with unfounded assumptions about what Jesus could and could not have actually said. In addition to rejecting the possibility of prophecy, it was assumed that Jesus would not have said certain things that sounded too much to the interpreters like later developments in the Church (never mind the fact that without the teachings of Jesus it becomes difficult to explain why the Church developed the way it did). The Quest for the Historical Jesus essentially attempts to sort out which sayings in the Gospels actually come from Jesus Himself (the "historical" Jesus), and which ones were likely added later (put in the mouth of Jesus by well-meaning editors of the Gospels who were really writing about "the Christ of faith"). This is a flawed methodology from the very beginning because one has to use the same unfounded assumptions in order to make decisions about which are the "authentic" sayings of Jesus. And like the myth of Q, scholars have built whole careers on this sorting game. Some scholars gathered to discuss their conclusions, and they even adopted a practice of voting on supposed levels of probability for the sayings of Jesus. They called themselves the Jesus Seminar.

When I was in seminary, one of my favorite professors told us a story. When the Jesus Seminar was first gathering, this professor, who was very well respected in the field, was invited to join. He went to the first meeting, and as soon as he found out what their methodology was to be, he promptly quit. The methodology is, at best, circular, and at worst, built on speculation and personal whim. And one has to think that at least for some of these scholars, the decision about whether a saying of Jesus was authentic was based in large part on whether they were comfortable with it — whether their idea of who and what Jesus *should* be fit with the saying in question. This led them to separate what they thought was the "real" (historical) Jesus from the *Christ of faith*, that is, the later Church's understanding of Christ.

The problem with this is it assumes that the later Church was wrong about who Jesus really was — that somehow the Jesus preached in the Church was an embellishment of the real Man. Of course, this would often include the assumption

[13] For a detailed treatment of the Quest in all its manifestations, and a thorough critique, see Johnson, *The Real Jesus*.

that the divinity of Christ was a later evolution of christology, and that the earliest Christians wouldn't have believed this. Often this goes hand in hand with the myth of acceptable pseudonymity, and a very late dating of the Gospels. In the end, it was not a search for the historical Jesus, but an attempt to recast Jesus in the image of skeptical scholars who rejected out of hand the possibility of His divinity. Had these scholars taken the Church Fathers seriously, they would have read Irenaeus's warning against separating the tangible Jesus from the spiritual Christ — something that some of the gnostics were doing at the time.[14] The scholars of the Quest did the same thing — they separated the human Jesus (the historical Jesus) from the spiritual idea of Christ, reducing their "Christ" to perhaps the Spirit (or the spirit) within a Jesus who was still just a mere man.

Stages of Development of the New Testament

Stage 1: The Writing of the Apostolic Documents

The first of the Christian documents to be written were the letters of Paul. In the fifties and sixties of the first century, Paul's ministry included writing letters to the Christians in various cities, many of whom were his own converts and disciples in churches he himself had founded. It is also possible that the Gospel of Mark was written as early as the fifties, based on the testimony of Peter.[15] It may be that the expulsion of Jews from Rome created the need for a written source that would give the remaining Gentile Christians in Rome access to the stories of the Gospel.[16] Also, given the way Christian liturgy included readings from the very beginning, it is hard to imagine the life of the Church going on for very long without texts from which the events of the life and ministry of Jesus (not to mention His passion and Resurrection) could be read in worship.

[14] Irenaeus of Lyons, *Against Heresies*, 3.11.7; see also 3.9.3.

[15] Eusebius of Caesarea, *Ecclesiastical History*, 3.3.4. Admittedly, Eusebius is not necessarily a reliable source on this subject, since he is only relating what he has heard, sometimes including contradictory traditions.

[16] Some have speculated that the birth narratives in Luke and Matthew were appended later, after the main part of the Gospels were written. It could be that the miraculous nature of Jesus' birth encouraged a docetic understanding of Christ, which made the mainstream Church worry about the use of the birth narratives. For example, see Tertullian, *Against Marcion*, 4.21, and *On the Flesh of Christ*, 23; cf. the *Protevangelion of James*. However, the very fact of a human birth would argue against docetism, so the docetics (including Marcionites and gnostics) tended not to talk about Jesus' birth. In any case, such a fear may explain why Mark, the first Gospel, has no birth narrative.

Some of the other apostolic letters may have been written at this time as well, possibly including Hebrews, James, Jude, and 1 Peter.[17] And as I have noted above, the two-volume set of Luke and Acts must have been completed by the mid- to late sixties, since Acts ends before the martyrdom of Peter and Paul.[18] Although there is some debate over this, there has never been any sufficient reason given for why the book of Acts would not include at least the martyrdom of Paul, if it had happened already when the document was written. On the other hand, by the time 2 Peter was written, we can see that people had already begun to think of Paul's letters as inspired Scripture (2 Pet. 3:14–16).[19] This could indicate that "our beloved brother Paul" had been martyred by the time 2 Peter was written (2 Pet. 3:15).

The question of whether Matthew was written before Luke, or the other way around, cannot be answered with any certainty—the only thing that is certain is that is it unnecessary to assume that one could not have copied from the other (and of course they both had access to Mark).[20] Several of the Church Fathers noted that Matthew was first written in Aramaic or Hebrew, and was then translated into Greek before being included in the canon, though this may be speculation based on the obvious fact that it was written for a Jewish Christian audience.[21] Irenaeus of Lyons notes that Matthew was written while Peter and Paul were still alive, in fact he says while they were in Rome.[22] Although some scholars date this Gospel as late as the eighties, this is usually based on the assumption that Jesus could not have predicted the fall of Jerusalem, as we noted above.[23] Therefore, a late date for Matthew and Luke is not necessary, and given the reality of apostolic travel, and the probability that Matthew also knew Mark and Luke personally, there is no reason to speculate

17 Eusebius of Caesarea, *Ecclesiastical History*, 2.23.25, 3.38.1–3.

18 Eusebius of Caesarea, *Ecclesiastical History*, 3.24.5–8; see also Pitre, *The Case for Jesus*, 47, 99.

19 Eusebius of Caesarea, *Ecclesiastical History*, 3.3.1. This is not the place to enter into the debate over the authorship or dating of New Testament letters, however, some issues related to authorship and early Christian reception will be dealt with below.

20 There is no historical or literary evidence for a so-called Q source. Though the early writers, including Eusebius, knew of other written Gospel sources from the fringes of the Church, there is no mention of a source that would explain the common elements in Matthew and Luke which are not also in Mark. A better explanation for those common elements is simply that Matthew copied Luke, or Luke copied Matthew.

21 Eusebius of Caesarea, *Ecclesiastical History*, 6.25; see Pitre, *The Case for Jesus*, 41–43.

22 Irenaeus of Lyons, *Against Heresies*, 3.1; Eusebius of Caesarea, *Ecclesiastical History*, 5.8.2; see Pitre, *The Case for Jesus*, 41–42.

23 Pitre, *The Case for Jesus*, 90–94.

about another mysterious Gospel source or require any significant time gap between the writing of these Gospels.[24]

The Johannine literature was the last to be written, in the nineties, though there are serious questions about the authorship of 2 John and 3 John, and some scholars believe they were written in the early second century.[25]

Stage 2: The Use of the Apostolic Documents

Already in the second half of the first century, apostolic documents were being copied, passed from church to church, and read aloud in worship meetings. The fact that multiple copies of these early documents were made while the originals still existed, combined with the fact that fragments of some very early manuscripts are still extant, lends a confidence of reliability that few other ancient documents share. It cannot be overstated that the proximity of the earliest manuscripts to the originals (we have manuscript fragments from the second century — only decades after the time the documents were written), combined with the reverence and care with which the apostolic documents were handled, make the books of the New Testament the most textually reliable documents from the ancient world, bar none.[26]

By the end of the first century, the letters of Paul (often including Hebrews) were circulating as a collection. One could also obtain a collection of the four Gospels, sometimes with the book of Acts. In fact, it is possible that the need to publish these Christian documents was part of the catalyst that led to the development (or at least the popularity) of the codex, or book.[27] Rather than copy documents on scrolls, which were rectangles of parchment glued together at the sides, it became more expedient simply to leave them as squares (pages), stack them and bind them on one side. This made it more convenient to put the material into one package, and some say it made it easier to find a particular passage in the middle of a document, though without the chapter and verse numbers that were added in the late Middle Ages, that is debatable. In any case, the fact that the documents which would be included in the New Testament were being read in worship demonstrates that they were already becoming authoritative and coming to be considered inspired Scripture on the level of the Old Testament.[28]

[24] Pitre, *The Case for Jesus*, 31–32.

[25] Eusebius of Caesarea, *Ecclesiastical History*, 3.24.17.

[26] See F. F. Bruce, *Jesus: Lord & Savior* (Downers Grove, IL: InterVarsity, 1986); see also Larry W. Hurtado, *The Earliest Christian Artifacts: Manuscripts and Christian Origins* (Grand Rapids: Eerdmans, 2006), 3.

[27] Hurtado, *The Earliest Christian Artifacts*, 5, 43–89.

[28] David S. Dockery, *Biblical Interpretation Then and Now: Contemporary Hermeneutics in Light of the Early Church* (Grand Rapids: Baker, 1992), 47.

By the middle of the second century, the term *gospels* (in the plural) is used as a category or literary genre.[29] At one time it was fashionable to say that the Gospels are neither history nor biography, or even that they represent a completely unique literary genre, though now scholars are beginning to acknowledge that it is more accurate to say that they are "historical biography," and that they do follow the pattern of ancient biographies (*lives*) with elements of ancient historical writings.[30] Justin Martyr referred to the Gospels as the "memoirs of the apostles," in contrast to the "archives" (the Old Testament).[31] Irenaeus commented that there must be four, and only four, Gospels.[32]

The first to attempt a standardized list of authoritative Christian documents (as far as we know) was the docetic heretic Marcion. He created a canon, or list of documents, which he thought should be the authoritative writings for his followers. However, since he was a docetic, he edited out anything that made Jesus sound too human, to the point where his canon was limited to edited versions of the Gospel of Luke and Paul's letters. He rejected the Old Testament entirely. In reality, it is probably the case that various bishops produced many different canonical lists for the Christians in their sees. The first that we know of to come from the mainstream Church is now called the Muratorian Canon, named after its discoverer. It may have been written by the Roman priest Caius at the turn of the third century. This particular list did not include some of the writings that are now in our New Testament, specifically Hebrews, James, 1 Peter, 2 Peter, and 3 John.[33] Nevertheless, by the end of the second century, or the beginning of the third, there was a generally acknowledged group of documents more or less like our New Testament, which was considered the Scripture of the Church, along with the Septuagint. Clement of Alexandria and Irenaeus had both used the term *New Testament* by the end of the second century, though sometimes it is unclear whether they are referring to the New Covenant which the documents reveal, or the documents themselves.[34]

[29] Justin Martyr, *1 Apology*, 66.3.

[30] Pitre, *The Case for Jesus*, 67–83.

[31] Justin Martyr, *1 Apology*, 67. The use of the term *archives* for the Old Testament goes back at least to Ignatius of Antioch. The phrase "memoirs of the apostles" may refer to the whole New Testament (Gospels and letters), the way that the "archives" would refer to the whole Old Testament (Law and Prophets).

[32] Irenaeus of Lyons, *Against Heresies*, 3.11.8.

[33] See the helpful chart in Shane Kapler, *The Epistle to the Hebrews and the Seven Core Beliefs of Catholics* (Kettering, OH: Angelico Press, 2016), 147.

[34] See Clement of Alexandria, *Who Is the Rich Man That Shall Be Saved?*, 3; *Miscellanies*, 1.5; and Irenaeus of Lyons, *Demonstration of the Apostolic Preaching*, 91; *Against Heresies*,

This naturally brings up the question: How did the bishops decide which documents to include in their lists of authoritative Christian books?

Criteria for Inclusion #1: Authorship

As the Church was considering which documents ought to be included in its New Testament, there were three basic criteria by which the documents were judged. Without a doubt, the most important was authorship. To be considered for inclusion, a document must have been written by an apostle or a close associate of an apostle.[35] Apparently, one degree of separation was the maximum allowable distance from those who knew Jesus personally. If the authorship of a document was called into question, the document itself was suspect. As noted above, if the authorship was deemed pseudonymous, the document was therefore not considered genuine and was rejected.[36] Of course, there was some debate and disagreements over the authorship of certain documents, which led to different lists with different documents included. However, it is important to remember that the gnostic documents (such as the *Gospel of Thomas* and the *Gospel of Peter*) were universally recognized as later pseudonymous or heretical writings and were never considered for inclusion in the canon by the mainstream Church.[37] Also note that there is no evidence of manuscripts of any gnostic documents from before the third century.[38]

The early Christians did understand the technical issues of debate surrounding the authorship of the first-century documents. In fact, the authorship of the letter to the Hebrews was a matter of great debate in the early Church. Eusebius said that the Roman Christians generally did not believe Hebrews was written by Paul.[39]

4.28.1–2, 4.32.1–2, 5.34.1. Note that in *Against Heresies*, 2.27.1–2, Irenaeus refers to the Gospels as Sacred Scripture; see also the *Didascalia Apostolorum*, 21.

35 Origen, *Commentary on John*, 1.5.

36 Ellis, "Pseudonymity and Canonicity of New Testament Documents," 217–219; see also Eusebius of Caesarea, *Ecclesiastical History*, 6.12, 6.25, and the *Apostolic Constitutions*, 6.3 (6.16).

37 See Eusebius of Caesarea, *Ecclesiastical History*, 6.12. Note that Eusebius knew that the *Gospel of Peter* had been rejected because it was the product of a docetic community. On the other hand, a few early canon lists did include a document known as *The Apocalypse of Peter*, but that is not a gnostic text. Note that manuscript evidence shows that the heretical groups were in fact in the minority on the fringes of the Church and that their documents were deviations from the mainstream; see Hurtado, *The Earliest Christian Artifacts*, 40–41.

38 See the chart in Hurtado, *The Earliest Christian Artifacts*, 228.

39 Eusebius of Caesarea, *Ecclesiastical History*, 6.20, 6.25. According to Eusebius, the Christians in Rome believed that Hebrews was written by Clement of Rome.

The Greek grammar was thought to be too good to be from Paul's pen.[40] However Eusebius knew of a tradition going back to Clement of Alexandria which said that Paul had written Hebrews in Aramaic as an apologetic (or evangelistic) treatise for Jews, and that it was later translated into Greek by Luke.[41] This would explain the different writing style. Paul's name was then presumably left off the document because his fellow Jews were suspicious of him. Eusebius himself believed that the letter was written by some disciple of Paul who wrote it from notes taken while listening to Paul's teaching. Perhaps this disciple was Luke, or Timothy, or perhaps another unknown disciple. In the end, though, Eusebius thinks it would be acceptable to consider the letter Pauline because the content comes from Paul.[42] However, as we have clarified, this does not mean that Eusebius would have found it acceptable for a disciple of Paul to write a letter and claim that Paul had written it, let alone invent a fictional greeting from Paul along with fictitious details like a forgotten coat (2 Tim. 4:13). Eusebius also tells us that the authorship of the catholic epistles (the letters of James, Jude, Peter, and John) was disputed.[43] However, it is interesting to note that no early Church writer ever questioned the Pauline authorship of the Pastoral Epistles or Ephesians, or the traditional authorship of the synoptic Gospels (Matthew, Mark, and Luke).[44] No canonical list ever omitted the Pastoral Epistles, or any one of the four Gospels, or includes any other gospel.[45]

Criteria for Inclusion #2: Liturgical Use

The second criterion for inclusion in the canon was the ability to stand the test of time and use in worship. As we have seen, the letters of Paul were originally written to be read in the assembly, and the Gospels quickly gained a place in Christian liturgy. As the apostolic documents were continually read in worship, they took their place alongside the Psalms and the Prophets as containing a divinely inspired message for the Church. For the most part, if a document was not suitable to be read in worship, it might not be considered acceptable as Christian Scripture. However, the criterion of

[40] On the other hand, the reader must keep in mind that normally Paul would have dictated his letters to a scribe. Changing the scribe could theoretically change the style of the letter, especially if Paul dictated in Aramaic and the scribe had to translate Paul's words into Greek.

[41] Eusebius of Caesarea, *Ecclesiastical History*, 6.13, 6.25.

[42] Eusebius of Caesarea, *Ecclesiastical History*, 6.25.

[43] Eusebius of Caesarea, *Ecclesiastical History*, 6.14.

[44] For an example of the assumption that Ephesians is apostolic, see Novatian, *On the Trinity*, 17.9.

[45] See the chart in Kapler, *The Epistle to the Hebrews*, 147–148.

apostolic authorship would trump this consideration, so that the Pauline authorship of Philemon and the Johannine authorship of Revelation would keep these documents on the list.[46] In the end, the very fact that these documents were included witnesses to the relatively universal acceptance of their apostolic authorship, as well as their perceived usefulness.

On the other hand, some documents had their advocates for inclusion in the canon, for example *1 Clement*, or even *The Shepherd*, but these proved unwieldy and unfruitful as liturgical texts, and that may be part of the reason why they were not included.

Criteria for Inclusion #3: Citation

The third criterion was citation by respected theologians. This is a bit of a chicken-and-egg situation, since in order for a document to be quoted by a theologian, it already must have had some measure of authority, or there would be no point in citing it to support an argument. However, the citation of a document by the theologians of the late second and third centuries cemented the authoritative status of the documents that would eventually be our New Testament. This brings us to stage three.

[46] By far most early Christians believed that the book of Revelation was by John, the disciple of Jesus. See Irenaeus of Lyons, *Against Heresies*, 4.21.11, 4.30.4; and Eusebius of Caesarea, *Ecclesiastical History*, 6.25. Papias, who claimed to have known John the Elder, is an exception, attributing it to that disciple of the apostle. However, the only serious challenge to the Johannine authorship in the early Church came from Dionysius of Alexandria, who was motivated to have the text excluded from the canon because of what he perceived as the danger of literal interpretation by an Egyptian bishop named Nepos. Dionysius of Alexandria argued that Revelation should not be included in the canon because it was not easily interpreted by the average person and thus lent itself to misinterpretation. See Eusebius of Caesarea, *Ecclesiastical History*, 7.24–25. Philip of Side (fifth century) had said that those who say John the Elder wrote Revelation are mistaken, and that Papias and Irenaeus's interpretation of the days of creation as one-thousand-year eras is also mistaken. George the Sinner (ninth century) also relates what he knew as the traditionally accepted belief, that Revelation was written by John the apostle in the time of Domitian, that the next emperor Nerva had released him, and that he had written his Gospel afterward, before being martyred; see Clement of Alexandria, *Who Is the Rich Man That Shall Be Saved?*, 42, where Clement says that John was in fact released after Domitian's death, and went back to Ephesus. Irenaeus says John lived into the reign of Trajan, so at least until AD 98, and also wrote the fourth Gospel; Irenaeus of Lyons, *Against Heresies*, 2.22.5, 3.3.4, 3.11.1, 5.18.2. If it seems unlikely that John could have lived to the turn of the second century, note that the Roman dole assumed recipients up to eighty years old, which would have been John's age at about that time. See Eusebius of Caesarea, *Ecclesiastical History*, 7.21. For more on the authorship and dating of Revelation, see Papandrea, *Wedding of the Lamb*.

Stage 3: The Authority of the Apostolic Documents

Important and influential theologians such as Irenaeus and Tertullian were determined to support their arguments with Scripture. They considered Scripture to be divine revelation, which was more reliable than human reason (i.e., philosophy).[47] Thus they assumed that the documents they quoted already held some weight with their readers as the teachings of the apostles. But by quoting them, they gave them even more credibility and authority than they may have already had. The theologians of the late second and third centuries implicitly refined the list of authoritative books by choosing which ones to quote (and not to quote, though the lack of a quotation from any particular book in extant writings does not prove a given author did not consider that book authoritative). Irenaeus quoted or referred to every book in our New Testament, except perhaps Philemon and 3 John. Tertullian quoted every book except 2 Peter. By the time of Novatian, these books were included, though Origen would still question the authenticity of 2 Peter.

Stage 4: Standardization of the Canon

Even though there was general agreement on most of the apostolic documents as early as the end of the first century, there was no universal consensus on a precise canonical list of New Testament documents. In fact, the first extant list of authoritative Christian documents that was exactly like our New Testament comes from the year AD 367. This was bishop Athanasius of Alexandria's Easter letter of that year. In his letter, he outlined which documents ought to be considered authoritative. This does not mean that the year AD 367 saw universal acceptance of Athanasius's list, or that other bishops would necessarily have had the same list, but since other bishops did defer to Athanasius on setting the date for Easter, it is natural to assume that his advice on the canon would carry weight beyond his see.[48] That said, there may have been lists that match our New Testament from earlier than AD 367, but which are no longer extant. Therefore, we cannot say that the Church did not have a New Testament until the fourth century, but we also cannot say that it had its Bible from the beginning.

In the year AD 382, Damasus of Rome (bishop AD 366–384) issued a letter that included the results of a council of Rome in which the current canonical New Testament list was affirmed. However, we still cannot assume from this that everyone across the entire worldwide Church accepted, or even received, this letter. Councils in North Africa in AD 393 (Hippo), AD 397 (Carthage), and AD 419 (Carthage) also confirmed the current New Testament list, but these were only regional councils,

[47] For the precedent, see Clement of Rome, *1 Clement*, 45, 63.

[48] Meyendorff, *Imperial Unity*, 113.

and so their decrees were not binding on the whole Church.[49] In AD 405, Innocent of Rome (bishop AD 401–417) endorsed the current list in a letter, and one of his successors endorsed the conclusions of the AD 419 Council of Carthage, and so these late fourth and early fifth century letters by the bishops of Rome served to solidify a consensus, at least in the West.

In the end, some of our New Testament books almost didn't make the cut. For reasons of contested authorship, Hebrews, James, 2 Peter, and 3 John took longer than most to gain acceptance.[50] As we have seen, 3 John and then 2 Peter were the last ones to be universally accepted. In the end, however, it was determined that their authorship was genuine.[51] The book of Revelation was also questioned as to its suitability for inclusion, although not for reasons of authorship, since almost everyone in the early Church believed it was written by John the apostle.[52] One problem with the book of Revelation, in addition to the obvious difficulty with the interpretation of the highly symbolic language and apocalyptic imagery, was the way that it was being interpreted and used by the certain influential theologians. Papias, Justin Martyr, Irenaeus, and Tertullian all seemed to interpret the so-called millennium of Revelation 20:1–3 as a literal reign of Christ on earth. These early writers are sometimes referred to as *chiliasts* or *millenarians* for their literal interpretation of the millennium, however this is a bit of an anachronism because they did not believe in any kind of *rapture* or modern-type millenarianism. As noted above, no one in the early or medieval Church had any concept of the *rapture*, since it is a concept that was invented in the modern age and is not actually mentioned in Scripture.[53] In any case, the majority of the Church Fathers were convinced that such an interpretation was

[49] See the chart in Kapler, *The Epistle to the Hebrews*, 147–148.

[50] Eusebius of Caesarea, *Ecclesiastical History*, 6.25. Eusebius says that 1 Peter is genuine, but admits that there was a dispute over the authorship of James, 2 Peter, 2 John, 3 John, and Jude. Jerome said that John the Elder wrote 2 John and 3 John; see Jerome, *Illustrious Men*, 18. Philip of Side (fifth century) said that the earliest Christians accepted only 1 John as from the apostle, and that the other two Johannine epistles were probably from John the Elder, a disciple of the apostle. That there was also debate over Jude and the other catholic epistles, see Eusebius of Caesarea, *Ecclesiastical History*, 6.13. Note that Eusebius also mentions Barnabas and the *Didache*.

[51] Admittedly, it could be argued that the more time went by, the easier it would be to ascribe genuine authorship to a pseudonymous document. However, this is where the second and third criteria would make up for any lingering uncertainty in the first.

[52] See n. 46 above.

[53] For more on this, and the early Church's more mainstream interpretation of the book of Revelation, see Papandrea, *The Wedding of the Lamb*.

missing the true, symbolic meaning of the text.[54] Most would come to a consensus that interpreted the millennium as the age of the Church, in which Christ reigned on earth through His Body, the Church. Nevertheless, several influential eastern theologians advocated keeping the book of Revelation out of the New Testament, and the Church almost had to deal with a situation where the West and East had two different New Testament canons. In the end, the book of Revelation was only rescued for the East by a couple of well-received commentaries written in the sixth and seventh centuries.

There were, of course, other early documents which were considered for inclusion in the canon, but which did not ultimately become part of our Bible. The *Didache*, *1 Clement*, and *The Shepherd* were all early contenders. Irenaeus apparently considered *The Shepherd* to be Scripture. Clement of Alexandria considered Clement of Rome's *1 Clement* to be Scripture, and some in the East were following his lead in doing exegesis on *1 Clement* well into the Middle Ages. The *Epistle of Barnabas* also got a few votes. But in the end the lack of apostolic authorship, along with the other factors already mentioned in chapter 3 above, led to their exclusion.

Patristic Exegesis

Exegesis is the "drawing out" of meaning from a text. When it comes to Scripture, it is never enough to know what the text *says*; one must take the next step and ask what the text *means*.[55] That is the task of interpretation, and the meaning of any text includes both the meaning in its original context (*What did it mean then? How was it received and understood by the original audience? How did those closest to it in time interpret it?*) as well as the relevance for the reader (*What does it mean now? To what extent is it*

[54] Jerome said that it was John the Elder who was responsible for the interpretation of Revelation that we first see in Papias; see Jerome, *Illustrious Men*, 18. Note that Jerome calls the literal interpretation of an earthly millennium the "Jewish tradition of the millennium," and he notes that not only Irenaeus (and Tertullian), but Victorinus of Petau, Lactantius, and Apollinarius also followed this interpretation. Eusebius criticized Papias's and Irenaeus's interpretation of Revelation, saying that it was a misunderstanding of the apostolic document, which should be understood as symbolic. Eusebius of Caesarea, *Ecclesiastical History*, 3.36–39. Photius of Constantinople (ninth century) said that Papias and Irenaeus did not represent the accepted traditional interpretation of Revelation. Finally, Justin Martyr, who himself interpreted the millennium as a literal one-thousand-year reign of Christ in a rebuilt earthly Jerusalem, admitted that many orthodox Christians disagreed with this interpretation. Justin Martyr, *Dialogue with Trypho*, 80.

[55] Martin, *Worship in the Early Church*, 87–88.

authoritative for the reader? How is it to be applied to the life of the Church?).[56] Therefore, even when the early Christians could agree on which documents were authoritative, that did not mean they always agreed on their meaning or their message for the Church. The ongoing debates of the early Church are obvious evidence of that fact. However, there were nine assumptions that the Church Fathers shared when it came to the interpretation of Scripture.

Assumption #1: The Divine Inspiration of the Sacred Texts, Including the New Testament

As we have seen, the author of 2 Peter referred to the letters of Paul as Scripture, on the same level of authority as the Old Testament (2 Pet. 3:14–16). Thus, the documents of the New Testament would come to be seen as having been inspired by the same Holy Spirit who inspired the prophets (John 14:26).[57] In fact, *Logos* christology affirmed that the text of Scripture was a written record of the voice of the divine *Logos*. To the early Christians, the written word was another incarnation of the living Word. Like the body of Jesus, the text of Scripture enfleshes the Word of God. And like Jesus Christ, the written word is both divine and human: divinely inspired yet written down by humans. The two natures of Christ are paralleled in the dual authorship of Scripture. The early Christians did take the aspects of human authorship seriously, however the ultimate author is God, and therefore every word in the text is there for a reason. As we will see, this conviction will lead some to look for spiritual meaning in even the smallest details of a biblical story. Finally, the same Holy Spirit who inspired the writing of Scripture would (with prayer) illuminate its interpretation.[58]

Assumption #2: Revelation Is Progressive

In the early Church, the concept of *progressive revelation* meant that God's intention for the human race gets clearer over time and as the needs of humanity change.

[56] In the early Church, there is no distinction between exegesis and hermeneutics; see Dockery, *Biblical Interpretation Then and Now*, 16.

[57] See Clement of Rome, *1 Clement*, 45, 63; and Irenaeus of Lyons, *Against Heresies*, 2.28.2, 2.30.6, 3.2.1. Irenaeus said that "the Scriptures are indeed perfect, since they were spoken by the Word of God and his Spirit," translation in *Ante-Nicene Fathers*, vol. 1, 399; see also Novatian, *On the Trinity*, 18.2; Cyprian of Carthage, *Epistles*, 51.6, 19–20, 27; and Augustine of Hippo, *On the Trinity*, 15.19.31; *Against the Donatists*, 2.4; and *On the Morals of the Catholic Church*, 29. Augustine argues that to say Christ's words in Scripture are not His is blasphemy.

[58] Irenaeus of Lyons, *Against Heresies*, 3.21.2.

Mysteries are revealed with time, so that in the Old Testament God the Father is presented clearly, but God the Son is veiled. In the New Testament, the Son of God is presented clearly, but the Holy Spirit is only partially revealed. Finally, the experience of the Church reveals the Spirit to us.[59] Therefore, as Christians consider and debate the meaning to be discerned from Scripture, each generation comes to greater clarity on the doctrines of christology, soteriology, and even ecclesiology.[60] However, this is not to say that those who live now are smarter than those who came before, or that a new interpretation could supersede an older one. New interpretations can build on, and further clarify, older ones, but they cannot contradict the conclusions of previous generations. Progressive revelation and apostolic succession were considered interdependent, which meant that the orthodoxy of one's ancestors in the Faith was the foundation on which to build the orthodoxy of the present day. Dionysius of Alexandria quoted Deuteronomy 19:14 as relevant on this point.[61] Just as one is not allowed to move the boundary markers set up by one's ancestors, one also does not contradict the accepted doctrines of the previous generations. These accepted doctrines are the very boundaries of what is acceptable in interpretation, and therefore are the safeguards of orthodoxy.

It is important to keep in mind that in the ancient world, that which is older is usually assumed to be better than whatever is newer.[62] The older, established, interpretation is the Tradition, which cannot be changed, it can only be further clarified. The writers of the patristic era would not want to be thought of as innovators. They would not want to be perceived as creating anything new, since what is new is automatically suspect as somehow disconnected from the Tradition. In other words, the burden of proof for truth is always on the latest interpretation. The Tradition, on the other hand, comes from those who were closest to the Source (Jesus), and it was of the utmost importance to remain consistent with the witness of the apostles.[63] In every generation, Tradition is what has been received from the ancestors of the Faith, and it is what the Faith is built on. It has stood the test of

[59] Gregory of Nazianzus, *Fifth Theological Oration in the Holy Spirit*, 25–26.

[60] Clement of Alexandria, *Exhortation to the Greeks*, 1. Clement says that divine revelation was originally through prophecy (in the Old Testament), but now (in the New Testament) it is revealed plainly. Cyprian implied that the reason revelation is progressive is that the return of Christ is drawing ever nearer; see Cyprian of Carthage, *Epistles*, 62.18.

[61] Dionysius of Alexandria, *Epistle to Philemon*.

[62] Tertullian, *Against Praxeas*, 2.

[63] On the concept of Tradition as an authority alongside Scripture, and helping to interpret it, see Irenaeus of Lyons, *Against Heresies*, 3.2.2, 4.33.8. See also Papandrea, *Handed Down*, chap. 1.

time, and it is the very stability of the Faith. Tradition informs the interpretation of revelation.

Today we talk about the *development* of doctrine. As St. John Henry Newman clarified in his essay *On the Development of Christian Doctrine,* there are positive developments of doctrine, which clarify and expand upon what was already known. Development is a kind of healthy growth. But there are also negative developments, which he calls corruptions. Corruptions are substantial, or extreme, changes of the kind that make something become what it was not. Orthodoxy is not static — it expands with time, growing with new insights to match new needs of the Church. But to change or to evolve, if change means a mutation, ceasing to be what it was and becoming something different, that would be a form of corruption — that is, a heresy. Development is growth; corruption is death.

To give just a few brief examples, throughout the rest of this book we will discover developments in the doctrine of the Trinity, especially with regard to pneumatology, which doesn't fully come into play until the fourth century. We will see developments in the doctrine of the Church (ecclesiology), and this includes the process of determining which documents would be considered authoritative Scripture. But when some will propose to change the essential basis on which all other doctrines are founded, such as the two natures of Jesus Christ, then that proposed change will have to be answered by opposing the corruption and clarifying (facilitating development) the orthodox doctrine. And if one should ask who has the authority to discern the difference between development and corruption (orthodoxy and heresy), the answer is, of course, the bishops, because they are the successors of the apostles.

As Newman said, "A true development, then, may be described as one which is conservative of the course of development which went before it, which is that development and something besides: it is an addition which illustrates, not obscures, corroborates, not corrects, the body of thought from which it proceeds; and this is its characteristic as contrasted with a corruption."[64]

Assumption #3: There Are Multiple Meanings in Any Given Text

Because the ultimate author of Scripture is God, the human author's intended meaning is not the only valid meaning to be gained from a text. Patristic exegesis allows for multiple meanings, and in fact the early Christians believed that God intended multiple meanings so that the Scriptures could never be completely mastered or

[64] St. John Henry Newman, *An Essay on the Development of Christian Doctrine* (London: W. Blanchard, 1845), 1.8, 87–88.

fully understood.[65] The Scriptures are a bottomless well, so that no one should think he had drunk his fill of them. Perhaps the best example of this principle would be the way that the Gospel writers attribute many of the details of the life of Jesus to the fulfillment of prophecy. It is one thing to say that generally acknowledged messianic prophecies were fulfilled in Jesus. But the apostles went so far as to say that Old Testament texts which were never thought of as messianic prophecies (such as Isaiah 53, the "suffering servant") were also fulfilled by Jesus. The early Christians therefore reasoned that even though the human author of an Old Testament text had one meaning in mind, God had another meaning in mind for the future Church.[66] Thus the suffering Messiah, an oxymoron to the Hebrew mind, is God's mystery revealed in Jesus Christ.

Assumption #4: Paradox Is to Be Embraced, Not Avoided

The Church Fathers said that the heretical groups on the fringes of the Church would pick and choose Scripture texts to support their christologies.[67] The Ebionites rejected texts that affirmed the divinity of Christ (such as Col. 2:9), while the docetics and gnostics rejected texts that affirmed His humanity (such as Luke 2:40). Another tactic was to reject certain texts by interpreting them in esoteric ways, so as to allegorize them into meaninglessness (a tactic still used to this day). For example, Ebionites and other adoptionists would take very literally Christ's statement, "The Father is greater than I" (John 14:28), but would diminish the force of His statement, "The Father and I are one" (John 10:30), by interpreting it metaphorically, or simply claiming that Jesus never said that. What the mainstream Church rejected, however, was the presumption of editing Scripture. Assuming divine inspiration, even apparently contradictory texts must be held together as true — one text cannot be ignored in favor of the other. Once the decision was made that a particular document was to be considered Scripture, the question was not *whether* the text is true, but *how* it is true in light of other biblical texts. To use the above example, the

[65] The idea that there could be only one correct meaning for any given biblical text is an invention of the Protestant Reformation. See Scott W. Hahn and Benjamin Walker, *Politicizing the Bible: The Roots of Historical Criticism and the Secularization of Scripture* (New York: Crossroad, 2013), 176.

[66] Irenaeus of Lyons, *Against Heresies*, 4.26.1. Irenaeus maintains that Christ is the hidden treasure in the Old Testament, which means that texts which refer to Him could not be properly interpreted before He came.

[67] Hippolytus, *Against Noetus*, 3; see also Cyprian of Carthage, who criticized this in his *Epistles*, 51.6, 19–20, 27.

mainstream approach to Scripture was not to ask which passage (John 10:30 or 14:28) was true, or even which one was more true, or more literally true, but to ask how to understand them both as true. The conclusion would be that Jesus Christ and the Father are one, but not the same. The Father is greater in authority, but not in divinity. The texts had to be interpreted in light of each other, with no attempt to minimize the mystery of it all. The heretics were seen as those who took Scripture out of context in order to maintain a more simplistic interpretation, while the orthodox were those who accepted mystery and embraced the paradox.[68] No doubt this is an idealistic and oversimplified comparison, but it was nevertheless the claim of the mainstream bishops.

Assumption #5: Patristic Exegesis Follows the Lead of Apostolic Exegesis

The apologists and theologians of the early Church accepted the methodology of Matthew and Paul when it came to interpreting the Old Testament. Like a Christian *midrash* (commentary), the New Testament interpreted the Old in light of the life and ministry of Jesus. The best interpretation was christocentric. This had the advantage of keeping the Church connected to the Old Testament (not only against docetism, but also to demonstrate that Christianity is not really something new, but the fulfillment of something older than philosophy), even while it allowed the Church to set aside certain aspects of Judaism such as animal sacrifices and dietary laws.[69]

As we have seen, the *Logos* christology of the second and third centuries affirmed the pre-Incarnation activity of the second Person of the Trinity. In other words, Christ appeared in the Old Testament. This was made necessary by the belief that "no one can see [God] and live" (Exod. 33:20), and yet there are times in the Old Testament where people do see a manifestation of the Divine. These theophanies were interpreted by the early Christians as appearances of the divine *Logos* in His pre-existent state. Hippolytus said that the reason the Messiah is referred to in Daniel 7 as "one *like* a son of man" (emphasis added) is because He was not yet the Son of Man, since He was not yet human.[70] In interpreting the Old Testament

[68] Dockery, *Biblical Interpretation Then and Now*, 69.

[69] Dockery, *Biblical Interpretation Then and Now*, 56, 65. The *Didascalia* maintains that there is a primary law in the Old Testament (the Ten Commandments) which is still in effect, but a secondary law (such as the dietary rules) which is no longer in effect since the ministry of Jesus; *Didascalia Apostolorum*, 26.

[70] Hippolytus, *Against Noetus*, 4.

christologically, the early Christians were not only doing what the apostles had done, they were doing what Jesus Himself had done (Luke 24; John 5).[71]

Assumption #6: Scripture Interprets Scripture

Since God is the author of both the Old and New Testaments, there is an assumed consistency of purpose and ultimate meaning across the two testaments.[72] This is, of course, necessary, not only to affirm that Christ is the fulfillment of the Old Testament, but also for the refutation of Marcionite rejection of the Old Testament. In practice, it means that obscure texts can be interpreted using other (presumably clearer) texts. There is an internal integrity of Scripture, regardless of differences in authorship and historical context, which allows the exegete to combine texts from different biblical documents and authors to look for a harmonized meaning.[73] This does not, however, imply that Scripture is to be interpreted using "Scripture alone." As we have seen, the Church Fathers believed that the tradition — that is, the exegetical conclusions of those who went before them — should also inform their interpretation of Scripture.

Assumption #7: In General, Interpretation of the Old Testament Was Non-Literal

Since there were two authors behind any text, God and the human author, the Church Fathers would say that most passages have at least two meanings. When it came to the interpretation of the Old Testament, the literal (historical) meaning of the human (i.e., Jewish) author was seen as secondary to the spiritual meaning that God had in mind for the Church. The early Christians reasoned that if all one had was the literal meaning, then the Old Testament would be irrelevant for the Church.[74] Therefore, the non-literal meaning(s) would be held up as the higher, or perhaps the deeper, meaning. The most important meaning is not the one on the surface, but the one hidden under the surface, since in the Old Testament Christ is veiled. The true meaning of the Old Testament could not be understood until Christ was revealed in His Incarnation.[75] In fact, to interpret the Old Testament literally would come to be criticized as a "Jewish"

[71] Dockery, *Biblical Interpretation Then and Now*, 24–25.

[72] Dockery, *Biblical Interpretation Then and Now*, 94; see Cyprian of Carthage, *Epistles*, 51.27.

[73] Justin Martyr, *Dialogue with Trypho*, 65.2; see also Cyprian of Carthage, *On the Lapsed*, 20, where Cyprian says that the gospel cannot be sound in one part and waver in another.

[74] This is an obvious hyperbole, though, since all the Church Fathers would agree that the Ten Commandments and other aspects of the Old Testament were still binding on all the people of God.

[75] Irenaeus of Lyons, *Against Heresies*, 4.26.1.

way of doing interpretation.[76] To focus on the literal or historical meaning of an Old Testament passage was to fail to take Christ into account. For example, a literal or historical interpretation of 2 Samuel 7:12 would focus on Solomon as the heir to David's throne and the one who would build the temple in Jerusalem. A spiritual (i.e., Christian) interpretation of that passage would focus on Jesus Christ as the descendant of David and the king of an eternal kingdom.

Technically speaking, there were two types of non-literal interpretation, typology and allegory. Typology is famously attributed to Irenaeus of Lyons, but really goes back to the apostle Paul, and even Jesus Himself (for examples, see Matt. 12:40 and 1 Cor. 15:44–47).[77] Using typology, Old Testament concepts and events are seen as foreshadowing or symbolizing details in the life and ministry of Christ. The Old Testament can then be interpreted as not only predicting Christ, but pointing to Him. Irenaeus wanted to counteract the docetic and gnostic rejection of the Old Testament, so he expanded the concept of typology, and the early Church followed his lead in looking for parallels between Old Testament and New Testament elements. The tree of the knowledge of good and evil is a type of the cross; Eve is a type of Mary; the crossing of the Red Sea and the water from the rock are types of Baptism; the manna in the desert is a type of the Eucharist.[78] In fact, over time, any mention of wood in the Old Testament became a reminder of the cross (cf. Wisd. 14:7), and any mention of water became a call to Christian Baptism.[79] It is noteworthy that, in pointing out Old Testament antetypes of the cross, the early Church Fathers give us some of the earliest references to the use of the cross as a symbol for the Church.[80] For example, already in the late first century the *Epistle of Barnabas* refers to the Greek letter Tau (T) as a sign of the cross.[81] Justin Martyr and Tertullian would

[76] Eusebius of Caesarea, *Ecclesiastical History*, 7.24–25. This is not entirely true, of course, since there were Jewish exegetes who interpreted the Old Testament non-literally, however, it nevertheless seems to be a generally held stereotype of the early Christians. Also, it must be pointed out that the ancient world's definition of what was "literal" differs significantly from the way we tend to think of what the word *literal* means.

[77] Dockery, *Biblical Interpretation Then and Now*, 24, 36, 39.

[78] Irenaeus of Lyons, *Against Heresies*, 3.22.4, 5.19.1, 5.21.2. Irenaeus also points out that Adam was tempted by food (but failed the test) and Jesus was tempted by food (but resisted the temptation and passed the test).

[79] Irenaeus of Lyons, *Against Heresies*, 4.5.4; see also Justin Martyr, *Dialogue with Trypho*, 138; and Clement of Alexandria, *The Instructor*, 1.5.

[80] See, for example, Justin Martyr, *1 Apology*, 60; Hurtado, *The Earliest Christian Artifacts*, 135–154.

[81] *Epistle of Barnabas*, 9.7–9; see Hurtado, *The Earliest Christian Artifacts*, 135–154.

both follow his lead and mention this as well, Tertullian revealing that Christians were making the Sign of the Cross on their foreheads.[82]

Allegory is often attributed to Origen, but actually comes from Greek philosophy. In an attempt to maintain the old mythologies in spite of the obvious anthropomorphisms (not to mention immoralities) of the gods, the philosophers advocated interpreting the myths as metaphors that would encourage virtue. In other words, the literal meaning of the myths left one with gods no one should emulate, let alone worship, but the philosophers believed the myths could be redeemed and reconciled with their own teachings through the use of allegory.[83] Working with Plato's dichotomy between the material and the spiritual, Philo of Alexandria articulated two levels of meaning to be found in a text. The literal meaning was analogous to Plato's material realm, which is not necessarily bad, but it is certainly inferior to the spiritual. The spiritual meaning was therefore the deeper meaning, more important, and indeed more *true*, than the literal.[84] And because the spiritual meaning had a divine origin, even the smallest details could be allegorized and interpreted as significant.[85]

With allegorical interpretation, the details of a biblical text come to represent abstract realities or moral virtues.[86] The point is that in this method of interpretation, the situation of the reader or interpreter becomes the focus, rather than the context of the author of a text.[87] For example, the Church allowed itself to forgo the Hebrew dietary laws by interpreting them allegorically.[88] The unclean animals

[82] Justin Martyr, *1 Apology*, 55; Tertullian, *Against Marcion*, 3.22; Hurtado, *The Earliest Christian Artifacts*, 135–154; see also Athanasius of Alexandria, *On the Incarnation of the Word*, 48, for the early Christian belief in the protection of the cross as symbol.

[83] Dockery, *Biblical Interpretation Then and Now*, 77.

[84] For example, see Clement of Alexandria, *Who Is the Rich Man That Shall Be Saved?*, 5. Clement wrote, "The Savior teaches nothing in a merely human way, but teaches all things to his own with divine and mystic wisdom. We must not listen to his utterances carnally, but with due investigation and intelligence must search out and learn the meaning hidden in them," translation in *Ante-Nicene Fathers*, vol. 2, 592. Although Clement is talking here about the New Testament, the quotation demonstrates the point well. Note that Clement interprets "Blessed are the poor in spirit" (Matt. 5:3) to mean "the poor are blessed in spirit." Clement of Alexandria, *Who Is the Rich Man That Shall Be Saved?*, 17.

[85] Dockery, *Biblical Interpretation Then and Now*, 78.

[86] For example, Clement of Alexandria interpreted the cleansing of the temple (connecting it to 1 Cor. 6:19) as a call to self-control; Clement of Alexandria, *Exhortation to the Greeks*, 11.

[87] Dockery, *Biblical Interpretation Then and Now*, 87.

[88] The best example of this is Novatian's *On Jewish Foods*. See also the *Epistle of Barnabas*, 10–12; Theophilus of Antioch, *To Autolycus*, 2.16; and Irenaeus of Lyons, *Against Heresies*, bks. 4 and 5.

become metaphors for human vices, so God doesn't really care whether you eat pork; God only cares that you don't act like a pig. The prohibition from eating weasels really means that God does not want us to act like weasels. Weasels are thieves, and so the message from God for the Church is: don't be a thief.[89] In the restriction to animals with cloven hooves, the two parts of the hoof represent the two testaments.[90] To have one testament only (the Old Testament, like the Jews; or the New Testament, like the Marcionites) would not be adequate. True faith requires two testaments, both the Old and the New.

Another kind of allegory is the so-called *vertical* (or *anagogical*) allegory. This assumes a continuity between what happens on earth and what happens in Heaven. Events in the material realm then become lessons about the spiritual realm (for example, see Luke 11:13).

Allegory might be built into the text, such as in a parable, or it might be used to interpret a text with no inherent allegory. Either way, the temptation to find meaning in every detail was sometimes too much for the early Christian exegete to resist. Theoretically, the principle of Scripture interpreting Scripture was supposed to provide some measure of checks and balances, but in actual practice some of the interpretations were so speculative as to be far-fetched.[91] As we will see, this will result in a backlash against allegorical interpretation in some circles.

In practice there was not always a clear distinction between typology and allegory. The primary difference between the two is that with typology, there seems to be an acceptance of the historicity of the Old Testament types, because God was at work in human history.[92] With allegory, on the other hand, there is no need for the details

[89] In addition to Novatian, *On Jewish Foods*, see Theophilus of Antioch, *To Autolycus*, 2.16, where he says that the prohibited animals (sea monsters, wild beasts, birds of prey) represent people (robbers, murderers, and godless people) because they prey on those weaker than themselves. See also Clement of Alexandria, *The Instructor*, 3.11.

[90] Novatian, *On Jewish Foods*, 3.10. Alternatively, the double hoof could represent accepting both the Father and the Son, according to the orthodox interpretation of the Trinity; see Irenaeus of Lyons, *Against Heresies*, 5.8.4.

[91] Some possible examples include Clement of Alexandria, *The Instructor*, 2.1, where he says that taking the coin out of the mouth of the fish in Matthew 17:27 represents taking greed out of our lives. Clement also says that Paul's words "when I was a child" in 1 Corinthians 13:11 should be taken to mean, "when I was a Jew." Clement of Alexandria, *The Instructor*, 1.6. Origen even speculated that God might intentionally put historical inaccuracies into the text of the Old Testament, as a red flag to the spiritual interpreter to stop looking at the surface and look for a deeper meaning.

[92] Dockery, *Biblical Interpretation Then and Now*, 81.

to be historical. We can see this in Jesus' parables. It is not necessary for the story of the Good Samaritan to have actually happened for Jesus' point to be made. But when Jesus uses typology and compares the coming tribulation to Old Testament events, He seems to assume the historical reality of those events.

Just as the philosophers saw allegorical interpretation as necessary for holding on to the Greco-Roman myths, the Christians knew that non-literal interpretation was necessary to redeem the Old Testament from its own anthropomorphisms of God.[93] The mainstream Christians knew that such anthropomorphisms could not be taken literally, however it was precisely the literal interpretation of the Old Testament that led the docetics and gnostics to reject it.[94] Non-literal interpretation was also necessary to interpret certain Old Testament promises as having been fulfilled in Jesus. Finally, a non-literal interpretation was seen as essential if the Church hoped to attract philosophically minded, educated Romans.

The point for the early Christians was that there is a spiritual meaning in the Old Testament that is deeper and more important than the literal meaning. The literal meaning might be good enough for the uneducated (or for those who do not put their faith in Christ) but those who are enlightened and who are serious about their Christian Faith and the Scriptures will not be satisfied with the literal meaning: they will look for the spiritual meaning. When it came to the Old Testament, then, the Church was left with two choices: Interpret it literally and reject it (as the Marcionites and gnostics did) as the product of an ignorant people or an untrustworthy demigod. Or interpret it non-literally and accept it (as the mainstream Church did) as a divine mystery that is only revealed in hindsight after the life, death, and Resurrection of Jesus Christ.

Assumption #8: In General, Interpretation of the New Testament Was Literal

The Old Testament and the New Testament were considered complementary, but while the deeper meaning was hidden in the Old Testament, spiritual meaning in the New Testament was thought to be closer to the surface. Therefore, one could read most

[93] Novatian, *On the Trinity*, 6.1, 5. Novatian interprets anthropomorphic elements as attributes of God, thus the feet (and wings) of God represent omnipresence (cf. Ps. 139), and the eyes and ears of God represent omniscience.

[94] Irenaeus of Lyons, *Against Heresies*, 4.3.1. Sometimes the gnostics did use allegory for the Old Testament when it suited them; see Irenaeus of Lyons, *Against Heresies*, 1.3, 3.2.1. Thus Irenaeus's critique is that the gnostics interpreted the anthropomorphisms of God literally (rejecting the God of the Old Testament), but in other cases they allegorized the text to make it say whatever they wanted it to.

of the New Testament literally, as recent history, and reserve non-literal methods of interpretation for when they were made necessary by the genre of the text (such as the parables and hyperbole used by Jesus, as well as the apocalyptic sections of the Gospels and the book of Revelation).[95]

As we have seen, the gnostics interpreted the Old Testament literally and used that as the reason to reject it and claim that the God of the Old Testament was not the God and Father of Jesus Christ. Ironically, the gnostics tended to interpret the New Testament non-literally, especially to discount the human nature of Christ, as well as Jesus' teaching on the Eucharist in the Bread of Life discourse in John 6.[96] The mainstream Church had the opposite approach to Scripture from the gnostics. It is no wonder that the gnostics would eventually separate from the Church, and even write their own scriptures. For the mainstream Church, it was not a simple question of literal versus non-literal, the key was knowing when to use a literal interpretation and when to use a non-literal. Thus, the mainstream Church tended to interpret the Old Testament non-literally, and the New Testament by using literal or historical interpretation whenever possible.

Assumption #9: Interpretation Is Meant to Be Done in the Context of Prayer

Finally, the early Church Fathers believed that the interpretation of Scripture is not an academic exercise, but part of a devotional life. Most of the early exegetes were pastors: bishops and priests who interpreted Scripture for the Church, not in an ivory tower, but as part of a community (2 Pet. 1:20). In fact, it could be said that interpreting Scripture was an act of worship, and therefore must be accompanied by

[95] There was some disagreement over the proper method of interpretation for the book of Revelation. It seems that both Irenaeus and Tertullian followed Papias in a literal interpretation of the millennium. However, this does not seem to have been the way the majority of Christians read Revelation. See Eusebius of Caesarea, *Ecclesiastical History*, 7.24–25. Interpreting the millennium literally was considered by the mainstream to be a "Jewish" (i.e., too literal) way of reading the text. Dionysius of Alexandria wrote against the literal interpretation in a document called *On Promises*, which was apparently a response to another document called *Refutation of the Allegorists* by an Egyptian bishop named Nepos. Dionysius of Alexandria did not claim to understand Revelation but knew that it could not be interpreted literally. He seems to have been motivated to have Revelation excluded from the New Testament canon, and to that end he tried to convince other bishops that Revelation was not written by John the apostle, though he did believe that the apostle had written the fourth Gospel and the letter of 1 John.

[96] Irenaeus of Lyons, *Against Heresies*, 3.12.11.

prayer. The same Holy Spirit who inspired the writing of the text must be invoked to inspire the reading of the text.[97] As Sts. Augustine and Anselm came to realize, faith must precede understanding.

The History of Patristic Exegesis

While all of the above was true in general, it is difficult to say whether it was all true all at once. Like most things, the Church's understanding of Scripture and its interpretation varied depending on time and place. And just as there were four stages of the development of the canon, there were also four stages of the development of interpretation, though we should not assume they were concurrent, or consistent, across the Church.

Stage 1: Two Levels of Meaning

In the second and third centuries, Irenaeus and Tertullian exemplify the first stage of patristic exegesis. Even though they claimed to reject philosophy, they were still sufficiently influenced by Platonism to assume that there was a spiritual meaning in Scripture that was more important than the literal meaning. Therefore, there were two levels of meaning in Scripture, the literal (or historical) and the spiritual. In the Old Testament, the historical meaning was not the spiritual meaning, so to find the spiritual meaning, one had to look beneath the literal, to the non-literal (the typological or allegorical). In the New Testament, the historical meaning *was* the spiritual meaning, but even then, the smallest of details in the narrative could be allegorized to find an even deeper meaning. The spiritual meaning was always the christological meaning, and the overall concern is that the interpretation lead one to faith in Christ as the Second Person of the Trinity. The basic rule of exegesis would be: if the literal interpretation of any text does not lead one to Christ, then one must look for a spiritual meaning.

Stage 2: Three Levels of Meaning

The second stage covers the third through the fifth centuries, though after the third century it is most prevalent in the West and Alexandria. This is traditionally said to be the legacy of Clement of Alexandria and Origen, and the catechetical school of Alexandria is often associated with the methodology of allegorical interpretation. Other notable examples of stage two include Ambrose of Milan and the early careers of Augustine and Jerome.

In this stage the interpretation of Scripture was compared to an ancient understanding of the human person, who was thought to have three parts: body, soul, and spirit (or mind). Thus there were three levels of meaning in Scripture. The literal

[97] Irenaeus of Lyons, *Against Heresies*, 3.21.2.

meaning was parallel to the body, grounded in the material world and therefore historical, but less valuable than the spiritual. The spiritual meaning was compared to the spirit, or mind. While there may be some value in the literal meaning, the most important meaning for the Church is the spiritual meaning, since that is where the Church gets its doctrine. As before, the spiritual meaning can come by typological or allegorical interpretation. But this stage adds a third level of meaning, in between the literal and the spiritual. Corresponding to the soul of the human is the moral meaning of the text. This is the practical relevance for Christian behavior. It is not as important as theology (the spiritual meaning) but it is more important than history (the literal meaning). Therefore, the three levels of meaning can be expressed in this way:

Literal (Historical) — What Jesus did
Moral (Ethical) — What we should do
Spiritual (Theological) — What we should believe

The three levels of meaning were described using an analogy of an egg. Just as an egg has three layers: shell, white, and yolk, so Scripture has three layers which need to be peeled back to reveal its deepest meanings. One has to begin with the shell (the literal meaning), but one cannot stop there. In reality, not every text even has a literal meaning (for example the highly symbolic book of Revelation). However, because of divine inspiration, every text has a spiritual meaning.[98] The serious student of Scripture cannot be satisfied with the surface meaning but must go on to the deeper meanings. For Origen, spiritual maturity meant seeing the spiritual meaning in Scripture.[99] Thus, he came to conclude that there may be things in the text which are not historically true but are nevertheless "truthful" in the sense of beneficial.[100]

98 Dockery, *Biblical Interpretation Then and Now*, 92; see Origen, *Against Celsus*, 4.49.

99 Thus the problems with reconciling a literal interpretation of the creation accounts in Genesis with science (even as Origen knew it) were overcome by claiming that God intentionally put historical inaccuracies into the text as a red flag to alert the spiritually mature reader to stop looking at the literal level and look for the deeper meaning.

100 Dockery, *Biblical Interpretation Then and Now*, 83, 92–93. See Origen, *Against Celsus*, 4.71. Note that Origen took this to the extreme, eventually saying that the spiritual meaning was only for a spiritual or intellectual elite. The literal meaning, on the other hand, was there to keep the common people occupied. In this way he comes close to the spiritual caste system of some gnostics who proposed that the three levels of the human person (body, soul, spirit) applied to three types of people (physical people, "soulish" people, and spiritual people). For these gnostics, full salvation was available only to the Spirituals.

Stage 3: Reaction Against Allegory — Back to Two Levels of Meaning

Stage three covers roughly the fourth and fifth centuries, primarily in the East (Antioch, Palestine, and Asia Minor). It is a reaction against allegorical interpretation (perceived as over-allegorizing) and a renewed appreciation for the literal meaning. This methodology is traditionally associated with the church in Antioch and contributes to the perception of a (often overexaggerated) rivalry between Antioch and Alexandria. It seems to begin officially with Lucian of Antioch (ca. AD 240–312) and his dislike of Origen, though it may go back as far as Theophilus.[101] In his later career, Jerome would also find affinity with this school of thought. If the Alexandrians were influenced by Plato, the Antiochenes were influenced more by Aristotle.[102] They wanted a more concrete interpretation and feared that the allegorical method would lead to excessive speculation, which would ultimately lead to heresy.[103] This was, in fact, one of the primary criticisms of Origen. Opponents of allegory argued that it could be used to make the text say anything the interpreter wants it to say. The allegorization of every detail in a biblical story was being used, they feared, to draw out messages that were not really there. In a sense, allegory had disengaged the text from its historical context, and (it was argued) like a ship without an anchor, it was left adrift in a sea of speculation.[104]

This does not mean that interpretation was no longer going to be christological. However, the Antiochenes recognized the necessity of taking the historical provenance of a text seriously, to the point of advocating study of the Old Testament on its own terms, apart from the New Testament.[105] Therefore, they gravitated toward the literal or historical interpretation as primary because they wanted to understand the intended meaning of the author of a text, before attempting to find a meaning for the Church.[106] In other words, to know what a text *means,* one first has to know what it *meant.*

[101] Theophilus had attempted to redeem a literal interpretation of the creation accounts in Genesis by saying that God had made the plants before the sun to show that it was not by natural causes that creation happened, but by the will of God; Theophilus of Antioch, *To Autolycus,* 2.15; see also Dockery, *Biblical Interpretation Then and Now,* 97, 106; and Grillmeier, *Christ in Christian Tradition, Volume 1,* 167–180.

[102] Dockery, *Biblical Interpretation Then and Now,* 115.

[103] Dockery, *Biblical Interpretation Then and Now,* 117.

[104] Dockery, *Biblical Interpretation Then and Now,* 72.

[105] Dockery, *Biblical Interpretation Then and Now,* 107.

[106] Dockery, *Biblical Interpretation Then and Now,* 103–105, 119. There is also the possibility that Jewish influence in Antioch and Palestine contributed to the eastern desire to emphasize the literal interpretation. This was certainly the case with Jerome. However, the characterization of literal interpretation as a Jewish methodology is something of a

Proponents of this reactionary movement advocated using the literal sense of the text whenever possible. If there was a moral meaning to be found, it would probably be found in the plain meaning on the surface, if not in the text at hand, then somewhere in the Bible. They reasoned that if God wants us to behave a certain way, He will tell us plainly. Allegorical interpretation was still a possibility but was to be used only when absolutely necessary. Even then, the spiritual meaning must always be consistent with the literal and must never contradict the plain meaning of the text anywhere in Scripture. Thus, this stage moved back toward two levels of meaning (literal or historical and spiritual), but with a preference for the literal.

Stage 4: The Middle Way — Four Levels of Meaning

The final stage of patristic exegesis represents a kind of middle way between extreme allegory and the rejection of allegory. This stage begins in the late fourth and early fifth centuries, and continues on into the Middle Ages. Its most famous advocate is Augustine of Hippo. Augustine would agree with the Antiochenes that the historical meaning of the Scriptures is the foundation for all other meaning, and that the spiritual meaning must be grounded in the historical.[107] Interpretation without a sense of tradition would always lead to heresy.[108] On the other hand, Augustine maintained that the historical meaning of the Old Testament was not always adequate for the Church, and that the Old Testament had to be read through the lens of the New. For Augustine, biblical history was for the purpose of prophecy, not history for its own sake.[109] Therefore, if the literal meaning did not point to Christ, a deeper meaning must be sought.

Augustine's interpretive touchstone was the law of love. Any interpretation of Scripture that did not lead one to love God and neighbor was incorrect.[110] Therefore if the literal/historical meaning did not accomplish this goal, one needed to look for other layers of meaning. Even the allegorization of minor details was fair game if it supported the rule of love.[111] Thus, Augustine incorporated what he saw as the best elements of the prior stages and brought the art of interpretation to a certain

---

caricature, since Jewish interpreters did use allegory and often saw multiple meanings in a text. See Dockery, *Biblical Interpretation Then and Now*, 27, 32, 76.

[107] Dockery, *Biblical Interpretation Then and Now*, 28.

[108] Dockery, *Biblical Interpretation Then and Now*, 71–72.

[109] Dockery, *Biblical Interpretation Then and Now*, 139; see Augustine of Hippo, *City of God*, 17.3.

[110] Augustine must have realized the danger of using allegory with such a hermeneutical presupposition. It is a short and slippery slope from "whatever does not promote love" to "whatever I don't agree with."

[111] Dockery, *Biblical Interpretation Then and Now*, 133–134.

plateau for the Church. As he understood it, there were four levels of meaning in Scripture, one literal and three spiritual.[112] The literal meaning includes not only the historical situation but also the original (human) author's intended meaning. The three levels of spiritual meaning are the analogical (which included both allegory and typology); the moral (what is expected of us, based on what we believe about Christ); and the anagogical (vertical allegory):[113]

Literal (Historical) — What happened
Analogical (Theological) — What we should believe
Moral (Ethical) — How we should behave
Anagogical (Eschatological) — What we hope for

[112] Dockery, *Biblical Interpretation Then and Now,* 145, 158–159.

[113] The moral interpretation is based on Jewish *midrash,* or commentary/homily. The anagogical interpretation is based on Jewish *pesher,* the interpretation of dreams and prophecy using metaphor. This assumes an apocalyptic promise-fulfillment format; see Dockery, *Biblical Interpretation Then and Now,* 29–31, 38.

Assumptions of Patristic Exegesis

"In matters of theology, absolute confidence is possible for only
two classes of people: saints and idiots."
— Origen, *Commentary on Genesis*

1. The Divine Inspiration of the Sacred Texts, Including the New Testament (2 Pet. 3:14–16)
   The texts are understood as inspired by the same Holy Spirit who inspired the prophets.
   The text of Scripture is the recorded voice of the divine Logos.
   Therefore, every word is there for a reason (this often leads to allegorizing all the details).
   The written word is another incarnation of the living Word.
   Like the body of Jesus, it enfleshes the Word of God.
   And like Jesus, it is both human and divine.

2. Revelation Is Progressive
   Things get clearer over time, and the New Testament is clearer than the Old Testament.
   New interpretations can build on, but cannot contradict, established ones.
   This assumes the authority of the Church through apostolic succession.

3. There Are Multiple Meanings in Any Given Text
   The human author's intended meaning is not the only valid meaning.
   This is because the ultimate author is really God.

4. Paradox Is to Be Embraced, Not Avoided
   Two apparently contradictory texts can be held in tension, where both are seen as true.
   Assuming divine inspiration, one set of texts cannot be ignored in favor of another.
   The question then becomes not whether a biblical text is true but *how* it is true.

5. Patristic Exegesis Follows the Lead of Apostolic Exegesis
   Interpreting the Old Testament in light of the life and ministry of Jesus, it is always christocentric.
   Even Old Testament passages that were never thought of as messianic become prophecies.
   Combining texts from different documents, such as the "Suffering Servant" (Isa. 53),
   with messianic prophecies to explain why Jesus as Messiah suffers death.

6. Scripture Interprets Scripture
   This assumes an internal integrity and consistency of message, even across the testaments.
   It is based on the assumption of divine inspiration.
   Interpreting one text by the application of other (clearer) texts.

7. In General, Interpretation of the Old Testament Was Non-Literal
    The most important (that is, christocentric) meaning is hidden under the surface.
    The two main types of non-literal interpretation are typology and allegory.

8. In General, Interpretation of the New Testament Was Literal
    While the (Christian) meaning was hidden in the Old Testament, it is usually plain in the New Testament.
    Some passages, such as parables and apocalyptic text, must still be interpreted nonliterally.
    The gnostics tended to interpret the Old Testament literally and the New Testament non-literally.

9. Interpretation Is Meant to Be Done in the Context of Prayer
    Interpretation is something done in community (2 Pet. 1:20), as part of a devotional life.
    Doing theology was not an academic exercise; it was part of the ministry of a pastor.
    Interpreting Scripture is an act of worship and must be accompanied by prayer.

The History of Patristic Exegesis

Stage 1: Two Levels of Meaning

Roughly the second and third centuries.

Interpretation is literal or non-literal (spiritual).

When the literal meaning does not point to Christ, look for a spiritual meaning.

Non-literal (spiritual) interpretation can be typology or allegory.

The higher/deeper meaning is the non-literal (based on a Platonic assumption that the spiritual is more real).

The key is Christ, and the best interpretation is always the christocentric interpretation.

- Literal versus spiritual (with the assumption that spiritual is better)

Stage 2: Three Levels of Meaning

Roughly the third through the fifth centuries, especially in the West and in Alexandria.

The legacy of Origen and the Alexandrian "school" (that is, methodology) of emphasis on allegory.

Based on ancient tripartite anthropology of body, soul, and spirit.

Scripture is like an egg, with a shell, white, and yolk.

To get the yolk, you have to start with the shell (the literal meaning, on the surface).

However, the serious student of the Bible cannot stop with the shell, but must go deeper.

Even more of an insistence that the spiritual (non-literal) meaning is more important.

- Literal (Historical/physical): What Jesus did
- Moral (Ethical/soul): What we should do
- Allegorical (Theological/spirit): What we should believe

Stage 3: Reaction against Allegory — Back to Two Levels of Meaning

Roughly the fourth and fifth centuries, especially in Antioch and the East.

Recognizing the problems of overallegorizing every detail.

Recognizing that allegory can be used to take the meaning out of an uncomfortable text.

A trend to shift away from the non-literal in favor of the literal meaning.

A new appreciation for studying the Old Testament in its Jewish/Hebrew context.

- Literal/Historical: To be used whenever possible
- Allegorical: To be used only when absolutely necessary, even then it must conform to the literal

Phase 4: Four Levels of Meaning — A Kind of Middle Way

An attempt at a middle way, or balance of the literal and non-literal.

Beginning in the fifth century and continuing into the Middle Ages.

Recognizing the necessity of taking the historical context seriously.

But also recognizing that the historical interpretation was not always adequate.

Also maintaining that the Old Testament had to be read through the lens of the New Testament to be relevant for the Church.

The spiritual was to be anchored in the literal/historical.

- Literal/Historical: What happened
- Spiritual (three types):
  - Analogical/Theological: What we should believe
  - Moral/Ethical: How we should behave
  - Anagogical (Vertical Allegory)/Eschatological: What we hope for

8

The Theologians and the Third Century

Irenaeus of Lyons

Born in the AD 120s in Asia Minor, he was probably from Smyrna. He was a student of his bishop, Polycarp, which makes him a third-generation bishop, only two steps away from the apostles themselves. Polycarp sent him to Gaul to be a priest under bishop Pothinus of Lyons. On the way, he may have spent some time in Rome, studying under Justin Martyr (or if not, he had certainly read Justin's writings and was a student of Justin through his works). As a priest in Lyons under bishop Pothinus, Irenaeus got involved in a controversy over the Montanists, who were being accused of heresy. Irenaeus was probably chosen to represent the church of Lyons on the issue because he was from Asia Minor, as the Montanists were, and in that capacity he traveled to Rome to hand deliver a letter to the bishop of Rome, Eleutherius (bishop AD 175–189).[1] While Irenaeus was in Rome, in the year AD 177, persecution escalated in Lyons and Vienne, and bishop Pothinus was martyred. Irenaeus returned to Lyons to find that he had been elected bishop. The account of the martyrs of Lyons and Vienne, written as the *Letter of the Churches of Vienne and Lyons to the Churches of Asia and Phrygia* (see below) was probably written by Irenaeus himself.

As bishop, Irenaeus also became involved in negotiations between the bishop of Rome and a faction from the East that was not celebrating Easter on a Sunday but was figuring the date for Easter based on the Passover date of the 14th of Nissan (see above). Called *Quartodecimans* (fourteeners), they saw themselves as sticking with the original method of calculating the date for Easter, when the rest of the Church was moving to a new way of calculating the date that would conform to Sunday worship. Victor of Rome (bishop AD 189–199) wanted to excommunicate the Quartodecimans in Rome (or perhaps all of them worldwide). Irenaeus talked

[1] The letter is preserved in Eusebius of Caesarea, *Ecclesiastical History*, 5.4.

him out of it, in part based on the argument that Victor's predecessors tolerated the practice, so to change that policy would be a departure from Tradition.[2]

Irenaeus wrote several works, of which only two are extant (three, if we count the martyr acts of Lyons and Viennes), nevertheless Irenaeus marks an important turning point in the history of the Church.[3] Before Irenaeus, the writers were catechists, ethicists, apologists, and philosophers. Although Irenaeus's work is heavily influenced by Justin Martyr, and to some extent Theophilus of Antioch, he surpasses them in the explanation of christology and in theology in general. Irenaeus was the first real theologian since the apostles, because he is intentional about supporting his arguments from Scripture rather than philosophy. He believed that reliance on human reason (philosophy) results in heresy, so for him, the Christian Faith must be founded on divine revelation, as opposed to human reason. With the transition from apology to theology, the primary audience for the documents in question is now Christian, so the goal of writing is no longer simply apologetics or even evangelization, but the rooting out of heresy and the clarification of orthodoxy. Correct belief matters, since to believe in the *wrong* Christ is to believe in no Christ at all.

Most of Irenaeus's quotations and references to Scripture are from the Old Testament, for two reasons. First, Irenaeus was arguing primarily against gnosticism, which rejected the Old Testament and its connection to Jesus Christ. Therefore, Irenaeus meant to show how the Old Testament pointed to Christ, and how the two testaments were connected. Second, the New Testament was still in its early stages of development, a development to which Irenaeus himself would contribute, as we have seen.

According to tradition, Irenaeus died a martyr in the year AD 202, which is reasonable to believe, since there was a significant escalation in persecution in that year. However, there is no evidence of a tradition of his martyrdom until about the fifth or sixth century, so that must remain somewhat uncertain. In any case, Irenaeus leaves us two of the most important early Church documents, and an extremely important legacy of influence on later theologians.

[2] See Eusebius of Caesarea, *Ecclesiastical History*, 5.23–24.

[3] In addition to the two treatises (and possibly the martyr acts of Lyons and Vienne), we do have a few letters written by Irenaeus, including the letters to the bishops of Rome, as well some other fragments preserved in the writings of later authors; see Eusebius of Caesarea, *Ecclesiastical History*, 5.1–4, 20, 24, 26.

Against Heresies

Written after AD 177 and before AD 189,[4] the actual title of this document is *The Refutation and Overthrowal of Knowledge Falsely So-Called,* however it came to be known by its shorter title already by the fourth century.[5] The "so-called knowledge" is a reference to gnosticism, named from the Greek word *gnosis,* which means "knowledge." As indicated above, gnosticism was actually a vast array of philosophical systems, based on an extreme dualism, but only loosely connected to each other by a similarity of concepts. While there were many different gnostic teachers on the fringes of the Church in the second century, Irenaeus attempts to explain and refute them all one by one, often going into great detail about the gnostic systems, which (while it can be tedious for the reader) is invaluable for the historian.[6]

The various forms of gnosticism incorporated complicated and elaborate cosmological myths, which Irenaeus attacks, and sometimes mocks. However, the most important problem with gnosticism was that it tended to deny, or at least diminish, the real humanity of Christ. For the gnostics, Christ was either a phantom who only appeared to be human, or a spirit who "possessed," or temporarily indwelt, a semi-tangible Jesus. For them, Christ had no connection to the Old Testament and His Father was not the God of the Hebrews. In fact, as we have seen, some taught that the creation of the material world was a cosmic blunder, and Christ came to save humanity from the inept (or evil) Creator God of the Old Testament. He would do this by bringing secret knowledge (*gnosis*), which would allow the enlightened to ascend to the highest levels of Heaven at the point of death.

Irenaeus countered the gnostics' claim to secret knowledge with the concept of apostolic succession. He reasoned that if Jesus had indeed brought secret knowledge, He would have told the apostles, who would in turn have told their successors, the bishops.[7] Since Irenaeus himself was a bishop, he argued that if there were any secret knowledge from Jesus, he would know it. He further criticized

4 See Irenaeus of Lyons, *Against Heresies,* 3.3.3, where he says that Eleutherius was bishop of Rome at the time it was written.

5 See Eusebius of Caesarea, *Ecclesiastical History,* 3.23.3.

6 We must keep in mind, of course, that gleaning information about an ancient religious system from the writings of its opponents is difficult, since we cannot take for granted that the orthodox writers were always accurate or fair in their representation of the heresy in question. On the other hand, ongoing discoveries of gnostic texts continue to demonstrate that Irenaeus did understand what the gnostics taught and although he criticizes it mercilessly, he does present it more or less faithfully. In any case, much of the information about gnosticism presented above is from Irenaeus's *Against Heresies.*

7 Irenaeus of Lyons, *Against Heresies,* 3.3.1–2.

the gnostics for claiming to know the secrets of God, while ignoring divine revelation.[8] To counteract the gnostic rejection of the Old Testament, Irenaeus showed the continuity between the Old and New Testaments. Creation was not a mistake, and in fact Christ was the agent of creation. The God of the Old Testament is the God and Father of the Lord Jesus Christ, and creation is good. Irenaeus further connected the Old Testament to the New by the use of typology. Old Testament types foreshadow parallel events in the life and ministry of Jesus and the early Church. For example, Adam was created from the virgin earth and was the first man; Christ was born of the Virgin and was the second Adam (1 Cor. 15:44–47). Eve disobeyed God and brought death into the world; Mary obeyed God and brought life by becoming the mother of Jesus.[9] Irenaeus described Mary as the Untier of Knots, because "the knot of Eve's disobedience was loosed by the obedience of Mary. For what the virgin Eve had bound fast through unbelief, this did the Virgin Mary set free through faith."[10] Also, the tree of the knowledge of good and evil in the Garden of Eden was the occasion for sin; the tree of Golgotha, the cross, was the remedy for sin. Thus, Christ can be seen in the Old Testament, which prepared the world for His arrival.

The Ebionites had reasoned that since Christ suffered, He could not be divine. The docetics and gnostics said that since He was divine, He could not have suffered. Ironically, both extremes were trying to safeguard the impassibility and immutability of divinity. The docetics and gnostics went so far as to reject the Old Testament because its anthropomorphisms seemed to describe a God who changes. Irenaeus, as a proponent of *Logos* christology, affirmed both the human and divine natures of Christ against these two extremes. For Irenaeus, the key is the Incarnation. The divine *Logos* became human, so the impassible became passible, by becoming human. Technically, the divine nature of Christ remains impassible, while the human nature can suffer and die for the sake of humanity's reconciliation with God. To be clear, this does not imply that Jesus is the name for the human nature and Christ is the name for the divine nature (as some had speculated), but that Jesus Christ is one Person who has both a human and a divine nature. For Irenaeus and the other writers of the late second through the early third centuries, the humanity of Christ is the Son of Man, or Son of David; the divinity of Christ is the Son of God. The Son of Man can suffer His passion, while the Son of God remains impassible.

[8] Irenaeus of Lyons, *Against Heresies*, 2.28.9, 4.6.4.

[9] Irenaeus of Lyons, *Against Heresies*, 3.22.4, 5.19.1.

[10] Irenaeus of Lyons, *Against Heresies*, 3.22.4, translation in *Ante-Nicene Fathers*, vol, 1, 455.

Finally, Irenaeus is a pioneer of what is often called the *wonderful exchange*, that is, a way of talking about the Incarnation that is based on Paul's words in 2 Corinthians 8:9, "For your sake he became poor although he was rich, so that by his poverty you might become rich," and Galatians 3:13–14. Paul wrote, "Christ ransomed us from the curse of the law by becoming a curse for us, for it is written, 'Cursed be everyone who hangs on a tree,' that the blessing of Abraham might be extended to the Gentiles through Christ Jesus, so that we might receive the promise of the Spirit through faith." In other words, while some were saying that the fact that Jesus was executed should disqualify Him as the Messiah, Paul did not deny the curse of Deuteronomy 21:23, but rather embraced it as part of God's plan for salvation. Jesus took on our curse (a curse He did not deserve) so that we could have His blessing (eternal life). Irenaeus, following Paul, wrote that "the Word of God, our Lord Jesus Christ, who did, through his transcendent love, become what we are, that he might bring us to even be what he is himself."[11] This is the wonderful exchange, that He became what we are — human — to make it possible that we could become what He is, a "son" (heir) of God, who will inherit immortality and eternal life.

Demonstration of the Apostolic Preaching

Sometimes translated *Proof of the Apostolic Preaching* (or *Teaching*), this much shorter document is a good recommendation for the student of early Christianity who wants a firsthand introduction to Irenaeus. It was probably written in the late AD 180s, definitely after *Against Heresies* since Irenaeus refers to that document in the text. It is addressed to a priest named Marcianus, who may have been Irenaeus's brother, and it amounts to a combination of internal apology and catechesis, written for a Christian audience. The literary form is that of a public letter, which means it was probably meant to be read out loud to a congregation.

Irenaeus's *Demonstration of the Apostolic Preaching* is in many ways a summary of orthodox Christian theology up to the end of the second century, and Irenaeus himself thought of it that way. Therefore, it is very valuable for the study of the early Church, in spite of the fact that Irenaeus got a bit of his history wrong, and believed that Jesus was crucified during the reign of Claudius. Nevertheless, for Irenaeus, all of human history is ordered and orchestrated toward making salvation possible

[11] Irenaeus of Lyons, *Against Heresies*, bk. 5, preface, translation in *Ante-Nicene Fathers*, vol. 1, 526. See also James L. Papandrea, "Loaning and Borrowing: Deification in Novatian of Rome" in *Deification in the Latin Patristic Tradition*, ed. Jared Ortiz (Washington, DC: Catholic University of America Press, 2019), for the connection between Christ's *kenosis* (Phil. 2:7) and the believer's *theosis* (2 Pet. 1:4).

(salvation history), and this is the *economy* of God, and so the treatise begins with an outline of the ways in which the coming of Christ was predicted in the prophetic writings of the Old Testament.[12]

The doctrinal content represents *Logos* christology, in which the pre-incarnate Word of God can be seen in the theophanies of the Old Testament. This is because God the Father cannot be localized in time and space (or *circumscribed*), so any appearance of God in the days before Jesus must be an appearance of the pre-incarnate Christ.[13] Therefore, it was God the Son, the pre-incarnate *Logos*, who walked in the Garden of Eden and talked with Adam, not God the Father.[14] And for Irenaeus, because the Son is the Word, it was also the Son who inspired and spoke through the prophets, rather than the Father or the Holy Spirit.[15]

A milestone of early Christian doctrine is apparent in this document, where Irenaeus becomes the first of the Church Fathers to clearly articulate that the Father and Son are of the same essence.[16] The principle behind this assertion is that the one who is begotten (or, *generated*) from God must also be God (i.e., divine). In other words, because the Son is begotten of (generated from) the Father, the Son shares the same divinity with the Father, and therefore also the same divine power. Thus, Irenaeus articulated the doctrine of *consubstantiality*, affirming that the Son is of the same divinity as the Father (Phil. 2:6; Col. 2:9).

Yet there is a distinction between the Father and Son, and an order, or hierarchy — also referred to as the *economy* of God — within the Trinity.[17] The distinction between the Father and Son is described in terms of relative approachability. The Father is utterly transcendent and invisible, and therefore is not directly approachable.

[12] The term *economy* refers to an order or arrangement. The concept of the *economy of God* is used in two distinct ways in the early Church Fathers. It can refer to the history of God's activity, which is seen as progressive and leading toward salvation (salvation history), or it can refer to the hierarchical arrangement of Persons within the Trinity: the Father, Son, and Holy Spirit (see below). The latter is an internal hierarchy of authority within the Trinity that is based on the relationship of the Father as unbegotten and the Son as begotten of the Father. This is not to be confused with the later concept of *economic Trinity*, which refers to external (*ad extra*) operations of the Trinity in human history. That definition of the term does not exist before the fourth century and, even then, only in the East.

[13] Irenaeus of Lyons, *Demonstration of the Apostolic Preaching*, 45; see also 30, 43, 51.

[14] Irenaeus of Lyons, *Demonstration of the Apostolic Preaching*, 12.

[15] Irenaeus of Lyons, *Demonstration of the Apostolic Preaching*, 49.

[16] Irenaeus of Lyons, *Demonstration of the Apostolic Preaching*, 47.

[17] Irenaeus of Lyons, *Demonstration of the Apostolic Preaching*, 7. See note 12 above.

The Son, on the other hand, can be visible and circumscribed, and therefore can appear in time and space, primarily in His Incarnation but also in the pre-Incarnation theophanies. This means that no one can approach the Father directly, but must approach the Father through the Son (John 14:6). Put another way, the Spirit brings us to the Son, and the Son brings us to the Father.[18]

Furthermore, there is a hierarchy of authority in the Trinity, in which the Son obeys the Father.[19] The Son is the Father's messenger, the agent of the Father who comes with the Father's authority but who nevertheless does the Father's will, not His own (John 6:38). This means that as the Sender, the Father has a level of authority above that of the Son, the Messenger.[20] In describing the Trinity, Irenaeus used an analogy of anointing. The Father is the one who anoints, the Son is the anointed one, and the Holy Spirit is the ointment. Thus, Irenaeus has set the stage for the third- and fourth-century descriptions of the Trinity.

For Irenaeus, the Father, Son, and Holy Spirit are the "three articles of our seal," a reference to Baptism in the triune name.[21] A correct understanding of the Trinity is important because it has implications for the sacraments, and especially Baptism, which makes one a Christian. Baptism was seen as spiritual rebirth, the "seal of regeneration," "the seal of eternal life," and the seal of adoption by God.[22] It was analogous to Jewish circumcision, which was also understood as a seal, or mark of membership in the community.[23] In Baptism (assuming that the rite also included Confirmation by the imposition of hands), one received the Holy Spirit, however for Irenaeus it was correct belief and morality that kept the Holy Spirit from leaving the individual after Baptism.[24] So Baptism is one's entrance into the family of God, but orthodoxy was required to maintain that membership. In other words, Baptism may be a rebirth and a sealing for eternal life, but one could lose one's salvation if one accepted a heretical view of Christ.

[18] Irenaeus of Lyons, *Demonstration of the Apostolic Preaching*, 7; *Against Heresies*, 5.36.1–2. In actual practice, it was believed that one could not get to the Father except through the Son, and one could not get to the Son except through the Church. It was within the Church that one would find the Holy Spirit.

[19] Irenaeus of Lyons, *Demonstration of the Apostolic Preaching*, 51.

[20] Irenaeus of Lyons, *Demonstration of the Apostolic Preaching*, 56.

[21] Irenaeus of Lyons, *Demonstration of the Apostolic Preaching*, 100.

[22] Irenaeus of Lyons, *Demonstration of the Apostolic Preaching*, 3.

[23] Irenaeus of Lyons, *Demonstration of the Apostolic Preaching*, 24.

[24] Irenaeus of Lyons, *Demonstration of the Apostolic Preaching*, 42; see also Hermas, *The Shepherd*, 33.3, 41. Hermas says that the Holy Spirit can be "choked out" of a person who invites evil into his or her life by harboring anger.

Tertullian

Septimius Tertullianus was born about AD 145–150 in North Africa, probably in Carthage.[25] As far as we can tell, he lived into the AD 220s. Since his writings come at or after the turn of the century, he is considered the first theologian of the third century. He was also the first Christian theologian to write in Latin, and he coined the Latin term for the Trinity, *Trinitas*. For these reasons, he is called the father of Latin theology.

Tertullian was raised in a pagan home and given the standard classical education.[26] It has traditionally been assumed that he was a lawyer, or at least had studied law, though this is far from certain. Eusebius tells us that he was "skilled in Roman law."[27] It is true that he is famous for having used Roman legal terminology to describe the Trinity, and his apologetics do contain some legal argumentation, but it is probably the case that any educated Roman would have known enough legal jargon and rhetoric to apply them to theology as he did.[28] Tertullian's genius was not in the world of law, but it emerged when he became a Christian in about AD 185. It seems Tertullian got married shortly after his Baptism, so it may be that his wife had something to do with his conversion. In any case, he took to the Church and became one of its most important proponents, even helping to define Christianity itself by way of its doctrines.

It is not clear whether Tertullian was ever ordained. There is a tradition that he was a priest in Rome before the turn of the century, however he seems to consider himself a lay person in some of his writings.[29] On the other hand, the documents in question were probably written after he left Rome, and other documents appear to be homilies. If he was a priest, he was never a bishop. Around the turn of the third century, he apparently had a falling out with the leadership in Rome, possibly over the bishop's rejection of the Montanists, with whom Tertullian had begun

[25] For a detailed life of Tertullian, see Barnes, *Tertullian*. Some sources give Tertullian's full name as Quintus Septimius Florens Tertullianus. Note that Barnes thinks he was born a bit later, around AD 170; see also Dunn, *Tertullian*, 3–11.

[26] Barnes, *Tertullian*, 246–247.

[27] Eusebius of Caesarea, *Ecclesiastical History*, 2.2.4.

[28] Barnes, *Tertullian*, 24–25.

[29] Barnes, *Tertullian*, 11, 58; Dunn, *Tertullian*, 3; see Tertullian, *On Exhortation to Chastity*, 7.3; *On Monogamy*, 12.2. The tradition that Tertullian was a priest is not attested to before Jerome. According to Barnes, there is no evidence that Tertullian was ever in Rome, however he seems to have at least visited Rome based on comments made in *On the Apparel of Women*, 1.7. Note that a priest in Rome at the end of the second century would not necessarily be expected to be celibate.

to associate.[30] It is possible that Tertullian had been a priest in Rome, but left the priesthood when he left Rome, and afterward considered himself a lay teacher.[31] This would be consistent with the Montanist movement, since their claim to the gift of prophecy often put them at odds with the hierarchy.

Tertullian was apparently drawn to the Montanists for their stricter morality, their emphasis on continuing charismatic inspiration, and for their millennialism. Their belief in ongoing prophecy combined with a conviction of the immanent return of Christ led to their ethical rigorism and millenarian interpretation of the book of Revelation.[32] For Tertullian, who was both a strict moralist and a devoted student of the writings of Irenaeus, the Montanists had it right, and they made the mainstream Church and its Roman leadership look morally lax. However, the reader of Tertullian's writings must never assume that he always speaks for Montanism, or that everything he writes is representative of Montanist teaching.[33]

Tertullian criticized the Roman bishops for allowing second marriages, which he said was the same as forgiving the sin of adultery (Matt. 19:9).[34] The Montanists, on the other hand, did not want to allow second marriages.[35] Because Tertullian came to disagree with the Roman bishops over matters of discipline, he concluded that authority was not necessarily in the bishops, but wherever the Holy Spirit is.[36] Thus, in practice, he apparently allowed that new prophetic revelation might take precedence over apostolic authority, though he maintained that prophecy would never contradict Scripture.

It is often stated that Tertullian "became" a Montanist in the first decade of the third century. He did return to Carthage, and he was influenced by the Montanists, however it is not accurate to describe this move as in any way leaving the mainstream

30 Tertullian, *Against Praxeas*, 1.7.

31 It has been argued that Tertullian's *On the Pallium*, 3–4 represents anti-Roman sentiment.

32 That is, early millenarians such as Papias, Irenaeus, and Tertullian believed in a literal reign of Christ on earth that was to come in the future, but before the final judgment and the establishment of the Kingdom of God. They did not believe in a "rapture," and in fact such an idea did not exist in the Church before the modern era. The Montanists were millenarians, which is probably one of the reasons Tertullian was attracted to them. As a student of Irenaeus, their interpretation of the book of Revelation matched Irenaeus's reading, not to mention his interpretation of the book of Genesis.

33 Tabbernee, "Montanism and the Cult of the Martyrs in Roman North Africa," 304.

34 Rankin, *Tertullian and the Church*, 28–29.

35 Tertullian, *On Modesty*, 1.2, 10.12. Note that Tertullian rejected *The Shepherd* as Scripture because it seemed to advocate forgiveness of adultery; cf. Cyprian of Carthage, *Epistles*, 55.21; see Rankin, *Tertullian and the Church*, 41–42, 46.

36 Rankin, *Tertullian and the Church*, 115, 195–196.

Church or converting to something new. The Montanists did not consider themselves a separate movement, and while there was some debate within the mainstream Church over whether Montanists should be considered heretics, the Montanist movement was not (yet) a schism.[37] Tertullian never thought of himself as leaving the Church, rather he saw himself as joining a prophetic reform movement that would critique the Church from within.[38]

Nevertheless, Tertullian is often considered a Montanist after about AD 207–208, though we cannot precisely date his move away from Rome (both literally and figuratively).[39] His ethical treatises reflect a stricter (rigorist or Montanist) morality, sometimes critical of the bishops who were more lenient than Tertullian would like when it came to the forgiveness of sins and the Reconciliation of sinners.[40] But his theological writings were thoroughly orthodox, and in fact helped define orthodoxy, both for his own time and for the future.[41] Tertullian takes the theology of Irenaeus to the next level by building on the concept of the one essence of divinity, and describing the Trinity in terms that would become standard for the western, Latin-speaking Church. In fact, it may have been the Montanist influence that brought Tertullian to clarify the full divine personhood of the Holy Spirit, in addition to the Father and Son.[42] Although Tertullian supported the idea of ongoing revelation through charismatic prophecy, his writings are at every turn grounded in Scripture and prior Tradition. For him, Scripture was still the primary authority, and the inspiration of the Holy Spirit would help interpret Scripture and Tradition, but would never contradict it.[43]

Unlike the apologists, Tertullian was a true theologian, and although he did write some apologetics, he followed Irenaeus in making a strict distinction between

[37] Rankin, *Tertullian and the Church*, 29–32; see also Tabbernee, *Fake Prophecy and Polluted Sacraments*, 404, 417–418. As Tabbernee says, "Montanism may never have existed apart from *within* 'mainstream' Christianity in North Africa" (emphasis his), however this is not necessarily the case for Montanism in other places. Tabbernee clarifies that Tertullian was only at the beginning of the period that would see the separation of Montanism into distinct congregations, and even then, it was largely due to the fact that they were being excommunicated from the mainstream Church. Still, there is no evidence that Tertullian belonged to a congregation that was exclusively Montanist.

[38] Rankin, *Tertullian and the Church*, 27ff, 41, 44.

[39] Rankin, *Tertullian and the Church*, xv, 3, 30; see Tertullian, *On the Soul*, 9.4.

[40] Barnes, *Tertullian*, 141.

[41] Dunn, *Tertullian*, 9.

[42] Rankin, *Tertullian and the Church*, 50.

[43] Tertullian, *On Monogamy*, 3.9.

theology and philosophy. He was outwardly very critical of philosophy, though he could not help but be influenced by it, as anyone who had received a classical education would.[44] But as a Christian he came to believe (like Irenaeus) that heresy comes from a misuse of philosophy. He famously said, "What indeed has Athens to do with Jerusalem? What concord is there between the Academy and the Church?"[45] For Tertullian, philosophy leads to paganism (i.e., polytheism), or, in the context of the Church, docetism and gnosticism. In fact, he criticized polytheism as illogical, saying that belief in multiple gods necessarily implies that those gods cannot be omnipotent or omnipresent if they have to make room for each other and leave certain spheres of influence to other gods. Thus the very definition of divinity (assuming omnipotence and omnipresence) requires monotheism.

As a writer, Tertullian was prolific, and it would be impossible within the scope of this book to cover all of his writings — in fact, with Tertullian we come to a point in the history of the Church where we cannot survey all of the important documents for the succeeding eras. However, for the present era there are three documents by Tertullian that are most important for the understanding of the development of the Church and its doctrine.

The Prescription against the Heretics

Possibly written while still at Rome, this is a standard internal apology. However, it is interesting for our purposes because of what Tertullian says about heresy in general, and how that illuminates the way that the early Christians of the mainstream Church saw their counterparts on the fringes.[46] According to Tertullian, heresy is the minority, while orthodoxy is the majority.[47] Just as there were followers of Jesus who left Him (John 6), heresy is the innovation that deviates from the established Tradition.[48] While orthodoxy is based on a solid foundation of apostolic succession, heresy seeks but never finds, and in fact delights in the intellectual wandering that takes no responsibility for any conclusions.[49] While orthodoxy interprets Scripture correctly, heresy takes Scripture out of context and uses it

[44] Dunn, *Tertullian*, 31–34.

[45] Tertullian, *The Prescription against the Heretics*, 7, translation in *Ante-Nicene Fathers*, vol 3, 246.

[46] Even if this document were written later, it is clear that in spite of his association with the Montanists, Tertullian considered himself theologically within the mainstream.

[47] Tertullian, *The Prescription against the Heretics*, 1.

[48] Tertullian, *The Prescription against the Heretics*, 3, 6.

[49] Tertullian, *The Prescription against the Heretics*, 10, 11, 14, 19–21, 28, 32. Tertullian is referring primarily to the gnostics.

to "prooftext" its own philosophical assumptions or speculations.[50] Yet heresy is necessary, because it becomes the occasion for orthodoxy to be clarified.[51] Still, this does not mean that heresy precedes orthodoxy, on the contrary, heresy is new (and therefore not trustworthy).[52] In the end heresy is dangerous because it is divisive, and maintaining orthodoxy is an urgent necessity for the sake of the unity of the Church.[53] In contrast to heresy, Tertullian included a version of an early creed to clarify *the rule of faith*, the definition of orthodoxy such as it was at the turn of the third century.[54] As Tertullian explains (possibly paraphrasing somewhat), this is what Christians believe:

> that there is only one God
> and that He is none other than the Creator of the world
> who produced all things out of nothing through His own Word, first of all sent forth,
> that this Word is called His Son, and under the name of God,
> was seen in diverse manners by the patriarchs,
> at last brought down by the Spirit and power of the Father into the Virgin Mary,
> was made flesh in her womb, and being born of her went forth as Jesus Christ,
> thenceforth He preached the new law and the new promise of the Kingdom of Heaven,
> worked miracles,
> having been crucified, He rose again the third day,
> having ascended into the heavens, He sat at the right hand of the Father
> sent instead of Himself the power of the Holy Spirit to lead those who believe,
> will come with glory
> to take the saints to the enjoyment of everlasting life and of the heavenly promises

50 Tertullian, *The Prescription against the Heretics*, 9, 14, 17.

51 Tertullian, *The Prescription against the Heretics*, 4, 30, 39.

52 Tertullian, *The Prescription against the Heretics*, 29, 31.

53 Tertullian, *The Prescription against the Heretics*, 20. More evidence that Tertullian did not see himself as belonging to a schism.

54 Tertullian, *The Prescription against the Heretics*, 13–14 translation of what follows is in *Ante-Nicene Fathers*, vol. 3, 249.

and to condemn the wicked to everlasting fire
after the resurrection of both of these groups shall have happened
together with the restoration of their flesh.

Apology

Following in the footsteps of Justin Martyr and Athenagoras, Tertullian wrote an apology for the Faith. The occasion of its writing may have been the edict of Septimius Severus in AD 202, which according to tradition was the year that Tertullian's hero Irenaeus was martyred.[55] Or it may have been the following year when persecution in Carthage led to the martyrdom of Perpetua and her catechism class. Tertullian's response to these events is, like the second-century apologists before him, to try to show that the Christian religion is reasonable and not a threat to the Roman way of life. In addition to demonstrating that the Christian Faith was not a threat to the empire, Tertullian also argued that there were now so many Christians in the empire that it would actually be bad for the empire to get rid of the Church.[56]

Tertullian's *Apology* contains many of the same elements and arguments as the second-century apologies. Belief in the Christian God is older, and therefore more reliable, than philosophy or paganism.[57] Pagan idols are inanimate objects made by humans, and in fact the ones made of precious metals need to be guarded.[58] In the old myths, the gods behaved badly, and so even the philosophers criticized the myths.[59] By contrast, Christians are held to a higher moral standard. They don't share their wives, seek revenge, or kill other humans (including abortion, exposure of infants, and participation in capital punishment).[60] According to Tertullian, Christians don't even cheat on their taxes![61] Other than that, he says, "We are just like you."[62] The implication is that, far from being a threat, the Church is good for the empire.

55 However, see Dunn, *Tertullian*, 17.

56 Tertullian, *Apology*, 1, 37.

57 Tertullian, *Apology*, 19, 47. The argument that Christianity is older than Greco-Roman philosophy and religion assumes that Christianity is based on the Old Testament prophets. In fact, the Christian apologists argued that anything worthwhile that the philosophers said was plagiarized from Moses and the prophets.

58 Tertullian, *Apology*, 5, 10, 12–13, 16, 25, 29. The contrast is often made between pagan gods, which are made by humans and need to be guarded by humans, and the actual God who made humans and who guards humans.

59 Tertullian, *Apology*, 11–12, 14, 46.

60 Tertullian, *Apology*, 6, 9, 37–39, 42, 44–46.

61 Tertullian, *Apology*, 42.

62 Tertullian, *Apology*, 39, 42.

In addition to the standard defense, Tertullian argued that polytheism is not logical, since if there are many gods, one cannot know about them all, let alone worship them all, and yet any gods not worshiped will be offended. If one is not afraid of the consequences of offending countless unknown gods, then those gods must have no real power.[63] In truth, the gods of the pagan pantheon are not gods, but rather demons.[64] Tertullian complained that the live-and-let-live attitude of pagan cults toward each other was not extended to the Church. Everyone else in the empire enjoyed religious freedom; why not the Christians?[65] Instead, he said, the Christians were being condemned without investigation. This is because if they were investigated, no crime would be found, and those who did the investigation would convert.[66] Are Christians accused of cannibalism? They don't even shed blood, let alone eat human flesh. Why not test them by offering them some human flesh to eat, rather than by trying to force them to make pagan sacrifices?[67] Are Christians accused of incest? There is more of a chance that those who expose their children will unknowingly marry a relative.[68] And why is it that Christians are tortured in an attempt to get them to *deny* their "crime," when at any other time, one tortures suspects to get them to confess?[69]

Tertullian further argued that it would be detrimental to the imperial economy to persecute Christians.[70] While it is true that they do not buy frankincense to be used as incense for pagan sacrifices, they do buy it for their funerals. And while it is true that they don't support the temple treasuries, they do give to the poor.[71] Finally, although it is true that (he claimed) Christians don't support the theaters, circuses, or athletic games in the arenas, they do wrestle with God in prayer for the peace of the empire.[72] In fact, Tertullian argued that in spite of the growing trend of blaming natural disasters on the presence of the Church, there were actually fewer disasters since the Christians started praying for the empire.[73] Therefore it is not in

63 Tertullian, *Apology*, 13, 24.

64 Tertullian, *Apology*, 22–23, 32.

65 Tertullian, *Apology*, 24, 28. This argument comes from Athenagoras; see Athenagoras, *A Plea for the Christians*, 1.

66 Tertullian, *Apology*, 1–2, 7. Tertullian knows of a story that Pontius Pilate converted to Christianity; see Tertullian, *Apology*, 21.

67 Tertullian, *Apology*, 9.

68 Tertullian, *Apology*, 9.

69 Tertullian, *Apology*, 2, 49.

70 Tertullian, *Apology*, 44.

71 Tertullian, *Apology*, 42.

72 Tertullian, *Apology*, 38.

73 Tertullian, *Apology*, 40.

the empire's best interest to kill Christians. Tertullian made a point to refer to the emperor Trajan's letter to Pliny, which forbade seeking out Christians.[74] He also quoted a story that the emperor Tiberius wanted to put a statue of Jesus Christ up in the Pantheon in Rome.[75] The point he was trying to make was that good emperors (like Tiberius) do not persecute the Church, but bad emperors (like the universally hated Nero) do persecute the Church.[76]

Against Praxeas

Tertullian's most important theological work is the treatise *Against Praxeas*. No one knows who Praxeas was, and in fact it might be a pseudonym. Whoever he was, he was apparently a confessor who was critical of the Montanists, and according to Tertullian, was at least partially responsible for the Roman church's rejection of Montanism as an acceptable expression of Christianity.[77] But the larger problem was that he was an adherent of *modalism*, a heresy which diminished the distinction between the Persons of the Trinity in an attempt to protect monotheism by emphasizing the oneness of God (see below). It could be that Praxeas was an early teacher of modalism, but it is equally possible that he was just a bit behind the times with regard to trinitarian theology, holding on to elements within early *Logos* christology that blurred the distinction between Son and Spirit. This may have been the case with the bishops of Rome whom Hippolytus criticized (see below), and in fact some have suggested that Praxeas might be a pseudonym for one of the bishops of Rome. In any case, we know that Tertullian opposed the bishops of Rome on disciplinary grounds, so it is not inconceivable that he opposed them on theological grounds as well. But the bishops of Rome were not really heretics (as evidenced by the fact that they excommunicated modalist teachers) and in the end the person of Praxeas is probably more of a straw man than a real man, Tertullian taking the opportunity of an enemy of Montanism as his foil to explain his understanding of the Trinity.

In *Against Praxeas*, Tertullian introduced two Latin terms, apparently from Roman legal usage, that would become the very definition of orthodoxy for describing the Trinity. The word *substantia* describes a property — something that

[74] Tertullian, *Apology*, 2.

[75] Tertullian, *Apology*, 5. Note that the Pantheon which stands in Rome today was not yet built in the time of Tiberius, however, it stands on the site of an earlier one. The current Pantheon was built by Hadrian, but the inscription that refers to Agrippa is an homage to the man responsible for the original.

[76] Tertullian, *Apology*, 5.

[77] Tertullian, *Against Praxeas*, 1.

can be owned — and is the Latin version of Irenaeus's concept of the shared divine essence.[78] The Father, Son, and Holy Spirit are one *substantia*.[79] This can be translated into English as *substance*, as long as one keeps in mind that it does not refer to material substance. The substance of the Trinity is divinity itself. The other term that Tertullian coined is *persona*, meaning an individual entity — legally, it meant someone who can own something.[80] This is translated into English as *person*, which refers to each of the three manifestations, or *Persons*, of the Trinity (Father, Son, and Holy Spirit). But note that the word *persons* is not the equivalent of "people," and we would not speak of three "people" of the Trinity. As it is used here, the word *persons* is a technical term that indicates the distinction between Father, Son, and Holy Spirit, while also maintaining the unity of the one God. Therefore God exists as one divine substance shared by three divine Persons.[81] The term *substance* describes the oneness of God, and the term *person* describes the fact that God is also three, providing a way of clarifying the distinction between the Father, Son, and Holy Spirit against modalism.[82]

As Irenaeus had indicated, the generation of the Son from the Father (that the Son is "begotten" from the Father) necessitates that the Son also be the same divine essence, or substance, as the Father.[83] The oneness of God requires it. As we have noted, the doctrine which affirms that the three Persons of the Trinity are all one substance is called *consubstantiality*. However, the immutability of the Divine also requires that the Father cannot become incarnate, let alone suffer and die. Therefore some distinction of Persons is necessary, even while maintaining the oneness. For Tertullian, the Father alone is the First Cause of all existence, and is ultimate transcendence, and uncircumscribable. The Son alone became incarnate, and only His

[78] For the traditional view, see J. Armitage Robinson, *The Meaning of Homoousios in the "Constantinopolitan" Creed* (Cambridge: Cambridge University Press, 1901), 21–23, 65–70. While the strictly legal definition of *substantia* has been rejected as a basis for the theological term, it is still the case that the concept of "property" is a suitable analogy, since property can be non-material, as in the case of intellectual property. See Eric Osborn, *Tertullian: First Theologian of the West* (Cambridge: Cambridge University Press, 1997), 131–132. Note that Tertullian calls the Gospel "the substance of the New Testament." *Against Praxeas*, 31.1.

[79] Tertullian, *Against Praxeas*, 2.

[80] Tertullian, *Against Praxeas*, 2; see Robinson, *The Meaning of Homoousios in the "Constantinopolitan" Creed*, 70–74, and Osborn, *Tertullian*, 132–133, 137.

[81] Tertullian, *Against Praxeas*, 12, 26.

[82] Tertullian, *Against Praxeas*, 26.

[83] Tertullian, *Against Praxeas*, 8.

human nature suffered. Tertullian followed Irenaeus in describing the hierarchy of the Trinity as one of Sender and Messenger. The Father is the Sender and the Son is His Messenger. This implies that in some way the Holy Spirit is also the Messenger of the Father and/or the Son. The hierarchy of the Trinity, then, is one of authority, specifically in terms of the internal relationships between the Persons, while the oneness of God is maintained by the single substance. Thus, Tertullian wrote, "These three [Persons] are one, but not one and the same, so that when [Jesus] said, 'I and my Father are one,' it means unity of substance, not a singular number."[84]

Tertullian criticized modalism for having a Trinity with too much "monarchy" (unity) and too little "economy" (distinction/hierarchy).[85] Ultimately, what the modalists propose is not really a Trinity at all, but a monad with three names. For the modalists, the only allowable distinction between the Persons of the Trinity was a label which described what God was doing at any given time. When God was the Creator, He was the Father. When God was the Savior, He was the Son, and when God was sustaining the Church, He was the Spirit. To put it another way, God was the Father in the Old Testament, the Son in the Gospels, and the Spirit in the Church. Among the many problems with this conception of the Trinity, it gives the appearance that the three Persons only exist one at a time. It also gives the impression that the distinction of Persons is only by task, or mode of operation (hence the name *modalism*). In fact, the mainstream Church would come to the conclusion that any operation of God is the activity of all three Persons of the Trinity, a doctrine called *inseparable operation*.[86] Therefore, popular reformulations of the triune name into formulas such as "Creator, Redeemer, Sustainer" are actually expressions of the heresy of modalism, because they contradict the doctrine of *inseparable operation* and imply a Trinity in which the Father does not save or sustain and the Son and Spirit do not create (cf. Jth. 16:14; John 1:3).

Tertullian also followed Irenaeus in emphasizing that Christ must have both a human and a divine nature in order to be the Savior. Against Marcionite docetism, he argued that "what is not assumed is not redeemed," and therefore if Christ did not have a real humanity, He could not be the Savior of humanity. For Tertullian, the birth of Christ demonstrated the two natures. That He had a birth at all proves His humanity against the docetics and gnostics who claimed Jesus had no birth or childhood. That His birth was miraculous in nature proves His divinity against the Ebionites. In fact, Tertullian demonstrates the very early devotion to Mary as

[84] Tertullian, *Against Praxeas*, 22, 25, translation by the present author.

[85] Tertullian, *Against Praxeas*, 8–9.

[86] Tertullian, *Against Praxeas*, 17; see also Ignatius of Antioch, *Letter to the Magnesians*, 7.

the Mother of God, and anticipates the conclusion of the fifth-century *Theotokos* controversy when he said that the divine *Logos* was circumscribed in Mary's womb, so that she was the Mother of the divine nature of Christ, not the human nature only. As the third ecumenical Council of Ephesus (AD 431) would later clarify, it is therefore appropriate to call Mary *Mother of God*. Tertullian also anticipated the definition of the fourth ecumenical Council of Chalcedon (AD 451) when he said that the two natures are "not confused, but united in one Person: Jesus, God and human ... the property of each [nature] is completely preserved."[87]

Hippolytus

Like Tertullian, Hippolytus was a disciple of Irenaeus, at least through his writings. But also like Tertullian, it is unclear what Hippolytus's status was in the Church. In fact, the person of Hippolytus is as much of an enigma as the Church has ever produced, to the point where some speculate there were two, or even three, "Hippolyti" responsible for the writings attributed to him.[88] Acknowledging the debate, and the problems associated with ascribing the Hippolytan documents to one person, we will

[87] Tertullian, *Against Praxeas*, 27, translation by the present author. Tertullian actually said, "The property of each *substance* is preserved." The term *substance* is synonymous with *nature*, since the two natures of Christ are actually two substances, one divine (the same divine substance as the Trinity) and one human.

[88] For a treatment of the debate surrounding the authorship of writings attributed to Hippolytus, see Allen Brent, "St. Hippolytus: Biblical Exegete, Roman Bishop and Martyr," *St. Vladimir's Theological Quarterly* 48:2 (2004): 207–231. For a detailed treatment of Hippolytus, see Brent, *Hippolytus and the Roman Church in the Third Century*. Many scholars do not believe that both *Refutation of All Heresies* and *Against Noetus* could be by the same author, however, I treat them together here in the conviction that they are at least the product of the same school of thought, originating in early third-century Rome. The differences between the two documents can be attributed to the passage of time between writings and to possible differences in audience and agenda; see Brent, *Hippolytus and the Roman Church in the Third Century*, 204–207, 217, 238, 249, 257. Although Brent agrees that the two documents represent the same school of thought, he argues that they are by different authors based on a perceived theological evolution from the *Refutation* to *Against Noetus*. Specifically, that on the one hand, *Against Noetus* is more trinitarian because of a more highly developed pneumatology, and on the other hand, it is in some ways a concession to the (supposed) milder modalism of Callistus as a tactic to combat the more extreme modalism of Noetus. See Brent, *Hippolytus and the Roman Church in the Third Century*, 208–211, 213–214, 240, 257. However, as I have indicated above, I do not believe that Callistus and the other Roman bishops were modalists, but that their christology may have included a holdover from an older form of *Logos* christology, which blurred the distinction between the pre-incarnate *Logos* and the Holy Spirit; see Papandrea, *Novatian of Rome*.

nevertheless treat them as a unit. If they are not from the same pen, they are at least from the same school of thought and represent the next stage in the development of doctrine, bridging the gap from Tertullian to Novatian.

Born around AD 170, Hippolytus was from the East, and therefore he wrote in Greek. At some point he came to Rome and was an influential presence during the time that Zephyrinus (AD 199–217), Callistus (AD 217–222), and their successors were bishops there. Eusebius says that Hippolytus was also a bishop but does not know of what city.[89] Hippolytus seems to refer to himself as a bishop in the preface to his *Refutation of All Heresies*. In the year 1551, a statue was found near the church of San Lorenzo, just outside the walls of Rome. The statue appeared to be of a figure seated in the position of a teacher (in a bishop's throne?). It had an inscription cataloguing the writings of Hippolytus, along with a list of the dates of Easter attributed to Hippolytus. Many have argued this was in fact a statue of Hippolytus as a bishop. Pope Pius IV (bishop 1559–1565) said that Hippolytus was the bishop of the coastal town of Portus, but there is no early evidence for this.[90]

Thus, Hippolytus may have been bishop of a smaller town near Rome. On the other hand, some have speculated that he may have been the leader of the eastern (Greek-speaking) Christians in Rome, functioning as their catechist, even possibly leading a separate catechetical school distinct from the Latin-speaking one under the authority of the official bishops of Rome, and thus he may have been like another bishop within Rome.[91] If this was the case, Hippolytus represented a group whose standards of morality and expectations for Reconciliation were stricter than the majority, and like Tertullian, Hippolytus criticized the bishops of Rome, especially for forgiving the sin of "adultery." This probably meant that they allowed second marriages and/or blessed the cohabitation of mixed-class couples who could not be married legally. The bishops of Rome also apparently allowed priests to marry and allowed divorced and remarried men to remain in the priesthood.[92] Hippolytus would complain that they even reconciled some who had been excommunicated by others, possibly even by Hippolytus himself.[93] Therefore, in spite of speculation that Hippolytus was a leader within the city of Rome, it seems most likely that he was the bishop of a smaller town near Rome, under the authority of the metropolitan bishop

[89] Eusebius of Caesarea, *Ecclesiastical History*, 6.20.

[90] Brent, *Hippolytus and the Roman Church in the Third Century*, 234–235.

[91] Hippolytus, *Refutation of All Heresies* 9.7. Note that Hippolytus refers to the *school* of Callistus.

[92] Hippolytus, *Refutation of All Heresies*, 9.7.

[93] Hippolytus, *Refutation of All Heresies*, 9.7.

of Rome. He had authority over discipline in his town, but the bishops of Rome could override his decisions, and reinstate those whom he had excommunicated.

Hippolytus also had conflicts with the bishops of Rome over theology. During the time that Zephyrinus was bishop and Callistus was his deacon (in charge of the catacombs that would later bear his name), a certain Noetus came to Rome from Smyrna. According to Hippolytus, Noetus was so influenced by eastern monism, he embraced a modalist version of Christianity and came to Rome to teach it.[94] At first, Zephyrinus was tolerant of Noetus teaching in Rome. Even though a modalist faction was developing in the church of Rome, Zephyrinus was apparently advised by Callistus to try to keep the peace, and so he was hesitant to excommunicate them. Hippolytus confronted the bishop and his deacon, and after some debate, Noetus was called before the council of priests.[95] At this point he denied that he was teaching modalism, however it soon became clear that he was, and so he was called before the council a second time. This time he had more support and held his ground. He was excommunicated, but continued teaching as the leader of a modalist school.

Callistus became the next bishop of Rome in AD 217.[96] Hippolytus had not forgotten that Callistus had been conciliatory toward Noetus, and eventually he accused the bishop himself of being a modalist.[97] For his part, Hippolytus may have overreacted against modalism to the extent that he emphasized the distinction between the Father and Son to the point of leaning too far toward adoptionism — and in fact he admits that Callistus accused him of worshiping two Gods.[98] In reality both Callistus and Hippolytus were probably within the realm of orthodoxy. As was the case with earlier bishops of Rome who were criticized by Tertullian, Callistus may have retained an early aspect of *Logos* christology that did not have a clearly defined distinction between the Persons of the Trinity, especially the Son and Spirit. This may have looked like modalism to Hippolytus. In addition, Tertullian's concept of consubstantiality, which Hippolytus had not picked up, might also have looked to him like a form of modalism.[99] While Hippolytus appears to accept the idea of a single essence from Irenaeus, he was apparently not comfortable with the way Callistus was expressing

[94] Hippolytus, *Refutation of All Heresies*, 9.2–5.

[95] Hippolytus, *Against Noetus*, 1.

[96] Apparently, it was not always necessary to move up through the "ranks" of ordination one at a time, and it was possible in some cases for a deacon to be elected bishop, on the assumption that he would be ordained priest and consecrated bishop at the same time.

[97] Hippolytus, *Refutation of All Heresies*, 9.7.

[98] Hippolytus, *Refutation of All Heresies*, 9.6–7.

[99] See Hippolytus, *Refutation of All Heresies*, 9.7, 10.13, 10.23.

it.[100] Callistus also appears to have taught early versions of *circumincessio* (also known as *perichoresis*, or *reciprocity*, the mutual interactivity of the three Persons of the Trinity) as well as *communicatio idiomatum* (the sharing of properties between the two natures of Christ).[101] Hippolytus rejected the latter because he thought it compromised the immutability of the divine nature.[102] In the end, it is clear that Callistus was not a modalist, because he excommunicated the modalist teacher Sabellius.[103] Callistus and Hippolytus both agreed that there was a distinction between the Father and Son, in that only the Son was begotten, and only the Son suffered and died. Eventually Hippolytus would inadvertently admit that Callistus represented the middle way between the Ebionites (Theodosius) and the modalists (Sabellius).[104]

Hippolytus continued to be a thorn in the side of two more bishops of Rome, until persecution returned to the city. In the year AD 235, both the bishop Pontian and Hippolytus were arrested and sent to the mines of Sardinia. Hippolytus died a martyr in AD 235 or 236.[105] According to one tradition he was drowned, however he may have died in the mines. He has left a valuable, if confusing, literary legacy. There are several important documents, most of which are the subject of intense debate as to their authorship. The most important for the student of the early Church are *Against Noetus* and the *Refutation of All Heresies*.

Against Noetus

Hippolytus admitted that Noetus was motivated by a desire to preserve the oneness of God.[106] Noetus had reasoned that if Christ was God, but not the Father, then that

[100] Hippolytus, *Refutation of All Heresies*, 10.29; see also Hippolytus, *On the Holy Theophany*, 7.

[101] On Callistus and the *communicatio idiomatum*, see Papandrea, "Loaning and Borrowing: Deification in Novatian."

[102] Hippolytus, *Refutation of All Heresies*, 9.7, 10.23; see also Hippolytus, *Expository Treatise Against the Jews*, 4; *On Christ and Antichrist*, 4; *Against Beron*, 1, 5–6. Hippolytus may have accepted the concept of *circumincessio*; see *Against Noetus*, 14. Note that there is ongoing debate over the authorship of the documents traditionally attributed to Hippolytus.

[103] Hippolytus, *Refutation of All Heresies*, 9.7.

[104] Hippolytus, *Refutation of All Heresies*, 9.7. Hippolytus actually accused Callistus of waffling between the two heresies, but in doing so, he betrays that Callistus was looking for the middle way between them.

[105] According to one tradition, Hippolytus and Pontian were buried in Rome on the same day. If they were executed together, this would certainly be possible, however Brent thinks that this tradition was invented to convey the impression that the two were reconciled; see Brent, *Hippolytus and the Roman Church in the Third Century*, 257.

[106] Hippolytus, *Against Noetus*, 2.

would imply two Gods, and compromise the monotheistic basis of Christianity.[107] If extreme dualism (as in docetism) led one to a strict dichotomy between spirit and matter, Noetus's monism led him to the opposite conclusion: that there was no distinction at all between spirit and matter. And if there is no distinction between spirit and matter, then there is no distinction between the divine and human in Christ, and ultimately no distinction between the Persons of the Trinity. Thus monism applied to Christianity leads to modalism. Therefore, Noetus taught that the Father became the Son in the Incarnation.[108] In other words, the Son is the Father come to earth. To the modalist, He is appropriately called the Father only before the Incarnation, and the Son only after the Incarnation.[109] This is a distinction of mode (time and activity), not a real distinction. Hippolytus responded by labeling Noetus's teaching *patripassionism*, "the suffering of the Father." In other words, Hippolytus reasoned that if Noetus was right, then the Father died on the cross.[110] Noetus answered the charge by taking a docetic view of the passion: Christ only appeared to suffer because God is immutable.[111]

Hippolytus began *Against Noetus* with an abbreviated statement of faith, which was presented as a challenge to Noetus by the council of priests.[112] He then went on to defend his understanding of orthodoxy by emphasizing the real distinction between the Father and the Son, against modalist monism.[113] For Hippolytus, this distinction did not compromise the oneness of God because God is still one, even though a Trinity (in Greek, *Triados*, a Triad).[114] Following Irenaeus, Hippolytus described the Trinity as one God and one divine power, but with a hierarchy (*economy*) of "three-fold manifestation."[115] The Father, Son, and the Holy Spirit are all equally worshiped, because together the three are the one God.[116]

[107] Hippolytus, *Against Noetus*, 2.

[108] Hippolytus, *Against Noetus*, 1, 7. This was the modalist interpretation of John 14:8–9, that the Son and the Father were one and the same; see also Hippolytus, *Refutation of All Heresies*, 9.5.

[109] Hippolytus, *Against Noetus*, 1–2; see also Hippolytus, *Refutation of All Heresies*, 9.5, 7. Note that Noetus and Callistus could agree on the concept of consubstantiality, which Hippolytus was slow to accept.

[110] Hippolytus, *Refutation of All Heresies*, 10.23.

[111] Hippolytus, *Refutation of All Heresies*, 9.5.

[112] Hippolytus, *Against Noetus*, 1.

[113] Hippolytus, *Against Noetus*, 10–11.

[114] Hippolytus, *Against Noetus*, 14.

[115] Hippolytus, *Against Noetus*, 3, 8, 11, 14.

[116] Hippolytus, *Against Noetus*, 12.

Hippolytus could see that modalism, assuming the immutability of the Father, and claiming that the Son *was* the Father incarnate, ultimately denies the real humanity of the Son, and makes him out to be more like the Christ of the docetics. Therefore, Hippolytus also defended the real humanity of Christ against the modalists' diminished humanity and docetic passion. Hippolytus made a point to say that Christ had His own human rational soul, emphasizing His full humanity.[117]

However, on other points, Hippolytus's christology was still partly in the second century. He does not have a clear distinction between the pre-incarnate *Logos* and the Holy Spirit.[118] He also follows Theophilus a bit too closely, saying that before the Word was begotten, the Father was alone — though he does try to correct (or redeem) Theophilus by saying that although God was alone, He existed in plurality.[119] So he said that the Word was God's reason, wisdom, and counsel, but the Word was not the Son before the Incarnation — something that would not be acceptable to later orthodoxy.[120]

In fact, Hippolytus understood two processions of the Word.[121] The first procession of the Word was the generation, when the Word was "begotten." At this point the Word of God was "uttered," or spoken forth to be the agent of creation. When the Word was begotten, He became distinct from the Father, moving from the reason or wisdom *in* God to the Word *with* God.[122] As with all the Church Fathers up to this point, it is implied that the generation of the Word was an *event* which marked a beginning to the distinction between Father and Son. Before the generation there was no distinction and no distinct personal existence of the Son. At the generation, the Word is extended out from the Father, God from God, power from power, like

[117] Hippolytus, *Against Noetus*, 17; see also Hippolytus, *Against Beron*, 8. Some have argued that certain elements in *Against Noetus* which anticipate later doctrinal controversies may have been added later by editors; see Brent, *Hippolytus and the Roman Church in the Third Century*, 224–225; cf. Irenaeus of Lyons, *Against Heresies*, 3.19.3. However, speculation that parts of extant texts were added later is often based on assumptions about the rate at which doctrine could (or could not) develop, but this always runs the risk of "needing" to say that part of a document was added later if the context contradicts conclusions about the state of development at that time. In other words, if one is reluctant to allow that the development of doctrine had come to a certain point at a certain time, then evidence of that supposedly later development in an earlier text becomes bracketed as a later addition on no other evidence that that it seems to be too far along in the development of doctrine.

[118] Hippolytus, *Against Noetus*, 16.

[119] Hippolytus, *Against Noetus*, 10–11.

[120] Hippolytus, *Against Noetus*, 10–11, 15.

[121] Hippolytus, *Against Noetus*, 17.

[122] Hippolytus, *Refutation of All Heresies*, 10.29.

rays from the sun or water from a spring.[123] This, too, will have to be nuanced later, since in a way it compromises the immutability of the Divine. The second procession is the Incarnation, when the Word becomes the Son, because He becomes human.

In addition to clarifying the distinction between the Father and the Son, the distinction between the divine and human natures in the Son was also important. Unlike Tertullian, Hippolytus did not believe that the divine nature could be circumscribed, so for Hippolytus, only the human nature was localized in time and space.[124] The divine nature remained infinite and omnipresent, since (he reasoned) to lack omnipresence is to have a need for movement, and movement is a kind of change, which would seem to compromise divine immutability. Hippolytus would not have agreed with Tertullian on the circumscription of the divine nature in the womb of Mary, and in this way he anticipated the heresy of Nestorianism (see below) which will propose too much of a separation between the two natures in the Person of Christ.

Refutation of All Heresies

Sometimes referred to as *Elenchus* or *Philosophumena*, this document was probably written in the last decade or so of Hippolytus's life, in the late AD 220s. It is in many ways a less clear version of Irenaeus's *Against Heresies* and borrows heavily from that document. Most of the *Refutation* is simply a catalogue of gnostic beliefs. What is interesting is that by this time the gnostics seem to have answered Irenaeus's charge that if there was secret knowledge the bishops would know about it. Some apparently responded by saying that the secret knowledge was not given to the apostles, but to Jesus' relatives, and was handed down through His stepbrother James.[125] For Hippolytus the danger of gnosticism was that it is a docetic syncretism that ultimately left Christ less than human, which called the crucifixion and Resurrection into question and thereby threatened salvation itself.[126]

Like the other theologians, Hippolytus also criticized philosophy, saying that heresy comes from a syncretism of Christianity with philosophy and/or astrology. Even so, while the pagans hold on to the old mythologies, Hippolytus pointed out

[123] Hippolytus, *Against Noetus*, 11, 16.

[124] See Hippolytus, *Against Beron*, 1; however, the authorship of this document is still a matter of debate.

[125] Hippolytus, *Refutation of All Heresies*, 5.2.

[126] Hippolytus, *Refutation of All Heresies*, 5.1, 7.15. It is interesting to note that Hippolytus mentions that the gnostics believed the human spirit to be situated in the brain; see Hippolytus, *Refutation of All Heresies*, 4.51.

that some of the philosophers were coming around to various forms of monotheism.[127] He claims it started with Pythagoras, who got a version of monotheism from the Egyptians.[128] But philosophy could not lead to salvation, since many of the philosophers taught versions of reincarnation, and some even believed in the transmigration of souls across species.[129] Others taught a version of evolution which assumed that matter was eternal and uncreated.[130] This, along with Plato's understanding that the material world was, at best, less real than the spiritual realm, seemed to contradict Genesis on the goodness of God's creation.[131]

The philosophers may have talked about a *logos*, but they often equated this *logos* with one of the gods of the Greco-Roman pantheon, such as Mercury. They saw the *logos* as an astrological figure, just one of many players in the cosmic drama.[132] Even when the *logos* of the philosophers was understood as the rational principle behind creation, or a quasi-divine figure who would be judge over the living and the dead, for Hippolytus this was still an inadequate understanding of the Christian *Logos* as (pre-incarnate) Christ.

Nevertheless, it is clear from the *Refutation* that there were certain philosophical concepts that Hippolytus (and the Church) accepted, as we have noted above. Christians and pagan philosophers alike shared the definition of deity as that which is eternal and immortal, with no beginning or end.[133] A strict distinction was made between that which is created (and is also therefore finite, corruptible, and perishable) and that which is uncreated (infinite, incorruptible, and imperishable).[134] Deity is assumed to be immutable, since change of any kind compromises perfection and leads to corruptibility. Deity is benevolent, therefore God is not the creator of evil, but evil comes from the misuse of free will.[135] Finally, deity is *simplex*, or indivisible.[136] Of course, all of this created a problem for the mainstream Christians, who affirmed both the divinity and the humanity of Christ, since the obvious mutability and passibility of the man Jesus seemed to contradict the assumption that divinity

[127] Hippolytus, *Refutation of All Heresies*, 1.2.

[128] Hippolytus, *Refutation of All Heresies*, 1.2, 4.43.

[129] Hippolytus, *Refutation of All Heresies*, 1.2–3.

[130] Hippolytus, *Refutation of All Heresies*, 1.5–7, 1.16.

[131] Hippolytus, *Refutation of All Heresies*, 1.16.

[132] Hippolytus, *Refutation of All Heresies*, 4.48–49.

[133] Hippolytus, *Refutation of All Heresies*, 1.1.

[134] Hippolytus, *Refutation of All Heresies*, 1.16, 4.43.

[135] Hippolytus, *Refutation of All Heresies*, 1.16; cf. Plato, *Phaedrus* 100.60. Evil is described by the philosophers as the result of going to extremes. It is a lack of self-control.

[136] Hippolytus, *Refutation of All Heresies*, 4.43.

must be immutable and impassible. The difficulty of interpretation of this paradox led to groups on the extremes rejecting one of the natures in favor of the other. The Ebionites, and later the adoptionists, denied the divinity in favor of the humanity. The docetics, gnostics, and then the modalists denied the humanity in favor of the divinity. The mainstream Church had to make a distinction between the divine and human natures in Christ, to clarify that only the divine nature is immutable, and only the human nature died. This parallels the distinction made between the Persons of the Trinity, such that only the Father is the unbegotten First Cause and ultimate Source of all existence, and only the Son is begotten and incarnate.[137]

Origen

Origen Adamantius was born about the year AD 186 in Alexandria, of Christian parents. He was a student of Clement of Alexandria and the philosopher Ammonius Saccas (the founder of Neoplatonism).[138] When he was fifteen or sixteen years old, in the year AD 202, persecution came to Alexandria and Origen's father was arrested and imprisoned. According to tradition, Origen would have followed his father and confessed his faith to the authorities, but his mother hid his clothes. Choosing modesty over martyrdom, Origen instead wrote a letter to his father in prison encouraging him not to deny the Faith on account of his family. His father was eventually beheaded, and Origen went from riches to rags when the family property was confiscated. After this time, he was supported by a wealthy woman who was a patron of Christian philosophers, however she also supported a theologian from Antioch named Paul, whom Origen considered a heretic. Origen and Paul debated the Faith, but Origen refused to pray with him.

At the age of eighteen, in the year AD 204, Origen succeeded his teacher Clement as the head of the catechetical school in Alexandria, in part because the persecution left no one else for the job. Since the school itself was a target, Origen only escaped arrest because he moved around from house to house (so we must not imagine the famous *school* as a fixed building or place). Eventually he sold all of his secular books for money to support himself, gave up teaching pagan literature, and devoted himself entirely to the school. Origen lived an ascetic lifestyle, sleeping on the floor, refusing to drink wine, wearing no shoes, and limiting his possessions. He fasted to the point of damaging his health. It is said that he also took Matthew 19:12 literally and castrated himself, presumably to avoid scandal if he were to teach women or have

[137] Hippolytus, *Refutation of All Heresies*, 1.18, 10.28–29; see also Hippolytus, *Against Noetus*, 11.

[138] The details of Origen's life, as far as we know them, come primarily from Eusebius of Caesarea, *Ecclesiastical History*, bk. 6, and Jerome, *Illustrious Men*, 54.

female patrons. Some scholars have questioned whether this story is true, however it is consistent with Origen's rigorism, and his enemies would have had other reasons to question the validity of his ordination, and so did not need to create the story of his self-mutilation.

Since Christianity was treated as a philosophy in Alexandria, it is possible that students came to the school as an "inquiry," not necessarily intending to be baptized. Many would probably have left before making a commitment to the moral standards of the Church. Still, the school attracted so many students that Origen himself attracted attention. During renewed persecution in Alexandria in the years AD 215–216, Origen fled to Jerusalem, and then to Caesarea. The bishops of Palestine invited him to teach, however this got him into trouble with his own bishop, who said that a lay person should not be teaching in the presence of bishops. He was eventually ordained a priest, but in Caesarea, not Alexandria, which only widened the rift between him and his bishop back in Alexandria. He continued teaching in Caesarea, attracting many loyal students, including the famous Gregory the Wonderworker. He became so famous as a Christian philosopher that around AD 225 he was summoned by Julia Mamaea, the mother of the emperor Severus Alexander. She sent a military escort to bring Origen to Antioch where she was staying so that he could explain Christianity to her. There is also a story that Origen corresponded with the emperor Philip (emperor AD 244–249).

Origen would eventually be excommunicated by a synod in Alexandria in AD 231. The synod interpreted Deuteronomy 23:1–2 as a prohibition against the ordination of anyone who was castrated, but the real reason for his condemnation had to do with the way his teachings incorporated elements of gnosticism (see below), and the fact that he had been ordained outside of his own city rather than by his bishop. However, Origen would never return to Alexandria, since the persecution caused him constantly to be on the run between Palestine and Asia Minor. He was finally arrested and imprisoned during the Decian persecution (see below), in about AD 250. He was tortured and eventually released, but his health was broken and he died soon after his release, probably between AD 253 and 255.

Origen was a prolific writer, but unfortunately many of his writings are lost or exist only in imperfect forms and fragments. He learned Hebrew so that he could translate and interpret the original language of the Old Testament. He created a parallel text called the *Hexapla*, which included six different versions of the Old Testament: the Hebrew text, the Hebrew transliterated into Greek characters, the Septuagint (the Old Testament translated into Greek), and three other translations, including one supposedly used by the Ebionites. At first, he limited his text of the Old Testament to the twenty-two books originally written in Hebrew, but later he added the deuterocanonical books that were included in the Septuagint. He also participated in a debate about the authenticity of the story of Susannah in the book of Daniel.

Always the philosopher, Origen wore the philosopher's pallium and interacted with pagan philosophy. As a student of Ammonius, he had known Ammonius's other famous students, Porphyry and Plotinus. He wrote a response to one of the most famous critiques of Christianity in his *Against Celsus*.[139] However, his interaction with philosophy led him into a speculative theology that would later get him into trouble and bring accusations of heresy.

On First Principles

Origen's most famous work was written while he was still in Alexandria.[140] Unfortunately, most of it only exists in a fourth-century Latin translation by Rufinus, who admitted that he had made changes to Origen's text, especially where Origen seemed heterodox by fourth-century (post-Nicene) standards. In truth, there is still plenty in the text that could be considered heretical, so one wonders what Rufinus took out. Ultimately, *On First Principles* as we have it is an unreliable source for discovering Origen's thought, except where fragments of the original Greek exist. In fact, the elements of the document that are most likely to have come from Origen are those which are the most speculative or heretical. The parts which are sometimes taken as a contribution to Christian theology were most likely edited or inserted after the Council of Nicaea, influenced by Rufinus's own theology, which comes from sources such as Novatian and Athanasius.[141]

In truth, Origen's genius and legacy is not as a theologian so much as a biblical exegete, though his heterodoxy comes through in his exegesis as well. He wrote many commentaries on Scripture, some of which still exist for sections of the Bible, including parts of the Gospels of Matthew and John. The commentaries were dictated as Origen composed as he spoke out loud, quoting Scripture from memory. The texts were taken down in shorthand, later to be written out by "girls skilled in penmanship," and then duplicated by copyists.[142] Origen is known as the most famous

[139] Among other things, Celsus had objected to the Christian belief in the divinity of Christ on the grounds that it compromised divine immutability. See Aloys Grillmeier, *Christ in Christian Tradition, Volume 1*, 105.

[140] Eusebius of Caesarea, *Ecclesiastical History*, 6.24.

[141] Rufinus read Novatian's *On the Trinity*, but thought it was written by Tertullian; see Jerome, *Apology Against Rufinus*, 2.19; see also Papandrea, *Novatian of Rome*.

[142] Eusebius of Caesarea, *Ecclesiastical History*, 6.23, in Lake, *Eusebius*, vol. 2, 69.

proponent of the allegorical method of interpretation. According to Eusebius, he was not satisfied with the literal meaning, and always looked for a deeper, more spiritual meaning in the text.[143] The philosopher Porphyry, in his *Third Treatise Against the Christians*, gave Origen credit for applying the allegorical method of interpretation to the Old Testament. Porphyry wrote, "While his manner of life was Christian ... in his opinions about material things and the Deity, he played the Greek, and introduced Greek ideas into foreign fables."[144] In other words, he applied Greek allegorical interpretation to Jewish writings. However, his attention to the spiritual meaning often led him to over-allegorize, and he would be criticized for finding meaning in the text that was never meant to be there.

Problematic Elements in Origen

Origen was condemned as a heretic several times after his death, including at a council in Alexandria in AD 400, and at the fifth ecumenical Council of Constantinople II in AD 553. The emperor Justinian even wrote an essay on the heresies of Origen.[145] Origen's theology was so intertwined with philosophy and so speculative that it is hard to distinguish what he really believed from what he was only proposing for further thought and debate. He seems to be the kind of person who "thinks out loud," except that his thoughts were recorded and held against him later. This is especially true of *On First Principles*, which was written while he was still relatively young. In the end, there are several points at which Origen is at odds with the orthodoxy of his own time, not to mention later orthodoxy.

Origen accepted a philosophical understanding of the human soul, which assumed that souls pre-existed their current bodies, and he probably believed in reincarnation and merit from pre-life existence.[146] This was seen as inconsistent with the Christian understanding of the soul as created for one life, after which there was death and resurrection, not reincarnation (Heb. 9:27). As applied to the human soul of Christ, Origen implied that his human nature was also pre-existent and that the Incarnation was simply the coming together of two eternal souls, the *Logos* and the human soul of Jesus. Although he is sometimes given credit for a

[143] Eusebius of Caesarea, *Ecclesiastical History*, 6.2, 6.19.

[144] Quoted in Eusebius of Caesarea, *Ecclesiastical History*, 6.19, in Lake, *Eusebius*, vol. 2, 59.

[145] Meyendorff, *Imperial Unity*, 232-234.

[146] See Origen, *On First Principles*, 2.2, 2.10. Origen's predecessor, Clement of Alexandria, had speculated that human souls were preexistent, at least by divine foreknowledge; Clement of Alexandria, *Exhortation to the Greeks*, 1. This may have contributed to Origen's philosophical speculation on the human soul.

doctrine of *eternal generation*, his concept of eternal generation applies not only to the divine nature of Christ in the *Logos*, but to all human souls.[147] This effectively negates the uniqueness of Christ among humanity. In fact, Origen seems to be saying that both the *Logos* and the Holy Spirit are created beings.[148] For Origen, it is unclear whether the Father and Son are consubstantial, and he questioned whether Christ should even be worshiped, saying that we should not pray to Jesus, because he had to pray.[149]

Finally, Origen accepted elements from philosophy which had been rejected by most Christians. He seems to have accepted the possibility of the existence of other gods, and speculated that John the baptist was an angel incarnate.[150] He also believed in a Stoic understanding of the eternal nature of all matter, and the end of the universe as a conflagration, only to be followed by a rebirth in which the universe would start all over again (thus a cyclical view of time, rather than the linear view of time that is revealed in the Judeo-Christian Scriptures). Origen's theology seems to be a curious combination of adoptionism (Christ is not essentially different from the rest of us) and gnosticism (all human souls are fallen divine sparks, except that Jesus Christ is the only one who didn't fall). Finally, Origen seemed to believe in universalism, that all people will ultimately receive salvation, a notion contradicted by Jesus Himself in no uncertain terms.

There were other accusations against Origen, some probably untrue or exaggerated, many leveled at him after his death when he could not defend himself. Nevertheless, it is clear that he may have been too smart for his own good, leaving a legacy tarnished by heresy. Whatever good Origen did would be overshadowed by the ways in which he went to extremes. And the proof of this is that his two most famous students, Dionysius of Alexandria and Gregory the Wonderworker (Gregory Thaumaturgus), both drifted into heresy, Dionysius into adoptionism (see below) and Gregory into modalism.[151] In fact, each of these students of Origen had opposed

[147] See Origen, *On First Principles*, 3.1.13. On eternal generation, see below. The first theologian to articulate this doctrine was Novatian.

[148] See Origen, *Commentary on John*, 1.23, 2.6.

[149] Origen, *On Prayer*, 10. See also, *Commentary on John*, 1.23, but cf. 2.18.

[150] See Origen, *Commentary on John*, 2.4, 2.25.

[151] See Gregory the Wonderworker, *To Philagrius*. Often subtitled, "On Consubstantiality," the word consubstantiality never occurs in the document. In this document Gregory seems to begin with the assumption that God can be either one (*simplex*) or three, but not both one and three. This leads him to refer to the three Persons of the Trinity as "names" for God, thus removing the distinction between Persons and reducing the Son and Spirit to mere emanations from the Father.

one heresy to the point of going to the opposite extreme. Dionysius's opposition to modalism led him into adoptionism, and Gregory's opposition to adoptionism (in the person of Paul of Samosata) apparently led him into modalism.

Novatian

Born around the turn of the third century, Novatian became a priest in Rome under bishop Fabian (bishop AD 236–250).[152] He probably wrote his most important work, *On the Trinity*, during this time. When Fabian was martyred in January of AD 250, the Roman church was not able to elect a successor, so Novatian's reputation as a theologian earned him the position of acting bishop of Rome. In this role he corresponded with Cyprian, bishop of Carthage, on behalf of the church at Rome. Three of his letters are preserved in the correspondence of Cyprian.

However, like Hippolytus and Tertullian before him, he was a moral rigorist, stricter than the majority of the Church, demanding a level of purity that was inevitably unrealistic. When persecution subsided briefly, and those who had denied the Faith to save their lives wanted to return to the Church, Novatian recommended excommunication. He became the leader of a rigorist faction and apparently had hoped to be elected as the next bishop of Rome. When the election was finally held in AD 251, Novatian lost to Cornelius, who represented a middle position between the rigorists and a faction of *laxists* who advocated easy access back into the Church for the fallen. Novatian was subsequently consecrated as a rival bishop of Rome by fellow rigorists, creating a schism which lasted for centuries. Novatian, taking the position of a bishop over a scattered flock, wrote two moral treatises (*On the Benefit of Purity* and *On the Spectacles*) as well as an allegorical treatment of Old Testament dietary laws (*On Jewish Foods*). More will be said about persecution and the schism in a chapter below, but for now it is enough to say that while Novatian's ecclesiology would not ultimately be acceptable to the mainstream Church, his theology was not only acceptable to the Church of the mid-third century, it took Tertullian's thought to its logical conclusions, and helped define orthodoxy for the third century and beyond. In spite of the fact that Cyprian would write that whatever he taught was irrelevant as long as he was outside the Church, Novatian's trinitarian theology would influence later theologians, some of whom did not realize whose treatise they were reading.[153]

[152] For a more detailed account of the life of Novatian, see Papandrea, *Novatian of Rome*, and James L. Papandrea, *The Trinitarian Theology of Novatian of Rome: A Study in Third-Century Orthodoxy* (New York: The Edwin Mellen Press, 2008).

[153] Cyprian of Carthage, *Epistles*, 51.24.

On the Trinity

Novatian wrote this document as a commentary on the "rule of truth," the Church's definition of trinitarian doctrine. It is an excellent summary of the state of Christian theology up to the mid-third century, and it even anticipates later standards of orthodoxy. Novatian is intentional about charting a course midway between the extremes of modalism on one side, and adoptionism (the legacy of the Ebionites) on the other. In fact, he said that Christ was being crucified again, "between two thieves," the true Christ in the middle between the extremes. Following Irenaeus and Tertullian, Novatian argued that both natures of Christ must be maintained, united in the Person of Jesus yet without any confusion that would blur the distinction between them. In his explanation of Christ, Novatian finally took the Church beyond the earlier *Logos* christology to a christology of *kenosis*. The term *kenosis* comes from the phrase "he emptied himself," in Philippians 2:7. The Incarnation is thus described as a descent, in which Novatian said the *Logos* emptied Himself of certain divine "powers" in order to become human.[154] However, this does not mean that the Son is any less divine during the time of the Incarnation, since Novatian made a distinction between divine powers, or attributes, and divine substance, or divinity itself. In other words, in the Incarnation the *Logos* maintains full divinity, however He must set aside the prerogative of, or access to, such divine "powers" as omnipresence and omnipotence in order to be fully human and truly experience the human condition.

Novatian also follows Irenaeus and Tertullian in the consubstantiality of the Persons of the Trinity, balanced with the hierarchy of authority in which the Father and Son are described as being in a relationship of Sender and Messenger. Taking these concepts to their logical conclusions, Novatian clarified that while there is a unity of substance (which was needed to maintain the oneness of the Trinity against adoptionism), there is also a subordination of authority (which was needed to refute the diminished distinction of Persons inherent in modalism, as well as the inherent polytheism implied in describing the three Persons as though they are three equal gods). Thus, Novatian's christology is properly expressed as a *dynamic subordination*, in which the subordination of the Son to the Father is not ontological, rather it is a subordination of authority that is both relational and voluntary.[155] Therefore

[154] Cf. Irenaeus of Lyons, *Demonstration of the Apostolic Preaching*, 64.

[155] Cf. Irenaeus of Lyons, *Demonstration of the Apostolic Preaching*, 69. Note that Novatian did not distinguish between power and authority, so although he would say that it was a hierarchy of power, he did not mean it in the sense of an adoptionist subordination of

Novatian had clarified the balance of unity (ontological equality) and distinction (hierarchy of authority) in the Trinity.

Novatian also moves beyond the understanding of the generation of the Word as an "event" to a true doctrine of *eternal generation*. Unlike previous writers, who conceived of the generation as an event, the point at which the Son becomes distinct from the Father, Novatian knew that there must be an eternal distinction in order to maintain the eternal personhood of the Son and the immutability of the Father. Therefore, the generation of the Son is described as an eternal state of being, in which both consubstantiality and distinction of persons are unchanging. In other words, the Son does not go from being *in* the Father to being *with* the Father. The Son is eternally in the Father and eternally with the Father.

Finally, Novatian also advanced the concept of *communicatio idiomatum*, which Callistus may have approached, by describing the ways that the two natures in Christ were united. In the union, the two natures retain their individual integrity, and yet each one "borrows" something from the other.[156] The divine nature received the frailty of humanity, allowing it to experience the human condition, while the human nature received the immortality of divinity, which makes salvation available to the rest of humanity. Therefore, Novatian was the first to successfully strike the balance of unity and distinction, both in the Persons of the Trinity and in the two natures of Christ. In this way, he brought theology to a plateau and set the stage for the ecumenical councils and creeds of the fourth century.[157]

---

divinity. Nevertheless, his description would have to be nuanced for future orthodoxy, in which power is associated with substance, so that it will be necessary to say that it is not a hierarchy of power, but it is a hierarchy of authority, the difference being that a hierarchy of authority is entirely voluntary on the part of the Son, even though it is based on the reality of the distinction between Begettor (First Cause) and Begotten (Generated). The problem in Novatian's time is that he understood the terms *potestas* and *auctoritas* to be synonyms, which did not allow him to make the distinction that would be necessary for later orthodoxy.

[156] See John of Damascus, *Exposition of the Orthodox Faith*, 3.4. Some later writers will speak of the *communicatio idiomatum* as though each nature communicates its idiomatic properties, not to the other nature, but to the singular Person. John of Damascus may represent a step on the road to this development, as he says that each nature communicates to the other nature, but through the subsistence of the Personhood. But this was not the original concept, and it runs the risk of turning the Person into a *tertium quid*, or worse, it runs the risk of the heresy of monoenergism (see below).

[157] For a more detailed exposition of Novatian's theology, see Papandrea, *Novatian of Rome*.

Christology and Theology in the Third Century

Modalism

As I have indicated above, the docetics and gnostics of the second century eventually migrated out of the Church, probably because of a combination of diverging beliefs and pressure from the orthodox bishops. These docetic and quasi-docetic movements continued in various forms for centuries, but they cannot properly be called heresies because they were no longer within the Church. They eventually created their own gospels and other writings, becoming in effect separate religions.[158] Continuing syncretism outside the Church would later result in a version of gnosticism known as Manicheism.[159] Yet anyone who leaned toward a docetic or hybrid christology and who stayed within the Church would probably have migrated toward the group known as *modalists*, sometimes called *modalistic monarchians*.[160] Modalism is not a development of gnosticism, but they share an affinity in the tendency to diminish or deny the real humanity of Jesus Christ.

Modalists are referred to as *monarchians*, because they were concerned for the monarchy, or oneness, of God. The modalists attempted to preserve the oneness of God by an extreme unity between Father and Son that effectively made them one and the same, and so diminished or denied a human nature in Christ. In other words, they rejected the idea of a plurality of Persons (possibly justified with passages such as Isa. 9:6–7), arguing instead that there was no distinction at all between the Father and Son. The Father was the Son and the Son was the Father. The Father became incarnate and the personhood of the Son was, in a sense, a "mask" worn by the Father to appear as Jesus. This christology (like gnostic christology before it)

[158] Contrary to popular myth, the gnostic gospels were never considered for the New Testament canon, since the communities that produced them were already separated from the mainstream Church by the time they were written. In fact, they were written *because* of the separation, and the perceived need for the gnostics to have gospels of their own. Therefore, it is not legitimate to refer to them (as some have) as the "lost books of the Bible."

[159] Epiphanius of Salamis, *Panarion*, 66. According to tradition, the founder of the Manicheans was a Persian named Mani, whose father was a gnostic. Mani was not satisfied with the gnosticism he inherited, however, and he added more syncretistic elements, including Persian Zoroastrianism, to create a new version of gnosticism. Eventually, Mani was exiled from Persia by the Magi (the priests of the Zoroastrian cult) and was forced to travel the world, spreading his ideas. In the late fourth century, Augustine of Hippo would join the Manichees for a time before becoming Christian.

[160] Note that in the Valentinian gnostic *Gospel of Truth*, the Son is called the "name of the Father." *Gospel of Truth*, 38.7–12, 39.24–26. This demonstrates the similarity between gnosticism and modalism; see Hurtado, *Lord Jesus Christ*, 544.

effectively negated the humanity of Jesus. However, the modalists were not necessarily docetics, in the sense of believing Jesus had no tangible body. They probably did believe that He had a body, but that it was simply God the Father who had put on a suit of flesh.[161]

We have already met Noetus of Smyrna in the writings of Hippolytus. Heavily influenced by philosophical monism, he apparently taught that maintaining the oneness of God (monotheism), required the denial of all distinction between Father and Son, saying that the Son is simply a temporary manifestation of the Father.[162] For him, Christ is the Father, who became His own Son in the Incarnation.[163] Therefore, God can only truly be called "Father" before the Incarnation. After the Incarnation, God must be called "Son," until the Ascension and Pentecost, when God becomes the Holy Spirit. This is a chronology-based distinction between Persons, which amounts to a distinction in name only and in which God can only be called by one of the three names at a time.

The opponents of Noetus (including Hippolytus) argued that this identification of the Son with the Father leaves God the Father dying on the cross, so they named this christology *patripassionism*, the suffering of the Father.[164] Apparently, Noetus countered this accusation by saying that the passion was not real, which confirms the conclusion that modalism solves the problem of monotheism by denying the humanity of Christ.[165] Therefore, for Noetus and the other modalists, the fact that God is one means that Jesus is not really human.

Noetus was probably the teacher of Tertullian's Praxeas (whoever he was) and of the more famous Sabellius, who expanded Noetus's teaching in the AD 220s, to the point where their opponents began to call the modalists by the name *Sabellians*, and modalism was called *Sabellianism*.[166] Like Noetus, Sabellius taught that *Father, Son,* and *Holy Spirit* were simply three different names for the one God.[167] These three names are only seen as relevant from the human perspective, as they are

[161] This was probably at least partly influenced by the imprecise language of some of the apologists who talked of the Incarnation as if Christ had "put on" flesh. It may also have been influenced by the hybrid christology of some gnostics, who acknowledged a tangible body of Jesus even while they denied a true human nature.

[162] Hippolytus, *Refutation of All Heresies,* 9.2–5; cf. Epiphanius of Salamis, *Panarion,* 57.

[163] Hippolytus, *Against Noetus,* 1–2; *Refutation of All Heresies,* 9.5.

[164] Hippolytus, *Against Noetus,* 1–2; see also *Refutation of All Heresies,* 10.23.

[165] Hippolytus, *Refutation of All Heresies,* 9.5.

[166] Epiphanius of Salamis, *Panarion,* 62.1–2.

[167] Epiphanius of Salamis, *Panarion,* 62.1.4. God is described by Sabellius as "three names in one *hypostasis,*" or one Person with three names.

three manifestations of the Father, or three ways that the one God reveals Himself to humanity. The three names are not, however, true distinctions within God (as a Trinity), nor do they imply relationships within the Godhead. It is as if the one God wears three different masks based on what God is doing, or when He is doing it.[168] This means that the three "names" for God become associated with divine activity, such that the *Father* is the name of God when God is Creator, the *Son* is the name of God when God is Savior, and the *Holy Spirit* is the name of God when God is Sanctifier. Therefore, the "threeness" of God only exists as artificial distinctions based on the *mode* of activity by which God is interacting with creation or humanity at any given time.[169] This distinction by labeling the "mode" of activity gave rise to the name *modalism*, or *modalistic monarchianism*. Therefore, the only distinction between Father and Son that is acceptable to modalism is a distinction of perception, from the human point of view, in which the perceived distinctions are described by function or activity.[170] Also implied is a temporal distinction; that God can be described as Father in the time of the Old Testament, as Son (or Jesus Christ) during the time of His earthly ministry, and as Holy Spirit in the age of the Church. The implication of this is that God can only be described by one name at a time.[171] In other words, for modalism, God is not three Persons in one substance but rather one Person with three names.

[168] It is not clear to what extent the proponents of modalism had the concept of the theater mask in mind. In Greek, the words for *person* could have a range of meaning to include the idea of "personality," or even "character." However, it is not as simple as saying that the three names for the Trinity are three "faces" of God, since the point is that in modalism the names refer to God's activity and/or the chronological distinction of Old Testament/New Testament/Church. A better analogy might be to suggest that the three different names for God in modalism are like three different hats that God wears, depending on the task at hand.

[169] Sabellius used some of the same analogies for the Trinity that the mainstream writers used, including the analogy of the sun (which Tertullian also used), where the star itself is like the Father, its light is like the Son, and its heat is like the Holy Spirit. However, Sabellius understood this in a way that removed any real distinction between the three, and it is a testimony to the imperfection of analogies that writers on both sides of the debate can use the same analogies to explain their differing christologies. In fact, what we observe is that it is not the analogy, but the explanation of it, that becomes the argument in favor of one version of christology or another.

[170] Ironically, this type of distinction is not acceptable to the orthodox, since it violates the principles of inseparable operation and appropriation.

[171] The implication of modalism is that God is not a Trinity, since modalists believe He can only be one *Person* at a time, rather like Peter Parker and Spider-Man — they cannot both

The mainstream Church would argue that God must be all three Persons at all times, always united in all activity (*inseparable operation*). However, the most important critique of modalism was that it assumes a Christ who is not really one of us. In this scheme, Christ is fully divine, but not fully human, since He is one and the same with the immutable and utterly transcendent Father (see the chart, *Christology and Theology in the Third Century* at the end of this chapter).

Adoptionism

The second-century Ebionite christology that saw Jesus as a mere human continued in the third century as a form of adoptionism that is sometimes called *dynamic monarchianism.*[172] Even though it is the opposite extreme from modalism, it is also a form of monarchianism because it is based on a well-intentioned attempt to protect the "monarchy," or oneness of God. It is called "*dynamic* monarchianism" because it assumes that divine *power* (*dunamis* in Greek) did not originally belong to Jesus but was received at His Baptism—limiting true divine power to the Father alone. This means that Jesus is the recipient of divine power, but not a source of divine power. In other words, God is one because Jesus is not God. In the early third century, an obscure teacher named Artemon (or Artemas), who is said to have been a student of Theodotus, was the bridge between the Ebionites and the most famous third-century adoptionist, Paul of Samosata.

Paul lived from about AD 200–275 and was the bishop of Antioch in Syria until he was deposed in AD 272. In spite of his condemnation, his christology would influence the Antiochene school of thought for centuries. Paul of Samosata taught that the *Logos* was the personification of God's will.[173] In this, he was probably influenced by his predecessor in Antioch, Theophilus, and the idea of the *Logos* as a thought in the mind of God. Therefore, Paul of Samosata reasoned that Jesus was a mere human who was indwelt by the *Logos* just as one might say the prophets were inspired by the Holy Spirit. Jesus conquered sin purely by resisting temptation and as a result, He was rewarded by God with an anointing, which amounted to the "cementing" of a permanent relationship between Jesus the man and the *Logos*, or the *will* of God. In other words, by conforming His will to the will of God so perfectly and consistently,

---

be in the same room at the same time. It is important to see that some analogies that are often used for the Trinity, such as H_2O (ice, water, steam) are actually analogies of a modalistic "Trinity," not an orthodox one. You cannot have both ice and steam at the same time.

[172] Behr, *The Way to Nicaea*, 138, esp. n. 1.

[173] Grillmeier, *Christ in Christian Tradition, Volume 1*, 165; cf. Epiphanius of Salamis, *Panarion*, 65.

Jesus was granted an eternal union of wills. This union took place at His Baptism, when the Father is heard to call Him *Son*. Jesus was not the Son of God by nature, but as a reward and therefore only by adoption. Adoptionists would argue that before His Baptism, it would be inappropriate to call Jesus the Son of God. After His adoption, He can be called "the son," as long as it is understood that although He was inspired, indwelt, and anointed, He was not really divine.

Adoptionism does not have an Incarnation, in the sense of the *descent* of the divine *Logos* who becomes human. Rather, it is the *ascent* of a mere human, who achieves an elevated status as the adopted son of God.[174] His sonship is not ontological, but volitional and vocational (cf. Jer. 1:1–10). The union between Jesus and Divinity is not a necessary union, but only a union of wills, which means it is a union that might not have been. Jesus was the first to be perfect, but anyone might have done it, in fact Jesus might not have done it. From the perspective of the mainstream Church, the idea that Jesus might have sinned meant that His status as Savior was tenuous. Thus for the orthodox the perfection of Jesus must be an essential element of His nature. But for the adoptionist, the perfection of Jesus is an achievement of personal discipline and obedience. Therefore, the adoptionist's Jesus (like the Ebionite's before) is fully human, but not divine. Divine power may be granted by virtue of His adoption, but it is really no more than the prophets had. Because of this, Paul of Samosata was outspoken against the worship of Christ, especially the singing of hymns in praise of Jesus.[175]

Paul of Samosata seems to have made a concession to the mainstream in that he did accept the virgin birth. Apparently, the universal acceptance of the birth narratives in the Gospels of Matthew and Luke forced him to account for a miraculous birth, which he did by attributing it to divine foreknowledge of Jesus' perfect obedience. In other words, because God knew that Jesus would be the one to achieve perfection, God granted him the gift of a miraculous birth. This gives the impression of a conundrum, because it seems to be an attempt to explain something that is not entirely consistent with adoptionist christology, but we do find this tendency in a branch of adoptionism sometimes called *angel adoptionism*.[176] In fact, Paul would use the same argument of divine foreknowledge to explain the preexistence of the *Logos* in John 1:1. He said that by divine foreknowledge the *Logos* could be *thought of* as preexistent, since God's will has always existed

[174] Eusebius of Caesarea, *Ecclesiastical History*, 7.30.

[175] Eusebius of Caesarea, *Ecclesiastical History*, 7.27–30; see also Malchion, *In the Name of the Synod of Antioch Against Paul of Samosata*.

[176] For a detailed treatment of the two kinds of adoptionism, see Papandrea, *The Earliest Christologies*.

in the mind of God, though He was not actually (i.e., substantially) preexistent. Paul would be the last of the adoptionists to deny a real preexistence of the *Logos*. Mainstream interpretation of John 1:1 (as well as Phil. 2) would force the fourth-century adoptionists to account for a preexistent *Logos* that is more than just a personification of God's will.[177]

Paul rejected the interpretation of the Incarnation as a christology of descent (as the orthodox interpreted "the Word became flesh," John 1:14).[178] It was said that he refused to accept that the Son of God "came down" from heaven.[179] In fact this reveals that for the adoptionists, Christ is not the product of an *incarnation* so much as an *elevation* through the indwelling of the *Logos*, whom Paul believed to be merely the personification of the will of God (as if to say, "the flesh earned the Word"). In other words, Jesus was filled with the Word of God, in much the same way that the prophets were filled with the Spirit of God. This is, then, a christology of ascent, in which a mere human earns the adoption by God, resulting in an elevated status. He was eventually confronted by one of his own priests, a man named Malchion. He was also accused of Nicolaitanism, that is, keeping a mistress while claiming to be celibate, however, this charge may have been invented to vilify him in the eyes of those who might not understand the intricacies of the theological debate.[180]

A synod was held in Antioch in the late AD 260s, at which both Malchion and Gregory the Wonderworker opposed Paul. (Remember that Gregory the Wonderworker, a student of Origen, had drifted into modalism, so adoptionism was, for him, the opposite extreme.) Paul of Samosata was declared a heretic by the council, excommunicated, and replaced as bishop, however he refused to leave the church at Antioch.[181] Apparently, the controversy caught the attention of the emperor Aurelian,

[177] Specifically, for Arius the *Logos* is a real preexistent entity — though not eternally preexistent, and created, not divine. While Arius is the fourth-century legacy of adoptionism, the fourth century will witness an evolution of adoptionism, to accept a qualified divinity in Christ. However, for Arius, the divinity of Christ was acquired, received as a reward, and it was a lesser degree of divinity than the Father, so that for him the Father and Son were not consubstantial.

[178] Eusebius of Caesarea, *Ecclesiastical History*, 7.30; see also Malchion, *In the Name of the Synod of Antioch Against Paul of Samosata*.

[179] Malchion, *In the Name of the Synod of Antioch Against Paul of Samosata*, 3.

[180] Eusebius of Caesarea, *Ecclesiastical History*, 7.30; see also Malchion, *In the Name of the Synod of Antioch Against Paul of Samosata*.

[181] Eusebius of Caesarea, *Ecclesiastical History*, 7.30. Eusebius's account includes a possible mention of a church building (*ekklesias oikou*) in Antioch. If this is a reference to a building, it would probably have been a house converted for worship. It is unlikely that there would have been any buildings built specifically as Christian houses of worship

who finally intervened in the year AD 272 to keep the peace. Aurelian (a pagan emperor) decreed that the church of Antioch belonged to whomever was in accord with the church of Rome.[182] This is significant because, although Christianity was not yet a legal religion, the emperor acknowledged that it existed throughout the empire and that there was some expectation of connection and consistency from one city to another. Also, the choice of Rome as the city with whom others must agree (though for the emperor it was probably only because Rome was the capital of the empire) contributed to the acceptance of the primacy of the bishop of Rome.

From the perspective of his opponents, Paul's adoptionist christology logically led to a soteriology that lacked sufficient divine intervention. In other words, if the adoptionsists were right, then Jesus first had to earn His own salvation (adoption) by being perfectly obedient to God's will. Therefore, as "Savior," He is only a pioneer who presents us with an example to follow, yet anyone else would still have to earn his or her adoption by achieving perfect obedience. The emphasis of adoptionist soteriology appeared to be on human effort, based on an optimism about human nature that assumes the possibility of human perfection. The majority of the bishops, by contrast, argued that salvation must be by divine initiative (through the divine nature of Christ), reasoning that if our adoption into the family of God depended on human righteousness we could not hope to have eternal life (see the chart, *Christology and Theology in the Third Century* at the end of this chapter).[183]

The Two Dionysii and the Orthodox Middle

Dionysius of Alexandria was the student and successor of Origen.[184] He took over the catechetical school at about the time that Origen was excommunicated in Alexandria, and he became the bishop there in AD 247. He was exiled in AD 257 during the

at this time, however there were dedicated worship spaces converted from domestic or other purposes. Before the Church was a legal entity, churches in some cities could own property as social organizations, such as the funerary societies which provided burial for their members. On the other hand, it could be an anachronism in Eusebius's fourth-century text.

[182] There was a growing consensus within the Church, based on apostolic succession, that all churches should agree with Rome, at least on matters of doctrine; for example, see Irenaeus of Lyons, *Against Heresies*, 3.3.2.

[183] Clement of Alexandria, *Who Is the Rich Man That Shall Be Saved?*, 8; Irenaeus of Lyons, *Against Heresies*, 3.20.3; Novatian, *On the Trinity*, 15.7–9.

[184] Eusebius of Caesarea, *Ecclesiastical History*, 6.29.

persecution of the emperor Valerian but returned to Alexandria a few years later.[185] He died in AD 264 or 265.

Dionysius of Alexandria saw Sabellian modalism as the Church's greatest threat, and so he reacted against it, at first by going to the other extreme. In his attempt to refute modalism's overemphasis on the unity of God, he proposed a distinction of Persons in the Trinity that crossed the line into adoptionism. He said that the Son of God was a created being, and implied that there was a time when He did not exist.

Dionysius of Rome (bishop AD 260–286) intervened to correct his Alexandrian counterpart. He wrote a document called *Against the Sabellians,* a title sure to catch the attention of Dionysius of Alexandria.[186] However, the treatise is really a warning against going too far in refutation against modalism and falling into adoptionism. It is addressed to the church of Alexandria, though it never mentions their bishop Dionysius by name. It does, however, accuse unnamed theologians of opposing one extreme with the other and missing the middle way. Following Irenaeus, Tertullian, and especially Novatian, Dionysius of Rome defended the mainstream against the two extremes of modalism and adoptionism. He argued for the consubstantiality of the Persons of the Trinity, and the eternal generation of the Son.[187] He clarified that the generation of the Son (that He is begotten) does not imply that He is created, and therefore there was no time when the Son of God did not exist.[188]

Dionysius of Alexandria wrote a response to Dionysius of Rome, in which he admitted that he should not have said that the Son was created. He also accepted the orthodoxy of eternal generation and consubstantiality, though he was uncomfortable with the latter because the Greek term used to describe it (*homoousios*) was not to be found in Scripture.[189]

This exchange is an interesting window into the process of the development of doctrine. On the one hand, the orthodoxy of any given time in the history of the Church is defined as that which is consistent with the orthodoxy of the previous generations, so therefore it is appropriate to speak of orthodoxy at various stages in

[185] Eusebius of Caesarea, *Ecclesiastical History,* 7.2.6–11.

[186] Grillmeier, *Christ in Christian Tradition, Volume 1,* 154–158. Dionysius of Rome may also have chosen to write the document this way because of accusations that he himself was a follower of Sabellius. While the accusation was unfounded, his own emphasis on the consubstantiality of the persons of the Trinity led some to accuse him of modalism.

[187] Ayres, *Nicaea and Its Legacy,* 94.

[188] Dionysius of Rome, *Against the Sabellians,* 2–3.

[189] Athanasius of Alexandria, *Defense of Dionysius,* 18, reprinted in J. Stevenson, *A New Eusebius: Documents Illustrating the History of the Church to AD 337* (London: SPCK, 1957, rev. ed. 1987), 254–255; see also Ayres, *Nicaea and Its Legacy,* 94.

the development of doctrine. On the other hand, the nuances of one generation's description of doctrine cannot be held to the standards of later generations. For example, the way that second-century apologists could sometimes blur the distinction between the pre-incarnate Christ and the Holy Spirit would not be acceptable to the theologians. Or the way Tertullian could speak of the Persons of the Trinity as "parts" of God would very quickly go by the wayside because of the importance of affirming divine simplicity and consubstantiality. And the way that the early theologians thought of the generation of the Son as an "event" would not be acceptable once Novatian clarified the doctrine of eternal generation. And Novatian's own way of describing the Incarnation as a *kenosis* in which the *Logos* empties Himself of certain divine attributes will not be entirely acceptable once Augustine of Hippo clarifies that God does not *have* attributes, but that God's attributes and powers are not distinct from God's substance. These subtle ways of describing doctrine would develop over time, in the back-and-forth swing of the pendulum of history, always adding nuance and clarity, and yet none of these developments represent anything that could be called an evolution, or a change in orthodoxy.

As we have seen, the early Church's understanding of progressive revelation rejected any deliberate deviation from the conclusions of past generations, but this did not prevent teachers, and even bishops, from testing the boundaries of what the mainstream Church could abide. The major heresies, then, are those philosophical and christological *extremes* that emphasize one aspect of theology by diminishing another. As Hippolytus had complained, the heretics accept one group of biblical passages, but reject another, based on their theological agenda.[190] To be fair, the canon itself was a developing concept, as we have seen, however the heretics were even choosing between texts by the same author, and within the same documents. Ideally, the mainstream Church revered all Scripture, accepting paradox and looking for a middle way between the extremes.[191] Novatian had said that the true Christ was to be found in the middle between the heresies, as if he was still being crucified by them, "between two thieves."[192]

Therefore, orthodoxy was, and was perceived as, the middle way between the extreme alternatives. While the Ebionites and adoptionists emphasized the humanity of Christ but denied His divinity, and the docetics, gnostics, and to a certain extent the modalists, emphasized the divinity of Christ and denied His humanity, the mainstream Church refused to choose and accepted both the full humanity and

[190] Hippolytus, *Against Noetus*, 3–4.

[191] Cyprian of Carthage, *Epistles*, 51.6, 19–20, 27.

[192] Novatian, *On the Trinity*, 11.5, 11.9, 30.6.

full divinity of Christ (see the chart, *Christology and Theology in the Third Century* at the end of this chapter). While adoptionism emphasized the distinction between Persons of the Trinity and denied an ontological union between the Father and Son, and modalism emphasized the unity of the Trinity but denied any real distinction of the Persons beyond functional labels, the mainstream Church embraced the paradox and looked for a balance of unity and distinction (see the chart, *Christological Options and Influences* at the end of chapter 12).[193]

Thus, the history of the Church is like a swinging pendulum. One teacher or group may test the boundaries on one extreme, causing the pendulum to swing wide to one side. Another teacher or group will perceive that this is too far from what can be tolerated, and reacts against it, but by going to the opposite extreme. Each generation produces its own version of the previous generation's extremes (and in some ways, this continues to this day). As the boundaries of acceptability are tested, the Church works to find its center of gravity, and so the pendulum swings back and forth across the decades and centuries, with each new generation supplying teachers and writers who are willing to react to heresy by going to the opposite extreme and cross the boundaries of orthodoxy into a heresy of an opposite kind. We will see this trend continue in the fourth and fifth centuries. Yet in each generation, "gravity" keeps bringing the pendulum back to the center, as the mainstream Church gains more and more clarity, finds more precise language to describe its theology, and (with the guidance of the Holy Spirit) comes to the conclusion that orthodoxy embraces the paradox by finding the place of balance. In other words, the truth is in the middle.

[193] For a more detailed treatment of the development of doctrine along these lines, see Papandrea, *Novatian of Rome.*

Christology and Theology in the Third Century

Adoptionism (Dynamic Monarchianism)

God is one because Jesus is not God (i.e., not divine).

Jesus Christ is human, but not really divine.

Jesus was a mere human; therefore, he is not preexistent.

He was the first human to achieve perfection.

As a reward for his perfect obedience, God adopted him.

The adoption took place at Jesus' Baptism.

Jesus did not have his own divine power (***dunamis***); rather, he received power.

Note the importance of adoption in Roman culture and in relation to the succession of Roman emperors; the emperor's successor is his adopted son.

Jesus is a son of God, but only by adoption.

We are also "sons" (heirs) of God by adoption

Objections of opposition:
It appears that Jesus had to be saved by his own obedience.

That implies that for the rest of humanity, salvation is also by human effort; that is, by following his example.

So Christ as "savior" is really only in the sense of pioneer.

The Theologians
Irenaeus
Tertullian
Hippolytus
Novatian

Jesus is God (that is, divine), but Jesus is not the Father.

The Father and Son are ***one*** (John 10:30), but the Father and Son are not ***one and the same*** (John 14:28).

Jesus Christ is the preexistent Logos who became human.

Jesus has his own divine power but limits himself for the Incarnation.

According to Novatian, the Incarnation is a voluntary and temporary emptying (***kenosis***) of divine "powers"/attributes.

The Trinity is a balance of:
Unity of substance/divinity
Distinction of Persons in a hierarchy of authority

The persons of the Trinity are ***consubstantial***, so the hierarchy of the Trinity is not ontological, but according to authority (Sender/Messenger).

The three persons of the Trinity cannot be distinguished by function since the unity of substance is also a unity of divine action (***inseparable operation***).

The Son of God is ***eternally generated.***

Jesus as Savior is the embodiment of both divine intervention ***and*** human representation.

Modalism (Modalistic Monarchianism, a.k.a. Patripassionism, or Sabellianism)

God is one because Jesus is not human; Jesus ***is*** the Father — the Father and Son are one and the same.

Jesus Christ is divine but not really human.

The multiple manifestations of God are only the different "masks" that God wears to reveal himself to humanity or to intervene in human history.

The different revelations of God are distinguished by "mode" of activity or by task/function.

The distinctions are more perceived than real.

Note that the implication is that God can be only one manifestation or mode of revelation at a time.

Objections of opposition:
If Jesus is identical with the Father, then God died on the cross (patripassionism).

More important, the identity of the Son with the Father effectively diminishes the humanity of Christ, and he is no longer really one of us; therefore, he cannot represent us on the cross, especially since his passion is diminished or denied to avoid patripassionism.

9

Early Ecclesiology

Ongoing Persecution

The Martyrs of Lyons and Viennes

During the persecution under the reign of Marcus Aurelius, public sentiment against the Christians in Gaul (modern France) led to violence. The year was AD 177. Polycarp had sent the priest Irenaeus to Lyons to assist bishop Pothinus. While Irenaeus was away in Rome to discuss the question of the Montanists, an angry mob took up arms and killed a group of Christians, desecrating their bodies and then refusing them burial (cf. Rev. 11:8–10). By this time, everything from failed crops to natural disasters could be blamed on the Christians, who were now a fair target for public rage. In some places it could be dangerous for Christians even to go about in public. Church leaders were, of course, a primary target, and bishop Pothinus was murdered. When Irenaeus returned to Lyons he found that his bishop was dead, and that he had been elected the new bishop. It is possible that Irenaeus himself wrote the account of the martyrs of Lyons and Viennes. It is certain that the event must have affected him, contributing to his skepticism of Roman virtue, reason, and philosophy.

In this martyr document, we meet the heroic Blandina. She is typical of many of the female martyrs, in that she meets her death with courage and dignity. She becomes the very image of Christian virtue, shaming the so-called virtue of the Romans. The interesting thing about this is that in both Greek and Latin, some words for virtue are based on the same roots as words for *strength* and *man*, which betrays the Roman bias that to be truly *virtuous*, one must be a man.[1] Yet in these martyr documents we see Christian women who exhibit a strength that puts Roman men

[1] In the *Martyrdom of Polycarp*, 9, the same idea is expressed in Greek. The Greek word *manly* (*andrizou*) is translated, *courageous*.

to shame.[2] It is presented as though these women are granted a charismatic gift of *manliness* to meet death with courage (cf. 2 Macc. 7:20-23), however there is more to it than that. On one hand, the point is to hint again at the apologists' argument that Christians are more virtuous than non-Christian Romans, as if to say, "Our women are stronger than your men." On the other hand, as the apostle Paul said, "there is not male and female; for you are all one in Christ Jesus" (Gal. 3:28). Therefore, it is not that these heroic women are turned into men, but that when it comes time to face death, men and women are equal as Christians. At first glance, some of this might seem similar to the stories of heroic women in the apocryphal acts. However, in the more mainstream martyr documents, their power to face death comes, not from celibacy or self-control, but from their faith, and ultimately, from Christ Himself.

The Scillitan Martyrs

This document tells the story of the martyrdom of a group of Christians from North Africa, who died in Carthage on July 17, AD 180. This was not long after the death of Marcus Aurelius, so their deaths would still be seen as justified under his edict. For our purposes it is enough to note just how far the persecution has come, and how bold the pagan mobs could be in committing acts of violence against their Christian neighbors. It is important to note that there was never a Christian call for violence or rebellion against their persecutors, never a Christian uprising against the pagans, and never a justification of the use of violence or retaliation during the times of persecution.

The Diary of Perpetua

Carthage in North Africa would also be the scene of the famous martyrdoms of Perpetua and Felicitas, which took place on March 7th, in the year AD 203. Vibia Perpetua was a young woman of the nobility, who was in catechesis preparing for Christian Baptism when she was arrested, along with her servant Felicitas (sometimes translated *Felicity*) and other members of her catechesis class. By this time, the right of a Roman citizen to a trial in Rome was gone. While in prison awaiting her execution, Perpetua kept a diary, which was later finished to include the account of her death and published, perhaps by Tertullian.[3] The diary is a very personal and poignant account of Perpetua's faith and her own father's attempts to convince her to denounce the Faith for the sake

[2] Clement of Rome, *1 Clement*, 55.

[3] See Dunn, *Tertullian*, 16–17, and Tabbernee, "Montanism and the Cult of the Martyrs in Roman North Africa," 301–302. Tabbernee does not think that Tertullian wrote the ending of the diary. He admits that it is possible it was written by a Montanist, but regardless, there is no hard evidence that Perpetua and her companions were Montanists.

of her newborn baby.[4] Like Blandina, Perpetua is given strength and courage from Christ to meet her death in the arena.

The account of Perpetua's martyrdom, which includes her dreams and her experience in the arena, is compelling for several reasons. In some ways, it uses apocalyptic imagery, much like the book of Revelation, to reinforce the idea that martyrdom is a victory over Satan. At one point, in a vision, in order to climb the ladder to Heaven, Perpetua must step on the head of a dragon (cf. Gen. 3:15; Rev. 12:1–6). The fact that Perpetua is a new mother symbolizes that martyrdom is both a birth, in the sense that the martyr is born to eternal life, and it is also a mother, in the sense that the Church is born through martyrdom.[5]

We can look back to the first Christian martyr Stephen, who followed the example of Jesus Himself when he prayed for the forgiveness of his killers, and compare that to Polycarp, who pointed at the crowd and said, "Away with the atheists!" and then one of the catechism classmates of Perpetua who would gesture to the crowd in the arena, as if to say, "What you do to us, God will do to you!" By the beginning of the third century, martyrdom had become a regular and dangerous, not to mention frustrating, part of the life of the Church. But submitting to martyrdom made a public statement. It was a faith statement, that the Christians believed in something bigger than life, and beyond this life. And it was a political statement, that as Paul had said, "There is neither Jew nor Greek, there is neither slave nor free person, there is not male and female; for you are all one in Christ Jesus" (Gal. 3:28), and so Perpetua is willing to die alongside her slave, equals in the sight of God without regard for social class, and in her willingness to give her life for her faith, she proves herself just as strong as any man.

The Persecution Escalates

By the end of the second century, Christians could be found at all levels of society, in every kind of job, including the military.[6] There had been Christians in some of the imperial households, and even the mistress of Commodus (emperor AD 180–192) was rumored to have been a Christian, or at least sympathetic to the Church. At the same time, accusations of anti-social behavior persisted. Pagan Romans feared that if

4 On the diary of Perpetua, see Joyce E. Salisbury, *Perpetua's Passion: The Death and Memory of a Young Roman Woman* (New York: Routledge, 1997).

5 Tertullian, *Apology*, 50. Here Tertullian famously says that the blood of the martyrs is the seed of the Church.

6 Tertullian, *Apology*, 1, 37. Of course, this supports Tertullian's argument and may be an exaggeration; see Sage, *Cyprian*, 47–48.

enough people joined the Church and stopped worshiping the traditional gods, these gods would remove their protection, which could mean the downfall of the empire. Any natural disaster could be blamed on the Church, and any military defeat could be blamed on the presence of Christians in the legions. As is shown by the martyrs of Lyons and Viennes, at any time an angry mob could form and take out their fears and frustrations on their "atheist" neighbors.[7]

We have already seen how emperors such as Marcus Aurelius and Septimius Severus had set the precedent of requiring sacrifice as a sign of loyalty. Christians were now being forced to choose between the self-proclaimed gods of the empire, or the God of the Church. In fact, the Church demanded loyalty even over family, if that family was not Christian. So the third century brings to the surface the choice: Caesar or Christ? Is the emperor the son of a god, or is Jesus the Son of God? Is the emperor the father (patron) of all, or is God the Father of all?

In the year AD 212, the emperor Caracalla (emperor AD 211–217) granted citizenship to all inhabitants of the empire. Until this time, Roman citizenship was a privilege, but now it had become a burden, since taxation was extended and loyalty could be demanded across the empire.[8] Later, Severus Alexander (emperor AD 222–235) would be tolerant of the Church, and it was his mother, Julia Mamea, who summoned Origen to Antioch to explain Christianity to her.[9] But this tolerance, along with the possibility of Christians in the imperial household, apparently caused Alexander's successor, Maximinus Thrax (emperor AD 235–238), to renew persecution. According to Eusebius of Caesarea, Maximinus's hatred for his predecessor

[7] Tertullian, *Apology*, 40.

[8] It seems that Caracalla required loyalty sacrifices for all (new) citizens, and while it was not his intention to persecute Christians, some may have been executed at this time for refusing to sacrifice.

[9] Eusebius of Caesarea, *Ecclesiastical History*, 6.21; see also the *Historia Augusta, Severus Alexander*, 22.4, 29.2, 43.6–7, 45.6–7, 49.6, 51.7. The reliability of the *Historia Augusta* has been questioned, however, even if stories of Alexander's preference for Christianity are exaggerated, his tolerance of the Church is based on historical events. Eusebius says that the emperor Philip (reigned AD 244–249) was also sympathetic to the Church, and that he actually had once attended an Easter service. See Eusebius of Caesarea, *Ecclesiastical History*, 6.19.15, 6.21.3–4, 6.36.3. The story of Philip attending Christian worship is probably apocryphal since it would be unlikely for an unbaptized person to attend worship before the end of the persecutions. However, the anecdote does tell us something of the precariousness of the Church's status within the empire before the fourth century—at the drop of a hat the Church could go back and forth from pursued to tolerated. It seems that Philip's reign was the calm before the storm.

led him to order Church leaders put to death.[10] These events set the stage for the persecutions of the mid-third century.

In the year AD 249, a new emperor would come to power, who would advocate a revival of traditional Roman religion. His name was Decius (emperor AD 249–251). Just two years before, Rome had celebrated its millennium.[11] But the empire was plagued by an economic recession in which previous emperors had devalued the coinage to supplement the imperial treasury. In addition, wars in the East had depleted resources and left the borders unstable. Decius himself, as a general, had left an eastern border undefended to come to Rome and claim the throne. The presence of the Christians only added insult to injury in the eyes of the emperor, and as far as he was concerned the Church stood in the way of Rome's return to its glory days. Like Maximinus, he hated the Christians, and he hated the fact that his predecessor was tolerant of the Church. In fact, there was a rumor (probably untrue) that Philip (emperor AD 244–249) may have even been a Christian.[12] Decius's solution was to call for renewed enthusiasm for the Roman gods, including sacrifices to Jupiter for the benefit of the empire, and in honor of the emperor. With this he would kill two birds with one stone: he would bring back the blessing of the gods, and he would force the Christians to give up their superstition. Thus, he initiated the first systematic, empire-wide persecution of the Church.

The Decian Persecution

As soon as Decius took the throne, persecution began in the provinces.[13] In late AD 249, Decius issued in edict which commanded all inhabitants of the empire to make a sacrifice on a certain date. The edict was heard by some in the Church as a fulfillment of Jesus' warnings of tribulation in the Gospels and in the book of Revelation.[14] Local councils were set up in each city to oversee the sacrifices. This was the first time that such an order was enforced systematically across the empire. Everyone who complied would receive a receipt, called a *libellus* (Latin for "little book," or pamphlet — imagine a sheet of papyrus about the size of an 8½-by-11-inch sheet of paper that would

[10] Eusebius of Caesarea, *Ecclesiastical History*, 6.28. It was said that Maximinus believed (or claimed) that an earthquake in Asia Minor was a sign from the gods, demonstrating their anger over the many conversions to Christianity. It was under Maximinus that Hippolytus and bishop Pontian of Rome were sentenced to the mines.

[11] The traditional date for the founding of the city of Rome is 753 BC. Thus, the one-thousand-year anniversary was in AD 247.

[12] Eusebius of Caesarea, *Ecclesiastical History*, 6.34, 39.

[13] Eusebius of Caesarea, *Ecclesiastical History*, 6.41.

[14] Eusebius of Caesarea, *Ecclesiastical History*, 6.41.

be folded into quarters). A person could be asked to show this *libellus* at any time as proof of compliance, and it could be required to buy and sell in the markets (cf. Rev. 13:16–17).[15] Failure to make the sacrifice would be considered an act of treason, punishable by death.

Exactly what was entailed in making a sacrifice depended on where one was in the empire, but could be as simple as burning some incense on a pagan altar, pouring out a libation offering of wine, or throwing some grain on a fire. It could mean sacrificing an animal (and this may have been Decius's original intention), but with everyone having to sacrifice, it is unlikely that very many cities made all their people go through a full animal sacrifice. If an animal was sacrificed, the person would most likely be expected to eat some of the sacrificial meat. A person would also be expected to swear an oath of allegiance to the emperor, and if one was suspected of being a Christian, the Roman official could also require a curse against Christ (cf. 1 Cor. 12:3). But even if one admitted to being a Christian at the beginning of the ordeal, simply renouncing the Faith and making the sacrifice would gain one's freedom.[16] Refusal to make the sacrifice could mean imprisonment, torture, exile with confiscation of property (a favorite of those governors who got to keep the property), or execution by decapitation, crucifixion, drowning, burning at the stake, or mauling by wild animals in the arena.[17] One could also be condemned to work in the mines, which was not much more than a prolonged death sentence, since prisoners were literally forced to work until they dropped dead. Eventually some Romans even took delight in devising especially barbarous methods of execution, such as tying a person to two trees bent over and held by ropes, so that when the ropes were cut, the trees would spring back to their original position, tearing the person in two.[18] Presumably, these more horrific methods of execution were meant to encourage other Christians to decide to make the sacrifice.

The response to Decius's edict was that Christians "ran eagerly towards the [pagan] altars."[19] Many refused to sacrifice on the basis that such a sacrifice was idolatry, and even worse, apostasy. But many others simply lined up to make the required sacrifices, reasoning that they knew in their hearts the pagan gods were not real,

[15] See Papandrea, *The Wedding of the Lamb*, 156–159.

[16] Eusebius of Caesarea, *Ecclesiastical History*, 8.11. Note that Eusebius says that some Marcionites were also the victims of this persecution; see Eusebius of Caesarea, *Ecclesiastical History*, 7.12.

[17] Eusebius of Caesarea, *Ecclesiastical History*, 8.7–8, 8.12.

[18] Eusebius of Caesarea, *Ecclesiastical History*, 8.9.

[19] Eusebius of Caesarea, *Ecclesiastical History*, 6.41, in Lake, *Eusebius*, vol. 2, 105; see also Cyprian of Carthage, *On the Lapsed*, 7–8.

and therefore it was acceptable to lie to the Romans and pretend to worship, going through the motions of a sacrifice. According to Cyprian they were motivated as much by a concern to protect their property and businesses as they were concerned for their lives.[20] Some denied they had ever been Christians (which was apparently not required).

Some fled the persecution, and of those captured, many sacrificed after imprisonment or torture. According to Eusebius, even women and children were tortured.[21] Torture could mean starvation, racking, beating, reeds pushed under the fingernails, eyes gouged out or feet hobbled to brand one as a criminal, or slowly pouring boiling tar or molten lead over the delicate parts of a person's body.[22] Christian women could expect to be raped as a matter of course.[23] The emperor's edict had endorsed the brutalization of Christians across the empire.[24] One can imagine that as more and more Christians died or fled, it became harder and harder for those who remained to stand firm, especially in the absence of their leaders.

In spite of the fact that many people denied their faith to save their lives, many were also martyred, among them bishop Fabian of Rome, who died in January of AD 250.[25] Many more were imprisoned, so that the prisons were full of Christians. Even some who *had* denied their faith to save their lives were left to starve to death in prison. However, far from destroying the Church, Decius had succeeded in giving the Church an opportunity for witness. Across the empire, pagans were converted, seeing that Christians would rather die than give up their faith. More documents like the early martyr acts made heroes of the martyrs, recounting their triumph over evil in the arenas. Just as before, these martyrologies contained embellishments, including stories of miraculous submission of the wild animals, which were often said to have refused to attack the Christians. The reality of the situation was that many Christians did not deny their faith, or even hide, but in fact reached out to

[20] Cyprian of Carthage, *On the Lapsed*, 6, 10; see also Hermas, *The Shepherd*, 14, which may have been in Cyprian's mind.

[21] Eusebius of Caesarea, *Ecclesiastical History*, 6.41.

[22] Eusebius of Caesarea, *Ecclesiastical History*, 6.5, 8.7–8, 8.12.

[23] Eusebius of Caesarea, *Ecclesiastical History*, 8.12.

[24] For an account of the persecution in Alexandria, see the letter of Dionysius of Alexandria to Stephen of Rome.

[25] Eusebius of Caesarea, *Ecclesiastical History*, 6.29. Eusebius records that Fabian was loved by the people of Rome because when he was elected a dove had landed on his head, mirroring Jesus' Baptism and signifying God's anointing. Cyprian said that the emperor Decius had remarked that he would rather confront a rival emperor than to see a new bishop installed in the church at Rome. Cyprian of Carthage, *Epistles*, 51.9.

minister to their brothers and sisters in prison, even at the risk of their own lives. This in itself was seen as a form of martyrdom.[26] Between outbreaks of persecution, the Christians continued to minister to the sick and imprisoned, and Romans continued to be moved by this to come into the Church. Decius had to go back to the eastern borders of the empire in AD 251 to repel an invasion. He was killed in battle, which many interpreted as God's vindication, and the persecution of Christians briefly subsided.

Novatian, Cyprian, and the Problem of the Lapsed

Thascius Caecilius Cyprianus (Cyprian) was bishop of Carthage in North Africa from AD 249 until his death in AD 258.[27] He had been ordained and elected bishop within only a few years after his conversion to Christianity. During the Decian persecution, he fled Carthage and attempted to care for his flock from a distance by writing letters, many of which are still extant.[28] Returning to Carthage in the spring of AD 251, Cyprian came back to a Church that had been broken by the persecution in more ways than one. When Cyprian realized that the very unity of the Church was threatened, he composed the treatise, *On the Unity of the Catholic Church* (sometimes called *On the Unity of the Church*). It is in this treatise that he famously wrote, "whoever does not have the Church for his mother, can no longer have God for his Father."[29] The reason that one cannot have God for a Father without the Church for a mother — in other words, the reason why there could be no salvation outside the Church — is that it is only within the Church where the valid sacraments are found. And it is only through the valid sacraments of the Church that one might hope to be saved. Cyprian also said, "whoever is outside the Church cannot be a martyr."[30]

In the aftermath of the persecution, two major problems arose. The first concerned the question of what to do about those who had denied the Faith to save their lives, known as the *lapsed*. Should they be allowed to return to the table of the Eucharist,

[26] Eusebius of Caesarea, *Ecclesiastical History*, 7.22.

[27] For a thorough treatment of Cyprian and the controversies of the third century, see Sage, *Cyprian*.

[28] *Epistles* 2 through 39 of Cyprian's correspondence were written from hiding. Later, Cyprian would write that fleeing persecution to avoid the temptation of idolatry was as good as being a confessor; see Cyprian of Carthage, *On the Lapsed*, 3. The Montanists, on the other hand, had said that to flee was to be unfaithful.

[29] Cyprian of Carthage, *On the Unity of the Catholic Church*, 6, translation by the present author.

[30] Cyprian of Carthage, *On the Unity of the Catholic Church*, 14, translation by the present author.

or would that be a slap in the face to those who endured torture, or whose loved ones had been executed? Some said mercy should be extended to the apostates. Others said they should be excommunicated. Still others looked for some middle ground between easy re-entry and permanent expulsion. Three factions emerged in this debate. The *laxists* advocated allowing the lapsed to come back into the Church with no penalty. This faction was led by one Fortunatus, who also had fled during the persecution.[31] His followers were primarily the lapsed themselves. The *rigorists* advocated excommunication for the lapsed. This group was led by a priest named Novatus in North Africa, and the theologian Novatian in Rome (see the previous chapter).[32] Cyprian had wanted to excommunicate Novatus, but Novatus fled to Rome to consolidate efforts with the rigorists there.[33] The remaining faction was simply everyone else, probably the majority, who couldn't be sure what to do about the problem.

From his place of hiding, Cyprian had counseled patience, saying that as long as the persecution continued, there was still the possibility that an apostate might undo his sin by getting a second chance at martyrdom.[34] But there were some priests back in Carthage who were already reconciling the lapsed and readmitting them to communion.[35] In addition, there were those who had refused to deny the Faith and were imprisoned and/or tortured, but who had not been executed. These *confessors* (called this because they had confessed the Faith at the risk of their lives) were seen by many Christians as having a prophetic authority on the basis of Jesus' words in Matthew 10:17–22: "When they hand you over, do not worry about how you are to speak or what you are to say. You will be given at that moment what you are to say. For it will not be you who speak but the Spirit of your Father speaking through you" (vv. 19–20).

So the lapsed were going to the confessors, even visiting them in prison, and begging for their forgiveness. The confessors, some of whom were lay people, were granting reconciliation without the authority of any bishop. Apparently lapsed Christians were returning to their congregations with letters of reconciliation written by the confessors. Some of these letters, called "*libelli* of peace," were written to cover

[31] Cyprian of Carthage, *Epistles*, 27, 54.9–10.

[32] Some of the early sources confuse these two men, as though they were the same person, but they were not. Novatus had been an enemy of Cyprian in North Africa for some time even before the controversy over the lapsed. See Cyprian of Carthage, *Epistles*, 42, 48.2. Cyprian accused Novatus of taking Luke 9:59–60 literally and failing in his duty to bury his own father.

[33] Cyprian of Carthage, *Epistles*, 48.2–3.

[34] Cyprian of Carthage, *Epistles*, 11.1–3, 13.2, 27.1–3, 51.3–4, 51.7; *On the Unity of the Catholic Church*, 19.

[35] Cyprian of Carthage, *Epistles*, 9.1–2, 11.2.

whole families.[36] As with the Montanists, here was a case of a confrontation between a kind of prophetic authority invested by the laity, and apostolic authority, specifically over Church discipline.[37] Cyprian tried to stop the confessors from granting reconciliation, but he could not directly refute their perceived prophetic authority.[38] He tried to argue that the *libelli* of peace would only be valid if the confessor who granted it was actually martyred, and it should only be honored after the end of the persecution. It should not be a general grant of reconciliation for a group of people, but should be for one person, named in the letter, who must be sincerely repentant.[39] In the end, however, Cyprian was unable to bring the situation under his control as long as he was personally absent from his see.

The second post-persecution problem concerned the episcopacy in Rome. When Fabian was martyred in January of AD 250, the Roman church was not able to elect a successor. Choosing a bishop at that point would have meant consigning that person to death, since it would not be possible to keep the identity of the bishop of Rome a secret for long. According to one story, the emperor Decius had commented that he would rather encounter a rival for his throne than see a new bishop installed in Rome. When the persecution subsided and the church of Rome was able to hold an election for bishop, Novatian must have expected to be elected. He had been the acting bishop for over a year, and his treatise *On the Trinity* had no doubt earned him a reputation as a first-rate theologian and the spokesman for Roman orthodoxy. However, he was a rigorist. To elect Novatian would have been to submit to the rigorist faction and endorse excommunication for all the lapsed. Therefore the more pastoral Cornelius was elected instead of the theologian. When Novatian lost the election, Novatus gathered three rigorist bishops from outside of Rome and had them consecrate Novatian as bishop of Rome in opposition to Cornelius.[40] Thus Novatian became "bishop" of the rigorists, claiming to be the bishop of Rome. Unless one counts Hippolytus, Novatian is therefore the first true *anti-pope*, or rival claimant to the office of bishop of Rome. A priest named Maximus would eventually become the leader of the rigorists in Carthage and claimed to be the legitimate bishop there, against Cyprian. Fortunatus was set up by the laxist party as their bishop in Carthage. The Church was in schism.

[36] Cyprian of Carthage, *Epistles*, 10.1–2, 10.4 (*et cum suis*), 12.1, 13.2, 26.1.

[37] See Rankin, *Tertullian and the Church*, 193–194.

[38] Cyprian of Carthage, *On the Unity of the Catholic Church*, 21.

[39] For Cyprian's description of the situation, see Cyprian of Carthage, *On the Lapsed*, 6–8, 10.

[40] Cyprian of Carthage, *Epistles*, 40.1, 48.2.

Soon after Cyprian returned to Carthage, he convened a synod. The first Council of Carthage was in April of AD 251 and was gathered to address the situation with the rival factions and their leaders claiming to be bishops. The rigorist and laxist leaders were excommunicated, along with their followers. To counteract the uncontrollable nature of confessor reconciliation, Cyprian said that only God can forgive the sin of apostasy (which of course in this situation included the sin of idolatry).[41] As Cyprian reasoned, this is because no one can judge the servant of another, only that servant's master can judge (Rom. 14:4).[42] However, a bishop (and only a bishop) might reconcile the lapsed to the Church, in the hope that God would ultimately ratify that decision.[43] But even Reconciliation by a bishop might not be enough without penance, so any who might reconcile the lapsed too easily would not be doing them a favor — in fact, they might be consigning them to damnation if it meant they would relax their penance.[44] Therefore, anyone who prematurely reconciled someone who had lapsed was threatened with excommunication.[45] The only acceptable exception would be if death was imminent.[46]

To determine a course of action regarding the lapsed, the council identified three categories of lapsed Christians. *Apostates* were those who made the required sacrifices. Any who paid or convinced a sympathetic neighbor to make the sacrifices on their behalf were still considered in this category, on the basis of Matthew 18:6 and parallels. *Libellateci* (*pamphleteers*, for lack of a better English translation) were those who bought a *libellus* or bribed a Roman official to obtain a *libellus* without making the sacrifice (cf. the story of Eleazar, who refused to pretend to eat pork, even to save his life, in 2 Macc. 6:18–28). *Traitors* were those who surrendered Scriptures to be burned or gave up church property to the authorities.[47] Thus the lapsed had to be dealt with individually, on a case-by-case basis, since the gravity of the sin (and

[41] Cyprian of Carthage, *On the Lapsed*, 17.

[42] Cyprian of Carthage, *Epistles*, 51.18.

[43] Cyprian of Carthage, *Epistles*, 26.1; *On the Lapsed*, 17. The granting of the authority to forgive sins in Matthew 16:18–19 was interpreted as having been given to all the apostles, not just Peter. Thus it was seen as extended to all bishops through apostolic succession. This authority could be granted by a bishop to the priests under his authority; see Cyprian of Carthage, *Epistles*, 58.1.

[44] Cyprian of Carthage, *Epistles*, 53.4; *On the Lapsed*, 14–15, 18.

[45] Cyprian of Carthage, *Epistles*, 27.3, 51.4, 54.4.

[46] Cyprian of Carthage, *Epistles*, 12.1–2, 51.5.

[47] The Latin word is *traditore*, which is where we get our English word *traitor*. However, it doesn't really have the connotation of *betrayer*, per se; it actually means one who hands something over.

therefore the extent of the penance) was dependent on the circumstances, including the intentions of the sinner.[48]

With regard to apostates, the council decided that they could not be reconciled until the point of death. They would remain in a state of excommunication, expected to be in perpetual penance, until death was imminent, and only then would they be reconciled. They might be reconciled earlier if they had sacrificed after being tortured, but only if they actually suffered torture; simply the threat of torture was not enough.[49] The *libellateci* and traitors could be reconciled with a significant time of penance, but priests or bishops who had lapsed would not be restored to their ministry.[50] No one would be reconciled unless sincere repentance was shown; repentance which would be demonstrated through penance. Even someone who fell gravely ill and was on the brink of death would not be reconciled if he or she had not shown sufficient repentance before becoming sick.[51]

A similar council was convened in the summer of AD 251 by Cornelius in Rome, attended by sixty bishops, and even more priests.[52] The Roman council basically agreed with the conclusions of Carthage. Thus, in both Rome and Carthage, the lapsed were not all excommunicated out of hand, but the rigorists were. The immediate result of this was that some of the Roman confessors became followers of Novatian.[53] Apparently, these rigorist confessors were offended that any of the lapsed would be reconciled, and were further scandalized by the fact that Cornelius and the Roman council had reconciled an entire group of apostates, a whole city church and its bishop who had sacrificed together.[54] Cyprian responded by commenting that confessors who separate from the Church should lose that title, and that even martyrdom outside the Church is meaningless and ineffective for salvation.[55]

48 Cyprian of Carthage, *Epistles*, 27.3, 51.4, 13, 16, 26; *On the Lapsed*, 14, 35. The early Christians did not believe that all sin was equal. Rather, they believed that some sins were worse than others (the worst being apostasy/idolatry and adultery). Therefore, the penance must fit the sin.

49 Cyprian of Carthage, *Epistles*, 52.2; *On the Lapsed*, 13–14.

50 Cyprian of Carthage, *Epistles*, 12.1–2, 51.5, 11, 17; *On the Lapsed*, 27.

51 Cyprian of Carthage, *Epistles*, 51.23.

52 Eusebius of Caesarea, *Ecclesiastical History*, 6.42–43.

53 Cyprian of Carthage, *Epistles*, 43, 54.9; see also Eusebius of Caesarea, *Ecclesiastical History*, 6.43.

54 Cyprian of Carthage, *Epistles*, 55.6, 17; see J. Patout Burns, "On Rebaptism: Social Organization in the Third Century Church," *Journal of Early Christian Studies* 1:4 (1993): 374–375, 395.

55 Cyprian of Carthage, *Epistles*, 48.1, 51.29, 53.4; cf. *On the Unity of the Catholic Church*, 14.

Novatian sent messengers to Carthage to try to establish himself as the legitimate bishop of Rome, but the messengers were rejected by Cyprian.[56] He then sent messengers with letters to other bishops across the empire to try to gain support.[57] Apparently he almost convinced bishop Fabius of Antioch to side with him, until Dionysius of Alexandria wrote to Fabius, who then held a synod in Antioch which excommunicated Novatian.[58] This is a bit ironic, since as we have seen, it was Novatian's *On the Trinity* that would influence the later bishop of Rome, Dionysius of Rome, and allow him to correct Dionysius of Alexandria on the doctrine of the Trinity.

When Cyprian officially took Cornelius's side, the Roman confessors realized they were outside the Church, and returned to Cornelius.[59] With the loss of the Roman confessors, Novatus went back to North Africa, and some of Novatian's faction (including Maximus, the rigorist bishop of Carthage), returned to the Catholic Church.[60] Even one of the bishops who had consecrated Novatian as the opposing bishop of Rome returned to the Church. Dionysius of Alexandria wrote to Novatian to try to convince him to come back to the Church and submit to Cornelius. The letter indicates that Novatian may have claimed that he was pushed to separate from the Church by the other rigorists, including Novatus. Dionysius wrote that by excommunicating the lapsed, Novatian "accuses our most compassionate Lord Jesus Christ of being without mercy."[61]

Cornelius sarcastically called Novatian "this master of doctrine," the "champion of the Church's discipline." He called his ordination as a priest into question by suggesting that his Baptism was irregular. He further accused Novatian of having refused his duties as a priest to avoid the persecution, and said that now he made his followers swear an oath to him in order to receive the Eucharist.[62] Most of this is probably not true, but was invented to discredit Novatian and prevent others from following him. Cyprian called Novatian "that wily and subtle man."[63] In about AD 257, the anonymous *Against Novatian* was written. It compared Novatian to Cain and

[56] Cyprian of Carthage, *Epistles*, 40.1.

[57] Cyprian of Carthage, *Epistles*, 40.2, 51.3.

[58] Eusebius of Caesarea, *Ecclesiastical History*, 6.42–46.

[59] Cyprian of Carthage, *Epistles*, 45.1–3, 51.

[60] Cyprian of Carthage, *Epistles*, 45.2, 47, 48.2; see also Eusebius of Caesarea, *Ecclesiastical History*, 6.43.

[61] For Dionysius of Alexandria's letter to Novatian, see Eusebius of Caesarea, *Ecclesiastical History*, 6.45, 7.7–8, translation in Lake, *Eusebius*, vol. 2, 147. It is also reprinted in Stevenson, *A New Eusebius*, 232–233.

[62] For Cornelius's letter, see Eusebius of Caesarea, *Ecclesiastical History*, 6.43.

[63] Cyprian of Carthage, *Epistles*, 45.1, translation in *Ante-Nicene Fathers*, vol. 5, 322.

Judas, and quoted to him the Scripture, "Stop judging, and you will not be judged" (Luke 6:37).[64] The author argued that the Church should welcome the lapsed to Reconciliation, just as Jesus had forgiven Peter. If Peter, who also denied the Faith out of fear, can be reconciled to Christ, so can the lapsed.[65]

Nevertheless, Novatian became the figurehead of the first lasting schism of the Church. Called *Novatianists* in the West, and *Purists* (*katharoi*) in the East, the sect grew and continued for centuries, with its own bishops and eventually even its own church buildings. At the first ecumenical Council of Nicaea in AD 325, a Novatianist bishop was present, and signed the creed. The Novatianists were therefore recognized as orthodox in their theology, even while being schismatics. It would be the first time a group would be formally recognized as Christian, but not Catholic.[66] The canons of the Council of Nicaea declared that Novatianist clergy could retain their ordained status if they returned to the Church. After the persecutions were over, the Christian emperors allowed the Novatianist churches to keep their property.[67]

A second Council of Carthage was held in May of AD 252, with a third in AD 253 and a fourth in AD 254.[68] In the end, the majority of the Church followed the lead of Carthage and decided to err on the side of mercy.[69] To excommunicate all the lapsed would decimate the Church, and would risk that those who were excommunicated would give up the Faith entirely rather than follow through on their penance. The rigorists were compared to those in the parable of the Good Samaritan who walked by the man on the road and refused to offer him help and healing.[70] In fact, because they were willing to consign the lapsed to possible damnation by denying them Reconciliation, they were no better than the thugs who beat the man and left him for dead. As Jesus had said, a good shepherd will leave the ninety-nine safe sheep to find the one that is lost. In the same way, the shepherds (bishops) of the Church should seek out the lost (the lapsed) and bring them back into the fold.[71]

[64] *Against Novatian*, 12–14.

[65] *Against Novatian*, 8.

[66] Acknowledging the distinction, Pacian of Barcelona (late fourth century) would later write, "Christian is my name, but Catholic is my surname ... by the one I am approved, by the other I am but marked." Pacian of Barcelona, *Epistles*, 1.5–8.

[67] See Stevenson, *A New Eusebius*, 320. The Novatianists were, however, persecuted by the Catholic bishops of the fourth and fifth centuries. For more detail, see Papandrea, *Novatian of Rome*.

[68] Stevenson, *A New Eusebius*, 224.

[69] Cyprian of Carthage, *Epistles*, 54.16.

[70] Cyprian of Carthage, *Epistles*, 51.19. See also *Against Novatian* 1.

[71] Cyprian of Carthage, *Epistles*, 51.15. See also *Against Novatian* 15.

Finally, since it was becoming clear that persecution would soon be renewed, all the lapsed who were willing to repent were offered amnesty to bring them into the Church to strengthen them for what was to come.[72] Still, this was not a guarantee of salvation. It was meant to prevent the lapsed from giving up hope and help them resist the temptation to sacrifice again, but for those who had committed apostasy, the only guarantee of the forgiveness of the sin of apostasy was another chance at martyrdom.[73]

Valerian became emperor in AD 253, but at first did not actively persecute the Church.[74] However, in AD 257, persecution was renewed and Cyprian was imprisoned. In July of that year, Valerian was apparently persuaded to revisit Decius's agenda, and he issued a letter to the senate which, in addition to the usual, forbade Christian assembly, specifically mentioning gatherings outside the city walls (i.e., in the catacombs and cemeteries).[75] Both Novatian and Cyprian were martyred during the persecution of Valerian, in AD 258. Valerian died in AD 260, his three-and-a-half-year persecution being compared to the forty-two months of blasphemy in Revelation 13:5.[76] Valerian's successor Gallienus ended the persecution with decrees of his own that discontinued the programs of Decius and Valerian, and even restored ownership of the cemeteries to the churches.[77]

Penance and Reconciliation

The persecution of the third century, with its subsequent controversy over the lapsed, forced the formalization of a system of penance. Confession had been a part of the eucharistic liturgy from very early on. It was probably originally a corporate prayer of confession, but the assumption that one should not receive the Eucharist without first confessing one's sins was held from the beginning (cf. 1 Cor. 11:27–32).[78] In addition, the possibility of excommunication had always existed in the Church (see 1 Cor. 5). The bishops were invested with the authority to proclaim the forgiveness of sins based on apostolic succession (from Matt. 16:19 and John 20:22–23), and eventually they would confer that authority on the priests as well. But this still left the question of

[72] Cyprian of Carthage, *Epistles*, 53.1–4; see also Burns, "On Rebaptism," 375.

[73] Cyprian of Carthage, *On the Unity of the Catholic Church*, 19.

[74] Eusebius of Caesarea, *Ecclesiastical History*, 7.10.

[75] Cyprian of Carthage, *Epistles*, 80.1; see also Eusebius of Caesarea, *Ecclesiastical History* 7.11. For an excellent overview of where the early Christians were meeting, see MacMullen, *The Second Church*.

[76] Eusebius of Caesarea, *Ecclesiastical History*, 7.10.

[77] Eusebius of Caesarea, *Ecclesiastical History*, 7.13.

[78] *Didache*, 14.1; Cyprian of Carthage, *Epistles*, 9.2, 10.1; *On the Lapsed*, 15, 26.

how one would be reconciled to communion after being excommunicated, or when one had, in effect, excommunicated oneself by sinful behavior.

The discipline of penance developed as a way to show the sincerity of one's repentance.[79] Penance was seen as an "outward and visible sign" of an inward reality. By the third century, Christians in different areas were experimenting with penitential systems which would specify certain acts of penance for particular sins. Because of the assumption that not all sins are equal and therefore the penance must fit the level of sin, and because of the need for consistency to avoid priestly favoritism, Celtic priests devised penitential books, which actually set down a standardized list of sins and the corresponding penance. There are extant examples of these *penitentials* from a later time, which demonstrate the perceived need for the formalization of the sacrament and the standardization of specific acts of penance.

To be clear, penance was not seen as way of earning salvation, or even forgiveness. Baptism was the sacrament that washed away the guilt of original sin, and any personal sin committed up until the time of Baptism.[80] But Christians in the early and medieval Church did not believe that Baptism washed away future sins, so any sins committed after Baptism were believed to be held against a person. Therefore, confession and penance became the way of dealing with post-baptismal sin.[81] Since it was assumed that a person could lose one's salvation by committing serious sins after Baptism, there was a sense in which regular confession and penance helped one retain one's salvation. In this way, confession and penance were understood to contribute to salvation, but more in the sense of demonstrating the sincerity of repentance than "making up for" the sin. In any case, salvation was always understood as more of a process than a foregone conclusion.[82]

In actual practice, penance usually meant a specified amount of time spent in prayer and fasting, as well as almsgiving (Tob. 4:10; Sir. 3:30).[83] During this time, the penitent would not receive the Eucharist, and may be expected to kneel at the back of the assembly during liturgy. When the time of penance was complete, a

[79] Cyprian of Carthage, *Epistles*, 54.13, 58.1. Note that penance here is a verb, to "do penance."

[80] Cyprian of Carthage, *Epistles*, 75.11; cf. *On Rebaptism*, 10.

[81] Cyprian of Carthage, *Epistles*, 51.22.

[82] *Against Novatian*, 10, 14, 1; see also Cyprian of Carthage, *On the Lapsed*, 17, 29, and the letter of Firmilian in Cyprian of Carthage, *Epistles*, 74.4.

[83] Polycarp, *Letter to the Philippians*, 10.2; Cyprian of Carthage, *On the Lapsed*, 35; see also Clement of Alexandria, *Who Is the Rich Man That Shall Be Saved?*; *2 Clement*, 16 (quoting 1 Pet. 4:8); and Hermas, *The Shepherd*, 50–51. Note that the *Didascalia* advises that if one cannot afford to give alms, one should fast and use the money that would have been spent on food to give alms; *Didascalia Apostolorum*, 19.

public confession would be made to the congregation, after which a person was granted *peace*, or Reconciliation, with the laying on of hands by the bishop.[84] The practice of private confession may go back to the confessors, who granted forgiveness on the basis of a visit from someone who had lapsed, and who confessed the sin of apostasy to one who was seen as having the prophetic authority to absolve that sin, precisely because he or she had not committed it. On the other hand, the existence of the Celtic penitential books is evidence that the practice could (and did, in some places) develop independently of the persecution.

As applied to the lapsed specifically, the Church devised stages of penance, leading one from excommunication back into full communion. The penitent began his or her time of penance as a *weeper*. Weepers were expected to remain outside of the worship space, dressed in mourning clothes, and begging their brothers and sisters to pray for them. After spending a prescribed amount of time as a weeper, the penitent became a *hearer*. Hearers were allowed to enter the worship space, but just inside the doors, not among the assembly. They may listen to the liturgy, but not participate. Next the penitent became a *kneeler*. Kneelers were admitted into the assembly among the people but must remain kneeling while the rest would stand. Finally, the last stage was to become a *co-stander*. Co-standers were allowed to stand with the rest, and participate in the liturgy, but could not receive the Eucharist.[85] Eventually, the co-stander would make his or her public confession and be reconciled. The whole process could take anything from a few weeks to over a decade, depending on the nature of the sin and the circumstances.

Ultimately it was determined that apostasy could be forgiven (but only by a bishop), since all serious sin is a kind of idolatry of one form or another.[86] And if adultery could be forgiven (though the rigorists would have argued it could not), then certainly the *libelliteci* and traitors could hope for reconciliation.[87] For the mainstream Church, the only truly unforgivable sin was schism, since by it the

[84] Cyprian of Carthage, *Epistles*, 9.2, 11.2, 45.2 (the Roman confessors' reconciliation), 58.1, 71.2.

[85] Eusebius of Caesarea, *Ecclesiastical History*, 6.42.

[86] Cyprian of Carthage, *Epistles*, 51.27. Although the mainstream Christians did not subscribe to the idea that all sins are equal in the eyes of God, some of the rigorists apparently did, and therefore Cyprian's comment in this letter may be a concession to a rigorist point. However, if the rigorists did hold the conviction that all sin is equal, it led them to create ever-growing lists of sins that could not be forgiven. For the Catholics, admitting that there is some truth to the concept that all sin is a form of idolatry led them to the opposite conclusion, that all sins could be forgiven.

[87] Cyprian of Carthage, *Epistles*, 51.20–22, 26.

schismatic separates himself from the Church, and from salvation.[88] Therefore schism is worse than apostasy, and Jesus' words in Matthew 7:23 ("I never knew you") were applied to the schismatics.[89]

The Controversy over Baptism and Rebaptism

The persecution and the problem of the lapsed led inevitably to a controversy over the validity of Baptism.[90] The issue was not infant Baptism (that was universally being done), but the validity of Baptisms done by clergy who had lapsed during the persecution, or by schismatic clergy.[91] The question was whether someone who had been baptized by a lapsed or schismatic bishop needed to be rebaptized. The original tradition had been that those coming back into the Church from a heretical group did not need to be rebaptized, they only needed Reconciliation with the imposition of hands.[92] However, Cyprian started rebaptizing people, apparently based on a more recent North African practice.[93] Councils were held in North Africa (presided over by Cyprian) in AD 255 and 256 which confirmed Cyprian's practice.[94]

Cyprian was opposed by Stephen of Rome (bishop AD 254–257), who wanted to keep the prior tradition of reconciling only.[95] In fact, Stephen wanted to excommunicate anyone who would rebaptize.[96] Eventually, Stephen would even break off

[88] Clement of Rome, *1 Clement*, 57; Ignatius of Antioch, *Letter to the Philadelphians*, 3. In the *Didascalia*, schism is referred to as a coveting of the "primacy" (i.e., of the bishop), which may be a reference to Novatian; *Didascalia Apostolorum*, 23.

[89] Cyprian of Carthage, *Epistles*, 72.16; *On the Unity of the Catholic Church*, 15, 19, 21; see also *Against Novatian*, 8, 10, 14. A century earlier, Irenaeus had written concerning other schismatics, "For no reformation of so great importance can be effected by them, as will compensate for the mischief arising from their schism." Irenaeus of Lyons, *Against Heresies*, 4.33.7, translation in *Ante-Nicene Fathers*, vol. 1, 508.

[90] Eusebius of Caesarea, *Ecclesiastical History*, 7.2–3.

[91] Cyprian of Carthage, *On the Lapsed*, 9.

[92] Eusebius of Caesarea, *Ecclesiastical History*, 7.2–3; cf. *Didascalia Apostolorum*, 10, 24; see also Burns, "On Rebaptism," 377, 398. There may have been some disagreement over whether the imposition of hands constituted Reconciliation or a re-Confirmation. If Cyprian saw it as Confirmation, then (in his mind) it would be the Confirmation of an invalid Baptism. See Cyprian of Carthage, *Epistles*, 75 and the letter of Firmilian in Cyprian of Carthage, *Epistles*, 74.

[93] Cyprian of Carthage, *Epistles*, 71.4, 72.3, 73.3.

[94] Cyprian of Carthage, *Epistles*, 58.3–6, 71.1, 72.1; see also Stevenson, *A New Eusebius*, 224.

[95] Cyprian of Carthage, *Epistles*, 71.1, 73.1–2; see also Eusebius of Caesarea, *Ecclesiastical History*, 7.2–3, 7–9. Note that the church of Alexandria agreed with Rome on this issue.

[96] Cyprian of Carthage, *Epistles*, 73.8.

communication with Cyprian, which gave the impression that he considered Cyprian excommunicated.[97] In reality, both bishops would agree that it was inappropriate to repeat a valid Baptism.[98] They simply disagreed on what constituted a valid Baptism.

The North African Understanding of Baptism

At the councils of Carthage it was argued that since Baptism effects the remission of sin, only those with the authority to forgive sins can perform a valid Baptism.[99] This would mean that any Baptism performed by someone outside of the succession of bishops, whether because of excommunication, heresy, or schism, could not be valid.[100] The principle at work here is that one cannot give what one does not have. The grace of forgiveness comes with the conferral of the Holy Spirit, but one who does not have the Holy Spirit cannot grant the Holy Spirit.[101] In this view, it is as though the presider is a conduit of grace from God to the receiver. If the presider has lapsed in his faith by making a pagan sacrifice, or if the presider has broken from the Catholic Church, or is guilty of mortal sin, then he has cut the conduit, and no grace can flow to the one who hopes to be baptized. Therefore, anyone baptized by Novatian, for example, was not really baptized, and if they wanted to come into the Catholic Church, they would need to be baptized.[102] According to Cyprian, he did not in fact *rebaptize*, because the recipients were never baptized in the first place.[103] For a Baptism to be valid, the presider must be beyond reproach.[104]

[97] Burns, "On Rebaptism," 377–378.

[98] Cyprian of Carthage, *Epistles*, 62.8, 70, 75.12–13. Note that Cyprian admits even a clinical (emergency) Baptism is not to be repeated, and the sacrament is not made any less valid by sprinkling or pouring. See also *On Rebaptism*, 10.

[99] Cyprian of Carthage, *Epistles*, 72.7, 75.11. The authority to forgive sins rested with the bishops, however, they could delegate this authority to the priests in their respective areas; see Cyprian of Carthage, *Epistles*, 58.1.

[100] Cyprian of Carthage, *Epistles*, 71.2, 72.6, 24, 73.7; *On the Unity of the Catholic Church*, 11, 13, 17. See also the letter of Firmilian in Cyprian of Carthage, *Epistles*, 74.26; and *Against Novatian*, 3. Note that all schismatic sacraments would be considered invalid. Ordination, especially, would also not be valid outside of the succession; see Cyprian of Carthage, *Epistles*, 48.2; *On the Unity of the Catholic Church*, 10.

[101] Cyprian of Carthage, *Epistles*, 58.2, 62.8; see also the letter of Firmilian in Cyprian of Carthage, *Epistles*, 74.8.

[102] Cyprian of Carthage, *Epistles*, 70.1, 71.1–5, 72.1.

[103] Cyprian of Carthage, *Epistles*, 70.1; see also the letter of Firmilian in Cyprian of Carthage, *Epistles*, 74.22.

[104] Cyprian of Carthage, *Epistles*, 71.2, 75.12.

Cyprian would argue that in fact it would be a disservice not to (re)baptize, since he believed that anyone not baptized could not be saved.[105] Not even martyrdom could save one who died for the wrong god.[106] He made no distinction between heretics and schismatics on this point: all risked damnation by removing themselves from the true Church.[107] What is more, the unity of the Church required that there could be only one Baptism.[108] Therefore, to consider a schismatic Baptism valid would be the equivalent of saying that the schismatics are also the Church, and therefore that they are not a schism at all.[109] On the contrary, Cyprian believed that to reconcile without rebaptism (which he considered simply Baptism) would be to commune with the excommunicated, which for him would make a mockery of the discipline of the Church.[110] And after all, he reasoned, didn't the apostles rebaptize those who had been baptized by John the baptist?[111]

This North African understanding of Baptism would continue in the Donatists, who in the fourth century would claim Cyprian as their precedent for the practice of rebaptism. Novatian apparently also shared this view of Baptism, since he rebaptized Catholics who came over to his schism.[112] Stephen of Rome would point to

[105] Cyprian of Carthage, *Epistles*, 72.3; see also the letter of Firmilian in Cyprian of Carthage, *Epistles*, 74.23.

[106] Cyprian of Carthage, *Epistles*, 72.16, 21. Cyprian paraphrases Paul in 1 Corinthians 13, that it profits nothing even to give one's body to be burned, if one dies for a heresy. Note that in this interpretation, the love of 1 Corinthians 13 is love for orthodoxy; cf. *On Rebaptism*, 13.

[107] Cyprian of Carthage, *Epistles*, 72.21, 75.1, 7–9. This was aimed specifically at Novatian. Cyprian acknowledged that his theology was orthodox but said that this did not excuse schism. Note that Montanists are also mentioned in the letter of Firmilian in Cyprian of Carthage, *Epistles*, 74.7, 19.

[108] Cyprian of Carthage, *On the Unity of the Catholic Church*, 11, 13, 17.

[109] Cyprian of Carthage, *Epistles*, 72.2, 72.6, 24; see also the letter of Firmilian in Cyprian of Carthage, *Epistles*, 74.26; and Burns, "On Rebaptism," 393.

[110] Cyprian of Carthage, *Epistles*, 72.19–20; see also the letter of Firmilian in Cyprian of Carthage, *Epistles*, 74.21–23.

[111] Cyprian of Carthage, *Epistles*, 72.24–25. In actual fact it is not clear whether the apostles baptized those who had been baptized by John, but since John's baptism would not have been a baptism in the name of the Trinity, it would not technically constitute a Christian Baptism.

[112] Cyprian of Carthage, *Epistles*, 72.2; see also Eusebius of Caesarea, *Ecclesiastical History*, 7.7, where the statement that Novatian "sets at naught the holy washing" may refer to his practice of rebaptism. In reality, Novatian was probably doing what we would now call "provisional Baptisms," since he probably did not rebaptize those baptized before the schism.

Novatian's practice and argue that the North Africans should not rebaptize, since that is what schismatics do.

The Roman Understanding of Baptism

Stephen of Rome, along with the anonymous author of the treatise, *On Rebaptism*, was the primary spokesman for the baptismal theology that would become the mainstream (Catholic) understanding. He argued that one should not ask *who* baptized, but only *how* the Baptism was performed.[113] The implication is that the spiritual state of the presider does not matter, because it is not the presider who baptizes, it is God who baptizes.[114] There is no conduit of grace from God that leads *through* the presider to the recipient. Grace flows directly from God to the one being baptized. Apostolic succession notwithstanding, a Baptism is valid no matter who performs it, as long as one is baptized into the right God, the Trinity. Therefore, to rebaptize is to presume to say that God's work was ineffective in the original Baptism, and thus rebaptism is an offense against God.[115]

On principle, Stephen also made no distinction between heretics and schismatics when it came to the validity of Baptism.[116] Any Baptism was valid as long as it was validly performed. Correct belief was not a requirement, since the disciples themselves had imperfect faith.[117] Even the method of Baptism (immersion versus pouring or sprinkling) did not matter, what mattered was that a person was baptized into Christ.[118] Eventually, the North Africans pressed the point, asking whether a person baptized by Marcion would in fact be baptized. In other words, what if someone were baptized into the wrong christ? Stephen would respond by clarifying that the Baptism must be performed in the name of the Trinity: Father, Son, and Holy Spirit (Matt. 28:19).[119] Thus even a Baptism performed by a heretical bishop would be valid (i.e., salvific) as long as the Baptism was done in the name of the Father, Son, and Holy Spirit.[120] Of course, this principle only applied if one was within the true Church, so that a schismatic or heretical Baptism could not save one if one *remained* outside the

[113] Cyprian of Carthage, *Epistles*, 72.4.

[114] *On Rebaptism*, 10.

[115] *On Rebaptism*, 10. According to the *Didascalia Apostolorum*, 26, rebaptism would "undo" the original Baptism.

[116] Cyprian of Carthage, *Epistles*, 73.2.

[117] *On Rebaptism*, 6, 9.

[118] Cyprian of Carthage, *Epistles*, 74.18; *On Rebaptism*, 10.

[119] Cyprian of Carthage, *Epistles*, 72.4–5, 12, 18.

[120] *On Rebaptism*, 10, 12. Any Baptism that was not trinitarian would not be considered valid, even by Stephen.

Church. The orthodoxy of the presider did not matter because the recipient of the Baptism could not be held responsible for the presider's faith, however the recipient was responsible to remain in the true Church for the Baptism to ultimately lead to salvation.[121] However, the point at issue was that if someone were to come over to the Catholic Church from a schism or heresy, that person's Baptism did not need to be redone, because of the conviction that God was at work in the Baptism — and God is faithful, even when church leaders are not. This Roman understanding of Baptism was confirmed at a synod in Rome.

Cyprian admitted that those who come from a heresy and are admitted without rebaptism are not necessarily damned, because it is not their fault if they were converted from paganism into a heretical sect or schism.[122] *Potens est Dominus misericordia sua, indulgentiam dare* (It is the Lord's prerogative to grant His mercy). However, he criticized Stephen, whom he thought should have known better, for preferring to excommunicate rebaptizers rather than heretics.[123] The more important problem for Cyprian, though, was that he reasoned that by considering a heretical or schismatic Baptism valid, the Church would seem to be validating the heresy or schism.[124] Thus, by not (re)baptizing, he accused Stephen of creating two Baptisms (schismatic and Catholic) where there should be only one (Eph. 4:5).

From Stephen's perspective, it looked like it was Cyprian who was turning one Baptism into two (two consecutive Baptisms). For him, it is rebaptism that violates the principle of "one Faith, one Baptism" (Eph. 4:5). Each bishop would argue that the other's baptismal theology actually cheapens Christian Baptism.

For the North Africans, one Baptism means *only one*. All other Baptisms are excluded because the unity of the Church depends on its purity. The Church is seen as more or less identical with the Kingdom, and so it is the duty of the Church to keep itself pure by excluding those who are not also in the Kingdom.[125] This is an ecclesiology of *unity through purity*. For the Romans, on the other hand, one

[121] *On Rebaptism*, 12.

[122] Cyprian of Carthage, *Epistles*, 72.23.

[123] Cyprian of Carthage, *Epistles*, 73.8.

[124] Cyprian of Carthage, *Epistles*, 70.1, 72.12, 20–21, 23–24, 75.3–4. For Cyprian, Baptism outside the Church is "adulterous water." See also the letter of Firmilian in Cyprian of Carthage, *Epistles*, 74.14, 23.

[125] However, Cyprian did apparently make a distinction between the visible Church and the true, or invisible, Church; see Cyprian of Carthage, *Epistles*, 48.4, 54.13. Note that there was a belief that the invisible Church was eternal, or at least preexistent (probably connected to the concept of the preexistence of Christ as *Logos*). It had been created before the sun and moon but was only revealed in the "last days" (the Church age) for the sake

Baptism means *all is one*. All Baptisms are included, as long as they are performed in the name of the Trinity — this is all that is needed to mark them as Christian. For the Romans, the Church on earth is not identical to the Kingdom. This is an ecclesiology of *unity through inclusion*. Thus, heretics and schismatics may not be destined for salvation, but this does not prevent God's saving grace from being at work in their Baptism, should they later join the true Church — in fact, the grace of their Baptism may lead them into the true Church. Of course, after the Baptism, the believer has a responsibility to remain in the true Church if he or she would hope for salvation, since continuing in a heresy or schism would be to separate oneself from the Church (and God), regardless of the validity of one's Baptism.[126] Stephen did admit that although he believed schismatic Baptism to be (theoretically) valid based on the operation of God, schismatic confirmation of the Baptism could not be valid since the bishop performing the confirmation was outside the succession.[127] Thus the principle that one cannot give what one does not have, which Cyprian applied to Baptism, Stephen applied to Confirmation.[128]

In the West (and only in the West), Confirmation would eventually become a separate sacrament distinct from Baptism. Perhaps this controversy contributed to that development. No doubt the growth of the Church, especially after its legalization, would make it difficult for one bishop to perform all of the Baptisms in a city. Thus the authority to baptize was delegated to priests, but the authority to confirm remained with the bishops (as it does to this day). Already by the end of the second century, Baptism and Confirmation were thought of as a double rite, or as twin rites, analogous to John the baptist's and Jesus' statements about Baptism

of salvation; see 2 *Clement*, 14; and Hermas, *The Shepherd*, 8.1. This strain of thought, running through Cyprian, may have contributed to Augustine's concept of election.

[126] *On Rebaptism*, 11–13.

[127] Cyprian of Carthage, *Epistles*, 75.10; see also the letter of Firmilian in Cyprian of Carthage, *Epistles*, 74.8.

[128] The reception of the Holy Spirit was associated with the imposition of hands in the Confirmation. Baptism and Confirmation were thought to be parallel to Baptism with water and baptism with the Holy Spirit (and fire); see Cyprian of Carthage, *Epistles*, 71.1, 73.7; and *On Rebaptism*, 3, 12, 17. Baptism and Confirmation were originally one rite, but by this time they were becoming two separate rites, perhaps in part because of the practice of infant Baptism, but more so because there were too many Baptisms in any given city for the one bishop to do them all, and yet only the bishop could preside over the Confirmations; see Cyprian of Carthage, *Epistles*, 71.1, 72.21. For the assumption that Baptism could be delegated to priests, but the Confirmation could only be done by a bishop; see Cyprian of Carthage, *Epistles*, 72.9; and *On Rebaptism*, 3.

with water versus Baptism with the Spirit and fire (Matt. 3:11; Mark 1:8; Luke 3:16; John 1:33; 3:5; Acts 1:5).

What, Then, Is the Church?

The church of Rome in the middle of the third century had forty-six priests, with seven deacons and seven subdeacons (perhaps based on the fourteen regions of the city, as divided by Augustus — one deacon covered two regions, with a subdeacon as his assistant).[129] There were also forty-two acolytes, fifty-two exorcists, along with other lay offices and over fifteen hundred widows and others supported by the church.[130] This implies a city church of almost fifty house-churches and perhaps as many as ten thousand members. But this begs the question, "What constitutes Church membership?" Indeed, what *makes one* a Christian? It is easy enough to begin by saying that Baptism defines the boundaries of Church membership, but we now know that does not really answer the question. On the one hand, some who were not yet baptized could consider themselves Christians (for example, Perpetua and other confessor catechumens).[131] On the other hand, some who were baptized might not be considered within the true Church.[132] As it was emerging in the third century, patristic ecclesiology developed along two definable lines.

The question became: Is the Church an enclave of the saved in a world of the damned, or is it a school for the soul? To put it another way: Is the Church a quarantine to protect the healthy from the sick; or is it a hospital for the sick who are becoming healthy?

The persecution of the third century caused a certain amount of circling of the wagons, and the rigorists emerged from that time determined to honor the martyrs by excommunicating the lapsed. The persecution also caused some to speculate that

[129] Eusebius of Caesarea, *Ecclesiastical History*, 6.43; see also *Apostolic Tradition*, 14.

[130] Eusebius of Caesarea, *Ecclesiastical History*, 6.43. Note that the office of exorcist is also mentioned in the letter of Firmilian in Cyprian of Carthage, *Epistles*, 74.10. The office of exorcist seems eventually to have been absorbed by the bishops, though exorcism (or precautionary exorcism) remained a part of the preparation for Baptism in many places.

[131] *On Rebaptism*, 11.

[132] Cyprian called Baptism the sacrament of unity; Cyprian of Carthage, *Epistles*, 75.6. As we have seen, the question of Baptism begs the question of rebaptism and baptismal validity. It was, of course, believed that in general Baptism defined Church membership; see the letter of Firmilian in Cyprian of Carthage, *Epistles*, 74.14, 17. However, a catechumen could be considered a Christian, as in the case of Perpetua. The term *hearer* described the catechumens, and the term *believer* seems to have been reserved for the baptized, except that a confessor was considered a believer, even if not yet baptized; see *On Rebaptism*, 11.

a presider's status within the Church could affect the validity of the sacraments. Thus there is some affinity between the rigorists and the North African baptismal theology, evidenced by the fact that both opposed Rome and its bishops. Hippolytus, Tertullian, and Novatian were some of the best theologians the early Church produced, and yet they were all rigorists. They had very high moral expectations for the baptized, and those who followed after them in their rigorism maintained ever-lengthening lists of the sins that could not be forgiven. It seems that for the Montanists, the Novatianists, and the Donatists after them, the primary task of the Church is to keep herself chaste, as the bride-to-be of Christ.[133] This would be done by identifying and excluding the unworthy, ultimately protecting the table of the Eucharist, but also ostensibly protecting those who might take the Eucharist unworthily.[134] At the risk of an oversimplification for the sake of convenient categories, we will call this a North African ecclesiology.

For the North African ecclesiology, the Church must be holy (i.e., perfect) to be effective. Diluting the purity of the Church might render it unable to save. Tolerance of heresy would inevitably lead to the ordination of heretical priests, the election of heretical bishops, and consequently invalid sacraments that could not offer salvation. Thus the rigorist ecclesiology is consistent with a sacramental theology which assumes that the faith of the presider effects the validity of the sacrament. This has implications especially for the reliability of not only Baptism and the Eucharist, but also confession, penance, and Reconciliation. How could the average Christian know if the clergy who granted absolution really had the power to grant it, if the Church was not pure? Thus, to reconcile the lapsed could ruin the Church for the faithful, so that the only way to help the lapsed was to excommunicate them.

A Roman ecclesiology, on the other hand, assumes that the Church is holy because Christ created it, and made it holy (Eph. 5:25–27). The Church is like the ark of Noah — to be saved from the flood one must be in it, but it contained both clean

[133] Rankin, *Tertullian and the Church*, 114.

[134] Those who might take the Eucharist unworthily included the uninitiated, who were to be protected from the Eucharist until they were ready, for their own good. It was believed by some that the unbaptized would risk damnation by taking the Eucharist, even out of ignorance; see the *Apostolic Constitutions*, 7.2 (7.25). In general, however, to receive the Eucharist without confession would be considered unworthy. By the third century, this included penance and Reconciliation; Cyprian of Carthage, *Epistles*, 9.2, 10.1; *On the Lapsed*, 15, 26. For the concept that the Eucharist would be ineffective if one held malice against another (Matt. 5:23–24), see the *Didascalia Apostolorum*, 11.

and unclean animals (cf. 1 Pet. 3:20–21).[135] Jesus' parable of the wheat and the weeds (Matt. 13) provided an analogy of the Church. The Church on earth (the visible Church) included both true Christians (the wheat) and false ones (the weeds). But it was meant to be that way until the judgment, when the weeds would be pulled up and thrown into the fire. To be fair, even Tertullian and Cyprian used this image for the Church, Cyprian saying it would be prideful to presume to separate the weeds while the Church sojourned on earth.[136] But Tertullian's Montanism and Cyprian's rebaptism reveal the direction their ecclesiology leans. Hippolytus had actually criticized Callistus for using this parable to describe the Church.[137]

Roman ecclesiology affirmed that the Church did not have to be perfect to be effective, it only had to be inclusive. The Church was not a cloister of the perfected, but a school for the imperfect who hoped to move toward perfection, in which catechesis and liturgy were the lessons. It was understood as a hospital for the soul, in which the Sacrament of Reconciliation is the medicine.[138] Thus, the Church was not identical with the Kingdom. The Church on earth (the visible Church) *included* the Church in Heaven (the invisible Church) but was not to be equated with it. The heavenly Church is the perfect one; the earthly Church must refrain from premature judgment. Therefore, Church membership makes salvation *possible*, but does not guarantee it. Baptism grants forgiveness, but does not guarantee perseverance. Baptism is a clean slate, but it is not a free ride.

For those who held a Roman ecclesiology, the Church was exemplified by the statement, "whoever is not against you is for you" (Luke 9:50). For the proponents of North African ecclesiology, the Church was exemplified by the statement, "Whoever is not with me is against me, and whoever does not gather with me, scatters" (Luke 11:23).[139] Roman ecclesiology is based on the assumption that purity might purify

[135] *Against Novatian*, 2, 5; see also Cyprian of Carthage, *Epistles*, 73.11–12, 75.2; *On the Unity of the Catholic Church*, 6. For Cyprian, the Church is the ark, and the persecution is the flood.

[136] Tertullian, *The Prescription against the Heretics*, 31, 33; Cyprian of Carthage, *Epistles*, 50.3, 51.13, 25. Cyprian was, of course, not a rigorist, and his argument here is aimed at the Novatianists. Cyprian said that rigorism came from a "too rigid philosophy"; Cyprian of Carthage, *Epistles*, 51.16.

[137] Hippolytus, *Refutation of All Heresies*, 9.7.

[138] Cyprian of Carthage, *Epistles*, 53.13; *On the Lapsed*, 15.

[139] Cyprian of Carthage, *Epistles*, 75.1. I am careful to distinguish what I am calling North African ecclesiology from the North Africans in general, since Cyprian would agree with significant elements of what I am calling the Roman ecclesiology. However, these categories, simplified though they may be, are proven useful by the ongoing controversy

impurity. North African ecclesiology is based on the assumption that impurity defiles purity. In the end, the Roman ecclesiology (and indeed the Roman sacramental theology) would become the standard in the Church, however the North African version would continue as long as Christianity itself continued in North Africa. In the controversy between Augustine and the Donatists, Augustine would be the proponent of the Roman ecclesiology against the Donatists.

Both lines of ecclesiological trajectory spring from the conviction that there is no salvation outside the Church. Cyprian famously said that one cannot hope to have God for a Father if one does not have the Church for a mother.[140] Thus true Christianity, and therefore salvation, was limited to those within the bounds of the Church. But it was precisely those bounds which were at issue. In the end, schism was perceived as worse than both heresy and apostasy, and the only truly unforgivable sin was to separate oneself from the Church.[141] To join a schism was to excommunicate oneself, because it was to step out of communion with the bishops in succession from the apostles (Matt. 18:17; 2 John 10–11). Eventually, the Catholic Church decided not to permanently excommunicate the lapsed, but it did excommunicate the schismatics.[142]

Therefore, the patristic definition of the Church ultimately rests on the foundation of apostolic succession. Apostolic succession drives both doctrine and discipline. True Christians are those who are connected to the apostles via the succession.[143] They believe the doctrines most consistent with the oldest tradition and accept the authoritative apostolic documents.[144] They receive the sacraments from bishops (and

---

between the Donatists of North Africa and Augustine, who, though he was North African, held to more of a Roman ecclesiology.

140 Cyprian of Carthage, *Epistles*, 72.21; *On the Unity of the Catholic Church*, 6; see also the letter of Firmilian in Cyprian of Carthage, *Epistles*, 74.18. On the Church as mother, see Cyprian of Carthage, *Epistles*, 9.3, 10.2, 40.2, 42; *On the Lapsed*, 9.

141 Cyprian of Carthage, *Epistles*, 54.21, 75.1, 9; *On the Unity of the Catholic Church*, 19, 21. See also the letter of Dionysius of Alexandria to Novatian in Eusebius of Caesarea, *Ecclesiastical History*, 6.45. Schism was compared to the split between northern and southern kingdoms in the Old Testament (2 Kings 17:20–21).

142 Eusebius of Caesarea, *Ecclesiastical History*, 6.43.

143 Tertullian, *The Prescription against the Heretics*, 20–21, 28, 32.

144 Tertullian had said that the Holy Spirit would prevent the true Church from going astray; see Tertullian, *The Prescription against the Heretics*, 28. In a sense, the Holy Spirit guarantees apostolic authority. This may be the earliest hint of what would become the doctrine of papal infallibility, since the infallibility of the bishop of Rome is essentially the infallibility of the Church, based on Matthew 16:18, "the gates of of the netherworld shall not prevail against it."

the priests to whom they give authority) in a direct line from the apostles.[145] They accept the discipline of their bishops, and listen to them as though they are listening to the apostles themselves. Heresy, apostasy, and schism are all divisive, but unity is found in the succession, and the succession is embodied in the bishops.[146] Thus, the very unity of the Church was seen to be centered in, and dependent upon, the authority of the bishops. As Ignatius had affirmed at the beginning of the second century, this meant that there could be only one bishop in each city.[147] But even more important than this is the fact that, for all the acknowledgement that Baptism is the sacrament of initiation into the Church, nevertheless the sacrament of the Eucharist is the sacrament of membership that completes Baptism (and Confirmation). And given the realities of Church discipline and the way that being in good standing in the Church meant being in communion, at the end of the day it is legitimate to say that for all intents and purposes, *the Church is the eucharistic table*. Therefore, membership in the Church finds its focus in the sacrament of the Eucharist, and is defined as those who gather at that table to receive the Body and Blood of the Lord. To remain in Christ (John 14–15) is to remain in the Church, specifically through regular reception of the Eucharist.

[145] Cyprian of Carthage, *Epistles*, 51.21, 53.2, 54.5. Both Baptism and Eucharist are considered sacraments of unity, and the Eucharist especially is described by Cyprian as the safeguard of unity. This is partly because the presider stands in the place of Christ Himself. Thus the unity of the Church is connected to the unity of the eucharistic table, which in turn is connected to the unity (and authority) of the episcopacy.

[146] Cyprian of Carthage, *Epistles*, 9.1, 3–4, 10.2, 11.2, 26.1; *On the Unity of the Catholic Church*, 5, 7; see also Tertullian, *The Prescription against the Heretics*, 20.

[147] Cyprian of Carthage, *Epistles*, 40.2; *On the Unity of the Catholic Church*, 5; see also Eusebius of Caesarea, *Ecclesiastical History*, 6.43. Cornelius, speaking sarcastically about Novatian, wrote, "this vindicator, then, of the Gospel did not know that there should be one bishop in a Catholic church." Translation in Lake, *Eusebius*, vol. 2, 119.

10

The Fourth Century and the Council of Nicaea

The Church and the Empire

Just at the time that the Church was clarifying its definition of itself, its relationship with the empire changed so drastically that from that time forward the Church and the empire each identified themselves in relation to each other. The early fourth century saw the extremes of the "Great Persecution" and then the first Christian emperor. More than any other time in the history of the Church, the end of the third century and beginning of the fourth century could be described as "tribulation."

In the forty years or so from the end of Valerian's persecution to the beginning of the Great Persecution, an atmosphere of mutual toleration gradually spread across the empire. Non-Christians generally tolerated the Christians, and the Christians even came to trust their non-Christian neighbors to a certain extent, so that being a Christian didn't seem quite so dangerous, and each side felt it was safe to assimilate some practices from the other. At the time, some non-Christians might even have interpreted it as a meeting in the middle, as philosophy moved toward a kind of monotheism, and it was thought that the only people who held on to the traditional Greco-Roman mythologies were those invested in government jobs, and the less educated folks out in the countryside. In fact, this is where we get the term *pagan*. It comes from the Latin, *pagani*, meaning rustic folk, or "country-dwellers."

Although the Church was still technically illegal, in some areas local churches existed as "corporations," possibly even registered with the government as funerary societies.[1] In this way the churches could own cemeteries and legally bury their dead. In this period, Christians also started to have dedicated church buildings, taking over or remodeling existing buildings, so that for the first time, one could point out

[1] Eusebius of Caesarea, *Ecclesiastical History*, 10.1, 5.

a building and say that is where the church meets.[2] What had begun as small groups meeting in people's homes had grown into converted spaces, then dedicated spaces, and eventually structures built specifically for worship. In Rome, the earliest church buildings (the so-called *title churches*) were converted (or perhaps built) on land donated by the owners of the original houses used for worship. In some cases, the remains of early Roman houses can be seen in the excavations under the present-day churches.[3] By the end of the third century, there were even some cities in the empire that had a population with a Christian majority. Many non-Christian Romans had come to a kind of resigned comfort with the Christians, and the Christians for their part had let down their guard. They did not see the Great Persecution coming.[4]

The Great Persecution

The emperor Diocletian had come to power in AD 285. Realizing that the empire was too large for one man to govern effectively, he created a *tetrarchy*, or a rule of four, in which the empire was divided in two (East and West) and each half had a senior ruler (called *Augustus*) and a second in command (called *Caesar*). In this way, Diocletian attempted to stabilize the borders on both sides of the empire, since each side would have its *Augustus* closer at hand. Diocletian retained for himself the highest authority, making himself the *Augustus* of the East. His second-in-command in the East was his son-in-law, Galerius. In the West, the *Augustus* was Maximian, and the *Caesar* was a general named Constantius (the father of Constantine).

Like Decius before him, Diocletian also tried to bring back the glory days of the empire's golden age through renewed enthusiasm for the old religion. However, by this time, the old religion was coming to be seen as outdated, even by some of the non-Christians who were more philosophically minded. But even more important

2 Eusebius of Caesarea, *Ecclesiastical History*, 8.1 The *Didascalia* describes the arrangement of worshipers within a basilica church (in this case the cathedral). The bishop's throne was at the eastern end, with the priests around the bishop. The lay men were situated closest to the priests, with the lay women in the back. The deacons functioned as ushers or *doorkeepers*, and visitors were questioned before being allowed to join the assembly; *Didascalia Apostolorum*, 12. For more detail on the early basilica churches, see MacMullen, *The Second Church*.

3 For example, this is probably the case with the churches of San Clemente and Santa Cecilia in Rome. Beneath the present church of Santa Cecilia are the remains of a Roman house that go back to the third century. According to tradition, the house was owned by the family of the martyr Cecilia, and after her death the land was dedicated for perpetual use by the Church. See Papandrea, *ROME*.

4 Eusebius of Caesarea, *Ecclesiastical History*, 7.23.

was the fact that the Christians had become comfortable enough with their place in Roman society that they felt it was safe to openly criticize the emperor's policies, if only by their actions. In fact, Diocletian would not have been the first emperor to have Christians in his own household, and it has been suggested that his wife and daughter (Galerius's wife) may have been Christians, or if not baptized, at least supporters of the Church. They, too, may have been openly disdainful of the old religion. At this point it seems that Galerius convinced Diocletian to renew persecution against the Christians.

The so-called Great Persecution began as a test of loyalty in the legions. It was believed by some that the presence of Christians in the military would negatively affect the ability of the Roman soothsayers to read the signs which would allow them to predict the best days on which to engage the enemy. According to tradition, Christian soldiers were seen crossing themselves, which was thought to negate the prophetic abilities of the pagan priests. So it was actually the Romans who asserted that one could not serve both Christ and the emperor, and based on prior precedents, pagan sacrifices were used as tests of loyalty and patriotism. Soldiers who would not make the sacrifices, or who were suspected of being Christians, were confronted and at least demoted, and some were eventually martyred.[5]

It was said that the emperor was annoyed that he could look out the window of his palace in the city of Nicomedia and see the building where the Christians met — perhaps even that he knew his wife and daughter were attending there. The first imperial edict of Diocletian against the Church was timed to be issued just before Easter of AD 303, and began with the demolition of the church building (he would have had it burned to the ground if it had not been so close to the palace).[6] More edicts came later in AD 303 and in AD 304. Christian worship was outlawed. Church buildings were ordered burned or destroyed. Christian Scriptures and other writings, as well as liturgical items were to be surrendered to the authorities — and based on the precedent of Septimius Severus's edict, Roman soldiers could conduct searches of homes without warning, arresting people and confiscating property. Any home where Christian Scriptures were found was to be burned down (probably on the assumption that it was a place of worship, though this could hardly be carried out in cases where the home in question was part of an apartment building). All Christians were ordered to demonstrate their loyalty to the emperors and to the state by making a pagan sacrifice. Refusal to comply meant prison, torture, condemnation to the mines, or execution.

[5] Eusebius of Caesarea, *Ecclesiastical History*, 8.4.

[6] Eusebius of Caesarea, *Ecclesiastical History*, 8.2.

The persecution was enforced more in the East than in the West, at least in part because Constantius was sympathetic to the Church and did not enforce the persecution in the areas under his control.[7] However, across the empire many Christian leaders were martyred. Others were imprisoned and tortured, or condemned to slavery (if they were of the lower classes). The number of apostates was far fewer than in the Decian persecution, to the point where the prisons were filled to capacity.[8] Although in many ways the Church had let down its guard in the decades following the Decian persecution, the problem of the lapsed had never really gone away. Some Christians even committed suicide to avoid the possibility of torture and the temptation to make an idolatrous sacrifice, though, of course, this would have been discouraged by the bishops.[9] Some were sent to meet the wild beasts in the arena.[10] If the Romans perceived that a whole town was Christian, the town was burned with the people in it.[11] Propaganda became a tool of persecution, as the Romans circulated documents such as the *Acts of Pilate*, an anti-Christian fictional account that made Pontius Pilate the hero of the story.[12]

Interestingly, Eusebius of Caesarea, in his *Ecclesiastical History*, treats the Great Persecution as though it was divine discipline for moral laxity and internal disputes which arose during the time of relative peace.[13] In this he is following the lead of Old Testament writers who saw the exile into Babylon as God's punishment for idolatry.

[7] Eusebius of Caesarea, *Ecclesiastical History*, 8.13. The reader should keep in mind Eusebius's agenda of supporting the dynasty of Constantine, so favorable assessments of Constantine's family must be taken with a grain of salt. On the other hand, Constantius may have secretly been a Christian; this could account for Constantine's exposure to the Faith. Accounts of Constantine's family do not all agree on whether Constantine's mother, now known to the Church as St. Helena, was a Christian before him or was converted because of him. Eusebius of Caesarea claims that she became a Christian because of Constantine, though that may be result of his attempt to give all the credit to Constantine. See *Life of Constantine*, 54–55. See also Raymond Van Dam, *Remembering Constantine at the Milvian Bridge* (Cambridge: Cambridge University Press, 2011), 69.

[8] Eusebius of Caesarea, *Ecclesiastical History*, 8.6. In the Roman world, prison was not meant to be a long-term sentence, but rather a holding place where one awaited either release or execution, or some other sentence such as condemnation to the mines. Therefore, the prisons were not large and did not hold a lot of people.

[9] Eusebius of Caesarea, *Ecclesiastical History*, 8.12

[10] Eusebius of Caesarea, *Ecclesiastical History*, 8.7.

[11] Eusebius of Caesarea, *Ecclesiastical History*, 8.11.

[12] Eusebius of Caesarea, *Ecclesiastical History*, 9.5. In the reign of Julian "the apostate" (emperor 361–363), the *Acts of Pilate* was made required reading in grammar schools.

[13] Eusebius of Caesarea, *Ecclesiastical History*, 8.1, 10.4.

Just as the Babylonians were to the Jews, the Romans were seen by some Christians as both the instruments of God's chastisement, and also the ungodly oppressors who would soon get what was coming to them. This is part of the message of the book of Revelation.[14] In fact, the untimely (and painful) deaths of the emperors would be seen as God's vindication, as Lactantius would later write in his *On the Manner in Which the Persecutors Died.*

Diocletian had retired in AD 305, leaving Galerius as the *Augustus* in the East. At the same time, Maximian was forced to step down, leaving Constantius as the *Augustus* in the West. Persecution continued primarily in the East, under Galerius, however it must be kept in mind that an emperor only has so much power to enforce (or prevent) persecution in all the places where the emperor cannot be personally present. In any case, Galerius, seen by the Church as the worst persecutor ever, became gravely ill. From his deathbed in AD 311, Galerius issued the *Edict of Toleration,* in which he admitted that the God of the Christians was indeed God, and promised to end the persecution if the Christians would pray for his recovery.[15] Permission was given to rebuild church buildings and for Christians to gather for worship. All Christian prisoners were to be released. However, when Galerius died (a horrible death as some Christian writers were happy to describe), persecution was then resumed under his successor. Christians were barred from visiting the cemeteries, and some were driven out of the cities where they lived.[16]

The First Christian Emperor

When Constantius died in the year AD 306, his son Constantine was proclaimed emperor by his loyal legions. Eusebius compared the young Constantine at this point to King David, anointed though not yet crowned.[17] Rule over the western half of the empire would come down to civil war between Constantine and Maxentius, the son of Maximian. Their legions met at the Milvian Bridge, over the river Tiber, on the northern boundary of the city of Rome, in AD 312. The Milvian Bridge itself had been destroyed to prevent Constantine's legions from marching into the city, and so Constantine camped across the river and waited. There are several versions of the story, however the basic tradition includes a dream or a vision, in which Constantine saw a Christian symbol emblazoned on the sky. The symbol was probably the so-called *Chi-Rho,* the monogram of Christ consisting of the Greek letter *chi* (which looks like

[14] See Papandrea, *The Wedding of the Lamb.*

[15] Eusebius of Caesarea, *Ecclesiastical History,* 8.16–17, 9.1–3; *Life of Constantine,* 1.57.

[16] Eusebius of Caesarea, *Ecclesiastical History,* 9.7.

[17] Eusebius of Caesarea, *Ecclesiastical History,* 8.13.

an "X") superimposed by the Greek letter *rho* (which looks like a "P"). These are the first two letters in the Greek spelling of *Christos*, or Christ.[18] Other (later) versions of the story say that Constantine saw a cross in the sky.[19] Upon seeing the symbol, Constantine heard the voice of God saying, *In hoc signo vinces* (In this sign, you will conquer). Constantine ordered his men to put the sign on their standards, and he and his legions would march into battle, literally under the banner of Christ. Eventually, this christogram would adorn Constantine's helmet and the shields of his men.

While Constantine was receiving a vision from God, Maxentius was consulting the pagan oracles. The Roman augurs predicted that if Maxentius went out to meet Constantine in battle, "the enemy of the Romans" would fall. Maxentius took that as good news, and a sign that he should engage Constantine in battle, but he should have asked who they meant by "the enemy of the Romans." He had his men create a makeshift bridge where the Milvian Bridge had been; a series of boats joined together to facilitate crossing the river. Constantine defeated Maxentius at what would come to be called *The Battle at the Milvian Bridge*, on October 28, AD 312, and October 28th would come to be celebrated as "Milvian Bridge Day." Maxentius himself was drowned in the Tiber, and Eusebius would compare his demise to that of the Egyptians who had pursued Moses: "horse and chariot he has cast into the sea" (Exod. 15:1).[20] Constantine was received in Rome as a liberator, and the grateful Romans (who had suffered under Maxentius and saw him as a tyrant) erected a statue of Constantine, and eventually also a triumphal arch, which still stands near the Colosseum. The inscription on the inside of the arch is a dedication

[18] Lactantius, *On the Manner in Which the Persecutors Died*, 44; Eusebius of Caesarea, *Life of Constantine*, 1.28–31.

[19] Since the cross was still being used as a method of execution (it would be Constantine himself who would end this practice), the Church's use of the cross as a symbol was not widespread, and of course only internal; therefore, it has been argued that the original version of the story must have been a vision of the Chi-Rho, not the cross. The earliest extant artistic depiction of the crucifixion is a carving on the wooden doors of the church of Santa Sabina in Rome. The door panels are original to the basilica, from the fifth century. On the other hand, both the Chi-Rho and the cross were used as Christian symbols before the fourth century. Some of the earliest extant Christian manuscripts include a *staurogram*, or crucifix-shaped symbol used as an abbreviation, and already in the second century Christian apologists were referring to the letter T (in Greek, *tau*) as a symbol of the cross. Tertullian mentions the already accepted tradition of Christians crossing themselves in *De Corona*, 3, and refers to the cross as an object of adoration in his *Apology*, 16. This was written in response to a pagan mockery of the crucifixion of Christ, which was a graffito of a man with a donkey's head on a cross.

[20] Eusebius of Caesarea, *Ecclesiastical History*, 9.8–9; *Life of Constantine*, 1.38.

to Constantine which reads, *Liberator Urbis — Fundator Quietis* (Liberator of the City — Founder of Peace). Constantine's triumphal parade included the bishop of Rome in a place of honor, as well as the bishops of surrounding cities, and upon entering Rome, he intentionally neglected the longstanding tradition of the victory sacrifice to the Roman god Jupiter.

In AD 313, Constantine and his eastern counterpart Licinius issued the *Edict of Milan*, which legalized Christianity (see the text of *The Edict of Milan* at the end of this chapter). Although it would only be enforced in the West at first, this is generally seen as the beginning of a Christian empire. It is important to note, however, that the Edict of Milan did not make Christianity the "official" religion of the empire, or even the *only* legal religion of the empire. It simply was meant to end the persecution. In fact, the edict itself was really a letter to the senators granting freedom of worship to all religions.[21] In the edict, Constantine specified that Church property was to be returned at no cost to the Christians. Thus, the Church would finally become a legal entity, with the right to own property under its own name and receive inheritances. Constantine ordered that reparations be paid to the Church for the time of persecution, that all Church property be restored, and eventually that imperial money would be used to build martyr shrines and the first basilica churches.[22] It is at this time that the typical Roman meeting hall, or *basilica*, was adapted for Christian use.[23] Constantine also exempted clergy and their dependents from taxes (the beginning of the tax-exempt status), and gave bishops the right to use the imperial transportation system. He would eventually end the use of crucifixion as a form of execution, make Sunday a day of rest from work (the origin of the *weekend*), and further exempt Christian clergy from civic duties.[24] He began to use some Christian symbolism on his coins, but he did not completely discontinue the use of pagan symbols.[25]

[21] Eusebius of Caesarea, *Ecclesiastical History*, 9.9, 10.5. The text of the Edict of Milan is also found in Lactantius, *On the Manner in Which the Persecutors Died*, 48.

[22] The word *basilica* refers to an architectural plan used by the Romans for the assembly of large numbers of people or for government or shopping center–type malls. It is essentially a large rectangle with an apse (niche) at one end, originally meant to hold a statue of a god or goddess. In the Christian context, the apse becomes the place for the altar, and later transept "arms" would be added to make the building cross-shaped.

[23] Eusebius of Caesarea, *Ecclesiastical History*, 10.4. Constantine built several basilica-style churches in and around Rome, some on the sites of earliest Christian worship there; see MacMullen, *The Second Church*.

[24] On Sunday as a day of rest, see the *Apostolic Constitutions*, 8.4 (8.33).

[25] It is not clear how much an emperor would be personally involved in the design and minting of coins. Many of the city mints had stopped making their own coins since the

When Constantine became emperor, he found that the Church was in some ways as divided as the empire. In the West, the Donatist controversy was threatening to split the Church in North Africa (on Donatism, see below). In AD 314, Constantine convened the Council of Arles, the first council of the Church convened by an emperor. At this council, rebaptism was condemned, and therefore the Donatists were considered not only schismatics but also heretics.[26] The Council of Arles also gave Christian bishops the same authority as civil magistrates, so that they could decide disputes between Christians. This would be the beginning of the clergy's right to register legal marriages. Constantine himself came to treat bishops as imperial advisers, though he also expected them to return the favor and consult him on ecclesiastical matters.

Constantine would eventually go to battle against Licinius for the sole rule of the entire empire. He defeated Licinius in AD 324, claiming that God had ordained his rise to power. But as soon as he took power in the East, he realized he had an even bigger problem than the Donatist controversy. The Arian controversy had erupted, which would lead to him convening the first *ecumenical*, or worldwide, council: the Council of Nicaea in AD 325. Constantine had hoped that the Church would help him unify the empire, but first he believed that he had to safeguard the unity of the Church.

Once he was the sole ruler of the empire, Constantine moved the imperial capital out of Rome. The senate was too powerful and too conservative (i.e., pagan) for him to make any significant moves toward a Christian empire as long as they were supposed to be his advisers. According to the story, he was told by God in a dream to move his capital to Byzantium, which he renamed *Nova Roma* (New Rome). Also called Constantinople, which means "Constantine's city," the project was begun in AD 326 and the new Christian city was dedicated in AD 330. No paganism would be allowed in New Rome. Temples were torn down or converted into churches. New church buildings were built. Pagan statues were destroyed or altered to look like biblical characters, or heroes of the Faith.[27] One important factor in the move from

---

recession of the third century, which may have consolidated more influence in the emperor, however the continuance of pagan imagery on coins minted during Constantine's reign does not necessarily tell us anything about his personal beliefs. It could also be that this was a concession to the still powerful (and pagan) senate.

[26] Constantine did not persecute the Novatianists. Although they also practiced rebaptism, at least at first, they were apparently not considered heretics by the official councils; see Stevenson, *A New Eusebius*, 320.

[27] There is a statue of Constantine's mother, St. Helena, in the church of Santa Croce in Gerusalemme in Rome. Most scholars believe that the statue was once a statue of a pagan

Rome to Constantinople was that the absence of the emperor in Rome left a power vacuum in the old capital that would eventually be filled by the bishop of Rome. This void would open the way for the bishop of Rome to become the most important and powerful man in the city of Rome and would contribute to the increasing authority of the bishop of Rome (the pope). Over the centuries, the bishops of Rome would take over some of the programs once run by the government, including feeding the poor and protecting the city from invaders. The people would come to trust in the bishop more than the government for their own security.

Before we move on to the Arian controversy, the question of Constantine's faith remains. Scholars and others have debated the issue, though it seems that for many people, their own agenda determines the outcome of their research. It must be pointed out that much of what is credited to (or blamed on) Constantine did not actually happen until the reign of emperor Theodosius I (AD 379–395). Constantine never ruled as a baptized Christian. Like many men of his time, he postponed Baptism until the end of his life, in part so that he would not be held to the moral standards of the Church (and the problem of post-baptismal sin). Constantine also did not make Christianity the "official religion" of the empire, or the only legal religion. Paganism was not outlawed until the time of Theodosius, when non-Christians were commanded to attend church.[28] Thus, Constantine did not invent the concept of a "state Church." In fact, there had never been such a thing as a "separation of Church and state." It had always been assumed that religion and government were interconnected, because religion was traditionally tied to one's nationality. In reality, of course, Constantine did favor Christianity and gave certain privileges to Christian clergy, and financially supported the Church. However, all he was doing was identifying with one religion (something many emperors did before him, with one cult or another), while allowing freedom of worship for the other religions.

As to his own personal faith, the question usually boils down to whether he was a sincere believer or simply an opportunist who tried to use the Church to his own political advantage. It seems clear that Constantine came from a Christian household. His father refused to persecute the Church wherever he ruled, and his mother is the one who would be known to the Church as St. Helena, though it is not certain whether she was a Christian before him. According to tradition, she made her first pilgrimage to the Holy Land between AD 324 and 327, as soon as such

---

goddess, but that it was altered and a cross was added, to honor St. Helena and the tradition that she found the True Cross of Jesus.

[28] Thus it was Theodosius, not Constantine, who tried to create a true Christian empire, in which citizenship was equivalent to Church membership.

travel was safe after her son had unified the empire. She located the sites of Jesus' birth, His death and Resurrection, and His Ascension, and she is said to have found many artifacts and religious relics, some of which she brought back to Rome.[29] She is also said to have found the True Cross of Jesus, in the tomb, where local tradition had handed down the location from generation to generation.[30] Constantine would build basilicas over the sites of Jesus' birth (the Church of the Nativity), His death and Resurrection (the Church of the Holy Sepulcher), and His Ascension (on the Mount of Olives). Eusebius called this the *New Jerusalem* of the book of Revelation. Constantine demolished pagan temples (including one formerly on the mount of Golgotha, where the Church of the Holy Sepulcher was built), and did other things that upset powerful pagans — he didn't need to do these things that afforded him no political advantage.[31]

In the end, we will never know whether Constantine grew up believing the Faith, or whether he had a conversion experience on the eve of the Battle at the Milvian Bridge. Either way, however, it seems clear that he reigned as one who believed in Jesus Christ, who believed that the Father of Christ was the God responsible for his rise to power, and who feared that God could take the empire away from him at any time if he proved unworthy. Nevertheless, he ruled with an iron hand and did not hesitate to murder his political enemies, even when they were members of his own family.[32] He looked to the Old Testament more than the New to guide him in running the empire, and he did not hesitate to use the Church to his advantage,

[29] The *Scala Santa,* or Holy Stairs, in Rome are said to be the stairs leading up to the Praetorium mentioned in the Gospels. This was part of the palace of Herod, later used by Pontius Pilate as his headquarters while in Jerusalem. Therefore, these would be the stairs Jesus ascended on the night of his trial before Pilate. Constantine had them removed and transported to Rome, where to this day, pilgrims ascend on their knees. See Papandrea, *ROME*, 184–187.

[30] Ambrose of Milan, *Obituary Sermon for Theodosius*, 40–51. With the True Cross, St. Helena is said to have found some nails and the *titulus*, the title plaque that Pilate had made, calling Jesus the King of the Jews. According to the story, the nails were sent to Constantinople, where they were built into Constantine's crown and his horse's bridle. To this day, in the Church of Santa Croce in Gerusalemme in Rome, one can see on display the relics of a nail and a large fragment of the *titulus*.

[31] In the early second century, the emperor Hadrian had built a temple to Venus on the site of Calvary/Golgotha and a temple to Jupiter over the site of the tomb of Jesus. In doing this, he shows that he knew that locals saw these sites as sacred, but ironically, by covering and building over the locations, he preserved them for later discovery in AD 326.

[32] In AD 326, Constantine had his own son and expected successor, Crispus, executed on the charge of conspiring with (or having an affair with) his own wife Fausta. When his

especially in an attempt to keep the empire unified.[33] So, was Constantine a sincere believer, or an opportunist? It seems the answer is that he was both: a sincere believer who also tried to use the Church for his advantage and for unifying the empire.[34]

Lactantius

In some ways one could say that Lactantius was the last of the apologists. He was actually not a philosopher, but a rhetorician, who tried his hand at both theology and history, with varying degrees of success. Born around AD 260 in North Africa, he had moved to the eastern capital of Nicomedia to teach rhetoric in the court of Diocletian. At this time, he must have met the future emperor Constantine, who would later hire him as tutor to his first son Crispus. But it was in Nicomedia that Lactantius (and indeed Constantine himself) would witness the Great Persecution at ground zero, and perhaps this led to Lactantius's conversion to Christianity. His most famous work was perhaps his *Divine Institutes*, written sometime after the start of the Great Persecution, but before the Edict of Milan. It is a work of apologetics that mostly copies those who wrote before him, and not always accurately. It is clear that he does not completely understand the theology of the Faith he is defending, but he has the zeal of a new convert. A few years later he wrote an *Epitome of the Divine Institutes*, both condensed and revised, possibly for Constantine and Crispus.

Lactantius's most important work is *On the Manner in Which the Persecutors Died*, written after the Edict of Milan. The details must be taken with a grain of salt, since like Eusebius, Lactantius's agenda is to justify and glorify Constantine as God's emperor. Nevertheless, the work is useful for tracing the history of Roman persecution of the Church from its beginnings with Nero to the end of persecution and the legalization of Christianity. Lactantius argues that not only are the persecutors bad emperors, but they are bad Romans, having forgotten the Roman virtues of peace and tolerance. Some, like Nero, even suffered the posthumous *damnatio memoriae*, meaning that even their fellow Romans condemned their memories after their deaths. In any case, Lactantius argues, they were not even sincere in their own religious convictions, because they often just used the persecutions to confiscate land and other possessions from the innocent, whether they were Christian or not. To be fair, it must be pointed out that not all persecution can be directly blamed on

mother, Helena, protested, he had Fausta executed as well. This was, in fact, the original basis for speculations that Constantine's Christian faith was not sincere.

33 Constantine knew what Diocletian had known, that the empire was too big for one man to rule. However, he must have hoped that he could do it with the help of the bishops.

34 Van Dam agrees. See *Remembering Constantine*, 15.

the emperor at any given time, since the farther one is from the capital, the more power a provincial governor would have had to choose to persecute Christians or leave them alone.

In any case, Lactancius was an eyewitness to the Great Persecution, and from inside the imperial court. He describes how Galerius's mother resented the Christians in the family (including her daughter-in-law?), and pressured Galerius to instigate the persecution. He also describes how Constantine's father Constantius did not persecute Christians, but rather only allowed the minimum of property damage in order to make it look like he was obeying the orders of his superiors. Of course, these events, not to mention the death of Constantius and the acclamation of Constantine as western Augustus, took place in far-off Britain, and so Lactantius was relying on second hand (possibly embellished) testimony.

He describes Galerius's illness and the Edict of Toleration in AD 311, at which time the Christian confessors were released from prison, including a confessor named Donatus, to whom he dedicated the work. And most important, he describes the events leading up to and including the Battle at the Milvian Bridge in AD 312 and the Edict of Milan in AD 313.[35] The text of the Edict of Milan included below is from this document. Lactantius died around the time of the Council of Nicaea.

The Arian Controversy

Adoptionism came to its most developed form in the early fourth century (see the chart, *Christology and Theology in the Fourth Century* at the end of this chapter). The *Logos* christology of Theophilus of Antioch, with its apparent lack of an eternally distinct existence of the Word, combined with quasi-gnostic influences found in Origen, and the christology of ascent found in the adoptionism of Paul of Samosata, all combined to create a christology in which the Word was not eternal and Jesus was a mere man who earned an adopted divinity.[36] In large part, adoptionism is as much an anthropology as it is a christology. As an anthropology, adoptionism begins with the optimistic

[35] Lactantius's account is the earlier one, written within a few years of the Battle at the Milvian Bridge. Lacatantius tells us that, the night before the battle, Constantine had a dream in which he saw the Chi-Rho christogram in the sky. Eusebius's account is later by as much as two decades. In that account, the dream has become a vision in the daytime, and the christogram has become the cross. See Robin M. Jensen, *The Cross: History, Art, and Constroversy* (Cambridge: Harvard University Press, 2017), 52–56.

[36] See Papandrea, *The Earliest Christologies*, 119–121; cf. also Grillmeier, *Christ in Christian Tradition, Volume 1*, 110. Another possible way to look at this is that Arius had combined elements of angel christology inherited from Lucian of Antioch with elements of the spirit christology of Paul of Samosata to create the fourth-century evolution of adoptionism.

assumption that human perfection is possible. Theophilus and some others of the Antiochene school of thought had rejected the idea of original sin, preferring instead to say that every human was born with a clean slate, and with the potential to be perfectly holy. This is consistent with a Stoic understanding of virtue as moral progress. It is also consistent with the Antiochene exegetical methodology that was perceived as being more congruous with Judaism, in which the essence of religion is following the Law. Thus, salvation was seen as the result of successfully striving for obedience to God. In other words, eternal life is the reward for an earthly life of righteousness.

In the development of doctrine as we see it in the early Church, christology and soteriology are interrelated. In other words, the conclusions one comes to regarding Christ and His relationship to the Father will guide one's conclusions about salvation, or vice versa. With Arianism, it could be argued that an optimistic anthropology leads to a soteriology that emphasizes human effort, which in turn drives an adoptionist christology.[37] Specifically, if salvation is a reward for obedience, then humans actually save themselves (or not) and the Savior is simply a pioneer, the first one to get it right, and the example to be followed. However, Arianism goes beyond the third-century version of adoptionism by allowing a certain level of acquired divinity as part of the Son's reward. Thus, Jesus was seen, not as God who became a human, but as a human who became a god, the first one to earn His elevation to a state of adopted divinity. However, this divinity is a lesser divinity than that of the Father, so the Father and Son are not united by consubstantiality, but rather by will (obedience), and therefore the Son is ultimately a created being.[38] The Arians interpreted Colossians 1:15, "firstborn of all creation," to mean that Christ was the first created being, created to be the agent of the rest of creation. For them, the fact that Christ was "begotten" (generated) meant that He was created. They believed there was a beginning to His existence and time before it, when He did not yet exist.

In contrast to this, most of the bishops of the Church assumed an anthropology which, though it did not deny free will, was sufficiently pessimistic to believe that no mere human could ever achieve a level of obedience that would allow him or her to "earn" salvation. Thus, Christ as Savior must be far more than an example to follow,

---

Apparently, Arius was heavily influenced by the Antiochenes; Theophilus, Lucian, and Paul; and perhaps also Origen as well.

37 In large part, I am indebted to my former professor, Dennis Groh, and his groundbreaking book. See Robert C. Gregg and Dennis E. Groh, *Early Arianism: A View of Salvation* (Philadelphia: Fortress Press, 1981). For a detailed treatment of the Arian controversy, see Ayres, *Nicaea and Its Legacy.*

38 In the year AD 260, Dionysius of Rome held a synod which condemned the idea that the Son and Spirit were created. See Grillmeier, *Christ in Christian Tradition, Volume 1,* 156.

and salvation must be more than human effort, it must ultimately be the result of divine intervention. Thus, as we have seen, mainstream (orthodox) christology was therefore a christology of descent, in which Christ is God who became human, not the other way around. These two opposite ways of looking at the intersection between anthropology, christology, and soteriology came face-to-face in the city of Alexandria.

Arius and Alexander

Arius (ca. AD 250–336) was a priest in Alexandria, under the authority of the bishop there, Alexander of Alexandria. Bishop Alexander was teaching the doctrine of eternal generation as Novatian had understood it.[39] However, for Arius (who apparently would have been more comfortable in the Antiochene school of Theophilus and Paul of Samosata), concepts such as eternal generation and consubstantiality seemed to overemphasize the connection and equality of the Father and the Son. To him these doctrines seemed to be either a form of modalism, or a form of polytheism that compromised monotheism by implying two gods. He reasoned that such an equality of Father and Son would make them no longer Father and Son, but "brothers." Arius reacted by going to the opposite extreme and teaching a modified form of adoptionism. He emphasized the distinction between Father and Son, to the point where the Son was not considered divine by nature but was a created being who acquired divinity. "There was a time when He was not" (i.e., did not exist) became the shorthand summary of Arius's teaching.

Arius could not completely deny the pre-existence of Christ, because of the Church's universal acceptance of John 1:1, so he admitted that the *Logos* was pre-existent, just not *eternally* preexistent. Following Paul of Samosata, he proposed that the *Logos* was not the pre-incarnate Jesus, but simply the personified wisdom of God, a created manifestation of God's mind extended for the purpose of creating the universe. However, even the *Logos* was not eternal, but was created just before the rest of creation. Divine foreknowledge of Jesus' perfect obedience led God to prepare the *Logos* to unite with the human soul of Jesus at His Baptism,[40] elevating the man Jesus to a level of quasi-divinity, higher than the rest of humanity but still

[39] See Papandrea, *Novatian of Rome*. Novatian is the first theologian to articulate the doctrine of eternal generation (though he does not call it by that name). Eternal generation was understood to mean that the Son's existence was caused by the Father (and so is contingent and dependent on the Father) but the Son is not created (so there is no beginning to His existence). This teaching probably made its way to the East through Dionysius of Rome and Dionysius of Alexandria.

[40] This part of Arius's teaching may be based on certain elements in Origen. The reader should note that most of what we think we know about what Arius taught comes to us as

lower than God the Father.[41] Thus Jesus Christ was an adopted son of God, just as we might become adopted children of God.[42] But He was not seen as the unique "natural" Son of God, united with the Father by a shared substance, as the mainstream bishops taught. For Arius, one might call Jesus the "son" of God after His Baptism, but one should not call Him the Son of God in an eternal or divine sense.[43] Both Arius and Alexander would agree that Christ was the mediator of God and humanity. However, for Arius, Christ was the mediator because He was *between* God and humanity, more divine than the rest of us, but less divine than the Father. But for Alexander and the mainstream Church, Christ is the mediator because He is *both* divine and human.[44] To be more specific, He is *fully divine* — that is, as divine as

---

reported by his opponents, so there is some uncertainty as to the accuracy of the report. There is precious little that survives from Arius's own pen.

[41] The possibility of degrees of divinity had already been rejected by the mainstream Church, when it was encountered in gnosticism; cf. the gnostic (Valentinian) *Letter to Flora* of Ptolemy. This contains the concept of a "lesser" divinity, which is begotten as a different essence from the unbegotten highest God. On the other hand, the precedent for the concept of degrees of divinity may also be found in Philo's *logos*, which could be interpreted as half divine and half created, thus a mediator that is in between Creator and creation. After the Council of Nicaea, the leader of the so-called Heterousian (or Anomoian) party, Eunomius, taught that there were degrees of createdness, such that the Son of God is created in relation to the Father, but Creator in relation to the rest of creation. The Eunomians were considered more Arian than Arius, and argued that the Son was "unlike" the Father, thus nudging those still on the fence to join the pro-Nicene party. For an excellent overview of the history of the Council of Nicaea and its aftermath, see Ayres, *Nicaea and Its Legacy*. Although Ayres does not give Novatian enough credit for his role as a pioneer in orthodox theology, there is no better book for understanding the fourth-century Arian controversy.

[42] Note again the influence of the Roman practice of adopting an heir in order to secure the succession of power. As we saw in the apologists, the Father and Son were compared by analogy to the emperor and his heir. Although Commodus was the natural son of Marcus Aurelius, most emperors who were not assassinated chose their successors by adopting the chosen men as their legal sons. Thus, adoption makes one an heir. Even Octavian (Augustus) was considered the son of Julius Caesar, though Caesar was actually his uncle. The mainstream Church understood adoption as analogous to the way we become children of God (John 1:12–13), but did not apply it to Jesus Christ, who is the *natural* Son of God, that is the Son of God by nature, which is the same as saying by the same substance (consubstantiality).

[43] The difference in capitalization of the word, *son/Son* is for clarity only. It is not meant to imply that Arius would have made this distinction. Such capitalization is a modern convention and was not part of ancient writing.

[44] Imagine a dispute between Canada and Mexico. If someone were to be chosen as a mediator, one might seek a mediator who is from the United States, between Canada and Mexico;

the Father, since the Father and Son (and the Spirit, though that comes later) are the same singular divinity, the same divine substance.

In about the year AD 319, Arius and Alexander confronted each other. Arius accused his bishop of teaching modalism. Alexander in turn accused the priest of dishonoring Christ by demoting Him from divine to created. At first the issue seemed to be concentrated on the title *Father* for God. Bishop Alexander pointed out that if there was a time when the Son did not exist, then there was a time when God was not a Father.[45] Paraphrasing Novatian, Alexander's counter-slogan became, "Always a Father, always a Son."[46] The implication is that if God changes from not being a Father to being a Father, this would compromise the immutability of God. For Arius, on the other hand, God was only potentially a Father before the creation of the Son. Arius was also concerned to preserve the immutability of the Divine, however for him the greater threat to divine immutability would be to ascribe a divine nature to one who was born as a baby, grew up and learned things, and even suffered and died. But ironically, in attempting to protect the immutability of God, Arius diminished it by implying a change in God, from not being a Father, to being a Father. Thus, Arius drew the line of createdness and mutability between the Father and the Son, whereas the mainstream bishops drew that line between the divine and human natures of Christ.[47]

The main differences between Arius, representing the fourth-century version of adoptionism, and Alexander, representing what would be clarified as the orthodox point of view, can be expressed as follows. For Arius, Jesus as *only-begotten* son of God means that He is God's favored and adopted son because of His perfect obedience, but ultimately He is created just like the rest of us. The connection between Father and son is one of cooperating wills, and the distinction between Father and son is a difference of substance, an ontological subordination in which any divinity that

---

or one might seek a mediator who has dual citizenship of Canada and Mexico. The former mediator is between Canada and Mexico, but neither Canadian nor Mexican. The latter mediator is both Canadian and Mexican. In the same way, the Arian Jesus is elevated to a state between God and humanity, but is neither God nor (arguably) human, since He has been elevated above humanity. The Nicene Christ is both divine and human.

[45] Clement of Alexandria had implied that before creation God was not a Creator, which may have provided Arius with a precedent for saying (or at least being comfortable implying) that there was a time before God was a Father; see Clement of Alexandria, *The Instructor*, 1.9.

[46] Novatian, *On the Trinity*, 31.3.

[47] The assumption on both sides would be that whatever is mutable must be created, and whatever is uncreated (i.e., divine) must be immutable. Augustine would later write that whatever is eternal must be immutable; Augustine of Hippo, *On the Trinity*, 1.2.

the son has is granted to Him and is not His own. Therefore, to call Jesus the Savior means that He is the pioneer of salvation, who first had to save Himself, before He could set the example for the rest of us to save ourselves through obedience to the will of God. For the Arians, there is no Trinity, per se, but such as it was in their eyes, the relationship between the Father and the son was an ontological hierarchy — a hierarchy of different levels of divinity — in which the son was neither consubstantial, nor co-eternal, with the Father.

For Alexander and the mainstream bishops, on the other hand, Christ as *only-begotten* means that He is uniquely and eternally generated.[48] As Novatian had taught, the Son's existence is dependent on the Father, but there was no time when the Son did not exist in reality as a distinct divine Person. The Father and the Son are of the same divine substance, and the divine nature is "natural" to the Son, it is not acquired or bestowed on Him by adoption. He is the only Son of God by nature — and while we may become adopted children of God by identification with the natural Son of God, Jesus Christ remains unique among humanity. His connection with the Father is therefore an ontological equality, and not a connection by will only. For the mainstream to call Jesus the Savior means that He is the embodiment (the *incarnation*) of divine intervention. He is not a pioneer, pulling Himself out of the same situation we find ourselves in, but rather a rescuer, coming to us from outside of our situation, who did not have to save Himself before He could save us.

Both sides knew that the human will of Jesus was submissive to the divine will (Luke 22:42). For the Arians, this submission of will constituted the only real *unity* between the Father and the Son, in that the human will of Jesus conformed to the will of God. But the christology of the mainstream majority affirmed that this submission of will demonstrated the *distinction* between the Father and Son, since it showed that the Father and Son are not one and the same Person, even though there is a unity of substance.[49] Therefore, to summarize, the Arian christology is

[48] For the Catholics, generation begets the same substance. But for Arius and his followers, the ungenerated (the Father) and the generated (the Son) could not be same substance. For him, unbegotten and begotten were parallel to (or even synonymous with) uncreated and created. For the Nicene bishops, both unbegotten and begotten are uncreated.

[49] It will later be clarified that the Person of Jesus Christ has two wills, a divine will of the divine nature, and a human will of the human nature. The divine will is not a different will from the will of the Father, since there is only one will in the Trinity. The divine will of Christ does not need to submit to the will of the Father because the divine will of Christ *is* the will of the Father. However, the human will of Christ does need to submit to the will of the Father (and does so by free will), but that is the same as saying that the human will of Christ submits to the divine will of Christ.

a christology of ascent, in which Jesus Christ is a man who becomes a god, setting an example of behavior, implying a salvation by will and works. Orthodox christology is a christology of descent, in which Jesus Christ is the divine Word who became human, who saves by divine intervention. In the year AD 324, bishop Alexander of Alexandria wrote a letter to the bishop of Byzantium (soon to be called Constantinople), whose name was also Alexander. In this letter, the bishop of Alexandria clarified the problems inherent in what Arius was teaching, and in the fourth-century version of adoptionism in general. The controversy would soon come to the attention of the new emperor.

The Council of Nicaea

The Arian controversy was a source of scandal in the Church, especially in the East. It is sometimes presented as though it truly threatened the existence of the Church, but that is an exaggeration. The controversy was nonexistent in the West at the time, and even in the East it would eventually become clear that orthodoxy was still in the majority. However, in the East the issue was a topic of heated discussion, even for the laity, and it would become a political football in the reigns of Constantine's successors. Both sides had significant supporters, and with salvation itself on the line, there was a sense of urgency to come to some conclusions about what the bishops would endorse. In the city of Alexandria, Arius's followers were threatening violence. The emperor Constantine knew that if he hoped to use the Church to help him keep the empire united, he needed to make sure this issue did not split the Church. He wrote letters to Arius and Alexander asking them to reconcile and sort out their differences, but to no avail, so Arius was excommunicated, and Constantine ordered all bishops to attend a council in the city of Nicaea, near the new city he was creating, just to the southeast of what would later become Constantinople.

The Council of Nicaea, in AD 325, was the first *ecumenical* (worldwide) council of the Church. It was attended by hundreds of bishops from all over the empire (though mostly from the East) as well as priests and lay people, including some hermits who came in from their desert cells to attend. Some confessors, who had been tortured in the Great Persecution, showed up, and they were treated with enormous respect. The question, as it was posed for debate, was whether there a time when the Son did not exist, or whether He is co-eternal with the Father. In other words, was the Son created, or was He eternally generated? Arius, and those like him, rejected the concept of eternal generation in favor of saying what Origen had said, that the Son was the product of the Father's will, not His essence.[50] The majority of bishops believed

[50] Ayres, *Nicaea and Its Legacy*, 53.

that the unity of Father and Son went deeper than only a union of will. However, when it came time to write a statement of faith that would express the belief of the orthodox majority, the task proved difficult. The Council itself had brought to light the existence of a variety of points of view, so that it was not a simple matter of two sides, one Arian and the other Catholic, one heretical and the other orthodox. It is not within the scope of this present book to outline the different factions in detail, however it is important to note that all of them claimed to be able to support their arguments with Scripture in one way or another. Thus, the task of writing a creed that could be taken by each bishop back to his home area, and which would not only teach the orthodox position but exclude the heretical, turned out to be more than anyone had anticipated.

The bishops who promoted the mainstream (orthodox) position believed that if they could find a way to describe Christ that would highlight His uniqueness (that He was not created or adopted like the rest of us), then Arianism (in all its variations) would be refuted. However, whenever biblical language was suggested, the Arians found it acceptable, implying that they could interpret it in such a way as to be consistent with their own christology. Ultimately, it became clear that the creed had to include the doctrine of the consubstantiality of the Father and Son. This was finally expressed with the Greek term, *homoousios*, meaning "of the same essence." In other words, the Son is of the same essence (or substance) as the Father, eternally generated, but not created. The Arians, of course, could not endorse this term, but the greater problem was that many of the other bishops were also reluctant to endorse it, since the word itself is not found in Scripture. And so it became clear that in this case, Scripture could not interpret itself. Scripture alone was not enough (*sola scriptura non satis est*), and the bishops had to look outside of Scripture to find a term that would sufficiently interpret Scripture in such a way as to articulate the teaching of the whole witness of Scripture, and provide the traditional orthodox interpretation, while ruling out the heretical one. Of course, the designation of orthodoxy and heresy as applied to one side of the debate or the other could only officially be determined at the outcome of the council, but in the end, the word *homoousios* and the doctrine of consubstantiality were confirmed as the most consistent with both Scripture and Tradition (prior orthodoxy). The creed was accepted (though reluctantly by some) and anyone who refused to sign it was excommunicated. Arius himself was exiled by the emperor for causing all the trouble — and so he found himself banished from the city of Alexandria.

To those who would not sign the creed, the term *homoousios* sounded like modalism, or worse, it sounded gnostic. The fact that the word is not found in Scripture did not make bringing the creed home any easier, so even some of the bishops who signed it would never use it. In fact, it was not required that every church use the creed. The creed was meant to be a standard by which other creeds would be measured, and as long as a bishop could say that the creed used in his see was in agreement with the creed of Nicaea, that was enough. Eventually, the creed would also become a tool of catechesis to teach new converts the correct understanding of the Person of Christ. By the late fourth century it would become a litmus test for orthodoxy. At the second ecumenical Council of Constantinople in AD 381, the creed was expanded to incorporate the outcome of the debate over the divinity of the Holy Spirit (we will examine this in the next chapter), and the statement of faith that we now know as the *Nicene Creed* was complete.[51]

Nicene orthodoxy insisted on a balance of unity and distinction in the relationship of the Father and Son. The unity is clarified by the affirmation that the Father and Son are consubstantial, as opposed to the adoptionist claim of a supposed ontological difference (degrees of divinity) between Father and Son. The distinction is clarified in the affirmation that the Father and Son are not identical, as the modalists had claimed. To be fair, Arianism also has both unity and distinction in the relationship of Father and Son, however the unity is one of cooperation only, and the distinction is actually an ontological separation — it is specifically in the assertion that the Father and Son are not consubstantial. The point is that *orthodoxy is the balance of unity and distinction*, while adoptionism and Arianism have too much distinction, to the point of separation (the Son is thought to be a created being), and modalism has too much unity (the Father and Son are thought to be one and the same).

The Arian controversy was not the only topic of discussion at the Council of Nicaea. Among other items on the agenda was the definition of metropolitan sees, in which Rome was confirmed as primary. This is significant that an ecumenical council (in the East, no less) would acknowledge the authority of the bishop of Rome, not only over other bishops in the surrounding areas, but also over the other metropolitans. Also, the correct calculation for the date of Easter was discussed. The decision was that all churches must conform to the calculation used in Rome, and although the ruling was not universally accepted or followed, this once again demonstrates that at least in theory the church of Rome held a certain primacy.

[51] The Nicene Creed is still the standard of orthodoxy for worldwide Christianity, except that the West has an added phrase. Where the Eastern version of the Creed affirms that the Holy Spirit proceeds from the Father, the Western version adds the phrase, "and the Son" (in Latin, *filioque*); that the Holy Spirit proceeds from the Father and the Son equally. This was added as an attempt to emphasize the equality of the Father and the Son against Arianism. See below, in chapter 13.

Athanasius of Alexandria and Nicene Orthodoxy

After the Council of Nicaea, the Arians and various *semi-Arian* factions did not entirely go away. Throughout the AD 330s and 340s there was a tennis match of smaller councils going back and forth, alternately dominated by one party or the other, each one excommunicating its opponents. Sometimes violence broke out, especially in Alexandria. Athanasius, who had been at the Council of Nicaea as a deacon and as Alexander's assistant, succeeded him as bishop of Alexandria (bishop from AD 328–373). Athanasius then became the primary spokesman for Nicene orthodoxy, championing eternal generation, and writing documents such as, *On the Incarnation of the Word, Defense of the Nicene Definition,* and *Against the Arians.*[52] When Athanasius became bishop of Alexandria, Arius himself was bold enough to complain to Constantine, resulting in an edict of AD 333 which ordered that all of Arius's writings must be burned. Consequently, apart from a couple of letters, Arius's writings no longer exist, except in fragments quoted by Athanasius and other opponents of Arianism.[53]

Some of the Arian bishops had signed the creed to keep themselves out of trouble, knowing that they could go back to their home sees and ignore it. Others refused to sign the creed. Nevertheless, Arian bishops would be alternately in and out of the good graces of Constantine and his sons over the next few decades. The Arian bishop Eusebius of Nicomedia would even be invited to become the bishop of Constantinople, in direct violation of one of the canons of the Council of Nicaea, which stated that bishops may not move from one see to another. In fact, it would be Eusebius of Nicomedia who would baptize the emperor Constantine at the end of his life. When the Arian bishops were able to gain power, they concentrated their efforts on getting

[52] On eternal generation, see Athanasius of Alexandria, *Defense of the Nicene Definition* (*De Decretis*), 10, 28–32; *Letter to the Clergy of Alexandria*, 52; see also Ayres, *Nicaea and Its Legacy*, 143–144. On the other hand, Athanasius's emphasis on the unity of will between Father and Son (by which he means a unity of activity, or inseparable operation) will leave the door open for both Apollinarius and Nestorius. Apollinarius would say that there is only one will between the Father and Son (that the human nature of Christ has no human will, so there is only one will in the Person of Christ), and Nestorius would say that while there are two wills, the union between the two natures is only a cooperation of wills; see Athanasius of Alexandria, *Discourse Against the Arians*, 3.25.10, 3.27–28, 3.30.59–67.

[53] Some have argued that there is so little that we can be sure is from Arius himself, that the very concept of *Arianism* is better understood as a creation of Athanasius. There is some merit to this point of view, however in the absence of a better way of talking about the controversy, we continue to use the term *Arianism* to describe the teachings of Arius and others who advocated this fourth-century version of adoptionism.

Athanasius removed from his see at Alexandria.[54] In all, he was exiled and reinstated five times. During times of exile, he was protected by the bishop of Rome, who sided with the Nicene bishops against the Arians and semi-Arians.

Arius himself was eventually recalled from exile and invited to Reconciliation with the Church, however, according to tradition, he died the night before he would have received Communion. This story is probably unreliable, but it shows how the opponents of Arius saw him as the arch-heretic whom God would rather kill than reconcile. It was not until after the Council of Constantinople in AD 381, when the Greek language used to describe the Trinity could be clarified and enough of the semi-Arians would come over to the Nicene side, that the Arian controversy would subside in the East. However, it would continue in the West into the fifth century, due to the missionizing efforts of the Arian bishops, and resurface again in the early Middle Ages.

On the Incarnation of the Word

This is actually the second of a two-part work, the first part being a more generic work known as *Against the Heathen*. Both were written before the Council of Nicaea, so *On the Incarnation* is not directly addressed to trinitarian heresies, per se, but it does outline Athanasius's understanding of the relationship of the Son to the Father, which would be the central issue at the Council. For Athanasius, since humans were originally created incorruptible, incorruption must be restored in order for us to receive salvation. The Incarnation is necessary for the restoration of human incorruption. So the one who was incapable of corruption took on corruptible flesh, so that we might become incorruptible again. The immortal had to become mortal, to make the mortal immortal. This is the continuation of Irenaeus's exchange formula. God became like us, so we could become like God — not that we become gods, but that we become god-like, in the sense that we were originally created to be. Athanasius called this process *theopoiesis*, but later it would come to be called *theosis*, or deification (cf. 2 Pet. 1:4).[55]

In Defense of the Nicene Council

Written almost twenty years after the Council, this is exactly what the title suggests, though it is also known by its Latin title, *De Decretis*. Here Athanasius gets to the heart of the matter of Nicaea, that is, opposing the trinitarian heresies of adoptionism and

[54] In order to get Constantine to exile Athanasius, his enemies (including Eusebius of Caesarea) falsely accused him of disrupting the grain supply coming out of Egypt. See Van Dam, *Remembering Constantine*, 60.

[55] See Ortiz, *Deification in the Latin Patristic Tradition*.

Arianism, and clarifying that the Son must be understood to be consubstantial and coeternal with the Father. Against Arianism (as it continued after the Council), Athanasius maintained that the generation (begetting) of the Son is not an event but is an eternal state of being (as Novatian had pointed out). Thus, eternal generation implies that the Father and Son are coeternal, and that there was no time when the Son did not exist, or when the Father was not a Father.

Furthermore, the Son's sonship is essential (natural), not adopted, because the generation (begetting) must result in the one begotten being of the same substance as the one who begets. In other words, being begotten does not mean created, and being unbegotten is not the same as uncreated, because both the Father (the unbegotten) and the Son (the only-begotten) are uncreated.

Eusebius of Caesarea and the *Ecclesiastical History*

In the time leading up to the Council of Nicaea, Eusebius of Caesarea (bishop ca. AD 314–340) was actually suspected of supporting an adoptionist or Arian christology. The accusations were probably true, though Eusebius was able to fly under the radar, and was never officially declared a heretic. He was ordered to appear before a council in Antioch in the spring of AD 325, and the creed he was using in Caesarea was examined for orthodoxy.[56] His creed was just vague enough to pass the examination, but it demonstrated the danger of having a creed that was not specific enough. Therefore, the issue was tabled until the Council of Nicaea, and at that time, Eusebius's creed may have been used as a starting point, or template, for the statement of faith that would be written there (see the comparison of creeds in the chart at the end of the next chapter).

In the aftermath of Nicaea, Eusebius was willing (though possibly reluctant) to get on board with mainstream orthodoxy, but what made him famous was that he would become known as the Church's first historian.

Ecclesiastical History

Eusebius's masterwork is our first written history of the Church. It is a compilation of all of the stories and traditions of the Church that were known to Eusebius, following the history of Christianity from its beginning down to his own day. Because Eusebius is relying on the materials available to him and is obviously not an eyewitness to most of what he records, we have to read his history keeping in mind his limitations and his agenda, which was to glorify the Constantinian dynasty. Often Eusebius will deal

[56] See Van Dam, *Remembering Constantine*, 59, who notes that a creed was attempted at this council, before Nicaea, but Eusebius rejected it. It seems that this, combined with the vagueness of his own creed, left the spring council at a stalemate.

with conflicting stories simply by relating multiple versions or differing opinions, almost side by side. Other times he presents what must be purely legendary material as though it is historical fact. Still, there is much that he preserves which we would not have otherwise, including important documents and fragments of documents from important writers, and so in the absence of contrary evidence we can receive his accounts as faithfully transmitting what early Christians believed happened, if not always what actually happened.

Life of Constantine

Even more than his history, Eusebius's *Life of Constantine* was meant to praise the first Christian emperor and raise him up as the new man of God in the world — almost as a second Messiah. He is presented as the savior of the Church, and of the world. And yet, there is historical value in the document, as it gives us details of Constantine's life that Eusebius would have no reason to fabricate. We are told that Constantine was raised in the court of the eastern emperors while his father was stationed in the West. We are told how Constantine, when he saw that his life was threatened, left Nicomedia and escaped to join his father in Britain, and how after his father's death, the legions raised up Constantine as their leader.[57]

Like Lactantius, Eusebius tells us that Constantine's father Constantius refused to persecute Christians. We also get another version of the events leading up the Battle at the Milvian Bridge, including the story of Constantine's vision — but now it is a cross that he saw emblazoned on the sky, rather than the christogram, or Chi-Rho. Eusebius claims to have seen with his own eyes a large golden jeweled cross that Constantine commissioned after his vision. Of course, Eusebius knows about the Chi-Rho symbol, calling it the symbol of the Savior's name superimposed over a cross, and relates how this sign was used on the standards of Constantine's legions. And not to be outdone by Lactantius, Eusebius also describes the punishment of the persecutors in the form of horrible illness, especially the illness of Galerius, which led him to issue the Edict of Toleration in AD 311.

Eusebius tells of Constantine's final victory over Licinius to become sole emperor, his reparations and concessions to the Church, and the events surrounding the Council of Nicaea. He also tells of Constantine's mother Helena, her pilgrimage

[57] See Van Dam, *Remembering Constantine*, 70–71, for the ways in which Eusebius embellished the story, including compressing the timeline to add drama, thereby making it seem as though Constantine arrived in Britain "in the nick of time," just in time to be present at the deathbed of his father.

to the Holy Land, the identification of the holy sites in Jerusalem and Bethlehem, and the building of the first churches on those sites.

Myths about Constantine

Did Constantine create a "marriage" of Church and state?

It is important to be clear that Constantine did not make Christianity the "official" religion of the Roman Empire, nor did he make it the only legal religion. He did not turn the tables and persecute the former persecutors. In fact, at no time did anyone in the Church ever take up arms against persecutors. Although it is fair to call Constantine the first Christian emperor — if by *Christian* we mean "believer" — he was not baptized until the end of his life. He did not rule as a member of the Church. He did favor the Church, even at the risk of his ability to cooperate with pagan senators, and with one notable exception, every emperor after him would also claim to be Christian (though some were Arians). But it was not until Theodosius I (reigned AD 379–395) that a baptized Christian ruled as emperor.[58] And even he was only baptized because he became gravely ill, and it was thought he might die — so he was given what is called a *clinical* Baptism, an emergency Baptism. But then he recovered and reigned as an initiated member of the Church. It was Theodosius who issued the *Edict of Thessalonica* in the year AD 380, which decreed that the official religion of the empire was "the faith delivered by Peter to the Romans."[59] A second edict in AD 381 made the practice of, or conversion to, paganism illegal, and required all citizens to be baptized.

In any case, far from creating a "state religion," Constantine granted freedom of worship to all religions, with the Edict of Milan. As we have noted above, religion and government had always been interdependent, and Constantine was (ironically, given the myth) a pioneer of religious freedom.

Did Constantine force the doctrine of the Trinity on the Church?

When we look at the history as we've seen it so far, we can see that the doctrine of the Trinity was part of the Church's DNA from the very beginning. In fact, the bishops of Nicaea would assume that it is *the* defining doctrine of the Church. It's what makes Christianity Christian. Jesus Himself told His apostles to baptize in the name of the

[58] Technically, Theodosius was emperor in the East. There was another emperor, Gratian (ruled 379–384), who reigned in the West at this time.

[59] *Codex Theodosianus*, 16.1.2. Interestingly, the edict mentions Alexandria (not Constantinople or Jerusalem) as secondary, as the see that represents the East in agreement with Rome.

Father, Son, and Holy Spirit.[60] From then on, the Church Fathers set about clarifying the doctrine, and by the middle of the third century, it was the very definition of orthodoxy in the mainstream Church.

And yet, there are some who say that the Church was not really clear on this (or even on the divinity of Christ) until the fourth century, and at the Council of Nicaea, the Emperor Constantine forced the bishops to (reluctantly) accept the doctrine just to keep the Church from splitting over it. Some go so far as to say that the Church didn't have a doctrine of the Trinity before the fourth century, but by now it should be clear that these myths are not true.

It is true that the controversy that led to the Council of Nicaea was a controversy over the doctrine of the Trinity, and it is true that some people thought the heretics had enough numbers to split the Church — but all that applies to the eastern half of the Church (and Empire). What most people don't realize is that even though the Council of Nicaea was an *ecumenical* (worldwide) council — and that does mean that all the bishops of the world were invited, and the Council's decisions would be binding on all of the universal Church — still very few bishops from the West showed up, because it just wasn't as much of a controversy in the West. The bishop of Rome did send a delegation, so Rome was represented. But the point is that (the exaggerations of certain Church Fathers notwithstanding) the Arian controversy could never have really destroyed the Church. It did not threaten to split the West, because the West had Tertullian (and Novatian).

The emperor Constantine did convene the Council of Nicaea, and he did attend, as a kind of facilitator. It is clear that he expected to be treated with the same respect as the bishops, but he did not take sides in the debate. In fact, his letters to Bishop Alexander and to Arius show us that before the Council he actually leaned toward the Arian side. And at least two of his sons also favored the heresy after him. So if he was going to push anything on the Council, it would have been the heresy. In any case, the outcome of the Council was a foregone conclusion before it ever met because even in the East the mainstream majority was orthodox, and there was no way that the council bishops were going to endorse anything but the established tradition.

Finally, some people claim that there was an observable shift in the Church from before Constantine to after Constantine, in which an emphasis on the humanity of Christ changed to an emphasis on the divinity of Christ. They will attribute this to Constantine's influence and suggest that he was bringing some form of paganism into the Church, endorsing a worship of Christ that either was not there before, or was in the minority. All of this can be an attempt by modern scholars and others to

[60] Matt. 28:19; see Papandrea, *Trinity 101*, 22–23.

downplay the divinity of Christ, as if an adoptionist interpretation of Christ would be getting back to a more original version of Christianity.

As the evidence shows, there is no observable change in the Church, but if there was, it would not be because of Constantine — after all, as we've seen, if he was going to "make" the Church go in any direction, it would be more toward the adoptionist emphasis on Christ's humanity. No, if there was such a perceived shift, the reason would be this: Before the time of Constantine, the greatest threats to the Church were the heresies of docetism, gnosticism, and modalism — and against these, the bishops and theologians did emphasize the humanity of Christ, in order to refute the heretics' belief that Jesus was not really human. But after the time of Constantine, the greater threat was Arianism, and so the Church had to emphasize the divinity of Christ to refute Arianism's diminished divinity. But in both cases, the Church was not emphasizing one nature over the other, but rather emphasizing what the heretics diminished in order to bring back the balance of orthodoxy — that Jesus is fully divine and truly human.

Did Constantine decide which books to put in the Bible?

By now the reader understands the process by which we got our Christian Bible, and especially the New Testament. However, there are some who have claimed that it was Constantine who forced the issue of which documents to include in the New Testament, or even that he personally chose which books to include. In Eusebius's *Life of Constantine*, we read that after the Council of Nicaea, the emperor commissioned fifty copies of the Scriptures to be made to accommodate the growing number of converts in Constantinople.[61] But the account says nothing about the actual contents of these books of Scripture. The idea that Constantine had anything to do with the "table of contents" of these Bibles is pure speculation, and completely without any supporting evidence.

Unity through Standardization

In addition to legalizing Christianity, Constantine had also reunited the two halves of the empire, which facilitated greater communication between bishops. The very concept of an ecumenical, or worldwide, council would have been impossible before Constantine. In other words, Nicaea could not have been authoritative for the whole Church without the attendance of a delegation from Rome, and the endorsement of the bishop of Rome (who had been too ill to attend himself). Constantine also built the first basilica churches, some of which would become the city *cathedrals*, the seats

[61] Eusebius, *Life of Constantine*, 4.36–37.

of the bishops (from *cathedra,* meaning "throne"). Thus, the stage was set for a new attention to standardization within the Church. Whereas the Church had formerly tolerated a greater amount of liturgical and disciplinary diversity, now the Church had the ability to work toward unity through standardization of practice. In addition, the ease of travel and communication highlighted differences from one city to another, which could sometimes be an embarrassment. And so the liturgical and devotional practices of the Church would begin to catch up to the doctrinal unity, in part facilitated by pilgrimage to places like Rome and Jerusalem — the latter having been inaugurated by Constantine's mother, Helena.

Christology and Theology in the Fourth Century

Arianism

Arius, priest of Alexandria

The legacy of adoptionism, but with a qualified (lesser degree of) divinity ascribed to the Son.

Only the Father is eternal.

If the Son were eternal, that would make two Gods.

The Logos was preexistent but not eternally so: "there was a time when he was not."

Jesus was a mere man who was rewarded for his obedience to God with the indwelling of the Logos.

Therefore, begotten means "created," and only-begotten means God's favorite, the "firstborn of all creation" (Col. 1:15).

This is an emphasis on the *distinction* between the Father and Son, to the point of a separation due to an ontological difference (difference of substance).

Arius accused Alexander of modalism.

Arianism is a christology of *ascent*: Jesus is a man who became a god.

Jesus as Savior means that he is the pioneer of salvation, the first to save himself and the one who sets the example for the rest of humanity.

Salvation is therefore by human effort, resulting in adoption.

The Councils of Nicaea (AD 325) and Constantinople (AD 381)

Alexander of Alexandria
(bishop AD 313–326)
Athanasius of Alexandria
(bishop AD 326–373)
The Cappadocians

Begotten means "generated" (caused) but not "created."

The Son is eternally generated, coeternal with the Father, and has no beginning: "Always a Father, always a Son."

Alexander accused Arius of demoting Christ.

Orthodoxy is a Christology of *descent*: Jesus is God (the Word) who became human.

Salvation is by divine intervention and human representation.

Jesus is unlike us in that he needs no salvation.

He is the only "natural" Son of God — the Son of God by nature; that is, substance.

We can be adopted by identifying with him.

The Holy Spirit is also divine and worthy of worship.

Note: The equality of substance within the Trinity means that anything that can be said about any of the three Persons must also be said about the other two, with only these exceptions:

The Father is unbegotten.

The Son is begotten, incarnate.

The Holy Spirit proceeds.

Apollinarianism

Apollinarius of Laodicea (over)reacted against Arianism, and against the possibility that Jesus might have sinned.

He emphasized the union of the two natures to the point of "overlap": the divine Logos replaces the human rational soul (mind/will), to ensure that Jesus would resist temptation.

This results in a diminished humanity, since the human nature of Jesus has no human mind or will.

It is as if the divine *Logos* is simply "wearing" a body, along with the soul that animates it, but with no human mind or will.

This is an emphasis on the unity of divine and human, but the divine overshadows the human.

Only one will (divine) in Christ is called "Monothelite."

The Edict of Milan: A Letter to the Senators, AD 313

from Lactantius, *On the Manner in Which the Persecutors Died,* 48

When we, Constantine and Licinius, emperors, came together in Milan, and conferred together with respect to the good and security of the public's welfare, it seemed to us that, among those things that are profitable to humanity in general, the reverence paid to the Divinity merited our first and chief attention, and that it was proper that the Christians and all others should have liberty to follow that mode of religion which to each of them appeared best; so that that God, who is seated in heaven, might be kind and favorable toward us, and to every one under our government. And therefore we judged ... that no one should be denied the freedom to attach himself to the rites of the Christians, or to whatever other religion his mind directed him, that thus the supreme Divinity, to whose worship we freely devote ourselves, might continue to grant His favor and kindness to us.

And accordingly ... all who choose [the Christian] religion are to be permitted, freely and absolutely, to remain in it, and not to be disturbed in any way, or interfered with. And ... at the same time the open and free exercise of their religion is granted to all others, as well as to the Christians. For it befits the well-ordered state and the tranquility of our times that each individual be allowed, according to his own choice, to worship the Divinity; and we mean not to derogate anything from the honor due to any religion or its votaries.

Moreover, with respect to the Christians ... concerning the places appropriated for their religious assemblies ... now we will that anyone who had purchased such places, either from our exchequer or from anyone else, do restore them to the Christians, without money demanded or price claimed, and that this be performed unconditionally and without question; and we will also, that they who have obtained any right to such places by form of gift do immediately restore them to the Christians.... And because it appears that, besides the places appropriated to religious worship, the Christians did possess other places, which belonged not to individuals, but to their society in general, that is, to their churches, we comprehend all such within the regulation aforesaid, and we will that you cause them all to be restored to the society or churches, and that without hesitation or controversy: Provided always, that the persons making restitution without a price paid shall be at liberty to seek indemnification from our bounty.

11

The Church after Constantine

The early fourth century, with the first Christian emperor and the first ecumenical council, is a turning point in the history of Christianity. Afterward, the sheer volume of Christian texts makes it impossible to examine them all at the level of detail with which we have looked at the documents of the second and third centuries. When we come to writers such as Augustine of Hippo, for example, the massive volume of their work prevents us from taking their thought as a unit, and requires us to talk about the progression of thought throughout their careers. Therefore, we cannot attempt to even mention every extant document by the Church Fathers introduced below (indeed, nor can we mention every one of the Church Fathers in our era). However, certain themes to which we have already been introduced continue the trends begun in the pre-Nicene era and can be traced as we look ahead to the later Fathers and Doctors of the Church.

In the second and third centuries, the doctrinal debates had surrounded two primary questions: the relationship of the Father and Son (the balance of unity and distinction of Persons in the Trinity); and the relationship of the two natures in Christ (that there is both divinity and humanity in the Second Person of the Trinity). Each of these questions continued to develop in the post-Nicene era. The first question was expanded to include the Holy Spirit (that the Holy Spirit is also consubstantial with the Father and the Son). The second question applied the categories of the first question to the Person of Christ (that is, the balance of unity and distinction of the two natures).

The Cappadocians

Also known as the *Cappadocian Fathers,* the term generally refers to three bishops from the Cappadocia region of Asia Minor: Basil of Caesarea (AD 329–379), his brother Gregory of Nyssa (ca. AD 330–385/386), and their friend Gregory of Nazianzus (AD

325–389). They continued the work begun by Alexander and Athanasius in solidifying the pro-Nicene position in the Church and bringing general acceptance of the creed. They did this by clarifying that consubstantiality (specifically the non-biblical term *homoousios*) did not imply a form of modalism. As Tertullian and Novatian had made clear in the first half of the third century in the West, the one substance did not imply that the Father and Son were one and the same, since the Father and Son maintained a personal distinction.[1]

However, the bishops at the Council of Nicaea had used the Greek words for *person* and *substance* interchangeably, which would create confusion in the interim between the first and second ecumenical councils. The Cappadocians were largely responsible for settling the question of which Greek terms should be used as the equivalents of Tertullian's *persona* and *substantia*.[2] Specifically, the Greek term that would be used as the equivalent of *persona* would be *hypostasis*, and the Greek term for *substantia* would be *ousia* (essence). Thus, the Greek East could clarify that the Trinity is three *hypostases* in one *ousia*. As we will see, the fact that Nestorius, the fifth-century bishop of Constantinople, did not conform to this convention of technical terms meant that more controversy was coming (see below). But for the time being, the work of the Cappadocians allowed some of the *semi-Arian* holdouts to come over to the Nicene side.

The Cappadocians also expanded the Church's understanding of the Trinity by applying Nicene conclusions about Christ to the Holy Spirit. In this, they were opposing a group known as *pneumatomachians* (*Spirit-fighters*), who denied the Holy Spirit's divinity, and therefore were opposed to the worship of the Spirit. Some of these may have been former Arians or semi-Arians who were willing to concede consubstantiality to the Son, but not to the Spirit. They apparently applied some of the Arian arguments about Christ to the Holy Spirit, in effect saying, "We may have to accept the divinity of the Son, but we can't accept the divinity of the Spirit." To them, calling the Holy Spirit *God* would be a form of polytheism.

Macrina the Younger (ca. AD 327–380)

Before we can meet the three Cappadocian fathers, we should first mention an important Cappadocian *mother*, actually the older sister of Basil and Gregory of Nyssa. When Macrina was twelve years old, and engaged to be married, her fiancé died. She

1 Ayres, *Nicaea and Its Legacy*, 190, 194, 216.

2 Hilary of Poitiers had written, "Much obscurity is caused by a translation from Greek into Latin, and to be absolutely literal is to be sometimes partly unintelligible." Hilary of Poitiers, *On the Councils*, 1(9), translation in *Nicene and Post-Nicene Fathers*, vol. 9, 6.

decided never to marry, and dedicated herself to a celibate life. Since the family was wealthy, Macrina was given a good education, and Macrina was, in fact, the driving force of the spiritual life in the household, and the first catechist of the famous bishop brothers.

Macrina would eventually convince their widowed mother to turn the estate into a kind of convent. The household was organized around complete equality with the noble ladies of the family working alongside their freed slaves as equals. Other widows joined them in the house, and they began to take in young women who might otherwise be homeless or destitute. Eventually Macrina herself became the *mother*, or abbess, of the household. After her death, her brother Gregory of Nyssa wrote the *Life of Macrina*: part biography, part hagiography, as an act of gratitude and praise of his saintly sister. She is also presented as the wise teacher in his treatise *On the Soul and Resurrection*.

Basil of Caesarea

Basil of Caesarea was apparently inspired by Macrina to make the commitment to a monastic life. He traveled to Egypt, Palestine, and Syria to meet with the desert hermits (see the section on early monasticism, below). Eventually he would write a rule for the monastic life that would influence all of both eastern and western monasticism. After observing the hermits, Basil came to the conclusion that a completely solitary life would always run the risk of becoming too focused on the individual's salvation, to the exclusion of any practice of loving one's neighbor. He wrote, in effect, "If you live alone, whose feet will you wash?"[3] Therefore, for him the monastic life could not be entirely a life of withdrawal from society. Even the apostles' attempt at communal life in Acts, chapter 2, was never meant to be a life of solitude. So rather than leave the city altogether, Basil's community of ascetics would live at the outskirts of the city, and minister to the poor. The virtue of voluntary poverty was not simply to *be* poor, but also to *help* the poor.

Basil also reasoned that one cannot grow in humility if there is no one to answer to, no one to submit to. Therefore, the community must have a hierarchy, with training in the virtue of obedience — all under the authority of the local bishop, not outside of that authority. Still, Basil recognized the validity of the vocation of marriage and family and did not consider those who could not accept the ascetic life as some kind of second-class citizens within the Church. He believed that anyone could practice compassion and the inner asceticism of struggle against evil and temptation.

[3] Basil of Caesarea, *Long Rule*, Question 7.

Basil wrote *On the Holy Spirit* against the pneumatomachians, affirming the validity of worshiping the Holy Spirit. He confirmed that the Holy Spirit is divine, in part based on the doctrine of inseparable operation. If all three Persons of the Trinity share the one divinity and are all involved in every divine activity, then all three must also be divine. The Holy Spirit is "giver of life" (not a receiver of life), language which found its way into the revision of the Nicene Creed that was competed at the Council of Constantinople in AD 381. The pneumatomachians responded by arguing that if all three Persons are divine, then that is really a form of tritheism, revealing that they had expanded their adoptionism to include the Holy Spirit, whom they believed to be a created being—and thus, they had rejected the doctrine of the Trinity. Against this point of view, Basil's work on the Spirit was continued by the two Gregorys.

Gregory of Nyssa

Gregory of Nyssa wrote *On Not Three Gods* to counter the accusation of tritheism, affirming that the doctrines of divine simplicity and inseparable operation (not to mention consubstantiality) rule out any kind of polytheism. Also, there could be no degrees of divinity, so the *economy*, or hierarchy within the Trinity cannot be ontological. Three *hypostases* (Persons) does not mean three gods, rather one *ousia* (essence or substance) means that the Trinity is one God.

Gregory also wrote *On the Holy Trinity*, in which he went even further than his brother had in affirming that the Holy Spirit is consubstantial and co-eternal with the Father. Thus, the conclusions of Nicaea about the Son were also applied to the Spirit. Gregory of Nyssa would become the resident theologian at the Council of Constantinople and would greatly influence the resulting Nicene Creed.

Gregory of Nazianzus

Gregory of Nazianzus, also known as Gregory the Theologian, would become bishop of Constantinople in the year AD 379, shortly after Theodosius became emperor. Theodosius was orthodox (anti-Arian), and so Gregory was chosen because he was pro-Nicene, and it was perceived that the capital city needed a firm orthodox hand to deal with the remaining opponents of Nicaea. The previous bishop had in fact been an Arian and had marginalized the orthodox Christians of the city by making them all pack into one small church. It took a year to remove the Arian bishop and turn the cathedral over to Gregory.

Gregory wrote the *Theological Orations*, including the *Fifth Theological Oration on the Holy Spirit*, in which he confirmed that it is appropriate to call the Holy Spirit *God*. He confirmed that the Holy Spirit is indeed consubstantial with the Father, as the Son is, which is to say that the Spirit is as divine as the Father and the Son. The Holy Spirit cannot be reduced to an activity or operation of God, because an operation is not of the essence of the operator, but the Holy Spirit is of the same essence as the Divine Operating Power. He also articulated the doctrine of *perichoresis*, that is, that the ultimate orientation of the Persons of the Trinity is toward the unity of the Trinity, and that this unity is guaranteed by the fact that each Person of the Trinity is *in* the other two Persons (John 14:11).[4]

Finally, Gregory clarified for the East that although the Trinity is one God, and one *ousia* (essence or substance), nevertheless there is distinction between the *hypostases* (Persons) such that the Father alone is unbegotten (ungenerated or uncaused); the Son alone is begotten (generated) and incarnate; and the Spirit alone proceeds. Beyond this, he said, it is a mystery, and we should not go further into speculation.

Together, the Cappadocians clarified that the Holy Spirit is of the same divine substance (consubstantial) with the Father and the Son and is therefore divine and is worthy of worship. Thus, the Holy Spirit cannot be a created being, or reduced to the personification of divine activity. Variations of these orthodox and Nicene clarifications had been affirmed in the West since Tertullian, and in the East at least since Athanasius, however the Cappadocians are credited with effectively ending the debate over the divinity of the Spirit and bringing the East around to an acceptance of the Greek technical terms to be used to describe the Trinity. Their work led to a revision of the creed at the Council of Constantinople in AD 381 that expanded the paragraph on the Holy Spirit to what it is today (with the exception of the western addition of *filioque*, "and the Son"; see below).

Apollinarius of Laodicea

With Apollinarius of Laodicea (sometimes spelled *Apollinaris*, AD 310–390), the pendulum swings to the other extreme from Arius (see the chart, *Christology and Theology in the Fourth Century*, at the end of the previous chapter). Apollinarius was a student of Athanasius and a supporter of Nicaea, who reacted against Arius's ontological separation of the Father and Son. He attempted to safeguard the unity and equality of the Son with the Father by emphasizing the divinity of the Son, as well as the unity between the divine and human in Christ.[5] However, in doing this, he described a Christ in which the divine nature overlapped and diminished the human nature. From the perspective of the mainstream bishops, it seemed that Apollinarius believed that the unity of the two natures was dependent on a human nature that had no free will.

[4] Gregory of Nazianzus, *Theological Orations*, 29, 42.15.

[5] Grillmeier, *Christ in Christian Tradition, Volume 1*, 334–337.

Apollinarius had rejected Arius's anthropological optimism and (like all Nicenes) reasoned that if Arian soteriology was correct, all hope would be lost, because no one could be obedient enough to be saved. In fact, he worried that if Jesus' sonship had depended on His human will power to follow the will of God, He very likely might have sinned, which would have disqualified Him as the Savior of humanity. Therefore, Apollinarius concluded that the only way Jesus could have been guaranteed to be without sin would be if there were no human will in Him at all, since it would be the human will that would give in to temptation. He speculated that in the Person of Christ, the human rational soul (the human mind) had been replaced by the *Logos*. So Apollinarius proposed a Christ who had no human will, but into whom the divine *Logos* was inserted to be the mind of the man Jesus. This was perceived by most bishops as unacceptable, because it seemed to diminish Christ's human nature — no human mind would mean that He was less than fully human. Although Apollinarius would have certainly denied it, his christology seemed to have less than two natures, and his Christ seemed to be somewhat gnostic, in the sense of being a divine entity in a human disguise. Apollinarius's christology was therefore rejected, because of the conviction that a Christ who is not fully human could not represent humanity and be the Savior of humanity.

Whereas the orthodox said *the Word became flesh*, and Arianism had said something like *the flesh earned the Word*, Apollinarius seemed to be suggesting that *the Word put on flesh*. The language of *putting on* flesh had been used by the apologists to describe the Incarnation, but in the fourth century it became important to clarify that it was not only a "suit of flesh" that the divine *Logos* wore, it was a full humanity. The problem is that Apollinarius had reacted against Arius's diminished divinity in Christ by overemphasizing the divinity to the point of diminishing the humanity. The Arians had, in effect, proposed a Christ with only one will (human), but Apollinarius went to the other extreme and ironically also proposed a Christ with only one will (but divine). A christology of one divine will is called *monothelite* (Greek for *one will*).[6] Although monothelite christology will resurface later, the majority of bishops would conclude that for Christ to have two natures, He must also have two wills, one divine (the same divine will as the Trinity) and one human.[7]

[6] Grillmeier, *Christ in Christian Tradition, Volume 1*, 339.

[7] See Hippolytus, *Against Noetus*, 17; *Against Beron*, 8. Hippolytus had already clarified that the full humanity of the Son meant that he did have a human rational soul (mind and will). This means that the Person of Christ has two wills, one divine and one human; see Roch Kereszty, *Jesus Christ: Fundamentals of Christology* (New York: Society of St.Paul/ Alba House, 2002), 365; cf. Ayres, *Nicaea and Its Legacy*, 296–297. Note that there is

The Edict of Thessalonica

In February of the year AD 380, Theodosius issued the edict that would make Christianity the official, and only legal, religion of the empire. But if any Arians or others outside the mainstream should ask, "What do you mean by Christianity?" the edict made it clear: *the Faith delivered by Peter to the Romans.* In the following year, another edict made conversion to paganism from Christianity illegal, and made Christian Baptism mandatory for all citizens of the empire. The marriage of Church and state, and indeed the conflation of membership in the Body of Christ with citizenship, were codified into law.

The Council of Constantinople

Gregory of Nazianzus was initially chosen to be the chair of the second ecumenical council, the Council of Constantinople, in AD 381. He was quickly disillusioned by what he perceived as politics and lobbying, and it soon became clear that there was reluctance among the majority of the bishops to insert the word *homoousios* (consubstantial) into the third paragraph of the creed as a descriptor of the Holy Spirit. It is not that the majority of bishops did not agree that the Holy Spirit is consubstantial with the Father (and the Son), but they knew that forcing the issue of putting that word into the creed again would alienate too many people, leading to a number of bishops refusing to sign the creed when they could otherwise sign it with less controversial language. Most of the bishops were looking for consensus — not to compromise, but to draw the boundary lines around orthodoxy as wide as possible, saying a bit less to

---

only one will in the Trinity. The three Persons of the Trinity do not have one will each for a total of three wills; this is made necessary by the assumption of monotheism, and is demonstrated by the concept of inseparable operation. The will is an attribute of the substance, not a personal property, so that there is one will in the divine substance of the Trinity, and one will in the human substance of the human nature of Christ. Therefore, the will of the divine nature of Christ *is* the will of the Trinity. When Jesus says, "not my will but yours be done" in the Garden of Gethsemane (Luke 22:42), it is just as accurate to say that the mind or will of the human nature in Christ conforms to the mind or will of the divine nature in Christ, as it is to say that the mind or will of the Son conforms to the mind or will of the Father. The mind or will of the divine nature of the Son *is* the mind or will of the Father; cf. Gregory of Nyssa, *Against Eunomius*, 1.34. Origen had also affirmed the human will in Christ, but apparently did not allow that the human nature of Christ had *free* will. He seems to have feared the same thing as Apollinarius, that a free human will in Jesus might result in sin, and then he would be disqualified as Savior. Whereas Origen had simply implied that the human will of Christ was not free, Apollinarius speculated that Christ had no human will.

include more people. So in the end, even the phrase "from the *ousia* of the Father" was left out, and Gregory resigned as chair of the Council (see the chart, *Comparison of Creeds,* at the end of this chapter).

Apollinarius's christology was condemned as heresy at the Council of Constantinople, as well as at a council in Rome of the same year. The conclusions of the Council of Nicaea were reaffirmed and Arianism was also condemned. Orthodoxy was implicitly defined as the middle way between Arianism and Apollinarianism. The creed produced at Nicaea was updated and expanded, including the extended paragraph on the Holy Spirit, which was the result of the Cappadocians' work. What we know as the Nicene Creed today is actually the result of both councils and it is properly called the Nicene-Constantinopolitan Creed. This is the creed still honored and recited in the universal Church to this day, except that the western version of the creed has the addition of the *filioque* clause (that the Holy Spirit proceeds from the Father *and the Son*; see chapter 13 below on the *filioque*).

Cyril of Jerusalem

Cyril of Jerusalem (AD 313–386) was born around the time of the Edict of Milan — one of our earliest Church Fathers actually born into a world where Christianity was legal. He could remember his childhood in Jerusalem, and he could remember the holy sites and what they looked like before Constantine's mother Helena identified them and commissioned their embellishment. He was a newly ordained deacon when the Church of the Holy Sepulcher was dedicated in AD 335. He was there for the festivities, with bishops from around the world. Later, he would have met Athanasius, as he passed through Jerusalem in AD 346. As bishop, he would host Basil of Caesarea in AD 357, and Egeria in the AD 380s.

We are not sure exactly when he was ordained a priest, but he was in that role by AD 348, when he preached a series of sermons known as his *Catechetical Homilies.* These include eighteen homilies for catechumens preparing for Baptism, and another five homilies *On the Mysteries,* that is, *mystagogical* reflections on the sacraments meant for those who had recently been baptized and were experiencing the Eucharist for the first time. As discussed above, early Christian preparation for Baptism often focused more on morality than theology, the assumption being that the meaning of the sacraments could not really be explained to anyone until after they had experienced them. The whole collection is sometimes referred to as the twenty-three *Catechetical Lectures* (so *Catechetical Lectures* 1–18 are the *Catechetical Homilies* and *Catechetical Lectures* 19–23 are the five *On the Mysteries*). In the mystagogical homilies, Cyril explained the regenerating grace of Baptism, the doctrine of transubstantiation (though he does not call it that), the Mystical Body of Christ, and the intercession of the saints. Giving advice to those who are about to receive communion, he says, "In approaching, therefore, do not come with your wrists extended, or your fingers spread; but make your left hand a throne for the right, as for that which is to receive a King. And having hallowed your palm [i.e., making the Sign of the Cross in your palm], receive the Body of Christ, saying over it, 'Amen.'"[8]

Cyril became bishop in the year AD 350, and shortly thereafter (on May 7, AD 351) the citizens of Jerusalem witnessed what Cyril took as a miraculous sign for the beginning of his episcopate. A cross of light appeared over the hill of Golgotha and lasted for several hours. Cyril, in his letter to the (Arian) emperor Constantius (son of Constantine, reigned AD 337–361), relates that the whole city came out to see it.[9] Although at first Cyril was reluctant to adopt the Nicene word *homoousios* (consubstantial), in this letter to Constantius he did use it, perhaps to school the Arian emperor and pressure him to embrace orthodoxy. Cyril's own orthodoxy is demonstrated in that he was hated by Arian bishops, who conspired against him. They reported to the emperor fabricated stories of Cyril's disrespect, and they were able to get him expelled from his see. In all, he was exiled three times, but was able to return to Jerusalem for good in AD 378. He attended the Council of Constantinople in AD 381, and there was no question of his orthodoxy.

John Chrysostom

John (AD 347–407) was born in Antioch, the son of an officer in the Syrian army. But his father died when he was very young, and his mother, widowed at the age of twenty, would remain unmarried the rest of her life. She created a kind of monastic atmosphere in their home, and John grew up in that environment. Even so, his mother did not have him baptized as an infant, probably because, like the mother of the Cappadocian brothers, she hoped that he would have a prosperous secular career. He did, in fact, become a very successful lawyer, and could have had a political career, but he couldn't stand the idea that he might get paid to use his skills to argue in favor of a morally inferior position — even less that he might be good at convincing people that something was true when it was not. And so at the age of twenty-three, he was baptized, and became a lector in the church at Antioch. It is noteworthy that, even after the legalization of Christianity, men who hoped for a career in politics would postpone their Baptism, and when they felt that they could postpone it no longer, they were baptized knowing that it meant a complete change of lifestyle.

8 Cyril of Jerusalem, *Catechetical Lectures*, 23.20 (*On the Mysteries*, 5.20), translation *Nicene and Post-Nicene Fathers*, vol. 7, 156 (translation adapted and updated by the present author).

9 Sozomen, *Ecclesiastical History*, 4.5.

John intended to become a monk, but his mother begged him not to leave home, saying, "do not make me a widow a second time."[10] So he continued living at home, practicing the monastic life, until his mother died. At that point, he left the city to live in a community of hermits in the mountains outside of Antioch. His earliest works were written as a kind of apology for the monastic life, probably in response to the Arian emperor Valens (reigned in the East, AD 364–378), who was trying to suppress monasticism and force the monks to do military service.

After a while, John's extreme asceticism affected his health, and he was forced to give up the hermit life and move back into the city. He was ordained a deacon by the bishop of Antioch in AD 381, the year of the Council of Constantinople, and it was in his role as deacon that he saw firsthand the needs of the common people, and how (as Basil had recognized) the life of a hermit does not allow one to be in ministry with people. When he was ordained a priest in Antioch in AD 386, he saw even more clearly the needs of people in the world, as well as the value of the family. Although Chrysostom has been criticized for his strong emphasis on the monastic life as the higher calling, he would come to appreciate the sacramental nature of the vocation of marriage, and eventually write an influential document, *On Marriage and Family Life*. In a world that had always viewed marriage as a transfer of property, and sex as the right of an owner of property (and in spite of his earlier writings on the superiority of celibacy), Chrysostom actually ended up leading the way in thinking of sexuality as something two equal partners do, to come together in the bond that is an image of the unity of Christ and His Church (Eph. 5:32).

At about this time, he wrote his most famous work, *On the Priesthood*, based on his conclusion that it was more important to be in the world than to withdraw from it. This document was extremely influential, and set the standard for the Church's thinking about the ministry of a pastor and preacher. In fact, it was his reputation as a preacher that earned him his nickname, *chrysostomos* (the *golden mouth*). His homilies were so popular, and drew such a crowd, that his audience had to be warned to look out for pickpockets. The people applauded his homilies, and when he told them not to applaud him, they applauded even more. He is also called John the Almsgiver, because of his endless exhortations to the people that the rich have a responsibility to care for the poor. His many extant homilies were written from notes taken by scribes as he preached, then later edited from his outlines.

Chrysostom preached against heresy, and against secular pursuits such as the gladiator and hunting games in the arena, as well as the chariot races in the circus, and the shows in the theater. He railed against the celebration of New Year's Day, the

[10] John Chrysostom, *On the Priesthood*, 1.5.

continuation of pagan traditions such as were part of most weddings, the practice of Jewish Christians continuing to observe Jewish rituals, and against occult practices and superstitions. He is also credited with converting most of the city of Antioch's remaining pagan citizens to Christianity by preaching through a time of crisis. In the year AD 387, the emperor Theodosius I (reigned AD 379–395) raised their taxes. In response, the people of Antioch rioted and smashed some statues, including one of the emperor's recently deceased wife. The emperor vowed to destroy the city in retaliation, but while Antioch's bishop Flavian went to Constantinople to intercede, John preached a series of twenty-one sermons, *On the Statues*, which brought peace and got the people through a very tense Lent. In the end, the emperor relented, and John was famous.

In AD 397, Chrysostom was "called" (virtually kidnapped) to become the next bishop of Constantinople. His consecration was delayed until the next year because Theophilus, the bishop of Alexandria, opposed it. Theophilus did not want to see the connection of Antioch with Constantinople strengthened in this way. But John did not have the personality to be the bishop of Constantinople. He was not diplomatic, and he had no hesitation to criticize people if he thought they needed it. He criticized bishops who would rather hang around the imperial court than be present in their sees to minister to the people. He opposed the abuses and moral laxity of the clergy, some of whom were neglecting their duties to live in luxury as part of the emperor's entourage. And he criticized the morality of the laity in and around the court. If he was the prophet of the poor in Antioch, he was even more so in the capital, pointing out the even greater gap between rich and poor. He refused to become a socialite, and he turned the bishop's residence into a monastic house, sold all the finery, and gave the money — along with most of his own salary — to the poor.

Nevertheless, he enjoyed popularity and influence for about a year. He treated everyone with compassion, including the immigrant Goths. He made sure they were cared for, preached to them through an interpreter, and even translated parts of the Bible for them. But his care for them would earn him enemies among those who were distrustful of the Gothic (Arian) soldiers stationed in the city, some of whom were harassing people. The empress Eudoxia supported John, that is until he started publicly criticizing her lifestyle. At that point she conspired with the bishop of Alexandria and the annoyed clergy of Constantinople to get John accused of false charges. He was exiled from the capital, but when he left, the common people rioted. That, along with a fortuitously timed earthquake that frightened Eudoxia, led to John's return.

But in AD 403, Eudoxia had a silver statue of herself put up in the square in front of the cathedral (the original Hagia Sophia church). The ceremony for its dedication included exotic dancers and a lot of noise during the liturgy. So Chrysostom criticized her again. It was reported to her that he had called her another Herodias in a sermon.

Whether or not it was true, she believed it, and in AD 404 he was dragged from the Easter vigil in the middle of the Baptisms. He was exiled again, this time even farther away so that he could not keep up correspondence with his friends, and his supporters in the city were persecuted. Chrysostom wrote to Pope Innocent I (bishop AD 401–417) for help. Innocent tried to intervene, along with the western emperor Honorius, but when the pope's ambassadors tried to enter Constantinople, they were turned away by soldiers. Chrysostom's captors tried to move him again, but his health was broken, and he died on a forced march in AD 407, and so he is considered a martyr. Details of his life come mostly from seventeen letters to a widow and deaconess named Olympias.

Like Cyril of Jerusalem, John Chrysostom preached homilies to the catechumens and the newly baptized that emphasized the miraculous nature of the sacraments — they are not simply human acts or symbolic commemorations of things that have already happened. Baptism effects a permanent change in the person being baptized, at the moment of Baptism. The Eucharist mystically re-presents the passion of Christ in a way that makes the recipient a participant in it. Marriage is also a sacrament, since it, too, effects a change in the couple, and is an image of the love of the Trinity.

Ambrose of Milan

Ambrose (AD 340–397) was born in Trier, but moved to Rome as a teenager, during the time that Liberius was bishop of Rome (AD 352–366). His older sister, known to the Church as St. Marcellina, entered the monastic life, and Ambrose went on to study law, and eventually became the provincial governor in Milan in about AD 372. At this time, the bishop of Milan was an Arian by the name of Auxentius, and the eastern emperor Valens favored Arianism. In AD 369, a council in Rome had excommunicated Auxentius, but he refused to leave his office and stayed in Milan with the support of the eastern emperor. Ambrose himself was outspoken in favor of Nicene orthodoxy, and consequently found himself temporarily exiled over the matter. Auxentius eventually signed an orthodox statement of faith but continued teaching a semi-Arian christology.

When Auxentius died in AD 374, the city of Milan was divided over whether the next bishop should be Arian or Nicene. A crowd gathered around the cathedral, which threatened to turn into a riotous mob. Ambrose rode into the middle of the crowd on his horse, to try to control the situation and prevent violence. According to the tradition, the crowd became quiet, and the voice of a child was heard, proclaiming Ambrose bishop. The crowd took this as a sign from God, and Ambrose was elected as the next bishop of Milan on the acclamation of the people — though he was only a catechumen at the time, not yet even baptized. In reality he was accepted because he was known to be pro-Nicene and had a reputation as an excellent speaker. He tried to refuse the job, but the western emperor Valentinian endorsed him, and within a week he was baptized, ordained, and consecrated a bishop.

Ambrose was bishop of Milan from AD 374 to 397. He was bishop when Theodosius issued the Edict of Thessalonica in AD 380, as well as during the time of the Council of Constantinople in AD 381, and he was bishop when the future St. Augustine arrived in Milan in AD 385. Ambrose was known for defending Nicene orthodoxy, and when an eastern emperor sent troops to attempt to take one of the basilicas in Milan by force, to make it into an Arian church, he inspired the lay people of Milan to occupy the basilica and prevent its capture. As a result, many of the Arian soldiers converted to orthodoxy.[11] On another occasion, he excommunicated the emperor Theodosius himself for ordering the massacre of citizens of Thessalonica who were in rebellion.[12] Ambrose also wrote hymns, made important developments in standardizing liturgy, and wrote his *On the Mysteries* on sacramental theology.

Theologically, Ambrose is less of an innovator and more of a collator and summarizer. He was influenced by all of the important western theologians, especially Tertullian and Novatian (via Hilary of Poitiers). But he had also traveled to the East, he could read Greek, and so he was able to integrate the influences of Athanasius and especially the Cappadocians into his work. Consequently, his document *On the Holy Spirit* (written in AD 381, the same year as the Council) is a more succinct and accessible treatise on pneumatology than one would get from trying to glean the information from all of the Cappadocian documents directly. Ambrose does take one step that goes beyond his predecessors. Whereas the Cappadocians had said that the Holy Spirit proceeds from the Father *through the Son*, Ambrose, in his attempt to emphasize the equality of the Father and the Son against Arianism, wrote that the Holy Spirit proceeds from the Father *and* the Son (in Latin, *and the Son* is one word, *filioque*).[13] For him, the doctrine of inseparable operation applies even to the procession of the Spirit, so that the Spirit must proceed from both Father and Son (just as the Son is sent by both the Father and the Spirit). This will influence Augustine's writing on the Trinity, which in turn will lead to the addition of the *filioque* clause into the creed in the West (see chapter 13, below).

Augustine and His Controversies

The questions of the third and fourth centuries continued on in new ways in the fifth century — to a large degree due to the aftermath of the persecutions of the third and

[11] Ambrose of Milan, *Epistle*, 20.

[12] The incident took place in AD 390. See Meyendorff, *Imperial Unity*, 37.

[13] Ambrose of Millan, *On the Holy Spirit*, 1.11, 3.1.

early fourth centuries. Specifically, the questions of ecclesiology and sacramental theology that were sparked by the Decian persecution re-emerged in the Donatist controversy of the fifth century. Also, the questions of anthropology (optimistic vs. pessimistic) which were raised by the Arian controversy were raised again in the Pelagian controversy. In some sense Pelagius answered those questions in ways that were similar to the way Arius would have answered them. In these controversies, the mainstream Church's primary spokesman and the major opponent of both Donatism and Pelagianism was the great saint, Augustine, bishop of Hippo Regius in North Africa.

Augustine of Hippo

Aurelius Augustinus (AD 354–430) was born in Thagaste, North Africa (modern Souk Ahras, Algeria), the child of a mixed marriage: a pagan father and a Christian mother. While his parents did not agree on religion, they did agree to give their son the best education they could. He passed through all the ranks of education that North Africa had to offer, eventually going to study in the capital city of Carthage, and then leaving for Rome to become a professor of rhetoric.

As a young man, Augustine had rejected his mother's Christianity because he thought that the Latin translation of the Bible in use in North Africa was crude; thus he equated a perceived lack of dignity in the writing style with a lack of truth in the content. Looking for answers elsewhere, Augustine joined the Manichees, a fourth-century version of gnosticism that was, in a way, the ancient world's equivalent to the Masonic lodge.[14] It was an outlawed secret society that claimed to be able to provide the answers to all of the questions of the universe. Augustine had hoped to find something to believe in, but was disappointed when the answers that the Manichees provided turned out to be unsatisfying.[15] The experience taught Augustine that he was approaching the prospect of faith backward. He was looking for answers, which would then give him something to believe in. However, after his disappointment with the Manichees, he came to conclude that it is not knowledge that leads to faith, but faith that leads to knowledge. In other words, first one has to make a commitment to believe by faith, then one can learn about one's faith. "We

[14] Dockery, *Biblical Interpretation Then and Now*, 136. Augustine joined the Manichees for the same reason that Marcion had gravitated toward docetism: an attempt to find a satisfying answer to the problem of evil.

[15] Eusebius criticized the syncretism of the Manichees, saying that their founder, Mani, had "stitched together" various doctrines and heresies; see Eusebius of Caesarea, *Ecclesiastical History*, 7.31.

believe in order that we may know, we do not know in order that we may believe."[16] This is summarized in the well-known phrase, *Credo ut intelligam* (I believe so that I may understand).

Augustine became disillusioned with his position in Rome, and especially with the students there. He used his Manichean contacts to land a position as professor of rhetoric in Milan. His mother Monica had followed him from North Africa to Rome, and she would also follow him as he left Rome and went to Milan. There she became friends with the bishop, Ambrose. It is said that when she asked Ambrose about how to handle the different liturgical and fasting traditions between North Africa, Rome, and Milan, Ambrose replied, "When in Rome, do as the Romans do." Augustine's mother is now known to the Church as St. Monica, and she has become the patron saint of mothers who pray for the conversion of their children. In addition, she has a presence in Augustine's autobiography that is a kind of personification of God's grace, which Augustine came to believe was relentless in its pursuit of a person, irresistible and ultimately never thwarted.

As the new professor of rhetoric, Augustine felt compelled to go and listen to the preaching of this bishop who had a reputation as a great speaker. He came for the style, but stayed for the message. Ambrose's non-literal interpretation of the Old Testament seemed liberating to Augustine, and he was eventually converted to Christianity, and was baptized in the year AD 386. As he recorded in his *Confessions,* he found himself in a garden, and mysteriously heard a child's voice, saying, "take it and read."[17] Augustine interpreted this as a message from God, telling him to take up the Scriptures and read for himself. He let the pages open wherever they fell, and read the words of Paul in Romans, chapter 13, and his heart was converted.

After his Baptism, Augustine decided to return to North Africa to form a religious community. Monica died on the way, in the port city of Ostia, outside of Rome. In one of the most poignant chapters of his *Confessions,* Augustine wrote of their last conversations, of her final illness and death, and the fact that she died happy, that she had lived to see her prayers answered and her son come to the Faith.[18] Upon returning to North Africa, Augustine settled in Hippo Regius (modern Annaba, Algeria), where he was ordained a priest. According to the story, Augustine was ordained against

[16] Augustine of Hippo, *Tractates on the Gospel of John,* 40.9, translation in *Nicene and Post-Nicene Fathers,* vol. 7, 228. Augustine seems to be referring to Isaiah 7:9, however his Latin version is based on the Greek translation in the Septuagint (LXX).

[17] Augustine of Hippo, *Confessions,* 8.12. Note the tradition of a child's voice in both Ambrose's selection as bishop of Milan and Augustine's conversion. Cf. Ps. 8:1–3; Matt. 21:16.

[18] Augustine of Hippo, *Confessions,* 9.

his will. He would have preferred a life of monastic solitude, however that was not to be. He became the right-hand man to the bishop, and eventually succeeded him as the next bishop of Hippo.

The very orthodox (anti-Arian) bishop, Ambrose of Milan, would be a significant influence on Augustine's theology, and subsequently Augustine himself would become the most influential pro-Nicene author in the West. Augustine's most important anti-Arian writing is *On the Trinity*, in which he expands upon the thought of Tertullian and Novatian (whose *On the Trinity* he would have read among the works of Tertullian). Augustine emphasized the equality of the Father and Son, especially in terms of consubstantiality and co-eternity, against Arianism. And although the creed of Nicaea had only said that the Holy Spirit proceeded from the Father, Augustine had learned from Ambrose that the Holy Spirit proceeded from the Father *and the Son* (*filioque*).[19] This would eventually make its way into the creed in the West, and cause friction between East and West, however the point at this time was to refute Arianism by demonstrating the equal divinity of the Son, emphasizing that He is equally the giver of the Holy Spirit along with the Father. Thus, Augustine made Nicene orthodoxy unquestionable in the West, just as Athanasius had done in the East.

Augustine advanced the articulation of the doctrine of the Trinity by saying that just as the generation of the Son is eternal, so the procession of the Spirit is also eternal, and not an event in time.[20] He also clarified that, with regard to divine attributes, God does not *have* attributes, as if they are distinct things that are not God, that God possesses, rather God simply *is* those attributes: they are descriptors of the very substance of God. Divine simplicity requires this, and in saying so, Augustine may have been correcting Novatian's tendency to speak of divine *powers* (attributes) as personal properties of the Son that could be set aside in the *kenosis*. Whereas Novatian used the Latin terms *power* (*potestas*) and *authority* (*auctoritas*) interchangeably, which led him to imply that divine power was a personal property specific to each of the three Persons of the Trinity, Augustine, on the other hand, made the implicit distinction between divine power (as an attribute of the one substance of divinity) and authority (which remains a personal property of each Person of the Trinity in the divine *economy* or hierarchy).

Augustine wrote his autobiography, the *Confessions*, around the turn of the fifth century. The publishing of this work was significant, since the ancient biography and autobiography were genres of literature in which glorifying the subject was more important than reporting the truth. Thus, the fact that Augustine did not refrain

[19] Novatian had hinted at this; see Novatian, *On the Trinity*, 29.6–11.

[20] Augustine of Hippo, *On the Trinity*, 15.17.27–28; see also Ayres, *Nicaea and Its Legacy*, 380.

from telling his readers of the embarrassing details and the regrets of his life made it both revolutionary and very popular. One incident in particular — a teenage prank of vandalism — stands out as especially telling. The young Augustine went along with a group of friends as they picked a bunch of pears, and threw them at some pigs. It might seem less than significant, but for Augustine, it was more than the theft of the pears — it revealed the human capacity for mob mentality and pointless destruction. Augustine commented, "I would not have done it on my own."[21] As Augustine looked back on his life, experiences of peer pressure and (in his own assessment) an inability to control his sexual desire led him to conclude that human perfection was not possible. Ironically, he was critical of himself for his shortcomings and at the same time confident enough to assume that if he couldn't do it right, no one could. Human habits and desires, as well as social pressure, were just too strong to expect that anyone could be consistently obedient to God. If salvation depended on self-control, there was no hope for anyone. Nor was there any hope for peace of mind. As Augustine famously begins his *Confessions*, "Our hearts find no peace until they rest in you."[22]

Keeping in mind that his mentor Ambrose was strongly anti-Arian, it could be argued that Augustine's own experience drove him to the extreme opposite of an Arian optimism, leaving him with a pessimism about human nature that could only see it as totally depraved. His disillusionment with Manichean philosophy only reinforced this pessimistic anthropology, driving him to depart from the classical understanding of virtue as perfectibility. Thus, the less he trusted human nature, the more he put all of the responsibility for salvation on God's grace, which he came to believe was irresistible. Even when it came to living up to the moral expectations of God, Augustine concluded that if God did not grant the ability to resist temptation, sin was inevitable. He admitted what perhaps many today can relate to: "In some strange way the very object which we covet becomes all the more pleasant when it is forbidden."[23]

For Augustine, to be happy (or blessed) required confidence in one's eternal destiny. In other words, if our salvation were up to us, we would lose it. The possibility of the loss of salvation created for Augustine an uncertainty that would make happiness

[21] Augustine of Hippo, *Confessions*, 2.8–9, translation in R. S. Pine-Coffin, *Saint Augustine Confessions* (New York: Penguin Books, 1961), 51–52. I am grateful to my former professor Dennis Groh for this insight, and indeed for many of my thoughts on Augustine.

[22] Augustine of Hippo, *Confessions*, 1.1, translation in Pine-Coffin, *Saint Augustine Confessions*, 21.

[23] Augustine of Hippo, *On the Spirit and the Letter*, 6, translation in *Nicene and Post-Nicene Fathers*, vol. 5, 85.

impossible. Therefore, Augustine reasoned that ultimately salvation was completely up to God, not at all up to us, and therefore if God had decided a person was to be saved, that salvation could not be lost, no matter what that person did. This represents a major shift from earlier writers who assumed that salvation could be lost through repeated disobedience or outright rejection of Christ. But Augustine reasoned that such a belief would lead to uncertainty and fear. The only alternative to living with this fear was to put all of one's trust in God, as opposed to one's own efforts.

If happiness means having what you desire, then to desire anything other than God would make happiness illusive, since anything other than God can be lost. To desire anything other than God would be to live with the fear of losing (or never acquiring) what we desire. Therefore, the only object of desire (or object of love) that could lead to happiness is God. But Augustine despaired that we cannot keep our love oriented toward God. He reasoned that the only way happiness is possible is if it is God who chooses us, since if it were up to us to choose God, we would ultimately fail. Therefore, Augustine made salvation entirely the work of God's choosing, or *election*, placing the emphasis on divine intervention over against human effort.

Pelagianism

Pelagius was a British monk who had come to Rome in about the year AD 405, and there he read some of Augustine's writings, especially the *Confessions*. Augustine had written, speaking to God, "Give me the grace to do as you command, and command me to do what you will."[24] In other words, "God, you can tell me to do whatever you want, as long as you give me the power to do it." Pelagius balked at what he perceived as an anthropology which exempted humans from moral responsibility. He reasoned that if the human will is ultimately incapable of obeying God without God helping (or as it seemed Augustine was saying, *making*) us obey, then how could God blame us when we don't obey? In fact, it would seem that sin itself is really to be blamed on God, since apparently God did not give us the ability to resist it. Pelagius (and his followers after him) would accuse Augustine of still being too influenced by the gnostic fatalism of the Manichees.[25]

Before the controversy with Pelagius, the Church Fathers seemed to be content with the tension between some form of original sin (based on Rom. 5) with a real human free will.[26] Now Augustine seemed to be taking original sin to an extreme,

[24] Augustine of Hippo, *Confessions*, 10.29, translation in Pine-Coffin, *Saint Augustine Confessions*, 233.

[25] On the Pelagian controversy, see Meyendorff, *Imperial Unity*, 135-139.

[26] For examples, see Justin Martyr, *1 Apology*, 43; Tatian, *Address to the Greeks*, 7; Theophilus of Antioch, *To Autolycus*, 2.27; Irenaeus of Lyons, *Against Heresies*, 4.37.1–4. Irenaeus says

and so Pelagius reacted by going to the other extreme. He rejected the concept of original sin completely, emphasizing free will to the extent that he seemed to be saying that humans could be good without God's help at all. Whereas Augustine had emphasized the role of God's grace (divine intervention, understood as election) almost to the exclusion of the role of the human will, Pelagius emphasized the role of the will (human effort) and seemed to be diminishing the importance of God's grace.

Pelagius was not an Arian; however, he promoted an optimistic anthropology that had some affinities with Arius.[27] After all, he was a monk, and if humans could not obey God through personal discipline and resisting temptation, then what would be the point of the monastic life? If Augustine was right, he reasoned, why even try to be good? One could justify sin simply by pointing out that God had obviously not granted the ability to avoid it. For Pelagius, not only is perfection possible, but it is expected of every believer.

Pelagius was eventually accused of heresy; specifically, he was charged with teaching against the doctrine of original sin, by saying that all humans are born sinless, and this was interpreted as though he was saying that there is no need for infant Baptism. He was also accused of having taught that a person does not need God's grace to do good and receive salvation. When confronted at a regional council in the East in the year AD 415 (the Synod of Diospolis), he was acquitted. This was partly because his eastern opponents missed the meeting, and there was no one there to articulate the accusations against him accurately. Pelagius did speak on his own behalf and ultimately avoided the charges by affirming that people do need God's grace.

---

that humans have free will because we are made in the image of God, and God has free will. However, note that angels also have free will; Justin Martyr, *2 Apology*, 7; *Dialogue with Trypho*, 141; Irenaeus of Lyons, *Against Heresies*, 4.37.1; but animals do not; Justin Martyr, *1 Apology*, 43; Theophilus of Antioch, *To Autolycus*, 1.6. The consensus among these writers is that if humans did not have free will, then there would be no moral responsibility and evil would be part of creation. That evil is not part of creation, and God as Creator is not responsible for evil, see Justin Martyr, *1 Apology*, 44; Tatian, *Address to the Greeks*, 11; Theophilus of Antioch, *To Autolycus*, 2.17; Clement of Alexandria, *Exhortation to the Greeks*, 6; Hippolytus, *Refutation of All Heresies*, 1.16. Therefore, whomever is rejected by God is rejected on the basis of God's foreknowledge of the individual's rejection of Christ by his or her own free will, not on the basis of predestination; Justin Martyr, *1 Apology*, 44; *Dialogue with Trypho*, 141; Irenaeus of Lyons, *Against Heresies*, 4.29.2, 4.39.4. As Theophilus had said, "It was not the tree, as some think, but the disobedience, which had death in it." Theophilus of Antioch, *To Autolycus*, 2.25, translation in *Ante-Nicene Fathers*, vol. 2, 104.

[27] Eastern Christianity was not influenced as much by Augustine, and so never lost this classical optimism. Therefore, the East seems to have retained the assumption of free will, resulting in less of an emphasis on original sin.

But back in the West, Augustine knew that Pelagius was only able to say this because he was working with a different definition of grace. Pelagius's definition of grace would be very much like Arius's definition. Grace is the example of Christ, along with his teachings as recorded in the Gospels. In other words, Jesus' summary of the Ten Commandments, along with the beatitudes, constituted everything a Christian needed to be good and obey God. For Pelagius, grace is a gift of God, in that it is the example to follow in order to be saved. Ultimately, though, this reduces grace to information. It is external to the human being, and it is *passive.*

For Augustine, grace is *active*; it is a force, which acts on the human person from the outside, but also from the inside. It is the very activity of God, pursuing the believer (the way Monica followed Augustine around Italy) and giving the Christian the power necessary to follow Christ. Without that power, we cannot resist the temptation to satisfy our selfish desires. Sin is a disease which infects the whole human race, and grace is the medicine that will heal our human nature. Although at times (especially toward the beginning of his career) Augustine affirmed the reality of free will, eventually he was pushed by the debate to say that on its own the human will is only free to sin.[28] God's grace frees the human will to do the will of God.[29]

Augustine responded to the challenges of Pelagius (and his followers) with many documents, now considered together as his anti-Pelagian writings. The same skepticism about human nature that made him an anti-Arian also makes him an anti-Pelagian. In *On the Spirit and the Letter,* Augustine makes the connection between Pelagius and Paul's Judaizers, who were said to be the first adoptionists and precursors to Arius.[30] Augustine says that we have free will only in the sense that we can will (i.e., *want*) to do what is right, but we are not actually able to do it without God's help (cf. Rom. 7:18).[31] The only thing one can do by free will is accept God's grace, but even that is really a work of God.[32] For Augustine (and as St. Paul admitted about himself), humans may have the will to do the right thing, but they do not have the ability. For Pelagius, humans have the ability, though they may not have the will to do the right thing, and may choose to do what is wrong (possibly based on a misunderstanding about what is right).

[28] Augustine of Hippo, *On the Spirit and the Letter,* 4.

[29] Augustine of Hippo, *On the Spirit and the Letter,* 52.

[30] Augustine of Hippo, *On the Spirit and the Letter,* 23.

[31] Augustine of Hippo, *On the Spirit and the Letter,* 25, 54. By contrast, Pelagius argued (from Plato) that if we know the good, we can do it. For Pelagius, what we need is information, to know what choices to make. For Augustine, what we need is inner healing from God.

[32] Augustine of Hippo, *On the Spirit and the Letter,* 60.

Other important anti-Pelagian documents include *On Nature and Grace, On the Proceedings of Pelagius*, and the *Enchiridion (Handbook) on Faith, Hope and Love*. The Pelagians had challenged Augustine with the question: If the responsibility for salvation is ultimately on God, and if grace is irresistible, then why are not all people saved? It is clearly God's will that all should be saved (1 Tim. 2:4). Augustine's response was his doctrine of election, which emphasized God's choice for who will be saved and who will be damned. Sometimes called *double predestination*, it is an unconditional election whereby God has decided the eternal fate of every human being, before they were born, and without the consideration of merit or even faith. Whether someone perseveres in faith is entirely a work of God based on divine election, so that if someone who professes faith should fall away and not be saved in the end, that would only mean that the person in question was never really among the elect. This implies that the atonement of Christ must be limited to the elect, or else the cross would be ineffective for some. Against the charge that the predestination of some to damnation seems cruel and unfair, Augustine would reply that all deserve that fate, and the fact that some are elect and predestined to salvation is a gift of God's mercy (cf. Matt. 20:1–16).

Pelagius's criticism of Augustine was essentially a criticism of his anthropology. Pelagius understood that Augustine was saying that the sin of Adam (the Fall) had changed human nature, and that it was, in a sense, broken, and in need of repair. But Pelagius argued that human nature was not broken, and it does not need grace to "fix" it. It is possible to avoid sin because the Fall did not damage our human nature. For Pelagius, grace helps those who help themselves. For Augustine, grace helps those who cannot help themselves.

Pelagius and his followers were finally condemned as heretics and excommunicated at the third ecumenical Council of Ephesus in AD 431, though Pelagianism continued as a rigorist faction, not surprisingly gaining the most acceptance in areas that had been open to Arianism. Between the extremes of Pelagius and Augustine, there emerged two attempts at a middle way (see the chart, *The Pelagian Controversy*, at the end of this chapter). John Cassian, who will be introduced in detail below, is usually credited with a *semi-Pelagianism*, that accepts an orthodox view of grace, but still put a lot of faith in human free will, to the extent that he implied that a person could do good works, even before any movement of grace.[33] This answer to the question would not be considered acceptable, since it did not emphasize strongly enough the need for grace to take the initiative, but Cassian was never considered a heretic. The other attempt at a middle way, the one that was accepted as a true middle way and the correct description of orthodoxy on free will and the providence of God, is

[33] John Cassian, *Conferences*, 13.7–10.

what we refer to as *semi-Augustinian*. This is the position that affirms that although the human will is free (and morally accountable), God's grace must take the initiative to empower any good works or spiritual growth.

It would take a century before the Church would sort out the teachings of Augustine and come to a conclusion on this controversy. At the Council of Orange in AD 529 (ninety-nine years after Augustine's death), the Church chose the *semi-Augustinian* approach to anthropology and soteriology. The chair of that council was the bishop, Caesarius of Arles, who is now seen as the champion of orthodoxy in this moment in history. The Council accepted Augustine's understanding of original sin, but rejected his understanding of election as a form of double predestination that implied a limited atonement. The Council accepted the Augustinian definition of grace but allowed that the human will is free to cooperate with grace, as long as it is clear that God's grace takes the initiative in inviting the human will to respond, and the human will could not act without that first invitation of grace. The Council accepted the Augustinian (i.e., Roman) view of the sacraments, but rejected the idea that perseverance for the elect was guaranteed and that their salvation could not be lost. Augustine himself is never named in the canons of the Council, but it is clear that not everything he wrote would be accepted simply because he wrote it. Augustine swung the pendulum too hard toward the side of putting everything on God's grace, and Pelagius had swung it too hard to the side of putting everything on the human will. In response to these two extremes, the Council affirmed the concept of *synergy*, which is a cooperation of the human will with God's grace.

Although not all aspects of Augustine's teachings were ultimately accepted by the mainstream Church, he is still considered one of the most important theologians of the West. His thought would influence the western world toward a skepticism about human nature that led to a spirituality of total dependence on God. By the end of his life he had moved away from the classical optimism that assumed the head could rule the heart. He came to believe that reason could not control the passions, and that the will is not free because it is not free of the strong powers of emotion, desire, habit, and social pressure. The only thing that could subdue these powers was the power of grace. The virtues of the classical world, based on the Stoic notion of moral progress, were gone and were replaced with submission to God's will as the one virtue that mattered. One could argue that Augustine marks the end of the classical world in the West. He was certainly a major contributor to the fifth-century changes which led to the beginning of what are often called the *dark ages*.[34] In terms

[34] However, see Rodney Stark, *The Victory of Reason: How Christianity Led to Freedom, Capitalism and Western Success* (New York: Random House, 2006), in which Stark argues

of anthropology, Augustine's debate with Pelagius set the stage for the question of original sin, free will, and predestination to be addressed again and again by Aquinas, Luther, Erasmus, Calvin, de Molina, Arminius, Wesley, and others.

Donatism

If the controversy with Pelagius was over a question of anthropology, the controversy with the Donatists was one of sacramental theology, which gets to the heart of ecclesiology, the Church's self-understanding. The Donatists were a rigorist faction in North Africa, who held to the North African view of the sacraments (the belief that the faith of the presider matters, and a lack of faith can invalidate the sacrament). They claimed Cyprian of Carthage as their spiritual father, since they practiced rebaptism. When Augustine became bishop of Hippo Regius, he was not the only bishop in the city. The Donatists had their own bishop, and they were to become a thorn in Augustine's side.

Just as the persecution in the third century had led to the emergence of rigorist factions and rebaptizing bishops, the Great Persecution at the beginning of the fourth century brought all of that back to North Africa. In AD 311, a new bishop of Carthage named Caecilian was elected. After the election it was discovered that he had been consecrated by another bishop named Felix, who (it was alleged) had lapsed in the persecution. Felix was not accused of being an apostate, but he was accused of being a *traitor*, having turned over some church property to the authorities. A rigorist faction rose up and opposed Caecilian on the grounds that his consecration as bishop was invalid. They feared, of course, that any sacraments over which he presided would also be invalid.

Therefore, the rigorists applied a North African understanding of Baptism to the sacrament of ordination, in this case specifically to the consecration of a bishop, which was understood as a conferral of the Holy Spirit, and with it, the authority of the Church. In other words, a lapsed bishop has forfeited the authority and expelled the Holy Spirit from himself, so therefore he could not confer the Holy Spirit on another, let alone grant authority. The rigorists raised up a rival bishop named Donatus. However, the Catholic Christians maintained that Caecilian was still the duly elected bishop and leader of the Church in Carthage.[35] From that point on, Carthage, and then North Africa, was split between the Catholics and the Donatists.

---

that the "dark ages" were not really as dark as we've been led to believe. Note that the fifth century also included the fall of the Roman Empire in the West.

[35] Just as we have seen during the third century, with the Novatianist faction, here it is appropriate to refer to the mainstream Church as Catholic (with a capital C) *as opposed to* the rival faction.

This split also tended to be along ethnic and class differences. The Catholics were generally Latin-speaking coastal people, whose ancestors came to North Africa from elsewhere (though Augustine himself would be an exception to this); while the Donatists were generally inland people, who were more indigenous and whose primary language was a Semitic derivative called Punic. The Catholics tended to be in the upper classes, but were consequently the minority.[36] The Donatists tended to be from the lower classes, and so constituted the majority, at least locally. When Augustine was bishop of Hippo, there were more Donatists there than Catholics.

As we have already noted, the emperor Constantine had declared that the Catholics were the true Church in that he had favored them over the Donatists when it came to restoring Church property and rebuilding churches after the persecution.[37] At the Council of Arles in AD 314, the Donatists had been condemned, and after that time they were the target of discrimination. Donatists evangelizing Catholics were subject to arrest.[38] In spite of this, the Donatists existed side by side with the Catholics in North Africa until the seventh century, when both forms of Christianity were driven out of North Africa by Islamic invasion.[39]

Augustine accepted the Roman understanding of the sacraments, and opposed the Donatists for their rigorism and their rebaptism. He wrote a series of anti-Donatist works, including *On Baptism Against the Donatists* and *The Correction of the Donatists.* Augustine's Roman view of the sacraments, along with his pessimism regarding human nature, inevitably led him to the Roman ecclesiology. In other words, if people cannot be perfect, neither can the Church, so we cannot expect to purify the Church by excluding the impure.[40] If grace is defined as a healing power, then the Church must be more like a hospital, inclusive even of the sick.[41] Therefore, we must be

[36] Though they were the minority in Hippo, and perhaps even in North Africa, in the bigger picture of the worldwide Church, the Catholics were the majority.

[37] Eusebius of Caesarea, *Ecclesiastical History,* 10.6.

[38] Eusebius of Caesarea, *Ecclesiastical History,* 10.6.

[39] For more detail on this, see Meyendorff, *Imperial Unity,* 147. After the barbarian invasion of North Africa, the Catholics were persecuted, and Catholicism was actually outlawed in AD 484, until the emperor Justinian liberated North Africa by defeating the Vandals in AD 533/534.

[40] Augustine assumed that the greater affects the lesser, implying that purity purifies the impure; Augustine of Hippo, *On the Trinity,* 6.8.

[41] Note that the relative uniqueness of Christ is related to ecclesiology as well. If, as the orthodox argued, Christ is unique among humanity, then the Church must be inclusive, since no one can be perfect like Christ. However, if Arius and Pelagius are right and Christ is more of an example to be followed than a Savior by divine intervention, perfection might be expected of His followers. The less unique Christ is understood to be, the

content to include everyone for the Church's time on earth and, like the parable of the wheat and the weeds, wait until the harvest (judgment) for God to sort out the real Christians from the false ones. In any case, once Christianity became the only legal religion, the Church had to be inclusive, since all citizens were expected to be baptized members. The Church that had been persecuted because it was counter-cultural had become the authority over the culture.

In the year AD 410, the city of Rome was sacked by invading Goths. Those who had resisted the move to a Christian empire blamed the fall of Rome on the Church, some saying that it was the failure to worship the old gods that led to the removal of their protection. Augustine responded by writing *The City of God*. This is really a tale of two cities, one a heavenly city and one an earthly city. A person's citizenship depends on the object of his or her love. If one loves the things of the world, then one is a citizen of the earthly city. However, one can never have real security in the earthly city, since the things one loves can always be taken away. If one loves God, on the other hand, then one is a citizen of the city of God, and one has real security, since in this case the object of love (God) can never be taken away. True security could never be found in the *pax Romana*, it could only be found in God, since it is God who maintains His hold on His elect. Assuming election, one who is elect could never lose God because the responsibility for perseverance is on God and God's grace. It must be so, Augustine reasoned, or no one would be saved, since humans are incapable of persevering unless it is a work of God.

Theodosius I (reigned AD 379–395) was the first emperor to attempt to create an empire in which all citizens were baptized Church members. Others would follow him, in effect trying to create the City of God on earth, including Charlemagne and John Calvin. However, it would generally be understood that as long as it sojourned on earth, the Church would always be an ark of clean and unclean, a field of wheat and weeds.

---

more is expected of believers, so it is arguably the case that for the Arians as well as the rigorists, the Church is meant to be exclusive, only for "true believers," which is to say only those who have achieved a certain level of perfection.

Comparison of Creeds

The Creed of Eusebius

We believe in one God, the Father almighty, maker of all things, both visible and invisible.

And in one Lord Jesus Christ, ***the Word of God,*** God from God, light from light, life from life, the only-begotten Son, the ***first-born of all creation,*** begotten of the Father before all ages; through whom also all things were made; who for our salvation ***was made flesh*** and lived among men, and suffered, and rose again the third day, and ascended to the Father, and shall come again in glory, to judge the living and dead.

And in the Holy Spirit.

The Creed of Nicaea (325)

We believe in one God, the Father almighty, maker of all things, visible and invisible.

And in one Lord Jesus Christ, the only begotten of the Father, that is, ***of the essence*** [***ek tes ousias***] of the Father, God from God, light from light, true God from true God, begotten ***not made,*** **of the same substance** with the Father [***homoousion to patri***], through whom all things were made both in heaven and on earth, who for us men and our salvation ***descended,*** was incarnate, ***and was made man,*** suffered and rose again the third day, ascended into heaven and comes to judge the living and the dead.

And in the Holy Spirit.

Those who say: There was a time when he was not, and he was not before he was begotten; and that he was made out of nothing [***ex ouk onton***]; or who maintain that he is of another hypostasis or another substance [than the Father], or that the Son of God is created, or mutable, or subject to change, [these] the Catholic and apostolic Church anathematizes.

The Nicene Creed (381)

We believe (I believe) in one God, the Father almighty, maker of heaven and earth, and of all things visible and invisible.

And (I believe) in one Lord Jesus Christ, the only begotten ***Son of God,*** born of the Father before all ages. God from God, light from light, true God from true God, begotten ***not made,*** **consubstantial** with the Father; through him all things were made. For us men and for our salvation he ***came down*** from heaven, and by the Holy Spirit was incarnate ***of the Virgin Mary and became man.*** For our sake he was crucified ***under Pontius Pilate,*** he suffered death and was buried, and rose again on the third **day *in accordance with the Scriptures.*** He ascended into heaven, and is seated at the right hand of the Father. He will come again in glory to judge the living and the dead and his Kingdom will have no end.

And (I believe) in the Holy Spirit, ***the Lord, the giver of life, who proceeds from the Father (and the Son), who with the Father and the Son is adored and glorified, who has spoken through the prophets.***

And (I believe) in one, holy, catholic, and apostolic Church. We confess (I confess) one baptism for the forgiveness of sins, and we look for (I look forward to) the resurrection of the dead and the life of the world to come. Amen.

The Pelagian Controversy

Augustine of Hippo (AD 354–430)

Anti-Arian

Rejection of optimistic anthropology
Pessimistic anthropology leads to emphasis on grace and election

Emphasized original sin: Humans are born fallen.

The human will is broken/ sick, enslaved — grace is the medicine that frees it.

The human will is only free to want what is right but not to do it; the power to do what is right is a gift of the Holy Spirit. Without grace, we are only free to sin.

Prayed: "Grant what you command, command what you will."

Salvation depends on election (double predestination).
Grace is active; it's a power.
The human will is passive.
Grace is irresistible.

Not heresy, but also not acceptable, according to the Council of Orange, AD 529.

ALL GRACE

Semi-Augustinian

Caesarius of Arles (AD 470–542/3)

Agreed with Augustine on everything (including original sin) except predestination

Emphasized that grace must be prior to any movement of the human will. The will is free to respond to grace but not free to take the initiative in turning toward God.

Atonement is not limited; grace is offered to all who are baptized.

Grace is resistible. The human will cooperates with grace (***synergy***).

***Both* grace and the human will are active,** but grace must take the initiative.

With Pelagius and Julian, declared heretics, this becomes the accepted middle way.

Accepted as the orthodox position at the Council of Orange, AD 529.

GRACE, THEN WILL

Semi-Pelagian

John Cassian (AD 360–435)

Monastic
Optimistic anthropology

Agreed with Augustine on grace as a power of God and a gift of the Holy Spirit.

But grace is resistible. And the human will can take the initiative to turn to God.

Grace cooperates with the human will.

This is an attempt at a middle way between Augustine and Pelagius, which accounts for both an emphasis on grace and allows for human free will.

This position was ultimately not acceptable because it gave too much freedom to the human will and implied that one could theoretically gain salvation without (or prior to) God's grace.

John Cassian was not considered a heretic; he was orthodox on other doctrines.

WILL, THEN GRACE

Pelagianism

Caelestius
Pelagius
Julian of Eclanum

Monastic
Optimistic anthropology
The human will is free to do what is right.

To deny free will negates moral responsibility and calls into question the monastic vocation.

Rejected original sin. Humans are born sinless.
This seemed to deny the need for infant Baptism.

Pelagius wrote: "Since perfection is possible … it is obligatory."

Salvation depends on an individual's use of free will.

Grace is the law and the example of Christ.
Grace is passive; it's information. **The human will is active.**

DECLARED HERESY at the Council of Ephesus, 431.

ALL WILL

12

The End of the Ancient World

Monasticism: The New Martyrdom

With the legalization of Christianity, martyrdom became almost nonexistent. However, the sacrifice of life inherent in martyrdom (and the *willingness* to sacrifice one's life that led some to become confessors) was replaced by the willingness to sacrifice lifestyle — that is, to voluntarily give up the comforts and conventions of family life in society. The idea of dying to oneself daily became a vocation, one dedicated to *asceticism*, from the Greek word *askesis*, meaning to struggle and strive, especially in the context of athletic training (see 1 Cor. 9:24–27; Heb. 12:1–3). Asceticism, therefore, is a lifestyle of simplicity, austerity, deprivation, and self-denial — training the physical body and mind for the spiritual life. This concept came to be combined with the Stoic virtue of *apathea* (not to be apathetic, but to be detached, dispassionate, and to exercise self-control over the emotions) and the result was a certain approach to life that seeks a radical rejection of worldliness for the sake of the Kingdom.

Therefore, monasticism (from the Greek word meaning "alone") is a choice to leave aside the normal connections of and to the world, in favor of an eschatological "watchfulness," such as Jesus advocated in the parable of the ten bridesmaids, sometimes called the ten virgins (Matt. 25:1–13, note that this is one of the parables that immediately precede the parable of the sheep and the goats, which is a parable about final judgment). Whereas the vocation of marriage and family fulfills God's call to bear and raise children, the ascetic vocation chooses celibacy as a witness to the conviction that Christians should live as though Jesus' return is imminent. To be one of the "wise virgins" was to live a life in anticipation of the resurrection, when people will "neither marry nor [be] given in marriage but are like the angels in heaven" (Matt. 22:30).[1]

[1] As we have seen, the fringe elements that produced the Apocryphal Acts often advocated celibacy for all Christians, as did the Marcionites, Encratites, and other heretical groups.

There were also some within the Church who believed that original sin was transmitted from one generation to the next via procreation (cf. Ps. 51:7), and therefore that sexuality, even within a marriage, was a necessary evil which would inevitably inhibit one's spiritual growth. Eventually, celibacy was seen by many as a higher calling than married life, and it came to be assumed that it was better if bishops and (in the West) priests remained unmarried (cf. 1 Cor. 7:7–9). As early as about AD 305, the Synod of Elvira, in Spain, declared that clergy must remain celibate.[2] In AD 385, bishop Siricius of Rome declared that everyone should "fast" from sexual relations for twenty-four hours before receiving the Eucharist, and therefore since any bishop or priest must be ready to preside over the sacrament every day, it is impossible for clergy to be married. Still, it would be centuries before these expectations were universally accepted.

Roman law had imposed taxes on adults who remained childless, for fear that the decline in population would result in insufficient numbers of men for the legions. So after legalizing Christianity, the emperor Constantine removed the legal barriers to celibacy so that Christians would not be hindered from taking up the ascetic lifestyle.

Early Monasticism

From as early as we can tell, the Church has always afforded some of its members (probably primarily women) the opportunity to devote their lives to full-time prayer

---

The difference between a heterodox or heretical approach to asceticism and the orthodox approach to asceticism is one of extremes versus moderation. In other words, the heterodox groups demanded celibacy for all members of the Church. For them, all sex was sin, and it had to be kept in ultimate separation from the Eucharist, effectively advocating excommunication for anyone in a physical relationship. For example, the *Acts of Thomas* includes a story of a man who, having had sexual intercourse with his wife the night before receiving the Eucharist, suffered the withering of his hands when he touched the consecrated host—reminiscent of the poor soul who died when he touched the Ark of the Covenant in 2 Samuel 6 and 1 Chronicles 13. So the heterodox or heretical groups preached a complete rejection of marriage, while the mainstream affirmed the validity of the vocation of marriage, even at times when it was assumed that celibacy was a higher calling. For the mainstream, the ascetics were spiritual heroes, but asceticism was not expected of everyone.

2 However, there is some debate among scholars as to whether the canons of Elvira all actually come from that council or whether some of the canons (Canon 33 on celibacy included) were added to the documents later. Even if the celibacy mandate was added later, Ambrose of Milan, writing in AD 386, considers a married clergy a very old custom. See Ambrose of Milan, *On the Duties of the Clergy*. Ambrose complained that some clergy in rural areas, where the Eucharist is offered less frequently, continue the older tradition. It may be that the growth of pilgrimages in cities such as Rome and Jerusalem increased the expectation that the Eucharist should be offered every day.

and service, as an alternative to the vocation of marriage and family life. At the beginning, these people were called consecrated *virgins*. Before long, this developed into a kind of lay office within the Church, as did the order of *widows*. The Church financially supported virgins and widows, who, as we have already noted, were seen as having a valuable ministry of prayer and visitation.

When Christianity was legalized, many people joined the Church, and it was no secret that some of them joined for all the wrong reasons. In a world where men would change their hairstyle or grow a beard just because the emperor did, one can imagine the impact that the stated conversion of the emperor would have on the perception of what was good for upward mobility. A few Christians responded to the influx of new members by leaving — not leaving the Church, per se, but leaving the cities, going out to the "deserted places" like Jesus did (Mark 6:31–32; Luke 5:16), and to try to follow Him more closely in solitude. Some reasoned that since "the Son of Man has nowhere to rest his head" (Matt. 8:20; Luke 9:58), therefore the best way to follow Jesus was to be homeless, and they, too, left the cities and moved out into the desert. Others took the opportunity to run from social responsibilities, taxes, or other problems, and followed the ascetics out into the desert in the hope of finding peace through radical simplicity of life. It is also possible that there were those who had run from the cities to avoid the Great Persecution and never returned. Eventually, once the way of pilgrimage to the Holy Land was opened up, some went on pilgrimage and never returned home. Whatever the motivation, these were the first hermits, who went out into the desert because Jesus went out into the desert, and that's where He faced demons, but also where angels ministered to Him. In fact, our English word *hermit* comes from the Greek word *eremos* for *desert*. And the lives of the hermits came to be seen as a prophetic act of separation from the world, a turning away from the cares and temptations of the world to focus on the Kingdom. To a large extent this meant a turning inward, to focus on personal holiness through prayer and contemplation.

So the ascetics became the spiritual successors to the martyrs and confessors. They were willing to die a daily martyrdom, as they died to themselves by their very lifestyle. And just as the confessors were invested with a kind of prophetic authority by the grassroots of the Church, so too the hermits were seen as especially holy people, from whom one might receive a blessing if one was willing to go out and find them. Sometimes this popular authority brought the hermits into conflict with the clergy, but most of the time, if they ventured back into the city for any reason, they were treated with great respect, as they were at the Council of Nicaea.

The development of early monasticism was a dynamic process with no clear-cut boundaries, but nevertheless, we can identify certain phases or movements that can illuminate its contribution to the Church.

The Anchorites

Anchoritic monasticism is a withdrawal from society, in fact a renunciation of the world, to live a life of isolation. Most of the first monastics withdrew from their social connections and went to live on the edge of civilization — that is, at the outskirts of a city or village. They built huts or other shelters against the city walls, living in plain sight of the rest who did not renounce society, and so they were (or at least saw themselves) as setting an example for the people of the village — a prophetic object lesson of solidarity with the poor and a critique of the rich. Some cities had multiple hermitages clinging to their walls. There was already some precedent for this kind of withdrawal in the pre-Christian world. The prophets of the Old Testament withdrew from their culture in order to critique it. The community of the Essenes lived on the edge of the desert, and it may be the case the John the baptist was one of them, or at least lived a similar lifestyle. Therefore, there were already some anchorites while Christianity was still illegal.

The Hermits

For the hermits, the edge of town was not far enough away from the world. To practice *eremitic* monasticism is to live out in the desert. This is the "wilderness" of Jesus' temptation, where spiritual battles are fought. To go out to the desert was understood to be a risk, since once the distractions of the world were stripped away, one could hear the voice of God more clearly, but one would also be more susceptible to the deceptions of the devil. The first hermits lived in caves, or in among the tombs of the necropolis outside the city. It would be the hermits' attempt at extreme isolationism which Basil of Caesarea would criticize for its inability to show love to any neighbor. Ironically, as these isolationists left the city behind to find solitude, that very act gave them great spiritual authority in the eyes of the average layperson, and people would travel out to find them, disturbing their solitude to ask their advice or beg a blessing.

The most famous of the hermits was Anthony of Egypt. His life dates are AD 251 to 356, and no that is not a typo, he lived to be over one hundred years old. He is often called the "father of monasticism," but it is clear from the *Life of Anthony* (written by Athanasius of Alexandria) that when Anthony decided to leave the city for the life of a hermit, he was following the example of those who had done so before him.

The Laurites

As more and more hermits migrated out to the deserts of Egypt, Palestine, and Syria, they began to form loose communities. A community of hermits may seem like an oxymoron, but this development was a kind of hybrid form of monasticism that is really a transitional stage on the path toward the next phase. In fact, the word *path* (in Greek, *laura*) gives this kind of monasticism its name, because of the walking paths that formed between the caves, tombs, or huts. Laurite monasticism was lived mostly in solitude, but with some concession for the hermits to gather, perhaps once a week for Eucharist, or to share resources, such as a common bread oven. The hermits could look out for each other, and care for any who were ill, and in this way they began to consider themselves brothers. One of their number was chosen to act as a kind of spiritual father, or *abba* (abbot).

The Cenobites

Cenobitic monasticism is solitude fully in community. The monastics are considered brothers, or sisters, who lead a common life, organized around a proscribed rhythm. The word *cenobitic* comes from the Greek word *koinonia* (fellowship), and it was assumed that the cenobites were living out the communalism intended by the original apostles in the book of Acts. Some cenobites maintained the solitude of individual *cells*, but with common buildings or rooms for worship and work. Others slept in dormitories and rarely left a single building or complex. This is the beginning of what we might call a monastery or a convent, but at first that might have been a converted home or donated estate. It might be in the city, or it might be outside the city in a rural area.

In most climates in the world, it is not practical, or even possible, to live outside all year round, and in some cases, to live the life of the poor too perfectly would be to risk one's life. The monk had to find the right balance of renouncing the comforts and pleasures of the world without disrespecting God's gift of life itself. To be cloistered, then, would provide protection from the elements and from dangerous animals and thieves, while also allowing the monks to remain closer to society without being corrupted by it. The monasteries also found it necessary to become self-supporting, so that they could fulfill Jesus' command to feed the hungry, not to mention avoid becoming a burden on the faithful around them. It was becoming clear that to fully follow Jesus, solitude alone would not be enough — contemplation would have to lead to action.

By the mid-fourth century, St. Pachomius had created a network of laurite communities united in one overarching community, and so he is generally given credit as the founder of cenobitic monasticism. Basil of Caesarea and Gregory of Nazianzus founded a monastery that was to include buildings for what we would call today a homeless shelter and a hospital, though we don't know to what extent their dream was realized. But the rule of life that Basil wrote for his community became the standard for eastern monasticism. Thus, the idea of the ascetic life had shifted from extreme isolation and solitude to a communal life with a balance of both solitude and collaboration. Eventually it would be expanded to include hospitality. The conventual life became attractive for women as an alternative to marriage, and for the very poorest of the poor, to join a religious community could actually be an increase in standard of living, possibly even providing an education.

Melania the Elder

Some of the wealthiest people in the Roman Empire were widows, who had inherited the fortunes of two families. When those widows were Christian, the result was sometimes the foundation of monastic communities. Melania the Elder (ca. AD 342–410) was one such woman. Widowed at age twenty-two, she took an entourage of women on a pilgrimage through the monastic communities of Egypt. She took up the ascetic life, and she would later be described as "that female man of God," meaning that by her commitment to asceticism, she had transcended her sex, or sexuality in general, as St. Paul had said, "there is not male and female" (Gal. 3:28). Just as the female martyrs were described in the martyr acts as "manly women," so now the female ascetics also were described as spiritual athletes, no less than the men, and as such, they are victorious over the flesh. In the year AD 373, Melania went to Jerusalem and founded a convent on the Mount of Olives. She also funded the monastery next door under the leadership of her friend, the theologian Rufinus.

The Pilgrimage Diary of Egeria

Egeria (sometimes spelled *Etheria*) was another example of a woman wealthy enough to make a long (at least three-year) pilgrimage to the holy land, and take a retinue with her. It is usually said that she was a nun, possibly an abbess, though we don't really know this for sure. Her so-called diary is actually a letter addressed to her *sisters* back home, probably in Spain, and that's what makes people assume she was in a religious community. However, the size of her entourage and the way she is treated as a dignitary by those who receive her in the Holy Land argues against her being a nun. She was probably a wealthy widow, the lady of a large estate — and perhaps in this context, if she had turned her house into a home for celibate women the way that Macrina's mother had — then perhaps we could think of her as the spiritual mother of a group of women who had taken up the monastic life.

Egeria went on a pilgrimage to the Holy Land in the years AD 381–384 (during the time that Cyril of Jerusalem was bishop), and much of what we know about the Holy Land, as well as the liturgy in Jerusalem at this time, comes from the extant part of her letter.[3] She mentions that there were already monks there, and they

[3] Egeria, *Pilgrimage Diary of Egeria*, see esp. chaps. 24–29.

were giving tours to the pilgrims. And we can see from her experience that the places where important things happened were themselves still important, and were treated as holy ground, even being included in the liturgies of Holy Week through the practice of processions and outdoor worship.

Marcella, Paula, Eustochium, and Jerome

Just as Melania and Rufinus had teamed up to found a convent and monastery on the Mount of Olives outside Jerusalem, so Paula and Jerome (ca. AD 345–420) did the same at Bethlehem. As it happens, Jerome and Rufinus had once been in the same monastic community in Aquileia, Italy — the community fell apart, and Jerome and Rufinus had a falling out. Throughout their entire careers, they were at odds over the fact that Rufinus was trying to rehabilitate the memory of Origen with a doctored translation of Origen's *On First Principles*, while Jerome was trying to expose the errors of Origen and secure Origen's place in history as a heretic. Jerome would become more famous than his colleague Rufinus, and would be known primarily for his translation of the Scriptures into Latin.

Jerome was friends with several wealthy female patrons. Marcella, another pioneer of the home convent, had become friends with Jerome during his time in Rome. She wrote to Jerome, asking such good questions that he considered her a dialogue partner, a fellow teacher, and his intellectual equal. He implies that her insights informed his own work. Among his extant correspondence, there are eighteen letters to her.[4] After Jerome left Rome, people started coming to her with their questions, since she had gained a reputation as a disciple of Jerome. She continued to promote monasticism (and oppose Origenism) in Rome. She died in the fall of Rome by the Goths in AD 410.

Paula (AD 347–404), the widow of a Roman senator, along with her daughter Eustochium, moved to the Holy Land to settle there, and to study Hebrew, Greek, and Latin. At one point, they wrote to Marcella, begging her to join them in Bethlehem. They founded (and funded) the monastery-convent in Bethlehem with Jerome, and supported his work.

Jerome had once written to Damasus of Rome (bishop AD 366–384) to get clarity from him on some matters of orthodoxy, and in the year AD 382, he found himself in Rome to attend a synod. There he met Damasus (and Athanasius), and became secretary to the bishop, and spiritual director to the wealthy patrons of the Church. One must keep in mind that, although Christianity was by now the religion of the empire, many men of the upper classes were still pagan, or if not, they postponed

[4] Jerome, *Epistles*, 127 is a kind of "life of Marcella," written to her student, Principia, a couple years after Marcella's death.

their Baptisms until retirement so that the expectations of a baptized member of the Church would not impede their careers. That means that in places like Rome it could still be the case that most wealthy Church members were women. This explains why Jerome and others like him seem to have had more significant relationships with female patrons, who were also his advisees.

Bishop Damasus asked Jerome to revise the Latin translation of the Bible that was in use at the time. Jerome began with the Gospels, which he finished in AD 384. He then went to work on the Old Testament, but he never finished that, and he never did the rest of the New Testament. Jerome is famous for having written a new Latin translation of the Bible called the *Vulgate*, but the truth is he was only revising the existing translation, not making a fresh translation, and he never actually completed the job. It is true that he went back to the Hebrew text for the Old Testament — something very few people could have done in his day — but that led him to some idiosyncratic choices about which books of the Bible he would include in his work. His decision to leave out the deuterocanonical books (presumably because they either were not originally written in Hebrew, or he could not find Hebrew manuscripts) meant that Augustine (whom he considered a friend, and whom he supported in the Pelagian controversy) would never accept his translation.

Damasus's successor was Siricius (bishop AD 384–399), who did not like Jerome, and apparently blamed him for the death of a young woman who, on Jerome's advice, engaged in overly strict ascetic practices until she died. Jerome left Rome in AD 385, bitter and resentful (a demeanor which he carried with him the rest of his life), and after a sojourn in Egypt settled in Bethlehem in AD 386. There he teamed up with Paula and Eustochium to create a monastic community that would care for the poor, offer hospitality to pilgrims, and provide the place and resources for Jerome to continue his work.

Jerome had originally been positive about Origen's works, even translating some of them into Latin, and recommending them to others. But when his friend Epiphanius of Salamis criticized Origen, Jerome was able to see the problems, and devoted much of the rest of his career to calling out the heresies inherent in Origen's writings. When pressed, Jerome would say that he could appreciate Origen for his exegetical works, but not for his theological works — a justification that is still used to this day by those who wish to maintain that Origen should be counted as one of the Church Fathers — however the same doctrinal problems are evident in Origen's commentaries as well. Rufinus and Jerome continued their debate until Rufinus died in AD 410.[5]

[5] Epiphanius had called Origen a heretic by AD 394. In AD 398, Rufinus published his Latin translation of Origen's *On First Principles*, which he admitted he had corrected to make

The important point for our purposes is that Jerome had reacted so strongly against the theological problems in Origen (and rightfully so) that he went to the other extreme — not unlike the way Augustine allowed himself to be pushed too far to the opposite extreme from Pelagius. Because Jerome thought that the allegorical interpretation of Scripture was to blame for Origen's heresies (never mind that he maintained that he could appreciate Origen as an exegete), Jerome entirely abandoned allegorical methods and went to what might be called an extreme Antiochene type of exegesis, that is to say, extreme literalism. So Jerome's commentaries tend to be very literal, and usually avoided any non-literal interpretation. This also meant that his Latin translation of Scripture tended toward the extreme literal (word for word), even at the expense of clarity of meaning, and therefore it was heavily criticized when it was published.

It is ironic that in preparing his translation, Jerome was like a second Origen, going back to the Hebrew for the Old Testament — in fact, he used Origen's *Hexapla*, in addition to consulting Jewish scholars, as Origen had, and yet he rejected Origen's reasons for doing so as well as his method — eventually rejecting the Septuagint and the deuterocanonical books, in spite of the fact that Jesus Himself quoted from them.[6] Jerome died in AD 419 or 420, under continual harassment from the Pelagians, whom he had criticized in support of Augustine.

John Cassian

We have already met John Cassian (AD 360–435), in the context of the Pelagian controversy. Here it is enough to say that his greater contribution to the Church is as a systematizer of monastic thought.[7] His *Institutes* catalogue his views on the monastic life, and the *Conferences* are based on conversations with eastern monastics, and preserve a lot of knowledge, not to mention wisdom, of the desert fathers. Perhaps most famous is the Fifth Conference, with Abbot Serapion, which details the "eight principal faults" that are the precursor to the Church's "seven deadly sins."

---

it orthodox. In the preface, he named Jerome as a supporter of Origen, which angered Jerome. Jerome made his own translation of *On First Principles*, which is no longer extant, but there are excerpts in his *Epistles*, 124, which he wrote to point out, not only the errors in Origen, but the problems in Rufinus's translation.

6 See, for example, Sir. 27:6, which Jesus paraphrases in Matt. 7:16–20; Sir. 28:1–4, which becomes the parable of the unmerciful servant; and Sir. 29:10–12, which is behind Jesus' statements about storing treasure in Heaven, e.g., Matt. 6:19–21. Cf. also Tob. 4:15 (Matt. 7:12); Jth. 11:19 (Matt. 9:36); and 1 Macc. 1–2 (Matt. 24:15–16). Also Paul, in Eph. 6 (the armor of God), probably has in mind Wisd. 5:17–22.

7 See Meyendorff, *Imperial Unity*, 87-88, 148.

In the earliest centuries of the Church, those sins which the apostles would have called *deadly sins* (1 John 5:16–17) were defined as any sin that broke one of the Ten Commandments. So, quite simply, the deadly sins were assumed to be idolatry, blasphemy, murder, adultery, and so on. Eventually, heresy and causing schism were added to list (and even moved to the top of the list). But if one is a hermit, and there is no one around to murder, or with whom one might commit adultery, is one safe from sin? The answer is no, because as Jesus had said, a person can commit adultery in the heart (Matt. 5:27–28), or can be guilty of a kind of murder in the form of anger (Matt. 5:21–22). So the monks began to talk about the ways in which someone might be tempted to these intangible sins — or put another way, the monks wanted to raise awareness of temptations to interior sinful thoughts that are really the motivations behind the kinds of sins that break the commandments. So the sin behind the sin of adultery is lust. The sin behind the sin of murder is hate, and so on.

Building from the work of Evagrius of Pontus, John Cassian wrote of the eight deadly thoughts: gluttony, lust, avarice, anger, dejection, acedia, vainglory, and pride. These are the eight vices that would later be consolidated into the seven deadly sins, attributed to Gregory the Great. However, it's not as simple as saying that one of the eight was removed, or two of the eight were combined, in order to get to seven. There is some overlap among them, and so it is worth taking a moment to define Cassian's eight faults more precisely.

- Gluttony — This is exactly what one might expect and corresponds to the deadly sin by the same name.
- Lust — This is also self-explanatory and directly matches the deadly sin of the same name.
- Avarice — Loosely translated *greed*, the concept includes covetousness, and can include envy. It corresponds to the deadly sin of avarice or greed.
- Anger — sometimes translated *wrath* in older texts, this is not a righteous anger, but the kind of resentment that holds a grudge. It is the refusal to forgive that Jesus criticized in the parable of the unmerciful servant (cf. also Sirach 28:1–5). Jesus also made it very clear, immediately after teaching His disciples the *Our Father*, that our own forgiveness (i.e., our very salvation) may depend on our willingness to forgive others (Matt. 6:14–15).
- Dejection — This is a self-indulgent sorrow, a hopeless sadness that leads to despair. It includes the bitterness that comes with being a sore loser. Ironically there is an element of pride in this, in the sense of a kind of lack of humility that would not allow one to move on from failures or disappointments. Dejection is not listed among the seven deadly sins but is somewhat conflated with acedia. Of course, the monks did not know about the reality of clinical

depression, so we should not assume that it is included here, when depression is outside of the control of the one afflicted with it.

- Acedia — Translated *sloth* in the old lists, this is not simply laziness, but a deeper aimlessness, a kind of intentional purposelessness that avoids work and responsibility. The abbess Mother Syncletica called it "sorrow without reason," which demonstrates how it can overlap with dejection. The point is that there is such a thing as justifiable sorrow, and there is even a kind of good sorrow, but acedia is a pointless sorrow, a destructive (or self-destructive) sorrow.
- Vainglory — Kind of a cross between pride and envy, vainglory is all about comparing oneself to others, either favorably (pride) or unfavorably (envy). It includes narcissism, boasting, calling attention to oneself, and self-glorification.
- Pride — As one would expect, this includes an inflated sense of self, but more important, it means that one has an unrealistic sense of one's place before God. In other words, it is a lack of humility that does not recognize one's dependence on God and one's utter lowliness in comparison to God's holiness. To go through life believing that one does not need God is a form of pride.

Cassian and the Controversy with Nestorius

In the controversy surrounding Nestorius of Constantinople, John Cassian was firmly on the side of orthodoxy, and it was the bishop of Rome who commissioned him to write his *Seven Books on the Incarnation of the Lord Against Nestorius,* the last part of which is a commentary on the Creed. The creed he is using is actually a creed of Antioch, updated to conform with the Nicene Creed. In this section, Cassian demonstrates that Nestorius's heresy has affinities with Arianism and Pelagianism before it.[8] Each, in their way, ended up diminishing the divinity of Christ, and as Cassian points out, Nestorius too (for different reasons) went down that same path.

Nestorius of Constantinople

The date of Nestorius's birth is unknown, but we do know that in his early career, he gained a reputation as a proven anti-Arian, and became bishop of Constantinople in AD 428. However, he seems to have overreacted against Apollinarius (swinging the pendulum once again) to the point where his christology has some affinity with Arian theology, in the sense that it emphasized distinction over unity — but not between the Persons of the Trinity, rather between the two natures in the Person of Christ (see the chart, *Christology and Theology in the Fifth Century*, at the end of this chapter).

[8] John Cassian, *Seven Books on the Incarnation of the Lord Against Nestorius*, 6.9, 14.

Understandably uncomfortable with the diminished humanity in Apollinarius's description of Christ, Nestorius attempted to preserve the full humanity of Christ, and at the same time preserve the immutability of the divine nature of Christ, by emphasizing the distinction between the two natures *over against the unity of natures*. He perceived that Apollinarius's emphasis on the unity of natures would inevitably lead to the detriment of both natures, since the humanity would be diminished and the divinity would be mutable. Thus, ironically like the Arians, he apparently rejected any kind of unity between divinity and humanity, other than a unity of wills. Whereas the Arians had said that the unity of Father and Son was a unity of cooperating wills, not a unity of essence; Nestorius would say that the unity of the two natures in Christ was (only) a unity of cooperating wills. In effect, Nestorius was saying the same thing about the two natures within Christ that Arius had said about the Father and Son. Nestorius and his followers were accused of taking this further than he ever really did, to the point where the two natures appeared to be two separate persons, only united because the human will in Christ cooperates with the divine will.[9]

The practical application of Nestorius's christology was apparent in his rejection of the title *Mother of God* (in Greek, *Theotokos*) as it was being used of Mary. For Nestorius, Mary could appropriately be called, *Mother of Christ* (*Christotokos*), but not *Mother of God*, since he argued that this title implied that the divine nature of Christ had a birth, and therefore a beginning. Of course, no one really thought that was what it meant. However, the title also implied that the divine nature was circumscribed in the womb of the Virgin, and in this case, the implication is correct. But since divinity is eternal and omnipresent, Nestorius could not embrace the paradox of circumscribed divinity, and so he did not want to allow people to use such a title that, for him, compromised the eternality and immutability of the Divine. It seemed to him that this title for Mary denied the very separation of natures that he was trying to emphasize. If both natures of Christ were circumscribed in the womb of Mary, that seemed like too much unity of the natures, and (he thought) risked the same problems as the christology of Apollinarius.

Nestorius was correct to insist (against Apollinarius) that Christ must have two wills (one divine, one human), but the way he described the submission of the human will to the divine will still had the effect of removing any true free will from

9 Nestorius's term for the two natures was *prosopon*, the same word others were using to talk about the whole Person of Christ. Because of this, Nestorianism is often characterized as dividing Christ into "two persons." But this is a good example of how a debate can be exacerbated by the fact that some people were using the same Greek word to mean different things, or in other cases, different words to mean the same thing.

Jesus. For Nestorius, the divine will controls the human will, and so even though he argued that there must be a human will in Christ, he rendered that will powerless to do anything other than submit. He also rejected the doctrine of *communicatio idiomatum*, arguing that the separation of the two natures made any communication of properties impossible (see the chart *Important Theological Concepts and Doctrines*, at the end of chapter 14). The two natures in Christ were, for Nestorius, like oil and vinegar in a bottle — they can never truly stay united, and one will always rise to the top, while the other will sink to the bottom. To his mainstream opponents, his description of Christ seemed less like he was talking about one Person with two natures, and more like two persons in one skin — like two people in a horse costume.

Cyril of Alexandria

Nestorius was opposed by Cyril of Alexandria (bishop AD 412–444), who argued that Mary was, in fact, the mother of the whole Person of Christ, including the divine nature, and therefore it is appropriate to call her the Mother of God.[10] For him, the unity of the two natures within the Person of Christ demanded that Mary was the mother of both natures. Cyril insisted that the union of natures was not simply a union of cooperating wills but was a union on the level of Christ's very personhood. While Nestorius seemed to be suggesting a volitional union, Cyril emphasized the personal (in Greek, *hypostatic*) union. In the ensuing debate (mostly by letters), Cyril won the support of Celestine, bishop of Rome, who recognized that the concept of the *hypostatic* union was consistent with the christology of the West, especially that of Tertullian, but as we have seen it was also consistent with Novatian.[11] A synod was held in Rome, which condemned Nestorius as a heretic, and another synod in Alexandria did the same. Therefore, it is fair to say that Cyril represents the orthodox middle between Apollinarius and Nestorius.[12]

On the Unity of Christ

In addition to some letters written by Cyril to (and about) Nestorius, Cyril's primary contribution to the controversy is his treatise (written in the form of a dialogue), *On the Unity of Christ*. Here he outlines why it is necessary to emphasize the singular personhood of Jesus, in opposition to the way that Nestorius was trying to keep the two natures separate. Cyril argues that if Nestorius was right, then the Word never

[10] On Cyril of Alexandria, see Meyendorff, *Imperial Unity*, 165–166.

[11] It is also consistent with the doctrine of *communicatio idiomatum* as we saw it in Novatian; see Novatian, *On the Trinity*, 13.5, 18.5, 22.9, 24.8–10.

[12] Grillmeier, *Christ in Christian Tradition, Volume 1*, 480.

really "became flesh." And if he never really became one of us, then we have no hope of salvation. Furthermore, Cyril maintained (against Apollinarius) that Jesus Christ must have had a full humanity with a human will. Against both extremes, Cyril emphasizes the unity of the two natures, to the point that we must not speak in a way that makes it sound like there are two sons, a divine Son of God and a human Son of Man, but rather we must speak of the one Son of God, who is the Son of Man, and who can be called both God and human. Therefore, it is dangerous to try to divide Jesus' words and actions, as though some were said and done by the divine *Logos*, and others by the human. Although there are still some things that can only be said to have happened to His humanity (birth, suffering, death), nevertheless, we have to ascribe all of His words and actions to His unified Personhood, a product of both the divine nature and the human life.

The Council of Ephesus

The third ecumenical council, the Council of Ephesus, was convened in AD 431 by the emperor Theodosius II (reigned AD 408–450). Bishop Celestine of Rome had given Cyril of Alexandria the authority to preside over the council, and John Cassian was in attendance as the pope's representative. Nestorius's supporters were delayed, and although the start of the council was postponed as long as possible, the council met before they could arrive, so Nestorius refused to defend himself, and it is probably the case that in his absence he was accused of teaching things that he never really believed or taught.[13] Nestorius left the council, and he and his supporters held their own separate council, which claimed to excommunicate Cyril. The emperor had both Nestorius and Cyril arrested until he could sort out the controversy. Cyril was released when it became clear that he was backed by Rome, and Nestorius was eventually exiled.

In the end, Nestorianism (as it was understood) was condemned as heresy, along with a reconfirmation of the condemnation of Apollinarius. The two-natures christology of Cyril was affirmed, assuming a hypostatic union of the two natures, and the fact that each nature has its own will was also affirmed. The use of the title *Mother of God* for Mary was confirmed as appropriate. It is important to keep in mind that, although *Mother of God* is a title for Mary, the issue behind it is one of christology, since the use of the title assumes that the two natures of Christ are united in such a way that even the divine nature was circumscribed within the womb of Mary.

[13] In a document known as the *Bazaar of Heraclides*, it is said that Nestorius agreed with Leo's *Tome* and the Chalcedonian Definition.

Thus, the Council of Ephesus implicitly saw orthodox christology as the middle way between Apollinarius and Nestorius. One way to think of it is that for Apollinarius, there was too little distinction between the two natures — the divine nature overlapped and overwhelmed the human nature, replacing part of the human nature and leaving less than a full human nature. With Nestorius, at the other extreme, there was too much distinction, to the point of a separation between the two natures, and a denial of the hypostatic union and the *communicatio idiomatum*. Therefore, while Nestorius recognized the two wills in Christ, the union of natures was *only* a union of the two wills, by the forced submission of the human nature to the divine. Orthodoxy, then, is the balance of unity and distinction of the two natures — more distinction than Apollinarius would allow, and more unity than Nestorius would allow.

Eutyches, Abbot of Constantinople

Eutyches (AD 378–454) was a monk, and the abbot of a monastery in Constantinople. He was not a bishop, nor even a theologian. Thinking that he was faithfully reflecting the teachings of Cyril, he overreacted against Nestorius and went even further from the mainstream than Apollinarius had (see the chart, *Christology and Theology in the Fifth Century*). Whereas Apollinarius had suggested what appeared to be an overlap of the divine nature of Christ overshadowing the human nature, Eutyches proposed a christology in which the divine nature completely absorbed the human nature, leaving no human nature after the Incarnation. Now it was not simply a matter of only one will in Christ (*monothelite*), it was a christology of only one nature (called *monophysite*). In Eutyches's description of Christ, though He may have theoretically had two natures which came together in the Incarnation, He had only one nature after the Incarnation, and that nature was divine. This is an extreme unity of natures in the Person of Christ which leaves room for no distinction at all, and ultimately absorbs and erases the human nature, leaving a Christ who is at best less than human, and at worst docetic. Thus Eutyches described Jesus as consubstantial with God, but not with humanity.

The mainstream Church had been affirming the reality of the two natures of Christ from the very beginning. Adoptionism, and then Arianism, had affirmed one nature only (human), and Apollinarius had responded with a christology that had more than one, but not quite two natures. Eutyches went even further than Apollinarius in the opposite direction from Arius, with a christology that once again reduced Christ to one nature, this time divine. But in emphasizing such a unity of natures, it appeared that the one nature that remained after the Incarnation was something that was not consistent with either of the two original natures. Eutyches's Christ was a *tertium quid* (a *third thing*) created from the amalgam of the two natures, but no longer either one.[14] Like an alloy, for example, brass is made of copper and zinc, and yet it is neither copper nor zinc. This implied a change in the divine nature that compromised divine immutability, and from the perspective of the mainstream resulted in a Trinity that was closer to a form of modalism. In any case, the one nature that resulted and remained was divine and had no real connection to humanity. The mainstream Church could not accept this, because if the humanity of Christ is absorbed to the point of loss, then it is no longer an incarnation.

Leo (the Great) of Rome

Leo had been archdeacon of Rome under Pope Celestine (bishop AD 422–432), and Cyril had communicated with him to secure Celestine's endorsement in the time leading up to the Council of Ephesus.[15] At about that same time, Leo had written *Authoritative Statements of Past Bishops of the Apostolic See on the Grace of God*, in support of Augustine's position against the Pelagians. Celestine sent this document around to the bishops of Gaul to make sure that they understood what was at stake with Pelagianism. Under the next bishop, Sixtus III (bishop AD 432–440), Leo continued the campaign against Pelagianism, advising the bishop in the case against one of Pelagius's disciples, Julian of Eclanum. Sixtus died while Leo was away on a reconciliation mission, and Leo was elected in his absence, and became Leo I of Rome (bishop AD 440–461).

Bishop Flavian of Constantinople excommunicated Eutyches at a council in AD 448. However, by this time Cyril of Alexandria had died and was succeeded by Dioscorus, who took Eutyches's side, in part for political reasons.[16] The debate now escalated into an argument between two metropolitan bishops, Flavian of Constantinople (who was orthodox) and Dioscorus of Alexandria (who was monophysite). Rome was consulted and Leo supported Flavian with a letter now known as the *Tome*.[17] Leo recognized the connections between Nestorius and adoptionism/Arianism on the one hand, and Eutyches and docetism/modalism on the other.[18] In his letter, Leo claimed the authority of apostolic succession, writing as if he spoke for Peter himself, with authority over the eastern metropolitans.

[14] Tertullian, *Against Praxeas*, 27; see also Osborn, *Tertullian*, 140.

[15] On Leo, see Meyendorff, *Imperial Unity*, 113–114, 148–152. With Leo, we come to the point where the title "pope" can be used for the bishop of Rome alone, without anachronism.

[16] For more detail on the political factors leading up to the Council of Chalcedon, see Meyendorff, *Imperial Unity*, 114, 156–157, 181ff.

[17] Leo of Rome, *Epistle*, 28.

[18] Grillmeier, *Christ in Christian Tradition, Volume 1*, 533.

A synod was held in Ephesus in AD 449. The emperor, Theodosius II, who supported Eutyches, allowed Dioscorus to chair the meeting, and all known opponents of Eutyches were barred from attending. Soldiers were called in to keep order, but chaos reigned. With Dioscorus presiding and Leo unable to attend, Leo's *Tome* was rejected without a hearing (possibly in part because there was no one there who could translate it from Latin into Greek) and both Flavian and Leo were excommunicated. Leo's delegation had to flee to escape, but Flavian was captured, beaten almost to death, thrown in prison, and soon afterward died in exile. This attempt at asserting the authority of Alexandria over both Rome and Constantinople (and with the emperor's intervention) was ultimately dubbed the *robber synod*.[19]

The Council of Chalcedon and the Chalcedonian Definition

In the year AD 450, Theodosius died, having been thrown from his horse. His sister Pulcheria took the throne, and she married Marcian, who was orthodox. Leo was able to convince him to convene another ecumenical council. The fourth ecumenical council, the Council of Chalcedon, met in AD 451. It met in Chalcedon rather than Constantinople, to be more convenient for the new emperor Marcian, who was busy with military campaigns against Attila the Hun. Leo of Rome was unable to attend, and in the following year would negotiate with Attila to save Rome from another devastating siege and sack.

The bishops of the council affirmed the creed of Nicaea-Constantinople and resolved not to create a new creed. They did, however, produce a statement of faith called the *Chalcedonian Definition* (see the text of the *Chalcedonian Definition*, at the end of this chapter). The *Definition* was meant to further clarify the christological and theological conclusions of the earlier councils. Dioscorus saw the writing on the wall and failed to show up. He was deposed from his see and excommunicated. Eutyches, too, was absent, and was condemned as a heretic.

Cyril's description of the *hypostatic* union was affirmed and Nestorius's condemnation reiterated. In addition, Leo's *Tome* was read and accepted, especially specific language that was taken as sufficient to refute Eutychian monophysitism. As Leo had phrased it (building on language from Tertullian, Novatian, and Augustine), Christ is one Person "in two natures."[20] This affirmed a full union of the two natures on

[19] Leo of Rome, *Epistle*, 95.

[20] Leo of Rome, *Epistle*, 28; cf. Novatian, *On the Trinity*, 13.3. In context, the phrase in the Tome is actually "in *both* natures," but it is, of course, clear that the word "both" refers to the two natures of divinity and humanity. The account of the acceptance of Leo's *Tome* changes depending who is telling the story. Official reports record that the *Tome* was

the level of Christ's very personhood (the hypostatic union), while at the same time maintaining a distinction between the two natures that left both natures intact. In other words, with the help of Cyril and Leo, the Church had articulated the balance of unity and distinction between the two natures in the Person of Christ to parallel the balance of unity and distinction between the Persons of the Trinity.

As Tertullian and Novatian had already taught, the Chalcedonian definition further clarified that the two natures of Christ must remain distinct, without change, confusion, or diminishing either nature or creating a third nature.[21] The divine nature must not be conceived of in any way that diminishes the human nature, and the human nature must not be conceived of in any way that diminishes the divine nature, or compromises divine immutability. In addition, the human nature of Christ is a full humanity with a rational soul (mind and will). Finally, it was reconfirmed that it is appropriate to refer to Mary as the Mother of God, since she is also the mother of Christ's divine nature. Thus, just as orthodoxy in the fourth century was a middle way between Arianism and Apollinarianism, orthodoxy in the fifth century was now defined as the middle way between Nestorianism and monophysitism.[22]

---

accepted unanimously, with shouts of "Leo speaks for Peter!" Other accounts claim that the bishops were pressured to accept it by the emperor as part of an attempt to secure the supremacy of Rome; see Matthias F. Wahba, *Monophysitism Reconsidered* (Sacramento, CA: St. Mary Coptic Orthodox Church, n.d.), 8–10. No doubt, as usual, the truth is somewhere in the middle.

[21] Tertullian, *Against Praxeas,* 27.11; *On the Flesh of Christ,* 13; Novatian, *On the Trinity,* 24.9; cf. Hippolytus, *On Christ and Antichrist,* 4; *Against Beron,* 1–2.

[22] There is some continuing legacy of traditional schools of thought in Alexandria and Antioch, which contribute to the differences in perspective. As Wahba points out, "While Antioch formulated its christology against Apollinarius and Eutyches, Alexandria did against Arius and Nestorius." Wahba, *Monophysitism Reconsidered,* 12. In other words, as authors often attempted to define christology in reaction to perceived heresy, the Antiochenes, building on the foundation of Theophilus, reacted against the Alexandrian emphasis on unity and proposed a distinction of natures. Thus, in the realm of theology Antioch tended to lean toward adoptionism, and in the realm of christology, Antioch tended to lean toward Nestorianism. On the other hand, the Alexandrians reacted against the Antiochene emphasis on distinction (perceived as too much separation) and proposed a unity of natures that confused the natures. Thus, in the realm of theology, Alexandria tended to lean toward modalism, and in the realm of christology, Alexandria tended to lean toward monophysitism. Even Cyril of Alexandria had at one time been influenced by Apollinarius. In the past it was conventional to say that the East emphasized distinction while the West emphasized unity. It has now been recognized that this is an oversimplification, if only because there are orthodox in both the East and the West. However, if one were to put Alexandria with the West, then there is still some truth to it.

With both the monophysites and the Nestorians condemned as heretics, the Council of Chalcedon had brought the Church to another plateau in the development of doctrine. By defining the doctrine of the Trinity and christology, the first four ecumenical councils had not only defined orthodoxy, they had defined Christianity itself. However, this was done at the expense of unity, since after Chalcedon both extremes refused to submit to the authority of the majority, and so they split from the Church and became separated ecclesial bodies, a division which still exists to this day.[23] The people of Alexandria would not accept the orthodox replacement for Dioscorus; in fact riots broke out there as well as in other major eastern cities, and the see of Alexandria would remain in turmoil until it was split into two. Clarifying the boundaries of orthodox christology naturally led to some being left on the outside of those boundaries, and although the Chalcedonian Christians would have claimed that the non-Chalcedonians were, by definition, not Christian, these groups nevertheless continued their worship of God in Christ according to their own understanding.

From the earliest decades of the Church, the authority of the bishops as successors of the apostles, as well as the development of the hierarchy, were meant to preserve the teaching and Tradition of the Church and maintain unity. However, in the post-Chalcedon Church, it was no longer as simple as saying those outside the mainstream were heretics, and therefore unchristian. Now there were those outside the mainstream who had sufficient numbers to survive as separate entities. The monophysites were centered in Egypt and became the Oriental Orthodox Churches (including the Coptic Church).[24] The Nestorians migrated to Persia and became the Assyrian Church of the East.

The Non-Chalcedonian Churches

Today the Chalcedonian and non-Chalcedonian churches have come to recognize each other as valid expressions of Christianity and have rescinded their mutual excommunications. Each of the two non-Chalcedonian groups have reconciled with the Roman Catholic Church, to the point of admitting that the other's christology is not a heresy, but is primarily a difference in emphasis. However, there is a long way to go before eucharistic unity can be achieved. The Assyrian Church of the East accepts

[23] There were some early (unsuccessful) attempts at reconciliation, most notably by the emperors Justinian and Zeno. See Meyendorff, *Imperial Unity*, chaps. 6–10.

[24] The Oriental Orthodox Church includes the Coptic Orthodox Church of Alexandria, as well as the Armenian, Syrian, Ethiopian, and Malankara Indian Churches; Wahba, *Monophysitism Reconsidered*, 3.

that, in theory, it is appropriate to call Mary the Mother of God (*Theotokos*), though they reserve the right not to use the title themselves. They have been recognized by the Vatican as a valid form of Christianity since 1994.

The Coptic Church, for its part, does not claim Eutyches as its founder (and rejects the term *monophysite*), but instead claims succession through Dioscorus of Alexandria, and maintains that it remains faithful to the teachings of Cyril of Alexandria.[25] For them, it seems, it is not so much that they object to the Chalcedonian definition, as it is that they do not acknowledge the Council of Chalcedon as an ecumenical council, mostly for ecclesial-political reasons. Coptics prefer to call their christology *miaphysite*, meaning one composite nature that retains the integrity of both natures, but emphasizes the hypostatic union.[26] The difference between *monophysite* and *miaphysite* could be described with an analogy. The Greek prefixes "mono-" and "mia-" both mean *one*, but with a difference similar to "mono-" and "uni-" in English. Monotone means only one tone, but unison implies more than one voice singing the same note. So, if we imagine two voices singing in unison as an analogy for *miaphysite* christology, the "mia-" in *miaphysite* means "both in one," as opposed to the *mono* in *monophysite*, which means "only one." On a more practical level, monophysite christology does not allow for the Son to be consubstantial with humanity, which miaphysite christology does. The Coptic Church has been recognized by the Vatican as a valid form of Christianity since 1973, when a joint statement on christology was issued by Pope St. Paul VI and Pope Shenouda III of Alexandria. It has been recognized by the Greek Orthodox Church since 1989, ratified by the signing of a joint statement on christology in 1990.[27]

The irony is that, in spite of an officially inclusive ecclesiology, the definition of orthodoxy and the clarification of the boundaries of doctrine ultimately led to exclusion of those who were only perceived as outside the boundaries, not so much because of different beliefs, but because of different ways of expressing their beliefs. In some ways, this was largely due to differences of language or disagreements over the definitions of words, and rivalries between metropolitans played no small part in the failure of factions to listen to each other. Thus, the Council of Chalcedon marks

[25] Wahba, *Monophysitism Reconsidered*, 12–14. The Coptics agree that Eutyches was a heretic.

[26] The phrase "in two natures" from Leo's *Tome* is still thought by the Coptics to leave too much room for a separation of natures. They prefer Cyril's phrase, "from (or out of) two natures." However, this phrase was rejected at Chalcedon because it was perceived as leaving too much room for a confusion of natures after the Incarnation.

[27] Wahba, *Monophysitism Reconsidered*, 15.

the end of an era, and for some, the date of AD 451 marks the end of the patristic period and the early Church.

Benedict of Norcia (Nursia)

St. Benedict (AD 480–547) was born a twin; his sister is known as St. Scholastica. In Rome, the humble little medieval church of San Benedetto is built on the foundation of their family home, and a side chapel preserves the family chapel where the twin saints prayed. From childhood, Benedict was said to be able to perform miracles, and the resulting fame led to an annoying lack of privacy for him and his family. That, along with the fact that he saw his peers as immature led him to leave the city and seek solitude. He lived in a cave for three years, with a monk as a mentor, and soon he became a famous hermit. Typical of the hermit's irony, others followed him, destroying his solitude, but forming a community. In the year AD 529 (the same year as the Council of Orange), he founded the monastery of Montecassino.

Benedict wanted monastic life to mirror family life — the monks would be considered brothers, with an abbot as their father. As in the greater Church, so in the monastery, unity required a hierarchy, with a single authority. Benedict would eventually found twelve other monasteries, all linked in a network much like Pachomius had done. He is often called the founder of western monasticism, but of course he was building on the work of others, including Augustine of Hippo.

Benedict is famous for the *Benedictine Rule,* the rule of life he wrote for his monasteries, which became the standard for all monastics after him. The Rule outlines the rhythm of prayer, work, and study that was to fill the hours, days, and years in the life of a monk. It includes the *canonical hours,* seven times of prayer that punctuate the day (now called the Divine Office), as well as detailed instructions on how to pray. Work must be part of every monk's life, if only to keep the monastery self-supporting, and so that any surplus can be given to the poor. The three traditional vows of poverty, chastity, and obedience are assumed, and Benedict added a fourth: stability. A monk was not to move around from one monastery to another but should stay in one place for the rest of his life. This forces brothers to learn to work out their differences and live together in peace.

Eventually Benedict decided that the monastic life should include education, and this was the beginning of the monastery school. Monasteries became the first seminaries, training the clergy and raising the standards for the education of bishops. Both the western and eastern church would come to rely on the monasteries to provide most of the bishops for many centuries. They also became almost like publishing houses, as monks copied manuscripts, including the Bible. And because of Benedict, western monasteries would preserve classical languages and literature during a time when illiteracy increased and many of the classical world's important documents might otherwise have been lost to history. Finally, modern western music begins in the monasteries, with the so-called Gregorian chant. Throughout the Middle Ages and into the renaissance, the history of music can be traced through the monasteries.

The monasteries began to expand out from the cities into the rural areas, not only doing their own farming, but helping neighboring farmers with clearing land, draining swamps, irrigation, and by teaching the locals new farming techniques. The poor were fed, the homeless and the traveler found shelter, and the sick were cared for. What Benedict had begun would eventually fulfill Basil of Caesarea's ideal of monastics caring for the poor, and make the transition for western monasticism from hermit to hospitality. The monasteries had literally invented the hostel, the hospital, and the concept of hospice.

As we will see, the monasteries will also become hubs and headquarters for the missionaries who will convert the rest of Europe to Christianity. Eventually the *mendicants* (beggars) would take the movement back into the cites where overcrowding and poverty meant there was a lot of work to be done. Francis of Assisi (1181/1182–1226) and his friars would bring the ministry of feeding the hungry and caring for the sick out of the cloister and take it to where the people were. Thus, monasticism would come full circle, back into society, back into the city. What began as withdrawal developed through community to hospitality to outreach.

Vincent of Lerins

Vincent of Lerins (d. ca. AD 445) is, in some ways, a transitional figure and one who sets the stage for the Middle Ages and medieval theology. Like Cassian before him, he was a semi-Pelagian monk, defending the Church against everything he saw as heresy (including Augustine!). So, therefore, he was not appreciated in his own time. Writing shortly after the Council of Ephesus (that is, in AD 434), he condemned Apollinarius and defended Mary as *Theotokos* against Nestorius. He also realized that, as the first three ecumenical councils had demonstrated, the Church could not afford to assume that Scripture was always self-interpreting, and there must be an authoritative method for interpreting Scripture in the context of the Church to avoid heresy. For him, the controversies of the early Church proved that we need Tradition to help us interpret Scripture. So, in answer to the question of how the Church must discern authoritative interpretation, Vincent wrote:

> We must, the Lord helping, fortify our own belief in two ways; *first, by the authority of the Divine Law, and then, by the tradition of the Catholic Church.*

> But here someone perhaps will ask, Since the canon of Scripture is complete, and sufficient of itself for everything, and more than sufficient, what need is there to join with it the authority of the Church's interpretation? For this reason — because, owing to the depth of Holy Scripture, all do not accept it in one and the same sense, but one understands its words in one way, another in another; so that it seems to be capable of as many interpretations as there are interpreters.[28]

Today, Vincent is probably most famous for his definition of orthodoxy, which is sometimes referred to as the *Vincentian Canon*:

> In the Catholic Church itself, all possible care must be taken, *that we hold that faith which has been believed everywhere, always, by all.* For that is truly and in the strictest sense "catholic," which, as the name itself and the reason of the thing declare, comprehends all universally. *This rule we shall observe if we follow universality, antiquity, consent.* We shall follow universality if we confess that one faith to be true, which the whole Church throughout the world confesses; antiquity, if we in no wise depart from those interpretations which it is manifest were notoriously held by our holy ancestors and fathers; consent, in like manner, if in antiquity itself we adhere to the consentient definitions and determinations of all, or at the least of almost all priests and doctors.[29]

Thus, Vincent writes that the Catholic Faith (that is, the orthodox Christian Faith) is the Faith that is *quod ubique, quod semper, et quod ab omnibus creditum est* — believed everywhere, and always, and by everyone. Of course, it is clear from the study of the history of the early Church that there are always dissenters, and that in reality, it is arguable whether anything was ever believed everywhere, always, and by all. But Vincent understood that. What he's talking about is the same definition of orthodoxy that we began with. That is, orthodoxy is the beliefs of the mainstream majority that are received from the mainstream majority in the previous generation. When we talk about what the Church Fathers believed and taught, we are talking about a consensus, and we are talking about the teachings that stand the test of time. And we are also talking about the beliefs that (we trust) are those endorsed by God

[28] Vincent of Lerins, *Commonitory*, 2, translation in *Nicene and Post-Nicene Fathers*, vol. 11, 132, emphasis added.

[29] Vincent of Lerins, *Commonitory*, 2, translation in *Nicene and Post-Nicene Fathers*, vol. 11, 132, emphasis added.

himself through the inspiration of the Holy Spirit.[30] This is Tradition, with a capital "T." And so Vincent concludes:

> It is the peculiar quality of Christian modesty and gravity, not to hand down to posterity its own accomplishments, but to preserve what it has received from our predecessors.[31]

And thus, the Church would conclude that its authority is both Scripture and Tradition. In one sense, Scripture is itself a subset of Tradition, since it is the Tradition that tells us what Scripture is. In another sense, Scripture is primary, since we believe it to be inspired on a level that the Church Fathers were not, and yet we cannot interpret Scripture faithfully without Tradition. And in each generation, as doctrine develops to become clearer over time (as we saw in our discussion of progressive revelation, above), the consensus of the Church Fathers becomes part of the Tradition of the Church.

[30] Tertullian, *The Prescription against the Heretics*, 28.

[31] Vincent of Lerins, *Commonitory*, 6, translation in *Nicene and Post-Nicene Fathers*, vol. 11, 135.

The Chalcedonian Definition (AD 451)

We, then, following the holy Fathers, all with one consent, teach everyone to confess one and the same Son, our Lord Jesus Christ, the same one perfect in divinity and also perfect in humanity; truly God and truly human, of a rational soul and body; consubstantial with the Father according to the divinity, and consubstantial with us according to the humanity; in all things like us, yet without sin; begotten before all ages [eternally generated] of the Father according to the divinity, and in these latter days, for us and for our salvation, born of the Virgin Mary, the Mother of God, according to the humanity; one and the same Christ, Son, Lord, only-begotten, to be acknowledged in two natures, unconfusedly, unchangeably, indivisibly, inseparably; the distinction of natures being by no means taken away by the union, but rather the property of each nature being preserved, and concurring in one Person and one subsistence, not parted or divided into two persons, but one and the same Son, and only begotten, God the Word, the Lord Jesus Christ; as the prophets from the beginning declared concerning Him, and the Lord Jesus Christ Himself has taught us, and the Creed of the holy Fathers has handed down to us.[32]

[32] Language updated for clarity by the present author.

Christology and Theology in the Fifth Century

Nestorianism	The Councils of Ephesus (AD 431) and Chalcedon (AD 451)	Monophysitism
Nestorius (over)reacted against Apollinarius, but it is not clear how far he went; however, his followers seem to have taken his ideas to the extreme. This is an emphasis on the ***distinction*** between the two natures, perceived as a ***separation*** of natures. The union of the divine and human in Christ is a union of action only, a moral union, or a cooperation of wills, but not a personal union — the point being that the union of natures was seen as too fragile because it was a union based on the obedience of the human will to the divine will. **The two natures are not only distinct: they are separate.** Therefore, Mary should not be called ***Theotokos*** (Mother of God) because she could not have been the mother of the divine nature of Christ. Nestorius himself had used language of personality to talk about the two natures, making it sound as if he thought Christ had a split personality. Later Nestorians pushed the separation of natures to the point where it sounded as if he were talking about two separate "persons." **Christ has:** **Two natures** **Two wills**	Cyril of Alexandria Leo of Rome The two natures of Christ are unified so that Mary gave birth to both natures, not the human nature only. Therefore, it is appropriate to call Mary ***Theotokos*** (Mother of God). The union of the two natures is described as a ***hypostatic*** (personal) union, a union on the level of Christ's very Personhood, and not a mere cooperation of wills, so the union is stable, permanent. Christ is "one Person in both natures." **The two natures are distinct, but not separate.** The two natures are ***unified, but not confused***. The union of natures does not cause either nature to be diminished or changed. **Christ has:** **Two natures** **Two wills** **He is one Person in a hypostatic union of both natures.**	Eutyches (over)reacted against Nestorius's separation of natures but went even further than Apollinarius to an extreme union of natures. This is a union of natures to the point of "absorption," in which the divine nature cancels out the human nature. No humanity remains after the Incarnation. Jesus is ***homoousios*** with the Father but not with humanity. **There is no distinction between the two natures after the union of incarnation.** This leaves only one nature (divine) in the person of Christ. "Monophysite" = single nature. The one nature is perceived as a ***tertium quid***, a "third thing," something that is not what either nature was. **Christ has:** **One nature** **One will**

Christological Options and Influences

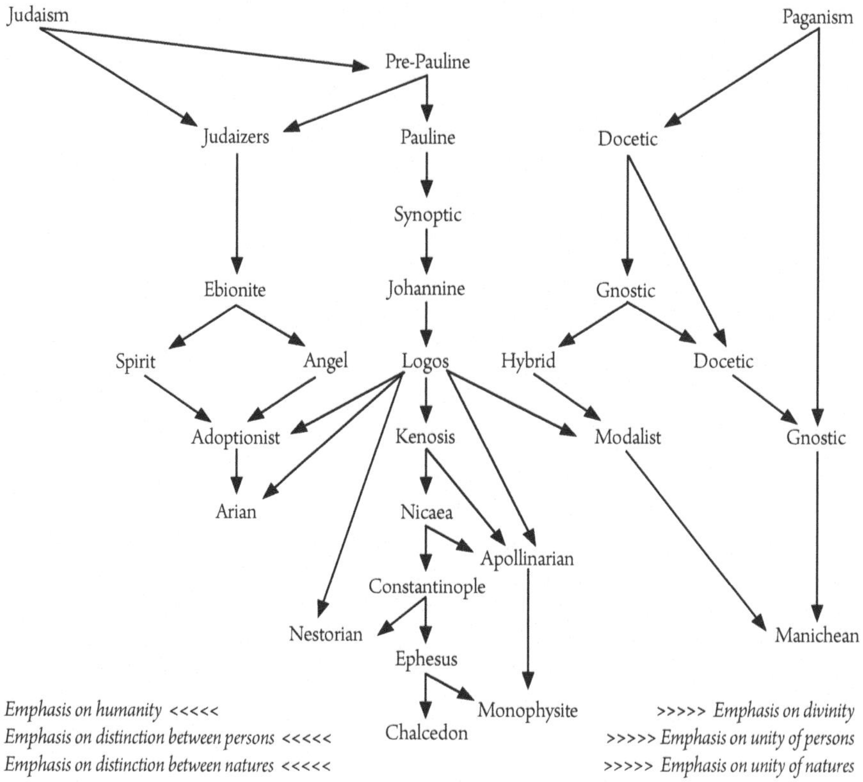

13

The End of the Early Church

Gregory the Great and the Conversion of Europe

With the two *greats*, Leo I (bishop of Rome AD 440–461) and Gregory I (bishop of Rome AD 590–604), we can see the shift in power in the western empire from emperor to pope. As we have already seen, on the basis of Peter's leadership of the apostles (Matt. 16:18–19; Acts 2:14–41) and the doctrine of apostolic succession, the early Church Fathers assumed that it was important to agree with the church in Rome on matters of theology. Even a pagan emperor had deferred to the bishop of Rome in the controversy over Paul of Samosata, and when Constantine moved the capital out of Rome, he effectively left the bishop in charge. The fourth-century ecumenical councils affirmed Rome's place as primary among the metropolitans, and the bishop of Rome's place as the ecclesiastical last court of appeals was confirmed in every controversy after the Church's legalization. The capstone of it all was arguably the acceptance of Leo's *Tome* as the definitive description of two-natures christology at the Council of Chalcedon. In the *Tome*, Leo clarifies that while the capital city of Constantinople may have royal authority, Rome has the apostolic authority.

Within Italy, the western emperors eventually became little more than figureheads — *exarchs* with their capital in Ravenna (on the Adriatic coast, south of Venice), where it was too marshy for the barbarians' horses to stage a proper siege. But the barbarian tribes would take over nevertheless, and the chieftains of those tribes became some of the kings of the early kingdoms of Europe. The last western emperor was (ironically) named Romulus. He was deposed in the year AD 476 by the gothic warlord Odoacer (Odovacer), who then made himself king of Italy. So we can say that, for all intents and purposes, the Roman Empire in the West fell for good in AD 476. Odoacer's reign was short lived, though. The eastern emperor orchestrated his assassination and put Theodoric the Ostrogoth on the throne, as a king who was theoretically supposed to be subject to the eastern (Byzantine) emperor. Theodoric ruled until about AD 527, but he was an Arian, and he persecuted orthodox Christians, and even put the bishop of Rome in prison. When Theodoric died, the Byzantine emperor Justinian (reigned AD 527–565) re-established Roman (Byzantine) control in the West, by invading and retaking Italy (he liberated Rome in AD 552), and then attempted to reinstate the two-emperor system, one for the East and one for the West. But it proved only temporary, and before long the idea of a unified empire was gone forever. Justinian had successfully driven the Goths out of Italy, only to leave it open for invasion by the Lombards, another barbarian tribe. By then, throughout much of Europe, especially in the south and West, a Catholic majority was ruled by an Arian (barbarian) minority. It would not be until late in the sixth century that the ruling families would convert to orthodox Christianity, but even after that, Arianism continued to be a problem in the West.

In the absence of a centralized government, the bishops of Rome took on the social responsibilities that the Empire had either never attended to or could no longer keep up. Thus, it was the Church, under the leadership of the bishop of Rome, that saw to it that the poor and sick were cared for, the dead were buried with respect, and the public was kept safe. Within a year of the Council of Chalcedon, Leo I had negotiated a peace with Attila the Hun, and prevented another invasion and sack of Rome. In the same way, Gregory I would negotiate peace with the Lombards, and eventually convert them to orthodox Christianity.

Gregory was born around the year AD 540, a native Roman from a wealthy family. But the Rome he grew up in was at best a shadow of its former glory. It was a broken, and broken-down, city, suffering the effects of significant population loss through plagues, and mass migrations to other cities, especially the up-and-coming cities like Milan. Gregory's father had been a senator, and so a career in politics seemed the obvious choice. Rather like Ambrose, Gregory had started out on a political career, and by the time he was thirty years old he became the urban prefect of the city of Rome — something like the mayor and the chief of police all rolled into one. But he became disillusioned with it all, and, convinced that he was living in the end times, he sold all of his possessions, gave away the money, and entered into the life of a monastic. He founded monasteries on his estates outside of Rome, and one within Rome, where he took up residence as a monk. The estate in Rome that once belonged to him is still a monastery and the site of the church named for him, the church of San Gregorio. He was eventually ordained a deacon and chosen to be the assistant to Benedict I (bishop of Rome AD 574–578), and became his right-hand man. The next bishop, Pelagius II (bishop AD 578–590) sent him to Constantinople as an ambassador. He came back to Rome in AD 585, and hoped to resume his monastic life, but like Leo before him, he ended up becoming the next bishop of Rome, in the year AD 590.

Pelagius II had died of bubonic plague, and Gregory's first task as the new bishop of Rome was to minister to the people in the midst of that plague. He encouraged the people to pray for an end to the plague and he organized processions to the seven pilgrim churches of Rome.[33] Legend has it that as the procession approached the old St. Peter's Basilica, the people saw a vision in the sky of the archangel Michael putting away his sword, representing the end of the plague. The vision occurred over the Roman mausoleum that was eventually built up as a castle, and called the Castle of the Holy Angel. Today there is a statue of St. Michael sheathing his sword on the top of the Castel Sant' Angelo in Rome. After the end of the plague, Gregory gained the reputation as one who made taking care of the people his greatest priority. He called himself the Servant of the Servants of God (*servus servorum Dei*), and the people understood that this applied not only to Gregory the man, but also to the office of bishop of Rome. Gregory established seven *deaconries*, or deacon stations for the distribution of food and resources to the poor. He mandated that offerings made to the Church "in kind," that is, offerings of resources like food, wine, and clothing, were to be given away to those in need.

In the year AD 593, Gregory did what Leo had done — negotiate for the safety of the city of Rome. This time the barbarian tribe was the Lombards, who had moved into Italy in the second half of the sixth century. Gregory made a peace treaty with the Lombard king Agilulf, which was seen as an offense to the Byzantine empire, but by this time the East was unable to provide any help in Italy, and in the end, this solidified the role of the bishop of Rome as a political leader and protector. When King Agilulf, an Arian, married Theodelinda, a Catholic, Gregory took the opportunity to evangelize the Lombards. In AD 602, Gregory welcomed them into the Catholic Church, and the following year, he baptized the heir to the throne, Prince Adaloald.

Gregory consolidated the monasteries of Europe into one network under his authority, and then he used them as hubs to send out missionaries all over Europe. These missionaries would convert the remaining pagans of northern Europe to Christianity, often by preaching in a town square and baptizing whole towns at a time (the concept of conversion as an individual decision was not prevalent before

[33] The seven original pilgrim stations were San Giovanni in Laterano (St. John Lateran, the Cathedral of Rome), San Pietro (St. Peter's — the original that was on the site of the present day St. Peter's Basilica), San Paolo Fuori la Mura (St. Paul's Outside the Walls), Santa Maria Maggiore (St. Mary Major), San Lorenzo Fuori la Mura (St. Lawrence Outside the Walls — at this time only the older half of what is there today), San Sebastiano (St. Sebastian, at the catacombs), and Santa Croce in Gerusalemme (Holy Cross in Jerusalem, St. Helena's church). For more information on these churches, see Papandrea, *ROME*.

the Protestant Reformation). When Ethelbert, the pagan king of Kent, went looking for a wife and found the Christian princess Bertha of the Franks, Gregory used the occasion of their marriage to send a missionary to Britain to bring Christianity to the kingdom of Kent. Ethelbert was baptized, along with many of his subjects. This missionary, named Augustine, would become the first bishop of Canterbury.

The literary legacy of Gregory the Great is primarily in his over eight hundred extant letters, which tell us much about the times in which he lived, the Church, society, and government. Of particular note is his letter to the patriarch John of Constantinople, on the occasion of John adding the word *ecumenical* to his title, calling himself *ecumenical* (worldwide or universal) *patriarch*. The word *ecumenical* used in this context implies that the patriarch would have the right to exercise his authority outside of his metropolitan region. John justified this on the basis of the Council of Chalcedon's canon 28, which made Constantinople the second most important metropolitan after Rome. Leo had objected to this canon, apparently seeing the problems it could cause, and now Gregory wrote to the patriarch, advising humility.[34] There are also a number of letters to the Frankish royalty, including discussions about the translation of relics — at one point Gregory has to write to the queen to refuse her request for him to send her the head of St. Paul![35] In another letter, he anticipates the controversy over icons, and spells out the very conclusion that later councils will come to on that issue (see below).[36]

Gregory's most famous work is his *Pastoral Rule*, on the life and commitments of a priest who is charged with the care of souls, written in part to justify why he originally did not want to be a bishop. It is heavily influenced by Chrysostom's *On the Priesthood*, and it was very influential in both the West and the East as a manual for clergy. Gregory wrote lectures on morality for his monks, and he wrote homilies and dialogues on the lives of the saints which were meant for the common people. He wrote prayers that would become the basis for the order of worship that bears his name, the *Gregorian Sacramentary*, and he may have written the first antiphons, or chants, that would become the basis for what would come to be called Gregorian Chant — though that may actually be named after Pope Gregory II (bishop 715–731), who founded the papal school of music.

In the development of the office of the papacy, it can be said that Gregory's pontificate is a turning point. On the world stage, Gregory's papacy completes a process that makes the bishop of Rome not only the leader of the Church, but also

[34] Gregory I, *Epistles*, 5.18; cf. also 5.21.

[35] Gregory I, *Epistles*, 4.30, 6.6, 6.50.

[36] Gregory I, *Epistles*, 11.13.

a political leader, and a social authority. Within the Church, Gregory clarified the roles of metropolitan bishops (what we would call archbishops, or patriarchs). The *pallium*, that is, the stole that symbolizes the mantle of authority which was once a vestment of government, and with the privileges of Constantine was extended to the bishops, became reserved for metropolitan bishops, who had authority over the other bishops in their region. And even with regard to councils, the western Church came to the conclusion that the bishop of Rome might not need to attend a council, but he did need to ratify the decisions of that council in order for them to be valid.

One final note is in order about the very word, *pope*. We have to keep in mind that this is an English word, meant to translate a form of the word for *father*, like *papa*. Because of the way individual house-churches were treated like an extended family, with the presider as the father figure, pastors have always been called *father*. This title would then naturally be extended to bishops, who always remain priests, but who were also seen as the *father* over a city or region of Christians. Eventually, the highest form of the word for *father*, what we call *pope*, came to be reserved for metropolitan bishops, and then solely for the bishop of Rome. So while it could be said that, with Leo and Gregory, the title *pope* comes to be reserved for the bishop of Rome, this is not necessarily something with which other metropolitans would agree (in the East they continue to be called by their version of the word *pope*), nor is it something that necessarily translates easily into languages other than English.

The Second Council of Constantinople (AD 553)

After the schism of the Church that resulted from the Council of Chalcedon in AD 451, numerous attempts were made by emperors, bishops, and theologians to reconcile with the non-Chalcedonians, especially with the miaphysite communions (who themselves agreed with the condemnation of Eutyches and did not consider themselves monophysite).[37] The fifth ecumenical council (the Second Council of Constantinople) was an attempt to bring the miaphysites back into the mainstream Church by reaffirming the condemnation of Nestorianism, thus proving that the mainstream middle was not (as the miaphysites feared) leaning too close to the other extreme, and by emphasizing that the Chalcedonian Definition was consistent with the christology of Cyril of Alexandria.[38] However, some hasty compromises were made in the way orthodox christology was articulated, and this only started a precedent of subtly

[37] Attempts at forcing unity through imperial intervention included edicts that forbade people from talking about controversial subjects, as well as proposals for compromise that traded one heresy for another. See Meyendorff, *Imperial Unity*, 384–352.

[38] Meyendorff, *Imperial Unity*, 18, 23, 243.

watering down orthodoxy to try to bring the miaphysites back in.[39] Also, by condemning Theodore of Mopsuestia (posthumously), the council alienated the Nestorians, who saw themselves as followers of Theodore. They responded by digging in their heels on the matter of "two hypostases"; this effectively widened the gap between them and the Chalcedonians.[40]

The ongoing controversy would also clarify the connection between monophysite and monothelite christology, causing some to caution against making compromises that might effectively undo Chalcedon. For all practical purposes, to be monophysite (to say that there is only one nature in Christ) is to be monthelite (to admit only one will in Christ). The Council of AD 553 also finally settled the matter of Origenism and condemned the heresies of Origen and his followers. In this, St. Jerome was finally vindicated.

Maximus the Confessor

St. Maximus (AD 580–662) was born in Constantinople, but his parents died when he was young, and so he found his way into a laurite community of monastics. Eventually his high intelligence brought him to the attention of the emperor Heraclius (reigned AD 610–641), who brought Maximus back into the city to be his personal secretary.[41] Before long, though, he left the imperial court, perhaps because he could see that the emperor was leaning toward heresy, and he took up the monastic life once again. In AD 626, Constantinople was attacked by the Persians, so Maximus fled to a monastery in North Africa, and by AD 632, he was in Carthage.

In the East, Christianity was being divided, both along geopolitical lines, and theological or christological lines. Non-Chalcedonian Christians who retreated into (Neo-)Persian territory found themselves under the rule of an anti-Christian dynasty. In the AD 630s, the Arabs began conquering surrounding territories and had captured Antioch, and then Jerusalem in AD 638. By AD 646, Egypt was taken, and by AD 651, the Arabs had completely consumed the Persian Empire. A failed attempt at a siege of Constantinople in AD 674-678 demonstrated just how much of the threat the Arabs were, and why the Eastern empire was too occupied to send

[39] Lars Thunberg, *Man and the Cosmos: The Vision of Maximus the Confessor* (Crestwood, NY: St. Vladimir's Seminary Press, 1985), 13.

[40] Meyendorff, *Imperial Unity*, 243, 288–289. On the "Three Chapters" (the condemnation of Theodore of Mopsuestia, Theodoret of Cyrus, and Ibas of Edessa), see Meyendorff, *Imperial Unity*, 235–243.

[41] Hans Urs von Balthasar, *Cosmic Liturgy: The Universe According to Maximus the Confessor*, trans. Brian E. Daley, S.J. (San Francisco: Ignatius Press, 2003), 74.

any help to the West. The conquerors were more tolerant of non-Chalcedonians because they were seen as having no loyalty to Constantinople, but it is not true that non-Chalcedonian Christians saw Arab colonizers as liberators.[42]

Within the Church, attempts continued to find some common ground between Chalcedonian and miaphysite christology. Maximus would become the Church's greatest opponent of these attempts at reconciliation, because he could see how they were chipping away at orthodoxy in the name of compromise.[43]

The emperor Heraclius championed a christology, proposed by the bishop Sergius of Constantinople, known as *monoenergism*, which means "one energy." It was argued that within the Person of Jesus Christ there could be only "one *theandric* (God-human) energy," that is, only one "mode of activity," or driving force for the activity of Christ.[44] On the surface this sounds good—like it is an affirmation of the hypostatic union. But it was clear to Maximus, as to the mainstream bishops, that this was little more than an attempt to bring back monothelitism (the idea that there is only one will in the Person of Christ) under another name. By saying "one energy," proponents hoped to draw in the miaphysites (and perhaps more radical monophysites) without committing to saying that there are two wills in Christ. But rather than avoid the conversation about how many wills are in Christ, it forced a renewed emphasis on just that question, and revealed that monoenergism was just another form of monothelitism.[45] In other words, monoenergism makes the works of Christ entirely works of His divine nature, with no real human element, and this is, at best, Apollinarianism, and at worst, a form of gnosticism.[46] Nevertheless, the Catholic bishop Cyrus of Alexandria accepted the concept in the hope that he could use it to reunite with the miaphysites in his region.[47] Pope Honorius of Rome (bishop 625-638) attempted to chime in on the controversy, but he had misunderstood Sergius, and his own letter's language was less than precise, and that got him wrongly accused of heresy.[48]

[42] Meyendorff, *Imperial Unity*, 27, 281-282.

[43] On this point, and on Maximus in general, see Meyendorff, *Imperial Unity*, 362f.

[44] von Balthasar, *Cosmic Liturgy*, 75.

[45] Thunberg, *Man and the Cosmos*, 20.; see John of Damascus, *Exposition of the Orthodox Faith*, 3.15, 19. John explains that each nature must have its own energy.

[46] von Balthasar, *Cosmic Liturgy*, 262–263. See also Meyendorff, *Imperial Unity*, 348, 362.

[47] von Balthasar, *Cosmic Liturgy*, 75.

[48] von Balthasar, *Cosmic Liturgy*, 76. See also Meyendorff, *Imperial Unity*, 352ff. It seems that Honorius wrote his letter in agreement with Sergius, thinking that Sergius was orthodox. In a moment of naïve zeal, Honorius advocated for what he thought would bring unity to the Church, without fully understanding what he was agreeing to. Sergius, in turn, took

Maximus came forward as the most articulate defender of orthodoxy. He argued for the *diothelite* (two-wills) christology as opposed to monothelite, and for *synergism* (the cooperation of the human will with the divine will in the Person of Jesus) against monoenergism.[49] A century earlier, the Council of Orange (AD 529) had confirmed that every individual person's human will must cooperate with the will of God and with grace (*synergy*), and in the same way, the human will of Jesus Christ cooperates with the divine will in His divine nature (*synergism*). For Maximus, in order to be faithful to the great Cyril of Alexandria, one must apply a kind of doctrine of inseparable operation to the two natures of Christ. The divine nature does not work without the human nature, and vice versa — and that means that the human will of Christ always submits to and cooperates with His divine will, and that this must be by *free* will.[50] Maximus could see that these attempts at reconciliation through compromise were taking the submission and cooperation of the human will too far, into something like suppression (Apollinarianism) or even complete annihilation (Eutychian monophysitism) of the human will, and thereby falling back into diminishing or denying His full and true humanity.[51]

As it turned out, the emperors and patriarchs in Constantinople would lean toward miaphysite and/or monothelite christology for the remainder of Maximus's life. Church and state alike would attempt to enact laws that would prevent any further discussion of the number of wills in the Person of Christ.[52] Eventually Pope Theodore I of Rome (bishop AD 642–649) publicly accused the bishop of Constantinople of

---

Honorius's letter as permission to move from monoenergism into full monothelitism. The result was that the See of Constantinople was monothelite from AD 638 to 681. Honorius died before he could clarify or defend himself, and he was posthumously excommunicated by the sixth ecumenical council in AD 681. In spite of the fact that later bishops, even bishops of Rome, have affirmed that council, it is not true that Honorius was a heretic. To this day, he is honored with his portrait in the apse mosaic of the Church of Sant' Agnese in Rome.

49 See Maximus the Confessor, *Opusculum*, 6. I am making a distinction between *synergy*, which is the cooperation of any person's will with the divine will and with grace, versus *synergism*, which is the cooperation of the human will of Jesus Christ with the divine will in the Person of Jesus.

50 Maximus the Confessor, *Ambigua*, 42; see also Paul M. Blowers and Robert Louis Wilken, eds., *On the Cosmic Mystery of Jesus Christ: Selected Writings from St. Maximus the Confessor* (Crestwood, NY: St. Vladimir's Seminary Press, 2003), 41, 93.

51 See Meyendorff, *Imperial Unity*, 337. Will and power are not separate, and so, since there are two wills in the Person of Christ, there must also be two powers, or two "energies," one divine and one human.

52 von Balthasar, *Cosmic Liturgy*, 79.

being a monothelite. In AD 649, Pope Martin I (bishop AD 649–655) held a synod in Rome, in which Maximus participated and which affirmed the conclusions of Chalcedon and condemned the heresies of monothelitism and monoenergism.[53] But this did not sit well with the eastern emperor, Constans II (reigned AD 641–668), who had both Pope Martin and Maximus captured and brought to Constantinople, where they were thrown into prison in AD 653.[54]

Martin's successor, Pope Eugene I (bishop AD 655–657) tried to make a deal with the bishop of Constantinople, and yet another attempt at a compromise was proposed. Could everyone agree to two *natural wills* (one will for each nature) in Christ, but only one *hypostatic will*, meaning one (composite?) will for the Person of Christ? Still in prison, Maximus was pressured to endorse this compromise, under threat of excommunication.[55] It was a question of the unity of the Church and the empire versus the truth with regard to christology, and Maximus did not cave under the pressure. He saw the proposal as creating a third will, a situation in which the medicine would be worse than the disease.[56] Maximus was finally able to talk Pope Eugene out of supporting this arrangement, but this victory was probably what sealed his fate. In AD 662, he was tried for heresy in Constantinople. His accusers cut off his right hand, and cut out his tongue, preventing him from opposing them in writing or in speech. He was exiled, but died before long, of complications from his wounds. He is considered a martyr, but he is known as *the Confessor* for the torture he suffered—not at the hands of an anti-Christian Roman persecutor, but at the hands of a self-described Christian, but heretical, emperor.

The Third Council of Constantinople (AD 680–681)

Maximus the Confessor was vindicated after his death, when at the sixth ecumenical council (the Third Council of Constantinople), diothelite (two wills) christology was

[53] Meyendorff, *Imperial Unity*, 365-367. The implication is that there must be the same number of "energies" as there are wills in the Person of Christ.

[54] von Balthasar, *Cosmic Liturgy*, 39. See Meyehdorff, *Imperial Unity*, 653. Pope Martin died in AD 655.

[55] von Balthasar, *Cosmic Liturgy*, 40.

[56] von Balthasar, *Cosmic Liturgy*, 80. It should be noted that this is the same mistake made by those who would argue that the *communicatio idiomatum* communicates, not from one nature to the other, but from each nature to the Person. In unnecessarily trying to protect the immutability of the divine nature, such contemporary theologians create a *tertium quid*, a *third thing*, a hypostasis apart from the two natures. Saying that the *communicatio* is "to the Person" is essentially a form of monoenergism.

formally affirmed, and Maximus's christology was confirmed as orthodox.[57] Nevertheless, this would prove to be the last hurrah for anything that could be called a unity of East and West in the universal Church.[58] Rather like Irenaeus before him, Maximus was an easterner who came to the West, and found that he fit in there. He accepted the primacy of Rome, and he endorsed the doctrine of the *filioque* (see below).[59]

Incidentally, it was also at the Third Council of Constantinople that the controversy over the book of Revelation was ended with the affirmation of its inclusion in the canon. Two commentaries on Revelation had been written in the East, one by a military officer named Oecumenius in the early sixth century, and one by Andrew of Caesarea (in Cappadocia), in the early seventh century. Both authors used their commentaries to affirm Chalcedonian orthodoxy and oppose Origenism, though it is interesting that Andrew felt he had to correct the errors of Oecumenius. In any case, though they interpreted the text of Revelation very differently in many ways, both authors affirmed the book's apostolic authorship, and ultimately served to rescue it from millenarian interpretations like those of Papias, Irenaeus, and Tertullian, and thus preserve it for the eastern church's canon, when it might otherwise have been excluded.

The Works and Legacy of Maximus

Maximus wrote most of his works during his time in North Africa. The primary works for his christology are two documents called *Quaestiones ad Thalassium* and the *Ambigua*. The actual title of the latter is (in English) *Explanations of Various Difficult Passages in the Works of Saints* [Pseudo]*Dionysius and Gregory* [of Nazianzus], which he wrote to demonstrate that these two authors were not falling into the heresies of Origen.[60]

Maximus is often numbered among the mystics, for his emphasis on mystical union with God as the ultimate goal of human life. Rejecting the way that monophysite and monothelite christology imply an absorption of the human into the Divine, which effectively negates the human, Maximus understood that all humanity was created to be glorified, that is, to experience *theosis*, or a kind of deification in which an individual human is transformed back into the likeness of God that the human

[57] Von Balthasar, *Cosmic Liturgy*, 44. It could be said that it was Maximus's christology that drove the council and kept it orthodox. Unfortunately, the reconciliation of Rome and Constantinople came at a steep price because they had to sacrifice the memory of Pope Honorius, along with the heretical patriarchs of Constantinople.

[58] Von Balthasar, *Cosmic Liturgy*, 56.

[59] Thunberg, *Man and the Cosmos*, 25–26, 33.

[60] See Thunberg, *Man and the Cosmos*, 32, 42.

race lost in the Fall.[61] This deification is the result of grace, and it is not unlike what westerners mean when they talk about sanctification. The Holy Spirit "converts the willing will toward deification."[62] This process leads the human person back to the incorruptibility, impassibility, and immortality — in short, the perfection — in which humans were originally created (see Wisd. 2:23).[63] The process is never completed in this life, and Maximus implies that it is never really completed even in eternity, since even in perfect union with God, no created being could ever reach a point of ultimate satisfaction.[64] Still, for Maximus, "the beginning and the end are one ... the goal of everything is given in its beginning."[65] Thus the deification of the individual is a microcosm of the redemption of the cosmos, and the redemption of the cosmos is a kind of deification of creation.[66] And the whole point of the Incarnation (following on from Irenaeus and Athanasius) is that Deity became human so that humans can become deified.[67]

The Filioque Controversy

The Nicene Creed, as it was updated at the Council of Constantinople, had said that the Holy Spirit proceeds "from the Father." More than that, the council Fathers were not willing to say, probably for the same reason they did not use the word *homoousios* to describe the Spirit. However, several of the Church Fathers, including the Cappadocians, had said that the Spirit proceeds "from the Father through the Son." Nevertheless, the creed itself said nothing of the Spirit's relationship to the Son relative to procession.

[61] Of course, humans do not actually become divine, since we were never created to be immutable and we could never go back in time and become uncreated; see Maximus the Confessor, *Ambigua*, 7.1. Also, humanity did not lose the *image* of God, in which we were created (Gen. 1:27; Wisd. 2:23), but it did lose the *likeness* of God. Another way to say this is that the image of God was not lost, but it was defaced, or obscured, until restored by Christ. See Ortiz, *Deification in the Latin Patristic Tradition*.

[62] Maximus the Confessor, *Quaestiones ad Thalassium*, 6, in Blowers and Wilken, eds., *On the Cosmic Mystery of Jesus Christ*, 103–104.

[63] Maximus the Confessor, *Ambigua*, 7.2–3; *Quaestiones ad Thalassium*, 2; see also Blowers and Wilken, eds., *On the Cosmic Mystery of Jesus Christ*, 30–32, 36, 38–39.

[64] Maximus the Confessor, *Ambigua*, 67, *Quaestiones ad Thalassium* 59, 65. This is to say that even in eternity, the human person could never tire of union with God.

[65] Maximus the Confessor, *Ambigua*, 7.2, quoted in Blowers and Wilken, eds., *On the Cosmic Mystery of Jesus Christ*, 59.

[66] Maximus the Confessor, *Ambigua*, 7.2.; see also Blowers and Wilken, eds., *On the Cosmic Mystery of Jesus Christ*, 38–39.

[67] Maximus the Confessor, *Ambigua*, 7.2–3.

As we have already noted, neither the Council of Nicaea nor the Council of Constantinople could make Arianism completely go away. Eventually Arianism moved to the West, for two reasons. First, the missionaries who converted the barbarian tribes of northern and eastern Europe to Christianity had been trained and commissioned by Arian bishops like Eusebius of Nicomedia. So while Arianism was being suppressed in the East in the aftermath of the fourth-century councils, the barbarian tribes were converted to Arianism, and brought it with them as they invaded western and southern Europe. Second, certain emperors, including the sons of Constantine, either favored or promoted Arianism, and we have already seen how an eastern emperor tried to confiscate a basilica in Milan in the hopes of creating an officially Arian place of worship, and it was only through the leadership of Ambrose that this was prevented. By the fifth century, there were actually two Arian congregations in Rome, and one of those church buildings remains today as the church of Sant' Agata dei Goti — that is, St. Agatha of the Goths, a nod to the Arian origins of the parish, even though it has been a Catholic church since the sixth century.

So although Arianism was not seen as a great threat in the West in the early fourth century, by the late fourth and early fifth centuries, it was. But now the mainstream Church had the creed, and the orthodox bishops and theologians knew that the way to combat Arianism was by emphasizing the consubstantiality of the Father and the Son — that is, their singular divinity and equal eternity. Romans chapter 8 makes it clear that the same Holy Spirit is the Spirit of the Father and the Spirit of the Son. Also, the Gospel of John and 1 Corinthians tell us that the Holy Spirit is the gift of both the Father and the Son. Based on this, Ambrose, and then Augustine, began to say that the Holy Spirit proceeds from both the Father *and the Son*. Because if the Spirit is as much the Spirit of the Son as the Spirit of the Father, and if the Son is as much the Sender of the Spirit as the Father is, then the Spirit proceeds from both. Therefore, that rules out Arianism, because the Son cannot be a created being if He is equally the Sender of the Spirit with the Father. And so it seems that as early as the end of the fourth century, some western churches were adding the phrase, "and the Son" (in Latin, *filioque*) to the creed.

The Visigoths (western Goths) had migrated into southwest Europe and had conquered parts of Spain. For a while they ruled as an Arian minority over a Catholic population. But in AD 586, they converted to orthodox Christianity. To prevent any backsliding, a regional council, the Third Council of Toledo in AD 589, mandated that the creed must include the *filioque*. Pope Gregory I endorsed its use but did not mandate it for Rome or for the greater Church. This may have been in deference to the eastern Christians, who he knew were not using it, but it is also the case that the

Nicene Creed was not yet a regular part of the Roman Mass, and so perhaps it was not seen as much of an urgency at this time. From Spain the tradition of adding the *filioque* to the creed spread to Ireland and England, and it was made official there at the Synod of Hatfield in England in AD 679.

During council meetings held to discuss the controversy over icons (see below), joint recitation of the creed by eastern and western leaders revealed that the westerners were adding something to the creed. This raised objections from the eastern delegations, not least because it was seen as an affront to the authority of the (eastern) ecumenical councils. At the Council of Gentilly in AD 767, eastern Christians raised the objection, implying that it was a barrier to any reconciliation or agreement over the issue of icons. Charlemagne, who was at this time King of the Franks, but not yet Holy Roman Emperor, took up the cause as a case of western pride, and waved the *filioque* as a banner in the face of the eastern Church. At the seventh ecumenical council, the Second Council of Nicaea, in AD 787, Pope Adrian I agreed that the eastern version of the creed was the official version, an act of reconciliation that was met by accusations of heresy from Charlemagne. The pope responded by saying that the eastern version of the creed could never be heresy, since it was the version published in AD 381, but from that time on, there have been those who would see the concept of *single procession* as an error.

By the end of the eighth century, Spain saw a resurgence of Arianism, which led to a renewed call for the use of the *filioque* in the creed, as well as a call for a more standardized expectation that the creed would be recited in every Mass across Europe. When eastern bishops objected once again that the western church had no right to change the creed written at the first two ecumenical councils, western bishops responded by saying that they were only doing to the creed of AD 381 what the council of AD 381 had done to the creed of AD 325.[68] At the Synod of Aachen in AD 809, Charlemagne — who had by this time been crowned Holy Roman Emperor — pushed for the affirmation of the western creed, with the *filioque*, as the official creed of the Holy Roman Empire, and he would encourage its use in all Masses as part of his program of standardizing liturgy across Europe. One of the last holdouts was actually the bishop of Rome. Charlemagne sent delegates to the pope, now Leo III (bishop AD 795–816) to try to convince him to officially add the *filioque* to the creed used at Rome. The pope refused, saying that not everything we believe has to be in the creed. Eventually, it was added at Rome, and by the middle of the eleventh century Rome was using the western creed in every Mass. This would exacerbate tensions between East and West, which would end in the

[68] Paulinus of Aquileia, at the Synod of Friuli (AD 796).

split of the eastern from the western church in AD 1054 (see below). In the end, the Nicene Creed with the *filioque* would replace the Apostles' Creed as the creed used with the Eucharist, and the Apostles' Creed would become the creed most associated with Baptism, and the Rosary.

It might seem like a small thing, and it might be hard for modern Christians to understand the controversy over the *filioque*, and yet even to this day some Christians still argue over *single procession* versus *double procession*, each side claiming the other side is a heresy. So what is really at stake here? The issue is this. As we have seen, the doctrines of inseparable operation and appropriation require that anything one can say to describe one Person of the Trinity must be true about the other two Persons, or about the Trinity "as a whole," that is, the substance of divinity. The divine attributes apply to all three Persons, because all three Persons are consubstantial. However, there are a few exceptions to this rule. Only the Father is unbegotten (ungenerated), and only the Son is begotten (generated), and incarnate. These must be true, because they flow logically from the biblical notion that the Son is *only-begotten*. But as we also noted, after the dust had somewhat settled in the aftermath of the Council of Nicaea, when it came to finding a term that was true of only the Holy Spirit, the Church was left with the concept of *procession* — but this was problematic for two reasons. First, the term had previously been used of the Son to talk about His generation from the Father, and second, it was not a precise biblical term like *only-begotten*. So while we can say that the Holy Spirit *proceeds*, what does that really mean?

For the Son, we have two terms that are unique to the Second Person. First, the Son is eternally generated, which describes His relationship of both dependence on, and distinction from, the Father. Second, the Son is incarnate, which describes His life as a human, but also it describes the way in which the Son is Messenger of the Father, who is Sender. The Son is the gift of the Father to humanity. That the Son is generated describes the relationship between the Father and the Son. That the Son is incarnate also describes the relationship between the Trinity and humanity. So here's the question: Does *proceeding* parallel for the Spirit what eternal generation is to the Son, or does it parallel what incarnation is to the Son? In other words, is the procession of the Spirit a description of the Spirit's eternal relationship to the Trinity, or a description of the way in which the Spirit is a gift of the Trinity to humanity? The answer is that it is actually both, but this is precisely what causes the confusion.[69]

[69] Part of the problem is that there are two Greek words that can mean eternal procession (*ekporeusis*) and temporal procession (*proienai*) respectively, but both of these Greek words get translated into one single word in Latin and English.

Eastern Christians think of the procession of the Spirit as parallel to the generation of the Son. Just as the Son is eternally generated from the Father, so the Spirit is eternally proceeding from the Father. Just as the Son's existence is contingent and dependent on the Father, but the Son is also an eternally distinct divine Person of the same substance and power as the Father, so also the Spirit's existence is contingent and dependent on the Father, yet the Spirit is an eternally distinct divine Person of the same substance and power as the Father. There was never a time when the Son did not exist, and there was never a time when the Spirit did not exist. But here's the rub: just as we would never say that the Son is eternally generated from the Father "and the Spirit" (which would paganize God, turning the Spirit into something like the mother of the Son, making the Son also the Son of the Spirit) — so the eastern Christians will correctly affirm that we cannot say that the Spirit eternally proceeds from the Father "and the Son" since the eternal existence of the Spirit is dependent on the Father alone.[70] So to the extent that procession of the Spirit is analogous to the eternal generation of the Son, the procession of the Spirit must be from the Father alone, or at most, from the Father through the Son.

Western Christians, on the other hand, tend to think of the procession of the Spirit as more of a parallel to the Incarnation of the Son, that is, the giving of the Spirit to humanity is like the giving of the Son to humanity. And in this, western Christians are correct to point to all the Scripture passages which make the Spirit the gift of both the Father and the Son. The heart of the problem is that the same word, *procession*, actually describes two distinct doctrines. The first is eternal procession, the eternal existence of the Holy Spirit and the Spirit's place in the Trinity, and this is what the easterners are thinking of when they insist that the Spirit proceeds from the Father alone. The second is temporal procession, the gift of the Spirit to humanity and to the Church, and this is what westerners are thinking of when they insist that the Spirit proceeds from the Father and the Son. Thus, the *filioque* itself (double procession) technically only applies to temporal procession. (See the chart *The Filioque*, at the end of this chapter).

[70] Augustine did actually say this. In his *On the Trinity*, he did say that the procession of the Spirit from the Father *and the Son* applies to both eternal procession and temporal procession. However, in this he went too far. In a situation rather like that of the Pelagian controversy, here Augustine allowed the argument to push him to an extreme that he would later have to nuance. See the response to this question by the Pontifical Council for the Promotion of Christian Unity, "The Greek and Latin Traditions Regarding the Procession of the Holy Spirit," published in *L'Osservatore Romano*, September 13, 1995.

The Iconoclasm Controversy and the Second Council of Nicaea (AD 787)

It's been said that icons (including stained-glass windows) are "the poor man's Bible," as though an illiterate person could learn theology from icons. The truth is that in the early Church, people did not own their own Bibles, so *everyone*, no matter how literate they were, learned their theology, not from seeing pictures, but from *hearing* the Scriptures read and explained in the liturgy. Icons are not stories told in images, like cartoons. Icons are symbols, tableaus, or vignettes that remind us of the stories we already know. They certainly do contain theology (and christology), but one would not learn any theology from the icon unless one knew what to look for.

It should be emphasized that the concept of an icon is not limited to the familiar Byzantine-style painting of Jesus or a saint. That is one kind of icon. But an icon can also be a symbol, including a cross or crucifix, a statue, a painting, a stained-glass window, or a mosaic. Even the fish-shaped sticker on a car bumper is an icon. Icons have been a part of Judeo-Christian religion and worship ever since God told Moses to put two golden cherubim on the lid of the Ark of the Covenant (Exod. 25:17–22). Later, God would instruct Moses to make a bronze snake and hold it up for people to look at and be healed (Num. 21:4–9), and the Church Fathers would see in this image a type of the cross, foreshadowing the time when Jesus Christ would be lifted up like that bronze serpent. In the catacombs in Rome, we can see from the frescoes of symbols and biblical scenes that visual images have been a part of the Christian Faith from the earliest centuries.

These visual images are icons, images that are not prohibited by the commandment against "graven images" because they are not idols to be worshiped, but rather they are what today we might call *devotional aids*. In other words, they are windows into the spiritual realm that focus the worshipers' attention, not on the icons themselves, but beyond them to God. They are a means to an end, not an end in themselves.[71] So if the word *icon* makes one think of a stylized Byzantine painting on a gold background, it is because that is one form of early Christian art that has been maintained, especially by the eastern churches, until this day. In fact, the mosaics in the oldest churches in Rome look very much like what we think of as *Byzantine* art, but that is just because it's early *Christian* art.

[71] Augustine of Hippo, *On Christian Doctrine* 3.9. Augustine wrote that if one uses or honors an icon, and understands its meaning, then one is really honoring not the sign but what it signifies.

So it may seem surprising that in the eighth century, it was the eastern church (or more accurately an eastern emperor) that tried to prohibit the use of icons.[72] In part because of contact with Islam, the emperor Leo the Syrian issued an edict declaring icons illegal. The bishop of Rome protested the edict, and southern Italy (with a population that included many Greek immigrants to Italy) erupted into unrest. The confusion over who held the final word on the issue lasted for over a century. Remember that in the East, the emperor had a higher authority than the patriarchs, but in the West, the bishop of Rome held more sway than even the emperor. Greeks living in the West started to worry about their salvation. In the East the monks (who loved the icons painted on the walls of their monasteries) fought for the icons, while politicians (who thought the monks had too much power) fought against them. John of Damascus (also sometimes called John Damascene, AD 675–749) wrote an important treatise that outlined the mainstream position of the Church, called, *Apologia Against Those Who Decry Holy Images*.[73] John argued that God historically works through material things, and to deny this is to deny the Incarnation itself, as well as the Eucharist.

Finally, in the year AD 787, the empress Irene of Athens (technically the queen mother of the young emperor Constantine VI), convened the seventh ecumenical council (the Second Council of Nicaea). There the issue was decided, based on the clarification of the Greek words for "worship" or "adore" (*latria*) versus "veneration" or "reverence" (*doulia*, or *proskunesis*). In other words, it was affirmed at the council that it is not appropriate to *worship* (*latria*) icons or the saints they depict, since worship is due to the Holy Trinity alone. However, it is appropriate to venerate (*doulia*), or show reverence (*proskunesis*), to icons and the saints they depict.[74] This is a similar kind of respect that we are commanded to show to our parents (Exod. 20:12; Eph. 6:1–3), and so it does not constitute a form of idolatry.[75] In spite of the decrees of

[72] See Jensen, *The Cross*, 123, 150-151. The cross was never considered an icon, per se, and so there was never any objection to it, though some worried about the crucifix, with its depiction of the body of Jesus.

[73] See also John of Damascus, *Exposition of the Orthodox Faith*, 4.16.

[74] The Church would eventually also say that there is a special reverence due to Mary, which is called *hyperdoulia*. One problem is that all of these words often get translated into English as "worship," especially when the translator does not understand theology, or when a text is coming into English "secondhand," through another language.

[75] New Testament examples of the reverence (honor) shown to those who are not divine include Romans 12:10; 13:7; Ephesians 6:2 (Exod. 20:12); 1 Timothy 5:3, 17. See Papandrea, *Handed Down*, 195–198.

the council, the controversy came back a few decades later, and was finally ended by another empress, Theodora, the wife of emperor Theophilus I.

Even though it seemed that the controversy was concluded by about the year AD 843, the distrust that it created between the eastern and western sides of the Church would contribute to the eventual split two centuries later. To this day, eastern Christians generally stick with two-dimensional highly stylized art, and avoid statues, in order to prevent any confusion that they might be the kind of images that would lead to idolatry. In the end, the Church's response to the use of icons is, as in most things, to take the middle way. Iconoclasm, that is, the complete rejection of icons, is seen as one extreme, and is really a form of gnosticism, rejecting the possibility that God and His grace can be mediated through the physical. At the other extreme is superstition, a fixation or obsession with images that comes with the fear of bad luck, and this can become a kind of idolatry if the icon is treated as an end in itself. As Christians, we neither reject icons nor worship them; we treat them as a means to an end, which is union with God through Christ, and not as an end in themselves.

The Filioque

	Father	Son (Jesus Christ)	Holy Spirit	
Internal Relationships of the Persons of the Trinity	Unbegotten (uncaused, ungenerated)	Eternally generated	Proceeds (meaning dependency, contingent existence)	Eternal State of Being
Relationship of the Trinity with Humanity/ the Church	Sender	Incarnate	Proceeds (meaning being sent to the Church, indwelling and empowering)	Event That Happens

14

Looking Ahead and Coming Full Circle

The Schism of West and East

The controversies over icons and the addition of the *filioque* to the creed created apparently insurmountable tensions between East and West. When the Roman liturgy finally came to include the western version of the creed in its Mass, it seems that this was the last straw for the eastern patriarchs. Other differences in the ways that the two halves of the Church had developed came to the forefront and exacerbated the situation. A partial list of serious differences would include:

- The language used for liturgy and theological writing (Latin vs. Greek).
- The growing authority of the bishop of Rome (the pope) as a singular point of authority to whom the eastern patriarchs did not want to have to defer.
- The growing authority of the bishop of Rome as a political power in Europe, now with lands and an army, and perceived as a higher authority than the emperor, especially when the eastern patriarchs had to defer to the emperor (in the year AD 800, Pope Leo III had, in fact, crowned Charlemagne Holy Roman Emperor, which solidified the pope's status as higher than an emperor, and was seen as an act of disrespect to the emperor in the East).
- The fact that western priests were expected to be celibate, while eastern priests were not, and yet the eastern patriarchs knew of widespread abuse of clergy offices in feudal Europe, complete with clergy keeping live-in "housekeepers" (mistresses), the buying and selling of ecclesiastical offices, and the practice of kings and lords choosing the clergy for their lands (known as lay investiture).
- The western Mass uses unleavened bread for its Eucharist, while the eastern liturgy uses leavened bread.
- The western church had begun withholding the cup from the laity, giving the Eucharist in the host only.

- Western Baptism was separated from Confirmation and First Communion, while the East kept all of these together as one ritual, even for infants.
- East and West had never gotten on the same page with regard to the date of Easter.

In the eleventh century, Islam was threatening the borders of the Christian East. The eastern emperor, Constantine IX, attempted to form an alliance with the West that would allow for military assistance. He acknowledged the Holy Roman Emperor, Henry III, as well as the bishop of Rome, Pope Leo IX, as his colleagues. The bishop of Constantinople was also included, but opposed the alliance, apparently out of fear that it would increase the power of the pope over himself. And so he used all of the differences between East and West mentioned above, and especially the western addition of *filioque* to the creed, to try to sabotage the alliance. Based on the charge that *double procession* was a heresy, the patriarch ordered that all Latin rite churches in Constantinople should be closed.

Pope Leo IX chose the worst person possible to send to Constantinople to negotiate with the patriarch. He sent a cardinal named Umberto (sometimes called Humbert), who was as theologically unsophisticated as he was arrogant. When Umberto got the cold shoulder from the patriarch, he started a war of words which culminated in a forged papal decree (Leo was already dead when Umberto wrote it) that presumed to excommunicate the patriarch of Constantinople. Umberto marched up the aisle of Hagia Sophia, the cathedral of Constantinople, and laid the document on the altar — in the middle of the liturgy. The decree was read and interpreted as though it excommunicated the patriarch and everyone under his authority, and so the patriarch returned the favor by excommunicating the pope and everyone under his authority — the whole of western Christianity. The year was AD 1054, and the Church was divided.

The mutual excommunications lasted until the twentieth century. Finally, in 1964, thanks to the work of Pope St. Paul VI, each side recognized the other as a valid expression of the true Faith. Talks continue, though progress toward eucharistic unity is slow. Part of the problem is the way in which both sides have further divided, the East into the national *autocephalous* (autonomously led) churches, and the West in the Protestant Reformation. And although the Roman Catholic Church has a singular point of authority — one person who can speak for the whole Church — the East has no such person, and so ecumenical dialogue is difficult.

Our survey of the history of Christianity, with its major writers and documents, has focused primarily on the early Church, when the Church was at least theoretically united. However, now we have seen that the major schisms of AD 451 and 1054 meant the end of that unity, though in the last century or so efforts toward recovering some measure of unity in the universal Church go on, and are considered extremely important. Pope St. John Paul II, in his encyclical *Ut Unum Sint* (*That They May be One*, from John 17), along with the creation of the Pontifical Council for the Promotion of Christian Unity, set the stage for ecumenism in the foreseeable future.

There remains one last topic to cover, which is to demonstrate the ways in which theology and christology come to a pinnacle, by coming full circle to where it all began: that is, with the two natures of Christ, and the implications that christology has for salvation.

Atonement: The Intersection of Christology and Soteriology

The convergence of anthropology and christology is *soteriology*, or the doctrine of salvation. As we have already seen, christology and soteriology are interdependent because what one believes about the Savior will affect what one believes about how salvation works. In addition, what one believes about humanity (anthropology) will determine what the human needs from God in order to be saved. Thus, as we have seen with Arianism, an optimistic anthropology (assuming human perfection is possible) leads to an emphasis on human effort, and to a soteriology in which all that is needed from Christ is to set a good example. On the other hand, Augustine's pessimistic anthropology (with its realism about habit, social pressure, and original sin) leads to an emphasis on divine intervention, but with a diminished view of human free will. The middle way that the Church eventually settled on was a semi-Augustinianism that began with a balanced view of human nature — fallen, but not totally depraved — and then a salvation that is a synergy of divine initiative and personal accountability. Divine grace invites, but the human will must respond to the invitation. How that actually works, the "nuts and bolts" of salvation, is the doctrine of the atonement, which answers the question of how the Savior saves.

Throughout the history of the early Church, there were several "theories" of atonement, which is to say, ways of describing the atonement and the role of Jesus Christ in salvation. These are not a matter of heresy versus orthodoxy, but rather several different ways of looking at the atonement, none of which is complete on its own. Some have fewer philosophical flaws than others, and a few might be considered heretical if taken on their own as though they are the last word, but in the big picture, the best understanding of atonement is to take them all together as different facets of the same gem. We will look at the historical theories of atonement, and then briefly look ahead to medieval atonement theories to round out our exploration. Incidentally, contrary to popular belief, the word *atonement* does not mean "at-one-ment." This is a meaning based on the English word, and although atonement does assume a reconciliation with God, the doctrine predates the English language. In the Septuagint, the Greek Old Testament, the word for atonement has the meaning of *cleansing*. The atonement is the purification of human nature, the restoration of the image of God, which was defaced by the Fall.

Ransom as Manumission

In the New Testament, the apostle Paul describes atonement in terms of freedom, specifically, the freeing of a slave, called *manumission*. Slavery was an uncontested part of Roman culture and society, but often slavery was not assumed to be a lifelong situation, and Roman law included several ways that a slave could become free. One of the most common ways was through manumission, the buying of a slave's freedom, either by the slave (slaves could earn their own money in the Roman Empire) or by someone else, usually a relative (see Lev. 25:48–49).[1] So for Paul, sin is a kind of slavery, which includes the futility of trying to escape it through human effort and the law. Adam sold all of his descendants into slavery at the Fall, and now we find ourselves in this situation where we are enslaved by our fallen human natures and the tendency to sin, which separates us from God, and leads to death (Rom. 6:23). Salvation, then, is a liberation — the *buying* of one's freedom — and Christ is our Savior in that He has purchased our freedom with his life (1 Cor. 6:20; Rev. 5:9). Christ is the second Adam, who offers freedom for all whom the first Adam had enslaved (Rom. 5:12–15; 1 Cor. 5:45–47). This is described as a *ransom* (Matt. 20:28; Mark 10:45; 1 Tim. 2:6; 1 Pet. 1:18–19). It can also be described as redemption, in the sense that we are *redeemed* as part of an exchange (Gal. 3:13–14).

Recapitulation

Building on what Paul and others said in the New Testament, Irenaeus of Lyons applied his method of interpretation through typology to the atonement. Recapitulation means a theme that returns, but in this case it refers specifically to the fact that the New Adam (Jesus Christ) fixes what the first Adam broke. By sacrificing His life, He was giving the most valuable thing that has ever existed (not simply life, but the life of the divine Son of God). By taking on our curse, that is, the death we deserve, He transferred His blessing to us (Gal. 3:13–14). In fact, when Jesus resisted the attempts of the devil to

[1] Michael Patrick Barber, *Salvation: What Every Catholic Should Know* (San Francisco: Ignatius Press, 2019), 38–39. Salvation as manumission is based on the Old Testament concept of the Jubilee, when slaves were freed. Jesus Himself said that He came to "proclaim liberty to captives" (Luke 4:16–21, v. 18, quoting Isa. 61:1–2). On this, see Thomas Weinandy, O.F.M. Cap., *Jesus Becoming Jesus: A Theological Interpretation of the Synoptic Gospels* (Washington, DC: Catholic University of America Press, 2018), 93.

tempt Him in the wilderness, He was proving that He could pass the same test that Adam failed. And so, as Irenaeus said, our Savior is "the Word of God, our Lord Jesus Christ, who did, through His transcendent love, become what we are, that He might bring us to be even what He is Himself."[2] Put more simply, He became one of us, so that we could become like Him (see 2 Pet. 1:4). This is what is sometimes referred to as the *wonderful exchange*. He submitted Himself to our limitations, and He gave His life, so that we could be free and have eternal life.

Ransom as Hostage Negotiation

Irenaeus also hints at what some of the Church Fathers would do with the idea of ransom and how that idea would develop and be criticized.[3] Several of the early Church Fathers reasoned that if humanity has been sold into captivity by the Fall, then we are all, in a sense, the victims of a kidnapping. The devil holds us hostage, and the life of Christ is the ransom paid for our release. In other words, in order to buy our freedom, Jesus Christ had to pay with His life. Christ was seen as the actual "ransom" itself, the payment that the Father was compelled to give in order to free the human race. It is important to understand that in the ancient world, it was commonplace for a colonizing emperor to take the son(s) of colonized nobility to his imperial court as hostages (see, for example, 1 Macc. 13:16). These "princes" were treated very well, and lived a life of privilege, education, and luxury. But they were still prisoners, essentially a guarantee against rebellion in their homeland. The rulers back home, client kings to their patron the emperor, would not rebel because it would put the lives of their sons in danger. When the time came, the emperor would choose which of the princes would go back home to rule as his loyal client king.

As the reader might already see, this way of looking at the atonement presented a philosophical problem. In the analogy, the devil is the emperor, holding humanity (the children of God) hostage. Therefore, it puts the devil in a position of power over God, and made the atonement something that the Father was compelled to do.[4] This is the well-known *ransom theory of atonement* that is often criticized, and for good reason. But as early as the Cappadocians, Church Fathers began to abandon

[2] Irenaeus of Lyons, *Against Heresies*, 5, preface, translation in *Ante-Nicene Fathers*, vol. 1, 526. On recapitulation in Irenaeus, see also 3.18.7, 3.21.9–10, 3.22.3, and 5.21.1. The anonymous *Epistle to Diognetus* did highlight the concept of *exchange* but did not articulate it quite in the way that Irenaeus and those who followed him would; see *Epistle to Diognetus*, 9.

[3] Irenaeus of Lyons, *Against Heresies*, 2.5.4.

[4] Irenaeus of Lyons, *Against Heresies*, 2.5.4. Irenaeus wrote that it is inappropriate to say that God is bound by anything.

this way of thinking about atonement, and as we will see, the medieval Scholastics will reject it entirely.[5]

The Fishhook

Since it was perceived as problematic that God could be compelled to pay a ransom, a new way of looking at the atonement was proposed by several of the Church Fathers, including Gregory of Nyssa (though we don't know who came up with it first).[6] If we imagine that humanity is held hostage, this theory can be thought of as more of a hostage trade, but with a catch — in fact one that could have been the origin of the phrase *bait and switch*. The human life of Jesus is offered as the bait. The devil thinks that by letting go of humanity, he can have an even greater prize — the Son of God (and thus have power over the Father by holding His Son hostage). But after the hostage trade, the devil finds out that he cannot hold Jesus Christ hostage after all, because of His divine nature. So while the devil saw the bait (the human nature) he did not see the hook (the divine nature), and far from being able to catch Jesus Christ, he was in fact caught by Him, and defeated. Augustine proposed a similar theory of atonement using an analogy of a mousetrap.[7] The human nature of Christ (actually His Blood) is the bait, and His divine nature is the spring of the trap.

Eventually, the fishhook and mousetrap theories were also criticized, because they seemed to make God deceptive, and it was argued that God would never deceive, not even Satan. Nevertheless, the point of these analogies is what is important. That is, both of Christ's natures are required for the atonement. Just as we have already noted in the controversies over the heresies, a savior who was a mere human could only "save" in the sense of setting an example. Such a human-only "savior" would first have to save himself (an impossible task) before saving anyone else. Similarly, a divine-only savior could theoretically bring divine intervention, but he could not pay the debt *we* owe, because he would not be one of us. So a savior who was not divine could not *save*, and a savior who was not human could not save *us*. Both natures are required: the Savior must be human in order to die for humanity (as a representative of humanity), but the Savior must also be divine in order to overcome death and rise in victory, making our resurrection possible. From this time on, the association of the two natures of Christ with salvation would be made explicit.

5 See Anselm of Canterbury, *Cur Deus Homo?*, 1.7.

6 See Gregory of Nyssa, *Great Catechism*, 24, quoted in Oakes, *Infinity Dwindled to Infancy*, 178–179.

7 Augustine of Hippo, *Sermon*, 263.1, quoted in Oakes, *Infinity Dwindled to Infancy*, 178–179.

Christus Victor

The title *Christus Victor* was not something that the Church Fathers used to describe the atonement. It was invented in the early twentieth century by scholars attempting to describe a general consensus in the way the Church Fathers would ultimately speak of salvation. Like the fishhook theory, it is another variation on the ransom theory, starting with the concept that humanity is being held hostage by evil powers. But here, the atonement is not a transaction with the devil, nor is it a hostage negotiation, or even a trick — Satan is not a mere hostage-taker, he is a terrorist with whom there can be no negotiation. Therefore, the atonement is an all-out rescue mission. Like Liam Neeson in the *Taken* films, Jesus Christ is a one-man Seal Team Six, who comes to earth to decisively defeat the enemy — but not with violence, of course, rather with self-sacrifice. By His Incarnation, He binds the "strong man" who holds us captive (Matt. 12:29; Mark 3:27; Luke 11:21–22; see also Rev. 20:2). This theory of atonement emphasizes that Jesus Christ in the Incarnation is the very embodiment of divine intervention, who overcomes the captivity of original sin and frees humanity to be once again the people of God. The image of God in us that was marred in the Fall is restored.[8] With *Christus Victor*, the patristic understanding of the atonement came to a kind of plateau. But it would take a group of medieval scholars known as the *Scholastics* to put the capstone on the Church's doctrine of the atonement.

The Scholastics

With Scholasticism, the value of philosophy (disparaged by theologians like Irenaeus and Tertullian) finally makes a comeback, in part influenced by the rediscovery of the writings of Aristotle. With the Scholastics, it is no longer a question of theology *or* philosophy. Instead, their work is based on the conviction that both faith and reason are gifts from God, and will complement each other, so philosophy can inform theology. In expanding upon the connection between anthropology, christology, and soteriology, the Scholastics would become the first systematic theologians.

Anselm of Canterbury

Anselm (1033/1034–1109) was influenced primarily by Augustine of Hippo. He took Augustine's *Credo ut intelligam* (I believe so that I may understand) and made it *Fides quaerens intellectum* (faith seeking understanding). In fact, Anselm put so much confidence in the ability of human reason and philosophy to come to an understanding

[8] Athanasius of Alexandria, *On the Incarnation*, 13.

of ultimate truths, that he argued it would have been theoretically possible to work out every major Christian doctrine, including the existence of God, the Trinity, and even the *filioque*, without appealing to Scripture at all.

Proslogion

In the *Proslogion*, Anselm proposes what is known as the *Ontological Proof* for the existence of God. This "argument from existence" goes like this: God is the being who must be beyond our imagination. And since we can imagine a god who doesn't exist, the real God must be greater than that, and therefore must exist. Put another way, since a God who exists is greater than a god who doesn't exist, then God must exist, since it would be impossible for the reality to be anything less than the greatest version of what Divinity is. This argument may seem a bit circular to us, and many people find it unconvincing for anyone who doesn't already believe in God. But Anselm was doing something important. He was using philosophy to back into the biggest questions of existence — questions we would pose more in terms like, "Why does anything exist at all? If there was ever a time when nothing existed, then how did anything come to exist without some outside force acting on it? How could nothing spontaneously turn into something? But if anything were eternal, why would we assume that it was inanimate rather than sentient? And if it is more likely that an entity exists that was eternal and intelligent, rather than to assume that nothing spontaneously became something, then God exists."

Cur Deus Homo?

In his most famous document, *Cur Deus Homo?* (Why the God-Man? — often incorrectly translated, "Why God Became Man"), Anselm followed the lead of the Church Fathers, in developing the argument that Christ had to be both divine and human in order to be the Savior of humanity.[9] The document is written as a dialogue between Anselm himself and a student named Boso. Anselm begins with an apparent dilemma faced by God. Humans are sinful and therefore deserve eternal separation from God. However, God loves humanity and wishes to save humans from the wages of sin. If God were simply to cancel the debt, God's justice would be mocked and an important part of God's nature would be compromised. On the other hand, if God were to condemn all of humanity, God's will to save humanity would go unfulfilled and another

9 Sometimes the title *Cur Deus Homo?* is translated "Why God Became Man"; however, there is no verb in the title, so a better translation is "Why the God-Man?" Ultimately it is not about the Incarnation, per se, but about the two natures of Christ, the "God-Man."

important part of God's nature (mercy) would not be realized.[10] The solution to this dilemma must be one in which the debt of justice is paid and humans are given the chance to be free of it.

Cur Deus Homo? demonstrates perfectly the connection between christology and soteriology. Anselm argued that the atonement works precisely because Christ has two natures. The human nature of Christ is required to pay the debt of justice on behalf of humanity (a human must pay the debt that humanity owes), and the divine nature is required because a mere human would have sins of his own and would not be able to pay the debt for himself, let alone the rest of humanity. This has been expressed in more modern times as, "Christ paid a debt He did not owe, because we owed a debt we could not pay." Thus, Jesus gave His life as satisfaction for the debt, or as the letter to the Hebrews describes it, a sacrifice — a once-and-for-all version of the animal sacrifices of the Old Testament. However, Anselm did not emphasize the sacrificial aspect of Christ's death. For him it was the payment of a debt — it is God's honor that is offended by sin, and that must be repaid.[11] In other words, since God is our Creator, we owe God our obedience. When we fail to obey God, we fall into a deficit of obedience, a debt — this is why the Latin version of the *Our Father* says, "forgive us our debts." For Anselm (as for the Church Fathers), it is not so much the *death* of Christ, but the *life* of Christ that matters. Since His life is the most valuable thing imaginable, it could be given as an overabundant payment for the debt of humanity. Therefore, it has more to do with Christ's giving of Himself than with a blood sacrifice. So, while Anselm's theory of atonement is sometimes referred to as the *substitution* theory, a better name is the *satisfaction* theory.[12]

According to Anselm, the most we could ever give to God would be our own lives, however that would be less than we already owed God, even before sin and

[10] On the balance of mercy and justice in God, see Clement of Alexandria, *The Instructor,* 1.8.

[11] Anselm was probably influenced by the concept of a debt of honor, the allegiance that would be owed to a landowner by his tenants in a feudal society. However, this concept is not completely new in the Middle Ages, and originally comes from the concept of the covenant and its expectation of loyalty (cf. Jer. 31), and is also tied to the concept of almsgiving; see Barber, *Salvation,* 26, 30, 40–41, 90–91.

[12] The label *satisfaction theory* is also preferable because it avoids confusion with a later theory of atonement known as *penal substitution*. The latter, a product of the Protestant Reformation, emphasized sin as a transgression of the law and requiring a *punishment* to appease God's wrath, over the idea of sin as a debt of honor requiring *payment*. It emphasized the cross over the Incarnation, and the death of Christ (as blood sacrifice) over His life as a gift. These Protestant emphases are not unbiblical, but they do represent a shift from patristic and medieval atonement theories.

apart from the debt. But Christ's life is without sin, and therefore it is a surplus payment, the credit being applied to humanity, and so forgiveness is granted. However, note that forgiveness is granted to human nature in general, since the problem of sin is a problem of human nature. Like Augustine, Anselm believed that the Fall had damaged human nature. The problem is that we as humans are consubstantial with Adam, and so his sin has corrupted our nature (Rom. 5:12; 1 Cor. 15:22). In Adam, the sin of the individual corrupts the entire human nature. In fact, each person's sin throughout the generations of history contributes to the corruption of human nature, which grows like a snowball rolling downhill, so that sin becomes inevitable.[13] The solution to the problem, then, is that Christ became consubstantial with us, so that in Him, the sinlessness of the individual heals the whole human nature.[14] When we say that Jesus Christ died "for" us, that doesn't just mean that His death was for our benefit — it means that He died in our place. This satisfies both God's justice and God's mercy because it incorporates both human representation (the human nature of Christ satisfies God's justice), and divine intervention (the divine nature of Christ brings God's mercy). Plus, as Anselm pointed out, if the Savior were anything other than divine, then we would owe our thanks and our allegiance to someone other than God.

Peter Abelard

Abelard (AD 1079–1142) began with an optimistic anthropology, much like Arius and Pelagius. Therefore, he rejected Augustine's understanding of original sin, and he also rejected Anselm's understanding of atonement as satisfaction. He argued that if grace is a gift of God, no one should have to pay for it, not even Christ. He further

[13] James L. Papandrea, *Spiritual Blueprint: How We Live, Work, Love, Pray, and Play* (Liguori, MO: Liguori Publications, 2010), 51–53.

[14] Note that the issue here is the question of whether Adam's sin affected only his person or his nature. Pelagius would argue that Adam's sin only affected him as an individual, not human nature in general. However, Anselm (and to a certain extent Augustine) would argue that since Adam and Eve constituted the whole of humanity at the time, when they sinned, their sin affected all of humanity through the universality of human nature. If Pelagius was right, and Adam's sin affected only his person, then there is no original sin, and Adam (and indeed Christ) influence us only by example. If, however, one applies the concept of consubstantiality to human nature, then Adam's sin affects us in a way that can only be counteracted by Christ's consubstantiality with humanity. This arguably demonstrates that Arian and Pelagian salvation is more of an individual salvation, while Augustine's and Anselm's soteriology leans more toward the corporate; see Augustine of Hippo, *On Original Sin*, 16; and Anselm of Canterbury, *On the Virgin Conception and Original Sin*.

maintained that since God had forgiven sin before the coming of Christ, then Christ Himself (as a sacrifice) was not needed to forgive sin. In his commentary on the book of Romans, Abelard refutes what appears to be a caricature of Anselm. He says, in effect, that God *can* save humanity simply by cancelling the debt. In fact, he argued that any other arrangement would have the same philosophical problem as the ransom theory, in that it seems to impose a necessity on God. Therefore, Abelard rejected the idea that Christ's death reconciles humanity to God, saying that if anything, the murder of the Son of God is the worst sin humanity has ever committed and it should make things worse. In this he anticipated some of the contemporary critiques of traditional atonement theories, saying that the very idea of a blood sacrifice seems cruel on the part of God. It seemed to him a great injustice that the innocent (Jesus) would have to die for the guilty. So Abelard proposed that it was not Christ's death that mattered, but His life. On the latter point, he and Anselm would probably agree. However, Abelard went so far as to say that the passion of Christ was not the satisfaction of a debt or a substitutionary sacrifice, but more of a wake-up call, or a motivational object lesson.

However, this got him into trouble because he was essentially saying that Christ did not need to die to make salvation possible. Ironically, Abelard proposed that those who killed Christ did not actually sin, since they thought they were doing God's will, and sincerely intended to do God's will. Apparently taking his cue from some of the teachings of Jesus in the Gospels (such as Matt. 5:27–28), Abelard made *intention* the criteria for what constituted sin. If one did not intend to sin (but did so inadvertently), the sin would not be held against that person. However, if one intended to sin, but was unable to carry it out, that person would still be guilty.[15] The point was whether one *intended* to follow the example of Christ.

Abelard is usually given credit for what is called the *moral influence* theory of atonement, which is often seen as similar to an Arian soteriology in that the Savior is an example to follow, and salvation is by human effort. In other words, it is not Christ's death that saves, but our reaction to it. Christ was the perfect example of self-sacrifice, and His suffering was an act of love for humanity. Therefore, the real question would be: Does it motivate us to repent and follow the example of Christ as one who loves unselfishly?[16] It could be argued that this is not really a theory of atonement, but a theory of how atonement was not necessary. However, just like

[15] Note that Clement of Alexandria had said that involuntary sin would not be held against a person. In fact, he said there were two types of involuntary sin; sins committed in ignorance, and sins committed through necessity; Clement of Alexandria, *Miscellanies*, 2.14.

[16] In this sense, Abelard was influenced by Augustine and his emphasis on love as the primary motivation.

Pelagius, Abelard was no Arian. He did not completely reject the idea of salvation as substitution, as he wrote in a letter to his beloved Heloise, "He [Christ] bought you and redeemed you with his own blood."[17] His was not really a salvation by works, but Abelard was probably a lot like Origen, in that he was too smart for his own good, and his pride led him to revel in hyperbole. He wrote that anyone could (theoretically?) escape the punishment of Hell by doing good works. Whether he meant this in a Pelagian or semi-Pelagian sense is unclear. In the end, he did reject the doctrine of original sin, and he emphasized human effort in defining salvation according to whether or not we follow the example of Christ. And so, he was accused of heresy (by St. Bernard of Clairvaux, among others), condemned as a heretic at councils in 1121 and 1140, and excommunicated. He found refuge at the monastery of Cluny, in Burgundy, and was reconciled to the Church by the abbot there shortly before his death, though it is unclear whether that was done with the sanction of any bishop.[18]

Nevertheless, Abelard's contribution to the development of atonement was to prevent the conversation from going too far toward the Augustinian extreme that would make salvation entirely an act of God's grace and leave no room for the participation of the individual. In doing this, though, he swung the pendulum hard to the Pelagian (or at least semi-Pelagian) side, diminishing the role of divine intervention in the atonement, and he paid the price for it. In fact, his entire life was characterized by flouting authority and making enemies everywhere he went (with tragic consequences), so consequently he moved around a lot. He chronicled the almost Shakespearean circumstances of his life in his autobiography, which he called, *The Story of My Misfortunes (Historia Calamitatum).*

Bernard of Clairvaux

Born in Burgundy to a family of knights, Bernard (AD 1090–1153) was critical of the ways in which *courtly love* was a romanticized justification of lust and adultery, and *chivalry* was an excuse for wealthy young men to engage in meaningless warfare between rival families. At the age of twenty-two, he joined the monastery of Citeaux, a reforming movement within the Benedictines that would come to be called the Cistercians. He would convince an uncle, his brothers, and his friends to join him

[17] Peter Abelard, *The Letters of Heloise and Abelard: A Translation of Their Collected Correspondence and Related Writings*, ed. and trans. Mary Martin McLaughlin and Bonnie Wheeler (New York: Palgrave Macmillan, 2009), 81.

[18] For the story of Abelard's life in his own words, see his autobiography, *The Story of My Misfortunes* (*Historia Calamitatum*). Abelard's relationship with Heloise is famous and has been the subject of numerous books and films.

there, and he demonstrated himself to be such a natural leader that in 1115 he was sent off with his followers to found the monastery of Clairvaux. By the end of his life he had founded sixty-eight monasteries, and had 164 (out of a total of 350 Cistercian houses) under his authority. In fact, this was a time when thousands of wealthy young men all over Europe would become disillusioned with the life of a knight and join the ranks of the monks.

In 1128, Bernard was present at the Council of Troyes, where he was instrumental in gaining approval for the Knights Templar, an order of monastic soldiers who were charged with protecting the Holy Land, and especially Jerusalem. The group had been founded by Bernard's cousin, Hugh de Payns, who asked Bernard to write the *Book in Praise of the New Militia*. In this book, Bernard criticized the secular knights, and said that monks are soldiers for peace. He also had to defend the idea of just war, which he did by arguing that what matters most is a person's motives and intentions. He would see the danger in this intentionalism when confronted with Peter Abelard.

Bernard's friend William of St. Thierry wrote to him to alert him to what Peter Abelard was teaching. According to tradition, Bernard saw how Abelard's intentionalism could lead to relativism, and responded with a version of the famous saying, "The road to hell is paved with good intentions." Bernard had used the emphasis on motivation in his defense of the monastic militia, but now he saw the danger in taking that concept to the extent of using it to avoid responsibility for sin. Bernard wrote *Against the Errors of Abelard* and was present at the Council of Sens in 1140, where Abelard was declared a heretic. That same year, Bernard had preached to the students of Paris, and many of them left the university to follow Bernard into the monastery—including some of Abelard's students.

In 1164, at the request of Pope Eugene III (bishop 1145–1153), Bernard embarked on a preaching tour to promote the second crusade (1145–1148), which was meant to liberate the city of Edessa. The crusaders never got that far, which shocked a Christian Europe that thought that since God was on their side, they could not lose. Bernard wrote several important mystical and contemplative works, as well as administrative writings to benefit the monastic orders, and lectures and sermons, which are preserved for us in the notes of his students.

Thomas Aquinas

Born Thomas of Aquino (AD 1224/1225–1274), he was the son of the Count of Aquino (between Rome and Naples). Thomas was educated by the Benedictines until age fourteen, when he went off to study at the new University of Naples (founded in the year he was born). Eventually he decided to join the Dominicans, because they were known to be teachers, and he went to Paris to study at the university there. In Paris, he was given the nickname *Dumb Ox* because he was a big guy, but quiet. The name is obviously "ironic," since he would soon be known as a great teacher and writer and is now considered one of most intelligent people in history. He turned down appointments as an abbot and an archbishop in order to pursue his vocation of teaching and writing.

Aquinas is most famous for his unfinished systematic theology, *Summa Theologica* (or *Summa Theologiae*). Aquinas, like the other Scholastics, affirmed that faith and reason are not contradictory, since both are gifts from God. However, he may have found a balance between the two that the others did not. If it could be said that Anselm leaned more toward faith (i.e., Augustine), and Abelard leaned more toward reason (i.e., philosophy), Aquinas presented the middle way, recognizing that while human rationality is a function of the image of God in the human person, it is nevertheless limited and therefore reason alone will not lead one to God — one also needs divine revelation. On the other hand, revelation requires reason to interpret it, and so each one needs the other. Aquinas combines Augustinian theology with a renewed (but measured) optimism about human nature which affirmed that people can know and do what is good, even if they cannot be perfect.

If the pendulum had swung toward the Augustinian side with St. Anselm, and to the Pelagian side with Abelard, St. Thomas Aquinas is the center of gravity where the Church would come to rest. Combining the best of the satisfaction and moral influence theories of atonement, Thomas brought the Church's *semi-Augustinian* anthropology to its logical conclusion and demonstrated how salvation requires divine intervention (God's grace is more than information, it is a power), human representation (Christ's human nature becomes the substitution for humanity), *and* human participation (the will of the individual cooperates with God's grace).[19] This would become the accepted Catholic understanding of atonement. Thomas's thought in general would come to be known as *Thomism*, and while it would be impossible to do justice to Thomas's contribution to the Church in the space available here, it will have to suffice to point out that few Christian writers, before or since, have come close to the legacy of Aquinas.

It is also important to note that in the Protestant Reformation, the reformers' reaction against the sale of indulgences led to an aversion to any talk of personal cooperation with grace (i.e., works), which made them move back toward Anselm and adopt a modified (more forensic, that is, law-oriented) version of the satisfaction theory that is often called the *penal substitution* theory (Anselm's *satisfaction* theory emphasizes *payment*, the reformers' *penal substitution* theory emphasizes *punishment*).

[19] See Thomas Aquinas, *Summa Theologica* III, q. 46, art. 1–3.

In any case, Thomas Aquinas had reclaimed a classical optimism about human nature, to such an extent that it set the stage for the Renaissance. For him, as for Augustine (not to mention Paul), God's grace is a power, the power to change direction in life. However, the human will must accept and respond to grace, which in turn merits more grace, a positive version of the snowball effect.

Soteriology, then, is the question of reconciliation with God, and how it is achieved. Can we reach out to God, or must God take the initiative and reach out to us first? The Council of Orange in AD 529 had concluded that although the human will can respond to grace, grace must move first. However, this still begged the question: How much can we contribute to our own salvation (Phil. 2:12)? How much does the human will cooperate with grace? What is the balance between grace (what God does) and free will (what we do)? The Church would accept Thomas Aquinas as the best interpreter of the atonement, that to connect with the Divine requires both divine power and willpower. It is not a question of either divine intervention or human effort, it requires both: the love, mercy, and compassion of a God who takes the initiative to reach out to humanity, as well as personal discipline and following the example of Christ. Thus, atonement is not one-sided, but is a divine-human dialogue which includes divine initiative (the Incarnation, revelation, and the grace of Baptism), human response (faith), divine intervention (the grace of healing and forgiveness), and human effort (prayer and good works).

So while Anselm had an important emphasis on divine intervention and human representation as the roles of the divine nature and human nature in Jesus Christ, and Abelard had an emphasis on individual participation in our salvation (though downplaying Anselm's emphases), Aquinas gives us a kind of "tripod" of atonement: divine intervention (the Incarnation), human representation (the cross), and individual participation (good works). In this way, the Church affirms *synergy*, the concept that we cooperate with God's grace and participate in our salvation by free will.

Conclusions

And so we come to the conclusion that each christological position assumes a certain anthropology and necessarily implies a certain soteriology. For example, adoptionism assumes an optimism about humanity which believes that humans could progress to perfection and earn their adoption by God. Adoptionist christology is one in which Christ is the pioneer of self-salvation. The Savior saves by setting the example for those who may follow in His footsteps. Adoptionist christology is a christology of ascent and therefore adoptionist soteriology is ultimately a salvation by human effort — it's what *we* do that saves us, not what Christ did. The grace of God is defined as God's gift of the teaching of Jesus and the example that He set for us. Against all of this, the mainstream Church reasoned that if the adoptionists were right, most (if not all) humans have little hope of salvation, and this is what gave the Arian controversy its urgency in the fourth century. It was one thing for theologians to argue whether Christ was co-eternal in the past with the Father, but many Christians worried that if salvation required earning God's favor, then all hope is lost.

On the other extreme, the soteriology implied by docetism, gnosticism, and modalism is a salvation of divine intervention, but without any human element. In each case, Christ is not really a human being, so His interaction with humanity is as divine revealer but not as representative of humanity. This is a version of a christology of descent, but one in which the descent only goes so far. Christ came only to bring secret knowledge or enlightenment, only to a spiritual elite who were predestined to it, or in the case of modalism the Father comes "in disguise," but in neither case does Christ truly experience the human condition. Thus, He is of God, but not one of us. In contrast to these extremes, the mainstream Church affirmed that for Christ to save us, He had to be both divine, and one of us. And as one of us, He made it clear that God's love and forgiveness are offered to all people, not just to an elite few.

Anthropology

For our present purposes, the question of anthropology is the question of what went wrong. What is broken in us that needs to be fixed? What is it about humanity that prevents us from achieving union with our Creator on our own power? Why do we need a Savior? Because if we think we do not need a Savior, then there is no point to our faith. As St. Paul said, "if Christ has not been raised, your faith is vain; you are still in your sins" (1 Cor. 15:17). So any Christian anthropology must take the reality of sin seriously. There is a reason why the moral influence theory of Abelard, taken by itself, would not be adequate to explain the atonement. It's because it lets people off the hook for sin and reduces the Savior to a good teacher. In a way, this is what both Arius and Pelagius did, and Abelard — though he made some positive contributions — highlighted the dangers of an overly optimistic anthropology. In fact, it could be argued that he anticipated the modern ploy of starting with adoptionism, but then just before it turns into works righteousness, falling back on universalism to double down on the avoidance of responsibility for sin. It would be easy, and convenient, and comfortable to be a universalist, but we cannot, because Jesus was not a universalist (see Matt. 7:21–23; 25:46).

On the other hand, we dare not go to the other extreme, which is a hyper-Augustinian pessimism that leads us to a Calvinist anthropology of total depravity. The truth is always in the middle, somewhere between the extremes of Pelagius and Augustine. We are fallen, but not totally depraved. We have free will, but it labors under the burden of original sin. Baptism cleanses us for a new start, but it does not guarantee perseverance to the end. God must take the initiative through the Incarnation and through grace, but we must respond in acceptance. We participate in our own salvation and sanctification through synergy — cooperation with God's grace (Phil. 2:12–13).[20]

It is also important to note that in order for God to fix what is wrong with us, the solution included the Incarnation, which is the embodiment of the Divine in a human life. In other words, He became one of us. To put it in the language of theological anthropology, He became *consubstantial* with humanity. But this only makes sense in the way that all humans are consubstantial with each other. In other words, if we define our humanity by markers that divide us — ethnicity, nationality, sex(uality), ability, and the like, then we imply that in Jesus God became like some of us, but not like others. Therefore, no matter how important it becomes to affirm the humanity of the oppressed and the marginalized, we must never lose sight of an anthropology of unity, which is to say that all humans are *one*, in the very sense that Jesus Christ became human. Therefore, we must define our humanity according to His humanity, making sure not to count as essential any aspect of human life that is not shared by all humans.

Christology

If anthropology tells us what went wrong, christology tells us how God is fixing it. If anthropology tells us why and how we are estranged from our Creator, christology tells us why and how God is reaching out to us in reconciliation. And yet, that reconciliation is not simply about being saved *from* something. It is also about being saved *for* something, which is life in the Body of Christ, and ultimately participation in the divine life (2 Pet. 1:4). He became like us, so we could become like Him. And we become a (re)new(ed) creation (2 Cor. 5:17–19).

From the very beginning, it was considered heresy to diminish either of the two natures of Christ. Christ must have two natures, or He is not Christ. And from our study of the theories of atonement and the Scholastics, we see the emphasis that atonement only works *because* Christ has two natures. The pendulum swung back and forth throughout the centuries, and no century was without some famous teacher or author who was so afraid of one extreme that he went to the other. But the truth is in the middle, and though they tried to crucify Him between the two thieves of adoptionism and docetism, or Arianism and modalism, or Nestorianism

[20] Barber, *Salvation*, 15, 26, 111.

and monothelitism or monophysitism, the true Christ remains in the place of balance, both arms outstretched to embrace the "both-and" answer to the christological questions.

Soteriology

We have looked at several "theories" of atonement, but it's worth noting again that in the New Testament, our tendency to sin is described in such strong terms as a kind of slavery. However we may describe Christ's work that gets us out of that predicament, the fact remains that we cannot get ourselves out. We are in it, and only someone from outside of it can pull us out. At the end of the day, salvation can only come by the descent of a Savior from without, by divine intervention. "You have been purchased at a price" (1 Cor. 6:20). If sin is slavery, then salvation is manumission.[21] On the other hand, it is interesting (and embarrassing) that it was not until the third century that the Church thought to condemn the institution of slavery. But that tells us that salvation was never really about overcoming injustice. In spite of Old Testament complaints and prophetic "speaking truth to power," salvation in the New Covenant is the reconciliation of the individual with her Creator by the mediation of Jesus Christ — it is about fixing what's wrong with *us*, not fixing what's wrong with the world.

For the early and medieval Church, salvation was also never just about forgiveness. It was not about being *declared innocent*, it was about being *healed* through the process of sanctification.[22] So atonement is not something that takes place in some heavenly courtroom and ends with the bang of a divine gavel. It is something more akin to what happens in a hospital. And in fact, that is how the Church Fathers saw the Church — as a hospital, with the sacraments as its medicine and the clergy as its doctors.

Ecclesiology

In the study of the history of the Church, it becomes clear that the Church was absolutely inclusive with regard to people. And we must not forget how rare this was in the ancient world. Most religions were based on the assumption that their membership was demographically determined. In most cases, a person believed in the gods of the culture in which she was raised. Foreigners had other gods, and nationality, such as it was, was not very distinct from religious affiliation. And when the foreign cults did cross borders, they were generally for one type of person: men, or women, or the wealthy, or the soldiers. But Christians could say that in Christ, there were no more

[21] Barber, *Salvation*, 45–46.

[22] Barber, *Salvation*, 69–82, 113.

distinctions of Jew or Gentile, male or female, even slave or free (see Gal. 3:28). To have a religion that welcomed all people without regard for ethnicity, sex, or social class was a radical way of thinking about a fellowship. This informed the Church's very identity, not to mention the self-identity of individual Christians, and it also contributed to the Church's growth.

Having said that, it has also become abundantly clear that the Church was not inclusive with regard to ideas. Within Christianity, truth is something that comes to us from God, as revelation. It does not come from "within" and we do not get to invent our own truth. Truth is received — first directly from God in the Scriptures and in the Incarnation — and then it is handed down to us by those who came before us. And so there are right and wrong answers to the important questions. There are correct interpretations (those most consistent with what has been handed down), and there are incorrect interpretations (those that deviate from what has been handed down). The former is called orthodoxy, and the latter is called heresy. And yet, orthodoxy *develops*. It is not static. It has been said that we are keeping a flame alive, we are not worshiping ashes. And so the important thing is always to distinguish between legitimate development, which allows for growth and even expansion, versus corruption, which is an illegitimate kind of change, an evolution in which a thing becomes something it was not. But the historic Church believed the promise of Jesus, that the Church would never become something it was not meant to be, that "the gates of the netherworld [would] not prevail against it" (Matt. 16:18).

Yet for all its structure, the Church is not an institution. Of course, it functions like an institution, with a hierarchy, and rules, and even sometimes suffering from the failures of human leaders. But the Church pre-exists the people in it. It is something greater than the sum of its parts, because it was instituted by God in Christ. It is sacramental, which is to say it is mystical, even miraculous. And in the early and medieval Church, Christianity's very self-identity was tied up with the sacraments — those ritual acts which convey God's grace to the believer and leave him or her changed forever. Certainly the Church is the community of the baptized, but that definition of membership cannot be pushed to a legalistic extreme, since we have seen how those who were not (yet) baptized could be considered Christians (for example the confessors and martyrs). And in any case, to say that the Church equals the baptized reduces the Church to the people in it, and it's more than that. This is why it is best to think of the Church in terms of the table of the Eucharist. The Church *is* the table because it welcomes its people to share in the fellowship of the Lord's Supper, but it is also a means of grace, for empowerment to the Christian life. And finally, it looks forward in anticipation to the fellowship of the heavenly

Kingdom, which means that it includes all of those who have gone before us, and who are with us at the table in a mystical way.

So what is unity, and at what cost is it to be sought after?

From the beginning it was assumed that the Church must be one. Therefore, it was desirable, even urgent, that the Church define the boundaries of acceptable teaching, and invest the authority over those boundaries in a hierarchy, for the sake of unity. But at least as early as the writing of the first letter of John, there were those who would not stay within the boundaries and who "went out from us" (1 John 2:19). Then, from the Marcionites in the second century, to the Novatianists in the third century, to the Donatists in the fourth century, to the Nestorians and miaphysites of the fifth century, there were always groups willing to separate from the mainstream Church to maintain their own identity and stand up for their divergent beliefs. How was the Church to balance orthodoxy and unity? How far could the Church go in accepting variations of doctrine before a particular teaching had moved far enough from the "center" that it could no longer be called Christianity?

For that matter, why not just let everyone believe what seemed right to them? The reason this would have been unthinkable was that the Church Fathers recognized that theology and christology always led to a particular soteriology, and they firmly believed that not every soteriology could actually save. Therefore, souls were at stake, and the heretic who insisted on teaching a divergent interpretation was in fact preaching "another gospel" (see Gal. 1:8), and one which would lead innocent people astray, and ultimately to their eternal damnation. Hence the need for the boundaries.

What is authority, and what are its limits?

The need for boundaries immediately raises the question of who has the authority to set the boundaries. As the hierarchy of the Church developed, authority became concentrated in the bishops, who were the keepers of the Church's doctrine and discipline. Apostolic succession assumes an institutionalization of authority, one that would ultimately be incompatible with the various forms of prophetic authority that were invested by the grassroots of the laity. Therefore, limiting the parameters of doctrine required limiting the authority. In the East, ultimate authority was placed in councils, but in the West, authority came to be consolidated in a single point at the top of the hierarchy, the bishop of Rome. Perhaps it is not a coincidence that the West inherited Augustine's pessimism with regard to humanity while the East never did. A pessimistic anthropology might have contributed to the idea that a centralized authority was needed for a people who could not really be trusted to know what was best for them. The East, on the other hand, with its (slightly) more optimistic anthropology and its continuing acceptance of human free will, could allow more participation in authority. In any case, the Council of Nicaea was the last ecumenical council to include participation by anyone other than bishops.

After Constantine legalized Christianity and made travel and communication between bishops more convenient, the Church also had to struggle with the question of standardization. In other words, how much diversity of practice (liturgy, ritual) should the one Church allow, so that it can still be considered one? Thus, it was not only doctrinal diversity but also liturgical diversity that caused concern.

What is the proper balance of unity and diversity, and how do we achieve it?

Just as the Church struggled to find the balance of unity and distinction among the three divine Persons of the Trinity, it also had to work toward a balance of unity and diversity in its practical life. Total unity was not possible, and to force it unnecessarily would create schism, which puts souls at risk no less than heresy. Therefore, how much diversity should the Church allow for the sake of unity, and at what point must the Church draw the line of definition for the sake of its own integrity? Put another way, conclusions about the relationship of the divine and human in Christ have implications for the Body of Christ, in which sincere believers seek a connection with the Divine. Of course, we have to be careful not to project our own ideas about "community" on God or make the Trinity some sort of analogy for human relationships, but the point is that what people truly need and want is access to the Divine. Salvation is nothing more or less than a relationship with God, through Christ, that continues into eternity. But here's the rub: the Church Fathers believed that one must have a relationship with the *right* Christ, or it would be ineffective to lead to salvation. A relationship with the christ of Marcion or Arius would not do it. The true Christ would not be found at the extremes, but would be found in the middle, in the center of gravity, in a place of balance.

The story of the early Church is therefore the story of the Church's struggle to define itself. Often Christians had to describe the Church in reference to its opposition, in other words, clarifying what Christianity *is* by pointing out what it is *not*. Therefore, an orthodox anthropology is not a completely pessimistic understanding of the human person as totally depraved, nor is it a completely optimistic understanding of humanity as capable of perfection. Orthodox ecclesiology is not so exclusive as to be purist, but it is also not so inclusive as to be universalist. Orthodox christology is not found in the extremes of gnosticism or adoptionism but affirms both the humanity and divinity of Christ. Nor is it found in the extremes of Arianism or modalism, but affirms both the unity and distinction in the Trinity. In fact, it is the hypostatic union of human and divine natures in the Person of Christ that is the very focal point of the union of humanity with God. And finally, orthodox soteriology is not all divine election without human participation, nor is it all human effort without divine intervention, but operates through divine initiative and synergy. The Church came to believe, and not only believe but wager eternity on this belief, that the truth is in the middle.

Important Theological Concepts and Doctrines

1. Divine Simplicity
    a. God is *simplex,* meaning non-composite: God does not have "parts"
    b. Parts would imply corruptibility, meaning that whatever is not *simplex* could be broken down
    c. Therefore, the three Persons of the Trinity are not each one-third of God
    d. Each Person of the Trinity is fully God/divine
    e. Not even the mind or will of God are distinct from God's substance/essence
    f. God does not *have* attributes, God simply is what God is
    g. So-called attributes of God are only descriptions of God's substance/essence
2. Immutability/Impassibility
    a. Immutability is changelessness, the inability to experience change
    b. Impassibility is the inability to suffer (suffering is a form of change, and implies a deficiency)
    c. Divine perfection requires immutability, since change would destroy perfection
    d. Divine omnipresence also requires immutability, since movement is a form of change
    e. Immutability does not mean inability to love, since God is immutably loving
    f. Impassibility does not mean lack of compassion; God is in solidarity with us in Jesus
3. Inseparable Operation
    a. A function of consubstantiality and divine simplicity
    b. All three Persons of the Trinity are unified in all divine activity
4. Appropriation
    a. Also a function of consubstantiality and divine simplicity
    b. What is said of one Person of the Trinity must be said of the others (with limited exceptions)
    c. What can be said of God/the Trinity can be said of each Person of the Trinity
5. *Perichoresis* (Latin: *Circumincessio*) or Reciprocity
    a. A function of divine simplicity, consubstantiality, and inseparable operation
    b. The mutual interexistence of the three Persons of the Trinity

   c. The interpenetration of the three Persons in action (movement toward the unity)
   d. The fact that each divine Person exists "in" the other divine Persons
6. Eternal Generation
   a. "Begotten" does not mean created
   b. What is generated is of the same substance as the Source of generation
   c. The generation (begetting) of the Son is not an "event" that "happened"
   d. The generation (begetting) of the Son is the eternal relationship with the Father
7. Consubstantiality (Greek: *homoousios*)
   a. A function of divine simplicity (whatever is not the same substance as God, is not God)
   b. All three Persons of the Trinity are the same substance
   c. The result of generation (in the case of the Son) and procession (in the case of the Holy Spirit)
   d. Describes the unity (oneness) of the Trinity
   e. The Son is also consubstantial with humanity by virtue of His human nature
8. Coeternality
   a. Goes hand in hand with consubstantiality and eternal generation
   b. There is no time lag before begetting or proceeding, no time when the Son did not exist
9. *Communicatio Idiomatum*
   a. As *perichoresis* is to the Trinity, *communicatio idiomatum* is to the two natures of Christ
   b. Properties idiomatic to each of Christ's natures are communicated to the other nature[23]

[23] There is a tendency among some contemporary theologians to claim that the *communicatio idiomatum* is only a one-way communication (from the divine nature to the human nature only), or that the *communicatio* is only a communication from each nature to the Person of Christ, but not to the other nature. The idea that the idiomatic properties are communicated *to the Person* of Christ (as opposed to being communicated directly to the other nature) is a later development, and in my opinion, one that was a concession that sacrificed the purity and precision of the original version of the doctrine to try to avoid some problems inherent in some contemporary "kenosis christology" (which is not to be confused with orthodox third-century *kenosis* christology). The issue, of course, is to describe this reality while maintaining the balance of unity and distinction between the two natures of Christ, and without implying any change in the divine nature that would compromise immutability, or implying a Nestorian separation of the natures. The divine

c. For example:
    i. By virtue of the union, the human nature receives glory and immortality
    ii. By virtue of the union, the divine nature experienced the human condition
    iii. But not to the extent of allowing passibility in the divine nature
d. The *communicatio idiomatum* is the solution to the paradox of "the immutable became mutable"
    i. It is a function of the *hypostatic* union, and describes a real personal union against Nestorianism
    ii. Yet it preserves the distinction of natures and thereby protects the immutability of the Divine

---

nature borrows, or receives, from the human nature the frailty of the human condition, so that Divinity can *experience* humanity, but always without implying any change or effect on the divine nature. See Maximus the Confessor, *Ad Thalasium*, 60, where he refers to knowledge as experiential. To say that "the Word became flesh" is to say that the divine *Logos* experienced humanity firsthand, yet without changing or in any way diminishing the divinity. All of this is by virtue of the hypostatic union and the *communicatio idiomatum*. By that same token, the human nature borrows, or receives, from the divine nature the glory and immortality that makes it possible for our human nature (which is consubstantial with His) to receive salvation and eternal life. The communication of idioms must be a two-way communication, with each nature communicating properties to the other nature, because one nature cannot communicate something *to the Person* without communicating it to the other nature (and of course one nature does not need to communicate anything to itself, so the other nature is the only thing left to communicate to). To say the communication is *to the Person* cuts the heart out of the point that the impassible became passible. The impassible can only mean the divine nature, which "becomes" passible by "borrowing" passibility from the human nature, in a way that both rules out change or need but also allows for experiential knowledge of the human condition. Also, to say the communication is *to the Person* implies a distinction of the Person from the natures, which effectively creates a christological *tertium quid*, a third thing with is neither nature — creating the false impression that there are three parts to Christ, two natures and the Person. But the Personhood is not distinct from the natures, the Person *is* the natures in the hypostatic union. To say that anything is communicated *to the Person* is a fiction meant to hedge around the divine nature and protect it from mutability and passibility — but that is not necessary if one understands the doctrine correctly. In fact, to say that each nature communicates *to the Person* but not directly to the other nature is either a form of Nestorianism (separating the two natures too much) or a form of monoenergism (see above, chapter 13). Thus, the divine nature can "experience" suffering, without actually suffering in a way that would imply change or need. Also, the distinction between *communicatio in concreto* versus *in abstracto* is, again, a later distinction based on categories not found in the early Church Fathers. The truth is that we can — and the Church Fathers did — speak of the communication of idioms from one nature to the other.

    iii. At the same time, it allows the divine nature to experience the human condition
    iv. This is how God can be in solidarity with humanity and remain immutable

10. Circumscribability (Localization, Spatial Limitation)
    a. The ability to be localized in time and space
    b. In the Incarnation, localization of the *Logos* in Christ required a *kenosis* of omnipresence
    c. Paradoxically, the divine nature of Christ was circumscribed in the womb of Mary
    d. Goes hand in hand with visibility

About the Author

Dr. James L. Papandrea is an award-winning author and professor of Church history and historical theology. His many books have been translated into multiple languages, and he has a significant presence on YouTube, including his video series, *The Original Church* (www.WhenTheChurchWasOne.com). A Catholic layperson and catechist, Jim has an M.Div. from Fuller Theological Seminary and a Ph.D. from Northwestern University in the history and theology of the early Christian church, with secondary concentrations in New Testament interpretation and the history of the Roman Empire. He has also studied Roman history at the American Academy in Rome. He is currently on the faculty at Garrett-Evangelical Theological Seminary and is recognized for his ecumenical work on behalf of the whole Body of Christ. He is a senior fellow of the St. Paul Center for Biblical Theology and was recently named a "Springtime Ambassador" by the Springtime of Faith Foundation, an organization facilitating ecumenical dialogue and Christian cooperation. Jim is a member of multiple professional organizations, including the Academy of Catholic Theology, the North American Patristics Society, and the Society of Biblical Literature. More information can be found via Jim's website: www.JimPapandrea.com, and his Amazon author page: www.DoctorJimsBooks.com.

Sophia Institute

Sophia Institute is a nonprofit institution that seeks to nurture the spiritual, moral, and cultural life of souls and to spread the Gospel of Christ in conformity with the authentic teachings of the Roman Catholic Church.

Sophia Institute Press fulfills this mission by offering translations, reprints, and new publications that afford readers a rich source of the enduring wisdom of mankind.

Sophia Institute also operates the popular online resource CatholicExchange.com. *Catholic Exchange* provides world news from a Catholic perspective as well as daily devotionals and articles that will help readers to grow in holiness and live a life consistent with the teachings of the Church.

In 2013, Sophia Institute launched Sophia Institute for Teachers to renew and rebuild Catholic culture through service to Catholic education. With the goal of nurturing the spiritual, moral, and cultural life of souls, and an abiding respect for the role and work of teachers, we strive to provide materials and programs that are at once enlightening to the mind and ennobling to the heart; faithful and complete, as well as useful and practical.

Sophia Institute gratefully recognizes the Solidarity Association for preserving and encouraging the growth of our apostolate over the course of many years. Without their generous and timely support, this book would not be in your hands.

www.SophiaInstitute.com
www.CatholicExchange.com
www.SophiaInstituteforTeachers.org